UNDERSTANDING ECONOMICS

THE MANCHESTER ECONOMICS PROJECT   Project Head C. Giles

Ginn & Co Ltd
London and Aylesbury

Acknowledgements

The publishers gratefully acknowledge the kindness of Manchester City Education Committee, and the Headmaster of Burnage High School, who granted the secondment of Mr. C. G. Giles. The name of the project not only recognises this, but also reflects the historical influence of that great City in the development of economic thought in Britain.

We are indebted to the Nuffield Resources for Learning Project for assistance, advice and encouragement, given through the persons of Mr. T. MacMullen and Mr. L. C. Taylor.

The Project's interest was not directly in the subject content of the course, but in the development of a style of presentation such that the student would not be continuously dependent on fully qualified teachers.

The early stages of the Pilot Scheme were administered by the National Extension College, Cambridge.

We are also grateful to H. M. Inspectorate, particularly to Mr. J. L. Gayler, who submitted the early project materials to the constructive criticism of a group of Principals and Vice-Principals of Colleges of Further Education, attending the Business Studies Course of the Department of Education and Science in Salisbury in 1969.

Understanding Economics and its satellite texts are based upon a plan devised by Mr. C. G. Giles, who initiated the Pilot Edition as Head of the Project and co-ordinated the planning of the satellites. The Pilot Edition was thoroughly tested in schools and colleges of further education. The present edition is the outcome of this testing programme. Major contributions to the Pilot Edition were made by Mr. G. Herbert of Northampton Grammar School and Mr. B. Fletcher of Newton Abbot Grammar School; together with Mr. D. Eltringham of Blyth Grammar School, and Mr. J. Nicholson of Sir James Smith's School, Camelford, they also contributed significantly to the present edition.

Mr. A. Charnley organised the school testing programme, collated the teachers' comments and planned the text of this edition.

To all the persons mentioned above, and the headmasters, staff and students of schools participating in the Pilot Scheme, we owe a considerable debt of gratitude.

This book is the result of a cooperative venture. We hope that it will so continue, and that those using the Manchester Economics Project materials will send us their opinions, and their suggestions for improvements.

Statistical material from Government publications is reproduced by permission of the Controller of Her Majesty's Stationery Office. Figure 6·3 and the table on page 182 are reproduced by permission of The Bank of England, figures 20·11 and 20·12 by permission of The Sunday Times, figure 6·2 by permission of The Union Discount House, and the table on page 21 by permission of Lloyd's Bank Ltd.

Diagrams were drawn by Ray Martin.

Third impression 1975 057501

Product No. 568545532 ISBN 0 602 21493 9

Published by Ginn and Company Ltd,
Elsinore House, Buckingham Street,
Aylesbury, Bucks HP20 2NQ

Printed by R. & R. Clark, Ltd, Edinburgh

The Consultative Committee

Professor C. T. Sandford *(Chairman)*	Professor of Political Economics, Bath University of Technology
G. G. Bamford	Principal Lecturer in Economics, Manchester College of Commerce
A. P. Budd	Visiting Professor of Economics, University of Pittsburgh; Department of Economics, University of Southampton
A. H. Charnley *(Project Adviser)*	Formerly of H.M. Inspectorate of Schools
C. G. Giles *(Project Head)*	Head of Department of Economics, Burnage High School, Manchester (Seconded to M.E.P. by Manchester Education Committee)
K. A. Hills	Formerly Managing Director, Ginn and Co. Ltd
G. O. M. Leith	Director, Phillips Research Institute in Department of Educational Technology, University of Sussex
R. J. Marriott	Formerly Economics Editor, Ginn & Co. Ltd.
I. T. McMullen & L. C. Taylor	Co-ordinating Directors, Nuffield Resources for Learning Project
A. E. Matten	Associated Examining Board
P. J. O'Leary	Chief Examiner in Advanced Level Economics, University of London Schools' Examination Board; Department of Economics, University of Bristol
R. F. R. Phillips	Secretary, Economics Association

Schools and colleges which tested the Pilot Edition

School or College	Head or Principal	Master in charge of testing
Aylesbury Grammar School	K. D. Smith, M.A.	R. E. Blaxter, B.Sc. (Econ.)
Barnstaple Grammar School	J. W. Morgan, B.Sc.	J. T. Baxter, B.A. (Econ.)
Burnage High School, Manchester	S. Hughes, M.A.	C. G. Giles, B.A. (Econ.) P. G. Williams, B.A. (Econ.)
Carisbrooke High School	S. G. Ward, B.A.	M. L. Rice, B.A. (Econ.)
Cheney School, Oxford	A. Wainwright, J. P., B.Sc.	M. N. Brayshaw, B.A. (Econ.)
Chichester High School for Boys	K. D. Anderson, M.A., B.Sc.	J. C. Powicke, B.A. (Econ.)
Cranbrook School	P. W. Rowe, M.A.	P. R. Allen, M.A., B.Sc. (Econ.)
Denstone College	D. Maland, M.A.	R. M. Williams, B.A. J. White, B.A.
Dover Grammar School for Boys	R. C. Colman, M.A.	W. G. King, B.Sc. (Econ.), B.Com.
Gordonstoun School	J. W. R. Kempe, M.A.	J. H. Day, B.Com., B.Ed., M.A., C.E.
Haileybury School	W. Stewart, M.C., M.A.	R. Rhodes-James, M.A.
Hanson Boys' Grammar School, Bradford	R. V. Dawson, M.A., M.Ed.	N. Donkin, B.Sc. (Econ.)
Haywards Heath Grammar School	E. C. Wynter, M.C., M.A.	R. D. Sargent, B.Sc. (Econ.)
Holte Grammar Commercial School, Birmingham	C. N. Mitchell, M.A.	A. G. H. Thompson, B.Com.
King George V School, Southport	G. F. Dixon, M.A.	M. E. Amer, B.A. (Econ.)
Lancing College	I. D. S. Beer, M.A.	J. H. McLachlan, M.A.
Lincoln School	J. C. Faull, B.Sc., A.R.C.S.	K. Haye, B.A. (Soc.) R. D. Traehearn, B.A.
Longsands Comprehensive School, St. Neots	T. A. Williams, M.A.	G. Shelton Fowler
Moreton Hall	Miss B. Lloyd-Williams	R. L. Coutts, B.A.
Morley Grammar School	J. R. Carr, M.A.	P. W. Dobson, B.A.
Newton Abbot Grammar	R. Cook, M.A.	B. W. Fletcher, B.Com. (Hons.)
Northampton Grammar School	H. J. C. Oliver, B.Sc.	G. Herbert, B.A. H. T. Ford, B.A.
Preston VI Form College	Miss M. I. Shanks, B.A.	K. Topping, M.A.
Queen Elizabeth's School, Crediton	O. B. Rigby, B.Sc.	Joan H. B. Skinner, B.Com. (E.P.S.) Raymond Skinner, Phd., F.R.S.A.
Ramsden Technical College, Huddersfield	H. T. Taylor, Ph.D., M.Sc. (Tech.), B.Sc.	M. R. Scott, M.Inst.P.S., A.M.B.I.M.
Teignmouth Grammar School	Dr. P. E. Thompson, M.A.	J. A. Stephenson, B.A.
St. Nicholas Grammar School	R. F. E. Watson, Ph.D., L.G.S.M.	M. A. Wilson, B.Sc., (Econ.) Ac., Dip.Ed.
St. Peter's School, York	P. D. R. Gardiner, M.A.	L. C. Le Tocq, T.D., M.A., B.Sc. (Econ.)
School of St. Mary and St. Anne, Abbots Bromley	Miss M. Roch, M.A.	R. M. Williams, B.A. J. White, B.A.
University College School	C. D. Black-Hawkins, M.A.	C. Williams, B.Sc. (Econ.)
Usworth Secondary School	T. M. Craig, B.A.	W. Richardson, F.C.B.I., F.S.C.T., A.C.P.

Introduction

The Manchester Economics Project materials are designed for those studying economics to the standard of G.C.E. 'A' level, or of equivalent professional examinations. They can be used as a conventional class text, but in preparing materials especial attention has been paid to the needs of those who are without a specialist teacher, or who attend a class perhaps once a week, or who pursue the sometimes lonely path of private study.

This book, *Understanding Economics,* is the central text of economic theory necessary to an 'A' level course. In reading it, your aim will be to understand the basic principles of economics, and many exercises are provided, especially in the early part of the course. By answering these, you will be able to check that you have understood the principles. Experience has shown that careful, conscientious work in the early sections is amply rewarded by faster progress later, when using principles to answer economic questions.

The *Satellite texts,* listed below, are short books designed to describe some aspect of the economic system, such as trade unions, or the financial institutions, or to show how economic principles may be applied when examining the workings of the system, as in the pricing of motor cars, or the forming of government policy. Each is a study course in its own right, and like the central text, contains questions to test understanding.

The *Study Guide* consists of a series of lessons, and is intended primarily for the private student. Each lesson contains an explanation and overall view of the topic to be studied, with suggestions for further reading, research, project work and essays. The *Study Guide* can also be used as a teacher's manual, and should be particularly helpful to the non-specialist charged with guiding economics students.

The three basic parts described above are the foundations of the M.E.P., but it is intended that other materials shall follow. Films are available from the Educational Films Unit of Bath University, and other visual aids are in course of development.

The Manchester Economics Project is designed to enable you to look at the world around you as an economist. Some of the theory may appear strange at first, but as you progress from section to section, and feel a sense of achievement as you master the subject, you will find a greater understanding of the events in a complex society.

Satellite texts

1 Arithmetical and Statistical Methods by G. G. Bamford

2 Financial Institutions by R. M. Williams

3 Industrial Relations by R. M. Grant

4 The Motor Vehicle Industry by A. Holme

5 Agriculture by D. Eltringham

6 Retail Trade and Distribution

7 Industry in the Public Sector by F. Perrott

8 The Management of the Economy by G. Herbert

9 Contemporary Problems of Foreign Exchange and Trade by J. Nicholson

10 Sample Studies of Financial Institutions by R. M. Williams

11 Monopoly and Restrictive Practices by G. Stanlake

Contents

THE ECONOMIC PROBLEM

STUDY SECTION **1**

What is the 'Economic Problem'?

You may be surprised to see the heading of this section being described as 'the' economic problem. There are, you may think, many economic problems, which are discussed regularly in the newspapers and on the television and radio. Problems such as the Balance of Payments, unofficial strikes, and rising prices, which concern most of us, are indeed economic problems but they are only a small part of 'the' economic problem which concerns all people living together in communities. Economics is a social science and as such is concerned with people. People cannot exist without obtaining food and water at the very least, and in most places they require clothes and shelter. Not only do people need essentials for survival but they also want comforts, where they can be provided. Here then is 'the' problem. These wants cannot be satisfied without sacrifice, either in the form of human effort or in the form of the using up of resources which are provided free, such as timber, water, minerals, etc. The problem is to use the resources at our disposal to their best advantage in order to satisfy as many of our wants as possible. It is worth remembering that whatever topic you study during this course, it will be related in some way to the basic economic problem.

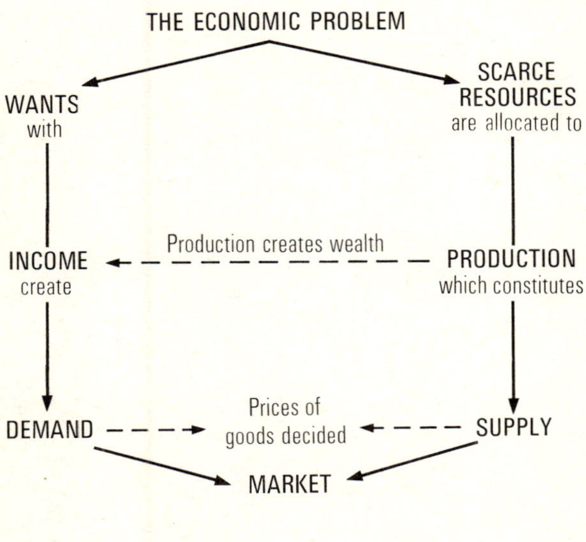

Figure 1·1

Work and pay

Consider the following information:

Country	Population 1967	km²
England	45 680 900	130 360
Scotland	5 186 600	78 772
Wales	2 709 900	20 761
N. Ireland	1 491 000	14 121
Total in United Kingdom	55 068 400	244 014

1·1

Which country in the U.K. has the highest density of population, that is population per square kilometre?

A Scotland? **C** Northern Ireland?
B England? **D** Wales?

Of this 55 million population about 24 million people are in employment, and in 1967 they produced goods and services which were worth about £34 025 million. They were paid £20 830 million in wages and salaries, £2 615 million was earned by those working for themselves, and £10 580 million was earned in the form of tents or profits.

The country would seem to be well off for goods and services, with plenty of money to spend on them. Most of you will say, 'Who's got the money? I haven't!' Immediately we have touched on one of the basic problems of economics. Practically everyone wants more money to buy the unlimited number of things he wants.

Wealth

The resources of an undeveloped country are almost entirely natural. There is the soil, its fertility, the minerals beneath the ground, forests, lakes, rivers, fish, wild animals, the climate, and so on. All these natural resources are called *land* by the economist. To them can be added the *labour* of the inhabitants. By themselves, land and labour produce a low standard of living—a hunting, fishing and food-gathering existence—and all societies, even the most primitive, have passed beyond it. People have houses, clothes, tools. These and other material possessions constitute *wealth*, a stock of assets resulting from past production. Modern industrial societies have vast accumulations of wealth; factories, roads, houses, machinery, stocks of food and clothing, libraries. All are the results of past production.

Some of this wealth is used for *consumption*, that is, it is used up to satisfy wants directly. Food is an obvious example—it satisfies our hunger. Clothing keeps us warm, cars move us from place to place. Note that when an economist speaks of consumption, he does not necessarily mean that the wealth is used up immediately. One cannot eat a meal twice, but clothing and cars can be expected to satisfy wants over a period of time.

Other forms of wealth satisfy wants indirectly. A plough enables food to be produced, and a factory makes cars, but it is not the plough which satisfies hunger, but food, and it is not the factory which moves us, but the car. Wealth used to produce more wealth is called *capital*.

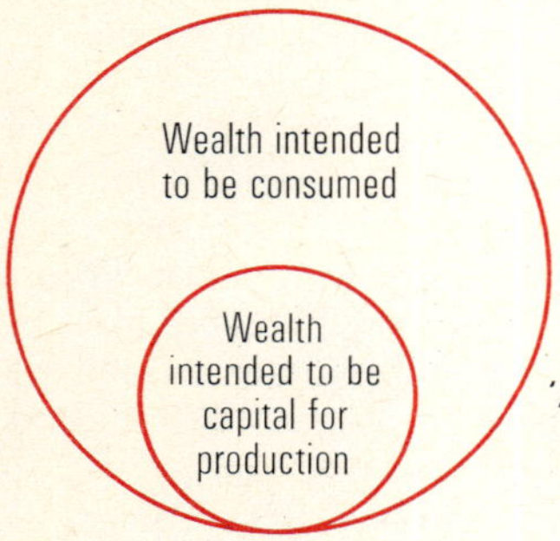

'All capital is wealth, not all wealth is intended to be used as capital.'

We commonly think of wealth as money, but as we have just seen, real wealth has the power either to satisfy wants, or to create more wealth. The pieces of metal or paper which form our money do not usually have such power. We cannot eat them or wear them, and they are of use only if we can exchange them for real wealth. How much real wealth is represented by statistics in money terms, such as those given in the preceding section, is one of the most important problems concerning economists. We shall study it later.

Income and expenditure

Most people receive their income in money form, though it is not uncommon for people to be provided with the use of a house, or a car, or overalls or uniform, as part of their wages. Money income can be exchanged freely for goods, and so we have a claim on the flow of production from factories, offices and business of all kinds. We can contrast this *flow* of income with the *stock* of wealth saved from past production.

1·2

a If the following goods belonged to you and formed your stock of wealth, which would you call capital?

A 1 kg of margarine in the pantry
B The novels on your bookshelf
C A tractor and plough on a farm
D A transistor radio in your bedroom
E A stock of goods in a shop

b **i** Write down the difference between capital and wealth.
ii Explain the difference between wealth and income.
iii Try measuring your wealth. How large is your stock of wealth compared with your annual income?

Let us look at your income and expenditure for a moment.

1·3

For individual students

The table below shows a fairly typical weekly income and expenditure pattern. Using this table as a guide, calculate your own figures for a weekly or monthly period. All items are expressed in new pence.

Income	£	**Expenditure**	£
Personal allowance	0·60	Magazines	0·20
Earnings	0·90	Travel	0·75
Gifts	0·50	Entertainment	1·00
Other	0·20	Other	0·05
	£2·20		£2·20

If you are working as a member of a group

Discuss these items and add other suitable items before anyone fills in any figures. Why should the totals on each side of the account be the same?

1·4

Show the relative sizes of the items in the income and expenditure, use a bar diagram or a pie chart for each side of the account. The results may be shown in several ways, and you should attempt each one. See satellite book *Arithmetical and Statistical Methods*, as a guide.

The results of exercise 1·4 might look something like this:

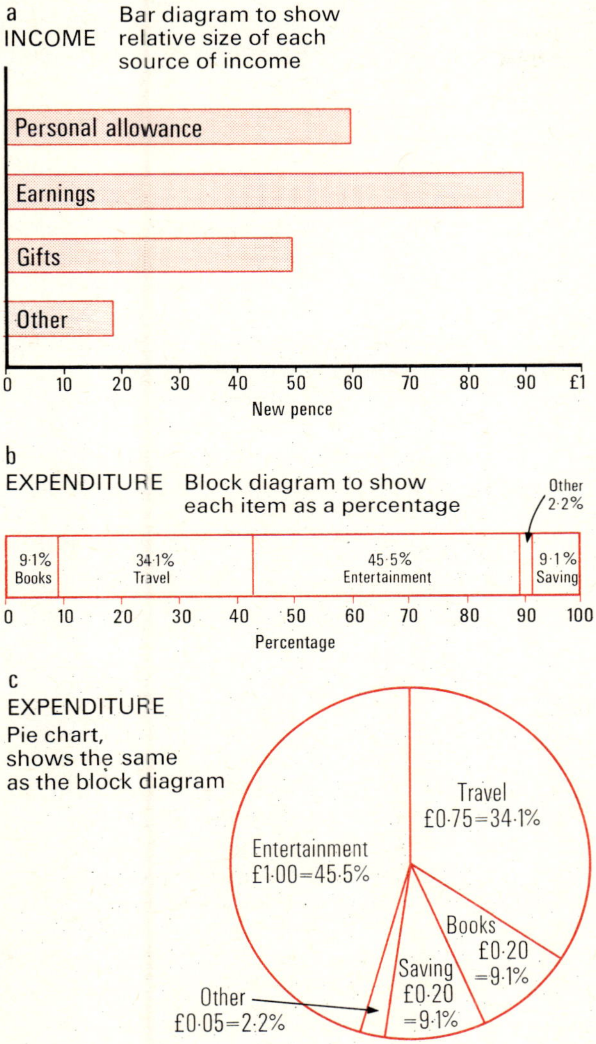

Figure 1·3

These figures show at a glance which are the most important items, which here means largest. Whether the largest items are really the most important is a matter of judgement. This must take account of one's values and ideas of what is important in life.

Family survey

Details of a national survey have been published in the Department of Economic Affairs (D.E.A.) reports for February and June 1966, August 1968 and the *Statistical News*, May 1968.

These publications show the way in which families spend their money. The results of the official studies of the Central Statistical Office (C.S.O.) are used by many government departments and are the basis of much economic planning. Before you try to analyse family income and expenditure, let us look briefly at some of the results of the C.S.O.'s investigations.

Income

The following figures refer to the U.K. population as a whole and illustrate the changing sources of personal income since 1955. Each figure shows the proportion of incomes coming from each source. The information is obtained from tax returns.

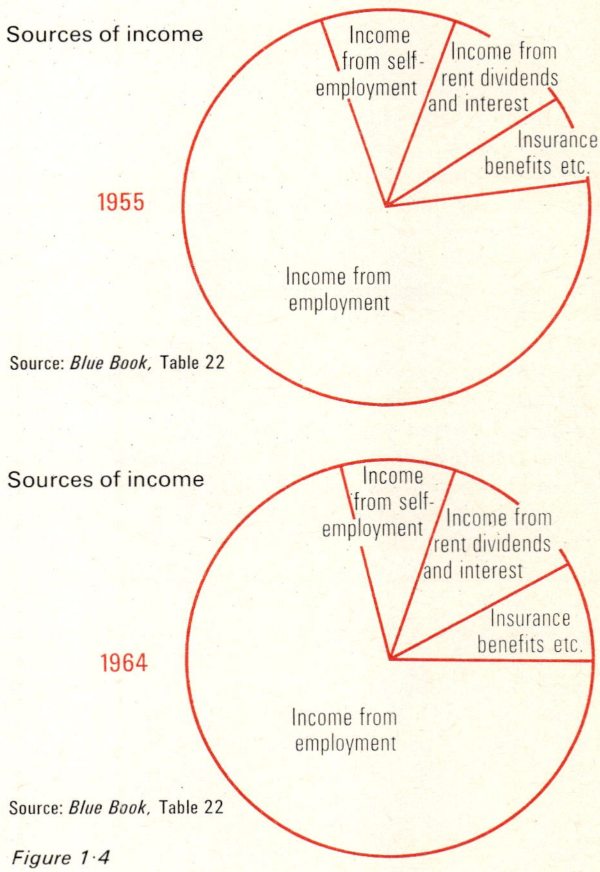

Figure 1·4

1·5

Using the copy of the table *Personal Income and Expenditure* (in the *Annual Abstract of Statistics*) of the figures from the current *National Income Blue Book*, draw up a list showing the same figures for the latest year available.

For the years shown in figure 1·4 calculate each item as a percentage of the total. (See satellite *Arithmetical and Statistical Methods*.) Show these items in a table like the one below. Do the same for the latest figures so that you have three columns of information which you can compare to answer the following questions.

	1955%	1965%	1970%
1 Income from employment			
2 Income from self-employment			
3 Dividends, rent and interest			
4 Insurance benefits, etc.			

a Write down those items which have declined in relative importance between 1955 and each succeeding year in the table.

b Write down those items which have become relatively more important between 1955 and each of the years in your table.

c The change in percentage does not show the whole picture. Draw up bar charts for each item.

1·6

Take the main items from the more detailed table of consumer's expenditure in the *Blue Book* (see figure 1·5) and your own household's expenditure under each of these headings and estimate for the past month. Add up the total under each heading, and calculate these totals as percentages of the household's monthly expenditure.

You have now collected some factual data showing what income you have available and how you have allocated your expenditure to satisfy your wants. In the process of allocation you have been making decisions and choosing the goods and services which *you* think are worth buying. Why have you to make a choice between different goods and services? The answer constitutes *the basic problem of economics, namely, that for both people and nations, resources are limited when compared with the goods and services which are desired.*

1·7

Apart from the things you actually spend your money on, list the ten next most important things you would buy if you had £50.

In deciding how you would spend £50, you will have encountered two important economic ideas. The first is the concept of a *scale of preferences*. All people have in their minds, more or less clearly, a number of things they would buy or do if and when they had the means. This applies not only to the sudden windfall, suggested in exercise 1·7, but also to the way in which they allocate their normal personal income. Such problems as whether to buy meat or fish, fruit or vegetables, a new coat or a pair of shoes are familiar to everyone. Some of the items are important to us, others less so.

The second concept is that of *price*. In deciding how to allocate our income to satisfy our wants, we have to consider the prices of the goods and services we wish to purchase, and if we are rational, we allocate our income to give us the maximum satisfaction.

Scarcity

If there is a limited supply of goods or services, they are said to be in *scarce* supply, relative to the potential demand for them. The actual demand for them is limited by their price. So prices ration out goods among competing buyers. For example, the price of a Renoir painting is so high that only a few wealthy people can afford to buy them. If the price were lower there would not be enough paintings to distribute among all those who could then afford them.

1·8

a Answer the following questions on resources by stating true or false:

A nation's resources are unlimited in amount.
True/False

The supply of goods and services to satisfy human wants is usually assumed to be limited in amount
True/False

b Which of the following rations out goods and services among competing buyers, under normal circumstances?

A Prices **B** Income **C** Supply

Wants

We speak of satisfying our 'wants'. This word has in economics a special meaning. A housewife may want a ruby and diamond necklace or a mink coat. Here the word is used in its everyday sense. If the housewife were also a wealthy actress she would be able to purchase these commodities, so that 'want' now has economic significance because the desire to buy is coupled to the ability to pay. Many of us have a series of wants—a want for a sports car, a desire for books, or records—but until we have the purchasing power necessary to satisfy these wants, we cannot engage in an economic activity.

Economic and free goods

We have seen so far that people have varying wants. They satisfy these by the consumption of commodities and services. Economists frequently use the term *goods* to cover both commodities and services. (Some even use 'good' in the singular, but we will avoid this usage.)

Some goods are free. This may be because, like the air we breathe, or the rain that falls, they are gifts of nature. It may be that like the services a mother gives her child, or the favour done by one friend to another, there is no question of payment involved, and no question of scarcity either. Free goods, therefore, are not part of the subject matter of economics. However, a little consideration will show that there are very few free goods, and that these exist only under carefully defined circumstances. Sunshine is free in the Sahara, but unless you happen to live there, you must, in order to enjoy some of this free sunshine, find the fare to the Sahara and the means to keep yourself alive while in the desert. Similarly water falls from the sky as rain, but to get a pure supply to the taps where households and industrial plants can use it, local authorities in the United Kingdom spend large sums of money (£54 million in 1965), which they recoup through a water rate. Most mothers wish to care for their children themselves, but a mother who happens to be a trained doctor may find that by doing so she is losing the opportunity to earn a considerable salary, and as soon as she considers the possibility of employing a home help, she is making an economic choice. However, since housewives do not receive wages, it is impossible to make a market evaluation of their services.

Those goods which are scarce, and which are normally exchanged for money, or are valued in money, are economic goods. We may conveniently divide them into commodities and services.

Commodities

Consumer goods are commodities which are consumed in a single occasion of use. Once they have satisfied a want they cannot be used again. For example, food once eaten has gone and matches can only be lit once.

1·9

List ten examples of consumer goods in your home.

Consumer durables are goods which satisfy wants over a period of time. They may be used many times over. China and cutlery may be used several times a day and will last for years. (Disposable cups and cutlery are of course designed to be used only once and then thrown away.) Bicycles, cars and houses satisfy their owners' wants over a long period of time, even with frequent or constant use. One of the largest groups of consumer durables are electrical goods—radios, heaters, etc. Eventually these items will need replacing.

1·10

List for yourself a further five examples of consumer durables.

Producer goods are the means by which other goods are made. They are wanted, not for themselves, but for the products they help to make. The largest groups of these goods are factory buildings, plant and machinery. They constitute the capital assets belonging to people or companies, or to the government. A table in the *Blue Book* shows *Gross Fixed Capital Formation*, that is the amount invested in capital items in the past.

Another table shows the *Net Capital Stock at Current Replacement Cost* which attempts to value the stock of capital assets which exist for each year.

1·11

From the *Blue Book* one can establish that expenditure on capital in 1965 was:

	£ million
Buses and coaches	39
Other road vehicles	408

	£ million
Railway rolling stock	46
Ships	98
Aircraft	34
Plant and machinery	2 347
Dwellings	1 285
Other new buildings and works	1 937
Transfer cost of land and buildings	58

a Data as above.

i How much was invested in transport in the U.K. in 1965?

A £625 million? **B** £579 million?

ii How much was invested in buildings in the U.K. in 1965?

C £5 627 million? **D** £3 222 million?

b Which was the largest item of fixed capital formation in the U.K. in 1965?

A Transport

B Plant and machinery

C Buildings

Remember to write the correct answers as *statements* in your notes.

Services

In all modern industrial societies services form an increasingly large part of the economy. Like commodities, they may be divided into consumer and producer services. In the former group are waiters, domestic servants, doctors and dentists; in the latter group architects, production engineers, advertising consultants.

It is frequently difficult to classify services. Does the local council provide a service, with its library and swimming pool, or does it provide the use of consumer durables? When we get a suit cleaned, do we hire the services of the cleaner, or the use of his machinery? The answer to such questions is not always clear. Usually it is impossible to use the facility without the services of the operative. We cannot borrow a book without the work of the librarian.

1·12

Classify the following list under the correct headings: Consumer goods, Consumer durables, Production goods, Services.

Ice cream, a steel girder, a bus journey, 100 kg cement, a pair of trousers, a Persian carpet, 2 kg beef, hairdressing, cash withdrawal at a bank, a television set, a theatre ticket, shoes, laundry, a stick of gelignite, a sailing boat, a bottle of whisky, a refrigerator, a lathe, a bicycle, welding equipment, 4 kg flour, a crane, 2 paper cups and a paper plate, a quarry, petrol.

1·13

Look again at figure 1.6. Add together the percentages spent on alcoholic drink and tobacco. Together they represent a larger percentage than any other single item apart from food. *Ought* they to spend this amount on these items? (Have you looked up subjective evaluation in a dictionary of economic terms?) Who should answer this question?

A An economist? **B** A moralist?

C A politician?

1·14

Which of the following definitions is accurate? Write your answers as statements.

a Consumer goods:

A are goods which are cheap and which everyone buys to satisfy his needs.

B are commodities or services used directly to satisfy human wants.

C are the commodities and services people and firms want.

b A consumer durable is:

A long-lasting commodity, used many times, yielding satisfaction over a period of time.

B used once only.

c Personal abilities as economic goods:

A consist of human skills exchanged for money.

B consist of natural human skills which make each person unique.

d Services as economic goods:

A are operations designed to keep product machinery efficient.

B are non-material economic goods produced by persons or firms for the benefit of others, and are usually consumed at the moment they are produced.

e Which of the following would you include in a definition of *economic goods?*

A They must be useful; that is yield satisfaction to man.

B They must be man-made.

C They can be material or non-material.

D People desire them.

E They must be scarce relative to demand.

Production

Economists use the term production to refer to any activity which satisfies human wants and which is paid for. Unless a payment is made it is nearly impossible to measure the value of a commodity or service. Can you think of any way in which one may measure these activities without using a standard like money? In practice economists are concerned with measurable transactions, although in theory they acknowledge that a housewife satisfies the wants of her family by cooking, cleaning and caring for them. However, as she is not normally paid, her services are usually ignored when adding up the total value of a country's production, even though a housewife is a producer, just as much as is her 'working' husband.

How the average family distributed its spending in 1964

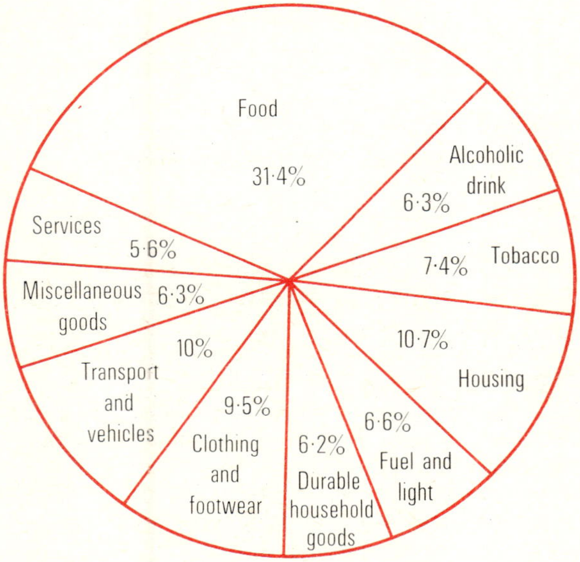

Figure 1·5

1·15

a Write true or false for each of the following statements:

- **i** Product means manufacturing goods. True/False.
- **ii** The waiter in the hotel is a producer. True/False.
- **iii** A civil servant is a producer. True/False.

b Production goods:

- **A** are anything which is used in a factory, such as machines.
- **B** consist of processes and techniques for making goods.
- **C** consist of goods used to produce further goods and services in the future.

This brings us full circle in our ideas. We saw earlier that wealth is a stock of assets which could be used for consumption purposes, or production purposes in the future. Now we have seen the origin of that wealth, namely past production. Later on the origin of production will be examined.

Production and money

Production provides a flow of goods and services. Although most people have some part to play in the process of production, for which they receive payment, this payment is in money.

Of course, people could be paid in the goods which they produce. This might be suitable for some farm workers, though it is unlikely. How would a spanner-maker find enough people willing to accept spanners in exchange for their goods? How would producers of services be paid? It is far easier to use some form of money which is a medium of exchange, acceptable to all people.

The use of money enables private individuals to amass a stock of currency if the flow of income to them is greater than the expenditure they make on consumption. In other words they can save. The savings are not necessarily held as money. Since savings are income 'not spent on consumption' they may be held as goods, for example, jewels; or as financial assets in stocks and shares; or as houses. Look again at the household budget you drew up in exercise 1·6. Did your household make any savings? If so, in what form were they held?

If savings are in money form they can be used in several ways. They can be used in exchange for goods or services whose price, in money terms, is too great to be met from current income. In other words, they can be used for future consumption, for example, a holiday, or may be used to buy a stock of goods, for example, a car, or furniture, or even a house. The stock of possessions and acquired skill, stocks and shares etc. gradually acquired by individuals is called *private wealth*. We may contrast this with libraries, hospitals, roads, harbours owned by the community as a whole. This is called *social or public wealth*.

Income

We receive income in return for our contributions to the process of producing goods and services. If we say we have insufficient income, this depends, in part, on the prices we are asked to pay for goods and services, and partly on our earnings, from whatever source. Since income of all kinds is measured in money terms, its 'real' value depends upon its purchasing power.

PURCHASING POWER OF THE POUND

taking the value as equivalent to 100p in various years. (All values shown in new pence)

1931	100p				
1938	98	100p			
1946	59	60	100p		
1956	$37\frac{1}{2}$	$38\frac{1}{2}$	64	100p	
1967	$28\frac{1}{2}$	29	48	$75\frac{1}{2}$	100p
19 · · ?					

To read this chart:
If you earned £1 per week in 1931, this would be worth only $28\frac{1}{2}$p in purchasing power in 1967 i.e. of the goods bought in 1931 for £1, you could have only $28\frac{1}{2}$p worth in 1967: try to extend this table to include this current year.

Figure 1·6

In 1968 the French Government decreed that all wages should rise by 10% and this happened. Were people any better off? What does one mean by 'better off'? Certainly the amount of money they had was greater than before. Could they buy more goods with it? That depends on the price of the goods they wanted to buy. Did these prices rise? Of course—manufacturers and shops had to find an extra 10% wages for all their employees. They put up their prices. Further, with everyone having more money to spend, profits were raised just a little, and no one noticed. Prices rose at the equivalent of 9% per annum. Were the people any better off? They were almost back where they started.

What is one's income worth? How does one measure this? Suppose the weekly family food bill is £8 now. If the prices of goods rise by 10% then the same basket of goods would cost you £8·80. In other words you would have to pay 80p more to consume the same amount of goods as before. Unless your income has gone up at least 80p then you would be worse off after the price rise in 'real' terms; that is, in terms of the bundle of purchases you can make. This distinction is a most important one. The value of your money income depends upon the prices you have to pay for goods. So the only way of measuring the value of your income is in 'real' terms.

Money income is the amount of currency, whose purchasing power varies, which you receive in return for productive effort.

Real income is the amount of goods and services which you could consume by using the money income.

1·16

a What happens to your real income as prices rise if you are on a fixed money income?

b If you have a fixed money income, and prices fall over the years, what happens to your real income?

FURTHER BASIC ECONOMIC CONCEPTS

There are a number of basic ideas in economics which will appear again and again but in different and more complex situations. These ideas are really very simple in themselves, but require careful study.

Opportunity cost

'You can't have your cake and eat it.' This is a popular version of a basic economic concept. Having chosen to spend our income on one thing we cannot use it for another. In terms of real output, having decided to use our resources to produce one thing, we cannot use the same resources to produce another.

1·17

A schoolboy has only $2\frac{1}{2}$p pocket money left. Icecreams and bars of chocolate are $2\frac{1}{2}$p each. The bus fare home is $2\frac{1}{2}$p. Which of the following actions are *not* open to him? Write the other items at the side as alternative actions which *are* open to him.

Will he be able to:

A buy icecream and a bar of chocolate?
B buy an icecream only?
C bus home and do without icecream and chocolate?
D buy chocolate only and keep the rest of his money?
E keep his pocket money and walk home?
F buy a bar of chocolate and bus home?
G buy a bar of chocolate only?

Check your answers.

Clearly he cannot both spend his money and keep it, nor can he spend it twice. This principle is called *opportunity cost:* by buying commodity x he has lost the opportunity of buying commodity y. Thus we can say that the loss of y is the opportunity cost of opting for x.

1·18

Let us look at the previous example again.

a If the boy buys chocolate what must he do without?

b If the boy buys transport home, what alternative must be foregone?

c What is the cost, in terms of foregone alternatives, of saving his money?

Frequently one finds 'letters to the Editor' in local newspapers demanding more housing, hospitals, libraries, buses, schools, etc. Where is the money to come from? The local community or council, will only raise so much by local taxation (through the rates system in the U.K.), for the council's political self-interest will limit the amount that it can tax the local electors. How does one decide how much is to be spent on housing, education or road improvements? If more is spent on housing where are economies made? Fewer schools perhaps? Fewer schools would then be the opportunity cost of more houses. (On the back of a rate-demand note, available from your local Rates Office, you will find a statement of the local rate, and the way in which it is spent.)

The same principle is true for the national accounts. If the national wealth is represented by a cake, then a larger slice for the armed forces must mean a smaller slice for, say, education or the social services. The only way to prevent cutting smaller slices is to make the cake larger and that raises problems to be discussed much later.

Opportunity cost arises because resources are limited in relation to wants.

The market

The market is another basic concept. It is any situation in which a buyer or a seller can exchange commodities or services. The buyer and seller may not even meet one another, since a letter, telephone or radio may enable them to communicate at a distance. So long as they can strike a bargain, that is an agreement, one to buy, one to sell, at an certain price, then a market exists. Very often the market may be managed by dealers and the buyer and seller arrange to exchange their products indirectly through these 'third parties'. The most familiar of these third parties are shop keepers. They act as intermediaries between producers of goods and their consumers.

The retail food market is familiar to all. This may be organised by farmers selling from roadside stalls, as many fruit growers do, or by selling through shops, or through a local 'market place' where the dealers (shopkeepers or stallholders) offer goods for sale. The price may be fixed or be open to bargaining, but in these circumstances price is normally expressed in money terms.

More involved still is the network of dealers in the commodity (wheat, tin, copper) markets, or in the market of foreign exchange in the City of London, or the Stock Exchange. Most of these use the telephone as the main means of communication. The essence of these market operations is speed.

However simple or complex the market is, it has certain features in common with other markets.

A market enables buyers (those with unsatisfied wants) to deal with sellers (those who offer goods for sale) and to agree on a mutually acceptable price (that is a rate of exchange).

But which is the buyer, and which is the seller?

Examine the following advertisements from a local newspaper:

> FOR SALE Secondhand sewing machine. Used twice. Accept £20 for quick sale. Box No. 279.
>
> FOR SALE 1971 Mini. Mint condition, only 5 000 miles. £425. Family emigrating. Box No. 352.

In each case both the advertiser and the person who answers the advertisement buys something and sells something. The person offering the sewing machine for £20 is trying to buy £20 cash with an asset which she wants *less urgently* than she wants the money. Similarly, the person answering the advertisement is buying a sewing machine which she wants *as much or more urgently* than the £20 in currency. Through the medium of the newspaper advertisement a market exists and exchange may take place. Both parties to the exchange are buyers and both are sellers. However, it is normal to call the person offering the goods for sale, a seller. The person who exchanges some form of money for the good which has been offered is called the buyer, but it is not necessarily true that the buyer offers money. He may offer other goods.

Specialisation

In most societies, however primitive, some specialisation is found. It may be that men go hunting and fishing, while women till the fields and make cloth, or it may be that one tribe makes axes, while another is noted for its fine canoes. Clearly there is some advantage to be gained from specialisation. Let us see if this advantage can be demonstrated in a precise fashion, using a simple model.

On an island, to the north-west of Scotland, live two men. John Anderson is an expert weaver of tartans. He can weave 20 m per week, but if he tries to go fishing for herring he is lucky if he can catch 100 kg per week.

Edward MacBrain, however, is an expert fisherman who can catch 250 kg per week; but, as a weaver he is not as good as John. The most he can weave is 10 m per week. These two men, working separately, spend alternate weeks on weaving and fishing. Suppose their output is recorded in the form of a production table:

	Cloth (m)	**Fish** (kg)
John	20	100
Edward	10	250
Total before specialisation, every two weeks	30	350

Would they be better off if they concentrated on the jobs at which they are more efficient, and then exchanged some of each other's products? At which job is each most efficient? While these figures give a fairly obvious answer, the working below will help you deal with the later exercises and test questions.

should specialise we must find out at which job each man is most efficient. Efficiency here means output per man per week. The relative efficiency of John compared with Edward is calculated by expressing John's production as a percentage of Edward's production, and vice versa, as follows:
John's relative efficiency at weaving =

$$\frac{20}{10} \times \frac{100}{1} = 200\%$$

So John's efficiency is 200% more at weaving than Edward.
John's relative efficiency at fishing =

$$\frac{100}{250} \times \frac{100}{1} = 40\%$$

So John's efficiency is only 40% of Edward's efficiency at fishing.
Edward's relative efficiency at weaving =

$$\frac{10}{20} \times \frac{100}{1} = 50\%$$

So Edward's efficiency is 50% of John's efficiency at weaving.
Edward's relative efficiency at fishing =

$$\frac{250}{100} \times \frac{100}{1} = 250\%$$

So Edward's efficiency is 250% of John's efficiency at fishing.

We have now shown that John is the most efficient at weaving and Edward at fishing. Now we can ask the first question again, 'Would it pay to specialise in the production of the goods at which they are most efficient?'

Stage 2 To find the gain in output compare the total output every two weeks before and after specialisation:

	Cloth (m)	**Fish** (kg)
Total before specialisation	30	350
Total after specialisation	(2 x 20) 40	(2 x 250) 500
Net gain from specialisation	10	150

Between them they have 10 m extra of cloth and 150 kg of extra fish every two weeks.

Stage 3 At what rate (price) will the goods be exchanged assuming that neither has any money.

	Cloth (m)	**Fish** (kg)
John	20	100
Edward	10	250

Every two weeks John could weave on his own 20 m cloth or catch 100 kg fish. That is a ratio of $\frac{20}{100} = 1{\cdot}5$. The opportunity cost of 5 kg fish is therefore 1 m cloth. So John would not consider giving Edward more than 1 m cloth in exchange for each 5 kg of fish, because he could catch 5 kg fish himself, if he sacrificed weaving 1 m cloth.

On the other hand Edward could, on his own, weave 10 m of cloth or catch 250 kg of fish every two weeks, that is a ratio of $\frac{10}{250} = 1{\cdot}25$. For Edward the opportunity cost of 1 m cloth is 25 kg fish.

Neither man will accept less than the opportunity cost of the product in which he specialises, so John will not give Edward more than 5 m of cloth for 25 kg of fish, and Edward will not accept from John less than 1 m of cloth for 25 kg of fish.

The rate of exchange must lie somewhere between 5 m and 1 m of cloth per 25 kg of fish. The better bargainer John is, or the more Edward wants cloth, the nearer the rate will be to 1 m of cloth per 25 kg of fish. Each party is better off after specialisation, if trade follows at a rate of exchange which is greater than the opportunity cost for each person involved.

Now you have seen how we start to work out the principles of the specialisation of labour.

1·19

Data: Two farmers are neighbours. Both grow potatoes. Percy makes excellent whisky from his crop but only has a few bags of potatoes for sale. Fred is not so good at brewing and distilling whisky, but he has more potatoes for sale.

Weekly output	Bottles whisky	Bags potatoes
Percy	6	4
Fred	2	8

a What is the relative efficiency of Percy compared to Fred in distilling whisky?

A 300% **B** 150%

b By how much would the total supply of bags of potatoes rise every two weeks if Fred specialises in potato production, and Percy specialises in whisky distilling?

C 200% **D** 33⅓%

Suppose that one of the two people concerned is more efficient in producing *both* goods. Would it still pay to specialise?

On the south coast of Cornwall live two fishermen. Peter—who is an inshore fisherman—and James who is an offshore fisherman. By fishing for mackerel and lobster on alternate days they catch:

Daily output before specialisation	Mackerel	Lobster
Peter	40	10
James	35	2
Total	75	12

Let us check on their relative efficiencies first. How efficient is Peter compared with James?

(a) in catching mackerel $\frac{40}{35} \times \frac{100}{1} = 114{\cdot}3\%$

(b) in catching lobster $\frac{10}{2} \times \frac{100}{1} = 500\%$

So Peter's relative efficiency is greater in lobsters. How efficient is James compared with Peter?

(c) in catching mackerel $\frac{35}{40} \times \frac{100}{1} = 87{\cdot}5\%$

(d) in catching lobster $\frac{2}{10} \times \frac{100}{1} = 20\%$

So James' relative *in*efficiency is least in catching mackerel.

If each man specialises in catching the fish where his relative efficiency is greatest (or relative inefficiency is least), then both men will be better off.

Daily output after specialisation	Mackerel	Lobster
Peter	—	20
James	70	—
New total	70	20
Gain	−5	+8

You will see that there are fewer mackerel caught but rather more lobsters caught. Is the sacrifice of 5 mackerel worth the gain of 8 lobsters?

From the table above you will see that Peter may catch 10 lobsters at the opportunity cost of 40 mackerel. This gives him a personal rate of exchange of 1:4. Similarly James has a personal rate of exchange of 1:17½. If Peter can trade with James at a rate exceeding 1:4 (say 1:6) he will be better off, but however strong his buying power, he will not be able to persuade James to give a better rate than 1:17½, for at this point James would be better off catching both products in his own time.

The minimum rate of exchange each man will accept is shown by the personal opportunity cost, or rate of exchange without specialisation.

Speciali ation in a more complex society

So far we have looked at three simple situations in which specialisation has taken place. These situations are called 'economic models'. The construction of any such model involves making assumptions about a situation in order to simplify it. This is done so that one can try to find out what are the basic principles which affect economic society.

Among other things, we have assumed that people's ability to produce goods and services varies, and so affects their efficiency in production relative to others. This is an assumption we will continue to make. We have also assumed that 'personal interest' of a selfish nature will dominate decisions about the rate of exchange, which although a valid assumption for most of the people for most of the time, is not always true. People do think of others, and this affects the way in which they behave.

People's behaviour, and therefore society's, is much more complex than our models describe, but we can increase our understanding of economics step by step by using economic models. We could, for example, easily construct a model with 6 or 7 different products, but the principle would be the same. People specialise in the production of goods and services in which they are relatively most efficient, or have the greatest comparative advantage. However in real life, the working of the principle of specialisation of labour is subject to severe modification by tradition, trade practices, safety and training requirements and many other factors which people consider to be more important than mathematical nicety.

Specialisation—the division of labour

People have always specialised in one occupation or another. This characteristic has been used in a modern industrial society to divide jobs into a series of operations in order to gain advantages. What are these advantages?

i Saving of time

By concentrating on one task a person usually gains in skill and speed. If he were required to do two or three tasks, he would have to readjust continually to the demands of each task, and therefore be less efficient. Thus a throat specialist can extract tonsils more quickly than a general practitioner.

ii Increase in output

In the early days of the motor industry, car engines were assembled individually. Perhaps only one man put together all the pieces in each engine, fitting and adjusting as he went. For example, Royce, a partner in Rolls-Royce, built his own relatively simple engine in a small workshop in Hulme, Manchester. Today the engine of a modern vehicle consists of components made by different firms all over the country, and assembled by hundreds of men, each specialising on one small task, such as fitting the flywheel. It is no longer a case of one car a month, but rather one every thirty seconds.

iii Improvement in quality

As each person specialises in a small range of activities he becomes an expert. 'Practice makes perfect'. A large firm may gain a better quality of management by employing experts; specialists in finance, production, sales, and labour relations.

iv Use of natural abilities

People are individual and have different talents and interests. They are more productive if they are happy in their work employing their abilities. Picasso can only be a full time artist because someone else produces his food and clothing.

People who are interested in their work tend to develop new ideas, or invent new processes or products. What kind of job do you think suits your ability?

v Reduction in cost per unit of output

Suppose a dentist who has been trained for five years sees 1 000 patients in his first year in practice, and also acts as his own secretary and receptionist. Assume that it cost £10 000 to train him. What is the cost per patient of training the dentist? Now, suppose he employs a secretary and a receptionist and sees 2 000 patients in the first year. What is the cost of training him per patient in the first year? It has dropped from £10 to £5 and the saving will probably pay for the wages of his assistants.

The three factors of production specialise to reduce costs in the following ways.

People are more productive when less time is wasted changing from one occupation to another. They learn to work faster, and thus the cost of employing them per unit of output is lower.

Land can be used in a specialised way in order to reduce costs. Farmers will plant their crops on the land most suited to them.

Capital in the form of specialised machinery is used. A yellow line painting machine is specific for this task. A passenger bus is specialised, and although it presumably could be designed as a multi-purpose vehicle, carrying bags of coal as well as people, we accept that separate buses and lorries are more useful than multi-purpose vehicles.

Consequently the average costs of producing every item are lower when the factors of production are specialised.

1·20

Try to find examples of each of the seven advantages of specialisation in your school or college. Write a brief explanation of each.

Disadvantages of division of labour

If we are to concentrate on one particular job, then we need to know what the job involves and whether we have the ability and kind of personality to do it. We have to choose correctly, for both a lack of ability and a lack of 'job-satisfaction' will result in unhappiness for ourselves, and low productivity for the economy.

Over-specialisation reduces our alternative opportunities for employment; highly specialised skills are of no use in other occupations.

Ability and personality are both important in making any kind of success in a job, and affect our economic worth to those employing us. If the firm has trained the wrong candidate, then the firm has incurred the opportunity cost of not training the right man.

Specialisation in some factories has reached the point where unimaginative people are preferred for simple repetitive tasks, as their attention is less likely to wander through boredom. Progressive employers usually try to avoid keeping persons for long periods on boring jobs, lest their interest and efficiency suffer.

Retraining and adaptability

There are two types of specialisation of labour which you should consider at this point.

Specialisation in depth. This kind of specialisation leads to a deeper understanding and a concentration on narrow fields of knowledge. This requires longer training for specialists, from four years at least for teachers to ten for medical consultants.

1·21

Is the longer training compensated by a higher salary? Find out the salary ranges and the period of training required for each of the following groups:

a teachers **b** architects **c** solicitors
d general practitioners (family doctors)
e medical consultants

The Burnham Scale for teachers is published; for the others salary scales are given in the advertisements in the quality daily press, or your careers' adviser should be able to help you.

Specialisation by process. The second kind of specialisation tends to make work simpler so that manual or clerical operations are eventually taken over by machines or computers. This tends to eliminate almost any form of training and requires adaptability from workers. It is currently estimated that most people now leaving school can expect to lead at least three different occupations during their working life.

The first kind of specialisation usually requires adaptability and retraining only occasionally.

1·22

List the advantages and disadvantages of specialisation, with brief notes on each to help your revision.

Exchange

Where specialisation exists man is no longer independent of others. The satisfaction of wants then requires the mutual exchange of goods.

Simple exchange—barter

'If you enter your car in the rally, John, then I will navigate', says Bill. This is a familiar example of exchange on a personal or family basis. Let us examine it more closely.

John		Bill	
Wants	Has	Wants	Has
Navigator	Car	Use of car	Ability to navigate

We can see that there is an important condition necessary for barter. Each person must want what the other person has to give and be prepared to give what the other wants. This principle is called *the double coincidence of wants*.

Multilateral exchange

'Multilateral' means many-sided. In a barter system involving many people, you have to solve the problem of double coincidence of wants, and end up with the right amount of the commodity required to exchange with the amount of the commodity you want. This may be shown by the following exercise.

1·23

In a Pennine village, cut off by snow, people cannot reach a bank to draw cash. They have to resort to bartering various items. Each person is identified by a number. The surplus of each is labelled 'S' and the item he wants to obtain is labelled 'W'.

1	**S**	7 kg potatoes	**5**	**S**	7 kg sugar
	W	Secondhand snowshoes		**W**	20 kg coal
2	**S**	Bottle of wine	**6**	**S**	2 kg tea
	W	A shovel		**W**	7 kg sugar
3	**S**	20 kg coal	**7**	**S**	4 kg chocolate
	W	Bottle of wine		**W**	7 kg potatoes
4	**S**	A shovel	**8**	**S**	Secondhand snowshoes
	W	4 kg chocolate		**W**	2 kg tea

How can **1** get the secondhand snowshoes?

Exercise 1·23 will show the difficulties of bartering and in most advanced economies it is usually confined within the family or among friends.

International barter sometimes occurs; for example, in a trade agreement with Russia in 1968, the U.K. exported steam turbines for electricity generating plant. In part payment a number of dumper trucks were received, which proved useful for building sections of the M6 motorway.

Exchange with money

When exchange takes place through the medium of money, there must be a price agreed between buyer and seller, this may be agreed before the time of sale, or fixed at the point of sale. Let us examine some common methods of arriving at a price.

Haggling

If you see a cutlass in a junk shop, without a price on it, you may ask the price. The amount the shop-keeper quotes will depend on what he thinks you will pay. (He may say 'Make me an offer.') Both of you will play a sort of psychological game before arriving at an agreed price, which will presumably give the shop-keeper a profit, and satisfy you. This process is called haggling, and is interesting as a simple single buyer and seller market procedure for setting a price.

1·24

How much would you pay for a cutlass? List the factors that would influence the price that you would pay.

However, in an area where there are many junk shops, and therefore sellers, you will be able to 'shop around' for the lowest price. Similarly, each shop-keeper will look for the most eager buyer.

In the Covent Garden or Smithfield type of market, it is generally found that when the retailers are less keen to buy, say, salad vegetables during a cool damp spell in summer, the prices fall. This is because the wholesalers in the market compete to sell off their stock before it rots.

The more urgently the sellers want to get rid of their goods the lower the price they will tend to accept. So the greater the competition between sellers the lower the prices tend to be. Under perfect market conditions (see S5) one single price acceptable to both buyers and sellers will prevail throu-out the market at any given time.

Auctions

The essence of an auction is that people make public offers (bids) in currency for the goods they want. The person offering the highest price gets the goods.

Normally, the price starts from a minimum which is set by the auctioneer. The person bidding the highest amount buys the goods, provided that his bid is above the 'reserve' or minimum price set by the seller or auctioneer.

Offers at fixed prices

This is the normal system in most Western countries; the price is stated and either you accept that price or do without the commodity.

Until the 1960s, Resale Price Maintenance (RPM) gave manufacturers the legal right to determine the retail price at which their goods were sold, giving the traders a fixed rate of profit. Price cutting would have made it unprofitable for small shops to continue to sell the goods and in these cases large numbers of small shops were the most important market for the manufacturers. It was argued that if the high volume of sales were lost, costs of production would rise, and so, then, prices would also tend to rise. Retailers liked RPM because it kept up their profit margins. If price cutting was allowed in retail shops, manufacturers were afraid that the number and geographical distribution of their retail outlets would be reduced by price competition. (For further explanations see *Satellites Monopolies and Restrictive Practices* and *Retail Trades and Distribution*.

1·25

Match the definitions to the terms:

A Offers at fixed prices	**1** The commodities are sold to the person offering the highest price.
B Haggling	**2** The money rate of exchange is fixed, with no opportunity for bargaining.
C An auction	**3** Several people make intermediate exchanges to achieve the double coincidence of wants.
D Multilateral barter	**4** Commodities or services are exchanged directly without the use of money.
E Simple barter	**5** The money rate of exchange is open for bargaining by offer.

By now you known that people have *wants* which they *satisfy* by consuming *goods* which they *exchange* with one another. The goods are made by *specialists* who depend upon exchange to obtain the things they want. You also know that the *price* of goods is the rate of exchange of money for goods, and that prices may be settled in various ways.

1·26

Who will be affected when the prices of goods change?

A The buyers only
B The sellers only
C Both buyers and sellers.

How buyers are affected by small price changes

Assume that you are a motorist with a fixed monthly income. How would you react to the price of petrol going up? Probably you would try to reduce the quantity you bought. Suppose you bought 30 litres per head and now decide to reduce your consumption by 1 litre. What is the importance to economists of your decision not to buy this last litre? Because it is the first litre you would do without when prices rise, it is in a sense the litre which is *least important* to you. This is the marginal unit of petrol. It is the first unit which you will cease to buy if price per unit rises.

The margin occurs where there is a change by one unit in an economic aggregate. A marginal consumer is one who either just juys a commodity, or just does not. Hence a marginal buyer is one who stops buying when price rises. What is important is *whether the units are marginal*. Thus if a person buys 10 litres of petrol, the 10th litre is the marginal litre. The previous 9 litres are *intra-marginal*, and the 11th and subsequent litres are *extra-marginal*. The margin moves as prices and consumers' preferences change. Therefore, if the price falls and the consumer buys 11 litres, the 11th litre is now the marginal litre.

The margin is one of the central concepts of economics and you shoud make sure that you thoroughly understand it.

The demand curve

As the price of a commodity rises, we probably buy less, and beyond a certain price do not buy at all. Consider the purchase of cream. You decide how much to buy according to the importance cream has to you (your scale of preferences), the price of the cream, and the opportunity cost of buying cream at any particular price. You have a

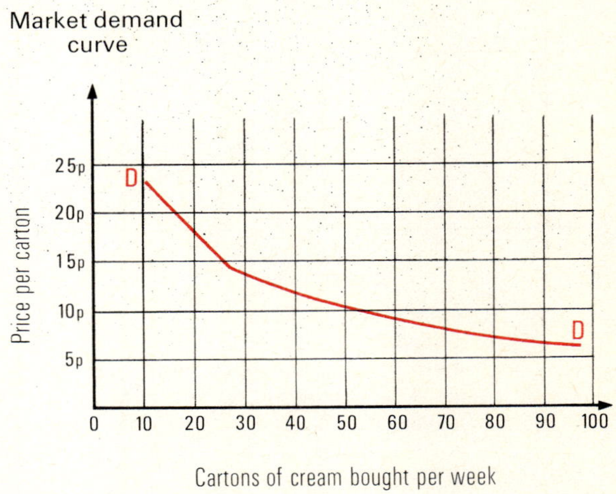

Figure 1·7

demand schedule: the amounts that you will buy at various prices.

If we take a group of people in the same market, and add together their demand schedules, we have a *market demand schedule*.

If we were to collect information from a group of housewives in a village, we might find that one housewife who does a great deal of fancy pastry-making always buys more cream than others. For example, even at 25p a carton she buys 10 cartons a week, though her normal purchase is 20 cartons a week at 10p each. Her demand is the amount she actually buys at any given price.

Her neighbours are not so wealthy, nor so keen on pastry-making. Nevertheless, the local dairy knows that as a whole, the village will buy:

Demand Schedule

20 cartons @ 20p a carton
30 cartons @ 15p a carton
45 cartons @ 12p a carton
60 cartons @ 10p a carton
100 cartons @ 7½p a carton

1·27

From the demand schedule plot your own graph like figure 1·17, showing how many cartons are bought at any given price. (To draw and read a demand curve see satellite book *Arithmetical and Statistical Methods*.

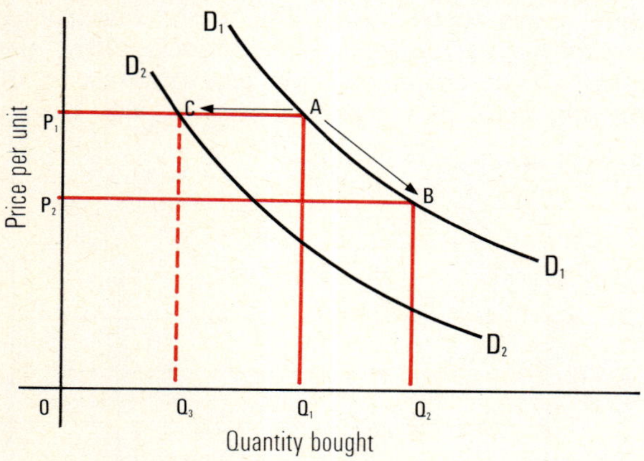

From A (Price P_1, Quantity Q_1) to B (Price P_2, Quantity Q_2) is movement along a curve, but from A to C (Price always P_1, but Quantity Q_1 to Q_3) requires a shift of the curve from D_1D_1 to D_2D_2

Figure 1·8

The line DD in the diagram is called a *market demand curve* and shows *the quantity of the economic commodity or service bought at each price in a given period of time*. More is usually bought when the market price is low and less is usually bought when the market price is high.

This is the definition of demand, so that a change in demand means that the whole schedule (and the curve drawn for it) will be different. *Students should be careful to distinguish between a movement along the curve (i.e. a change in the quantity demanded as price alters) and a change in the position of the curve itself that is, a change in demand (see S8).*

1·28

Data: your graph of Market Demand Curve.

a How many cartons would be brought if the market price was 11p per carton?
A 56 **B** 42

b If the Dairy wants people to buy 70 cartons per week, at what price should it offer cream for sale?
C 19p **D** 8p

c If the price is 10p, which unit is the marginal unit?
E The 50th **F** The 60th

d At a price of 10p, how many units are intra-marginal?
G 59 **H** 60

You can see that at any market price there will be consumers, who will marginally reduce their consumption or drop out of the market (that is, stop buying) as soon as the price rises.

You should not read on unless you are absolutely satisfied that you understand the concept of the margin. Check your understanding by using the satellite *Arithmetical and Statistical Methods*.

For those who prefer a mathematical explanation, the concept of the margin can be illustrated by the following diagram.

Number of units purchased:

M
1, 2, ... n, n+1, n+2, . .
M

The line MM represents the margin, and n is the marginal unit, the last unit bought. The unit n+1 can also be considered a marginal unit, in the sense that it is the first to be added to our purchases if price falls. Units before n are intra-marginal. Units after n (or n+1) are extra-marginal.

How a change in price affects producers and sellers

You will have to read S11 to understand the whole of this problem. At this stage we will simply say that under most circumstances (though not all) more of a commodity will be offered for sale when prices rise, and less when prices fall. This is a rather over-simplified statement. The main point which we need to make here is that *the term 'supply' means the 'quantity' offered for sale at various prices in a given period of time*. The usual graph of quantity offered for sale plotted against prices, looks like this:

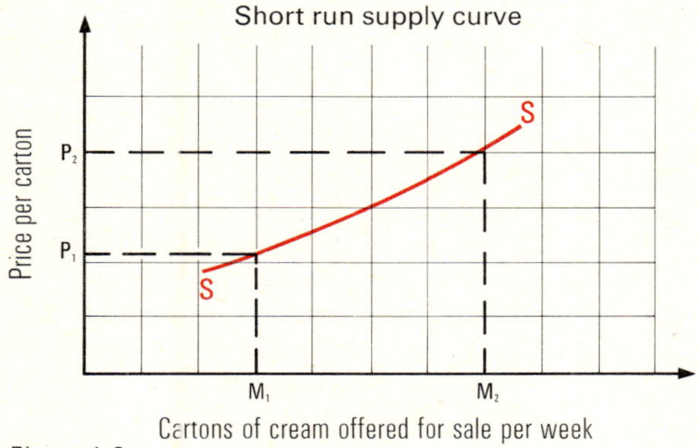

Figure 1·9

If the price in the market rises from OP_1 to OP_2, then the quantity offered for sale will extend from OM_1 to OM_2 and vice versa.

Supply and demand

The important thing to remember here is that there is no such thing as 'the supply of' or 'the demand for' economic goods except in relation to price. Both the quantity offered for sale and the amount bought *vary according to the price* in the market.

The amount sold varies with price, and so does the quantity offered for sale: *the supply schedule of a commodity shows the quantity offered for sale at various prices. The demand schedule for a commodity shows the quantity which would be bought at various prices.*

Market price

Figure 1·7 shows us a market demand curve, and figure 1·9 shows us a short-run supply curve. If we now superimpose the two curves on the same grid, we can determine *market price*, which is that at which the amount of a commodity or service which is offered by sellers equals the amount which will be accepted by the buyers. (This is an important concept in economics, and the reader is warned that there are assumptions made which will be explored fully in later study sections.)

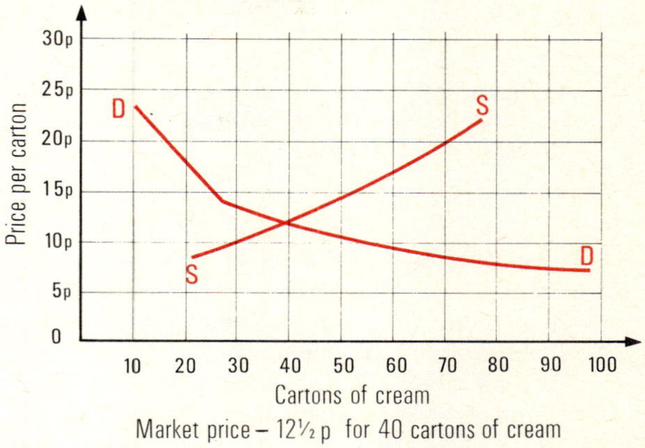

Figure 1·10

1·29

With this book closed, define the terms 'supply' and 'demand'. Check your answer before going any further.

We have seen (in exercise 1·7) that we all have wants, which we may or not be able to satisfy. The study of what our wants are and why we have them is the field of the psychologist and market researcher. Once we have some resources at our disposal and are able to take action to satisfy our wants we are in the field of economics. This was expressed by Lord Robbins, when he wrote 'economics is the science which studies human behaviour as a relationship between ends and scarce means which have alternative uses'. In other words he assumed that economic goods are scarce relative to wants ('ends'). The economic problem is how to allocate scarce goods ('means') in the most satisfying way.

As a matter of convenience economics has been divided into various branches which we will encounter in the succeeding study sections:

Micro-economics studies how the individual producer and consumer attempt to solve their economic problems.

Macro-economics studies the relations between national totals of employment, incomes and production.

Econometrics studies the workings of the economy using statistical techniques.

ANSWERS

1·1

Correct **B**

For the latest figures see *Whitaker's Almanac* or the *Annual Abstract of Statistics,* published by H.M.S.O. —available in most libraries.

1·2

a Correct **C**, **E**. Mistaken **A**, **B**, **D** consumer goods.

b **i** Wealth consists of assets held by consumers and producers. Capital is that part of wealth held for future production.

ii Wealth is a *stock* of assets. Income is a *flow.*

iii Write down your personal income and personal stock of wealth.

1·3

Exercise on personal income and expenditure table: totals must balance because any income not spent on consumption is recorded as savings, so expenditure must equal income.

1·4

Bar diagram and pie chart for 1 3.

1·5

According to data.

1·6

Home expenditure details on the same basis as table in the National Income *Blue Book.* Individual and Group Charts.

1·7

List ten *desired* items.

1·8

a Correct **B**. Mistaken **A**: resources *are* limited. Correct **C**. Mistaken **D**: supply *is* limited.

b Correct **A**. Mistaken **B**: any income is enough if prices are low. Mistaken **C**: the supply sets a limit, it does not *allocate*.

1·9

Own list.

1·10

Own list.

1·11

a iA iiD

b C

1·12

Physical economic goods		Non-material economic goods	
Consumer Goods	Consumer Durables	Production	Services
Ice cream 2 kg beef Whisky Petrol 4 kg flour Paper plate and cups	Television set Pair of trousers Bicycle 2 left shoes Sailing boat Persian carpet Refrigerator	Crane 100 kg cement Stick of gelignite Quarry Lathe Welding equipment Steel girder	Bus journey Cash withdrawal at a Bank Hairdressing Laundry Theatre ticket

1:13

If you think that this high expenditure would lead to a loss in production then perhaps the economist should try to answer the question. If you think that the term 'ought' concerns morals then the moralist should answer. If you think that politics is about the well being of people, including economic factors as well as morals, then perhaps it is the politician who should seek to answer this question.

1·14

a Correct **B.** Mistaken **A**: consumer goods are not necessarily cheap. Mistaken **C**: there are goods other than consumer goods which are wanted.

b Correct **A.** Mistaken **B**: An insufficient definition.

c Correct **A.** Mistaken **B**: these are not necessarily economic goods unless exchanged for money.

d Correct **B.** Mistaken **A. C.** Mistaken **B**: natural goods can have economic value.

e Correct **A, C, D, E.**

1·15

a **i** False. The satisfaction of want involves distribution of goods and provision of services, as well as manufacturing.

ii True
iii True

b Correct **C**, mistaken **A**: factories are not the only places in which production takes place. Mistaken **B**: processes and techniques are not physical goods.

1·16

a Real income falls.
b Real income rises.

1·17

Possible **B, C, E, G.** Not possible **A, D, F.**

1·18

a Icecream, or bus journey.
b Icecream, or chocolate.
c Goods and services which are not bought.

1·19

a Correct **A**. Mistaken **B**: you have taken the wrong ratios.
b Correct **D.** Mistaken **C.**

1·20

Your own list: metalwork room, art teacher, etc.

1·21

Personal research.

1·22

See text.

1·23

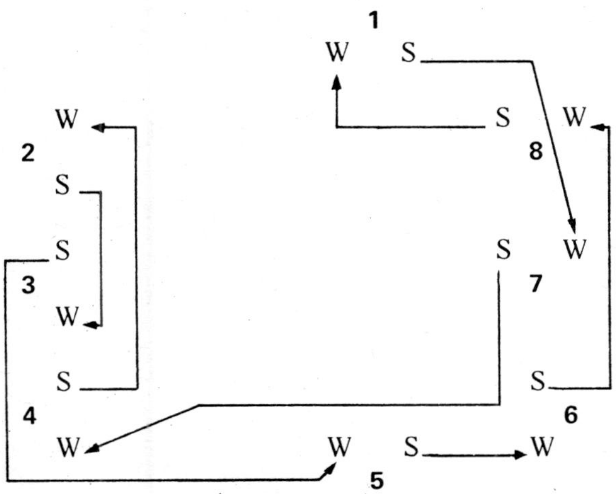

1·24

Price—variable:
Factors:
(a) Condition of cutlass (estimated market value)
(b) Amount of money you have (income)
(c) Your interest in old weapons (scale of preferences)
(d) Opportunity cost of acquiring cutlass.

1·25

Match the definitions to the terms: **A2; B5; C1; D3; E4.**

1·26

Correct **C.** Mistaken **A, B.**

1·27

a Yes
b Yes

1·28

a Correct **B**: 42 cartons @ 11p.
b Correct **C**: 70 cartons @ 8p.
c Correct **F**.
d 59 are *within* the margin, the 60th carton is *on* the margin.

1·29

Demand for a commodity or service at any time is the amount of it that will be bought at each given price.

The supply of a commodity or service at any given time is the amount of it that will be offered for sale at each given price. Note that the *quantity demanded* is the actual amount that will be bought at a given price. Likewise the *quantity supplied* is the amount that will be supplied at a given price.

The nation's assets are used to produce economic goods. The people who produce the commodities and services are paid wages which form their money income. The income may be spent either on consuming goods or may be saved. Let us assume for the time being that the resources not used up in producing goods and services for consumption

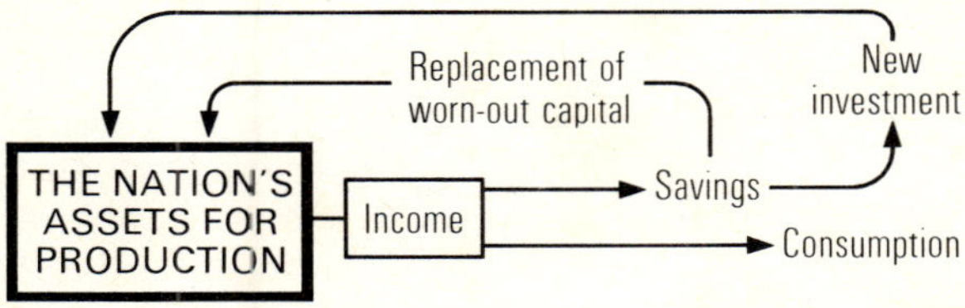

Figure 2·1

may be used to make producers goods, either to replace worn-out capital, or to add to the existing stock of capital goods and that this accounts for that part of expenditure not consumed, i.e. saved.

For any production to take place, even in the most primitive circumstances one must have the land, the human beings, and the time to do the work.

Primitive production—land, labour and capital

At some stage primitive man turned from being a hunter to being a farmer. To do this required some seed and a hoe to till the soil. To obtain seed necessitated spending time collecting ripe seed from wild grain, storing it, tilling the ground and sowing the seed. Having made a hoe, primitive man had an enormous advantage—he could plant and cultivate his crops properly—but someone had to spend time collecting suitable materials to make the hoe and that involved a further opportunity cost.

Making the hoe and saving up seeds used labour which could have been used to collect seeds for immediate consumption, but the hoe saves weeks of work collecting wild grain, by making cultivation possible.

This agriculture required more than just land and labour. It required 'saved up' labour in the form of the hoe.

The hoe is capital; it enables even more food to be produced although it cannot be eaten. It can be used again and again to produce further wealth (grain) in the future. Production of goods and services requires therefore three resources, or *factors of production.*

Labour — the human resource.
Land — the natural resource.
Capital — the man made resource.

It is essential to remember that production usually involves the joint use of these three factors. In order to achieve this there is a fourth factor, *enterprise*, or management. Without its organisation the other factors of production would lie idle and unused, as explained later in the section.

Labour as a factor of production

Every person is unique, in character, appearance and abilities. When regarded as productive resources, people provide two assets; physical work, that is, muscle power, and mental or intellectual power. Everyone uses some of each asset, but in varying degrees. As technology changes, then production processes seem likely to demand more and more thinking power and less physical strength.

The quality of labour depends, it would seem, partly on inherited intelligence, partly on home background, both physical and emotional aspects, and partly on the provision and quality of educational opportunities and how well these opportunities are grasped.

Labour may also produce the non-material economic goods, i.e. services, as well as the physical goods of which one normally thinks.

Manpower for G.B. (i.e. excluding N. Ireland)

	1958	1967	Current Year
Total employed	23 129	24 440	
Men	15 303	15 609	
Women	7 826	8 831	
Wholly unemployed	368	466	
Vacancies	213	281	

All figures are 000's

This information is taken from *The British Economy in Figures* (Lloyd's Bank).

2·1

Plot the data above in the form of a diagram like figure 2·2.

The working population has to support the total population. This does not mean that all the rest do not work; large amounts of work are done voluntarily and go unrecorded, and so are not included in the statistics. However, our standard of living depends to some degree on these unmeasured activities, so one should not ignore them altogether.

Every unit of labour is unique. Everyone is different, not only in appearance but in ability, in the extent to which ability is used, in character and so on. Some people work hard, some prefer less work and more leisure. It is of economic importance that no one is a perfect substitute for another person. If one worker leaves a firm, he can probably be replaced, but the new man will not be quite the same, for he may be more skilled or less hard working.

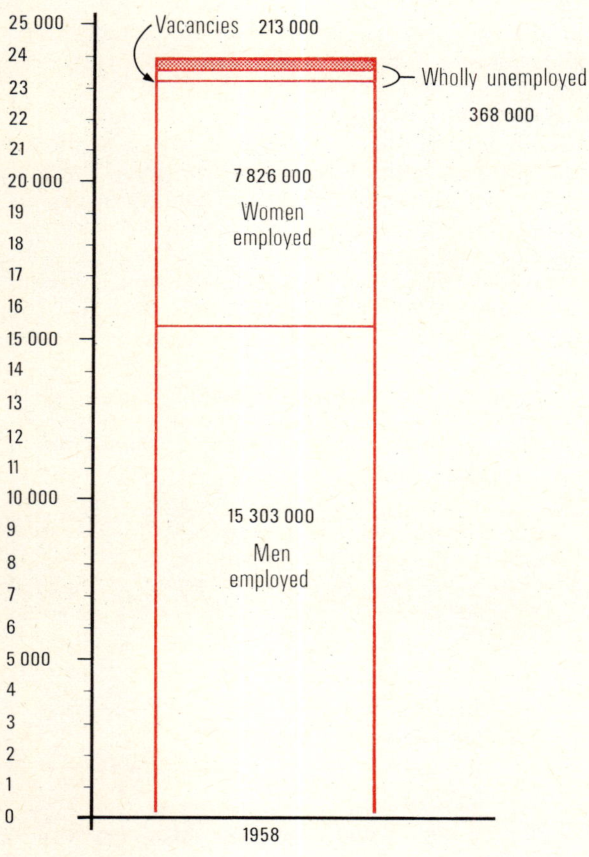

Figure 2 2

Untrained people are not substitutes for trained people. This is why, in figure 2·2, there were in 1967, 281 000 vacant jobs and 466 000 unemployed. The vacancies were unfilled because people are not perfect substitutes for one another. If an employer needs, say, an extra weaver, he cannot hire an unemployed miner without incurring training costs. Moreover, vacant jobs are also due to geographical and occupational immobility.

Regular use

Labour deteriorates through lack of use. Periods of unemployment depress mankind, for psychologically people seem to need work, if only because it shows that they are valued as people. Labour is most efficient when in regular use, for after a period of unemployment skills may have to be relearned. (See satellite *Industrial Relations*.)

Mobility of labour

Labour is said to be mobile when people change jobs. Land and capital may be used for alternative purposes without considering anything other than technical difficulties, but obliging people to change jobs involves personal problems. The need to change jobs will inevitably occur because any productive process is subject to change. The market may demand more or less than the present production level at current prices. That may mean using more or less labour somewhere in the process; if labour is required in new places then people must move, since people and their labour are inseparable. Financial or other incentives are used to induce labour to be mobile and to respond to changing economic circumstances. Resistance to mobility of labour arises from such causes as cost of movement, language barriers, social inertia (the desire to stay within one's familiar community) and immigration laws.

Effort and reward

To increase output you can either increase the number employed, or pay extra for extra work done, but if you say that more pay will produce more work, you are assuming that pay and effort are directly related. Some of the circumstances which affect this relationship are outlined below.

i The opportunity cost of work. The opportunity cost of working a longer day is the leisure time workers might otherwise have. If the earnings from the extra time worked are worth more to the worker than the leisure foregone, then more overtime work will be done.

Certain influences may make leisure time more or less attractive compared with the potential earnings. You may have a second, 'spare-time' job which will pay better than overtime. Engineers may do car repairs in their back-yard, teachers may teach in evening classes and so on. The opportunity for leisure enjoyment may be limited so that the opportunity cost of overtime work is minimal. On the other hand, local entertainments and the proximity of enjoyable leisure facilities could tend to make the opportunity cost of overtime work higher than the extra earnings offered.

ii Working harder or faster. Instead of working for a longer time you may be able to earn more by working harder or faster, so increasing your output, but, of course, there are physical and mental limits to this. Most people will find some level of maximum sustainable effort, and extra pay will induce extra effort only occasionally. Working circumstances will set upper and lower limits to one's work. For example, if you are on a production line, although you must keep up with the work load, you cannot work any faster than the moving line permits. A desire to remain acceptable to other members of a working group is understandable; in some jobs social conformity is an important factor in setting the level of effort made.

iii Hidden rest. If the work is boring, and most unautomated routine manufacturing is, then workers may take 'hidden rests'. Neither they, nor their management, may be aware of the extent of this. Unnecessary cleaning and readjustment of equipment will undoubtedly lower the rate of production.

iv Job satisfaction. The question of job satisfaction is increasingly being recognised as important in all kinds of work. If the work yields a continuing sense of pride, and a feeling that it matters to the boss, then the level of effort made may well be quite out of proportion to the pay earned; the effectiveness of the organisers' and administrators' work may also be greater.

v Social morale. The results of community events may be reflected in production levels. In one English town where the majority of workers is employed by a single large firm, it was discovered that 'Monday morning blues', following a defeat of the town football team seriously reduced production, to the extent that it paid the firm to offer financial support to the club to recruit better players and reduce the number of defeats. The opportunity cost of supporting the team was less in terms of lost production.

vi Taxation. Whatever other influences play a part in the relation between effort and reward, taxation is certainly important. The total earnings before tax is called *gross earnings*. After deduction of tax (sometimes about 33% of gross pay) and other items you are left with *net earnings*. If the net earnings of an extra hour's work is judged to be too small, then the foregone leisure may be of greater value than the net extra earnings.

These factors reflect the human character of labour. Other influences which affect efficiency of working are discussed in S9.

Offer curve of labour

If we plot on a graph the offer or individual supply curve of labour, we often get a curious shape. The reasons indicated above suggest why the offer curve is this shape.

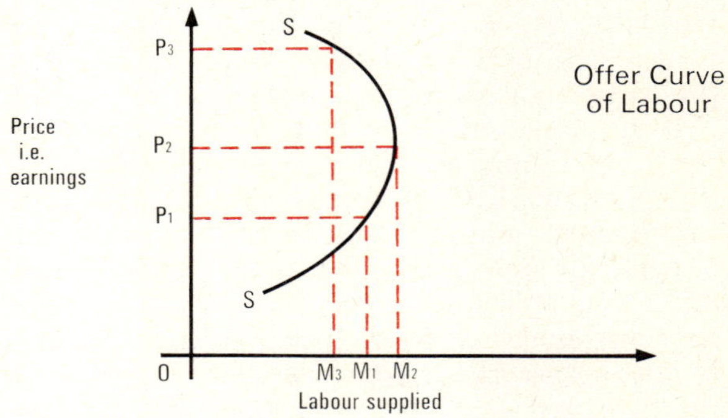

Figure 2·3

The curve SS shows the amount of effort offered by labour to employers at various prices (levels of earnings). If you start at the level of earnings OP_1 then OM_1 of effort will be offered for sale. More and more time or effort will be offered in return for higher earnings up to a point OM_2. At this level OP_2 is earned. Despite higher earnings less effort will be offered by labour at any earnings above OP_2. The maximum effort—OM_2 is set by physical and mental limits, and the opportunity cost of work.

At the earnings level above OP_2 the customary standard of living may be maintained with less effort. The leisure foregone may be increasingly important and the high earnings will allow greater leisure activities. Any more effort may be subject to tax dis-incentive effects.

For these and other reasons discussed above the offer curve may slope backwards above a certain level of earnings (OP_2). Technical progress may permit a shorter working week, (OM_3), at a much higher level of earnings, (OP_3), due to automation and improved management and organisation.

Wages and the supply of labour

Malthus wrote in 1798 that if the poor were paid higher wages they would have larger families and so increase the supply of labour available. This would depress wages, people would then starve to death and the supply of labour would be reduced. Wages would eventually rise again and the process would be repeated. In all 'western industrialised' countries this pattern of events has not occurred and as the standard of living has risen the average size of family has tended to fall.

There is a distinction between the total employable population and those actually working. Given the existing employed population, wages can normally only be raised if productivity per worker is increased, of if the suppliers of other factors of production will accept less for their factors.

If the employed population can be varied, then there is a simple relationship between wages and supply of workers. Existing wage rates may be high enough to attract immigrants, or low enough to persuade some people that they would be better off seeking their fortunes overseas. A rise in wages may encourage married women and retired persons to return to work, or young persons to start work rather than continue their education; a fall in wages may have the reverse effect.

Specific and non-specific labour

As you discovered in S1, specialisation may lead to two kinds of results, specialisation in depth and specialisation by process. Tasks requiring a long period of training or a high degree of mental ability tend to increase the specificity of the labour, whereas tasks resulting from the division of a manufacturing process leave that labour adaptable within that type of work. Thus it may be easier for a labourer to become a factory worker than for a doctor to become a lawyer.

On the other hand many jobs fall between these two extremes. An accountant or a lawyer may well become a manager.

Specific labour has, virtually, one use only. Non-specific labour has a range of alternative uses. Generally speaking *specificity* increases as the degree of specialisation increases.

2·2

Which three of the following would you rate as being the most specific forms of labour?

- **A** A nuclear physicist
- **B** An electrical engineer
- **C** A shop assistant
- **D** An engineering fitter
- **E** A trawler captain

Land as a factor of production

Land provides the materials with which man can satisfy his wants, that is, all the resources to which we have access and can use for production. Some of these resources—the sunshine, wind and rain are free goods for the most part (they have no opportunity cost). Economists use the term land to describe not only the earth's surface, but also the seas and lakes upon it, the minerals under it, and the climate in which it stands.

Wherever land is exchanged for money (which assumes that someone claims ownership) then it is regarded as an economic commodity, that is, it incurs an opportunity cost.

Nowadays the land, as we know it, is rarely land pure and simple. It has had generations of labour to alter it, to change its use and characteristics, and it therefore contains capital.

2·3

Which of the following would you include as part of the factor 'land'?

- **A** Water supplied by the local water board.
- **B** Gas from under the North Sea.
- **C** The sand dunes at a seaside holiday resort.
- **D** Iron ore quarried near Corby.
- **E** Seaweed in S. Wales used for making laver bread.

Productive character of specific land

If land as such has no cost of production, why are people prepared to pay for it? Firstly, because a parcel of land has a unique set of natural characteristics. Some is fertile, some subject to flooding, some too steep to cultivate, some gets too much sun or rain, some too little. Every plot is therefore scarce relative to the alternative uses to which it can be put. Secondly, the natural characteristics may be changed by the activity of man in accordance with his ability and his needs. Land can be drained, fertilised and levelled. Even if the characteristics are not ideal, the land available to any individual may be the best in the circumstances.

Since people claim ownership of land, it is not freely available to anyone who wants it; thus the unique qualities become scarce relative to the demand for them. The land then acquires a market price at which it changes hands—the price which the entrepreneur had to pay to buy the land.

Land has a range of alternative uses, all of which produce goods, or services, which will satisfy human wants, and which may be sold and so yield an income, in money or in kind, to the owner of the land. The more productive the land, the greater the income to the owner and the greater the demand for that land will be. Since economic situations are always changing, the greater the range of alternative uses which enables the owner to respond to market changes, the more lucrative the land will be in the long run. Again this adds to the demand for the land.

Heterogeneous land

The productive qualities of land are largely natural in origin, though often substantially amended over time by man. Remember that at *any given time* land is specific to one use, but the use can be changed over the long period. Moreover, no two pieces of land can be identical, because they must have different locations. Location is often the most important characteristic of land, as it is the one that cannot be changed. Moreover, location is accompanied by a certain climate, which may also be an important factor in deciding the most profitable use for the land.

2·4

Examine house prices in your neighbourhood. How are they affected by the position of the land on which the houses stand?

The general effect of location upon the enterprise situated upon any particular piece of land may be summed up by the costs arising from that location. Briefly, these are the costs of transporting raw materials to the factory, and of carrying away the finished product to the market, and the costs of providing labour. This latter may involve providing a works bus, or offering some additional payment or other benefit to induce workers to travel.

From time to time particular costs may arise from location. An otherwise suitable site may be on weak soil, and pile-driving may be necessary before building can commence. Factories in country areas may have to plant screening trees, to preserve the amenities. The combinations of costs arising from location are very many, and are the especial concern of economic geographers.

Capital

Capital is a part of the *stock* of wealth existing at any given time. It is produced by combining labour and land and possibly *existing* capital. Producing capital involves the postponement of present consumption in order to create goods to be used in future production and consumption.

For this reason stocks of unsold goods are regarded as capital. They represent an investment and a corresponding 'storing-up' of labour and capital by the producer, and until they reach the consumer they do not satisfy any wants.

Formation of capital

No one can create real capital just by saving money (i.e. not using it for consumption). If savings are used to buy existing shares or existing (i.e. second-hand) machinery, the country's productive capacity is not increased; only the ownership has changed. The country's stock of capital is increased when *new* real assets are created.

The country benefits only when new capital is created, since this will add to the total productive capacity, and thence to an increase in wealth, by increasing the output of goods and services available.

The nature of capital

We have seen that capital is a commodity which will produce future wealth. It can be divided into three forms, non-material capital, real assets, and financial assets.

i Non-material capital. This is simply personal skill acquired through training, for example, the surgeon's skill. It is difficult to measure or transfer this skill.

ii Real assets. These are commonly divided into fixed and working capital.

Fixed capital consists of physical assets which, once purchased, exist for a long period of time. Factory buildings, shop premises and public works such as roads, bridges, docks, etc., last the longest. Plant normally consists of mobile parts of production facilities such as cranes, bulldozers, forklift trucks, assembly lines and so on. Machinery refers to equipment directly used to make things, such as lathes, drills, and presses for shaping sheet metal. These terms are not formal definitions but terms commonly used to describe broad categories of goods used in production.

Working or circulating capital is a stock of goods and cash. In a manufacturing concern part of the firm's capital is in the form of raw materials and components (see satellite *The Motor Vehicle Industry*). While these are being processed to make the final product they are called 'work-in-progress'. Stocks of finished goods are held to meet large orders, to prepare for extra large sales, say at Christmas, just waiting to go to wholesalers, or for export.

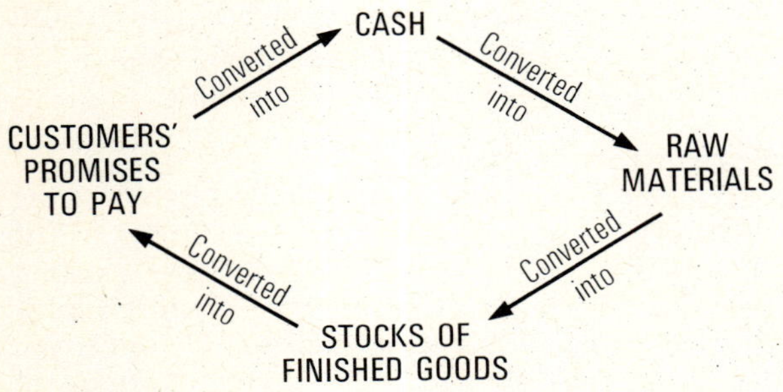

Figure 2·4

iii Financial assets. These are the various documents which give the owner a claim on a real asset. Unlike the assets they represent, they can easily be transferred from one person to another. The most familiar types of financial assets are stocks, shares, debentures, cash.

Stocks are usually a claim on the government, shares a share in the profit of a firm, debentures a right to receive a fixed rate of interest, and cash, of course, can be a claim on any commodity or service. A man who is the sole owner of a factory will receive all the profit, but may find it difficult to dispose of his capital asset. One of 10 000 shareholders in a company will receive a smaller profit, but will find it relatively easy to dispose of his share of the company's assets. The owner of a £1 note can switch his claim on resources at will: he can buy anything he wishes.

This power to change the form in which assets are held comes from their quality of *liquidity*. Many real assets, such as factories, ships, railways, are not easy to sell. Stocks of goods are perhaps easier to dispose of, and financial assets are simplest of all to realise, i.e. turn into cash. Cash itself is, of course, the most liquid of all assets. It is important to note that apart from that section of capital which circulates as cash, financial assets merely represent ownership of real capital. From the national viewpoint, therefore, paper claims held by persons and firms cannot be counted as capital, because this would involve counting both the claim and the real capital.

Financial assets are a means of separating the ownership from the control of real assets. Many thousands of individual people own capital assets, without ever seeing them. These are the investors who do without current satisfaction of wants but lend their money in return for the payment of profit and interest. (See satellite *Financial Institutions*.)

Trade capital

Sometimes businessmen use the expression 'trade capital', which consists of working capital, and 'cash in hand' used for day to day business expenses. Some firms go bankrupt because they have insufficient working capital to cover all these needs. They may have the fixed capital and plenty of goods in progress or ready for sale, but they may run short of cash to pay for the previous stock of raw material (bought on credit) because all their money is in the goods waiting to be sold. Such a firm is said to be in an illiquid position.

In the retail trade, the premises are often rented. Most of the capital of the shop keeper is held as stocks of goods. As he sells the goods, the capital becomes liquid again and can then be re-invested in new stocks. If the shop and its fittings are the property of the shop keeper, then these items form his fixed capital, and his stock and till money are working capital.

Both private individuals and society at large own capital. The ownership of society's capital assets may be organised through nationalised industries or public corporations. The profits supply revenue to pay for services organised and provided by the government. Losses are made good from taxation.

Private individuals own capital because they hope for an income from it. The consumption they do without is, therefore, less important to them than the hoped-for future satisfaction which will be provided by the profits on the invested capital.

2·5

Classify the following types of capital belonging to a small firm making fibreglass boats:

i £5 000 in a bank account.
ii Small factory building (700 m²).
iii Mobile crane and fork lift truck.
iv Fittings and components.
v Fibreglass and resin. Timber for moulds.
vi Spray guns, electric drills and tools.
vii Dyes and glue.

In addition to the capital belonging to the firm, there is also capital which belongs to the nation as a whole—roads, railways, airports, power stations—such capital is often called the economic infrastructure.

Characteristics of capital—a summary

Capital is wealth used for production. Capital is created not for itself but for what it will eventually produce.

Capital originates from savings—income not used in consumption.

Income is paid to the supplier of land, capital and labour, and that part of it which is not consumed is savings.

The proportion of total production which is not consumed is used for further production so capital exists as:

(a) Production goods—buildings, machinery, etc.
(b) Stocks of goods held for facilitating production.

Capital requires continuous maintenance and replacement because it wears out—this is called 'capital consumption' or depreciation, and this requires a continued excess of current production over consumption.

Enterprise

At this point we should enquire whether enterprise can, or should, be separated from labour.

Does enterprise perform a different economic function from that done by labour? If enterprise means organisation it may be argued that all labour—management and men—have to organise themselves and their work. The only difference is one of degree not type. Management spends a lot of its time in organisation. The workers spend most of their time working to orders and only a little in the organisation of others.

On the other hand, there are at least two different kinds of organisation which do not take place on the shop floor of the factory. One is co-ordination of the factors of production by deciding how much of each factor is needed, how they are to be combined to make the most profit and how the work should be performed or regulated. The second is the anticipation of the demand for the goods which are made—which is a most uncertain procedure.

Although everyone takes risks, there are two different kinds; (a) physical risks, say, injury or fire and even unemployment, which can be insured against to mitigate the effects; (b) the risks which are peculiar to enterprise—called business 'uncertainties'. These market uncertainties, which cannot be insured against, concern the setting of a selling price and deciding how many of the goods to make. Insurance is not possible for these because they are not the measurable kind of risk which can be calculated in terms of mathematical probability tables. Uncertainty necessitates making decisions of a policy nature, which is not the same type of decision as the shop floor worker is required to take.

The reward to enterprise is also of a different nature. Rent payments made for the use of land, wages for labour and interest on borrowed capital are all contractual payments fixed by agreement. Profit is not agreed in advance: it is always a residual amount—what is left over when all the bills have been paid and expenses met. It is a reward for dealing with uncertainty. The basis of payment, as a residual quantity, is therefore different from that of wages, so enterprise may be said to be a separate factor.

As a firm grows, other people may provide finance. Shareholders then own the firm, and the ownership will be separated from management. Managers deal with the uncertainties, and perhaps risk losing their jobs, but it is the owners who risk their capital. Thus it is difficult to say who is the entrepreneur—he does not exist as a single person.

Because you cannot identify a single person as the entrepreneur, it does not follow that enterprise is not a separate factor. Land, labour and capital are in a sense passive resources which need an active catalyst to make them productive. They are of little economic significance until production takes place. Enterprise is the active factor of production, and thus we may say that there are four factors of production.

2·6

Name the four factors of production, and match the principal source of reward for each factor. (N.B. This is an over-simplification of the allocation of rewards.)

Natural Resource	Profit
Human Resource	Interest
Man-made Resource	Rent
Enterprise	Wages

Capitalistic production

It is essential that you do not confuse the economic and political aspects of capitalism. In the economic sense, all advanced societies are capitalistic, because capital is required to produce and sustain a large flow of manufactured goods. Industrial production, as we know it, would not be possible without large accumulations of capital. The political argument comes from the ownership of capital and land. We shall see later how the price of factors of production is determined, but for the moment will merely note that in general in an economy where capital and land are privately owned, this ownership attracts a reward regardless of whether the owner does any work. This reward may be substantial. On the other hand, workers only receive payment for labour performed. This is the basis of the political argument against capitalism, and the reason why, in certain countries, capital and land are state-owned. Nevertheless, even where capital is not owned by individuals, it still exists.

ANSWERS

2·1

Own graph.

2·2

Correct **A**, **B**, E. Mistaken **C**, **D**: these can do a wider variety of jobs.

2·3

Correct **A**, **B**, **C**, **D**, **E**: note that **A**, **B**, **D**, **E**, also include other factors of production before reaching the consumer.

2·4

Own research. Note view, social 'tone' of neighbourhood, amenities, nearness to shops and bus routes.

2·5

i Financial Asset—Cash in hand.
ii Building—Fixed capital.
iii Plant—Fixed capital.
iv Stocks—Working capital.
v Stocks—Working capital.
vi Machinery. Fixed capital.
vii Stocks—Working capital.

2·6

Land
Labour
Capital
Enterprise

Land—Rent. Labour—Wages.
Capital—Interest. Enterprise—Profit.

POPULATION

STUDY SECTION **3**

A full Census of Population for England, Wales and Scotland has been made every 10 years since 1801 (except 1941). Because it takes several years to process the information, annual mid-year estimates are made.

Total population

Two sets of population statistics are available. The *de facto*, or *home* population is the number of people actually present in the U.K., and the *total* population is the home population, excluding foreign forces stationed in Britain and including British forces serving overseas.

3·1

a What was the home population of the U.K.?
 i in 1961?
 ii in the latest year for which you have data?
b Is there an increase or decrease in the home population between the two years?

Causes of change in total population

The most important influence is the difference between the birth rate and the death rate—the difference is called the *rate of natural increase* or *decrease* of the population.

The *birth rate* is the number of live births for every 1 000 persons in a given place in a given period; in 1965 there were 18·3 births per thousand of the U.K. population. Similarly the *death rate* is the number of deaths for every 1 000 persons per annum.

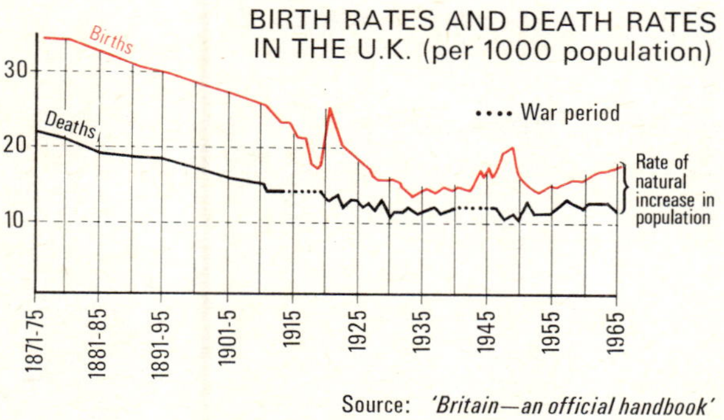

Figure 3·1

3·2

Imagine a small country of 20 million people. If the birth rate was 15 and the death rate was 10 in a given year, by how much would the population change in that year?

3·3

For the U.K. the following figures are given:

	Birth rate	Death rate	Home population
1964	18·7	11·35	54 066 000
1965	18·3	11·55	54 436 000

What is the difference between the natural increase in population in 1965 and the natural increase in population in 1964?

A +370 000 **C** +367 600
B +397 100 **D** + 29 500

Remember that these figures are rounded.

3·4

Draw on graph paper your own diagrams similar to 3·1 using the latest data from the *Annual Abstract.*

You should find tables for: total home population, male and female totals, immigration and emigration. The birth rate (total births per 1 000 of the population), the death rate (deaths per 1 000 of the population showing males and females separately).

The crude birth rate is a reflection of the fertility rate: the number of births per 1 000 women in the fertile age range (assumed to be from 15–45 years old). Selected figures are given in the *Annual Abstract,* from 1870.

The fertility rate is the result of social, economic and medical influences, such as the standard of living, the duration of full-time education and the quality of that education, and the desire of married women to return to work.

As the average age of marriage falls, women of the fertile age group are more likely to have children. Fertility is higher at the younger ages so that the number of pregnancies may rise; thus, the average number of children per family will increase.

A desire for a high standard of living in the first years of marriage may delay the start of a family. In western society most young people want to start married life at a material standard of living as high as that of their parents, who have reached that level only after twenty years or more. Such economic forces tend to keep young wives at work for a number of years before starting a family and thus the birth rate may be accordingly reduced.

The increasing use of birth control techniques may tend to reduce the average size of families, or may simply space the births of children over the fertile period but not affect the total number per family.

Religious and social customs influence the birth rate since they affect the marriage age, the attitudes towards material wealth, the size of a family and possible use of birth control techniques.

The provision of medical services may influence the fertility rate, especially among the better-educated.

3·5

Plot this data as a bar diagram.

Number of Marriages				
	Males		Females	
Age	1956	1965	1956	1965
Under 21	36 147	65 146	129 328	171 695
22–24	158 890	175 281	145 580	144 589
25–29	107 655	94 468	59 195	45 769
30–34	39 764	30 554	24 366	17 271

Source: *Annual Abstract of Statistics*

For a given fertility rate the population will grow faster as marriage age falls, since each generation is born progressively sooner. There will be more generations per century.

3·6

Note the year of birth of yourself, your parents, grandparents and great grandparents. Calculate the number of years between the births of the first (eldest) member of each generation.

The death rate contains two elements. One is deaths due to disease, accident or old age; the other is *infant mortality*, the deaths of children under 1 year of age. Because infant mortality has such a strong influence upon the rate of population increase, it is expressed as deaths per 1 000 live births.

In some developing countries today, and as recently as 1870 in the U.K., infant mortality was as high as 150. The development of medical services and antenatal care, together with superior diets and better hygiene, have reduced this mortality rate in the U.K. to 19·6 in 1965.

3·7

Draw your own graph from this data.

Infant Mortality		Infant Mortality	
1870	150	1940	61
1890	145	1950	31·2
1910	110	1960	22·4
1930	67	1966	19·6

Source: *Annual Abstract of Statistics*

As medical science improves there has been a rapid fall in the death rate at all ages and an extension of life expectancy.

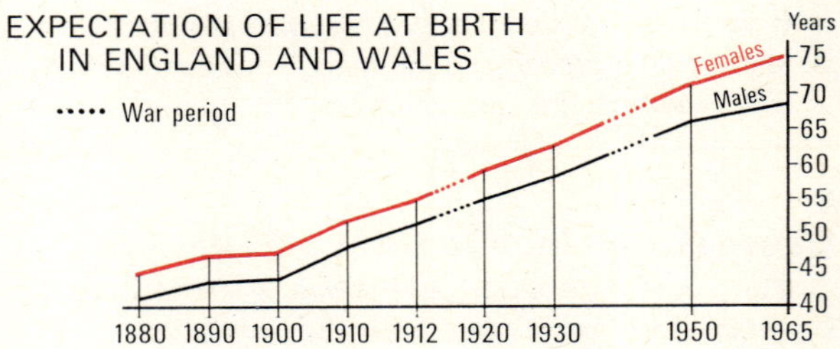

Figure 3·2

Improvements in the standard of living, particularly in nutrition, have improved health and reduced death rates. Better housing and public health services have been very important, notably in the field of providing pure water supplies, improved sanitation, sewage disposal and vaccination facilities.

Tables of life expectancy are available in the *Annual Abstract of Statistics*. Such tables have an economic importance, for they form the basis of life assurance calculations.

3·8

Examine publications of life assurance companies. What premium do they require for an assurance £1 000, payable on death or at age 65, for a man aged (a) 20 years, (b) 30 years, (c) 40 years?

The many varied influences on population growth may be summed up by the *reproduction rate*, which is the extent to which females in the fertile age group are replaced in the next generation.

The last influence upon total population that you should note is migration. Despite the considerable publicity given to migration in recent years, the numbers involved are relatively small compared with natural increase.

3·9

Chart the immigration and emigration figures for several recent years to see whether there is on balance a population inflow or outflow from the U.K.

Changes over time

POPULATION OF ENGLAND AND WALES FROM 1801 (millions)				
Census	Persons	Males	Females	U.K. Total
1801 March 9/10	8·8	4·2	4·6	
1951 March 30/31	17·9	8·8	9·1	22·2
1901 March 31/ April 1	32·5	15·7	16·8	38·2
1931 April 26/27	39·9	19·1	20·8	46·0
1951 April 8/9	43·7	21·0	22·7	50·2
1966 (mid year estimate)	48·0	23·3	24·7	54·7

Source: *Annual Abstract of Statistics*

Figure 3·3

Despite large scale emigration to the New World and the Empire, the population of England and Wales continued to grow at 1–1½% in the latter part of the nineteenth century, due to the relatively high, though falling, birth rate, and the great advances in medicine and public health.

3·10

The clearest way to show most changes over time is to put them in diagramatic form. From the data in figure 3·3 above, draw your own graph of the population of the British Isles.

3·11

a Compare the birth rates of 1886–90 with 1918. Express the difference as a percentage of 1886–90.

b Compare 1918 birth rate with that of 1939 (i.e. before the Second World War had its effect) and express as a percentage of 1918.

c How does 1965 compare with the reduced birth rate during the First World War?

Age distribution of the population

Every population has a certain pattern of distribution between the various age groups. The usual method of showing this distribution is by means of a bell graph as in figure 3·0. The longer the bar, the greater the proportion in each age group; as a certain number of all ages die each year, the older groups contain fewer people.

AGE AND SEX DISTRIBUTION OF HOME POPULATION OF UK IN 1965

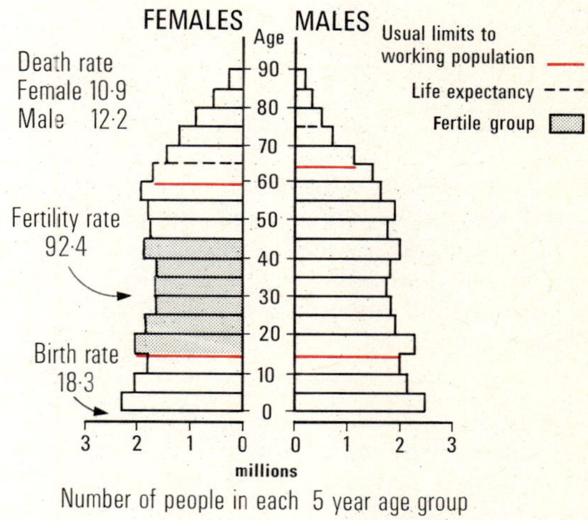

Total population 54 457 000
Annual Abstract Statistics

Figure 3·4

If the expectation of life increases, or the birth rate falls, or both, the average age of the population will increase and the top of the 'bell' is relatively wide. If there is a sudden increase in the birth rate, the foot of the bell will be much wider than the rest, indicating a high proportion of children. Even wars may leave their mark, and bell graphs for the populations of Britain and France in the 1930s clearly show the loss of men in the First World War.

Examine the 15–20 age group in 1965 (born 1945–50, the immediate post-war group). They are known as the 'post-war bulge'. As they grow older this bulge moves up figure 3·4. The bulge will remain even though it gets smaller as this group ages and dies. At each stage from babyhood,

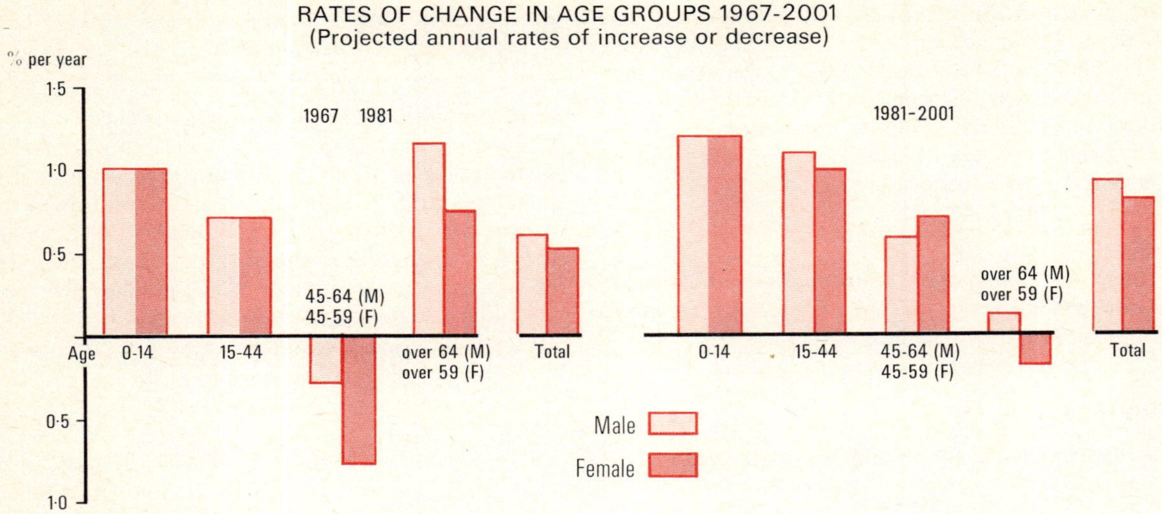

Figure 3·5(a)

Figure 3·5(b)

school, further education and employment, there will inevitably be a change in demand for the kinds of goods and services required by that age group. The age distribution of population is thus not a constant but something moving through time with each generation.

3·12

Using the *Annual Abstract of Statistics,* draw an up-to-date bell-chart of the British population.

3·13

a Estimate from your own figure:
- **i** the proportion of the total which consists of children (under 15).
- **ii** the proportion of the total which consists of the retired groups.
- **iii** the proportion of the total which is the 'working population'.

b
- **i** Define 'working population' as shown in the figure.
- **ii** In 1965 there were in total more females than males, but there were more boys than girls. Examine the figure carefully and find out in what age group women begin to outnumber men.
- **iii** Compare 1965 with your details for the latest year. Is the number of young men greater than the number of young women in your age group?

Effects of population changes

The population provides both the labour force, and the market for the products of industry. Any change in population will affect the economy. For example, a rise in the total population of a given country necessitates a rise in the national income of that country even to maintain existing material standards of living. Somehow, the total real income must be increased to satisfy the needs of current and future consumption and production. If natural resources are in fixed supply, then they will have to be used more productively to overcome the tendency to diminishing returns. More of the current resources will have to be devoted to the creation of physical capital and to providing better education (to improve human capital) in order to create the means to supply goods and services in the future.

However, we have seen that a change in total population is almost always accompanied by a change in age structure, and it is generally this age structure change that has the greater effect upon the economy.

The most important feature of the age structure is the relation between the population of working age and the number it has to support. As the length of full time education continues to grow, the impact on the actual number of wage and salary earners is even greater than the chart suggests. The number of retired people is growing more rapidly than the working population as life expectancy rises.

Increasing numbers of people live to enjoy a long retirement.

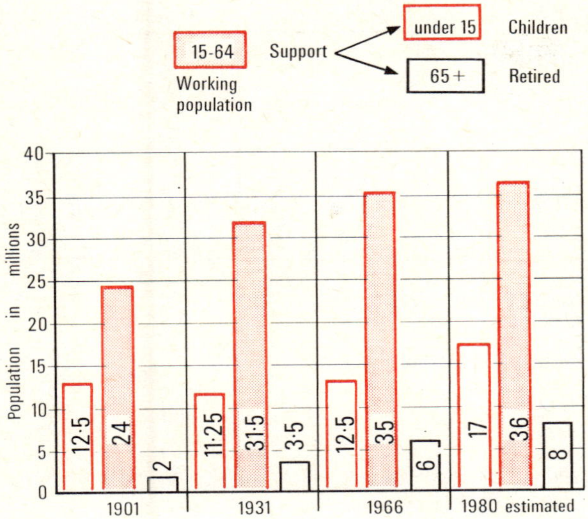

AGE DISTRIBUTION OF U.K. POPULATION

Figure 3·6

The proportion of the population currently producing the supply of goods and services is going to decline as the under-15 and over-65 age groups increase more rapidly than the 16–64 group. Thus the working population will have to become more productive to maintain the population as a whole, at the present standard of living.

The size of the working population

Economists are interested in the total labour force available to the community. From the population within the age limits 15–64 (about 37 million) are deducted those who are not available; mothers at home, the sick and unemployable, students, the armed forces, the retired. The working population (about 26 million) consists of those in full-time employment (estimated from National Insurance cards) and those registered at Labour Exchanges as unemployed and available for work.

The factors determining the size of the labour force are therefore those which determine:

(a) The number of people in each age group and the frequency with which each generation reproduces itself, e.g. age of marriage, birth rate, size of family.

(b) The age at which young people start work, which is largely determined by length of compulsory schooling, and the opportunities for further education.

(c) The age at which people retire, which is influenced by provisions of pensions and formal arrangements whereby some men may be retired from, say, the police force at well below the age of 65. Even though women have a greater life expectancy they usually retire 5 years earlier than men; this is, however, quite an arbitrary arrangement.

(d) The net gains or losses as a result of emigration and immigration.

The population, however, is not only the producer of goods, but is also the consumer. The demand for many types of goods is peculiar to certain age groups. Any change in the number of people in each age group will rapidly affect the pattern of demand, and have considerable effects upon the economy.

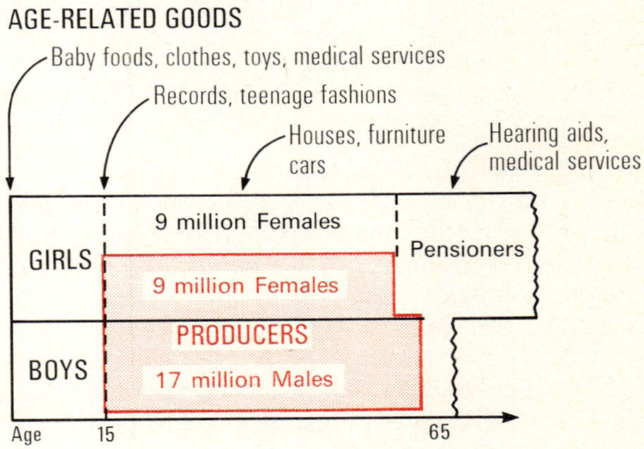

Source: *Annual Abstract of Statistics*

THE POPULATION OF CONSUMERS AND PRODUCERS

Figure 3·7

An expanding population, with a high birth rate will have a considerable demand for baby foods, prams, schools and educational materials. If the expectation of life is increasing, there will be a demand for welfare services, old people's homes, hearing aids. All these will have to be produced by the efforts of the working population.

Family size

The size of the family unit is affected by a great many social factors. Up to the middle nineteenth century low standards of living and high infant mortality meant that families had to be large (an average of six surviving beyond infancy would ensure that two lived to adulthood to replace their parents). Since then the average size of family has tended to fall until the 1950s. In upper income groups large families of five or more children currently seem to be more fashionable, as parental income is high enough to maintain both a large family and a high standard of living. However, a problem in many countries is the prevalence of large families among the poorer sections of the community, least able to afford the large houses the need. This may lead to the provision of publically subsidised housing.

REGIONAL MIGRATION IN ENGLAND AND WALES

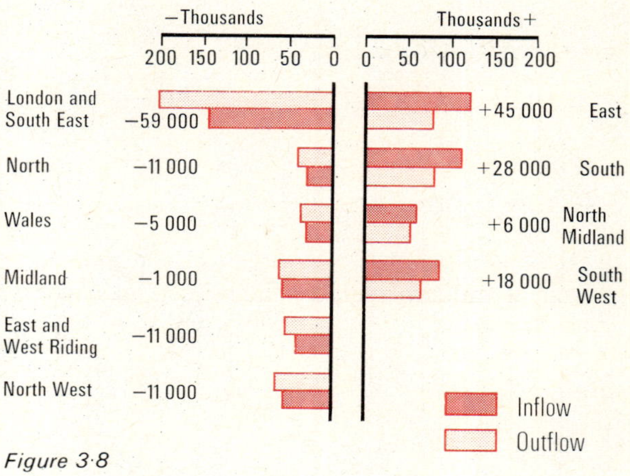

Figure 3·8

3·14

Which of the following changes in population structure will lead to an increase in state expenditure?

- **A** An increase in the number of old age pensioners
- **B** A falling family size
- **C** A stationary birth rate
- **D** An increase in the proportion of female births

Population distribution

The causes of differing densities of population are perhaps more the concern of the geographer than the economist, but we should note that in many countries, changes in density may be accompanied by changes in age structure. For example, in some regions of the U.K. population is decreasing—notably the Northwest Highlands and Southern Uplands of Scotland and in Mid-Wales—as the more mobile elements (young men and women) move away to seek work. They leave an even younger generation which, in time, will also move, and an ageing population which will remain. As the proportion of the older people increases so does the need for medical services and social welfare. Industry tends to decline, then employment and trade slackens and material progress may cease.

It should also be noted that there is a world wide tendency for population to be concentrated in towns. The world's population is rising steadily, and is now approximately 3 500 million. By the year 2000 it will probably exceed 6 250 million. There are now over 1 700 towns exceeding 100 000 in population. Nearly 20% of the world's population lives in towns.

In Britain, it is estimated that by the year 2000, the density of population will increase from about 230 to about 380 persons per km^2, and that as a result, the country's built-up areas will be doubled.

3·15

a By how much is it estimated that population density will increase by 2000 A.D.?

b If U.K. population rises from 54 millions to 72 millions between 1970 and 2000, how many more cities of 500 000 population will be needed?

Optimum population

The question is often posed, whether this or that part of the word is over-populated: what exactly does this term mean? We have seen that the factors of production must be combined in the correct proportions to achieve the maximum output. To the economist, the optimum population is that number of people, which, when combined with *existing* land and capital, will produce the maximum output per head of the population. Hence we can only say that India is overpopulated if we believe that a diminution of population would lead to an increase in output per head of the population. Neither is the Sahara Desert *under*-populated. Given the existing resources of land and capital an increase in population would probably lead to a fall in output per head. On the other hand, in those parts of the Sahara where oil has been found, and it has been possible to borrow capital, an increase of output per head has been possible.

World variations

In most of the discussion on population above, examples have been drawn from the U.K. Other countries have different patterns.

In general, where the standard of living is low, in India, Africa and some parts of South America, the birth rate is high, infant mortality is high, and the expectation of life short. The immediate impact of modern medical facilities is to cause a sharp decline in infant mortality, and to lower the death rate. As a result, there is a rapid increase in population. At a later stage, the desire to achieve a higher standard of living, and an increased level of literacy and education may cause a decline in the birth rate, as birth control techniques are accepted. Many of the developing nations are moving, often rather slowly, towards this stage.

Countries deficient in natural resources often find that their work force emigrates. Ireland has long provided many workers for the rest of the British Isles. Since many were bachelors, and others left their wives in Ireland, sending money home, this caused an imbalance of population in Ireland.

Money sent home by emigré workers plays an important part in the international finance of several countries.

3·16

Using the data in the *United Nations Demographic Year Book* or the *Oxford Economic Atlas* make out a chart to scale showing life expectancy in various countries. How does the U.K. compare with other countries?

Future developments

It is important to understand the dynamic (constantly changing) pattern of population, for all government and industrial plans must take account of likely population growth. Figures 3·9 and 3·10 show estimated past and projected future changes in numbers and age structure of the United Kingdom population (including forces overseas) between 1951 and 2001.

An important point is that people of present normal 'working age', 15–64 for men and 15–59 for women, have declined as a proportion of the population since 1951 and, on present projections, form a smaller proportion still in 1981, but between 1981 and 2001 they again form an increasing proportion.

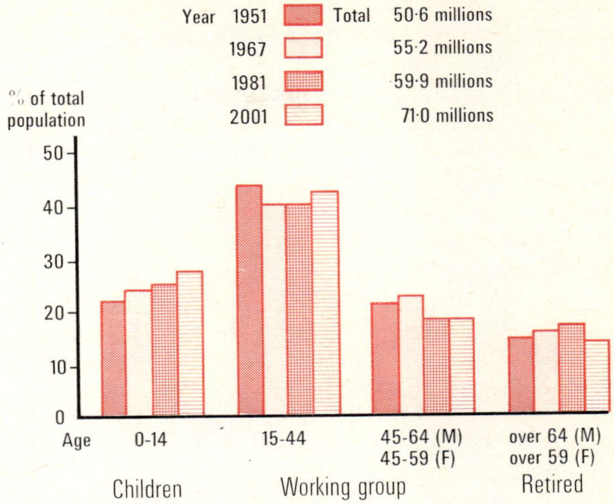

Figure 3·9

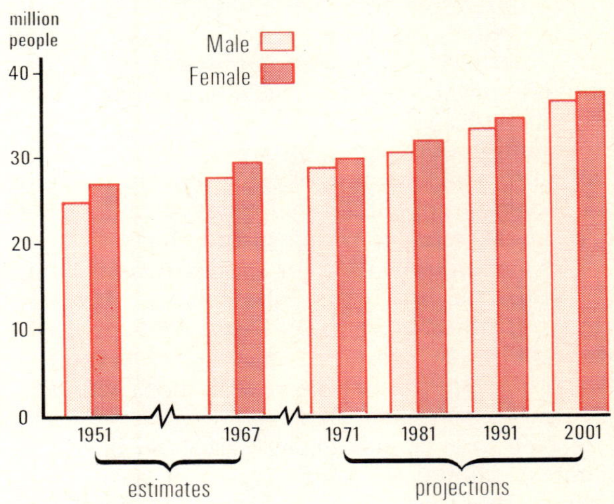

Figure 3·10

Between 1965 and 1985 it is expected that the number of people in the following age groups will change:

I 20–40 age groups will rise by about 15%
II 40–64 age groups will rise by about 5%
III 65 and over age groups will rise by about 28%

Group I consists of families with mostly young children.
Group II consists of families with teenage children and grandchildren.
Group III contain the retired people.

From figure 3·9 you will see that between 1967 and 1981 the number of 'workers' increases by only about 5% of the total population, while the number of people over present retiring age increases by 14%; but, between 1981 and 2001, 'workers' increase by 20% while 'retired' people are slightly down in number. During both periods there is a steady increase in the numbers being educated who do not produce goods or services; under-15s will increase by 16% by 1981 and (given present trends) a further 28% by 2001. The raising of the school leaving age will add further to the numbers at school.

The number of men over retirement age is relatively low now, mainly because of World War I casualties; the number of both men and women over 45 is, and will for many years, be affected by the low birth rates between the wars.

By 2001, most people born between the wars will be retired and those born in the more 'fertile' years after 1945 will be working. About 69% of the population will be under 45 in 2001, compared with 64% in 1967.

Assumptions of future birth rates are, of course, subject to a wide margin of error; but the forecast for the adult population in 1981 is quite accurate because this refers to people already born.

The assumptions used for the projections from mid-1967 are briefly described in the *Monthly Digest of Statistics*, No. 268 April 1968, HMSO. Projections are prepared by the Government Actuary's Department in consultation with the General Register Office.

As the total population has risen, so have the numbers employed. However, there have been considerable changes. At a distance in time, it is easy to see that harness-makers and saddlers were bound to be in declining demand, and that garage mechanics and tyre makers would be required as the motor industry developed. Such technological changes are obvious, but closer to our own time it is not always clear to us which industries are in long term decline, and which are merely undergoing a period of bad trade, or readjustment to market demand.

Generally speaking the numbers employed in an industry will depend on the following factors.

i Changes in the efficient use of manpower which lowers the number required for the same output of commodities and services.
ii The local supply of suitably qualified, or experienced workers (or the opportunity for migration or retraining).
iii Changes in techniques of production which may raise output by employing more capital but use the same amount of, or less labour (becoming more capital intensive).
iv The level of demand for the products of the industry.
v Competition from imports which affects home market demands, or success in exporting, which raises the level of production.
vi Short-term fluctuations of business activity which in turn depend on trade cycles and government policies.

Industry group	1959	1965	Latest Year
Agriculture, forestry, fishing	656	497	
Mining and quarrying	834	629	
Manufacturing			
Food, drink, tobacco	808	839	
Chemicals	518	518	
Metal Manufacturing	574	632	
Engineering and elec. engineer	1 927	2 287	
Shipbuilding and marine engineering	291	219	
Vehicles	870	870	
Metal goods	506	591	
Textiles	900	819	
Leather, leather goods and fur	64	61	
Clothing and footwear	572	558	
Bricks, pottery, glass, cement	337	358	
Timber, furniture	284	301	
Paper, printing, publishing	575	639	
Other manufacturing	279	335	
Construction	1 418	1 700	
Gas, electricity, water	381	419	
Transport and communication	1 712	1 655	
Distributive trades	2 755	3 023	
Financial, professional and scientific services	2 494	3 108	
Catering, hotels	580	622	
Miscellaneous services	1 413	1 604	
National govt. service	526	566	
Local govt. service	748	772	

Figure 3·11 Source: *Annual Abstract of Statistics*

Occupational changes

Figure 3·11 shows the broad distribution of the working population between industries. A more detailed classification is given in the Standard Industrial Classification, which lists over 30 000 occupations, and official statistics are published in the *Employment and Productivity Gazette* each year.

As some industries decline, and others expand, there may be regional shifts in employment. Since the end of the First World War, the older British industries, largely based on coalfields, have declined, and the newer, lighter industries, have grown up close to the markets formed by centres of population. This has resulted in a drift to the Midlands and the southeast of England, these two areas attracting the more mobile members of the working population from elsewhere. Thus the factors of industrial change, population growth and change of population age structure give rise to the problem of congestion in some areas, and unemployment in others.

We may note also the growth of industries requiring skilled workers. Older persons, made redundant by declining industries, may find retraining extremely difficult. Unskilled, unadaptable labour tends to remain unemployed longest.

3·17

Using a large sheet of graph paper, draw a vertical bar chart to illustrate the relative size of each occupational group in figure 3·11. (For rounding of numbers—see satellite *Arithmetical and Statistical Methods*.)

3·18

Examine figure 3·11. Which industries are expanding their labour force? Which are contracting?

ANSWERS

3·1

a Home population for 1961:
  i 52 709 000
  ii latest year?

b Almost certainly there will be an increase in population.

3·2

Total population 20 000 000
Birth rate $15^{0}/_{00}$
Death rate $10^{0}/_{00}$
Net increase $5^{0}/_{00}$
$5^{0}/_{00}$ of 20 000 000 = 100 000

3·3

Correct **D**.

Mistaken **A**: this is the change in *total* population which includes the net migration and is not the *natural* increase in population.

Mistaken **B**: this is the natural increase for 1964.
Mistaken **C**: this is the natural increase for 1965.

3·4

Own graphs.

3·5

Own bar diagram.

3·6

Own research.

3·7

Own graph.

3·8

For a man in good health, about:
(a) £25 p.a. (b) £32 p.a. (c) £45 p.a.

3·9

Own chart.

3·10

Own graph.

3·11

a 1886–1889, 30 per 1 000
1918 18 per 1 000
The difference is 40% that is, the birth rate fell by 40% between 1886/90 and 1918.

b The birth rate fell by about 15·4% between 1918 and 1939.

c The birth rate in 1965 was only about 7·7% higher than the 'low' of 1918.

3·12

Own chart.

3·13

a Estimates from recent data:

i $\frac{\text{the number of children under 15}}{\text{home population}} \times \frac{100}{1}$

ii $\frac{\text{the number of retired people}}{\text{home population}} \times \frac{100}{1}$

iii $\frac{\text{the number of people 16–59/64}}{\text{home population}} \times \frac{100}{1}$

b i The working population is the number of females between 16 and 59 plus the number of males between 16 and 64 who work for pay, or are registered as available for work.

ii About 50.

iii Variable answer according to age.

3·14

Correct **A**: however, **B** and **C** may also lead to an increase in the proportion of elderly persons in the population, and therefore is **A**.

3·15

a 150 persons per km²

b 36′

3·16

Own chart.

U.K. life expectancy is among the world's highest.

3·17

Own chart.

3·18

Expanding: engineering, construction, distribution trades, financial and professional services.

Contracting: mining, agriculture, textiles.

FIRMS: FORMATION AND LOCATION

STUDY SECTION 4

Production creates commodities and services which satisfy material or non-material wants. Three resources, land, labour and capital, organised by entrepreneurs, are used to produce economic goods. The organisation which produces economic goods is called a firm—one term which covers the range from the one-man retailers to the large scale public or private corporations.

We will now examine the ways in which various types of firms are organised in the United Kingdom. This is necessary because the legal form they take has economic consequences: for example, a sole trader takes all the risk whereas partners or shareholders share both risks and control, and of course, the profits.

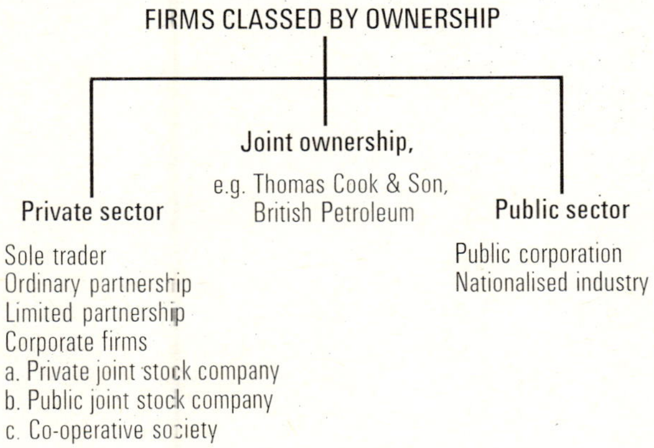

Figure 4·1

Private sector

'Private enterprise' refers to firms entirely or almost entirely financed by private individuals. Various government investments, grants or loans, may be accepted by private enterprise.

The normal assumption is that entrepreneurs go into business to make maximum profits. Certainly business would cease to function without profits, but rarely are maximum profits extracted from the market. Entrepreneurs of all sizes of business tend to have mixed motives. A desire for personal power, and a response to a feeling that they know how a business ought to be run, or an interest in the trade, are common features of top executives. Nevertheless a profitable business is the only one which can provide stable employment for its workers, and national wealth and efficiency are largely based on the aggregate efficiency of individual firms.

The plant, the firm, and the industry

A *firm* may be any business unit—a sole trader, a partnership or a company. It may have one or more *plants* or factories, which are separate units of production facilities.

A *company* is the financial organisation for a particular kind of firm (normally joint stock and with limited liability).

Several firms producing similar commodities or services form an *industry*. If any one firm can control the supply or the market price of a commodity, it is called a *monopoly*. This term, which describes the state of the market, is examined in the next chapter.

Size of firm

There are three basic ways to judge the size of a firm.

i The number of employees. This should be compared with the size of both the national labour force, and the numbers employed in the industry in question.

ii The value of the capital assets. Some firms, such as the major oil companies, own vast amounts of equipment and machinery, others, such as advertising agencies, own little more than office equipment.

iii The value of their output. This should be related to national and industry totals. The application of these concepts may be seen in the satellite texts *The Motor Vehicle Industry* and *Agriculture*.

The sole trader

This is the simplest kind of firm, typified by small retail businesses, window cleaners or jobbing builders.

Generally, sole traders, as people, are not specialists since they have to cope with all aspects of running the business. Normally the firms are small, and limited in their scope for development or improvement by lack of capital. The amount of capital required depends on the size of stock, and the rate at which it sells and so returns the working capital in liquid form for reinvestment. Usual sources of new capital are personal savings, savings of friends, bank loans or overdrafts (secured against title deeds to his property or a life assurance) and, most of all, trade credit i.e. buying goods on credit and hoping to sell them before the supplier has to be paid. This latter involves considerable risk for all concerned, and the closing of credit can bring even large but illiquid firms to bankruptcy if the cash flowing from sales is insufficient to pay accounts on the date agreed.

4·1

Which of the following do you think are the advantages of being a sole trader?

- **A** The ability to take business decisions without delay.
- **B** A plentiful supply of capital.
- **C** Direct contact with customers and suppliers.
- **D** The supplying of credit to long term customers.
- **E** The ability to specialise in certain management functions.

Ordinary partnerships

People may set up a *partnership,* subscribe various amounts of capital and share the profits.

The number of partners in most cases is limited to twenty. The advantages and disadvantages are similar to those of sole traders, except that new partners can be taken on to provide more capital, and ensure the survival of the firm. A partner who takes no part in management may become a *limited partner*: if the firm becomes bankrupt he loses no more than the capital he has contributed.

Corporate firms with limited liability

Sole traders and partners often find difficulties in raising capital, and with the exception just noted, have *unlimited liability* for the debts of their businesses. To avoid these disadvantages, corporate firms (companies) can be set up, to which many *shareholders* can contribute capital, but with *limited liability* for the debts of the company. In the case of the failure of a limited company, the owner or shareholders lose only the amount of the capital they have invested, and the company's creditors cannot touch their personal possessions. Thus a shareholder in a limited company can decide how much to invest, and therefore put at risk. Without limited liability, companies would not be able to borrow the money savings of persons with low incomes.

A company is formed (incorporated) in various ways. Chartered companies were established by Royal Charter, as were the East India Co., and the Hudson's Bay Co. The Bank of England was first chartered in 1694. The charter was renewed as necessary until it was nationalised in 1947.

Statutory companies were formed under Acts of Parliament (statutes). Railway and canal companies were usually formed this way to prevent undesirable duplication and unnecessary competition in public utilities.

Registered companies, registered with the Registrar for Joint Stock Companies, in accordance with the Companies Act, normally are companies limited by shares. This is the usual 'A. Jones & Co. Ltd.' type of company.

The joint stock principle

This means of sharing business uncertainties and risks has been known at least since the fourteenth century. It simply means that each of a number of people contributes a share of the company's capital. This entitles them to equivalent share of the profits (or losses).

The *stock* (in this sense of the word) is the stock of capital owned *jointly* by the stock-holders (or shareholders). With limited liability, your investment is all that you are putting at risk. The receipt for the capital invested is the share certificate which is a document of title (i.e. proves ownership). Since it is easy for individuals to invest new capital in joint stock companies without really knowing all the details of the company, it is important that misleading or fraudulent claims are not made by the company's promoters. It is the responsibility of the Registrar for Joint Stock Companies to examine the prospectus which every company issues as an advertisement asking the public to subscribe for shares. The Registrar also examines the accounts to ensure that fraud has not been perpetrated during the past year.

Private joint stock company

Not only does this give all of a group of investors limited liability but it also permits up to 50 shareholders plus any number of past employees, instead of only 20 as in the partnership. Shareholders cannot, however, transfer (sell) their shares to other people without consent of the other shareholders. This prevents outsiders buying up 51% of the shares and taking control against the wishes of the company. In the days of mergers and amalgamation this can be important since outside investors may provide additional capital but can be prevented from taking control. In public joint stock companies the need for additional capital may effectively surrender the company to someone else's control because shares in these companies are bought and sold without restriction. In recent years there have been a number of cases where even millionaires have lost control of the companies they founded. The private company is not allowed to make a public appeal for new shareholders. In general the limited number of shareholders means that these companies are moderate in size with relatively limited amounts of capital. There are over 300 000 of these companies, most of which are family businesses. In order to gain the advantages of limited liability many sole traders form private companies, usually enlisting friends and relatives as shareholders.

Public joint stock companies

In some countries these are called 'corporations', but not in the United Kingdom. Government public sector enterprises such as the Post Office are constituted as 'Public Corporations', which is an entirely different kind of firm.

The public joint stock company has to have at least seven shareholders and may have an unlimited number of shareholders—100 000 in some cases. The number of shareholders depends on the amount of capital which the company has and how it is divided.

Suppose the share capital is £10 000. This might be divided into

10 000 × £1 shares; up to 10 000 shareholders
40 000 × 25p shares; up to 40 000 shareholders
2 000 × £5 shares; up to 2 000 shareholders

Rarely do shareholders hold one single share. Various kinds of shares are discussed below.

4·2

A private joint stock company, founded 40 years ago by the chairman of the board, badly needs more capital. A friend has offered to invest the additional money but there are already 50 shareholders. Which option would you advise them to take, assuming that permission to increase the capital has been obtained from the Registrar of Joint Stock Companies?

A Buy the chairman's shares and force him to retire so leaving room for the new shareholder.

B Retire the chairman and allow the new man to buy up the chairman's shares.

C Make the new man a 'sleeping partner'.

D Allow the chairman to retire from employment by the firm, without having to sell his shares, and then permit the new man to make his investment.

Forming a public company

The first step to be taken is for at least seven people to sign a memorandum of association, which gives certain essential information:

Name of company: J. Enterprise & Co. Ltd.
Registered office: Mermaid St., Rye, Sussex.
Objects of the company: Manufacture of hovercraft.
Liability of shareholders: Limited.
Nominal capital: £14 250.

(Nominal capital is also known as *authorised capital* which means the amount the company is authorised to raise; or as *registered capital*—the amount registered with the Registrar for Joint Stock Companies).

Next, the company must draw up its articles of association, or adopt a model set from the Companies Act (Table A). These articles govern the internal working of the company.

The third step is to formally register the company, and obtain a *Certificate of Incorporation*. This will be issued by the Registrar for Joint Stock Companies when he receives:

(a) the list of directors' names;
(b) a solicitor's declaration that the Companies Act has been complied with;
(c) a statement of nominal capital;
(d) payment of fees and stamp duties for registration.

The certificate of incorporation authorises the company to appeal to the public to invest in their company's shares.

The fourth step in forming a company is to issue a *Prospectus*. This is an invitation to the public to subscribe for shares. It details the company's proposed business and supplies information on the expected profits. It has to be accurate and to prevent fraud a copy is filed with the Registrar.

Types of shares

A company sometimes only issues one kind of share—the ordinary share (or equity). These shares entitle the holder to vote at the annual general meeting of the company. Votes are primarily used for the election of directors of the firm. In cases of policy disputes shareholders may elect a new board of directors provided that the directors do not use their own shares to out-vote the other shareholders.

Shareholders exercise the risk-taking element of entrepreneurship, and the management element is exercised by directors. Like anyone else, shareholders may wish to balance the degree of control they exercise against the risk they take. Though liability is limited, risk can be even further reduced by buying certain shares which involve less risk, but which usually pay a lower rate of dividend. The dividend paid depends on the profits made by the company, the amount retained in reserves and the taxes levied on profits. Economists distinguish, in principle, two elements in dividends; interest on the capital invested, and a share of profit. No such distinction is made in real life.

Risk for the shareholder may be reduced by giving his shares preference when it comes to distributing dividends, but these shares usually pay only a fixed rate, assuming that some dividend is declared.

Preference Shares. These entitle the owner to have his (fixed) dividend paid before other shareholders are paid.

Cumulative Preference Shares. Like ordinary preference shares, these entitle the holder to be paid before ordinary shares receive any dividend. If no dividend is declared in a given year, then for example, a 5% cumulative preference share would have to earn the arrears in the next year, i.e. 10%. Whenever dividend is not paid, the arrears accumulate to the holder until dividends are declared.

Ordinary shares (Equity). These bear most of the risk since they only attract dividends after the preference shareholders have been paid. Dividends on equity, however, are often much larger than the fixed rate on the preference shares. Hence their attraction as a source of investment income, apart from the voting power they confer on holders.

There are also non-voting ordinary shares (often called 'A' shares), which provide the hope of large dividends, but offer no control element (much like a limited partner).

Although a company may have a large nominal capital, it need not issue shares to this amount immediately, but may start by raising the capital needed for initial operations, and making further issues later.

Note that once shares are issued, they are never repurchased by the issuing company, i.e. they are not redeemable. The shareholder has to sell his share to some other person.

Loan capital

Capital acquired by the issue of shares is known as *risk capital,* because shareholders share the risks of the firm. Sometimes capital is borrowed by the issue of *debentures,* of *loan stock.* These are loans, not shares. They are repaid (redeemed) after a certain date, and the fixed rate of interest which is paid to lenders is a prior charge which must be paid before shareholders receive any dividends.

The capital of the firm

Nominal capital is the maximum capital which can be raised—as stated in the Memorandum of Association. Part of this may be *issued capital,* that is, the amount to be issued in shares as advertised in the Prospectus. The rest may be issued later as required to extend the business.

Shareholders may not be required to pay the whole value of the share straight away. If only half is required then the company will have 'called up' half the issued capital. The shareholders must be able to supply the balance of the issued capital when required by the company, i.e. the amount the company requires immediately is *called up* capital. The amount they have received is *paid up* capital.

4·3

The following information about a public company is known:

i Half the nominal capital has been issued.
ii Two thirds of issued capital has been called-up.
iii Issued capital is valued at £50 000. What is the value of the nominal capital?

A £100 000 **B** £33 333 **C** £25 000

A new venture which is attractive to would-be investors may have more shareholders wanting shares than there are shares available. Such a share issue is termed *over-subscribed.* The shares are usually allotted *pro rata,* i.e. in ratio to the number applied for, but the applicant must send in the whole value of the shares.

Once the shares are allotted and the directors have paid for their shares, the Registrar will issue the *Certificate to Commence Business.*

4·4

Which of the following would be helpful in deciding whether a firm is a public or private joint stock company?

A A copy of the prospectus.
B A statement of number of shareholders.
C Stock Exchange quotation of share value.
D A statement that liability is limited.
E The name of the family controlling a majority of the equity.

4·5

Put in order from least to greatest the risk borne by the holders of the following types of shares:
I Preference shares. II Cumulative preference shares. III Ordinary shares. IV Participating preference shares.

A I II III IV
B II I III IV
C III IV I II
D III IV II I
E II I IV III

4·6

a Which kind of shares in a public company would give you voting power?
A Preference shares **B** Ordinary shares
b What proportion of equity would you need to control in order to dominate company policy?
C 51% **D** 90%

Control of the firm

One of the attractions of the private company used to be that the founders could keep details of turnover (value of sales per year) secret from other firms who might want to take them over as a means of expanding business.

The 1967 Finance Act removed this advantage because copies of the accounts and balance sheet must now be sent to the Registrar. For a small fee anyone may see a copy in the Registrar's Office. If turnover is more than £50 000 then this must be stated. Such information may attract unwelcome bids by other firms. If 51% or more of the private company's shareholders are willing to sell, they must give first refusal to the other shareholders. If these cannot or will not buy the shares then the 51% may sell their shares and control passes out of the hands of the firm's founder (usually against his wishes and with a possibility that he may find himself out of work). Since the shares have been sold to the public, section 28 of the 1948 Companies Act has been violated and company loses its private status.

In a public company control rests with the majority of equity shareholders. In some cases, where shares are spread thinly over a large number of shareholders, any individual with a block of shares may effectively keep control because of the difficulty of assembling a voting power greater than that individual block.

The advantages of joint-stock companies

The amount of capital available is more than individuals can supply.

Risks are spread among many shareholders, and the various types of shares spread the degree of risk even further.

The capital cannot be withdrawn from the company, yet ownership may be transferred to others. This is a major advantage of public companies: the stock exchange in London and other large cities are markets for existing share capital. The price at which shares are bought and sold does not directly affect the company concerned since it is merely a change of ownership which is involved. The existence of the stock exchange gives liquidity to a shareholder's investment, should he or she need to obtain cash rapidly.

As a firm grows, the founder can 'buy' managerial expertise without having to lose control of the firm. Though the risks of ownership of the company are spread among large numbers of shareholders, day-to-day control still rests with the directors. Once the directors have been elected by the shareholders they manage the firm for the next year. Though *ownership* may be spread widely, actual *control* may be concentrated in a small group or family of directors owning a majority holding, or, if most shareholders do not vote, minority holdings may exercise power.

Unlike partnerships which must be dissolved when one partner leaves or dies, joint-stock companies continue in being, until the shareholders decide to liquidate the company.

Disadvantages of a joint stock company

Shareholders and financial columnists in newspapers judge company success by the size of dividends. In the long run other criteria, such as working conditions for employees, pricing and marketing policies, export performance, investment policy, modernisation of techniques, etc., may be more important.

Many shareholders may invest in very risky ventures without any knowledge of how the business is run or the nature of the activities in which it is engaged. However, Unit Trusts and Investment Trusts are forms of investment available which reduce the risks. These 'institutional investors' have to know a great deal about the firms in which they invest.

Some public companies are very large and complex in their organisation, sometimes owning hundreds of subsidiary companies. As few shareholders have the expertise to disentangle the patterns of organisation, many cease to exercise their right of control by voting. Annual general meetings of large companies are usually poorly attended.

Where companies are very large the delegation of authority may be poorly delineated and the human factor ignored. Modern managements recognise that personal job satisfaction and good labour relations tend to raise efficiency and profits.

The significance of share prices

When British Petroleum announced that it had struck oil in Alaska its ordinary shares rose by 3/6d. (17½p) so adding £60 millions to the stock market valuation of the company on the day after the announcement. Was this important? It did not affect BP directly because shares are only titles to capital—and the price at which owners buy and sell these 'titles' cannot add to or subtract from the physical capital in the hands of BP. On the other hand, investors in aggregate estimated that the 'oil-strike' should lead to additional dividends being paid out—otherwise they would not have paid this much extra to obtain the shares.

In the longer run the market price indicates the level of demand for shares and, by inference, the level of demand which might be expected if BP offered a block of new shares for sale in order to raise more capital for use in the Alaskan oilfield.

To existing holders of BP shares such a price rise in the market represents an increase in the market value of their holdings, but to potential buyers the price rise means that they have to find more cash to purchase the shares. They will do this only if they estimate that the increased future dividends will make the purchase, at the higher price, worthwhile.

The problem of estimating what will happen in the future to each company in whose shares one invests is at the heart of Stock Exchange dealings.

Capitalisation or scrip issues

If a public company has very large reserve funds which have swollen for some reason, it may decide to convert a proportion into share capital. In a sense it uses the reserve fund to buy new shares in the company for all of its present shareholders instead of giving them a bonus in money form. They will then receive a free issue of shares (in proportion to shares currently held, as for rights issues). They are usually regarded as a bonus issue and provide a dividend income to shareholders in the same way as other shares.

Such issues are usually made in order to bring the capital structure (i.e. pattern of shares issued) into line with the true value of the company's assets.

If you had two hundred £1 shares and received a scrip issue at a rate of 1 for 2 you would then have three hundred shares. Assuming that the same amount of total profit is distributed to the enlarged number of shares, the market value of the three hundred shares will remain at £200, and each share's market value will fall to £0·66. The principle of 'cum' and 'ex-dividend' (the latter is written 'xd' in the financial press) applies to rights issues and to capitalisation issues.

4·7

Select two public companies from the Stock Exchange list of quoted shares.

a Trace the valuation of all the quoted shares on a daily or weekly basis for the next six months.

b Make an imaginary investment in each firm and work out each week the gross gain or loss from the sale of your shares.

c Your six months should cover the annual dividend on shares. Note when you buy them whether they are 'cum' or 'ex-dividend' i.e. with dividend or without dividend.

d Work out at the end of the six months whether you have made a profitable investment in each company.

N.B. Choose fairly well-known companies, one of which should be a candidate for takeover and keep a look out for reference to your companies in *The Times, Financial Times, Guardian* or *Economist.* and any other sources available to you. In this way you will be able to build a picture of the company at work.

Your data should be plotted:

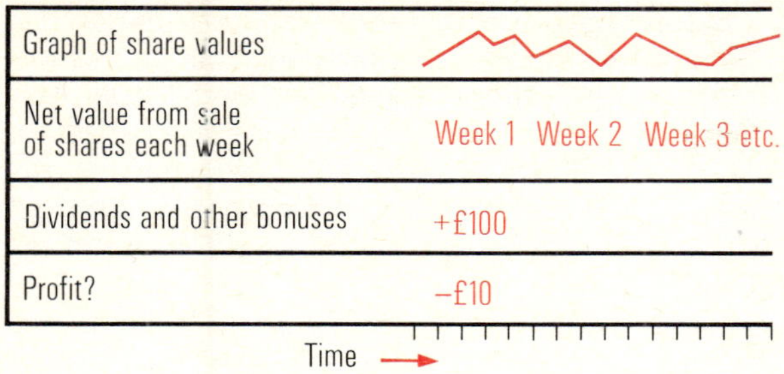

The Stock Exchange

The Stock Exchange is a specialised market in *existing* stocks and shares (securities). New issues of shares are rarely sold through it. Four groups of people are involved—the investors, for example, members of the general public, and various financial institutions; the brokers, usually partnerships of ten or a dozen; the jobbers on the Stock Exchange, also usually partnerships; and the joint-stock companies.

Brokers deal with the general public on one side and with jobbers on the other. They provide an advisory service to their clients and make a living on $1\frac{1}{4}\%$ brokerage (commission) on the deals they arrange for them. It is their job to sell at the highest price or buy at the lowest price they can find on the market, according to the clients' best interests. (See satellite *Financial Institutions*.)

Jobbers only deal with brokers: they do not deal directly with the general public. They specialise in dealing in particular markets, e.g. the market in oil shares, in gold shares, in 'blue chip' (mainly banks), etc. They hold supplies of shares which investors have sold, but which have not yet been re-sold to other investors. (Note that 'investor' in this case means a buyer of securities. In this sense the term is not directly connected with real capital investment, and must not be confused with it.)

Jobbers act as a kind of reservoir for stocks and shares. They make a living by buying shares from brokers (selling on their clients' instructions), at a price slightly lower than the price at which they re-sell shares to brokers (who are buying on behalf of their clients). The difference between these two prices is called the Jobbers Turn. It is costly and risky to hold shares on this basis and, hence, jobbers have to be wealthy.

The public joint-stock companies have to maintain an up-to-date Register of Shareholders, and they are informed of changes in ownership by means of a stock transfer form sent to them by brokers. It is to registered shareholders that dividends are paid out.

Prices on the Stock Exchange vary from hour to hour and day to day. Unravelling the causes of price changes and the difference between prices can be an investor's full-time occupation. For example you might find this kind of comment in the City columns of your newspaper:

'Money Market men are convinced that a bid is to be made for this electronics firm. This, runs the argument, is why the ordinary shares, which carry the votes, have increased in price while the non-voting 'A' ordinary shares have

DEALING IN SHARES

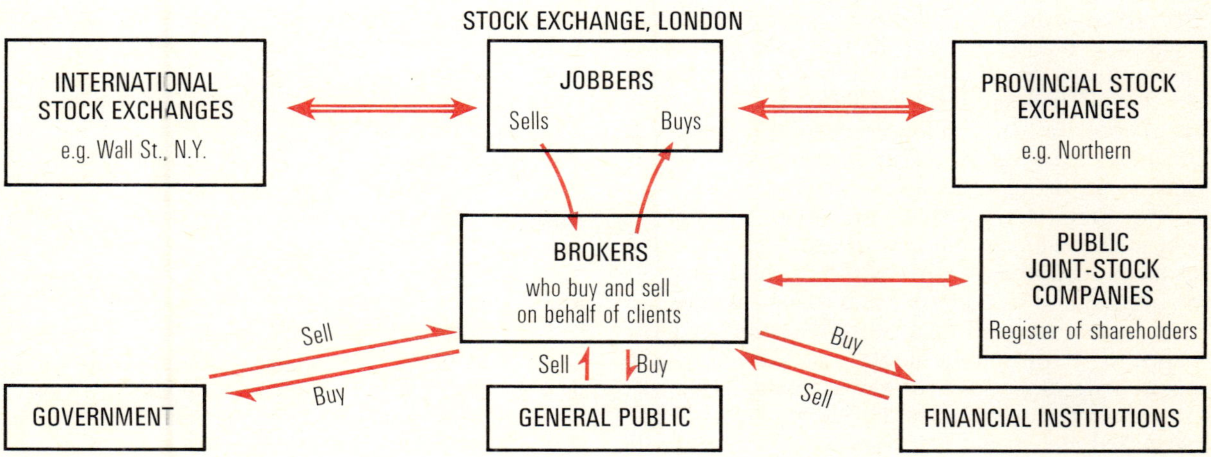

Figure 4·2

drifted back so that the difference in price between the two is no less than 91p. Normally the price differential is only a matter of pence.

The feeling is that a bidder is building up a block of voting shares in a preliminary to making a takeover offer for the whole equity capital, including the 'A' ordinary shares.

The firm of course, has been a take-over hope for many months, but never before has the price differential been so great'.

Functions of the Stock Exchange

These may be summarised as follows.

It is a market in *existing* shares, i.e. it is not the usual market through which new shares are offered for sale.

It confers liquidity to investments, i.e. shareholders are more willing to invest in industry through shares if they know that they can readily convert shares into cash.

The Stock Exchange provides a means by which relatively small investors (from about £500 upwards) can obtain a share in industrial liquidity. Without the Stock Exchange such small investors would be denied the opportunity and industry would be denied very large total sums from 'small' savers. (See satellite *Financial Institutions*.)

It provides a means of valuing companies, since the value of the company's shares indicates peoples opinions of the company's success. For taxation purposes, e.g. capital gains tax and estate duty, stock exchange valuations are often necessary.

About half of the deals done on the Stock Exchange involve government bonds and stock. These are the principal instruments through which the government borrows short term money. (It is needed to finance the gap between the receipt of taxation and the daily expenditure on providing the social services and other items.) The government borrows by selling securities; these are attractive because they can be sold for cash, if necessary, through the Stock Exchange.

The Stock Exchange is the major institution whose development has contributed to the growth of an industrial economy. Most of the industrial revolution and its consequences (the growth of the U.K. into a major world power) would not have happened if the public joint stock company had not been developed as a form of industrial organisation. Only the existence of the Stock Exchange has permitted the growth of very large amounts of share capital.

The public sector

Before the 1939–45 World War some public corporations had been established but it was not until the 1945–49 series of Nationalisation Acts that any pattern in their constitutions was established. There are considerable variations in the degree of power which the responsible Minister has over the governing bodies (the Boards) of the corporations.

The ownership and control of the nationalised industries is vested in the Public Corporations, examples of which are:

Atomic Energy: United Kingdom Atomic Energy Authority (UKAEA)
Banking: Bank of England
Broadcasting: BBC and ITA
Gas: Gas Council, Area Gas Boards
Telecommunications, mail and banking services: Post Office.

The Chairman and members of each Board are appointed (and dismissed) by the Minister.

There are other national corporations which are not nationalised industries, for example, the English Industrial Estates Corporation (and Scottish and Welsh equivalents).

The Minister, on behalf of the government, may give general directives as to how the industry should be run (but he is not supposed to interfere in day to day management). Usually major policy decisions are made in consultation with the responsible Minister, so formal directives are not common. The Minister can also specify corporations' minimum financial targets. (For an example see satellite *Industries in the Public Sector*.) Statistical information must be given to the Minister as required.

Ownership and control

These industries are publicly owned, i.e. owned by the nation as a whole and run for the benefit of the nation. The government policy in respect of nationalised industries is subject to parliamentary approval. The reports and accounts of the corporations are examined by a House of Commons Select Committee, which then reports its findings to Parliament.

Investment funds for these industries are, mainly, drawn from the 'public purse', that is, taxation. Profits from these industries (normally called 'trading surpluses') are paid to the Treasury. If these public corporations were in private enterprise most of them would be regarded as monopolies. They are among some of the largest 'firms' in the country.

Public corporations are not government departments, but are special statutory bodies with fairly clearly defined and specific responsibilities. The managing boards are not staffed by civil servants, but the men and women appointed are chosen for their experience and competence in their field of activity, and are usually the best available people from the industry itself.

Few of these corporations comprise all of their industry, though most of the firms left outside in private hands are small enterprises.

In economic terms the case for nationalisation rests on three important premises:
(a) Public ownership prevents exploitation of the general public by private monopoly.
(b) Public ownership may be the only effective way of modernising an essential industry by concentrating it in larger and more efficient units.
(c) Where certain basic industries or transport services may decline or fail to serve society's needs adequately then public ownership and subsidy may be cheaper than *not* nationalising.

Joint ownership

Successive governments have acquired a controlling interest in various private firms. Some have been acquired incidentally as part of the nationalisation of a particular industry. This is why the N.C.B. is the largest brick manufacturer in Britain. Other firms may have had capital invested in them to encourage major development programmes which are regarded as being in the national interest. (See satellite *Monopolies and Restrictive Practices*.)

THE LOCATION OF INDUSTRY

When an entrepreneur sets up a factory or other production plant, he seeks a location where his costs of production and marketing will be minimised. He must pay attention to a number of *locational factors*, which are discussed below, and which, in practice, are inter-related.

Land

The cost of a site is important, since it may be so high that it may have to be spread over several years. If not purchased site rent can be a significant overhead.

Where the land is not flat and well drained, site preparation is an expensive preliminary to building operations.

A growing firm will try to purchase land where there is room for subsequent expansion and the cost of holding unused land for several years will have to be taken into account.

Labour

No industry can exist without workers, and although in some cases a new plant may import workers from elsewhere, this is unusual.

Raw materials

Supplies of wool from Cotswold sheep, iron ore near Sheffield, coal on the Pennine flanks, are simple examples of local supplies of raw materials which gave birth to great industries. Most raw materials have a higher volume and greater weight than the goods made from them. Many are, therefore, more expensive to transport than finished products, but are less valuable, so that it does not pay to transport these raw materials very far.

Where many raw materials are involved, the processing or manufacturing plant will be located at a point where the effect of transport costs is minimised.

Power supplies

In the days of steam and water power, industry tended to concentrate upon coal fields and rivers, as the case might be, but now that fuel and power are supplied by pipeline or cable, there is far less attraction to the point of power production.

Safety

A number of industries must be located away from large concentrations of population for safety reasons. Atomic power stations and explosives factories are two examples.

Waste disposal

Certain industries produce considerable waste products, and the difficulties of disposing of these may have a significant effect upon location.

Marketing

For many consumer goods, the cost of delivery form the point of production to the point of sale is a significant part of production cost. Therefore there is a striking tendency for large centres of population to attract all kinds of consumer goods industries. These in turn attract the industries which provide them with producer goods.

Transportation

You will probably have realised that several of the factors already described are dependent upon transportation. If a factory or plant lies close to a road, railway, river, coast, it will be a great deal easier to assemble the factors of production, to market the goods and dispose of waste materials. Which particular form of transport is most appropriate in each case is often as much a matter of technology as of economics. The transport may be provided by the entrepreneur, as when a works provides buses for the workers, or builds a dock to unload raw materials, or it may be provided by the community, as in the case of the thousands of London factories and offices which rely upon the public transport systems to get their employees to work.

The role of transport costs in the location of industry

We have assumed that planned location is designed to reduce known costs to a minimum. For the purposes of this part of the discussion, these costs may be divided into, costs of raw materials, costs of manufacture or processing, costs of distributing the product to its markets. Most manufacturing is now free from the pull of power sources which dominated the location of industry in the early nineteenth century.

Raw materials

The cost of raw materials to the manufacturer is not only affected by the distance and cost of transport, for the value of the commodities also has an important effect on the ability of the manufacturer to afford transport costs.

Raw materials such as low grade iron ore or crude oil have a relatively low *value* compared with the products made from them. The processing of these materials reduces their *bulk* by a large percentage (ore may contain only 25% of iron) and so transporting the processed materials is cheaper than transporting the finished product. This is not all, for the value of the finished product is much higher than the raw material so even the same cost of transport, say £1 000 per train load, would have a greater effect on the cost of £10 000 worth of ore than on £50 000 worth of steel, e.g.

$$\frac{1\,000}{10\,000} = 10\% \text{ increase in cost of raw material}$$

$$\frac{1\,000}{50\,000} = 2\% \text{ increase in cost of finished product}$$

Where a product has a high bulk/value ratio then transport costs will raise its price by a much larger percentage than where there is a low bulk/value ratio.

Market density

A parallel argument applies to market density. The costs of delivery per unit of the product are reduced if most of the firm's output is distributed within a small area. The smaller the proportion of output or the larger the area, the higher will be unit costs of distribution.

4·8

Assuming manufacturing costs are similar in any location, in which direction will industry be attracted to locate in the following circumstances?

	Raw materials	Finished product	Location
i	High bulk/ low value	High bulk/ low value	A B or C?
ii	High bulk/ low value	Low bulk/ high value	A B or C?
iii	Low bulk/ high value	Low bulk/ high value	A B or C?
iv	Low bulk/ high value	High bulk/ low value	A B or C?

Location **A**—near localised supply of raw materials
Location **B**—in between A and C
Location **C**—near a high density market

The more dispersed are the sources of raw material or the lower the market density, then the smaller will be their influence on the location of manufacturing industry.

When raw materials are imported and the first stage of processing reduces the bulk and raises the value of the processed products, then location will tend to be at the point of 'break of bulk', hence the establishment of oil refineries and iron and steel works on coastal sites. Such locations also satisfy the need for large areas of flat land.

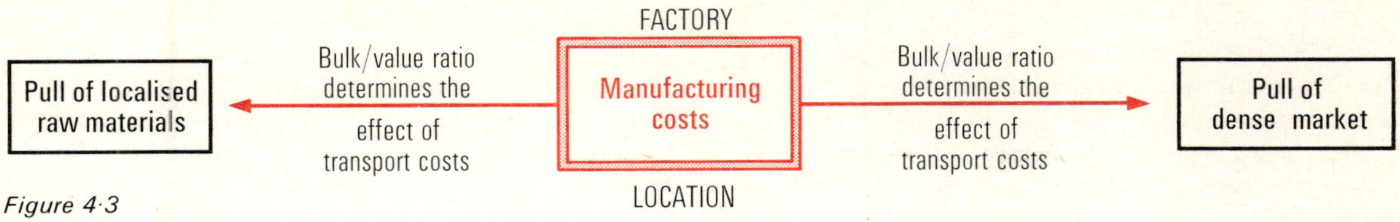

Figure 4·3

LOCATIONAL INFLUENCES

A model of transportation costs

A theoretical model may be constructed to show how the cost of assembling factors of production will influence the location of industry.

Example 1 Two supplies of raw materials are 7 km apart. Assume they are both required in equal quantities but commodity A costs £5 per tonne per kilometre and commodity B costs £10 per tonne per kilometre to transport. Using a pair of compasses, mark off a series of arcs at 1 cm intervals to represent distances of 1 km, 2 km, etc. to 7 km. Label the starting point A. It costs £5 per ton per km to transport commodity A, so each successive arc in your diagram will represent an extra £5 in transport costs as shown in black in figure 4·4. Transport costs of commodity B are shown in red. Assume all other costs are unaffected by the location. Where will transport costs be minimised?

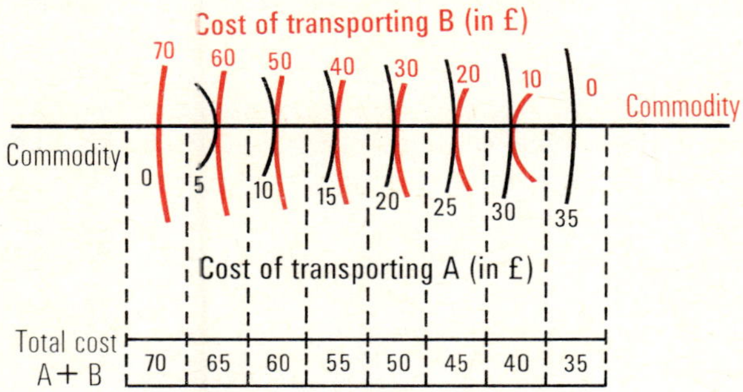

Figure 4·4

The plant using these commodities should be located at the site of B to minimise transport costs.

4·9

Given two raw materials produced 12 kilometres apart, material X costing £7 per tonne/kilometre and material Y costing £9 per tonne/kilometre to transport, how far from the site of X will transport costs be minimised for the plant which is to use them?

A 12 kilometres **B** 0 kilometres
C 6 kilometres

Example 2 Three raw materials are used to make pig iron.

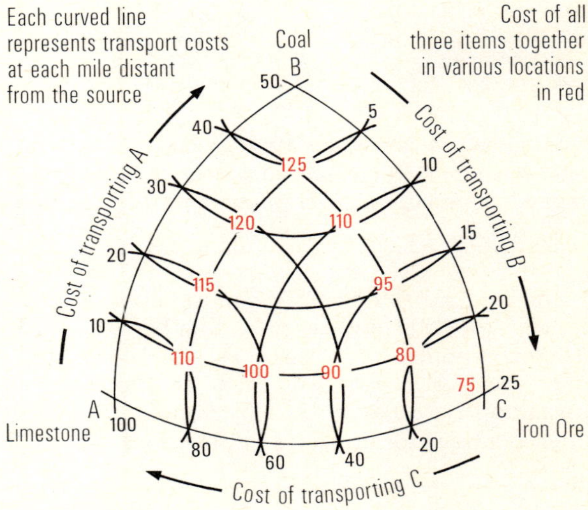

Figure 4·5

A suitable coal mine, limestone quarry and iron ore mine are five km from each other. Costs per tonne/kilometre for transport are; limestone £10, coal £5, iron ore £20. Assume that they are used in equal proportions in a blast furnace to make pig iron, where would transport costs be minimised? Transport costs would be minimised by transporting the limestone and coal to the iron ore mine and setting up blast furnaces there.

4·10

However, the raw materials would not necessarily be used in equal quantities. If they were used in a ratio of 3 tonnes iron ore : 2 tonnes coal : 1 tonne limestone, costs would be increased proportionately. By drawing a new version of figure 4·4 estimate where the blast furnaces should be located to minimise costs.

A 1 km from A, 4 km from B, 4 km from C
B 4 km from A, 4 km from B, 1 km from C
C 5 km from A, 5 km from B, on site C

4·11

Even this does not show the cost of these raw materials to the user, since these transport costs must be added to the costs of the materials. There are then at least three variables to consider—cost of materials, cost of transport, distance of raw materials from one another.

Mine Product	Cost per tonne	Amount used per week	Transport costs per Tonne/km
A Coal	£10	2 000 tonnes	£5
B Limestone	£4	1 000 tonnes	£4
C Iron Ore	£6	3 000 tonnes	£5

Assume the mines are 10 kilometres equidistant. At what point would raw materials costs be minimised? State your answer in terms of distance from A, B and C.

Imagine working out a more sophisticated 'model' for 200 suppliers providing between them 3 000 components to a single user and located all over the U.K. or U.S.A. Such an exercise can nowadays be accomplished by computer, and is often the basis for decisions in plant location.

4·12

Taking each factor of location in turn, consider how it applies to (a) the motor industry, (b) the shipbuilding industry, (c) oil refining.

Regional advantages which reduce costs

Regional specialisation is an extension of the general principle of specialisation. It is the tendency of some regions to specialise in certain industrial activities. At its extreme it can produce mono-industrial areas, that is, areas whose industrial structure (and employment) is bound up with the fortunes of a single industry. Barrow-in-Furness is dominated not only by a single industry, shipbuilding, but by a single firm, Vickers Ltd. A high percentage of a region's work force may be employed in one industry, but the industry may also be found in all other regions. In this case the region is highly specialised but the industry is not very localized.

Localization of an industry is the tendency for some industries to concentrate most of their activities in certain areas where their costs are minimised. It may originally occur because of the overwhelming influence of one of the three natural advantages outlined above. It may continue as a result of industrial inertia—which means that all the original raw materials or other advantages have gone but the industry persists. The classic examples are cutlery in Sheffield and pottery and china in Staffordshire. The produce of these industries depends far more on the skill of the work force than on other factors. It is cheaper to bring in all the industrial raw materials than to move the people. Even if an industry is highly localized, it may not mean that those regions in which it is located, specialises only in that industry; there may be other larger industries there.

Regional advantages acquired over time

Localisation grows gradually and often depends on various advantages which develop over time and which accrue to particular industries in the region. The following five advantages which reduce costs are normally *external* to any particular firm, but are essential to the development of an industry.

i Regional transport. Where local transport facilities are good, the costs of transport of raw materials to the manufacturers, and his distribution costs to the local market, are reduced. A lack of transport may inhibit industrial development on particular sites. Inter-regional transport is essential to regional specialisation because of the necessary exchange of products which subsequently takes place. In the absence of outstanding natural advantages, industry is discouraged from these areas because of inadequate or seasonally congested transport systems.

4·13

Select a local industrial estate or industrial area of a town and find out;

- i ease of access to industrial sites,
- ii congestion or delay in transport,
- iii connections with regional markets,
- iv its inter-regional connections,
- v the availability of Freightliner or container transport services by British Rail.

ii Skilled labour. As an industry grows in an area, the labour force employed by that industry is gradually trained in particular skills. These skills may be deliberately fostered.

When regions specialise in particular industries, local colleges may develop special resources of knowledge and research which ultimately benefit local industry. Government retraining centres assist in the process of retraining labour for new skills which are in demand by local industry. This is particularly important in areas of persistently high unemployment.

iii Research and capital. Regional specialisation may produce a sufficient demand to set up and support research institutions. Originally the Shirley Institute was established in Manchester to serve the research needs of the cotton industry, but its scope has widened to cover a larger range of textile technology. Increasingly university and college research departments are becoming concerned with the needs of industry. They produce both industrial research and a highly specialised and skilled kind of labour.

Just as important in furthering the growth of a region's industry is the local supply of capital, both for the extension of industrial enterprises and for investment in research.

iv Commercial facilities. Typical examples in the past have been the establishment of organised markets such as the Baltic Exchange in London; and the development of specialised knowledge and skills by local banking and insurance services. These make a very real difference to the costs of firms, which are external to the process of production. Savings in these are called *external economies.* At ports, the provision of specialised handling facilities for, say, timber or containers, may involve multi-million pound investments, but reduce costs borne by individual local firms.

An informal market in knowledge and commercial expertise tends to develop in clubs and societies in a local town. Cambridge is a centre for science-based industries, not only because of the University research facilities but because of the cross-fertilisation of ideas between people who live in the area. New entrepreneurs in this kind of industry are clearly attracted by the desire to establish their firm among a like-minded society.

v Subsidiary industries. Not only may the region specialise but firms will specialise among themselves. In Birmingham today some firms make gold wire, others make ring blanks or undertake engraving, and form a subsidiary industry to the Birmingham jewellery trade. However, the general tendency is for firms in subsidiary industries to be integrated with those in the main industry under one ownership of unit of control—the integrated firm.

Specialisation among firms reduces costs by increasing productivity and net output in the same was as did specialisation of labour in S1.

4·14

Which of the following are advantages which may accrue to a highly localized industry?

A An organised market through which to sell the product
B A local supply of skilled labour
C Subsidiary industry
D Good local transport
E Local supply of capital

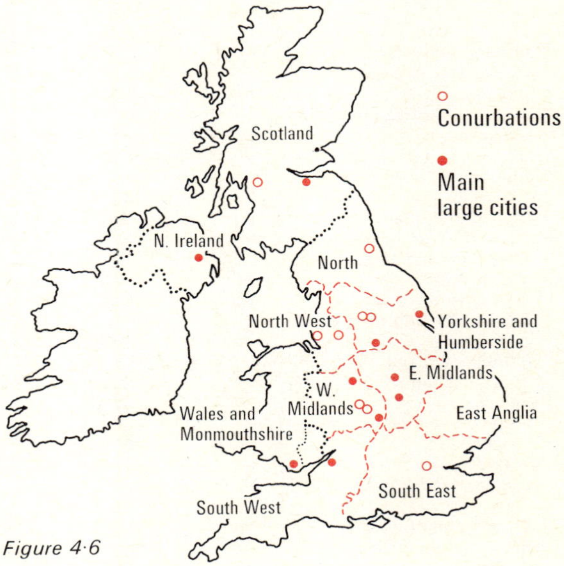

Figure 4·6

NEW STANDARD REGIONS

Standard regions

At this point it may be advantageous to refer to a book of economic geography, or an economic atlas, to refresh your knowledge of the distribution of industry in Britain. In studying the distribution of industry our work overlaps a good deal with that of geographers, and we can make much use of their materials.

Geographers try to define regions, but the administrative areas into which Britain is divided for various purposes do not always coincide with economic regions defined by geographers or economists.

By grouping administrative areas into Standard Regions, which correspond as closely as is practicable to economic regions, it is possible to produce statistics which are more useful than those based on, say, towns or counties alone.

Measuring regional specialisation

Modern economics makes great use of statistical and mathematical techniques, and it is advisable to have some understanding of these. Below are given the methods used to calculate the location quotient and the coefficient of localisation, using the data given in figure 4·7.

Location quotient

Regional specialisation is measured using the location quotient, which compares the extent to which a region's employment is concentrated in a

EMPLOYMENT **Employees in employment in June 1967**
New Standard Regions **Thousands**

	Standard Industrial Classification orders	United Kingdom	North	Yorkshire and Humberside	East Midlands	East Anglia	South East	South West	Wales	West Midlands	North West	Scotland	Northern Ireland
Males and females													
Total all industries and services	I–XXIV	23 303*	1 279	2 034	1 424	606	7 881	1 315	952	2 300	2 926	2 100	477
Total index of production industries	II–XVIII	11 453	679	1 157	837	256	3 216	560	493	1 437	1 580	1 004	235
Total manufacturing industries	III–XVI	8 877	456	877	624	193	2 545	410	321	1 215	1 327	732	178
Agriculture, forestry and fishing	I	443	22	35	35	56	103	48	16	31	19	67	10
Mining and quarrying	II	554	98	112	98	2	18	16	75	43	34	55	4
Food, drink and tobacco	III	853	37	83	49	41	227	65	21	71	128	103	28
Chemicals and allied industries	IV	518	55	46	19	11	170	13	26	27	117	33	3
Metal manufacture	V	592	53	110	46	3	50	6	92	143	37	50	—
Engineering and electrical goods	VI	2 348	123	169	149	56	849	110	58	309	314	184	28
Shipbuilding and marine engineering	VII	208	42	8	1	3	41	18	3	1	31	48	11
Vehicles	VIII	823	11	44	53	16	251	60	20	204	117	40	8
Metal goods not elsewhere specified	IX	569	14	70	22	4	129	12	23	208	61	25	3
Textiles	X	751	20	170	123	3	34	15	17	36	195	91	50
Leather, leather goods and fur	XI	57	2	6	4	1	19	4	2	6	9	4	1
Clothing and footwear	XII	523	34	56	75	14	139	25	15	23	88	31	25
Bricks, pottery, glass, cement, etc.	XIII	353	19	36	24	8	87	11	11	83	47	24	4
Timber, furniture, etc.	XIV	306	15	27	18	11	122	19	7	34	34	25	5
Paper, printing and publishing	XV	640	17	40	26	17	304	37	12	33	90	58	7
Other manufacturing industries	XVI	337	17	12	17	7	125	16	15	47	60	17	5
Construction	XVII	1 590	102	130	90	49	505	103	73	141	168	185	45
Gas, electricity and water	XVIII	433	23	38	26	12	149	31	24	39	51	33	8
Transport and communication	XIX	1 629	80	123	71	38	656	88	68	107	217	154	26
Distributive trades	XX	2 857	153	230	163	69	1 081	166	97	211	359	271	59
Insurance, banking and finance	XXI	658	20	37	20	13	368	27	16	36	67	45	10
Professional and scientific services	XXII	2 681	141	212	137	74	962	176	117	224	314	263	61
Miscellaneous services	XXIII	2 153	108	148	95	60	929	145	77	152	225	175	39
Public administration	XXIV	1 428*	77	92	66	40	565	105	68	101	145	121	37

* Including some civil servants stationed overseas not allocated to regions

Source: *Abstract of Regional Statistics*

Figure 4·7

given industry with the extent to which the nation's employment is concentrated in that industry.

Location quotient =

$$\frac{\%\text{ of the region's work force in the industry}}{\%\text{ of the nation's work force in the industry}}$$

For example, measure the location quotient of textiles in North West Region.

1 Number of employees in

$$\frac{\text{N.W. Region in textiles}}{\text{Total employees in N.W. Region in all industries}} \times \frac{100}{1}\ \%$$

$$= \frac{195\,000}{2\,926\,000} \times \frac{100}{1} = \frac{19\,500}{2\,926} = 6{\cdot}8\%$$

2 Number of employees in U.K. in

$$\frac{\text{Textiles}}{\text{Total employees in U.K. in all industries and services}} \times \frac{100}{1}\ \%$$

$$= \frac{751\,000}{23\,303\,000} \times \frac{100}{1} = \frac{75\,100}{23\,303} = 3{\cdot}2\%$$

Location quotient

$$= \frac{\%\text{ of regional employees in the industry}}{\%\text{ of nations' employees in the industry}}$$

$$= \frac{a}{b} = \frac{6{\cdot}8}{3{\cdot}2} = 2{\cdot}125$$

Location quotient for N.W. Region in textiles = 2·125

4·15

Calculate the location quotient for the North West region for chemicals, agriculture.

4·16

Calculate the location quotient for the industries in exercise 4·17 for your region, or if you live in the North West region, compare with another region of your choice. (Groups should arrange to cover all the regions.)

Coefficient of localisation

The coefficient of localisation measures the extent to which an industry is localised in a particular part of the country. If all industries were spread evenly, then an area employing, say, 10% of the nation's workforce, would also employ 10% of the workers in each industry. If the region employs 40% of the workers in the industry under consideration, there is a deviation of +30%. If it only employs 4% of the workers in the industry, there is a deviation of −6%.

The method of making the complete calculation is set out in figure 4·8. There are two stages to the calculation.

i For each region calculate the percentage of the employment there in the given industry. Subtract from this the percentage of the nation's work force employed in this region in all manufactures and services. A plus deviation is an indication of concentration; a minus deviation indicates a lack of concentration and should be ignored.

ii All plus deviations are added, and divided by 100. We now have a coefficient of localisation

NEW STANDARD REGIONS	% of the selected industry which is employed in each region	% of all manufacturers and services employed in each region	Plus deviations
	Col. 1	Col. 2	Col. 3
North	1·34%	5·49%	
Yorks and Humberside			
E. Midlands			
E. Anglia			
South East			
South West			
Wales			
W. Midlands	24·78%	9·87%	14·91%
North West			
Scotland			
N. Ireland			
	100%	100%	

Figure 4·8

for the industry. The higher the coefficient, the greater the degree of localisation. Note, however, that the coefficient does not tell us *where* the industry is localised. This is shown by comparing the regions' deviations.

As an example, let us work out stage **i** for the vehicle industry. Using data from figure 4·7, complete the entries in figure 4·8.

(a) Find the percentage of the vehicle industry's employees working in the Northern Region

$$= \frac{\text{Total number which 'vehicle' industry employs in Northern Region}}{\text{Total number which 'vehicle' industry employs in U.K.}} \times \frac{100}{}$$

$$= \frac{11\,000}{823\,000} \times \frac{100}{1} = \frac{1\,100}{823} = 1{\cdot}34\%$$

(entered in Col. 1)

(b) Find the percentage of 'all industries and services' employees working in the Northern Region

$$= \frac{\text{Total number which 'all industries \& services' employ in Northern Region}}{\text{Total number which 'all industries \& services' employ in U.K.}} \times \frac{100}{1}$$

$$= \frac{1\,279\,000}{23\,303\,000} \times \frac{100}{1} = \frac{127\,900}{23\,303} = 5{\cdot}49\%$$

(entered in Col. 2)

(c) Repeat (a) and (b) for each Standard Region add, and divide by 100. Enter in Col. 3 all the plus deviations.

Now check this second example for the vehicle industry in the West Midlands Region

Stage 1

(a) $\frac{204\,000}{823\,000} \times \frac{100}{1} = \frac{20\,400}{823} = 24{\cdot}78\%$ (entered in Col. 1)

(b) $\frac{2\,300\,000}{23\,303\,000} \times \frac{100}{1} = \frac{230\,000}{23\,303} = 9{\cdot}87\%$ (entered in Col. 2)

(c) In this case the plus deviation =
24·78—9·87 = 14·91—entered in Col. 3

Col. 1 should total 100% since all of the industry must be employed somewhere in the regions. A similar argument applies to Col. 2. The coefficient of localisation can be calculated for each industry in figure 4·6, but you should understand the process by which these figures can be obtained.

4·17

(This question should only be attempted if you have mechanical computing aids; otherwise it is time-consuming.)

Refer to figure 4·6

a Which are the four most highly localised industries?

b Which are the four most dispersed industries?

Regional specialisation and localized industries

i Localized industry in a specialised region

Some areas have offered so many cost-reducing advantages to one or two industries that these industries have absorbed nearly all the local factors of production. Not only is the industry highly localized but the majority of the working population is employed by that industry in that region, and so both the location quotient and the coefficient of localization will be high.

ii Localized industry in a non-specialised region

Some industries are very highly localized but the location quotient of the region in which it is located may be small if the industry only employs a small proportion of the regions' work force.

Comparative advantages which reduce industrial costs

Why do industries so dominate regions? Partly it is because of cost advantages in particular areas and partly because other regions do *not* offer so many advantages.

Regions specialise in those activities in which their relative efficiency is greatest, that is, in those activities in which they have a *comparative* advantage.

Theory of comparative costs applied to regions

Take for example some entirely imaginary figures for two regions A and B.

The table shows the cost in terms of *units of productive effort* (UPE) which are needed for each unit of output.

Region	Cotton Textiles	Ship-building	Steel	Engineering
A	60	50	100	80
B	40	20	20	60

A unit of productive effort includes all the costs, not just labour, of producing a unit of output.

4·18

a In which industry has each region an absolute advantage i.e. where its costs are lowest per unit of output? (Data above)

Region A

A Cotton | **B** Shipbuilding
C Steel | **D** Engineering

Region B

A Cotton | **B** Shipbuilding
C Steel | **D** Engineering

Check this answer—it is very important.

The law of comparative costs says that a region 'will specialise in those activities in which it has a comparative advantage', that is, where its relative efficiency is greatest.

4·19

Remember that where the use of effort is smallest the efficiency is greatest.

a In which two industries has B the greatest *comparative* advantage, i.e. where its relative efficiency is greatest?

A Cotton | **B** Shipbuilding
C Steel | **D** Engineering

b In which two industries is A's relative *in*efficiency the least?

A Cotton | **B** Shipbuilding
C Steel | **D** Engineering

4·20

a If we assume that each region will specialise in *two* industries, in which two industries will B specialise?

A Cotton | **B** Shipbuilding
C Steel | **D** Engineering

b If B specialises in *three* of these industries, in which will it specialise?

A Cotton | **B** Shipbuilding
C Steel | **D** Engineering

If B can supply the national needs for the products of its two main industries the tendency will be for B to compete so effectively with other regions that, apart from the effect of transport costs, it will find those industries localised only in the B region. If the industries grew to dominate the employment of the region then the fortunes of one or two industries would be the fortunes of the entire region (and there would be a high location quotient.)

The regional problem

Every region, except the south east, suffered very high rates of unemployment during the world economic depression of 1930, but the worst hit areas were those in which one industry predominated, for example the Northeast (shipbuilding), and South Wales (coal mining).

In these 'mono-industrial' areas the majority of the region's work force was employed by the main industry or its subsidiary industries. If the main industry could not sell its products, or get orders for more goods, then the work force was dismissed from employment. Unemployment benefits were small and were reduced by the government as an economy measure. There were in these areas no other industries which could employ the work force. The effect of the failure of the staple industries was so great that eventually the government decided that some means should be found to encourage firms to set up business in these depressed areas. Young people emigrated in search of work in the south east or abroad. These depressed areas tended to have an ageing and less adaptable work force and a reputation for difficult labour relations engendered by fears of unemployment and insecure jobs.

Voluntary relocation

The 'image' which a region has in other parts of the country may completely inhibit voluntary relocation. Not only must the management be satisfied on economic grounds that their costs will be no higher in a new area, but they must also be satisfied that the area is pleasant, cultured and able to provide educational facilities and other amenities. Social factors and personal attitudes have a large influence on management decisions. For example, a Board of Trade investigation indicated the surprise of many management executives and their families that there was any countryside at all in the north.

The costs of congestion

Congestion in the Southeast and Midlands costs money. It overloads community services such as schools, telephone services, and transport. The costs of solving congestion problems are increased as population and, therefore, housing density is increased. Congestion compels workers to demand higher wages because of travelling costs and the higher price of accommodation caused by local scarcity.

If industry expands in the south east and Midlands then either the additional demands for labour will not be met (and wages will rise because men provide a scarce service) or even more people will travel long distances to work, adding further to congestion. The biggest single cause of wage inflation since the post war period has been the 'unsatisfied demand for labour in the Midlands', according to the Department of Employment and Productivity.

The under-employment of manpower is just as wasteful, and the Confederation of British Industries says that much more should be spent on training and retraining in the North to supply relocated industry with the skilled manpower it requires.

Policy objectives

Legislation has concentrated on two aspects. The first is to provide a variety of means by which the costs of new firms (and later of existing firms) should be reduced. This causes a locational pull to new firms or firms wanting to build new plants. The second aspect is the system of denying permission to build new factories in areas which already have more jobs than people in the local work force.

Apart from the negative influence of denying development permission by withholding Industrial Development Certificates (I.D.C.s), nearly all post war legislation has aimed at attracting industry to certain areas by reducing some aspect of their cost. There was comparatively little success before the 1939–45 war in moving people to areas which had job vacancies. Such policies did little for those left in depressed areas and only added to congestion and housing problems elsewhere. Most legislation has aimed at solving the problems of *localized unemployment*.

There is a second problem—the uneven distribution of industry. This has been mentioned already in the discussion of the geographical distribution of population and occupations, and at the beginning of this section on the location of firms and industries. Legislation dealing with new towns and town developments (see *Strategy for the Southeast*, H.M.S.O.) involves, partly, a policy of *re-distribution of industry* and, partly, relief of regional unemployment problems (e.g. new towns in the Northeast and central Scotland).

The full costs of the concentration of industry, services and populations in the Southeast and Midlands has not been estimated. Economists lack a measure for human happiness, and need the assistance of administrators, sociologists, etc., to co-ordinate a policy for the distribution of industry. Recent policy concerning regional unemployment and congestion is discussed in the satellite *The Management of the Economy*.

Legislation in the last 40 years

Before 1939. Legislation before the war was largely confined to persuasion. This was not very successful because there was little incentive for industry to move to the depressed areas and little or no assistance for unemployed people to move to those areas where there was work.

1939–50. The Barlow Report changed the emphasis to moving industry to the people. This tends to reduce the social costs of moving the unemployed. It does help reduce poverty and human misery in the depressed areas where so many were unemployed and it saves wasting human productive resources and social capital in the form of houses, roads, municipal services and transport etc.

Part of the means of persuasion was a system of grants available in certain areas designated Development Areas, and provision of government sponsored industrial estates like that at Team Valley, Gateshead, established in 1936. The other main weapon was the building licence, which was necessary for all industrial buildings of more than 465 m^2 in area. The permission for development contained in the licence could be withheld if the development was not in the 'interest of the nation' and could more usefully take place elsewhere. Licences were freely available in Development Areas.

1951–60. This was a period when legislation lapsed and persuasion was again tried. Control over office development was established but not enforced, with the consequent surplus of unused offices in London, but an acute shortage of housing. Extra assistance for setting up industry by grants and investmant allowances (whereby £100 000 of capital could be depreciated against tax liability and so cost the equivalent of £30 000) was selectively used to assist small areas of particularly high unemployment outside the development areas.

1960–64. Under the Local Employment Acts the Development Areas were replaced by a number of smaller Development Districts within which assistance was available to assist in reducing pockets of unemployment. More assistance was available to provide factories for industry, grants for those who built their own, and some help for the first time in non-industrial buildings, for example, warehouses.

Standard grants of 25% of industrial buildings and 10% of cost of acquiring and installing plant and machinery were also introduced so that the size of grant aid became predictable.

1965 & 66. Industrial Development Acts strengthened the control by Industrial Development Certificate (I.D.C.) and strengthened investment incentives in Development Areas (which superseded the Development Districts) and widened the criteria on which the Board of Trade established these Areas. These were 'all circumstances, actual or potential, including the state of employment and unemployment, population changes, migration and the objectives of Regional Policies'. Industrial Development Certificates (under the 1966 Act) could have various conditions added which were then included in the planning permission.

By 1969 up to 35% of the cost of a new building in a development area could be met by grants. Investment grants on new plant were 40% (twice the rate for other parts of Britain) and general grants could be made towards the cost of new capital assets and the need for working capital. Other help included grants for unusual initial cost in setting up in development areas, low rents for buildings in government sponsored estates (and remember rents in the Home Counties may be three or more times normal rents in the North). Some assistance in training of labour and in housing key workers was also available.

Industrial estates

These may be sponsored by private companies, local authorities, New Town Corporations, or the Industrial Estates Corporations (one each in England, Scotland and Wales) which are national corporations set up in 1960, government sponsored, for the establishment and administration of industrial estates all over the country.

The first was established as a private venture at Trafford Park, Manchester, in 1896, based on a dock side location at the third largest port in Britain. It had rail and road services to the industrial hinterland of south east Lancashire, and the port of Manchester was, and is, the gateway to export markets. This estate was primarily a heavy industrial estate.

Diversification of local industry

The first estate for light industry, which still exists, was a private venture by Slough Estates Limited. It built factory buildings which new firms could rent instead of buying outright. Power and water came from the Estate's own power station and artesian wells. Setting up a factory was, therefore, much cheaper than was possible before. Slough Estates was enormously successful and today houses over 400 light industrial firms. The principles upon which these estates were built were extended to Government-sponsored estates, first in the North East and South Wales, and later, all over the country. Team Valley, Gateshead (1936) was the first government-sponsored estate established under the 1934 Special Areas (Development and Improvement) Act. Here the English Industrial Estates Corporation (established in 1960) has its headquarters. Over 116 000 people are employed on government financed estates and sites in England alone.

The aim is to diversify industry in mono-industrial areas (so reducing the location quotient in these areas for the dominant industry) and thus reduce local unemployment and achieve a less highly localized industrial pattern in the U.K.

Local authority industrial estates

Among the first local authorities to set up industrial estates were Liverpool and Manchester. Their motive, like those who have followed their example, was to increase local employment opportunities, to control industrial development and the location of industry in their areas, and to derive the benefit of a higher rate income which such estates provide.

Board of Trade industrial estates

These are operated as part of the regional policies of the government, especially in New Towns and 'overspill areas'. As many of the old slum and industrial areas of the nineteenth century are cleared from the centres of the conurbations, new industrial sites are required (a) to house industry which supplies local as well as national markets, and (b) to provide the displaced populations with employment. 'An unemployed man is a wasted national asset, just as much as is unemployed machinery.'

'Advance' factories were built in advance of requirements. In 1968 twenty-four were still unoccupied.

B. of T. Factories built

	1965	1966	1967	1968
Northern England	3	7	12	11
N.W. England	0	1	1	2
S.W. England	0	5	0	1
Scotland	5	10	18	15

Private estates

A single developer established over 50 industrial estates in England between 1955 and 1969; a factory or warehouse completed every week for 14 years! A sum of £50 million was invested in another 23 industrial estates in Scotland by the same firm. This rather overshadows the Board of Trade's advance factory development.

New towns

New towns and town development plans are a combined approach to the dispersal of population and the dispersal of industry. They involve, usually, the establishment of industrial estates, and in certain areas special tax and other concessions are offered to encourage firms to move to these areas.

Conflict of policies

Industrial development is subject to control by I.D.C.s. Some new towns are in development areas and so receive I.D.C.s fairly easily, and the New Town Development Corporations can also offer the attractions of grants, buildings and other assistance. Where a new town is not in a Development Area the Board of Trade may refuse I.D.C.s on the grounds that the development should be elsewhere. This directly conflicts with the specific objectives of the New Town Development Corporations. On the other hand, many Development Areas lack the modern estates and accompanying conditions with which to attract industrialists but they can offer the financial incentives, provided under various acts of legislation.

Part of the problem is the distinction, noted earlier, between a policy designed to distribute industry more evenly and a policy designed to diversify more industrial areas and to reduce the waste due to localized unemployment.

ANSWERS

4·1

Correct **A, C, E**: these are the advantages:

Mistaken **B**: the sole trader usually lacks the capital to expand business.

Mistaken **D**: sole traders usually lack the financial resources to lend for a long period.

Mistaken **E**: sole traders have to provide labour and management together.

4·2

Correct **D.**

Mistaken **A**: this is not necessary.

Mistaken **B**: this option does not add new capital, it only changes the ownership of existing capital.

Mistaken **C**: there is no such thing in a private company.

4·3

Correct **A.**

Mistaken **B**: this is two thirds of the issued capital.

Mistaken **C**: the issued capital is part of the nominal capital, not the other way round.

4·4

Correct **A**: only a public company has a prospectus.

Correct **C**: only a public company has a stock exchange quotation because private companies cannot sell their shares publicly. However, not all public companies have stock exchange quotations.

Mistaken **B**: though private companies may have only fifty shareholders, more may be added if they are past employees, without negating private status.

Mistaken **D**: both private and public companies have limited liability.

Mistaken **E**: the public sale of even one percent of shares will make a company public. Many large public companies, for example, Marks & Spencer, Pilkingtons, G.E.C./A.E.I. and many merchant banks are still controlled by families.

4·5

Correct **E**: the risk is reduced by having preference.

Mistaken **A, B, C, D.**

4·6

a Correct **B.**

Mistaken **A**: re-read the text.

b Correct **C.**

Mistaken **D**: 51% enables you to out-vote everyone else.

4·7

Own research.

4·8

i Correct **B.**
ii Correct **A.**
iii Correct **B.**
iv Correct **C.**

4·9

Correct **A**: total transport costs would be (7 x 12) plus (9 x 0) = £84.

Mistaken **B**: total transport costs would be (9 x 12) plus (7 x 0) = £108.

Mistaken **C**: total transport costs would be (9 x 6) plus (7 x 6) = £96.

4·10

Correct **C**: the total cost per unit of coal plus limestone plus iron = £100.

Mistaken **A**: £10 plus £40 plus £240 = £290.

Mistaken **B**: £40 plus £40 plus £60 = £140.

4·11

Costs will be minimised at C the site of the iron ore mine, 10 km from A and 10 km from B.

Coal	£20 000
Transport	£100 000
Limestone	£4 000
Transport	£40 000
Iron Ore	£18 000
	£182 000

4·12

The motor industry

Production depends upon many small specialist units, each supplying components to an assembly plant. Transport costs are a vital item. Labour need only be semi-skilled.

The shipbuilding industry

The local supply of raw materials is less important than formerly. A suitable physical location is essential. Skilled labour is required.

Oil refining

Refineries require large areas, and must be located near to the point of import. The tankers must have a suitable anchorage, but labour requirements are slight.

4·13

Own research.

4·14

Correct **A, B, C, D, E**: all these are possible.

a	Mining and quarrying	·46
	Textiles	·45
	Metal manufacture	·41
	Shipbuilding, etc.	·37
b	Professional and scientifical services	·04
	Gas, electricity and water	·04
	Distributive trades	·05
	Construction	·06

4·15

The location quotient for the North West Region:
for chemicals = 1·7
for agriculture = ·34

4·16

Results variable.

4·17

Highly localised

Mining	·46
Textiles	·45
Metal manufacture	·41
Shipbuilding	·37

Dispersed

Gas, electricity and water	·04
Professional services	·04
Distributive trades	·05
Construction	·06

4·18

a A has an absolute disadvantage in everything B has an absolute advantage because it uses the *least* amount of effort per unit of output in each industry.

4·19

a Correct **B, C.**
b Correct **A, D.**

4·20

a Correct **B, C.**
b Correct **A, B, C.**

MARKETS

STUDY SECTION **5**

A market exists in any situation in which exchange between buyers and sellers takes place. In everyday speech we usually refer to a place—the cattle market, the produce market—where buyers and sellers congregate at regular intervals. In economics the term market is used more widely. The London Stock Exchange is a market place for shares, because here members of the Stock Exchange meet to buy and sell, but they do so largely on behalf of clients, who may live anywhere in Britain, or even abroad. The market for shares consists of those persons owning them and those persons wishing to sell them, who make contact with each other through the Stock Exchange, and their respective stockbrokers. Thus this market consists of a group of people. Similarly we may refer to the teenage market for records, the market for cigars, the Birmingham market for women's fashions. Any group of people having a common interest in a certain type of commodity may be identified as a market, and as communications improve, it becomes less necessary that the group should ever gather in one place. Central London contains at least fifty camera shops, and clearly it can be considered a market place for cameras, but the magazine *Amateur Photographer* carriers advertisements from many shops: it creates a market situation wherever it circulates.

The extent of the market can thus be delimited by knowledge. Most markets, in fact, exist not as places, but as organisations, or even as publications, through which buyers and sellers make contact.

Economists analyse market situations according to the state of competition within them. One measuring rod is a rather artificial and very simplified concept known as *perfect competition*. It is an economic model with which one can compare real situations. The model makes use of a number of assumptions, any number of which may not apply in a given situation. It is these exceptions which distinguish various types of *imperfect* competition. There is nothing idealistic or necessarily desirable about a state of perfect competition. Indeed some near approaches in real life can be very wasteful of resources. The opposite extreme to perfect competition is *absolute monopoly* where one firm produces the whole supply of a given commodity. Like competition, it is not necessarily either good or bad.

Common examples of markets

The most familiar example is the ordinary *retail* market where the housewife buys vegetables, meat and other foodstuffs, clothing, household goods, etc. Where perishable goods are involved, sellers are often anxious to clear their stocks by the end of the day. Stalls are close together, and the buyer has the opportunity to compare prices asked by various sellers. They, for their part, have full knowledge of what their competitors are asking for their goods. If one man drops the price of tomatoes, for example, his neighbour will probably find it necessary to follow suit.

The large *wholesale* markets of London are well-known and serve a wide area—Smithfield (meat), Billingsgate (fish) and Covent Garden (fruit and vegetables)—but most large provincial cities also have produce markets where retail shopkeepers buy their stocks. Of a similar nature are the country cattle markets, where butchers buy their beef from the farmers.

A large organisation, such as a hotel chain or supermarket, may have buyers in several wholesale markets, in touch by telephone or telex. Thus buying can be switched to the cheapest point.

The market for *labour* in its widest sense consists of all employers' organisations and trade unions, the Labour Exchanges, and the 'Situations Vacant' columns of newspapers and magazines. Through these buyers make known their wants, and suppliers of labour make known their availability. As a result, a general level of wages emerges. A market for a particular type of labour must be far more carefully defined. For example, at any given moment there is a fixed quantity of qualified teachers. They are represented by five unions. Their services are bought by the local education authorities, and private schools. The vacant posts are advertised in about six magazines and three or four daily newspapers. Though the wage level is fixed in the short term by negotiation (in the Burnham Committee), in the long term it will depend upon the number of teachers required to fill posts, and the salary necessary to attract new entrants who will thereby add to the supply of teachers.

The *capital* market is described in S6 and the satellite book *Financial Institutions*, but we must remember that as well as the Stock Exchange and the various banking organisations, it includes the

Press, particularly the 'city' pages. An investor may ask his bank to buy shares for him, but his decision to invest money in a new company may have come through knowledge gained in his newspaper, or a radio or television broadcast.

Land cannot be moved, so there can clearly be no one place where it is offered for sale. It is usually sold through estate agents and press advertisements. Building plots may be offered in local newspapers, but farms and factory sites would be advertised in appropriate trade magazines.

Even *enterprise* has its market, as the numerous firms of management consultants show. These consultants give general advice to firms, but also act as intermediaries between those firms requiring managerial skills, and those individuals who, possessing these skills, wish to sell them.

5·1

If you wished to buy or sell the following, through which organisations or publications would you obtain market information?

i A second-hand car
ii A racing pigeon
iii A mansion and country estate
iv A boatyard
v A caravan holiday

Supply and demand in the market

A vegetable produce market, where buyers and sellers meet face to face offers a clear example of the workings of supply and demand to produce a market price, and is worth examining in some detail. Let us see what might happen in a vegetable market during the course of one day. Figure 5·1 shows the demand and supply curves prevailing for lettuce.

At the start of the day the lettuce growers expect the price to be 5p per lettuce, at which price they are only prepared to bring 200 lettuces. However, to their surprise and delight, they find that the hoteliers and shopkeepers who buy their lettuces are willing to pay 30p per lettuce if only 200 are available. Those sellers with initiative telephone their farms to arrange for extra supplies of lettuce to be sent. As these arrive, the quantity supplied to the market rises to 360, which they are prepared to sell at 12p. However, buyers are prepared to pay 16p so further supplies are still put on the market until a situation is reached where the quantity of lettuces supplied equals 440.

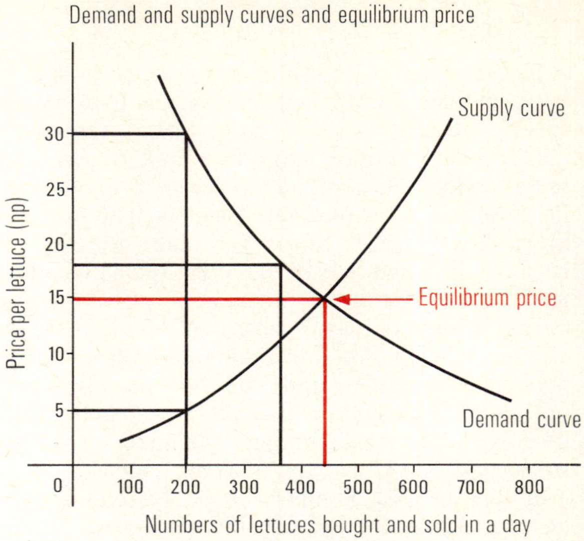

Figure 5·1

Thus supply is a function of price, i.e. the amount supplied varies as the price changes. At this price the quantities supplied and demanded are balanced. If the price fell further, buyers would be willing to purchase more than 440, but sellers will not offer more lettuces, as at this price they consider it not worth the bother and cost of picking them.

Thus at a price 15p and quantity 440 lettuces we have an equilibrium price and quantity, that is, a position of balance where the quantity supplied equals the quantity demanded.

5·2

How much money would be paid by the buyers to the sellers if the market price had been fixed at 15p during the whole day's trading?

5·3

Demand curves usually slope downwards towards the right, because at lower prices the consumer is able and willing to buy more.
True/False.

5·4

The demand curve for lettuce links the various quantities of lettuces a consumer would buy at different prices if every other influence on demand remained unchanged.
True/False.

5·5

Supply curves slope upwards to the right because the lettuce growers must usually be recompensed for the extra costs of bringing extra supplies to the market.
True/False.

5·6

If the price of lettuces falls below 15p suppliers will pick more lettuces from their fields and transport them to the market.
True/False.

Perfect competition

The assumptions for perfect competition are:
i large numbers of both sellers and buyers,
ii product homogeneity, which means that there is no real or imagined difference between the outputs of different producers,
iii freedom of entry for buyers and sellers into the market,
iv a responsive market, that is, there is nothing to hinder an immediate response to any price changes.

Let us examine these assumptions in detail.

i Large numbers No single buyer or seller can have any influence on the amount bought or offered for sale in the market, nor can he influence the price.

No consumer buys enough to affect the market price by buying more or by buying less. The number of sellers is so large that no supplier offers for sale more than a small percentage of the total, and, therefore, any change in the individual firm's output does not affect the market enough to affect the price. It sells all its output at a price set by external market forces. In other words it is a 'price taker'. Depicted graphically, the demand curve facing each firm will be horizontal as in figure 5·2.

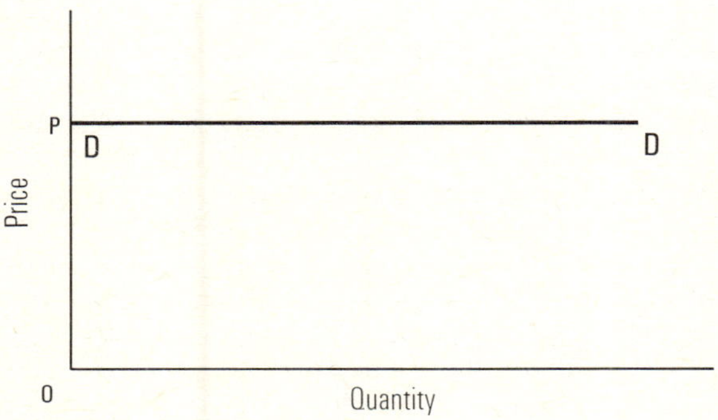

Figure 5·2

At price OP the demand for the individual firm's products is unlimited. This condition is called perfectly elastic demand, and will be explained later.

ii Product homogeneity Consumers must believe that each supplier's product is identical to those of other suppliers, and that they are, therefore, perfect substitutes for one another. If consumers believe that the products are not perfect substitutes, then they will be prepared to pay a higher price for those which they believe to be superior.

The consumers will have no 'favourite' shop or supplier if the product is really identical. The circumstances under which the sale takes place must not give any apparent superiority to the product sold by one shop as compared with another shop, or else price differences appear and perfect competition will cease to exist. Since consumers will be indifferent as to who sells the product, any slight price fall in one place will attract all the consumers, and the price will tend to rise back to its market level. Any price rise will deter any consumers from buying from that shop or supplier.

Sellers are assumed to have no favourite clients to whom they give preferential prices or price reductions on large orders. Suppliers will be indifferent as to who buys their products.

Consequently, you also have to assume that there is no persuasive advertising (that is, the kind which attempts to show the unique or special qualities of a certain brand of goods). Branding and other artificial means of differentiating between products is clearly incompatible with the perfect market.

iii Freedom of entry into the market If the free market price is to be established and maintained, no buyer must be prevented from competing in the market. Legal and physical limits on consumers will not exist in the perfect market.

In the factor market, manufacturers are assumed to be free to buy factors without any artificial barriers such as the need for membership of particular unions or, in land, the need for an Industrial Development Certificate or planning permission.

Suppliers are also free to enter the market without barriers, such as refusal of distributors to carry their product, or patents preventing manufacture of certain goods. Financial barriers will not prevent entry of marginal firms into a perfect market. Each firm will be supplying a small percentage of the market requirements, but that does not mean the firm will have to be small, because the market may be very large.

It is assumed that the price of factors does not rise as the output of firms increases, or the number of firms in the industry increases. This means either that some resources are currently unemployed, or that resources are completely mobile in that they can change to a new use without hindrance. We shall see later that this condition is described as a perfectly elastic supply of factors. The result of this assumption is that all firms have the same costs and compete on equal terms.

Freedom for buyers and sellers to leave the market is also assumed.

iv A responsive market This is the assumption that there are almost immediate market responses by sellers and buyers to any change in price.

Buyers and sellers must have *perfect knowledge* of the market, that is, any slight change in price in the market would result in immediate reaction. If they do not know the price at every point of sale, then they might, unknowingly, pay more or ask more than the market price ruling elsewhere.

Transport costs have to be assumed to be insignificant, so that there are no geographical barriers to prevent consumers taking advantage of price differences.

Suppliers of commodities to the market are assumed to know what is the profit rate of each competitor, so that they may react to changing circumstances. Higher than normal profits will tend to attract new firms into the market.

The conditions of a large number of buyers and sellers competing on equal terms, with perfect knowledge, negligible transport costs and no government intervention in the operation of the price mechanism, are often considered to be the conditions necessary for a *perfect market*. This limited concept must not be confused with the wider concept of perfect competition. The market describes the relation between buyers and sellers, whereas competition describes the relation between both buyers and buyers, and sellers and sellers.

5·7

Construct a summary table in three columns. Column 1 should list the conditions of the perfect market **i, ii, iii, iv**. Column 2 should show their effect on buyers 1a, 2a, 3a, 4a. Column 3 their effect on sellers 1b, 2b, 3b, 4b.

5·8

Chart at least one example for each section, which illustrates a breakdown of the assumptions made. Each one will represent some degree of imperfection in the market.

Monopoly among suppliers and monopsony among buyers

As a contrast to perfect competition we can look at *monopoly* which, at its limit, may be represented by a single producer supplying a product for which there is no close substitute. A consumer who buys the entire output of a commodity is a *monopsonist*, the only common example of which is the government. (Monopsony is also called a buyers' monopoly).

Monopoly

Trying to decide whether or not any particular firm is a monopoly first requires you to define what you mean by a 'product', and whether or not there is a close substitute for the product. A real monopolist will produce something which is unique, and which, therefore, is the only product which will satisfy a particular want. In practice there is nearly always some alternative commodity which will satisfy a want, even if only indirectly. Such a product or service is a substitute, but can it be said to be a different product from the original one if it is used as a substitute? Suppose you have a *want* for entertainment: *Entertainments*—sport, television, radio, books, theatre, music.

Each one is an indirect substitute satisfying the same *want*. Suppose you opt for music, which kind will you buy? Traditional jazz, modern jazz, country and western, blues, 'pop', classical orchestral, opera, ballet?

By which means will you satisfy the want for music? Listening to records, tape, radio or television or by participating in a small ensemble, group, in a band or orchestra?

If you listen to records, which 'label' will suit your taste in music? Each label is a close subsititute for others, although a great deal of advertising is simply designed to persuade you otherwise.

At each stage, you are selecting from a range of substitutes, however indirect. At what point should the line be drawn to distinguish one product or service from another? The answer is indeterminate and poses one of the problems of defining a monopolist.

The demand curve in imperfect competition and monopoly

In all kinds of imperfect competition, including monopoly, the output which a single firm produces will affect the price of the product. Because of the differences, however slight, between one firm's product and another's, each firm can be said to have a monopoly of its own product, and in order to sell more output, the firm must lower the price at which it is offered. Therefore the demand curve of each firm in imperfect competition slopes downwards towards the right (figure 1·7).

Legislation in the U.K. which seeks to limit monopolies assumes monopoly powers may exist where 33·3% of the total sales of a given product are controlled by one person (or firm), or by restrictive agreements between firms, or by firms who organise themselves in such a way as to restrict competition.

The real test is whether profits are abnormally high compared with the rest of the industry, or whether there is a significant degree of price control by the firm or firms concerned (see satellite *Monopolies and Restrictive Practices*).

The most monopolistic situation in real life would be one in which there is *one* dominant firm which does not have to consider the short-run effects of its actions on the producers who directly or indirectly produce substitutes for its product, is not immediately or significantly affected by the actions of other firms, and is in a position to prevent new firms from entering the industry.

Sources of monopoly power

These are often based on the *control* of supplies of raw material and/or of the means of distribution by which competitors may be denied supplies altogether, or may be forced to pay high prices in order to obtain them.

Other sources of power rest on various forms of agreement, which may be written (where the parties to the agreement want to ensure that everyone keeps to the agreement) or it may just be an 'understanding' or 'gentleman's agreement' which is based only on trust in the other party. The agreements may cover price policy, or the quantity offered for sale (an attempt to create artificial scarcity), or a market-sharing system by which geographical areas are shared out in such a way that each individual seller only 'competes' actively in areas which the others miss out!

Monopolies may come into being in several ways. Some are created when sellers believe that by acting together they can obtain a better price than by competing. This belief gives rise to the agreements just described.

Other monopolies are created by statute. The laws concerning copyright and patents enable artists, photographers, composers and inventors to have exclusive rights to the exploitation of their creations. Nationalised industries are usually legal monopolies, and so are certain professions. The National Coal Board has the sole right to mine coal in Britain, and only solicitors and barristers can carry out legal work. Other legal monopolies, such as the licensing of taxi cabs, are created for reasons of public safety, and to avoid wasteful competition.

Some firms become monopolies through commercial processes. If they are outstandingly successful, they may buy up their competitors, or drive them out of business. Firms which have an early start in an industry often become so large that later arrivals find it impossible to amass enough capital or capture enough sales to compete effectively.

Few entrepreneurs enjoy competition. If they are successful, events tend to create a monopoly. When times are hard, competitors tend to get together for survival. Behind a trade association's talk of 'public safety', 'maintaining standards' or 'regulating entry to the profession' (trade or industry), there is often a desire to eliminate competition. The 'national interest' may be invoked to eliminate overseas competitors, by means of quotas and tariffs. A quota is a fixed quantity of goods which is allowed to be imported, whereas a tariff is a tax on imports which has the effect of raising the price for the consumer, though the importer may import as large a quantity as he wishes. (See satellite *Agriculture*.)

Within the factor market, unions may negotiate a 'closed shop' policy under which all workers in a firm must be members of the appropriate union before the firm will employ them. The union then acts as a monopoly in the negotiation of the price at which labour is hired. Some unions, such as the British Medical Association, not only operate a 'closed shop' but undertake the control of entry into the profession, and also maintain standards of work and discipline.

Forms of trade restriction which are illegal are detailed in the Restrictive Trade Practices Act, 1956, and various judgements have been made by the Restrictive Practices Court. Recommendations of the Monopolies Commission are made in its Reports which should be available through your local library.

5·9

Imagine you are a manufacturer of certain consumer goods. How many ways are there to 'spoil' the market to your own advantage? Are your methods legal? Read the satellite text *Monopolies and Restrictive Practices* and *Agriculture*.

Monopsony

Private sector examples are not common. In some instances a retail chain of stores may require a supply of goods which is greater than any individual manufacturer can produce. To any individual firm, the retail stores buying organisation is a monopsonist because it can take the whole of the producers' output. To some extent the monopsonist can dictate price, quality and design, but it is in the interest of both parties to see that the manufacturer makes a reasonable level of profit, to keep him in that line of business.

In the domestic market, government departments or nationalised industries may be the major buyers of products such as mining equipment, aircraft of telephones. The government has a monopsony because there is no alternative buyer, while there may be an alternative supplier (or the government could create one as a public corporation, e.g. the Post Office could make its own telephones).

A special form of monopsony is the agricultural marketing board. Partly because agricultural production is liable to vary from year to year with the weather, and partly because many farms are too small to afford efficient marketing techniques, it has become customary to set up marketing boards. To the farmers they are a monopsony; to the buyers of produce a monopoly. The boards usually try to set a steady price, so that in years of good crops the farmers receive more, and in years of scarcity less, than they would under freely competitive conditions. In some years the boards make profits, in others losses. Overall, they must balance their profits against their losses.

Marketing boards have had a chequered history. Some, like the Milk Marketing Board, have been successful, others, like the Tomato and Cucumber, and Egg Marketing Boards, have been disbanded. Much seems to depend upon the farmers confidence. If they consider that they can get better prices by not selling through the Boards, they will do so, and the system will break down.

A curious position exists where government intervenes in industrial production. Some projects, such as the construction of space rockets, or the development of supersonic aircraft, involve such enormous research costs that without a government contract or finance, they would not be undertaken. Where the government is the purchaser of the product, a state of true monopsony exists.

Market information

Organisations such as the Consumer's Association, publishers of *Which,* are aiming to create a more perfect market situation, by the dissemination of accurate information.

All markets in which the buyers are collectors, e.g. of stamps, coins, antiques, whether they are genuine collectors or speculators, depend upon the availability of information on the current prices at which deals are made. Under conditions in which large numbers of people speculate that prices will rise, the prices do tend to rise because the demand for the goods has risen rapidly, while the supply may well be fixed or even diminishing. Speculation is subject to '*self-fulfilling expectation*', that is, the reaction of speculators to market situations tends to produce the results they fear or anticipate.

Remember then, that the state of competition between buyers not only describes their situation but is also the situation which sellers face in the market, and which may be exploited for reasons of profit. Equally, the competitive situation which exists between sellers, which describes the conditions under which supply takes place, is also the situation with which buyers are faced. Under perfect competition or under monopsony *consumers sovereignty* reigns, but in almost any imperfect market, consumers are not sovereign because market imperfections may more easily be exploited by producers than by the individual consumers themselves.

5·10

What does 'consumer sovereignty' mean?

A Consumers can buy whatever they please.

B Consumers' decisions in purchasing (or not purchasing) ultimately determine the selection of goods which will be produced.

C Consumers are most powerful in the market because there are more of them than there are manufacturers.

5·11

If the manufacturer is a monopolist who operates in a market which has imperfections in the competition between buyers, what is likely to happen to the market price if more is offered for sale?

The market price tends:

A To rise **B** To fall
C To remain constant

5·12

Look at a current car advertisement and say how many ways in which it seeks to mar the perfect market. *Groups of students* should seek to find the 'advertisement of the day', or for the week, which uses the greatest number of techniques to 'spoil' the perfect market.

5·13

A firm finds that it has to pay higher wages in order to attract additional labour. Where in the factor market may the imperfections lie?

ANSWERS

5·1

i *Glass's Guide.* Dealers. Newspapers.
ii *Racing Pigeon. Pigeon Racing News.* Pigeon clubs.
iii *Country Life. Times. Sunday Times.* Estate agent.
iv Industrial estate agent. *Motor Boat. Ship and Boat Builder. Yachting Monthly* Local newspapers.
v Local newspapers, newagent's display card. *Modern Caravan. Caravan Sites.*

5·2

6 600p.

5·3

True.

5·4

True.

5·5

True.

5·6

False.

5·7

	Buyers	**Sellers**
Large numbers	No influence on price	Only offers small % of market
Product homogeneity	Products are perfect substitutes. No favourite shops	No favourite clients
Freedom of entry	No limits on entry	Marginal firms may enter
Responsive market	Perfect knowledge Frequent purchases. No transport barriers	Know own and other profits Perfect knowledge

5·8

	Buyers	**Sellers**
Large numbers	Post office buys van	Kodak sells 90% of colour film in U.K.
Product homogeneity	Loyalty to shops and brands	Discounts for large customers
Freedom of entry	Licence needed to purchase gun	Wholesalers sell only to the trade
Responsive market	May be unaware that supply price has fallen and be willing to pay usual rate	Not always aware that customers willing to pay more

5·9

Buy up competitors.

Advertise to create consumer preference.

Accept low profits to undercut competitors and drive them out of business.

Come to exclusive arrangements with suppliers of raw materials, or buy them up.

All above are legal.

5·10

Correct **B.**

Mistaken **A**: consumers can buy only what is offered for sale.

Mistaken **C**: it is only what people buy or do not buy which determines what will be produced.

5·11

Correct **B.**

Mistaken **A**: people tend to buy *less* when prices rise.

Mistaken **C**: when more of the product is made available, this is unlikely.

5·12

Group activity.

5·13

Closed shop policy, immobility of factors, imperfect knowledge of alternative work, fixed or limited supply of labour, etc.

MONEY AND FINANCIAL INSTITUTIONS

STUDY SECTION **6**

In this section we shall examine the part played by money in an economic system. Money is used not because it contains value in itself, but because it performs certain essential functions in an economy. Before examining the part played by money within our economic system, however, we should be quite certain of our definition of the term 'money'.

Can you imagine a society in which money plays no part? Probably you will immediately think of a primitive society. Such a society has a barter economy, barter being the principal means by which people exchange the goods and services which they contribute to the community's total production. In such a system complications arise as soon as trade is attempted. A man who has specialised in making spears will need to provide his food wants by exchanging the spears he has produced for different items of food. He has to find someone who not only has food to exchange but also wants spears in exchange. This is called a double coincidence of wants. The pattern of trade is such that these societies hold regular gatherings where everyone who has produced a commodity must take it to market in the hope of finding someone with whom to exchange. Any great degree of specialisation is positively discouraged, and everyone tends to provide completely for his own wants and the advantages from specialisation are foregone.

Inevitably, even primitive societies discovered that some commodities are acceptable to everyone. Salt, ivory, precious stones and metals, rare sea shells are all attractive and scarce enough in themselves to be acceptable in payment for all other goods in primitive societies. These items have therefore served as an intermediary between buyer and seller. Our spear manufacturer, for instance, could exchange spears for, say, salt. He could then store the salt safe in the knowledge that he could always exchange the salt for any food he needed. There does not have to exist a double coincidence of wants, therefore, for trade to take place. People can specialise and feel safe in the knowledge that they will be able to exchange the goods they have produced. In this instance salt is acting as a medium of exchange, and it is the money of the society in which it is used.

Anything which performs the functions of money, such as salt in the previous example, *is* money. Let us examine these functions.

i A medium of exchange. Anything which functions as money in a society can be used in payment for goods which are required. In this role money allows specialisation to take place and removes the need for a double coincidence of wants. It can be compared to the oil which circulates around a car engine. The function of the oil is to reduce the friction between moving parts; the function of the medium of exchange is to reduce the friction between potential buyers and sellers.

ii A measure of value. Money acts as the unit in which accounts are kept, costs are calculated and prices are stated. How would our man quote the price of one of his spears? He might price it at one pound of salt or three fish or one length of rope, and so on. Thus without money a commodity or service does not have a single price but a series of exchange values.

iii A store of value. The existence of a commodity which is acceptable in payment for anything else allows anyone who produces more than he needs immediately to store the wealth he has created, safe in the knowledge that when he comes to spend it in the future, it will have kept its value. A hunter may catch in a week more than he can eat. If he can sell the surplus, he can store the money and buy food at a later date.

iv A standard for deferred payments. Where a transaction is agreed upon now, but payment is to be made in the future, each party to the agreement must be sure that terms in the future will be the same. Otherwise no deal will be possible and no credit will be allowed. Since the value of money is usually stable over a period of time, both buyer and seller can feel happy that the terms of the agreement will remain the same.

Any commodity which performs the above functions is acting as money and therefore *is* money. Generally speaking precious metals have become universally the accepted materials for money, because they have certain qualities. Perhaps you can find which qualities these are by answering the following questions.

6·1

Why would dollars be unsuitable for use as money in the United Kingdom?

6·2

Why would pebbles from the sea shore be unsuitable?

6·3

Why would iron be unsuitable for coinage?

6·4

Why would old postage stamps be unsuitable?

6·5

Why would lumps of granite be unsuitable?

6·6

Why would large diamonds be unsuitable?

6·7

Why would small diamond chippings be unsuitable?

Check your answers before proceeding.

It is not difficult to see why gold has been universally adopted as money. It has all the qualities necessary to enable it to perform all four functions of money.

The supply of money in the U.K.

i Notes and coins. Roughly 28% of the money in use in the U.K. is in the form of currency. This consists of bank notes and metal coins. At one time the bullion value of the coins was equal to the face value but nowadays they are no more than tokens. Our money is thus known as token money. Its only value lies in exchange. It has no value in itself.

'Legal tender' refers to money forms which you are legally obliged to accept in full settlement of debt. No one can refuse to accept legal tender. Bank of England notes are legal tender up to any amount, but 2p coins are only legal tender up to 20p worth and coins up to 10p are only legal tender up to £5. Coins of 50p are legal tender up to £10.

ii Bank deposits. The major part of the supply of money in the U.K. is made up of bank deposits. Where a person has a deposit with a bank he does not necessarily have to draw out cash in order to make payments. If he has a current account, which entitles him to a cheque book, he can simply make out a cheque payable to another person, and part of his deposit will be transferred from his account to the other person's account. A cheque is thus an order to a bank to transfer money from one account to another. The cheque is not money: it is the bank deposit which is money.

More and more payments are made by cheque these days and the banks are seeking ways of speeding up the clearing of these cheques, which have to travel physically from one person to another, then to a bank and from there back to the bank of origin. En route some accounts are credited and other accounts are debited. The application of computers to the recording of transactions and the automatic crediting and debiting of accounts is greatly accelerating the process. In 1967 six hundred and nine million cheques were 'cleared'; such is the pressing need for mechanisation of the process. Since it is the bank deposit which is being transferred then any method of doing this will be a substitute for cash transactions. Thus the credit card, which in the U.S.A. is a widely accepted means of payment, is gaining ground here in the U.K. Do not confuse the method of transfer with the deposit it represents.

The table below shows the money supply in the U.K. in September 1970.

MONEY SUPPLY	£ millions
Notes and coins in circulation with the public	3 154
Bank Deposits	10 869
TOTAL MONEY SUPPLY	14 023

Source: *Bank of England Quarterly Bulletin Sept. 1970*

6·8

Calculate the proportion of total money supply made up by currency.

Liquid assets and near money

Near money is not quite money in that it is not immediately spendable. There is a small time lapse before this particular form of wealth can become as spendable as money itself.

Any asset or part of your wealth that you can immediately exchange for goods is called a liquid asset. The most liquid of all assets is cash, that is to say notes and coin. You may, however, choose to hold your wealth in the form of an interest-bearing loan certificate such as a government bond. If this loan to the Government is not repayable for a period of five years then your wealth is said to be in an illiquid form: it is not immediately spendable. Where you choose to hold your wealth in illiquid form you can earn interest on it by lending it. Holding wealth in liquid form thus involves an opportunity cost; the interest which you could have earned on your wealth if you had invested it. It follows, therefore, that the more liquid your assets are, the less interest you are likely to earn on them.

Banking institutions are faced with the problem of earning interest on the money deposited with them while also keeping enough cash for their customers when it is demanded over the counter. They are public companies accountable to their shareholders for a profit each year, but they are also accountable to their customers who demand to be paid in cash on demand. The bank's problem is thus referred to as one of 'profitability versus liquidity'. The more liquid they keep the money deposited with them, the less interest they earn for their profits. The more money they lend out, the less likely they will be able to meet their customers' demands for cash.

In order to overcome this problem the banks hold their assets in a form which not only earns them interest, but also retains some liquidity. One way in which they can do this is to buy commercial bills of exchange. In buying these bills they are earning interest by lending their money for periods of three months, but they know they can sell them to other institutions at a moment's notice. Thus they have the best of both worlds. Their money is in near-liquid form and is earning interest. These bills are an example of near money.

Bills of exchange have long been used in commerce to provide credit of three months to buyers of goods. The seller of goods draws up the bill in which the buyer of goods promises to pay the sum due on a stated day in 3 months' time (usually 91 days). The buyer of the goods then has to 'accept' liability for the bill by signing it. The bill is made payable to the seller of goods by the holder (called the bearer) at the time the bill is due for payment. If the buyer of the goods is very creditworthy, which means that no one in the trade doubts his ability to pay the bill, then the seller of the goods can obtain cash, by selling the bill to a *discount house*. (There are about a dozen large discount houses and about the same number of small ones which make up the discount market.) If there is any doubt or a lack of knowledge about the credit status of the buyer of the goods then the bill will have to be 'accepted' by a merchant bank or some other reputable institution (see below).

The seller of goods does not pay a fee to the discount house for cashing the bill. Instead he sells it at 'discount', that is, he receives less than the amount which will be paid in 91 days' time. For example, a British exporter may sell £10 000 worth of tractors and spares to a European importer who signs a 91 bill for the £10 000, expecting that in 91 days he will be able to pay. Meanwhile the exporter may require money so he sells the bill to a discount house for slightly less than £10 000, say for £9 500. The discount house will then claim the full £10 000 at the end of 91 days and the £500 discount is regarded as interest earned on £10 000 for 91 days (which is equivalent to 5% for 91 days or 20% per annum). This income is often called the *yield* on a bill.

For another example, assume a bill is for £100, the discount rate is 5% per annum, and the bill is for 91 days. (Assume simple interest.)

5% discount on £100 = £5 per year.

1·25% discount on £100 = £1·25 for 91 days.

Therefore the seller of goods will receive:

£100·00—£1·25 = £98·75.

6·9

How much would a seller of goods, who draws a 91 days bill for £10 000 on the buyer of goods, obtain from a discount house, if the discount rate of 8% per annum simple interest?

A £980 **B** £920 **C** £973

In effect the buyer of goods obtains 3 months' credit, and the seller obtains his money immediately (minus a small discount) instead of having to wait for 3 months. In this way the seller maintains his liquidity and can commence fresh business operations, whilst the discounter has a claim, payable in three months. Since the claim can be sold by the discount houses to someone else, this transferability makes commercial bills very liquid.

6·10

Why does not the seller of goods borrow money from the bank for his business, instead of discounting his bill of exchange?

Commercial bills were much more important before commercial banks provided extensive facilities for lending money as advances. They are still important for domestic and international trade. Commercial bills are normally *self-liquidating* in the sense that they finance trade which will produce the finance to repay the money.

Bills may be used almost as cash if the drawer (the firm selling the goods) can get a bank to guarantee that it will pay the bill if the drawee (the buyer of the goods) defaulted. Giving the guarantee by accepting liability is called 'acceptance' of the bill. Most banks do some accepting work but certain merchant banks have specialised in this work because their knowledge of the creditworthiness of overseas firms puts them in a favourable position to judge the risk of default. These merchant banks are members of the Accepting Houses Committee, and they are often called 'accepting houses'. They make part of their living by charging a small fee for accepting liability for the bills. Bills accepted by a bank are called *bank bills,* those accepted by other traders, usually large and well known firms, are called *trade bills*.

Treasury bills

The Government often needs to borrow money for short periods of time. Suppose that in the first week of the financial year, the Ministry of Transport has to pay out a bill of £50 million to a contractor who has just completed a motorway contract. It is possible that, with other calls on different Ministries for similar payments, the receipts from taxation and other revenues fail to match the expenditure in that week. Rather than go into debt the Government chooses to borrow for a short period of time. Each week it estimates how much will be needed and the Bank of England 'sells' Treasury bills to the general public. These are finance bills which simply promise to repay money after 91 days.

In practice all Treasury bills are normally bought by financial institutions since they come in multiples of £5 000 (£25 000 is a common value). They are bought at a discount by the discount houses who guarantee to buy up all those issued if other institutions do not want them. Thus they guarantee to lend to the government the money it needs in the short term.

Treasury bills are completely creditworthy and need not be accepted by the accepting houses. They are a short term loan to the government and a profitable short term investment for the institutions that discount them. Furthermore Treasury bills are completely liquid since they can either be rediscounted with other institutions or resold to the Bank of England which will discount them at the current Bank rate. The formal definition of the Bank rate is 'The rate at which the Bank of England will discount first class bills'. First class bills are bills which have been accepted by an accepting house. In the case of Treasury bills however they do not need accepting to be regarded as first class.

The money market

We are now equipped to look at the London money market. This is the market for short term loans. It consists of a network of institutions including the Bank of England, the discount houses, the banks both British and foreign and the merchant banks or accepting houses. The discount houses occupy a central position in this market which deals in loans ranging from overnight to one year in length. Refer to figure 6·1 while we discuss the work of the main institutions in the money market, the market for short term loans.

The work of the discount houses

Discount houses, which are unique to Britain, are public joint stock companies whose principal business is the discounting of Treasury and commercial bills. Their business depends very much upon the supply of these bills which tend to be subject to the government's credit discisions and government borrowing. The general level of interest rates is a vital factor in their work, since they are constantly borrowing at one rate and lending at a higher rate. They occupy a key position in the City of London, as they are the only institutions which may borrow directly from the Bank of England. They borrow funds for very short periods of time, such as a day or a week, mainly from the banks, and lend them out for periods of about three months to the government or to industry. This is how they make their profits. The rate of interest on money borrowed for a week is less than that payable on money lent out for three months.

There are twelve London discount houses and in order to study their business in detail it is necessary to examine a typical balance sheet. Figure 6·2 shows the way a discount house uses the money it borrows. Its borrowing is listed

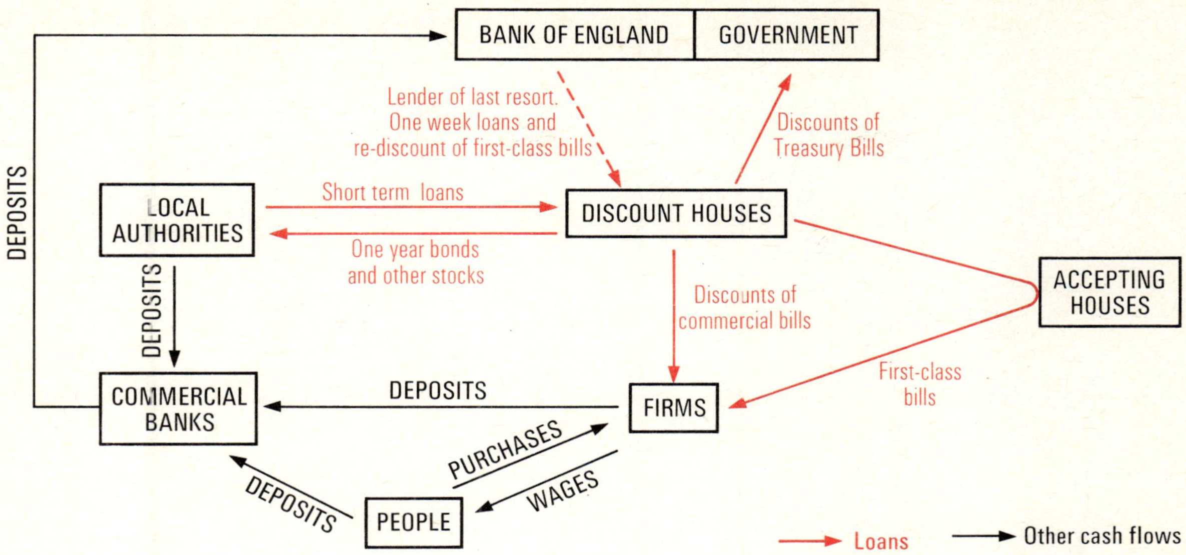

Figure 6·1

as Liabilities while its lending is detailed as Assets. A few explanatory notes will be helpful.

Liabilities

Most of the money used for trading is borrowed, secured against the company's assets. Its share capital is small. The banks can recall some of their loans whenever they are short of cash, and the discount houses are forced to replace this loss by borrowing from the Bank of England.

Assets

i *Cash at bankers and in hand* is self explanatory.

ii *Bills discounted* are those bills which will mature in three months and are earning interest.

iii *Sterling negotiable certificates of deposit* are special claims on sterling which have been sold to the discount house at a discount and which the house will cash in due course.

iv *Securities or Bonds* are certificates of indebtedness which promise to pay a specified sum on a given future date. They have written on them the rate of interest payable, the conditions and date of repayment. The government, other public bodies and firms may issue these in order to raise money for long periods of time.

The discount house, like any other sensible firm, must balance the security of liquidity against the desire to maximise its profitability. Thus it does not hold all its assets in any one particular form.

6·11

a What proportion of total liabilities is held in cash?
A 76·2% **B** 8·2% **C** 13%

b List the following assets in order of their size, using figure 6·2.
1 Cash **2** Bills discounted
3 Sterling negotiable certificates of deposit
4 Securities **5** Other quoted investments
6 Loans

c How much was on loan by the discount house to the government at 31st December 1968, in discounted Treasury Bills?
A £124 563 257
B £209 331 783
C £163 863 005

Functions of the discount houses

i They create short term loans for commercial enterprises by discounting commercial bills, and for the government by discounting Treasury bills.

ii As exclusive borrowers from the Bank of England they provide the channel by which it enters the money market. Since the Bank of England does not lend directly to commercial banks, it acts as lender of last resort to the banking system via the discount houses (see page 80).

The Union Discount Company of London, United and Subsidiary Companies
CONSOLIDATED BALANCE SHEET, 31st December, 1968

CAPITAL

	(£)	(£)
ISSUED		7 500 000
RESERVE		4 000 000
		11 500 000
PROFIT AND LOSS ACCOUNT		1 218 322
		12 718 322
LOANS secured on assets of the Company	381 074 566	
DEPOSITS, OTHER LIABILITIES AND RESERVE FOR CONTINGENCIES	14 805 232	
MINORITY INTERESTS	38 597	
PROPOSED FINAL DIVIDEND	562 500	
		396 480 895
		£409 199 217

NOTES:
(1) There is a contingent liability in respect of Bills re-discounted (excluding Treasury Bills) of £15 683 681 (1967: £20 319 400).
(2) The amount now recoverable in respect of income tax suffered in excess of taxation upon profits to date has been included in Loans and Amounts Receivable

CURRENT ASSETS

	(£)	(£)
CASH AT BANKERS AND IN HAND		5 368 940
BILLS DISCOUNTED *less* rebate and reserve:		
British Government Treasury Bills	124 563 257	
Commercial and other bills	84 768 526	
		209 331 783
STERLING NEGOTIABLE CERTIFICATES OF DEPOSIT at less than cost		6 973 070
SECURITIES:		
(a) Quoted at less than market value:		
British Government Corporation, Local Authority and Commonwealth Government bonds	163 863 005	
(b) Unquoted, at less than cost:		
British Corporation and Local Authority mortgages and bonds	14 396 845	
		178 259 850
OTHER QUOTED INVESTMENTS at less than market value		1 658 471
LOANS AND AMOUNTS RECEIVABLE		7 420 152
FIXED ASSETS		409 012 266
FREEHOLD PREMISES, furniture and fittings at cost *less* amounts written off		186 951
		£409 199 217

Figure 6·2

iii Their activities in the money market tend to equalise the demand for and supply of short term loans, and this has a stabilising effect on interest rates.

iv By providing an efficient short loan system they attract lenders from both overseas and within the British Isles.

The balance sheet of commercial banks

Examination of a balance sheet will help to explain a commercial bank's activities. The notes below should be read in association with the table opposite (figure 6·3) which shows a combined balance sheet of the London clearing banks. For our purposes the percentages of total deposits shown in the third column are more important than the absolute totals.

Liabilities

Deposits (customers' claims on the banks) form over 95% of banks' liabilities. Most deposits are held in either the form of current accounts, which can be transferred by cheque or converted into cash, or deposit accounts from which withdrawals are not usually allowed without notice. The banks charge a fee for handling current accounts, but pay interest on deposit accounts. However, the Bank of England makes no distinction between current and deposit account liabilities when specifying the reserve requirements explained below.

Assets

The distribution of a bank's assets will be determined by three considerations; liquidity,

BALANCE SHEET OF THE LONDON CLEARING BANKS, AUGUST 1969

Liabilities (other people's claims on banks)	£m	Assets (banks' claims on other people)	£m		as % of gross deposits
Deposits		Cash		874	8·2
Current accounts	5 200	(Till money	625)		
Deposit accounts	4 353	(Bankers' balances	249)		
Other accounts	1 043				
		Money at call and short notice		1 412	13·3
Total deposits	10 596	Bills discounted		722	6·9
		(U.K. commercial	267)		
		(Treasury bills	124)		
		(Other	331)		
		Subtotal Liquid Assets		3 008	28·4
		Special Deposits		214	2·8
		Investments		1 162	11·0
		Advances		5 562	52·5
		*Total		9 946	

Source: *Bank of England Quarterly Bulletin*

* Capital and reserves owed to the shareholders are omitted on the liabilities side, and cheques in course of collection and the value of banks' property are omitted on the assets side. The items listed in the table are those required to explain the banks' commercial operations.

Figure 6·3

profitability, and security. Among its assets it must always have enough cash to meet customers' demands for conversion of their deposits into notes and coin. They realise that only a small proportion of total deposits will be converted into cash during any day or week, and some cash will become available from customers paying in cash. In fact cash holdings will be kept to the minimum necessary, because cash holdings earn no interest. If loans can be made which are immediately recallable, the need for holding cash will be reduced.

We have already seen that longer term loans are less liquid but more profitable, because higher interest rates can be charged. However, banks will not lend money for very risky ventures, although high interest rates could be charged, because customers would soon withdraw their deposits from a bank which had been lending to firms which failed.

Liquid assets

i Cash, by agreement with the Bank of England, is kept by commercial banks to at least 8% of the value of total deposits, in order to meet all the likely demands of their customers for cash. We say that the required *cash ratio is 8%*. The larger part of this cash is kept as till money in the banks, the remainder as balances at the Bank of England. The banks can operate on such a low cash ratio because they hold the very liquid non-cash assets described below.

ii Money at call and short notice represents loans to the discount houses. Money at call can be recalled immediately, and earns a lower rate of interest than money at short notice which is recoverable, if necessary, after about a week. Money at short notice can earn interest 2% below Bank rate.

iii Commercial bills are bought from the discount houses in bundles maturing at dates convenient for the banks. They represent short-term loans, which earn interest for the banks but which can be resold to the other buyers for cash if necessary.

iv Treasury bills are also bought from the discount houses. The yield (rate of interest) on Treasury bills and commercial bills will be slightly lower than Bank rate.

6·12

Why will the yield on Treasury bills be slightly lower than the yield on commercial bills?

The liquidity ratio

By agreement with the Bank of England the value of liquid assets (including cash) held by the commercial banks must be no less than 28% of the value of total deposits. Therefore the minimum liquid assets ratio, or *liquidity ratio is 28%*; for most of the year the banks will keep the liquidity ratio slightly higher.

Illiquid assets

v Special deposits are the extra deposits which the Bank of England sometimes requires from the commercial banks, when it wishes to reduce the banks' ability to lend. Banks are required to deposit extra balances, not to be counted as part of the cash assets, equal to a small percentage of their previous month's deposits. First introduced in 1960, the maximum percentage called by 1970 was $3\frac{1}{2}\%$. Calling special deposits has the effect of reducing the banks' cash and liquid assets, and as will be explained in S 12, they have to reduce their total deposits to maintain the required liquidity ratio.

vi Investments are gilt-edged securities (bonds issued by the British government and some Commonwealth governments). Holders receive a fixed sum in interest per year, but since the market price of these securities varies, the effective yield on the securities varies according to the changes in the market price (see S16). The yield on the securities which the banks hold, and which usually have less than five years to run until maturity, will vary around the level of Bank rate.

Because of the risk attached to this type of investment, banks do not hold industrial shares. They can be reasonably certain that governments will redeem their bonds, and the bonds can be easily sold to another buyer on the Stock Exchange. However, the *capital value* of the bond may fluctuate as economic conditions within the country change, so bonds, although easily convertible into cash, cannot be counted as part of liquid assets.

vi Advances are the banks' loans to their customers, which must eventually be repaid to the banks. In the meantime customers have the use of the bank deposits created in their favour. Making loans, either by a loan contract for a certain period (e.g. two years), or by allowing overdraft facilities, usually renewable every six months, is the most profitable of banks' activities. The charge for overdrafts varies from $\frac{1}{2}\%$ above Bank rate for nationalised industries to about 4% above for private individuals borrowing small amounts.

Advances are loans for periods up to five years. They are profitable, but illiquid, and British banks have been unwilling to lend for longer periods.

6·13

Given that liquid assets are £280 000, and are at the minimum required ratio to deposits, construct a simple balance sheet of a commercial bank, including deposits, cash at the minimum necessary amount, money at call, bills discounted, special deposits at 2% of total deposits, investments, and advances at 50% of total deposits.

6·14

If a customer opens a new account by bringing £100 cash into a bank what will be the effect on

i the bank's liabilities
ii the bank's assets
iii the bank's liquidity ratio.

6·15

If a customer opens a new account by borrowing £100, i.e. a new deposit of £100 is created in his favour, what will be the effect on

i the bank's liabilities
ii the bank's assets
iii the bank's liquidity ratio

6·16

Which of the following would cause a fall in the liquid assets of a bank?

A Payment of tax by its customers to the government.
B Debt interest paid by the government to the bank's customers.
C A call for special deposits by the Bank of England.
D Payment of bills by the bank's customers to customers of other banks.
E Increased lending to discount houses.

Banks and the creation of money

We have mentioned that banks can create money for customers by making loans. This is a very important activity which we must examine carefully.

The original bankers were merchants who accepted gold for safe-keeping, and issued notes (I.O.U.s) in exchange. These notes were convertible into gold; a relic of these times is the now meaningless promise on Bank of England notes 'I promise to pay the bearer'. When banknotes were accepted as money and were transferred between people as a medium of exchange, bankers found that a large proportion of the notes they issued were never presented to them for conversion back into gold. Therefore the bankers did not need to hold enough gold to back all their notes, but only an amount sufficient to enable them to exchange gold for that proportion which was presented, say 50%. Thus the cash assets (gold coin) would be 50% of liabilities (notes issued). In other words, bankers could issue notes to a value in excess of the gold coin they held, by making loans to customers. In such a simple bank, the balance sheet might have looked like this:

Liabilities	£	Assets	£
Notes issued	100 000	Gold coin	50 000
		Advances	50 000
			100 000

In this case the bank created money by issuing notes. It was limited by the need to have gold equal to 50% of the notes issued, and the need for security in lending. The people to whom the bank lent had to be credit-worthy. Exactly the same analysis applies in the present day, but the liabilities are no longer notes, but bank deposits, and the most important limit to making loans is the need to preserve the 28% liquidity ratio.

The creation of bank deposits

We have already explained that nowadays bank deposits are used as money, i.e. they are transferred between people without being converted into cash. There are two ways in which bank deposits are created.

i A customer exchanges cash for a deposit

If a customer brings in £100 in cash to open an account, the bank receives cash and enters the equivalent amount in the customer's account. In this case there is no immediate increase in the public's holding of money, because the customer has exchanged cash for a bank deposit, and the change in the bank's balance sheet is as follows:

Liabilities	£	Assets	£
Deposits	+100	Cash	+100

ii A customer exchanges a promise to pay for a deposit

A customer may ask for a loan of £100, i.e. for a deposit of £100 to be created in his favour. The bank manager will not lend unless he is sure that the loan will be repaid. He may ask for certain collateral to be given to the bank, such as an assurance policy which the bank would keep if the debt was not repaid, but often the promise to repay is sufficient. In such a case the supply of money in the hands of the public has increased, since in exchange for the customer's illiquid asset (his promise, backed if necessary by a collateral security) the bank has created money—a new bank deposit. The bank's balance sheet will change in the following way.

Liabilities	£	Assets	£
Deposits	+100	Advances	+100

If the customer sold a government security to the bank the effect would be similar; the customer would gain a deposit, and the bank would increase its illiquid assets, this time its investments.

Limits to the creation of bank deposits

Banks do not have unlimited power to create deposits by lending (i.e. creating credit). They must always ensure that they hold adequate cash and liquid assets to back their deposits, to meet their customers' requirements for cash, and they will require adequate security for their loans, to reduce as far as is possible the risk that the debtor will default. Let us analyse the process of credit creation, using first of all the limit of the cash ratio.

i The cash ratio

If there were only one bank, with a system of branches serving the whole country, and the required cash ratio were 8%, this bank would know that when it received extra cash it could increase deposits by the ratio 100:8, i.e. deposits could increase by 12½ times the increase in cash assets. If an original deposit of £100 were made in the name of a customer who brought in cash, then £1 150 extra deposits could be created by lending. In such a case the bank's balance sheet would change in the following way:

Liabilities	£	Assets	£
Deposits	+1 250	Cash	+ 100
		Advances	+1 150
			1 250

We must note that if this national bank suffered a loss in cash, then it would have to reduce its deposits to maintain the required cash ratio of 8%. This would require the bank to reduce its deposits by 12½ times the reduction in cash assets, i.e. by £100 for every £8 reduction in cash. $\left(\frac{100}{8} = 12\frac{1}{2}\right)$

6·17

Assume that the national bank's assets fall by £50. Draw up the new balance sheet to show the changes in deposits and assets, in a manner similar to the table above.

If there were several banks in the country, no single bank could increase its deposits by $12\frac{1}{2}$ times as soon as it received an increase of cash. Why? As soon as the new deposits were used, most would be transferred to customers of other banks, and to settle the inter-bank debt, the first bank would have to transfer cash. This transfer of cash would then require an immediate reduction in deposits by $12\frac{1}{2}$ times the reduction in cash assets.

However, the extra cash, which originally came into one bank, will be distributed between the various banks as customers transfer their deposits. Eventually the banking system as a whole gains more cash. Assuming that this increase in cash assets is a permanent gain to the banking system, and working on a cash ratio of 8%, the banks collectively can make loans which result in total deposits rising by $12\frac{1}{2}$ times the increase in cash. Which particular banks increase their cash, and therefore the loans, and which do not, will depend on their size, skill in attracting customers, and their customers' need for loans, but these differences will average out over the entire system to a $12\frac{1}{2}$ times increase in loans.

ii The liquidity ratio

We have seen that the amount that a bank can lend by creating bank deposits is related to the cash available. It is also related to the method of lending. Liquid assets are easily convertible into cash, and can therefore be called upon to replace any loss of cash. In the U.K. it is customary to maintain liquid assets at a value of 28% of total deposits. If, as a result of an outflow of cash, the cash ratio falls below 8%, some liquid assets can be turned into cash to restore it. This in turn causes the liquidity ratio to fall. To bring the liquidity ratio back to 28% the bank could sell some illiquid assets and convert them into liquid assets, but this is not easily or quickly done, and so the liquidity ratio is adjusted by reducing the creation of deposits (or by calling in advances) until deposits are again $3\frac{1}{2}$ times liquid assets ($100:28 \simeq 3\frac{1}{2}:1$). In recent years the liquidity ratio has become a more important limit to credit creation than the cash ratio.

It is therefore the volume of liquid assets, and the need to keep a minimum ratio of liquid assets to deposits of 28%, which determine the amount of bank lending-credit creation. It is by increasing or decreasing the amount of liquid assets held by the banks that the Bank of England attempts to control the money supply. An increase in liquid assets will encourage a multiple expansion of deposits, and a reduction in liquid assets can force a multiple contraction of deposits. This will be explained in S12.

Now let us look at the remaining institutions in the money market.

The merchant banks

This term covers a variety of institutions which cover a very wide range of banking and other financial activities. Most of them originated as merchants who bought and sold goods in the normal way but particularly in overseas markets. As they built up their specialist knowledge of overseas trade and its financial requirements, they gradually dropped their own trading to concentrate on the financing of other merchants' trade. They are mostly joint stock companies and have an important function in the money market because of their wide knowledge of firms who trade on an international basis. It was almost inevitable therefore, that they should take on the role of accepting houses in backing commercial bills of exchange issued by foreign firms. Rothschild's, Baring Bros., and Hambros are famous among the merchant banks. In addition to their function as accepting houses they also finance business deals such as mergers and take-overs, act as bankers to some large firms and offer specialist advice to their customers in the field of industry and commerce.

The National Giro

The National Giro is primarily a centralised and computer operated system for transferring money from one body to another without the use of currency, postal orders or money orders. However, it has recently added to its operations the making of advances, and may be regarded as a government bank. The branches of the Post Office are its collecting points and any one will provide you with a booklet on the details of its operation.

Foreign banks

Banks of other countries have branches in London to facilitate foreign trade. The Bank of

Spain, for example, has a branch near Covent Garden market.

The Bank of England

The Bank of England is the Central Bank for the United Kingdom. It originated as far back as 1694 when a group of businessmen answered an appeal from the government of the day for funds and in return secured sole right of handling the government's financial business.

i It is the government's bank. Since it was nationalised in 1944 the Governor of the Bank of England has worked even more closely with the Chancellor of the Exchequer in implementing the government's monetary policy. In this capacity:

(a) The Bank manages the government's accounts, receiving tax and other revenue and paying for the goods and services received by the government. It manages the National Debt, registering stock transfers, and paying interest.

(b) It advises the government on matters concerned with internal monetary policy, such as the desirability of influencing the volume of credit that is being created, or the level of interest rates.

(c) It acts as the Treasury's agent in carrying out external monetary policies in co-ordination with other central banks and international monetary institutions such as the International Monetary Fund. It manages the Exchange Equalisation Account to maintain the value of the pound sterling.

(d) It raises loans on behalf of the government by selling Treasury bills and short term bonds in the money market, and by selling long term bonds in the capital market, which we will deal with later. As we shall see, this activity in the money market enables the Bank of England to influence the supply and demand for credit. Let us describe the process now and leave the implications for later study.

To raise short term loans on behalf of the Treasury, the Bank of England issues Treasury bills by tender. Those buyers offering the lowest discount obtain the bills. Discount houses form a syndicate to compete with other bidders for the bills. If the other bidders, for example, a foreign government, offer a higher price for the bills then the discount houses would receive none, but in practice the syndicate usually offers a price which will secure them most of the total allotment. In effect they would take up the entire issue of Treasury bills ('cover the tender') if there were no other bidders and this guarantees the Bank of England will always have the cash it needs for the Treasury.

6·18

If the Government sells the bills at a lower price to the discount houses than it did last week, what has happened to the rate of interest in the short term credit market?

Government departments, the Bank of England, the National Insurance Fund and the Post Office Savings Bank also want to hold Treasury bills as a short term investment for their surplus funds. To avoid unfair competition with the discount houses some bills are sold to them directly ('through the tap'). Thus a distinction is made between Tender and Tap bills.

Through the regular sale of Treasury bills the Bank of England is in a position to exert an influence on the interest rates in the money market. By offering more Treasury bills (which remember the discount houses guarantee to take up), it draws in more cash from the market in return for bills which are simply I.O.U.s payable in 91 days' time. The discount houses are prepared to take up the extra bills but only if they are offered a higher rate of interest. The rate of interest will thus rise. Now when a firm wishes to sell a commercial bill of exchange to the discount market it will be asked to accept a lower price (a higher rate of discount) because the discount houses are relatively short of funds. So all short term money rates will rise and this will restrict the demand for short term credit.

The Bank of England also raises funds for the government on a long term basis. It sells new issues of government stock on the Stock Exchange. These government bonds carry a fixed rate of interest and can have a repayment term of anything from 5 years to 30 years. In some cases no date is fixed for their redemption. By selling stock to the public the Bank of England can reduce the public's holdings of money (bank deposits). On the other hand when the Bank buys back its securities (repays its debts) it increases the public's holding of money. The principle at work here is that when an institution or member of the public buys these securities his money is tied up for a period of time and he is therefore less liquid. He cannot spend his wealth because he is not holding it in liquid form. Thus whether the government wishes to increase or reduce the total spending of the nation, it can in part achieve this through its activities on the Stock Exchange. These operations are known as *open market operations*.

6·19

If I sell a government bond has my wealth become more or less liquid?

(e) The Bank of England is the sole note issuer for England and Wales. It prints notes and authorises the minting of coins by the Royal Mint. New notes and coins get into circulation in return for old ones which are removed by the commercial banks as they deteriorate.

ii It is the bankers' bank. All the commercial banks hold deposits with the Bank of England. Normally they hold two-thirds of their total cash holdings in their tills and a third with the Bank. Where the banks have to settle debts between themselves they effect a transfer of part of the deposit they hold at the Bank of England. When the commercial banks wish to hold a proportion of their assets in the form of Treasury bills they do not buy directly from the Bank but rather they buy from the discount market itself; hence the commercial banks never borrow directly from the Bank of England. This rule prevents the commercial banks being especially favoured, for by dealing through the discount houses, the Bank deals with the whole banking system.

iii It is 'Lender of Last Resort' to the discount market. When the discount houses find themselves without sufficient cash to meet their regular needs they are 'forced into the Bank'. Here the Bank of England guarantees to lend them money by buying or rediscounting first class bills at a discount rate known as the Bank Rate. It is called 'last resort' borrowing by the discount houses since the rate of interest they will have to pay is higher than any other in the money market, so that in the last resort the Bank of England is the final source of funds: The Bank cannot be bankrupt. If the Bank of England does not wish interest rates in the money market to rise, then it will lend at prevailing market rates.

iv It is central banker to the Sterling Area. Many countries choose to hold their national reserves of currency in the form of sterling. Not unnaturally they deposit currency with the Bank of England which guarantees to operate a scheme to iron out fluctuations in the value of sterling in exchange for other currencies. The scheme works to the benefit of Britain which gains from the foreign currency deposited here and to the benefit of members of the Sterling Area who are content in the knowledge that the value of their reserves will remain relatively stable as the price of sterling is fixed. Much more will be said of this later.

We have now looked at all the institutions in the money market. All that remains is for us to tie together the links between them.

The money market at work

Refer again to Figure 6·1.

i Cash originates from the Bank of England.
ii People and firms deposit cash with banks.
iii Banks lend to customers by creating deposits in their favour, but to meet possible demands for conversion of deposits into cash, they must keep cash equal to 8% of total deposits, and liquid assets equal to 28% of total deposits.
iv Banks lend money at call and short notice to the discount houses.
v Discount houses borrow short and lend for longer periods of time to the commercial and industrial sectors by buying bills at a discount. They also provide short term funds for the public sector by buying Treasury bills at a discount.
vi Merchant banks acting as accepting houses enable the process of discounting to continue since they act as guarantors for commercial bills.
vii The Bank of England supports the whole system by guaranteeing to lend to the discount houses at the current Bank rate should the discount market have an urgent need for cash.

6·20

If the public were suddenly to demand more cash than usual from their banks, where would the banks raise the extra cash? By

A calling in money lent at call to the discount houses.
B borrowing from the Bank of England?
C borrowing from foreign banks?
D issuing more shares?

6·21

When the banks call in the money they have on loan to the discount houses at call and short notice, where do the discount houses raise the cash they need?

A from other discount houses?
B from the Bank of England?
C from the Accepting houses?

6·22

When the government wishes to increase the spending power of the public will it

A sell Treasury bills?

B buy Treasury bills?

C sell a new issue of bonds?

D buy bonds on the Stock Exchange?

We will leave our discussion of the money market at this point with a reminder that we shall return to it in S12 when we discuss how the total supply of money can be influenced by the Bank of England. Now let us turn our attention to the capital market.

The capital market

This is the market which deals in loans having a life longer than the typical 91 day loans dealt with by the money market. All medium and long term loans are raised on the capital market. It consists of institutions such as the assurance and insurance companies, the Stock Exchange, investment trusts, unit trusts, building societies, finance companies and finance corporations. Details of these institutions can be found in the satellite text *Financial Institutions* but let us look now at the main functions of each.

Insurance companies. These receive annual premiums on policies which cover periods of 15–25 years and cover risks to commodities and property. They also provide cover for risks to life (the assurance business). They are important institutions in the capital market since nearly half of all personal savings in the U.K. is made in the form of premiums paid to assurance companies on policies which will mature after a set period of time. If you were to take out an endowment policy for say, £1 000, which matured in 20 years' time you would be required to pay annual premiums for that period. You might pay £600 in all over that time, the bonus you receive being the interest the company is prepared to pay you for the use of your money.

These companies are faced with the task of investing the money paid to them in premiums and in doing so they take a very active part in the capital market. They are large buyers of existing stocks and shares, take up new issues of shares and invest largely in fixed interest government securities. The stock of investments held by insurance companies amounts to about £7 000 million so you can see that they have a considerable effect on the demand, when they are buying, and on the supply, when they are selling, of securities in the market.

Pension funds. Companies, local authorities, the government and trade unions all operate pension funds for their employees. These funds are invested in bonds, shares and property in order to earn an income on the fund and to increase the value of the fund. The better managed the fund, is the better pensions can be offered to members of the scheme.

Building societies. Members of the public can either become shareholders of a building society or simply deposit money as one might with a commercial bank. The funds are then invested by the society in property by granting mortgages to people who wish to purchase their own house or other property. The most common repayment term for a mortgage is 20 to 25 years. Security for the loans lies in the deeds to the property, and each loan is regarded as self-liquidating in that it is repaid monthly together with the interest rather than waiting for the loan term to end and then having a large sum repaid in total.

Finance houses. These provide the money for hire-purchase agreements which are used to finance the purchasing of goods. A large proportion of their money comes from the commercial banks, and industrial and commercial enterprises which deposit money on three to six months' notice of withdrawal. Individuals also become depositors in some of the smaller finance houses.

Nearly 70% of all hire-purchase loans made to individuals are for the purpose of buying cars. The Chancellor of the Exchequer has the power to fix or to alter at any time the initial deposit required from a customer before an agreement can be arranged, and also the length of time over which the loan must be repaid. In this way the government can strengthen its control over the public's demand for goods and services throughout the country.

Finance corporations. These bodies are set up to lend money to industry. Banks, insurance companies and other firms all subscribe to their funds and each corporation tends to have a specialist function. Thus the Industrial Reorganisation Corporation (1966–70) was set up by the government to lend to firms where positive economic benefits were possible as in the case of mergers. The I.R.C. was able to encourage and speed up the merger between British Motor Holdings and the Leyland Motor Company and so reduce the time taken for the reorganisation to take place.

Investment trusts. These are joint stock companies which are not engaged in the production of a commodity or a service like most companies, but in the buying and selling of other companies' shares. They themselves issue shares to the public through the Stock Exchange and use the capital so raised to buy shares and gilt edged securities on which they will be paid dividends and enjoy appreciation of their value.

The risks involved in such activity are minimised by spreading the purchases of shares over the whole field of enterprise. Some shares in the portfolio may do well, others may do badly, but providing that on average they earn a respectable income and a capital gain, the Investment Trust will earn profits, and with these it will vote dividends to its own shareholders.

Unit trusts. The activities of these institutions are similar to those of investment trusts except that they are not public companies but trusts run by an independent group of managers. When you buy a unit you are not buying a share in a company but a fraction of the total holding of shares valued at their current market price. You may choose to invest in one which offers a high income or one which aims to offer capital growth. Since the units are not shares the Stock Exchange does not cater for their buying and selling which is normally done by the managers' advertising in newspapers. Many other financial institutions have banded together to float new unit trusts. The trust usually has a fixed life after which it is wound up. A small rate of discount is charged for the expenses of administering the trust.

The best way to understand what each of these trusts has to offer is to study the advertisements which appear regularly in the 'quality' Sunday newspapers.

6·23

Find one unit trust offering a high income and one offering a high capital growth. Compare the yield offered if you were to hold £100 worth for a period of five years. See how this compares with the yield offered by an investment trust which you can find quoted.

When the value of shares is falling generally and the profits of firms are insufficient to pay high dividends, both the income yield and the capital growth of unit trusts muct be adversely affected. In times like these, other methods are sought of providing both income and capital growth for investors. One such method is to organise a sort of unit trust which invests in property. The managing body buys a selection of properties and the individual investor buys a tiny part of the whole. The income from the trust comes from rents on the properties, and the capital growth comes from the appreciation in property values.

Trustee Savings Bank and Post Office Savings Bank. These exist for small savers who wish to have their money savings relatively liquid and at the same time earn a small rate of interest.

The Stock Exchange. Details of the working of the Stock Exchange were given in S4. It is the market for *existing* capital. Government bonds, local authority stock and public companies' share are freely bought and sold on the Stock Exchange. The great contribution it makes to the field of raising capital for industry is that investors are secure in the knowledge that if they want to convert their shares into cash they can do so at a moment's notice by selling them to jobbers on the Exchange at the current market price. The buyers of shares know, therefore, the market value of their assets, and that a market exists, where at a price, they can turn an illiquid asset, a share, into a liquid asset.

The Stock Exchange investigates companies thoroughly before it will permit their shares to be 'quoted'. At any hint of insolvency, fraud, or other situations which might cause the public to be sold shares which were worthless, it will suspend dealings. This gives the public a certain degree of protection.

The immediate response of share prices to the changes in the demand and supply of shares gives a very quick guide to the state of health of industry generally. Where high profits are being earned generally, shares will be in great demand and the prices of shares generally will rise. On the other hand the opposite may occur. Thus the general movement in share prices is said to act as a sort of barometer, denoting the economic climate of the country. Again this acts as a guide to investors. Since the market for any particular share is nearly perfect an investor does not have to waste time shopping around for a more favourable price.

Finally, the organisation of the market allows

the financial institutions that we have been describing to invest on a scale that would otherwise have been impossible.

The new issues market. Merchant banks also act as *issuing houses* in order to launch new shares or new issues of established shares on to the new issues market. They advise firms on the amount to be raised, the type of shares to offer, and guarantee to buy all of the new shares if they cannot be sold immediately to the public. Thus a firm can be confident of raising the capital quickly and surely.

These then are the institutions of the capital market which provide funds for people and firms requiring them for periods of one to thirty years. As you will already have noticed many of the institutions we have described in this section deal in both the money market and the capital market. Since all financial institutions are faced with the problem of liquidity versus profitability they will choose to spread their assets over different periods of time. Thus they may not only lend for five or ten years but also hold Treasury bills as a short term investment.

The capital market is a complex study and one in which the interaction of the various institutions has considerable effect on the economy as a whole. As we shall discover in S12, the level of interest rates, and therefore the cost of investment, is determined by this interplay. The supply of money and therefore the stimulus for investment and consumption is also largely determined within the system we have just described. The volume of credit used to finance trade has a vital effect on the national spending with far-reaching effects on the price level, the level of economic activity and the Balance of Payments. This is why we must understand what the institutions do and how they do it. In S12 we shall examine the effects of their actions and the measures which the government can take to control the monetary system.

To test your understanding of the part played by the capital market in the economy answer the following questions.

6·24

You are the managing director of a small private company and you need £1 000 quickly. Where would you raise the capital?

6·25

In the above situation where would you raise £100 000

i for short term purposes

ii for long term purposes (fixed capital)?

6·26

How would you attempt to raise £1 million for business purposes?

6·27

Through which medium would you borrow the money to purchase a specific item of equipment costing £10 000?

6·28

Where would an individual raise the capital to

i purchase a house

ii improve the structure of a house he already owns?

6·29

To which organisation would you go for advice on taking over another firm?

6·30

As a large company to whom would you turn for financial assistance in order to develop a new process, or a wider market?

6·31

What is the Exchange Equalisation Account?

ANSWERS

6·1

Because it would not be normally acceptable to shopkeepers, and money must be acceptable to everyone.

6·2

Because they are not scarce enough.

6·3

Because it is not scarce enough.

6·4

Because some might be rarer than others and thus more valuable than others. All units of money must be homogeneous, that is identical in every respect.

6·5

All units of money must be portable.

6·6

Because you could not split them up to pay small bills without the diamonds losing their value. Money must be divisible.

6·7

They are not easily distinguishable. Other stone chippings may be substituted for them. Money must be recognisable.

6·8

Approximately 22%.

6·9

Correct **A**

6·10

If it is cheaper to go to the bank he will, but this is unlikely: discount houses as specialists, are usually cheaper.

6·11

a C **b** 5–1–3–6–2–4 **c** C

6·12

Because Treasury bills are normally less risky than commercial bills.

Liabilities	£	**Assets**	£
Deposits	1 000 000	Cash	80 000
		Money at Call	100 000
		Bills discounted	100 000
		Liquid assets	280 000
		Special deposits	20 000
		Investments	200 000
		Advances	500 000
			1 000 000

6·14

a rise by £100—new deposit of customer
b rise by £100—cash received
c rise—extra cash means extra liquid assets

6·15

a rise by £100—new deposit of customer
b rise by £100—*advances* on illiquid asset
c declines. No new liquid assets acquired, but deposits have risen.

A,C,D.

6·17

Liabilities	£	**Assets**	£
Deposits	625	Cash	−50
			−575
			625

6·18

The rate of interest has risen.

6·19

My assets are more liquid.

6·20

Correct **A**: it was lent to the discount houses on this understanding.

6·21

Correct **B**: they are 'forced into the Bank', i.e. to borrow from it.

6·22

Correct **D**: these are open market operations. The public receives money in exchange for bonds. Purchases or sales of Treasury bills do not have a direct effect on the spending power of the public. They affect the short term rate of interest.

6·23

Own research.

6·24

Providing you want the money for less than 5 years you will go to a bank.

6·25

a From your bank, or another lending institution such as a merchant bank.
By attracting an additional shareholder (n.b. your shares are not on sale to the public).

6·26

By becoming a public company and selling shares to the public.

6·27

Hire purchase.

6·28

i A building society
ii From the same source but this time re-mortgaging your existing property.

6·29

A merchant bank.

6·30

You would raise money by an issue of shares (risk capital) or debentures (loan capital).

6·31

The Exchange Equalisation Account is used by the Treasury for the purchase and sale of gold and foreign currencies, i.e. it holds our reserves of international money.

FOREIGN MARKETS

Why do countries trade with one another?

Firms and individuals within England, Scotland, Northern Ireland and Wales trade with one another. The reasons for this have already been discussed in the section on specialisation. We know, for example, that most cars bought in Wales are made in England, and that most of the whisky consumed in England is made in Scotland. Such an exchange of commodities, occurring within the boundaries of one state, is called *domestic trade*, and results from the uneven distribution of natural resources, the uneven distribution of talent and abilities, and the immobility of factors of production.

If British traders, on the other hand, buy French wine or German cars, or sell Scotch whisky to the U.S.A., this is called *international trade*. The essential reasons for international trade are the same as those for domestic trade, but there are certain complications which are of interest to the economist. Different countries have different languages, and different political and monetary systems. These give rise to economic differences. The mobility of labour is hindered by language differences and by migration laws; markets are made less perfect by customs duties, import prohibitions and the problems of advertising in strange languages; capital movements are subject to government regulations. Even entrepreneurs may find it difficult to exercise their skills in an unfamiliar social setting. Perhaps the most obvious difficulty is that virtually all international trade involves the use of two or more currencies. A British car exporter may be paid in dollars, but if his wife wishes to buy her groceries, or he wishes to pay his workers, these dollars must be converted into pounds sterling.

7·1

a Which of the following factors affect the demand for goods in the international market?
- **A** The lack of adequate domestic supplies of essential commodities.
- **B** Relative prices for goods made overseas.
- **C** The production of goods surplus to domestic requirements.
- **D** The desire to conserve domestic supplies.

b Which of the following influences may lead to goods being offered for sale on the international market?
- **A** The need to earn supplies of overseas currency.
- **B** Domestic production costs being lower than those abroad.
- **C** The production of goods surplus to domestic requirements.

c Which of the following tend to limit international trade?
- **A** Import duties.
- **B** Differences in relative efficiency of producers.
- **C** Import quotas.
- **D** Political and economic embargos.

Foreign exchange

How do we pay for the goods which are bought abroad in countries which have their own currencies? Let us examine a very simple economic model. We assume a world of two countries, A and B, trading in one commodity, and using a common currency or gold as the medium of exchange. Suppose A has a surplus of wheat and B wants wheat, they can exchange wheat for a payment of gold.

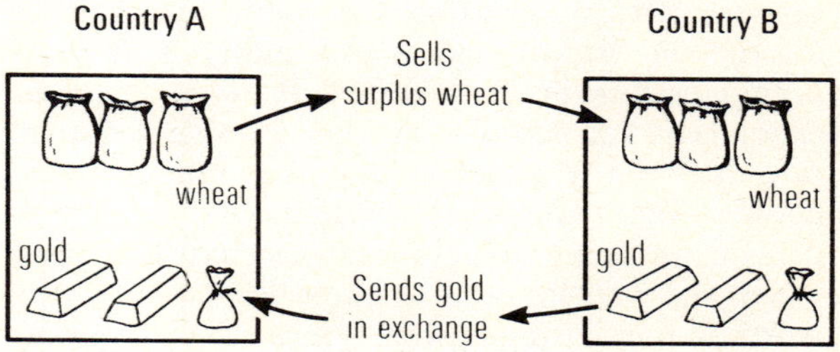

Figure 7·1

If trade continues, A will accumulate gold and B will be reducing its gold reserves.

The gold is of little direct use to A unless she can spend it. So A will seek to buy from B, say, railways. The gold will be sent back to B in exchange for railways sent over to A. So long as the double coincidence of wants applies, some trade will be possible. The gold will simply be shipped back and forth. Notice that B has to make railways specifically for export. One does not produce surplus quantities of railways on a casual basis.

Now taking the same circumstances, we can create a more complex model, where each country only uses its own currency. Let us assume that A uses dollars, and B uses pounds. In the first instance when A sells surplus wheat, B can only offer pounds in exchange. But no-one in country A can spend pounds. So a fund is held by B's banks, standing to the credit of A, which A can spend when she wants to.

When A decides to buy railways she does not need to ship gold to B but simply pays the manufacturers of railways in B with the pound sterling credits, having pounds transferred from the bank account which stands to A's credit, to the railway manufacturers. The manufacturer has been paid in his own currency. Country A has obtained her railways.

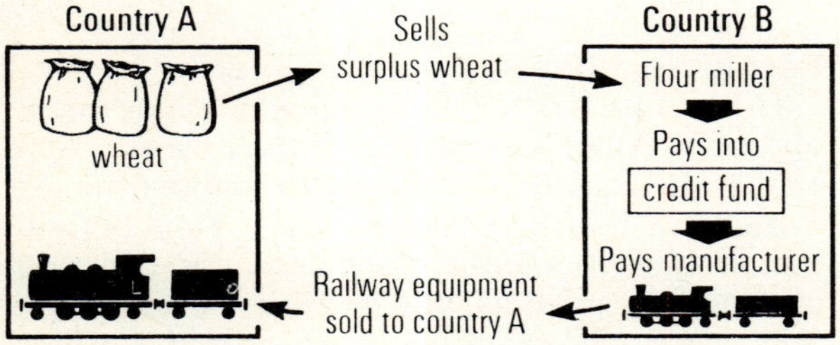

Figure 7·2

All this is possible, despite the fact that each country uses a separate currency; but it does depend on the willingness of country A to hold pound credits in the country B. This, in turn, depends on various assumptions: a stable exchange rate between the currencies and mutual trust between the countries. Only then can country A depend on being able to use the credits as, and when, she wants, and also know what the fund is worth in purchasing power. The purchasing power must be constant both in pounds sterling terms and in real value in country B.

These assumptions may be modified in real life. Meanwhile, we can note that the pound credits are claims to goods and may be bought, or sold, in the foreign exchange market.

7·2

In the simplified example in figure 7·2.

a What is the cost of the railway to country A?

b What is the cost of the wheat to country B?

By a process similar to that outlined above, country B may build up dollar credits in country A. As international trade continues each country will build up credits or debits with other countries. The situation is summarised at the end of each financial year in a government account called the Balance of Payments. Is international trade profitable?

The answer to this question depends on what is meant by 'profitable', and to whom the profits accrue.

If 'profitable' refers to normal trading profits, then, presumably, international trade is profitable to the firms involved, otherwise they would cease to trade. Exporters must have found markets and importers must have found sources of supply. They must also have obtained the foreign currency with which to trade, from commercial or merchant banks.

If 'profitable' refers to the interests of the country as a whole, we have to look much deeper into the problem. How much of the country's domestic resources is used to make the goods exported? How much of the domestic resources could be used to make, at home, the goods which are actually imported? It it worthwhile to make the exchange of exports for imports? Does the import of a commodity prevent the expansion of a domestic industry also producing that commodity? What is the measure of worthwhileness?

International trade is only worthwhile if we can export goods which we produce relatively more efficiently (i.e., in whose production we have a comparative advantage) and import goods of which we are relatively less efficient producers. In this way fewer resources are used in the production of goods because each country can concentrate on those goods in which it is, relatively, most efficient. More goods can be made at less cost.

We can now look at the principle of specialisation as applied to international trade.

International specialisation

The elementary analysis of international specialisation assumes that we can treat countries as single corporate bodies. As such they specialise in a relatively simple and direct way. You have seen how specialisation can arise in simple communities (S1) and how it has developed between regions in more complex communities (S4). We continue to make most of the same assumptions, and assume also that the desire to trade is there and can be made effective. From a national point of view *'trade will be advantageous if each of two countries specialises in the production of those goods in which it has a comparative advantage or in which it has the least comparative disadvantage'*: this is the *Law of Comparative Advantage*.

Model 1

Assume a 'world' of two countries. Both can produce wheat and cloth, but the use of one UPE (Unit of productive effort = labour + land + capital) will produce different quantities of each product.

In Country A, one UPE would produce	16 units of wheat *or* 4 units of cloth
In Country B, one UPE would produce	14 units of wheat *or* 6 units of cloth

If each devotes two UPEs to production we assume that they will produce *both* goods; e.g. Country A will produce 16 units of wheat *and* 4 units of cloth.

In Country A two UPEs produce	16 units of wheat +4 units of cloth
In Country B two UPEs produce	14 units of wheat +6 units of cloth
Total 'world' production is	30 units of wheat +10 units of cloth

To compare relative efficiences in the production of wheat:

$$\frac{\text{wheat units per UPE in A}}{\text{wheat units per UPE in B}} \times \frac{100}{1}$$

$$= \frac{16}{14} \times \frac{100}{1} = 114\%$$

Therefore Country A is 14% more efficient than Country B in the production of wheat. (If the countries were equally efficient the ratio would be 100%—and neither country would be more efficient).

To compare relative efficiences in the production of cloth:

$$\frac{\text{cloth units per UPE in A}}{\text{cloth units per UPE in B}} \times \frac{100}{1}$$

$$= \frac{4}{6} \times \frac{100}{1} = 66\%$$

Therefore Country A is less efficient than Country B in the production of cloth. Comparing the relative efficiencies, we see that Country A has a greater relative efficiency, or comparative advantage in the production of wheat: 1 UPE produces 114% of B's output of wheat, and only 66% of B's output of cloth.

If each country specialises in the production of the goods in which it has a comparative advantage, then:

Country A will produce	16 x 2 = 32 units of wheat
Country B will produce	6 x 2 = 12 units of cloth

7·3

By how much has the 'world' total production been raised as a result of international specialisation?

We now assume trade takes place, each country exchanging the product of one UPE.

Country A trades 16 units of wheat for 6 units of cloth.

Country B trades 6 units of cloth for 16 units of wheat.

As a result of specialising and then trading, Country A has gained an extra 2 units of cloth and Country B has gained an extra 2 units of wheat.

7·4

Country X and Y each has 2 UPEs. In each country 1 UPE is used for the production of coffee, and 1 UPE for the production of cameras. As a result each country's output is:

Country	Coffee units	Camera units
X	36	20
Y	30	24

Calculate the gain in world total production if each specialises in accordance with the law of comparative advantage.

Model 2

Assume a world of two countries, each able to produce the same two goods. As before, they differ in their relative efficiencies. But in this model Country R has an absolute advantage in both goods: it can produce more than Country Q of both goods for the same input of resources.

We need not know how many UPEs each country has. All we need to know is whether specialisation and trade benefit both countries.

Output of 1 UPE	Cheese units	Radio units
Country R	200 or	120
Country Q	150 or	100

Is there any point in trying to trade? A country has a comparative advantage if its relative efficiency at producing one of the goods is greater than the relative efficiency of the other country.

To measure relative efficiency of Country R compared with Country Q in the production of cheese:

$$\frac{\text{Cheese units per unit of productive effort in R}}{\text{Cheese units per unit of productive effort in Q}} \times \frac{100}{1} = \frac{200}{150} \times \frac{100}{1} = 133\tfrac{1}{3}\%$$

Country R is $33\frac{1}{3}\%$ more efficient than Country Q in the production of cheese.

To compare the relative efficiency of Country R with Country Q in the production of radios:

$$\frac{\text{Radio units per unit of productive effort in R}}{\text{Radio units per unit of productive effort in Q}} \times \frac{100}{1} = \frac{120}{100} \times \frac{100}{1} = 120\%$$

Country R is 20% more efficient than Country Q in the production of radios.

According to the law of comparative advantage, Country R should specialise in cheese because it is comparatively more efficient in cheese than in radios (i.e. $33\frac{1}{3}\%$ is greater than 20%). Country Q should specialise in the production of radios, in which it has the least comparative disadvantage.

The gain from specialisation

If the countries begin to specialise, in R UPEs will be shifted from radio production into cheese production, and in Q UPEs will be shifted from cheese to radio production

Change in output as factors are shifted:

	Cheese units	Radio units
In R 9 UPEs shifted	+1 800	−1 080
In Q 11 UPEs shifted	−1 650	+1 100
Gain in output from specialisation	+ 150	+ 20

This example shows that if trade is possible, countries can increase their output of both commodities by specialisation according to the principle of comparative advantage, even when one country may have a comparative advantage in both products.

Model 3

Suppose the output per UPE in each country was shown by the following table:

Output per UPE	Cheese units	Radio units
Country R	180	120
Country Q	150	100

7·5

a Which country has an absolute advantage in the production of cheese?

b Which country has an absolute advantage in the production of radios?

c Which country has a comparative advantage in the production of cheese?

d Which country has a comparative advantage in the production of radios?

e Will there be any gain from specialisation and trade?

If you have answered question 7·5 correctly, you will see that specialisation and trade will be beneficial only when one country has a comparative advantage over another in the production of a commodity. It is *comparative* advantages, and not absolute advantages which matter.

The limitations of this analysis

i Free Trade. Perhaps the most obvious assumption being made is that trade between the two countries is free of restrictions imposed by governments such as tariffs, quotas and customs duties, political embargos and restrictions to avoid transmitting diseases (e.g. U.S. refusal to trade with China, measures to prevent foot and mouth disease, or rabies). Only if free trade and perfect competition exist will the difference in relative efficiencies be felt to the full and the benefits of that trade realised.

ii Transport costs. These may offset the gains analysed in Models 1 and 2, since they raise the cost of production (or lower the relative efficiency) in terms of the productive effort required to get the goods to their market. Similarly, perishability of goods may make transport much more expensive, or even pointless, if the goods have gone bad.

iii Is demand reciprocal? The analysis so far assumes that the double coincidence of wants exists in respect of the two goods concerned. Details about quality, design and suitability of goods are ignored.

iv Structural changes in industry. If each country specialises exclusively in the goods at which it is most efficient, it is automatically dependent on the other country for the supply of the other goods. This means that its industrial structure is permanently changed. Strategic, military or economic considerations may make a country hesitate to take the risk of depending entirely on others for certain goods. International specialisation may be less complete than the theory suggests.

v Mobility of factors. This analysis assumes that the factors of production previously used in different industries are free to move entirely into the specialist line. Furthermore the substitution of new factors into the specialist industry may well upset relative efficiencies and remove the advantages of international specialisation.

vi Returns to scale. If a firm doubles its sales by exporting say, silk ties, it may then pay to use machines instead of printing by hand. At a greater output costs may fall more than proportionately.

The analysis ignores the effect of an expanded market. Not only may it affect relative efficiencies but it will almost certainly affect returns to scale in the industry which specialises. (See S9 for Law of Proportionate Returns.) Increasing returns may apply in manufacturing industries, especially if they use a large proportion of capital. It is quite common to plan production for the home market, and to produce extra quantities for export at a lower price provided that the additional variable costs are covered by these extra sales (see S11 for fixed and variable costs).

Decreasing returns may apply when expansion of the industry means using less efficient factors of production, especially in agriculturally based industries or where a high proportion of labour is used.

vii Full employment. If one assumes full employment then the factors previously employed in the industry which has to disappear as a result of specialisation must find some employment or, as they will not be able to buy the goods produced abroad, the market for the overseas country will be limited. Trade may not, then, expand as a result of the specialisation which has taken place.

The models assume that in specialising, all the resources employed in the abandoned industry are transferred to the industry of specialisation. If, for example, the United Kingdom ceased aircraft production and specialised in car manufacture, all the land, labour and capital formerly employed in aircraft manufacture should be transferred to car making. Hence, the opportunity cost of car making would be the loss of aircraft production. If there is full employment this might perhaps be 1 000 cars: 1 aircraft and a gain or loss could be calculated. However, suppose that after specialisation some of the aircraft industry's resources are unemployed. Then, the opportunity cost of 1 000 cars is 1 aircraft + x unemployed. There is no way of calculating the cost of unemployment, and therefore it is difficult to calculate the true gains from trade when some unemployment is created.

viii Perfect market. In an international perfect market it has to be assumed that:

(a) there is perfect knowledge of each market by the other country, so that cost differences can be calculated and advantage can be taken of the benefits of specialisation;

(b) no producer is in a position to influence price, by advertising or by restricting supply. How, for example, can anyone calculate the cost of diamonds, when almost the entire supply is controlled by one firm? International cartels or monopolies do exist, and so does discriminating monopoly.

A failure in any of these two assumptions will mean that the rate of exchange of the products may be unfavourable to one of the countries and its gains from international specialisation eroded.

ix Benefits. Models can be constructed to show that, at worst, one country may be no better off than it was before, whilst the other country gains all the benefits. In most cases there is some gain for both countries. However, the rich countries may gain more than the poorer countries, hence the gap between them may widen. The analysis takes no account of social and political aspects of trade. Many trading groups, such as the Commonwealth, or Comecon, have been set up as much for political reasons as economic ones.

x Specific products. Once specialisation has taken place, countries are producing commodities especially for export. This means structural changes in the allocation of domestic resources, which in turn affects costs and relative efficiencies. For example, a British publisher producing the Bible in Swahili cannot direct his product to the British market, nor switch his specialised editorial staff to other books.

xi Units of productive effort (UPE). The unit of productive effort, used as the tool in this analysis cannot be calculated in any real situation, for besides land, labour and capital, it includes social factors, such as education.

The closest that economists have come to defining a UPE is by calculating wage costs per unit of output.

xii Restrictions on the convertibility of currencies. Currency problems are assumed not to exist at this stage, but for many political and economic reasons countries restrict the conversion of their currencies, and so reduce the freedom to trade of their importers and exporters.

7·6

State the law of comparative advantage. Summarise the criticisms of this law, giving examples from the contemporary economic scene.

7·7

As a check on your understanding of the argument and the assumptions made in discussing international trade above, answer the following questions.

a What savings may follow specialisation?

b What happens to the markets available to producers?

c Why would you expect economic resources to be more fully utilised?

d What would you expect to happen to the level of industrial costs and prices after international specialisation has occurred?

e Would you expect the volume of goods traded to increase or decrease?

f Why is mobility of labour a problem in this sphere of economics?

g What effects would you expect international trade to have on the cultural and political relationships between countries?

h Will the wealth gap between developed and developing nations be closed by international trade? What will the effect be?

i Will international specialisation affect consumer spending patterns? If yes, what ways, if not, why not?

j Will specialisation by a given industry eliminate that industry in the other country, if not, why not?

Terms of Trade

The Terms of Trade show the ratio at which two countries exchange their goods. In real life it is worked out in money terms, but for the moment we will ignore money.

Return to Model 1 where for each unit of productive effort:

Country	Wheat units or Cloth units		
A	16	or	4
B	14	or	~~4~~ 6

The Theory of Comparative Advantage has already shown that by specialising the 'world' total production can be increased.

To discover whether trade would be worthwhile, we need to know the terms on which each country trades, i.e. the relative value of Wheat : Cloth.

Setting the limits

With a given unit of productive effort Country A can produce 16 units of wheat for every 4 units of cloth—a production ratio of 4 : 1. So after specialisation A would not exchange wheat for cloth at any ratio greater than 4 : 1, i.e. A will never give more than 4 wheat units for every 1 cloth unit B wants to sell.

Country B will not accept less than 14 units wheat for 6 units of cloth, i.e. a ratio or opportunity cost 7 : 3, because it can do as well as this for itself, using its own units of productive effort.

The terms at which trade is done, the rate of exchange, must lie between the two domestic opportunity cost ratios, i.e. between 4 : 1 and 7 : 3 or 2·33 : 1.

7·8

Take the data from Model 2 and calculate the range for the terms of trade.

Now, by dropping the assumption which ignored money, and measuring the value of goods in money terms (by taking the U.S. dollar as an international measure), we can calculate the actual terms of trade.

So far we have dealt with the exchange of commodities. If we take, say 5 cars for 10 motor boats, and each car and each motor boat is valued at £1 000, then the price exchange ratio equals the physical exchange ratio, i.e. 5 000 : 10 000 or 5 : 10

or 1:2. Suppose that motor boats are now £500 each. To exchange 5 cars for £1 000 worth of boats now means that £5 000 worth of cars are now exchanged for 20 motor boats. Now suppose that for some reason the price of motor boats falls to £250, so that £5 000 worth of cars will now buy 40 motor boats. Thus for the same effort of producing 5 cars, the one country has had the chance of obtaining first 10 motor boats, then 20, then 40. Thus the terms of trade have moved in favour of this country.

We have only considered trade in one currency, sterling. Suppose that the motor boat producer's currency is the franc, and that it changes in value from £1 = 20 francs to £1 = 30 francs, although the prices of the goods remain the same. Whereas £5 000 worth of cars previously bought 10 motor boats, it will now buy 15 motor boats.

Thus the terms of trade can change because
(a) a change in the domestic price of either commodity will affect the physical rate at which it exchanges for the other, and
(b) a change in the rate of exchange of the two currencies will also affect the physical rate at which one commodity will exchange for the other.

The terms of trade index

It is essential for the government to have some idea of the terms of trade in order to manage the economy. It has available figures of quantities and values of exports and imports collected by Customs officials. The statistical problem is to compare total imports with total exports. It is clearly impossible to compile a *quantity* total for either, since we cannot add up gallons of wines, cubic feet of timber, yards of cloth, and so on, for all the thousands of different items and units of measurements. Neither can we add the total values, because we would be ignoring the price change of each item during the period under consideration, and by so doing also ignoring the fact that if price changes, so does the amount of real goods represented by a given total value. We therefore have to devise a weighted index system.

Essentially, the terms of trade are compared in terms of commodity prices, which are 'weighted' according to the quantities involved. Hence jumbo jets, imported occasionally, have a lesser weighting than foodstuffs. (For a fuller explanation of weighting, see satellite *Arithmetical and Statistical Methods*.)

The United Kingdom terms of trade have been calculated since 1963 according to the following formula.

$$\frac{\text{Index of Export Prices}}{\text{Index of Import Prices}} \times 100 = \text{Terms of trade Index}$$

Thus if the index of export prices changes to 150, and the index of import prices changes to 50, then, $\frac{150}{50} \times 100 = 300$, which means that our exports are exchanged for three times as many imports as in the base year, when the index was 100.

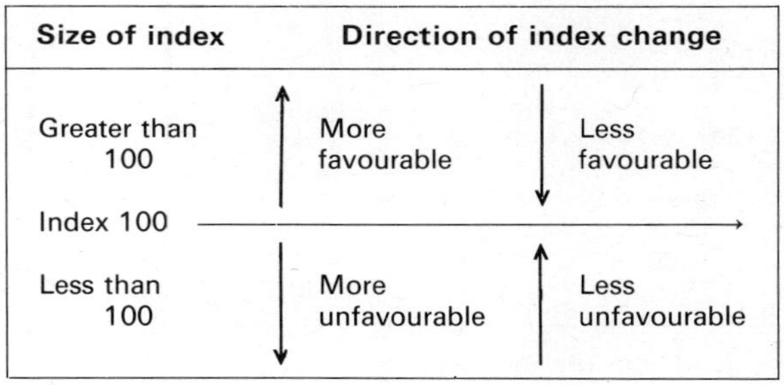

Figure 7·3

If the Index rises then it will indicate a trend favourable to the U.K. in world prices. If it falls, the trend is unfavourable because the prices of the U.K.'s imports will have risen in comparison with the prices paid for U.K. exports.

An index greater than 100 is a favourable one.

An index less than 100 is an unfavourable one.

A change of index up towards 100, e.g. 73 to 86, means that the index is now less unfavourable than before.

A change of index down towards 100, e.g. 106 to 102, means that the index is now less favourable than before. (See figure 7·3.)

However, a favourable movement in the terms of trade does not mean that there will be a favourable movement in the balance of trade or balance of payments.

7·9

Which of the following might result in an increase in the amount of imports?

- **A** The threat of war
- **B** A dock strike
- **C** Higher income tax
- **D** An increase in immigration
- **E** An increase in the standard of living (i.e. real income per head)
- **F** A decrease in import duties
- **G** An increase in subsidies to farmers.

7·10

Which of the following might lead to an increase in exports?

- **A** A threatened dock strike
- **B** Technological improvements in domestic industry
- **C** Creation of a free trade area
- **D** Political revolution
- **E** An increase in the standard of living of the customer overseas.
- **F** A trade depression overseas.

7·11

1961 = 100	Import Price Index	Export Price Index	Terms of Trade
1958	103	99	
1966	109	112	
1967	109	114	

Consider the data above.

a Calculate the terms of trade for each year.

b How did the terms of trade in 1967 compare with 1958?

- **A** more favourable
- **B** less favourable
- **C** more unfavourable
- **D** less unfavourable

c By how much did the terms of trade index change between 1958 and 1967?

- **A** +9 points
- **B** −9 points

7·12

What does a favourable change in the index mean?

- **A** Prices of imports rise relative to the prices of exports
- **B** Prices of exports fall relative to the price of imports
- **C** Prices of imports fall relative to the price of exports.
- **D** Prices of exports rise relative to the price of imports.

Having dealt with the terms of trade index which shows the relation between the prices of imports and exports, we can now turn to the *balance of trade* which shows the total volumes of exports and imports. The total balance of trade is only part of the balance of payments account of a nation, but at present it is sufficient just to look at it alone, and examine its constituent parts.

The balance of visible trade

This refers to the value of imports and exports of *goods*. In the United Kingdom exports are valued *free on board* (f.o.b.), which assumes that the exporter receives in sterling an amount covering the cost of the goods and does not have to pay the cost of transport and insurance, which are paid by the importer. Imports to the U.K. are shown as including cost, insurance and freight (c.i.f.). Hence the United Kingdom's trade figures tend to over-value the total amount spent on imports.

The balance of invisible trade

Most invisible export comes from the sale of services to foreigners. Some services, like shipping, may be provided abroad; others like banking and hotel accommodation, are provided in the U.K., but since they are sold to persons other than residents of the U.K., they are exported.

In the same way, when a British citizen takes a holiday abroad, and cashes his cheques in a foreign bank to pay for his holiday meals, he is 'importing' services.

Also included in invisible trade are government expenditure and payments of interest, profits and dividends.

Let us look at that part of the balance of payments account which constitutes the balance of total trade (see *Annual Abstract of Statistics*).

Part of the balance of payments account for the U.K. dealing with the balance of total trade only (£mn)

	1969
Imports (c.i.f.)	−7 202
Exports and re-exports (f.o.b.)	+7 061
Balance of visible trade	−141
Balance of invisible trade	+557
Payments to U.S.A. for military aircraft	−61
Current balance (Balance of visible trade + balance of invisible trade)	+416

Source: *Annual Abstract of Statistics*

Thus during the accounting period 1968 we had a surplus (+) on the total balance of trade amounting to £416m, and a balance on visible account of −£141m. From 1970 there were changes in the presentation of the Balance of Payments Accounts, but no change was made in this section of the accounts, except that both imports and exports are now f.o.b.

7·13

a From the current *Abstract of Statistics,* complete a table for this year, similar to the one above.

b How could we rectify a deficit, referring only to the items of this account and the information given in this chapter?

c From the *Balance of Payments Accounts* draw two charts, one for imports and one for exports for 1970 and for the latest year for which you can obtain data. Make notes on the changes observed.

d From the *Annual Abstract of Statistics* you can conveniently identify the countries which supply U.K. imports. By grouping appropriate countries together and expressing the value of goods imported from these countries as a percentage of the total, construct bar diagrams to show the relative importance of sources of imports.

e From the *Annual Abstract of Statistics* you should construct a set of diagrams for exports, comparable to those worked out for section d.

ANSWERS

7·1

a Correct **A, B, D.**
Mistaken **C**: a surplus does not create a demand, it merely provides a supply.

b Correct **A, B, C.**

c Correct **A, C, D.**
Mistaken **B**: differences in relative efficiency in production do not prevent trade, they encourage it.

7·2

a Surplus of wheat exported.

b Railway stock bartered for wheat—credit fund merely an intermediary.

7·3

World production has risen. 2 Wheat units—2 Cloth.

7·4

After specialisation, X produces 72 coffee units, Y produces 48 camera units. Gain is therefore 6 coffee and 4 camera units.

7·5

a Country R

b Country R

c Neither country

d Neither country

e No gain from specialisation.

7·6

State Law of Comparative Advantage.

'Trade will be advantageous if each of two countries specialise in the production of those goods in which it has a comparative advantage or in which it has the least comparative disadvantage.'

Summary of criticisms—from headings.

7·7

a Economies of scale in production and marketing.

b Markets are widened after specialisation.

c A fuller use of resources because of wider markets therefore greater sales. More efficient production because of specialisation.

d Costs and prices should tend to fall because of greater efficiency from specialisation.

e Other things being equal, the volume of goods traded will rise.

f Immobility of labour may reduce the ease with which resources are redeployed during process of specialisation. Without mobility, rewards to labour may vary from country to country.

g Cultural and political relationships should be closer and more interdependent.

h International trade *may* close wealth gap. Though both may be better off, wealthy nations may benefit even more and relative gap widen.

i Consumer spending will be affected because of changes in relative price of goods.

j Specialisation in one country in a given industry may not eliminate that industry in another country because of size of the market, economic barriers, strategic reasons.

7·8

Country R's production ratio, or domestic opportunity cost, is

200 cheese to 120 radios $= 1\frac{2}{3}:1$

Country Q's production ratio, or domestic opportunity cost, is

150 cheese to 100 radios $= 1\frac{1}{2}:1$

Therefore the terms will be between $1\frac{2}{3}$ and $1\frac{1}{2}$ units of cheese for 1 radio.

7·9

A Correct: essential commodities will be stockpiled.

B Incorrect: imports of commodities in bulk by sea will be impossible.

C No certain connection: individuals have less to spend but governments may spend more, and so increase demand for imports.

D Correct: more people usually lead to more trade.

E Correct: this usually leads to a greater variety of goods being demanded.

F Correct: the prices of imports will fall.

G Indeterminate: the cost of home-produced food falls to the consumer, thereby saving imports, but farmers have more money to spend, say, on imported animal foods.

7·10

A Correct: exporters will try to send goods before the strike occurs.

B Correct: this will lead to a decrease in export prices which, one assumes, will attract more buyers.

C Indeterminate: its effect depends on whether the exporter and his customer is in the free trade area.

D Indeterminate: its effect will vary according to the political beliefs of the various parties in power in exporting and importing countries, and their relations with each other. It is a political event, but its effect on economic affairs may be far-reaching.

E Correct: the customer will be able to afford more goods.

F Incorrect: this will usually lead to a decline in trade.

7·11

a Terms of Trade

1958	96
1966	103
1967	105

b The terms of trade in 1967 were more favourable than they were in 1958.

c The index changed by 9 points between 1958 and 1967.

7·12

Correct **C, D**: a favourable change in the terms of trade index means that prices of imports fall relative to prices of exports or that prices of exports rise relative to prices of imports.

Mistaken **A, B**: re-read the text.

7·13

a Graphical exercises.

b
- **i** Increase exports and/or decrease imports of visible trade.
- **ii** Increase tourism to U.K.
- **iii** Decrease foreign travel by U.K. residents.
- **iv** Increase flow of dividends, profit and interest to U.K.
- **v** Manufacture own military aircraft.
- **vi** Hope for favourable change in terms of trade.

c Own research.

d Own research.

e Own research.

DEMAND

In S1 and S5 you were shown what a demand curve looked like under normal circumstances. The purpose of this study section is to show why economists usually assume the demand curve has this shape.

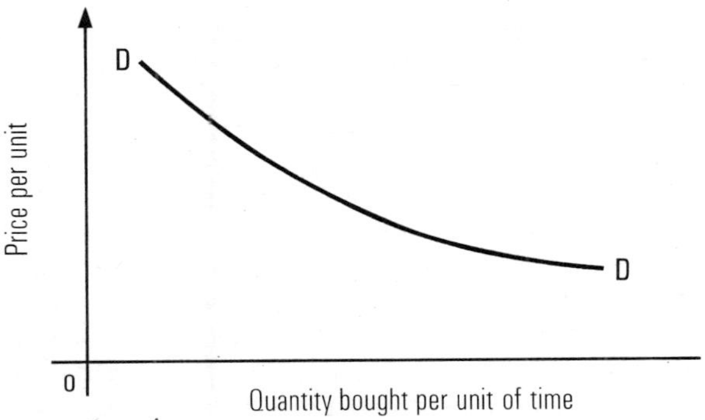

Figure 8·1

Choice is a process of decision making. If you choose to buy one commodity rather than another then you add to the amount bought of one commodity, leaving the other unconsumed. Your wants for goods are generally assumed to be unlimited but the means to satisfy those wants are limited, hence the need to make choices. Rational consumers will tend to make choices on the basis of obtaining the greatest 'value for money', i.e. maximising the satisfaction they can obtain with their income. Each choice involves an opportunity cost. Each choice will also involve making *marginal additions or subtractions* to the amount of a product they consume, i.e. a change of one unit in the amount consumed. The marginal unit is the unit just added to or subtracted from the amount consumed.

Scarcity and utility

As we have seen, to be of interest to an economist, a commodity or service must be scarce. If there is no scarcity, there is no point in anyone paying money for that commodity or service. Consider how you spent your money in the last few days. The pattern you discern shows the net result of decision making. Unless you wish you had spent your money in some different way, you can assume that the resulting allocation gave as much satisfaction as you could obtain from your income. It is not enough to say 'I would rather have bought cigarettes than pay bus fares because cigarettes give more satisfaction'. In fact you have shown, by paying bus fares, that you preferred bus fares to cigarettes. This is the sense in which economists use the word 'satisfaction'.

Those expenditures to which you give priority are assumed to yield the greatest amount of extra satisfaction in terms of fulfilling your wants. It is usual to use the word *'utility'* to refer to the power of any economic commodity to satisfy wants. Utility is a useful concept, but there is neither means of measuring it nor units in which it can be counted.

Marginal utility

The value, or utility, which consumers place upon commodities is entirely subjective, and varies according to circumstances. If diamonds are scarce and you only have one, you will tend to value that unit very highly. If, however, you could pick them up like pebbles and you had a large quantity, you would not value an extra one very highly.

If we call the subjective satisfaction from each diamond its utility, then the *extra* satisfaction to be derived from owning an *extra* diamond is its marginal utility. If you have a large number of diamonds the utility gained from each extra one will tend to diminish. This tendency is the law of diminishing marginal utility which states, 'As successive units of a commodity are purchased to satisfy an economic want, the utility gained from each additional unit will diminish, other things remaining the same.'

The *total* utility from possessing a given stock of a commodity will grow each time you pruchase another unit, but it grows by a smaller and smaller amount as the marginal utility diminishes.

Consider a student buying pens. If the cost of each extra pen is the same as the previous one, i.e. the price is constant, then there will come a time when the extra satisfaction is only just worth the cost of the extra unit. If he then bought another pen its utility to him would be less than he could obtain by spending that money on something else. In this case the marginal utility of pens would have fallen below the opportunity cost so he would not, in fact, buy an extra pen. In a perfect market one tends to go on buying until the marginal utility equals the price for each commodity bought. The marginal satisfaction gained from each commodity is then proportional to its price.

Marginal utility

$$\frac{\text{Margin of utility of cheese}}{\text{Price of cheese}} = \frac{\text{Margin of utility of tomatoes}}{\text{Price of tomatoes}} = \frac{\text{Margin of utility of bacon}}{\text{Price of bacon}}$$

If the ratio of marginal utility, to price of cheese does *not* equal the ratio of marginal utility to the price of tomatoes, and so on for bacon and the whole range of goods and services bought by a consumer, then he will readjust his extra expenditure until the ratios *are* the same. This process is known as achieving a point of *equi-marginal satisfaction,* where no alternative allocation of expenditure will increase total utility so that at the point of equi-marginal satisfaction total satisfaction is maximised.

Suppose we make a table showing three commodities at present purchased by a housewife. For the purposes of illustration we will give a numerical value to the marginal utility of each.

	Cheese	Tomatoes	Bacon
M.U.	2	1	3
Price	4p	2p	6p

In this situation her ratio of marginal utility to price is consistently 1 : 2, and any further purchasing would be equally divided between the three goods.

If the housewife decided that she would prefer to have more salad meals than usual, then she would buy tomatoes in preference to other goods until the marginal utility of tomatoes to price again reached 1 : 2.

Suppose that the price of cheese doubled to 8p. She would stop buying cheese until its marginal utility rose to 4, in which case the ratio of marginal utility to price would again be in balance with the other goods.

Difference between marginal utility and total utility

We can now see why in Europe water, which is essential to life, has such a low value in money terms, while diamonds or pearls, which are of little use, have a high money value, for, to the economist, the word 'value' means a relationship between the subjective value (utility) of a commodity and its objective value (price). Water is, in the U.K. and most of Europe, a relatively abundant commodity. The subjective value of an extra bucket of water is therefore small because it is not scarce, i.e. the marginal utility of a bucket of water is very low. Diamonds, however, are very scarce and the subjective value of an extra few diamonds is very high, i.e. the marginal utility of a diamond is high. The opportunity cost of giving up a diamond necklace is very high indeed. Since it would not readily be given up, it will command a high market price.

In other continents pure fresh water is a scarce commodity (as the World Health Organisation constantly emphasises). Purchasing drinks of fresh water from water carriers is an everyday affair, for example, in Morocco. Many Europeans, particularly British tourists, find this a curious state of affairs—again a subjective evaluation.

For each individual, then, the demand for each commodity or service he buys can be explained in terms of the relationship between its marginal utility to him and its price. The aggregate of all personal decisions therefore forms the market demand for that commodity at that price.

8·1

Which of the following factors will affect the marginal utility of a commodity or service?

- **A** The market price.
- **B** The relative scarcity.
- **C** Subjective tastes or preferences.
- **D** Changes in circumstances such as climatic seasons or fashions.
- **E** Travelling abroad.

The demand curve

We have shown how each consumer has a scale of marginal utility derived from each extra unit of a commodity or service which normally tends to diminish. This being so, to persuade an individual to buy more of a commodity or service, in view of this falling marginal utility, price must be lowered. Consider a consumer who has established a marginal utility/price ratio of 2 : 7 among the range of goods he purchased. He can only be persuaded to buy one commodity to the point where marginal utility falls to 1 if the price falls to $3\frac{1}{2}$, to maintain the ratio and the equi-marginal equilibrium. This is confirmed by common observation: most people buy more when the price falls, so that demand curves normally slope downwards.

8·2

Why do people usually buy less as the price rises?

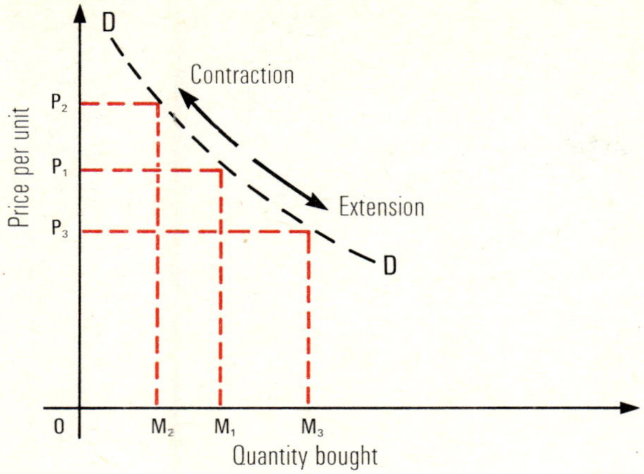

Figure 8·2

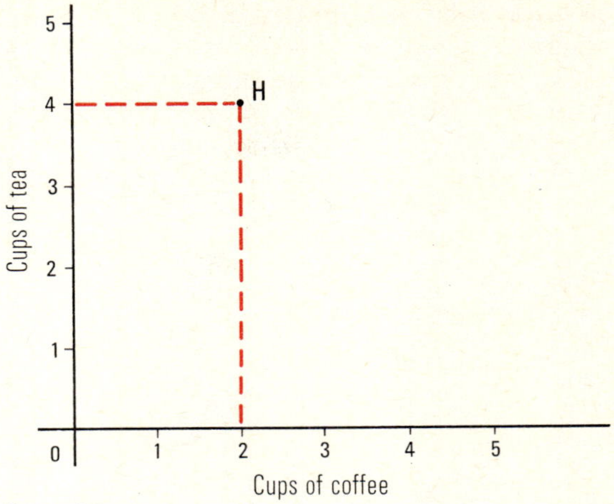

Figure 8·3

So far we have considered the economic behaviour of one person. The behaviour of a group of consumers is the sum of their individual demand schedules, and results in a *market demand curve* as in figure 8·2.

At price OP_1 quantity OM_1 is bought. If the price rises to OP_2 then the price rises out of proportion to the satisfaction obtained by marginal consumers. They therefore buy less or cease to buy. Consequently, as demand *contracts,* less will be bought (OM_2) at the higher price. If, however, the market price had fallen from OP_1 to OP_3 then some consumers will be willing to purchase some units of this commodity and other consumers will tend to buy a little more. Demand *extends* from OM_1 to OM_3 as price falls.

A continuous series of small price changes can be taken and the resulting extensions and contractions can be plotted to form a demand curve which simply shows the relationship between the price per unit of a commodity or service and the quantity which would be bought.

Indifference analysis

An alternative analysis of consumer behaviour is known as *indifference curve analysis.* A consumer purchases a certain combination of cups of tea and coffee per day (figure 8·3).

Position H is a point of indifference where the consumer purchases four cups of tea and two cups of coffee per day. He has no desire to change this situation, which we assume represents a given level of satisfaction to him.

If we now assume that he must give up one cup of tea, how much extra coffee will he require to leave him just as satisfied as before, i.e. indifferent to which situation he is in?

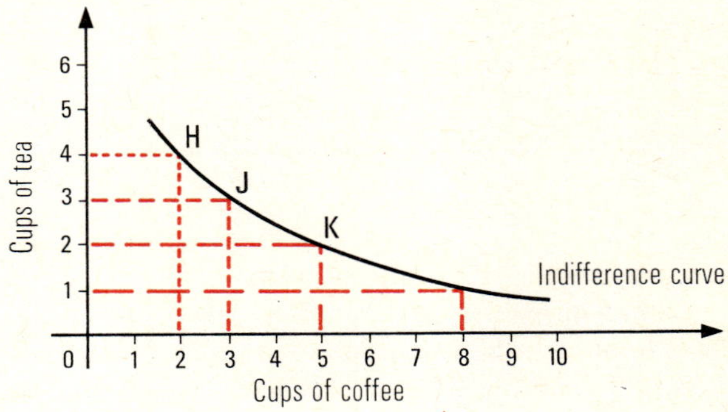

Figure 8·4

At first he does not mind giving up one cup of tea, provided that he can replace it with one cup of coffee (J). Assume he is denied yet another cup of tea, so that he now has only two instead of four. He will then demand an extra two cups of coffee to compensate for the loss of another cup of tea (K). So long as the compensation is adequate, this consumer's level of satisfaction remains constant. A line joining a series of points of indifference is called an indifference curve. It represents a varying combination of products consumed but a constant level of satisfaction.

As he loses each cup of tea he requires an increasing amount of compensation to restore him to the previous level of satisfaction and thus, to a position of indifference. This is because he values the remaining cups of tea more highly the scarcer they become, and because marginal additions to cups of coffee yield less and less extra satisfaction.

Marginal rate of substitution

Examine figure 8·5. Here the consumer is satisfied with a combination of 5 cups of tea and $4\frac{1}{3}$ cups of coffee at point A. Suppose he wishes to change this combination. How much tea will he give up to gain another cup of coffee, i.e. what will be his rate of substitution if he moves from point A?

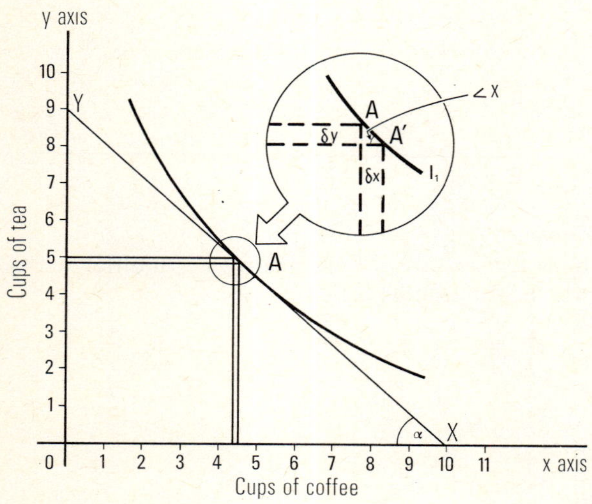

Figure 8·5

We see in the inset a magnified view of the curve near point A. The small decrease in tea consumption is δy, and the corresponding increase in coffee consumption is δx. Remembering that A is a point, the side AA′ is represented by a tangent to the curve at A. (Non-mathematicians may find it helpful to imagine that δy and δx are shrinking. As they diminish, so will AA′, until the line AA′ is the point A.)

How much tea is sacrificed for coffee in moving from point A? It is $\frac{\delta y}{\delta x}$, but by referring to the figure, we see that $\frac{\delta y}{\delta x}$ is the tangent of ∠x, and since the small triangle δy δx AA′ is similar to the triangle OXY, formed by the tangent and the axes, then ∠x = ∠α, and tan x = tan α. In this case, tan α = $\frac{9}{10}$ = ·9, and this is the rate of substitution at point A.

Note that we have assumed that the consumer is moving from point A. He is changing his pattern of consumption. Unless we make this assumption, we cannot measure the rate of substitution. Because of the change in quantities consumed, we are measuring a marginal rate of substitution.

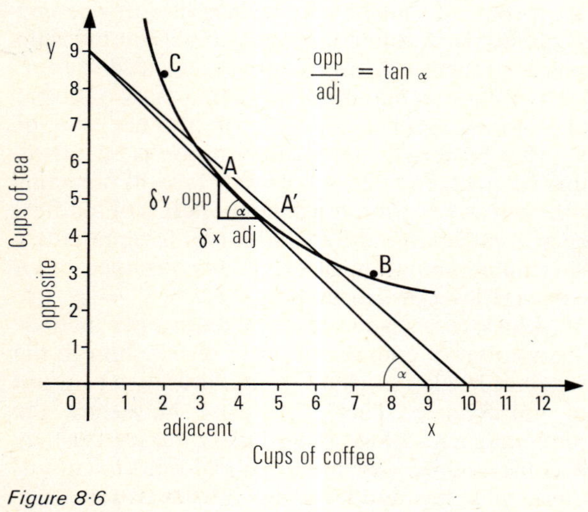

Figure 8·6

The law of diminishing marginal substitution

Now refer to diagram 8·6. Point A is fairly centrally placed on the indifference curve, points B and C are towards the ends of the curve. If you measure the rate of substitution (tan α) at these two points, you will find in one case that it is greater than at A, in the other case less.

8·3

At point B, is tan α greater or lesser than at A?

The alteration in tan α along the indifference curve illustrates the law of diminishing marginal substitution. In simple terms, the more cups of coffee we have, the less tea we will sacrifice to gain still more coffee.

8·4

Assume each of the following combinations of soft drinks and ice cream yields the same level of satisfaction as other combinations. Plot these values on graph paper and draw in the indifference curve which passes through the points i to vi.

	x axis	y axis
Point	**Soft drinks**	**Ice creams**
i	2	9
ii	3	7
iii	4	5·5
iv	5	4·5
v	7	3
vi	10	2

a Assume this consumer normally purchases 9 ice creams and 2 soft drinks. How much ice cream would he sacrifice in order to obtain an extra drink (a third) without altering his level of satisfaction?

b If this consumer wishes to substitute another drink for ice cream (he now purchases 4 drinks), how much ice cream will he be prepared to sacrifice without affecting his level of satisfaction?

c How much ice cream will be sacrificed for a fifth drink and still leave him indifferent?

d Suppose yet another (sixth) drink is substituted for ice cream, how much ice cream will be given up without altering his level of satisfaction?

Indifference maps

A single indifference curve represents an assumed level of satisfaction. If we want to represent a higher level of satisfaction then we can draw in a new curve further from the origin of the graph—l_2 in figure 8·8.

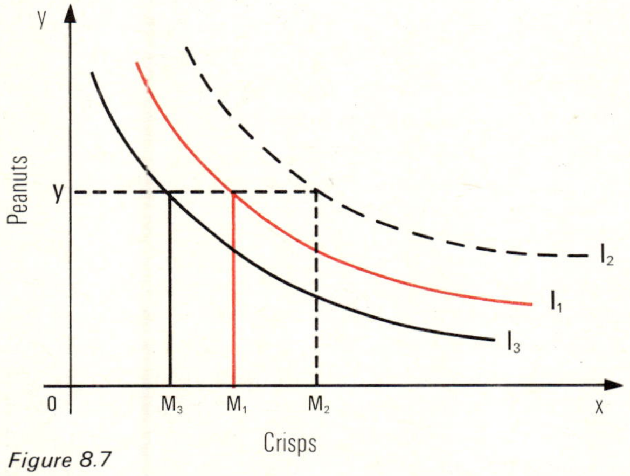

Figure 8.7

All points on l_2 represent a higher level of satisfaction than l_1. If we assume the consumer has OY packets of peanuts, then on l_1 he has only OM_1 of crisps, but he has OM_2 of crisps in combination with OY peanuts when he is on l_2. Similarly l_3 represents a lower level of satisfaction than l_1.

An *indifference map* represents a series of indifference curves, the pattern of which is set by the individual preferences of consumers.
in figure 8·8.

8·5

A student is interviewed about varying combinations of peanuts and potato crisps he would like to consume in a week. Three sets of combinations result, each set representing a different level of satisfaction. (Scale: 1 cm to 1 unit x; 2 cm to 1 unit y.)

Satisfaction Level 1		Satisfaction Level 2		Satisfaction Level 3	
x axis Crisps	**y axis Peanuts**	**x axis Crisps**	**y axis Peanuts**	**x axis Crisps**	**y axis Peanuts**
1	9	4	11	8	11
3	6	5	8	9	9·5
5	4	6	7	12	6·5
8	2	9	4	16	4
10	1	13	2		

a Draw the three indifference curves 1_1, 1_2, 1_3 corresponding to the three levels of satisfaction. If he enjoys only the first level of satisfaction, how many packets of crisps will he wish to consume in combination with 7 packets of peanuts?
A 2·2 **B** 6 **C** 11·4 **D** 2·5

b If this consumer is able to enjoy the second level of satisfaction, how many packets of peanuts will he wish to consume in combination with 10 packets of crisps?
A 4·2 **B** 1 **C** 3·4 **D** 8·3

c Assume now that the consumer enjoys the highest of the three levels of satisfaction. If he consumes, normally, 10 packets of peanuts and 8·6 packets of crisps, by how much will his consumption of crisps rise if he gives up 2 packets of peanuts?
A 10·4 **B** 1·8 **C** 1 **D** 5

d Suppose the consumer is enjoying the second level of satisfaction and consumes 13 packets of crisps per week. By how much will his consumption of peanuts change if he substitutes peanuts for 3 of his packets of crisps? Assume his level of satisfaction is unchanged.
A −1·4 **B** +3·4 **C** −1 **D** +1·4

e Calculate the marginal rate of substitution of crisps for peanuts on 1_1 where 4 packets of peanuts are consumed.
A 2·5 **B** 0·8 **C** 0·35

f Calculate the marginal rate of substitution of crisps for peanuts:
  i on 1_2 where 9 packets of crisps are consumed.
  ii on 1_3 where 6·5 packets of peanuts are consumed.

Allocation of personal resources

Two factors are involved in the allocation of personal resources; personal preferences and the market. In this analysis we have already seen that personal preference determines the rate at which one commodity will be substituted for another, which in turn determines the shape of indifference curves and thus the pattern shown on an indifference map. There are many indifference curves between those drawn, but it would be too crowded to attempt to put them on the figure. Indifference curves do not cross one another, since at a point of intersection both curves would have the same values. This is incompatible with the concept that each curve represents a different level of satisfaction.

The market determines the relative price of any two commodities and so determines how much of each commodity could be bought with a given income.

8·6

Suppose we look more closely at the student who buys peanuts and crisps. Let us assume he has 80p per week for these items, and also assume that peanuts are 5p per packet and crisps are 8p per packet.

a How many packets of peanuts could he purchase if all his money was spent on this item?

b How many packets of crisps could he buy with his 80p?

Plot the answers to **a** and **b** on graph paper like figure 8·8.

With his money the student can purchase either OA of peanuts or OB of crisps, *or* he can purchase any combination of crisps and peanuts which are on the *budget line* AB. The position of the budget line is determined by the relative prices of the goods and the size of income which can be spent.

8·7

Data as for exercise 8·6.

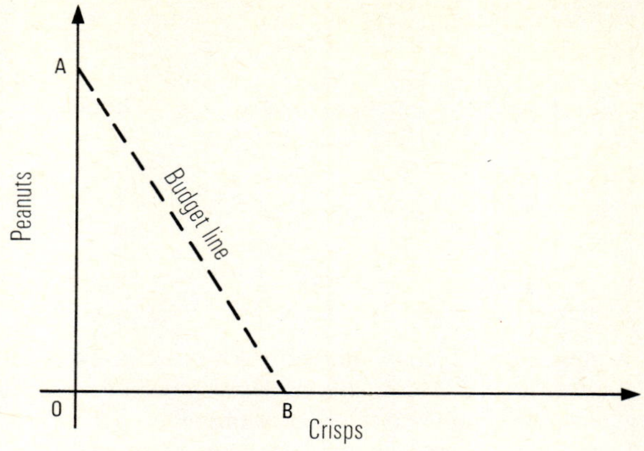

Figure 8·8

a If he purchases 5 bags of crisps, how many packets of peanuts can he afford?

b If he purchases 8 packets of peanuts, how many bags of crisps can he buy?

Now, we can combine what is desired, as shown by indifference curves, with what is possible in this market, with the stated amount of money, as shown by the budget line. We can then examine how the student allocates his resources to maximise his level of satisfaction.

8·8

a Plot the indifference curve 1_2 from exercise 8·5 on to your graph for exercise 8·6. It should be tangential to the budget line where 8 packets of peanuts and 5 bags of crisps are bought.

b Plot the other two indifference curves from exercise 8·5 on to the same graph.

You should complete this exercise before proceeding further.

Examine figure 8·9. The maximum level of satisfaction this student desires is indicated by indifference curve 1_3. But, of all the combinations of crisps and peanuts open to him along the budget line, none is the same as any combination along 1_3. He can only just reach 1_2, the next highest level of satisfaction shown, where at Q, a possible combination and a desirable combination do coincide. Point Q is where the budget line is tangential to the indifference curve. The highest level of satisfaction which the student can achieve, given his present income is on I_2 where he can just afford to buy 8 packets of peanuts and 5 bags of crisps. In the circumstances this combination will yield more satisfaction than any other. It uses up all his available money so he could not buy, say, an extra packet of peanuts without giving up some crisps. But to do that would leave him on a lower indifference curve than I_2.

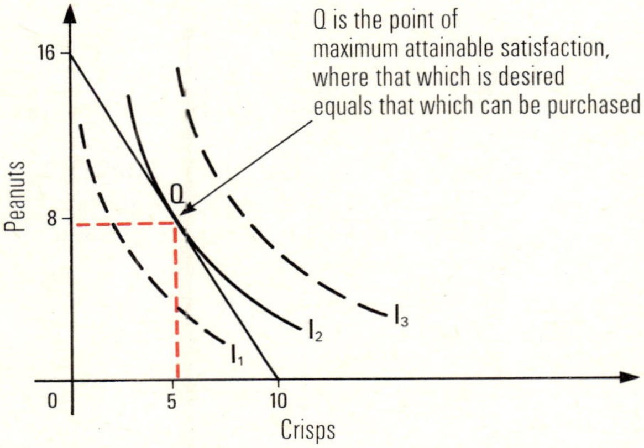

Figure 8·9

8·9

a Assume this student wants to buy 9 packets of peanuts and 5 bags of crisps. Plot this on your graph for exercise 8·8.

b Calculate the cost of this combination from the prices given in exercise 8·6.

c Can he buy this combination with his 80p?

8·10

Assume now this student tries to buy only four bags of crisps and nine packets of peanuts.

a Can he afford this combination of goods?

b Does this yield more or less satisfaction than does Q; in other words is this point when plotted above I_2 (between I_2 and I_3) or below I_2 (between I_2 and I_1)?

The point where the budget line and an indifference curve are tangential represents the maximum satisfaction attainable and shows which combination of goods will be purchased.

Maximum satisfaction

We continue to use the data from exercise 8·6 as an example from which to draw general conclusions.

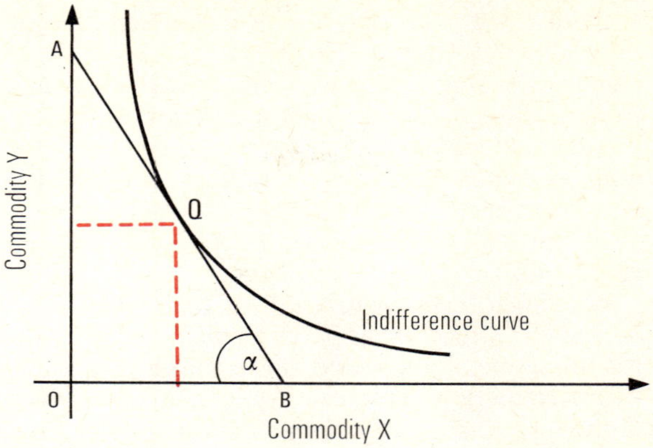

Figure 8·10

The ratio of the prices of the two goods is shown by the amount of each which can be bought with the fixed amount of money:

$$\text{Ratio of prices} = \frac{OA}{OB} = \frac{16}{10} = 1{\cdot}6:1$$

The slope of the budget line AB is tan α

$$= \frac{\text{opp.}}{\text{adj.}} = \frac{OA}{OB} = 1{\cdot}6$$

therefore the slope of the budget line measures the ratio of the two prices.

At Q the slope of the indifference curve is the same as the slope of the budget line because they are tangential at Q. The slope of the indifference curve measures the marginal rate of substitution of commodity X for commodity Y which is

$$\tan\alpha = \frac{OA}{OB} = 1{\cdot}6$$

Therefore at Q the marginal rate of substitution equals the ratio of the prices of commodities X and Y. This is the point of maximum satisfaction.

Two theories—why?

Under indifference curve analysis the point of maximum satisfaction, Q, is where *the marginal rate of substitution* of one commodity for another *is equal to the ratio between the prices.* This position can be measured.

In the marginal utility theory the point of maximum satisfaction is where the *marginal utility* of each commodity *is proportional to the relative prices.* This position cannot be measured.

You will already have realised in the discussion on the marginal utility theory that utility cannot be measured. It may appear that the indifference curve theory which does assume not a measurable scale of satisfaction but a choice between alternatives, does give rise to a quantitative analysis. In fact it does not; a student interviewed may have some idea of his preferences between chicken and cheese sandwiches over a narrow range, but it is quite impossible for him to give accurate preferences between water-skiing and study for an examination—there are far too many imponderable factors.

Why then have we studied these two theories? Marginal utility is a psychological explanation for the shape of a demand curve, and is also a useful introduction to other aspects of economics. However, this theory deals with two elements, utility and price, and except at an advanced level, ignores income. The advantage of indifference curve analysis is that it is possible to show geometrically the effect of price and income changes. These will shortly be considered.

The analysis of demand

8·11

Suppose a man is laying in a stock of wine for future use. His preference for red and white wine are expressed as follows:

x axis Red wine	y axis White wine
5	37·50
15	25·00
30	15·00
50	7·50
80	2·50

Draw the indifference curve corresponding to this data.

Just to check that you have the curve correctly drawn:

a How many bottles of white wine will he buy in combination with 40 bottles of red wine?

b How many bottles of red wine would he buy in combination with 20 bottles of white wine?

c If his purchase of red wine changed from 62 to 10, by how much would his purchase of white wine change?

We can now ask how many bottles of red wine he will buy if both cost him £1 per bottle. The answer is worked out in the following way.

The pattern of his preferences is known from the indifference curve: We assume, as usual, that he will buy that combination of goods which will maximise his satisfaction, i.e. where his budget line is tangential to the indifference curve.

As both cost £1 per bottle, then the opportunity cost of each £1 spent on white wine is one bottle of red wine. The price ratio is, here, £1:£1.

Therefore the budget line must have a slope of 1:1. To construct this line on your graph, use a ruler at a slope of 1:1, i.e. for every unit moved up the y axis, you must move one unit along the x axis, and move up the graph until the budget line, drawn along the ruler, is tangential to the indifference curve. (On a graph whose axis scales are the same, a ratio of 1:1, whose tangent = 1, is 45°.)

In this instance you will find that the budget line cuts both the x and y axes at the 40 mark.

The combination which yields maximum satisfaction at this price ratio is then read off from the point of tangency; 25 bottles of white wine and 15 bottles of red wine.

8·12

Data as for 8·11.

a Suppose that the price of red wine was 50p and white wine is still £1.

i What is the ratio of the price of white wine to red wine?

ii What is the tangent of the gradient of the budget line in degrees?

Draw in the budget line at the point of maximum satisfaction.

iii At what values does the budget line cut the x and y axes?

iv What combination of white and red wine will yield maximum satisfaction at this price ratio?

b If the price of white wine is unchanged and red wine was 25p per bottle, what combination would yield maximum satisfaction to the hotelier?

The substitution effect

We assume that the wine purchaser is free to reallocate his expenditure as relative prices change, but we also assume he maintains a constant level of satisfaction.

The result of exercises 8·11 and 8·12 should produce a graph similar to figure 8·11.

You will notice that the effect of a change in relative prices is to change the slope of the budget line. The consumer's position of maximum satisfaction therefore moves along the indifference curve (in figure 8·11 from A through B to C). This

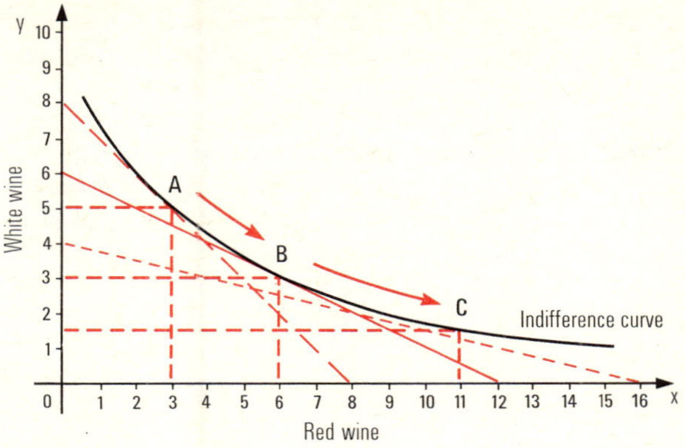

Figure 8·11

movement is the *substitution effect* and shows that the consumer will tend to substitute some of the relatively cheaper commodity (i.e. the one whose price has fallen) for some of the relatively expensive product.

The income effect

The effect of a rise in *real* income is to raise the consumer from one indifference curve to a higher one. To isolate this effect in our graphs we must assume that relative prices do not change (otherwise the substitution effect will occur).

x axis Lamb (kg)	y axis Chicken (kg)	x axis Lamb (kg)	y axis Chicken (kg)
0·5	8·5	2·0	10·0
1·5	5·0	2·3	8·0
3·0	3·0	3·0	6·0
6·0	1·0	5·0	3·5
		7·0	2·0

8·13

A housewife's preferences for chicken and lamb in kilos per week is shown in the table above. Two sets of preferences are indicated in the table.

a Draw the indifference curves corresponding to this data.

Suppose the housewife has £4 per week for purchasing meat. Assume the price of chicken is 50p per kilo and lamb is £1 per kilo.

b Draw in her budget line for meat.

c At what value does the budget line cut the y and x axes?

d What combination of chicken and lamb yields maximum satisfaction?

8·14

Data as for exercise 8·13.

Assume that this housewife's purchasing power has risen to £6 per week for meat, in other words her real income has risen. (The prices of chicken and lamb are unchanged.)

a If all her money was spent on chicken, how many kilos would she buy per week?

b Alternatively, if all her money was spent on lamb, how many kilos per week would she buy?

c Draw in the new budget line between the points calculated for (a) and for (b).

d After the rise in money income available for spend-on meat, what combination of chicken and lamb will yield maximum satisfaction?

The effect of a rise in real income is, therefore, seen as a parallel shift in the budget line in figure 8·12. The level of satisfaction achieved is higher, as represented by the point of tangency with a higher indifference curve. A reduction in real income would have the reverse effect.

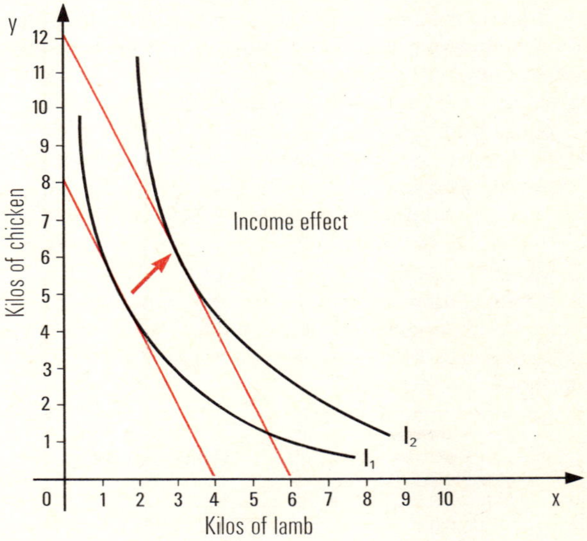

Figure 8·12

Real income rises for two reasons; either money income rises and prices remain the same, or prices of both goods fall and so with a given amount of money more of each commodity can be bought.

A change in absolute price—the price effect

How does a change in the price of a commodity affect the consumer?

8·15

If we examine the consumption of petrol by a housewife, we discover that her preferences for money to spend on general shopping and the weekly purchase of petrol shows the patterns set out in the table.

a Draw the indifference curves for this data.

b Assume this housewife has £12 per week for general shopping. If petrol is 12p per litre and all the money was spent on petrol, how much could she buy?

x axis Petrol litres	y axis Money income £
20	14
30	10
38	8
50	6
70	4
110	2

Draw in the budget line to show the combinations of general expenditure and petrol which are *possible* when petrol is 12p per litre.

c What combination of general expenditure and petrol purchases will yield maximum satisfaction?

d How much of the housewife's money is spent on petrol? Measure this on the y axis.

A £6·50 **B** £5·50

8·16

While continuing to assume that money income does not change, let us now consider a change in the price of petrol. Suppose the price of petrol rises to 24p per litre.

x axis Petrol litres	y axis Money income £
10	12
15	9·50
21	7
35	4·40
60	2
80	1

a How many litres could this housewife purchase if all her money was spent on petrol at the new price?

b What combination of general expenditure and petrol will yield maximum satisfaction at the new price?

c When the price of petrol changes from 12p per litre to 24p per litre, by how much does petrol consumption change?

The effect of a change in absolute prices can be seen as a change in slope of the price line and a shift in the consumer's position from one indifference curve to another as in figure 8·13.

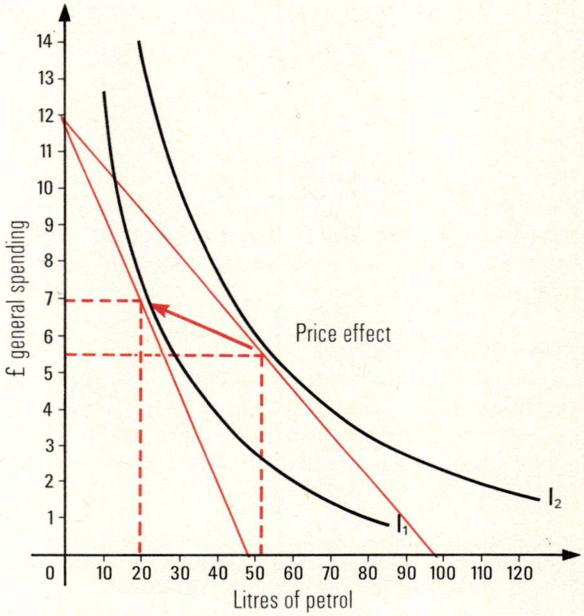

Figure 8·13

Further analysis of the price effect

A change in the price of one commodity means that the ratio of the price of that product relative to all others is changed. There is therefore a substitution effect. At the same time, if the price of that product rises, it means that the consumer has less money left for other things, i.e. real income has fallen even though money income is constant. This causes an income effect. The extent to which the price effect is due to each factor can be analysed in the following manner.

If the price had changed, but the real income had not fallen, then the slope of the new budget line would be the same slope as YM_2, i.e. parallel to YM_2 (in figure 8·14) and tangential to I_1, i.e. the original level of satisfaction.

The change in price results in a substitution effect from position A to position B_1.

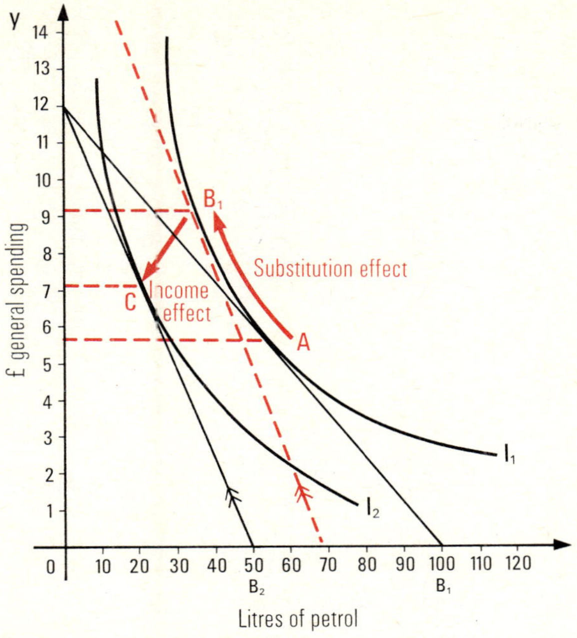

Figure 8·14

8·17

a How much petrol was bought at 12p per litre?
b If the real income had not fallen, how much petrol would have been bought at 24p per litre? (Position B_1 in figure 8·14.)
c What is the substitution effect in this instance?

The result of the fall in real income due to the rise in price is shown by the movement from one indifference curve to the other (from position B_1 to position C).

8·18

Measure the extent of the income effect by comparing the amount of petrol bought at B_1 with the amount bought at C.

An alternative method

If the price change is large the alternative method of considering the substitution and income effects in reverse order will produce a slightly different measurement for each effect.

If we consider the income effect first, we argue that a rise in price of a commodity lowers the real income of the consumer. A fall in real income, without the price change, would shift the budget line YM_1 in figure 8·15 from its original position to a parallel one, tangential to the indifference curve I_2, i.e. at the lower real income level.

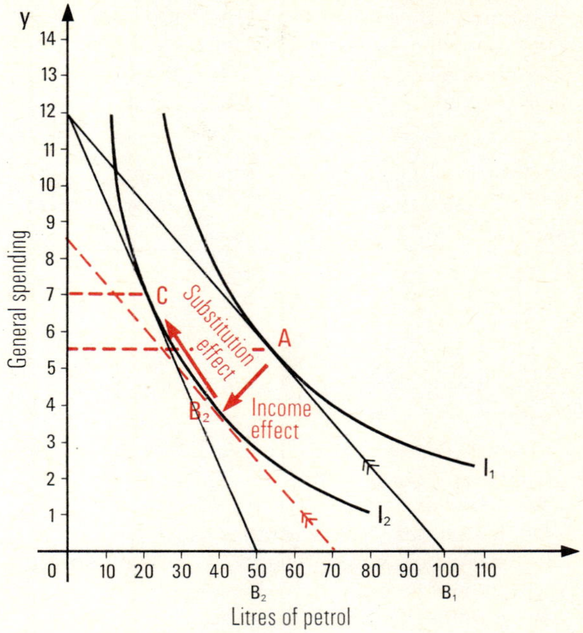

Figure 8·15

8·19

a How much petrol was bought at 12p per litre?
b At the reduced real income level, how much petrol is bought? (Position B_2 in figure 8·15.)
c What is the extent of the income effect measured by this analysis?

The consumer will reduce her expenditure on the petrol and substitute some other aspects of general expenditure for petrol. The substitution effect is seen in figure 8·15 as a move along the indifference curve from B_2 to C.

8·20

Measure the extent of the substitution effect as shown by this method.

Neither of these two methods of measuring the extent of the income and substitution effects as components of the price effect is more correct than the other.

8·21

A young businessman allocates £11 of his income per month to entertainment. His preferences for whisky and other forms of entertainment are shown in the following two sets of figures, each showing a different level of satisfaction. Draw the indifference curve map.

x axis Whisky bottles	y axis Money on entertainment (£)	x axis Whisky bottles	y axis Money on entertainment (£)
0·5	12·0	2·2	12·0
1·5	7·0	3·0	9·0
2·9	5·0	4·1	7·0
4·5	3·5	5·0	6·0
7·0	2·0	7·0	4·5
10	1·0	10·0	3·0

a If whisky costs him £2·75 per bottle, how much will he buy per month?
A 4 bottles **B** 7·7 bottles
C 1·2 bottles **D** 7 bottles

b If the price of whisky falls to £1, how much more whisky will he buy?
A 5 bottles **B** 6·0 bottles
C 1·7 bottles **D** 3·8 bottles

c How much of the increased purchase of whisky is due to the income effect of the change in price? (Measure the income effect first.)
A 2·8 bottles **B** 1·6 bottles
C 4·2 bottles **D** 2·2 bottles

A rise in money income

8·22

In the table below are recorded three sets of preferences for income held in money form compared with money spent on office space.

y axis Money Income per month £	x axis Office space M²	x axis Money Income per month £	y axis Office space M²	x aixs Money Income per month £	y axis Office space M²
60	5	85	15	130	15
40	10	65	19	100	25
20	20	50	23·5	80	40
10	35	35	30	65	60
5	60	25	38	55	85
		10	70	50	100

Assume this man's income is £40 per month.

a How much will he spend on office space at £1 per square metre (M²)?
A £10 **B** £20 **C** £35 **D** £40

Suppose this consumer's income now rises to £120 per month.

b If the price of offices does not change, how much will he now spend on office accommodation?
A £23 **B** £40 **C** £50 **D** £80

c How many square metres would he now purchase?
A 30m² **B** 33m² **C** 40m² **D** 360m²

Assume the price of office space now rises to three times its former level.

Construct the new budget line to show the effect of the rise in price of office accommodation.

d How much will the consumer have in money after meeting his expenditure on his offices?
A 23·3 m² **B** 40 m². **C** £50 **D** £120

The income consumption curve

8·23

A young businessman is interviewed about his preferences for monthly income and overseas travel. Three sets of preferences emerge. The y axis measures monthly income, the x axis days of overseas travel.

y	x	y	x	y	x
80	2	144	6	160	9
64	3	110	7·75	140	10
40	5	70	11·25	110	12
20	8·5	40	16·25	80	15
10	12	26	20	52	20
				30	26

a Draw the indifference curves corresponding to this data.

Assume overseas travel costs £8 per day on average.

b If the businessman's income is £80 per month, how many days overseas travel will he buy?
A 5 **B** 10 **C** 40 **D** 80

c If the cost of overseas travel does not change and the businessman's income rises to £160 per month, how many more days of travel will he take?
A 20 **B** 15 **C** 11·25 **D** 6·25

d Assume now that the businessman's income rises to £200 per month. By what percentage will his overseas travel increase?
A 3·75 **B** 30 **C** 33·34 **D** 133·4

Plot on your graph a line joining the points of tangency of the successive budget lines with the indifference curves.

These should pass through

x axis	y axis
5	40
11·25	70
15	80

This line is an income consumption curve (ICC) and shows how consumption changes with a rise in income. For most commodities it is normal for more to be bought as income rises, as shown in figure 8·16.

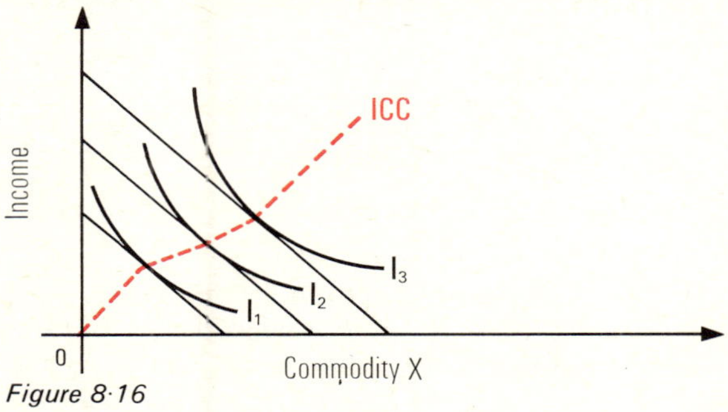

Figure 8·16

8·24

The preference for income in money form and loaves, for a certain family, are shown in the table (y axis shows income in new pence, x axis shows loaves bought per week).

a Construct the indifference map corresponding to the data below.

Assume this family has £1 per week for this group of foods.

b If loaves cost 5p each, how many will be bought?

c If the price of loaves now rises to $7\frac{1}{2}$p each, how many will this family buy?

d Suppose the price of loaves now rises to 10p, how many loaves will be bought?

e Account for the increase in bread purchases when real income has fallen (because of the price increase).

y new pence	x	y new pence	x	y new pence	x
80	4	100	4	80	5
60	5	73	5	70	6
45	6	50	7	68	7
20	8	38	9	63	9
10	10	28	12		

The normal price consumption curve

8·25

The following data refers to a family's pattern of preferences for holiday spending money per day and ice creams per day. (The y axis, as usual, shows money in £, the x axis, the ice cream.)

x	y	x	y	x	y
6	1·10	7	1·58	8	2·18
7	0·66	9	1·20	11	1·66
8	0·40	11	0·91	13	1·42
9	0·24	12	0·80	15	1·26
11	0·06	14	0·63	17	1·16
		17	0·48	20	1·05
				24	0·99

a Plot this data to show the indifference map.

b Assuming this family has £2 per day to spend, how many ice creams will they buy at each of the following prices?
i 5p each **ii** 10p each **iii** 20p each

c Plot the price consumption curve through the points of maximum satisfaction. The price consumption curve shows how consumption varies as price changes.

Deriving a demand curve

A demand curve shows the quantity of a commodity which is bought at any given price.

8·26

Plot the price of ice creams from exercise 8·25 on the y axis and the quantity bought on the x axis. The price you know from the budget lines (or given one, you can derive the others as proportions). The quantity bought at each price is read at the point of maximum satisfaction on each budget line, i.e. the price consumption curve.

The demand curve shows the relationship between price per unit and the amount bought at each price.

The shape of the demand curve

In due course you will discover that most demand curves are similar in shape to that in figure 8·17. This is described as 'convex to the origin', sloping downwards from left to right.

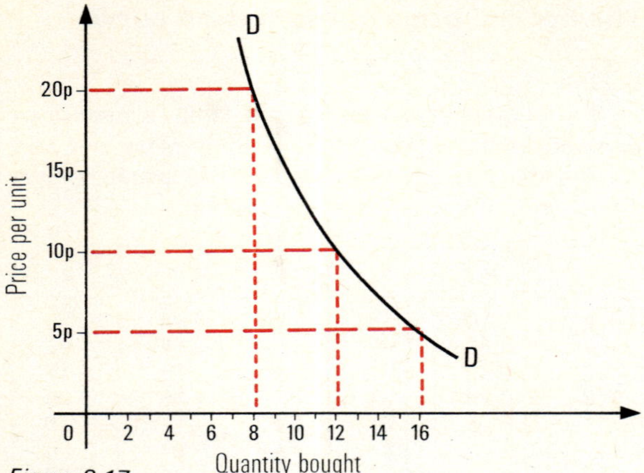

Figure 8·17

The demand curve shows that, as the price of the commodity falls, all other things being equal more tends to be bought. Marginal consumers play a key role here, since they will tend to buy more as price falls.

Why do marginal consumers buy more? The law of diminishing marginal utility and the law of diminishing marginal rate of substitution shows that when the price of the commodity falls the ratio of satisfaction to price is altered. Additional units are then purchased until the consumer reaches the equi-marginal satisfaction position again. This is the point at which the rate of marginal substitution is proportional to the prices of each commodity bought.

When the prices of normal goods change, there will be first of all a substitution effect as people switch into the cheaper alternative goods. Secondly, a fall in any price is equivalent to an increase in real income, so there will be an income effect (see figure 8·12).

Notice that the demand curve does not explicitly demonstrate the difference of the two effects (figure 8·14), whereas the indifference curve analysis does show each effect (figure 8·15).

8·27

Draw a demand curve for bread derived from exercise 8·24.

a If the price of bread rose to 12½p per loaf, how many loaves would the family buy?

b If they were buying 6·4 loaves per week on average, what would you expect the market price of bread to be?

Two theoretical extremes to the usual shape of the demand curve are shown in figures 8 18 and 8·19.

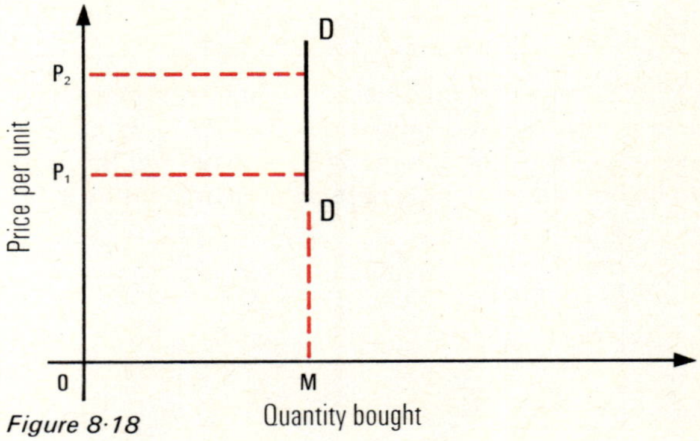

Figure 8·18

Figure 8·18 shows a commodity for which there are no substitutes. No matter what the price, OP_1, OP_2, etc. people will buy the same quantity OM. For example, a person would pay a surgeon, for a life-saving operation, any price within the limits of his income.

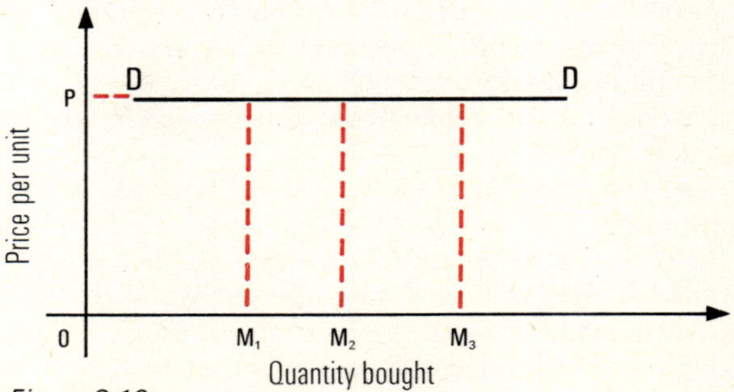

Figure 8·19

Figure 8·19 shows the demand curve for a commodity where, in the range shown on the x axis of the graph, people will buy everything offered for sale at price OP. A manufacturer who produced a 50 cm colour television set to sell at £5, would face such a demand curve!

ANSWERS

8·1

Correct **B, C, D, E.**

Mistaken **A**: the market price may affect the quantity bought, but not the utility.

8·2

If the price rises, marginal utility must also rise to maintain the marginal utility : price ratio. This is achieved by buying less.

8·3

At point B, tan α is less than at point A.

8·4

a $\frac{\delta y}{\delta x} = 2$ b $\frac{1 \cdot 5}{1} = 1 \cdot 5$ c $\frac{1}{1} = 1$

d $\frac{0 \cdot 8}{1} = 0 \cdot 8$

8·5

a Correct **A.**
Mistaken **B**: this is on 1_2.
Mistaken **C**: this is on 1_3.
Mistaken **D**: you have read peanuts on the wrong axis.

b Correct **C.**
Mistaken **A**: you have measured peanuts on the wrong axis.
Mistaken **B**: this is on 1_1 instead of 1_2.
Mistaken **D**: this is on 1_3 instead of 1_2.

c Correct **B.**
Mistaken **A**: this is the number of crisps bought, not the *change* in his consumption.
Mistaken **C**: you are reading the change in numbers from 1_2 instead of 1_3.
Mistaken **D**: you have read the number from 1_2 instead of 1_3.

d Correct **D.**
Mistaken **A**: he consumes more (+) not less peanuts.
Mistaken **B**: this is his new level of peanut consumption, not the *change* in consumption.
Mistaken **C**: you have probably read this change from 1_1, instead of 1_2.

e Correct **B**: the tangent should produce an angle of about 39°.
Mistaken **A**: your graph has a scale on the x axis half that of the y axis. By halving this scale your tangent is at an angle of about 68° instead of 39°.
Mistaken **C**: you have a scale on the y axis half that of the x axis so producing a tangent angle of about 19°.
If your graph is not drawn with equal scales on x and y axes you must calculate $\frac{\delta y}{\delta x}$ at the point of tangency in order to answer section (f).

f **i** Approximately 0·71 (33°).
ii Approximately 0·7 (35°).

8·6

a 16 packets peanuts—point A, y axis, figure 8·8
b 10 bags of crisps—point B, on x axis

8·7

a 5 bags of crisps @ 8p = 40p. This leaves 40p for peanuts @ 5p per packet. ∴ 8 packets of peanuts can be purchased.
b 5 bags of crisps can be bought.

8·8

Plotting graphs.

8·9

a Plot point.
b

Total cost of 9 pkt peanuts @ 5p	=	45p
Total cost of 5 bags crisps @ 8p	=	40p
		85p

c This is not possible for the student because he only has 80p.

8·10

a

4 bags of crisps @ 8p	=	32p
9 bags of peanuts @ 5p	=	45p
The student can afford		77p

b This combination yields less satisfaction than the point of maximum satisfaction Q.

8·11

Indifference curve.
i 11 bottles of white wine
ii 22 bottles of red wine
iii From 5 to 31 bottles of white wine = +26 bottles.

8·12

a **i** 2:1
ii 2 = 63° 30′
iii y axis: 30 bottles; x axis: 60 bottles
iv 15 bottles white wine; 30 bottles red wine.
b 7·50 bottles white wine; 50 bottles red wine.

8·13

a Indifference curve.
b Budget line.
c y axis is cut at 8 kilos of chicken.
x axis is cut at 4 kilos of lamb.
d 5 kilos of chicken and 1·5 kilos lamb per week.

8·14

a 12 kilos chicken per week.

b 6 kilos lamb per week.

c New budget line.

d 6 kilos of chicken and 3 kilos of lamb per week.

8·15

a Indifference curves.

b 100 litres.

c £5·50 general spending 54 litres of petrol.

d Correct **A**: this is the amount of money given in exchange for petrol.
Mistaken **B**: this is the amount of money left *after* buying petrol.

8·16

a 50 litres.

b £7 general spending
21 litres petrol.

c At 12p, 54 litres are bought.
At 24p, 21 litres are bought.
Change is therefore minus 33 litres.

8·17

a 54 litres.

b 33 litres.

c The substitution effect is minus 21 litres.

8·18

The income effect is minus 12 litres.

8·19

a 54 litres.

b 40 litres.

c The income effect is minus 14 litres.

8·20

The substitution effect is minus 19 litres.

8·21

a Correct **C.**
Mistaken **A**: this is the number he *could* buy if all his entertainment money goes on whisky.
Mistaken **B**: this is the money he spends on other forms of entertainment.
Mistaken **D**: have you labelled your axes correctly?

b Correct **D.**
Mistaken **A**: this is the number he buys, not the change in amount.
Mistaken **B**: this is the amount of money he spends on other entertainment.
Mistaken **C**: this is the change in the amount of money he spends on other entertainment.

c Correct **B.**
Mistaken **A**: this is the level of purchase of whisky due to the income effect, not the change from 1·2 bottles which was his original purchase.
Mistaken **C**: this does not answer the question since it is the substitution effect measured along the indifference curve, instead of along the axis.
Mistaken **D**: this is the substitution effect instead of the income effect.

8·22

a Correct **B.**
Mistaken **A**: the amount he will spend on office space is indicated by the point of tangency of the budget line.
Mistaken **C**: are you guessing?
Mistaken **D**: this is the amount he would purchase if all his money went on office space.

b Correct **B.**
Mistaken **A** and **C**: the budget line does not change its slope since the price of housing is assumed constant.
Mistaken **D**: this is the amount of income left for other expenditure after paying £40 for office space.

c Correct **C.**
Mistaken **A**: you have not divided 120m^2 correctly.
Mistaken **B**: a distractor.
Mistaken **D**: 120 is divided by 3 not multiplied by 3.

d Correct **C.**
Mistaken **A**: he purchases 23·33m^2 of office space at the new price.
Mistaken **B**: 40m^2 is the maximum he *could* buy at the new price.
Mistaken **D**: this is his total income.

A rise in money income moves the budget line to a new position parallel to its original one but at a higher level of satisfaction.

If the rise in income (3 times its original value) is offset by a rise in price of the commodity concerned (by 3 times), the budget line changes its slope as shown in figure 8·20.

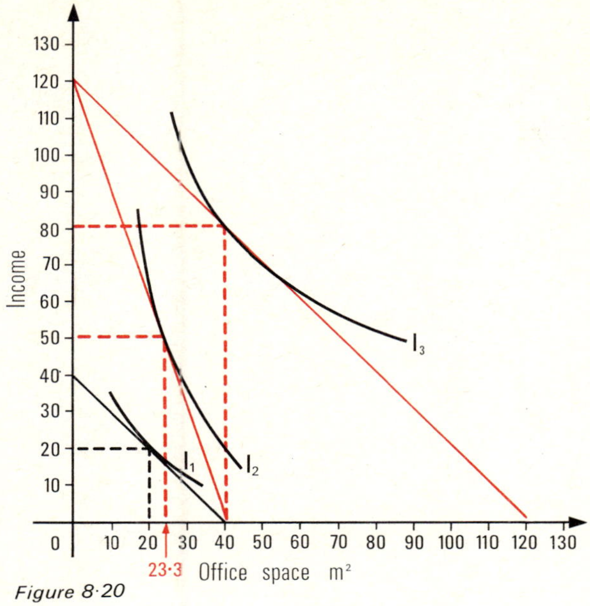

Figure 8·20

8·23

a Indifference curves.

b Correct **B**. Mistaken **A, C, D.**

c Correct **C.** Mistaken **A, B, D.**

d Correct **C.** Mistaken **A.** This is the number of extra days, not the percentage increase.
Mistaken **B**: percentage calculation inverted.
Mistaken **D**: wrong figures for percentage.

8·24

a Indifference map.

b At 5p, 6 loaves are bought.

c At 7½p, 7 loaves are bought.

d At 10p, 8 loaves are bought.
As real income falls, if you follow down the PCC curve towards the origin, you will see that more loaves are bought. This is so because at lower real incomes bread is substituted for dearer foods. The substitution effect is overcome by the income effect.

8·25

a Indifference map.

b **i** At 5p, they buy 16 ices per day.
ii At 10p, they buy 12 ices per day.
iii At 20p, they buy 8 ices per day.

c Demand curve which shows the relation between price and the quantity bought at each price.

8·26

Price consumption curve or demand schedule. See figure 8·17.

8·27

a 9 loaves.

b 6p per loaf.
This is the unusual case where the income effect outweighs the price effect.

LABOUR

In this section we attempt to answer three questions; what determines the supply of labour? How do entrepreneurs decide how much labour to employ? What determines the payments to labour?

The supply of labour

To economists, the supply of labour is the working population referred to in a previous study section. What determines the size of this? Most of us own neither land nor capital and must therefore sell our labour in order to purchase the necessities of life. In the short run, wage rates will influence the number of people offering their labour, but in the long run the size of the working population depends upon basic demographic trends—birth rates, death rates, migration rates and mobility rates. In general the population is expanding in all countries. This is the natural result of advances in medical science so that more children survive infancy and adults live longer. Nevertheless, in some countries, labour is still in short supply and this is so because labour is normally used in conjunction with land and capital. Unless there is sufficient labour to combine with land and capital, an entrepreneur cannot expand production as much as he would like. People have always moved in search of work and the advance in the technology of transport has made this migration both faster and easier, though, to some extent, political nationalism has tended to restrict this normal movement of workers from country to country. Let us study the mobility of labour to the other factors of production and consider the movement of the other factors of production towards labour later.

9·1

In the nineteenth century some economists (Malthus in particular) believed that population growth would be checked by famine, disease and other disasters. Why has population growth not led to world wide famine?

The mobility of labour

Why do people move? Many are born in places where there is simply not enough work for them. For many years, people have left Ireland, Southern Italy and Jamaica, because there was little prospect of finding work in their homeland. On the other hand, people have left relatively wealthy countries like the United Kingdom in seach of better payment. For example, doctors trained in the United Kingdom, began in 1960 to emigrate to the United States, where the remuneration for doctors is phenomenally high, although in the United Kingdom they were well paid, compared with the rest of the working population.

Migration is not simply an international phenomenon. Most executives, teachers and other professional people accept that they will need to move from area to area to gain promotion. Industry changes; factories find that their products are no longer in demand and cease production, mines are worked out and have to be closed down. Sometimes entrepreneurs make errors in gauging the market and the resulting bankruptcy means that their workers are dismissed.

Barriers to the mobility of labour

When workers are left jobless it is desirable that some should be mobile. As the case for mobility is so obvious, why are there pockets of unemployment? Local ties are strong, and a man whose family has been resident in one locality for many years will have many friends, relatives and social connections in that area. He likes living where he does and will try to avoid moving to another region. Even if a person is prepared to move he may find difficulty in learning about vacancies in other areas. Professional men are usually well served by advertisements in the national and trade press, but in general a worker such as a bricklayer will find it difficult to learn of opportunities more than fifty miles away. Sometimes, mobility between industries is restricted by union regulations which are there to defend the standard of living of their present membership. People may be unable to move in search of work because they cannot afford to travel in order to seek employment, or to move their families if they obtain employment. Furthermore, there are political barriers to movement, some states just will not grant work permits to foreigners.

We have dealt mainly with the problem of geographical mobility but there is also the mobility between occupations to be considered. Usually the more skilled or specific the training of the workman, the more difficult it is for him to find a new job. For example, an airline pilot would find it difficult to become a ship's captain. Nowadays, it is not sufficient to be able to do a job, but it is necessary to hold a certificate, diploma or union card to obtain employment. Nevertheless, there is an area of unskilled jobs which require little training and where labour at the margin can move comparatively easily from one occupation to another. A dustman can easily become a jobbing gardener. Other barriers to occupational mobility are prejudice, against women, for example, or against members of particular races or religions, and the cost of the lengthy training required in some cases.

The need for mobility can be reduced because as workers retire they need not be replaced and as school leavers enter industries they can be directed into those occupations which are growing.

Aids to mobility

Large sums of money are spent by employers advertising vacancies. Advertisements range from cards placed in the windows of small shops ('Office cleaner wanted') to advertisements in local newspapers, and to expensive advertisements in the national and trade papers. The government is responsible for the Labour Exchanges which provide information and the Government also provides financial assistance for people wishing to train for other jobs and to people wishing to move. In fact, resettlement grants cover such expenses as lodging whilst looking for work or accommodation, household removal costs and even legal fees incurred when buying a house. Education through Technical Colleges and Industrial Training Boards is provided free or at low cost and ensures that workers may learn the skills which the contemporary economy requires. In major cities and especially in Development Areas there are government Training Centres where unemployed persons can learn a new trade. However, wages are low during a retraining period, and men with families to support cannot always afford to take a retraining course.

Does mobility mean that only labour should move?

All the above may suggest to you that it is the duty of workers to move to a new job or a new area. Let us examine the need for a worker to move to a new occupation. In Scotland there is a trained pool of ship-building workers. If the firm employing them were to become bankrupt, should the government expect these workers to either move or retrain themselves? It all depends on the value of their specific skill to the community. Thus, it may be of more benefit to the nation as a whole to retain their skills and to provide alternative work within the same occupation. Hence the ship workers in Scotland may be given defence contracts to build submarines in order to retain their skill in the hope that they will be able to return to building oil-tankers in the future. Another example is the pressure put on a national airline to buy aeroplanes produced in that country even though foreign produced planes may be cheaper. The real crux of this problem is that the fall in demand may be temporary but the loss of the skills should the labour force be dispersed may be permanent. When a community becomes established, it acquires social capital such as schools, roads, libraries, parks, amateur organisations and so on. This represents a considerable accumulation of wealth and if large numbers of workers and their dependents move, this capital may seriously depreciate; furthermore the nation will have to build a duplicate set of social facilities in the areas to which they move. In such circumstances, there may be more social benefit and less social cost if the government, either directly, or by encouraging entrepreneurs, creates jobs in areas of unemployment. This is the reasoning behind the government's activities in the Development Areas. It is more efficient in some cases to bring capital to labour even if capitalists have to be given grants and subsidies to tempt them to build factories in these areas.

9·2

Find out how much unemployment pay and supplementary benefits a married man with two children is entitled to for a period of six months.

a How far would this go towards removal costs if the man was able to go to another area and take up a job at the current average rate of earnings?

b How much cheaper would it be to pay removal costs for a 200 km removal than to pay unemployment benefits?

The demand for labour

The demand for labour is derived from the demand for goods and services. In other words it is wanted not for itself but for what it will produce. Normally labour is used in combination with other factors of production, but output does not usually increase in proportion to the amount of labour used. Will your family car be cleaned twice as quickly if two people clean it, a hundred times more quickly if a hundred people clean it?

This question could be posed in another way. Suppose you were running a small window cleaning business so that your capital item consisted of one long and one short ladder. If you, as the owner, did all the window cleaning yourself, then presumably only one ladder would be used at a time. If you hired an assistant and, thereby, increased the labour force by one, leaving your capital item (two ladders) fixed, then presumably, one of you can clean the upper windows and the other the lower windows so that the windows of each house will be cleaned twice as fast. Now suppose you hired another assistant. The second assistant would not be able to use the ladder; indeed, if he tried to do so the result would be loss of time. Thus, by increasing the labour force of the window cleaner and by keeping the capital item (two ladders) fixed, we find first of all an increase in efficiency and then a diminution of efficiency.

Because this tendency seems to apply whenever one factor of production is increased and another factor of production remains fixed, economists have made a generalised statement which they call a 'law'. All this means is that there have been sufficient instances in real life to make economists believe that they can make a statement which will, in similar circumstances, truthfully describe the course of events. Because we all know that more people can be employed by a firm, or that people can be dismissed by a firm, we can approach this part of economic theory by assuming that the other factors, land or capital will remain fixed, and that we will be able to alter the quantity of labour.

It will be useful to start this study by asking a question and then by seeing if the application of this 'law' helps us to find an answer. When do you replace labour by other factors of production, or, how do you combine labour with the other factors of production?

The law of variable proportions or diminishing returns

This law states the relationship between the input of factors of productions and the consequent returns (output). In this context *returns* means both the average and the marginal product.

Suppose you continue to put extra men to work on a plot of land; ultimately the increase in total output due to each extra man will diminish, other things remaining the same, if for no other reason than that they get in one another's way.

More formally, the law states that although increasing returns may occur at first if extra units of a variable factor are added to fixed factors of production, the marginal, then the average product will ultimately diminish, other things remaining the same.

The plot of land is regarded in this case as the factor which is fixed in amount. The men are the variable factor, i.e. variable in quantity, but we assume their quality is constant so that we can eliminate the effect of employing less efficient

Variable factor Col. 1	Fixed factor Col. 2	Total output per day Col. 3	Average output per variable factor Col. 4	Increase in total output Col. 5
Units of labour (the variable factor in this example)	Sets of fibreglass moulds	Hovertruck parts	Physical product	Marginal product of labour
0	1	0	0	
1	1	5	5·0	5
2	1	15	7·5	10
3	1	35	11·7	20
4	1	53	13·25	18
5	1	65	13·0	12
6	1	72	12·0	7
7	1	72	10·4	0
8	1	70	8·8	–2

workers. The increase in total from employing an additional man is called the *marginal product of labour*. The techniques of production, the quality of the factors and the degree of specialisation of labour remain unchanged. Of course, labour could be a fixed factor, and land or capital could be varied, in which case we would be considering the marginal product of land or capital.

The law when the fixed factor is intensively used

Assume an entrepreneur has just one set of moulds for manufacturing fibreglass bodies for hover-trucks. They are to be used as intensively as possible by adding, one by one, marginal units of labour. (This assumes that each man works a fixed number of hours per day.) We must ask two questions; (a) what is the technical optimum output (i.e. the point at which output per man is a maximum) with a fixed quantity of moulds; (b) what is the maximum worth employing?

The *variable factor* is normally increased by marginal amounts, in this case, by additives of one man.

The *fixed factor* is constant in amount in the short run.

Total product is either given or may be calculated from the other data:

a Col. 1 × Col. 4

or b From Col. 5—the first man adds 5 to the total of zero, total must be 5; the second man adds another 10 to the previous total so the total is now 5 + 10 = 15 and so on.

Average product = Col. 3 ÷ Col. 1, i.e. number of labour units divided into their total product. When the average product per unit of the variable factor is at a maximum, the combination of factors is at the *technical optimum*.

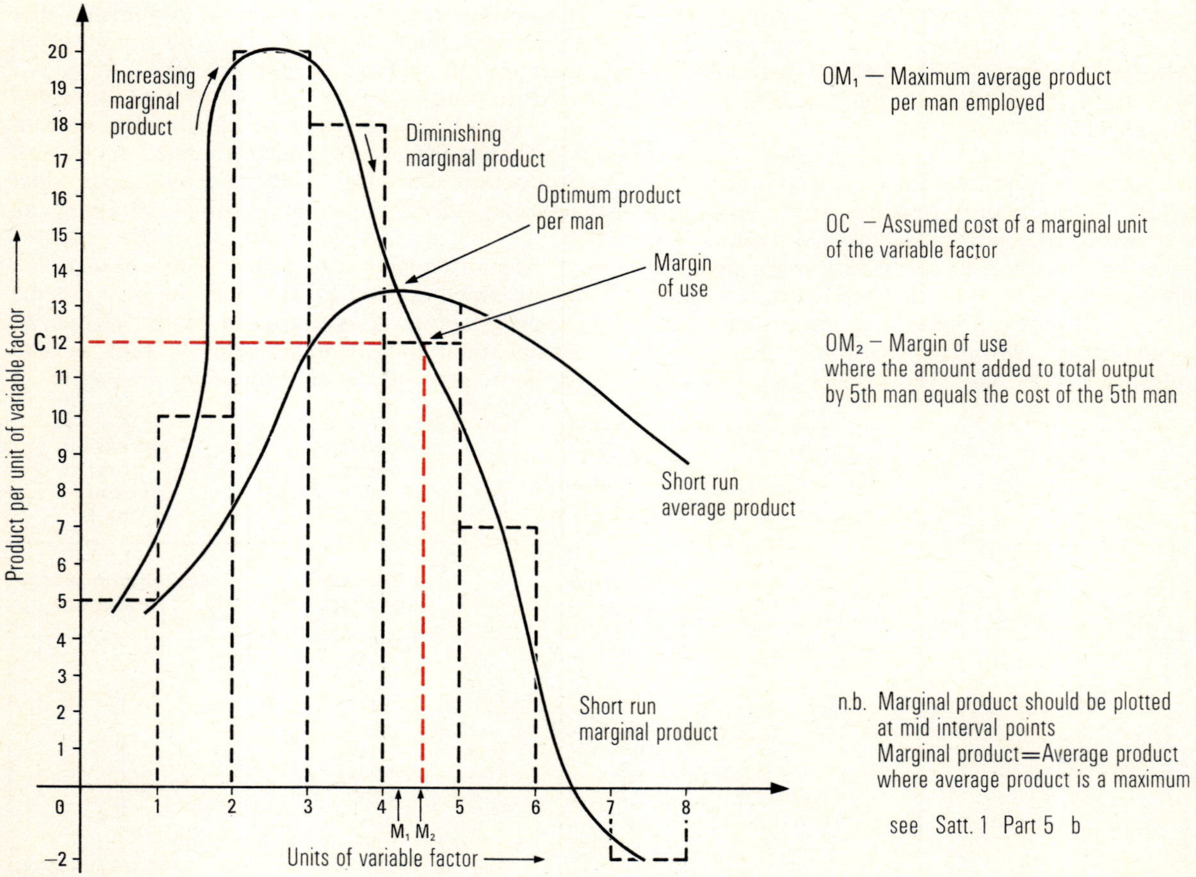

Figure 9·2

Marginal product is the increase in total product which results from a marginal increase in the variable factor, i.e. it is the amount added to the total by each extra man in turn. Therefore the marginal figures are written at the mid-point between the total product figures.

Col. 3	Col. 4	Col. 5
0	0	
		→5
5	5·0	
		→10
15	7·5	

Marginal product may be written as:
(Total physical product of (n + 1) men minus.)
(Total physical product of (n) men.)

The relationship between average and marginal output

So long as an extra man adds more than the average amount to the total (i.e. while marginal product is higher than average product) the new average will rise. Once an extra unit of the variable factor adds less than the average to the total product, then the new average will fall. If marginal product equals average product the average is constant, neither rising nor falling, and is at a maximum. (Further explanation is in the satellite *Arithmetical and Statistical Methods*).

9·3

a When the second man has been employed what is the average product?
A 7·5 units **B** 15 units

b How much does the third man add to the total (i.e. his marginal product)?
C 35 units **D** 20 units

9·4

a By how much does the employment of the third man raise the average product?
A 4·2 units **B** 2·55 units

b Does the employment of the fifth man raise or lower the average product?
C Raises **D** Lowers

9·5

Draw your own graph from table above, large enough to include the total product curve.

Returns—the product per unit of the variable factor

Read these comments in conjunction with your graph.

Increasing returns. Up to the point where four men are employed, average product increases as the optimum ratio of factors is approached. Up to this point the fixed factor is under-utilised—there is more than the men can properly cope with and this acts as a constraint. The marginal product begins to fall after three men are employed, but so long as marginal product is greater than average product, the average continues to rise.

Maximum returns per variable factor. This applies when the optimum ratio of fixed to variable factors is being used (1:4) i.e. 1 unit of fixed to 4 of variable factor. At the point OM_1, where the average product per man is at a maximum, average product equals marginal product.

Diminishing returns. Ultimately, as the law says, average product will diminish. As more men are added, the total product still rises but by a smaller and smaller amount. Marginal product falls as each additional man adds less to the total than his predecessor. (Remember he is just as efficient but the fixed factor is now being overworked in combination with the variable factor.) Once the marginal product is less than the average, the average falls, i.e. from the fifth and subsequent men. The seventh man adds nothing.

Negative marginal returns. If another man is employed, he will so get in the way of the others that total product will actually fall (from 72 to 70) because marginal product of the variable factor is negative (−2).

9·6

a How many men can be employed until the marginal product diminishes?
A 3 **B** 4

b How many men can be employed before their average product begins to fall?
C 4 **D** 5

Limitations of the law of variable proportions

The main assumption of a limiting nature is that of 'other things remaining the same'. They seldom do: no business remains frozen while one factor is varied. Diminishing returns to the variable factor will inevitably result whenever the amount of one factor or more is fixed. Technical innovations, especially those which change the *quality* of a factor, will change the proportions in which the factors are used and may delay the operation of the law. The above examination of the Law of Variable Proportions has only referred to physical returns, i.e. actual units of product. The physical optimum does not tell the entrepreneur which is the most profitable number of men to employ since he knows neither costs nor revenues at this stage (Profit = Revenue − Costs). *The point where average product per man is a maximum is not necessarily the point of maximum profit* (figure 9·2).

If you turn to the maximum product per man OM_2 is just after the employment of four men. Suppose this figure described the output of a small market garden. If the owner could only sell the production of three men, then it is quite obvious that he would not employ a fourth man to reach the position of maximum product per variable factor. It is easy to see the distinction between the technical optimum combination of factors and the most profitable combination if you imagine that the market garden produced tomatoes and that there were a dock strike stopping the import of tomatoes. In such a case, the price of home produced tomatoes would go up so that the market gardener would employ as many men as were required to produce the maximum number of tomatoes, even though the output per man was below the optimum. In economic terms, a firm will not employ an extra unit of a factor of production unless it adds to the *value* of total production at least enough to cover the cost of employing it. We must now discuss this problem in detail.

The marginal productivity theory

The value of the marginal product of labour is defined as the net addition to the entrepreneur's total revenues arising from the employment of a marginal unit of labour. (This assumes, of course, that the extra output is all sold.)

No rational employer will pay in wages more to a man than he adds to the firm's revenue. In other words the demand for labour in any firm depends on how much any extra man is worth in terms of earning extra revenue for the firm. An entrepreneur will continue to employ additional units of a factor until its *marginal revenue product* (mrp) equals the price of that factor. It is assumed that all units of labour are equally efficient (they are homogeneous) so that we can assume that the wages paid (the price of labour) are the same for each unit.

As more men are employed, the marginal revenue product eventually falls in accordance with the law of variable proportions.

9·7

Fill in the blank columns in the table below. The price of labour (wages) and the marginal revenue product of labour are important *elements* in determining the amount of labour in any kind of industry.

9·8

a Show the data given in exercise 9·7 on a graph. Plot the marginal revenue product on the y axis and the number employed on the x axis. (Marginal revenue product is plotted at mid-interval points.) Draw in the marginal revenue product curve.

b Measure wage rates on the y axis on the same scale as the marginal revenue product. If wage rate in the labour market is £24, how many men would this firm want to employ?

A 52 **B** 53 **C** 54

c If the wage rate rose to £30·50, how many fewer men would the firm wish to employ?

A 1 **B** 2 **C** 3

d Assume the wage rate of £27 and only 51 men are employed

Number employed	Commodity selling price	Output/ Sales	Marginal physical product	Total revenue £	Marginal revenue product £
50	50p	2 567			
51	50p	2 631			
52	50p	2 690			
53	50p	2 744			
54	50p	2 794			
55	50p	2 841			

i how much does the 51st man add to the firm's revenues?

ii how much does the 51st man add to the wage bills?

iii if another man is employed, does he add more, or less, to the firm's revenues than he does to its wage bill?

The marginal revenue product curve

As the marginal revenue product is the marginal physical product multiplied by the extra revenue from the sale of an extra unit (if the marginal man produces 6 units which are sold at £1 each, his marginal revenue product is £6), the law of variable properties or diminishing marginal returns will apply to marginal revenue product. Thus, the marginal revenue product curve will follow the same pattern as the marginal physical product, first rising as output increases, then tending to fall as further additions are made to output. It naturally falls if the price of the units sold has to be reduced in order to sell more; which is usually the case because a demand curve is normally sloping downwards.

The effect of rise in wages

The dismissal of men when wage rates increase is, in practice, unlikely. Redundancy arrangements and union pressure may reduce the freedom of firms to sack men at will.

It is more likely that the management will negotiate with unions some means of increasing the marginal physical productivity of labour, which will then raise the marginal revenue product high enough to pay higher wage rates. Some technical innovation or reorganisation of working methods are common bargaining points. Alternatively, the selling price of the commodity might be raised so that the marginal revenue product is raised, assuming that the rise in price does not reduce the quantity bought by the firm's customers.

Variation of marginal revenue product

To represent the above argument diagrammatically, see figure 9·6. If we assume a wage rate OW_1 and a state of perfect competition in the product or commodity market then if the union insists on a new wage rate OW_2 given the mrp curve, the labour force must contract to ON_2. If a method can be found to increase productivity to mrp_2 then ON_1 labour force can be paid OW_2 wages as the increase in productivity CA covers the increase in wages.

On the other hand, if the firm is in a monopolistic position and can increase the selling price of the product, this means that the revenue added by the marginal man is automatically also increased so that an increase in selling price is equivalent to a move of mrp, to the position mrp_2.

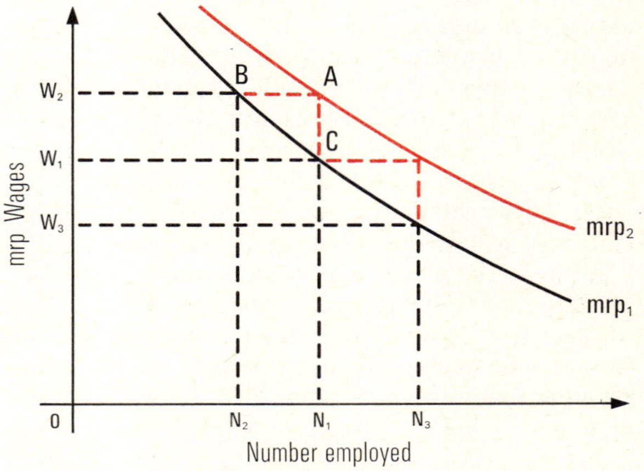

Figure 9·3

9·9

Is the theory of marginal revenue productivity a sufficient explanation of the determination of wage rates?

Limitations of the marginal revenue product theory

Although this theory can be applied to any factor of production, it only deals with the entrepreneur's demand for them. For example, it says that given that an extra man costs £20 per week then he will be employed if his marginal revenue product is likely to be £21 per week. However, why does he cost £20 per week? What were the supply conditions which led this worker to ask for £20 per week? As a theory about what individual firms do and why they do it mrp is a good general principle but wages are paid by people to people and many non-economic influences enter into such bargains.

Employers are not as sensitive to changes in productivity or wage rates as the theory suggests. Most of them do not have this kind of information available and the technical requirements of so many men per machine may over-rule some of these considerations. If a machine will not work unless it is tended by eight men, then an employer cannot reduce the number by one or two to seven or six men.

The theory does not account directly for the effects on the productivity of labour of the quality of entrepreneurship, the quantity and quality of capital or the effects of imperfections in the factor and commodity markets. The efficiency of any one factor is, in practice, bound up with the other factors with which it is used, though the theory assumes one can deal with any chosen factor in isolation.

Labour is not homogeneous and of equal efficiency. This partly explains why labour of varying efficiency will be employed at different wage rates.

How is the marginal revenue productivity of public services such as medicine and education to be measured? What determines rates of pay in service industries? The answer to these questions are much more complex than this theory suggests.

9·10

The only situation in which it will not pay the farmer to change the amount of labour hired and output produced is where marginal revenue product of the last unit hired is

A less than
B equal to } the cost of hiring that unit.
C greater than

Number employed	Output/Sales A	Output/Sales B	Commodity Selling price
40	1 178	1 178	50p
41	1 208	1 211	50p
42	1 234	1 241	50p
43	1 258	1 268	50p
44	1 280	1 294	50p
45	1 298	1 318	50p

9·11

The data in the table above is shown for a manufacturer.

a Calculate the marginal revenue productivity for output/sales A, and draw the curve on graph paper.

b How many will be employed if the wage rate is £13?
A 41 **B** 42 **C** 43

c Suppose a change in working methods would raise output to the figures shown in Col. B, calculate the marginal revenue productivity for this data.

d Assume the wage rate is still £13, how many more people would be employed?
A 44 **B** 43 **C** 2

e If the more productive working method was adopted (Col. B) and there was no increase in the number employed because of a union closed shop, by how much would the union force the wage rate to rise (if all the increased revenue was paid out as wages)?
A £15 **B** £3 **C** £2

Wages and salaries

We normally use the term wage for a cash payment on a weekly basis. Wage earners sometimes receive few benefits beyond their cash payment, but we should note that actual earnings may be considerably larger than the nominal wage because of overtime payments, productivity bonuses, etc. The salary earner is usually paid monthly, often by cheque or bank transfer. Although the salary earner may participate in profit sharing or receive an annual bonus he normally receives extra benefits in the form of security of tenure, longer notice before dismissal and possibly better conditions of work, i.e. canteens, private offices, company cars, longer holidays, etc. Salesmen often receive a commission on sales in addition to their salary.

Basis of payment

Wages may be paid as a rate per hour worked (a time rate) or as a rate per number of items produced or processed (a piece rate) or a combination of both. Time rates may also be expressed as rates per week or per shift. Salaries are usually paid with less reference to time, other than a minimum working day. They are paid for a job to be done, however much time it may entail.

The negotiation of wages and salaries

The most familiar method of wage determination is that between trade unions and employers' associations. The power of unions is particularly affected by the personalities of, and personal relationship between, the negotiators on both sides and the extent to which the shop floor and union leaders are closely in touch. Strikes (the complete withdrawal of the supply of labour) are weapons for use as a last resort, and are most effective if employers lose money, or the public brings pressure on the government to seek a settlement.

National level negotiations usually produce

agreements on minimum rates of pay and conditions of work. It is left to the local or plant negotiators to settle details and terms for any earnings in addition to the nationally agreed wage rates.

During the early 1960s the dominant theme for wage claims was *comparability*, i.e. claims were intended to secure increases at least similar to those obtained by other groups of workers. Once one group made a successful claim for increased wages on the grounds of comparability, the differential between them and other groups was upset. Other groups then claimed an increase in wages. A spiral of wage claims started, each claim justified by a comparison with the new increased wage in the other industry. Such claims make no reference to marginal revenue productivity. The tendency was for the higher wage costs to be passed on as higher prices to consumers, with the result that prices rose rapidly during this period. The alternative policy for employers of employing fewer men and women was not considered at a time when more people had ever increasing amounts of money to spend and an expanding market for most manufacturers' products existed. In the late 1960s, *productivity* succeeded comparability as a more appropriate basis for determining whether a wage increase should be granted or not.

One of the first productivity deals which involved 'buying up the union rule book' was made at the Fawley oil refinery in 1960. This agreement replaced the set of working agreements and rules in the union rule book, which had previously been in use, by a much more flexible set of arrangements. The productivity of labour was increased and in return higher pay and greater job security was given to the workers.

Wage drift

The difference between nominal wage rates and actual earnings is called wage drift. Generally it occurs as a result of locally-negotiated rates of pay in excess of nationally agreed minima. It is not, therefore, evenly spread among the population. In areas where labour shortages occur (the South-east and Midlands), employers must pay 'above the rate' in order to keep their labour force or to attract new labour.

Actual earnings may exceed wage rates for three reasons; firstly, because more people work overtime. This effect is specifically excluded from figure 9·4. Secondly, the average per head may go

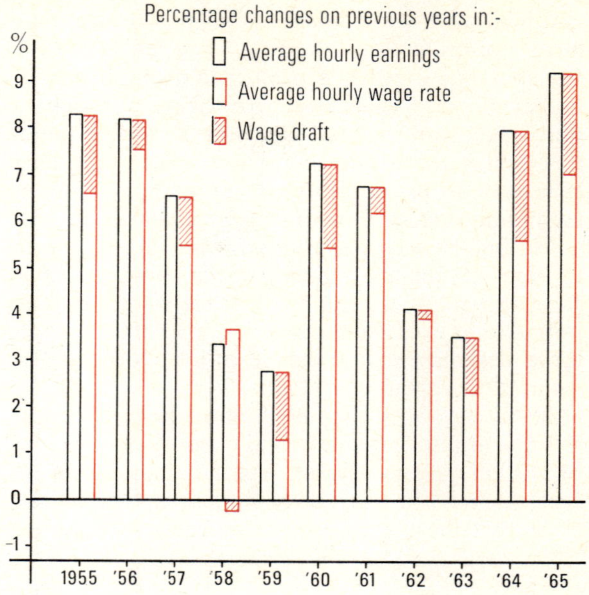

Figure 9·4

up as people move to higher paid jobs. More people may be paid on a piece work plant basis. Thirdly, negotiations, reflecting a relative scarcity of labour or higher productivity, may cause a wage drift. The second effect cannot easily be separated from a general wage drift.

Where wage drift is a particular feature of a growth industry or expanding firm, this may be the prime mechanism by which labour is attracted well before wage rates are renegotiated nationally.

9·12

Which of the following most accurately defines wages drift?

A Any earnings above nationally agreed wage rates.
B Annual increases in wages.
C The effect of overtime earnings on wages.
D The difference between average hourly earnings and average hourly wage rate.
E The difference between average salaries and average wage rates.

Why are there differences in earnings?

Rates of pay for people of similar efficiency or doing similar work vary because wage drift raises earnings on a local basis, or some workers may have non-monetary benefits, such as free fuel, transport, or foodstuffs from employers, in lieu of higher wages. Luncheon vouchers, non-contributory pension schemes, discount shopping facilities, extra holidays, company cars, company houses and opportunities to buy company shares are common additions to wages or salaries.

Many jobs offer advantages which are preferred in lieu of higher money wages, for example, agreeable work, the opportunity for using personal initiative or exercising power over others, prestige, these also may attract people to jobs with modest salaries or wages.

In fact, labour is not homogeneous: people differ in ability, education and training. Some types of workers are in greater demand than others. In fact, such is the variety of human aptitudes and skills that there is a series of markets for labour.

What are the long run influences on wages?

i The size of the real national income. This depends not only on labour, but on the country's natural resources, technology and managerial skills.

ii The size of the working population. This determines the number of people there will be available to produce commodities and services.

iii Social and political systems. Some societies are commercially active and exploit their natural resources, or engage in trade. Others perhaps put religious considerations before economic aims in ordering their life. How the national income shall be 'shared out' is a major consideration in most political philosophies.

9·13

How do you apply the *mrp* theory to land?

ANSWERS

9·1

Improve seed strains, new fertilisers, the use of machinery and other agricultural developments have increased the yields of crops. Better literary and general education have spread this knowledge to many farmers. Improvements in transport have enabled food surpluses to be moved to areas of high population density.

9·2

Own research. Results variable with rate and price changes.

9·3

a Correct **A.** Mistaken **B.**
b Correct **D.** Mistaken **C.**

9·4

a Correct **A.** Mistaken **B.**
b Correct **D.** Mistaken **C.**

9:5

Graph. See satellite 1, part 5 b

9·6

a Correct **A.** Mistaken **B.**
b Correct **C.** Mistaken **D.**

9·7

See below.

Number employed	Commodity selling price	Output/ Sales	m.p.p.	Total revenue £	m.r.p. £
50	50p	2 567		1 283·50	
			64		32
51	50p	2 631		1 315·50	
			59		29·50
52	50p	2 690		1 345	
			54		27
53	50p	2 744		1 372	
			50		25
54	50p	2 794		1 397	
			47		23·50
55	50p	2 841		1 420·50	

9·8

a Graph.

b Correct **C**: the 54th man adds £25 to total revenue so it is just worth employing him.
Mistaken **A**: have you plotted mrp at mid-interval values? See satellite *Arithmetical and Statistical Techniques.*
Mistaken **B**: the 53rd man adds £27 to total revenue. To stop here means a loss of potential output and sales.

c Correct **B.**

d **i** £32.
ii £27.
iii Where wages are less than the marginal revenue productivity, the employment of an extra man adds more to revenues than he does to the wage bill.

9·9

No, because

(a) a worker cannot be separated from his tools—a lumberjack needs an axe, a secretary needs a typewriter,

(b) the keeping of detailed records is likely to be more expensive than the benefit resulting from the statistics,

(c) by the time that the calculations are complete everything will have changed and thus the figures will be irrelevant, the mrp theory cannot be applied exactly in real life.

Nevertheless to some degree the wage that an employer can pay is obviously related to the net output per worker and in industries where large amounts of capital are used, i.e. labour is the relatively scarce factor, labour tends to be highly paid. Similarly countries which use large amounts of capital relative to labour tend to have high wages.

9·10

Correct **B.**

At **A** it is worth hiring more units.

At **C** each unit costs more than it produces in revenue.

9·11

a

Number employed	mrp A	mrp B
40		
41	15	16·50
42	13	15
43	12	13·50
44	11	13
45	9	12

b Correct **B**: 42 men will be employed.
Mistaken **A**: it is the 42nd man who adds £13 to total revenue not the 41st man.
Mistaken **C.**

d Correct **C.**
Mistaken **A**: this is the number which will be employed, not the *increase.*
Mistaken **B.**

e Correct **C.**
Mistaken **A**: this is the new wage level not the increase in wages.
Mistaken **B**: your mrp curve is not drawn at mid-interval points.

9·12

Correct **D.**

Mistaken **A, B, C, E**: re-read the text.

9·13

There is a margin of use of land; if you look at Welsh hillside farms, you often see cultivation extending further up the hillside as economic conditions improve—say wool prices rise.

If the price of gas increases, it is worth even extracting it from the North Sea bed—i.e. the mrp of the undersea fields is such that capital and labour are now applied to land.

THE SIZE OF FIRMS

STUDY SECTION **10**

If we assume that firms aim to earn maximum profits, then we shall expect firms to increase their output for as long as an increase in output increases profits. The limits to expansion will be either rising costs of production as the law of variable proportions operates, a sheer lack of the required factors of production, or falling prices. If a firm has to reduce the price of its product in order to sell more, it will eventually reach a position where a further increase in output will add more to costs than it does to revenue. So a further increase in output will not be worthwhile.

In this section we are concerned with the advantages of growth (which arise from economies of scale), the direction in which growth takes place (the various forms of integration), the form of organisation for large combinations of firms, the methods by which growth may take place, and the reasons for the survival of small firms.

The relative size of firms

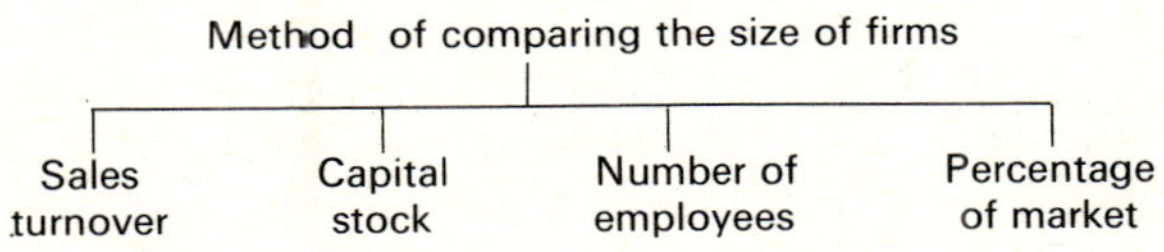

Each of the four methods of comparing the size of firms given above has advantages or disadvantages, principally because the use of any single method ignores the other three. Let us examine each criterion.

The sales turnover is the total amount of money paid to the firm by its customers per year, or a firm's total annual revenue. A firm may have few employees, like a discount house, but have a turnover of several million pounds which is equivalent to the turnover of a chain of supermarkets employing thousands of assistants.

The capital stock may be the market value of the shares issued by a firm, or it may be the real value of the assets owned by the firm. Usually the market value of the shares will indicate the value of the company's net assets, but sometimes the two diverge, perhaps because shareholders have inadequate financial information. It is obviously difficult to value private companies and unincorporated businesses, and until their real capital is sold on the open market no-one really knows the market price. Thus, to estimate the importance of a firm, we normally use either the number of employees as a measure of comparison or its share of the market. Firms which employ less than 100 employees are normally called small firms, firms with 100 to 499 employees are called medium sized and those with more than 500 may be described as large, but these figures are arbitrary. You should specify precisely what you mean when you use the terms, small, large or medium sized.

Finally when considering the importance of a firm within an industry, we normally say that a firm whose output accounts for more than one third of the sales of that commodity is in a monopolistic position, so any firm with more than about one fifth of the market would be regarded as large within that industry. Again, these figures are arbitrary. In making a judgment as to whether or not a firm is large, you should find out first the easiest figure to obtain, the number of employees, and then look at the other criteria to ensure that you have a complete picture of its economic importance.

A firm may be large in terms of the number of people it employs but still be a small firm in relation to the industry of which it is part; or, it may be relatively small in terms of turnover, but labour intensive, and so employ large numbers of people. It is important, therefore, to consider the nature of both the firm and the industry when assessing the relative size of any individual firm. The amount of capital used for the production processes may be large, as in the iron and steel and heavy engineering industries. Nevertheless, the turnover (i.e., the value of total sales per year) of such industries may be no greater than a merchant bank which uses very little capital equipment and employs only a hundred people. In terms of influence on the market the larger firms will be those which sell the greatest proportion of total sales of the product. The relative size of car manufacturers is usually expressed in terms of percentage of the market, partly because accurate national statistics are easy to obtain and, partly, because this is a real measure of competitiveness.

10·1

a Examine the table. What percentage of all manufacturing firms employs less than 500 persons?
A 10·55 **B** 22·1 **C** 23·3 **D** 94·7

Numbers employed	11–24	25–99	100–499	500–999	1 000–1 999	2 000 +	Total
No. of establishments	12 571	27 478	12 213	1 693	777	429	55 161
No. of employees (thousands)	222	1 420	2 552	1 163	1 078	1 743	8 178

b What proportion of manufacturing industry's work force did these firms employ?

A 2·7 **B** 5·29 **C** 20·0 **D** 38·9

Your answer to **a** tells you the proportion of manufacturing firms which employs the percentage of employees in answer **b**.

10·2

a Draw a bar diagram to show the distribution of different sizes of firms in manufacturing industry, using data from the table above.

b Draw another bar diagram to show the distribution of employment among different sizes of firm.

If you are making studies of any particular industry group, e.g. textiles, motor vehicles etc., you should repeat exercise 10·1 for that industry using the *Annual Abstract.*

Factors affecting the size of firms

If two firms start with the same resources and are in a similar market situation, the size of the firm depends mainly on the attitudes and skill of its management. On the production side, the size of the firm is largely determined by the extent to which various kinds of cost-reducing economics are employed. If economies result from the substitution of capital for labour, the size of the firm, in respect of numbers employed, may be reduced, but the size, in terms of the value of capital, may increase.

i Internal economies of scale. Internal economies of scale are reductions in the average cost of production which can be achieved by an individual firm as it increases its output. When a firm is formed, the owner or the manager is the fixed factor, or, perhaps, the capital in the factory and the size of the plot of land upon which the factory is built, may also be regarded as the fixed factor in the short run. As output is increased more intensive use is made of the fixed capital and other fixed factors, so the fixed costs of production are spread over a larger number of units. Also the variable costs per unit of output are reduced as the average product per variable factor increases. For these reasons, as output is increased the average cost of producing each unit will fall initially, and then rise, in accordance with the law of variable proportions. Strictly speaking, most reductions in average cost as output increases arise from varying the proportions of the factors, e.g. using more men and raw materials in conjunction with the fixed factors, land, equipment, and the entrepreneur, but such economies of varying proportions are usually included under the general heading, economies of scale. The shape of the average cost curve is discussed more fully in S11. However, no entrepreneur will determine the precise level of output by looking only at his cost structure. His aim is to maximise profits, which means that he will plan a level of production at which the difference between total receipts and total costs is greatest. Hence the economic level of output depends not only on the level of total costs but also on the level of total receipts. In S11 we shall deal with receipts; in the meanwhile let us see precisely how firms can achieve reductions in average cost as they increase their output.

ii The economies of skill. The most obvious economy is due to the specialisation and division of labour. Long runs of making the same product tend to increase workers' skill and so reduce the time required for the job. Co-ordination of the factors of productions and production control can be achieved with greater precision so that costs per unit of output may be substantially reduced. Efficiently organised management can handle much larger plants with little increase in the salary bill. Large firms can economise on that scarce resource —enterprise.

iii Technical economies. Some goods can be made more quickly or cheaply by machinery but in most cases, the machinery can only be paid for if the scale of output is large. For example, aspirin tablets can be made by a chemist or produced in a drug factory. There are also goods which can, for purely technical reasons, only be made through the use of large and complicated units of capital, for example, plastic bowls and nylon tights. Unless large quantities were produced the cost of using these machines would be prohibitive.

Firms which are large enough can make economic use of internal data-processing equipment and computers. Instantaneous calculations and access to the information required may permit decisions which cut costs directly.

As the scale of output increases in manufacturing industry, it is usually possible to introduce different techniques which will reduce the cost per unit of output. This usually means substituting more capital for labour by bringing in semi-automatic machinery. Already computers control machine tools which cut and form machine components or plate steel for prefabricating ships. Iron or aluminium castings can be turned into engine blocks for cars by automatic machinery, and a dozen men may now do the work of, perhaps, 350. This does not always cause unemployment, since reductions in costs may result in reductions in the price of the product, an increase in sales and output, and the men being transferred to other parts of the production process.

The large, expensive items of capital, such as computers, which can only be used at a low cost if output is very high, are called *indivisible factors*. Small scale machines of this kind either cannot be made, or are much less efficient.

iv The economies of increased dimensions. This may be illustrated by examining the costs of transporting crude oil, which has tended to fall as the size of oil tankers has grown.

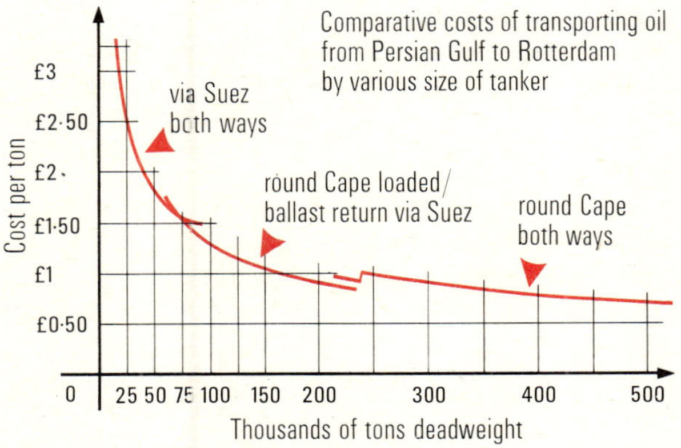

Figure 10·1

	Deadweight tons
Post War	16 500
Mid 1950's	50 000
1960	100 000
Mid 1960's	250 000
1970	372 000

v Economies of linked processes. Increasing scales of output allied to product standardisation usually means that some form of volume- or mass-production will be undertaken. Economies can then be achieved by physically linking each succeeding process. The time and cost of handling materials and the amount of money tied up as work-in-progress or in stock is reduced. Hence car firms may hold stocks of components for only a day's output or stocks of tyres for a few hours' production. A more far-reaching process called integration may follow as part of the search for economies of linked processes. The basic principle is, once again, specialisation and the division of function. The use of production lines, typified by the car assembly industry, is the usual result (see satellite, *The Motor Vehicles Industry*). Figure 10·2 illustrates an integrated firm.

vi Economies in purchasing. When production is on a large scale, the bulk buying of raw materials or components is possible. Discounts are made possible because economies of scale apply equally to suppliers of materials, e.g. a large refinery can buy its oil cheaper per ton because it can take full large tanker loads. Monopsony power may also be used by purchasers of raw materials to reduce the price per unit of the goods supplied.

vii Stochastic economies. The statistical laws of large numbers imply that as the scale of operations increases it is possible to predict certain changes and so produce economies. These so-called stochastic economies of scale depend on laws of probability. Suppose an engineering firm carries enough spare parts to cope with 90% of breakdowns in its machinery. Although it cannot rule out the possibility that all the machines will break down at once, it would be expensive to carry all the spares for all the machines. Since it is probable that only a few machines will break down at any one time it is unlikely that spares for every machine will be needed at the same time. If the firm doubles the number of machines it uses, it will not need twice the stock of spare parts or twice the number of maintenance engineers. The firm can predict, on past experience, what things are most likely to be needed and how many breakdowns are likely to occur.

If three garages merge their spare parts services, the total stock of spare parts will fall since previously each one had to carry the full range of items. Economies can then be achieved by minimising the stock of parts consistent with providing an adequate service to customers. (Remember that although stocks must be held, the money used to purchase them is not earning anything. Carrying unnecessary stocks is an expensive business, and involves, of course, an opportunity cost.)

viii Economies in finance. Large firms can reduce the cost of finance in many ways. A large firm can raise new capital more easily, and on more favourable terms because it will have access to the capital market through the new issues market. Also the large public company can usually raise additional capital through the Stock Exchange on more favourable terms than small companies. Legal and other charges will form a smaller proportion of the total amount raised.

A large firm will be able to borrow from a bank at a lower rate of interest than small firms or private individuals. The overdraft interest for large firms is 1% above Bank rate, whereas for very small firms and individuals the charge is $2\frac{1}{2}$% above Bank rate.

ix Economies in marketing. Marketing involves the whole process of investigating consumer preferences, design, the provision of alternatives to meet the need for consumer choice, through to sales, delivery and after sales service.

As output increases the marketing force need not be increased proportionately. The sales made by one salesman can double. Distribution costs can be reduced if larger quantities are carried to each destination at any one time. For example, firms producing enough goods to fill several railway containers, or even a whole train, will find that the freight charges per unit are very low.

These economies arise out of the large economies of increased dimensions of large lorries, ships and aircraft, and railway wagons. The opportunity to use facilities to capacity in large scale movements of materials and finished products is important to the cement, coal and oil industries. A full train-load of oil costs little more to move than a half train-load.

The economical use of container systems is based on filling them to capacity, reducing the costs of handling, and increasing the speed of turn-round. By increasing the number of journeys per year of the carrier, idle time is reduced. Transport charges per unit can be reduced, and earnings may be increased.

10·3

Data: Costs calculated for a United Nations symposium on the iron and steel industry for Latin America.

Cost of flat rolled steel in hypothetical plants of different sizes

	Annual output capacity of plant of finished products (thousands of tonnes)			
	100	400	800	1 500
	U.S. Dollars			
Item				
Ferrous material	120·71	92·58	82·94	75·47
Salaries and wages	15·52	6·22	4·51	3·30
Other costs	12·30	10·67	8·60	7·30
Total direct cost	148·53	109·47	96·05	86·07
Capital costs	43·46	29·70	19·80	17·37
Total cost per ton S	191·99	139·17	115·85	103·44

This information illustrates quite clearly the effect of economies of scale, but it does assume that the increased output can be sold. At the time these calculations were made, imported flat steel products cost about $182 per tonne in Latin America.

As the scale of output rises you will notice there is a substantial reallocation of the factors of production.

For comparison, the Shotton plant of British Steel Corporation has a capacity of 2 000 000 tonnes flat rolled steel per annum.

a Calculate the fall in the cost per tonne of each item expressed both in dollars and as a percentage, when the plant capacity is raised from 100 000 tonnes p.a. to 1 500 000 tonnes p.a.

b List the savings in percentage order.

Diseconomies of scale

Sooner or later a firm reaches a stage of output where one factor of production is again fixed in supply: the fixed factor may be land, buildings, machinery, or simply the ability of human beings to control a large enterprise. When this point is reached, the effect of the law of variable proportions is felt, and the further increases in output from employing more variable factors result in rising average cost per unit. These rises in average costs are called diseconomies of scale. In the long run, when it is possible to alter the amount of all the factors employed, i.e. increase the scale of operations, the central management will be the fixed factor. Therefore in the long run the basic reason for rising average costs is that the firm may become too complex to manage or administer from one centre. Management becomes over-specialised and cannot react to new opportunities: administrative costs rise rapidly. Such diseconomies can be called decreasing returns to scale.

10·4

Do large trade unions suffer from diseconomies of scale? (Refer to the satellite *Industrial Relations.*)

External economies of scale

External economies of scale are reductions in average costs which become available to all firms in an industry or an area as the number of firms increase. In turn, such external economies attract more firms into the area: they represent the *acquired advantages* of an area. The reductions in average cost of production are due to the following.

i Economies of concentration. When an industry is concentrated in an area a pool of skilled labour will develop and local colleges may well run special training courses for young people and for existing employees in that industry. (To check, examine the prospectus of your local technical college.) In some industries, e.g. in the Yorkshire woollen industry, firms will specialise in particular processes, such as spinning, weaving, dyeing, and making the finished product.

ii Economies of shared services. Banks and other financial institutions in the area will develop special facilities for financing the trade or the industries concentrated in that area. As the area develops the local authorities will be encouraged to improve road communications, so reducing transport costs. Firms which are too small to provide these expensive facilities for themselves may set up joint research establishments and use computers on a time sharing basis. Other common services which will develop are firms providing machinery, repair and maintenance firms, firms making use of waste products, and packaging and transport firms.

Note that external diseconomies of scale may develop if an area becomes too congested. Delays cause rising transport costs, and land costs rise rapidly.

Integration: the direction of growth

Integration takes place when two or more established firms join together to form one new firm, and are under unified control as a result of a merger, or take-over of share capital. When two or more plants bring together a whole series of consecutive or related processes, which in the past have each been the concern of separate firms, this is called integration.

Economists distinguish between several kinds of integration to describe different patterns in the flow of products from the raw materials stage to the market.

Horizontal integration describes the growth of a firm by the bringing together of two or more firms who process the *same* product or who are engaged in the *same* stage of production. For example, two commercial banks may integrate, thus expanding the number of branches under one control. This may lead to economies in accounting, by making the use of a computer economical.

Lateral integration brings together related but not competitive products or processes. British Leyland was formed by merging Leyland Motors (lorries and buses) with British Motor Holdings (cars and vans); the merged General Electric Company and Associated Electrical Industries group manufactures almost every kind of electrical product (e.g. light bulbs and fittings, refrigerators, electric cables, transformers, power station turbines and generating equipment). The firm's motive for integration may be to create the situation in which it is able to offer clients a complete range of industrial equipment without the need to subcontract.

Vertical integration links processes in the order in which products are manufactured. The principal motive for integration is to ensure an adequate supply of materials.

Territorial integration involves the merging of firms in different regions or countries to expand the market served by the controlling firm. The polycentric international (or multi-national) firm is found in the oil, aero-space, motor vehicles and chemical industries. Although product specialisation is not always necessary for large scale manufacturing (shipbuilding, for example, very often produces 'one-off' jobs) territorial integration often leads to product standardisation as a means to

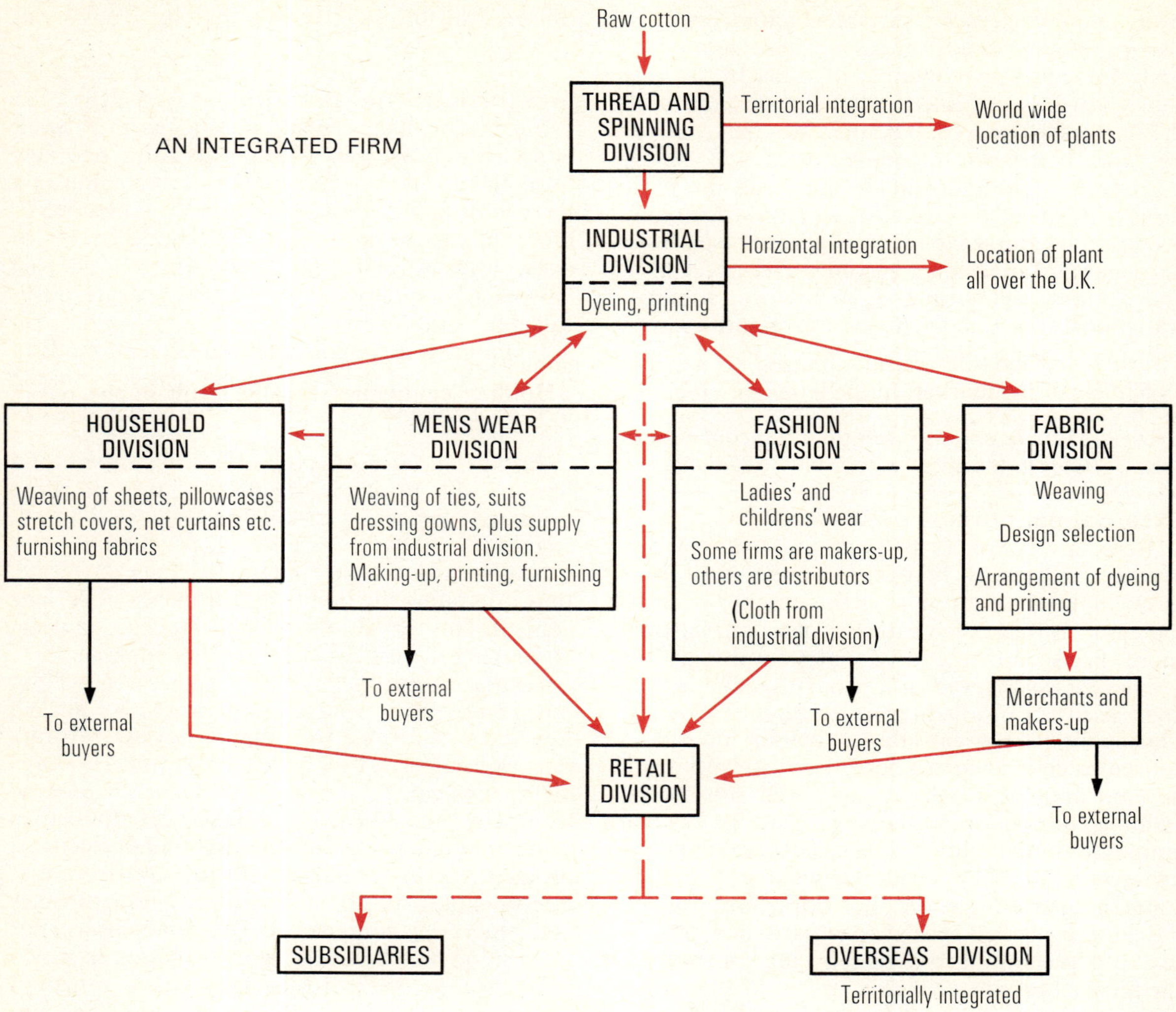

Figure 10·2

creating volume- or mass-production plants.

Diagonal integration usually means that ancillary processes or services are brought under the control of the firm's principal customer, for example, cardboard box manufacturers may be integrated with confectionary firms. In a library consult *Who owns Whom*, and examine the range of companies and activities controlled by Unilever, I.C.I., Reed-International.

Figure 10·2 shows a large integrated textile firm controlling every process from buying raw cotton to selling finished products in its own stores. It supplies semi-finished goods, e.g. yarns and cloth, and also finished goods to other firms. The basic organisation is based on vertical integration. The product divisions form lateral integration. Within each product group are a number of firms (trading under different names) which are horizontally integrated. Territorial integration exists particularly in world-wide subsidiary firms in the thread and spinning division and in the overseas division; many of the latter are raw materials producers, merchants, and retail groups. In terms of control, most of the firms in each division are fully owned subsidiaries of the parent company.

One main problem is to balance the output of

each stage of an integrated firm with the input required for succeeding stages.

Co-operation without integration

i Manufacturers' associations. These organisations are formed by independent firms in order to pool information and ideas.

Common pricing policies may be agreed, both for minimum agreed prices or for fixed pricing arrangements even though the latter is illegal in the U.K. Quotas are sometimes operated whereby each manufacturer agrees to produce a fixed quantity of goods or restricts himself to a fixed percentage of the market. In the latter case there is still some motivation for firms to expand their output. Market sharing on the basis of products or geographical division is quite common.

ii The cartel. The cartel is an arrangement for organising and enforcing a common pricing policy or an agreed pattern of output levels. It enables the member firms of the cartel to retain their separate identities whilst removing the effects of competition. In particular it avoids a price-cutting war, which may end only when one or more firms so cut prices that they go bankrupt.

Industrial cartels commonly set up a central selling agency to service the member firms, or parcel out markets so that the allotted firm only competes actively in areas where no one else does. Maximum output levels are often agreed so that the selling agency may control the supply.

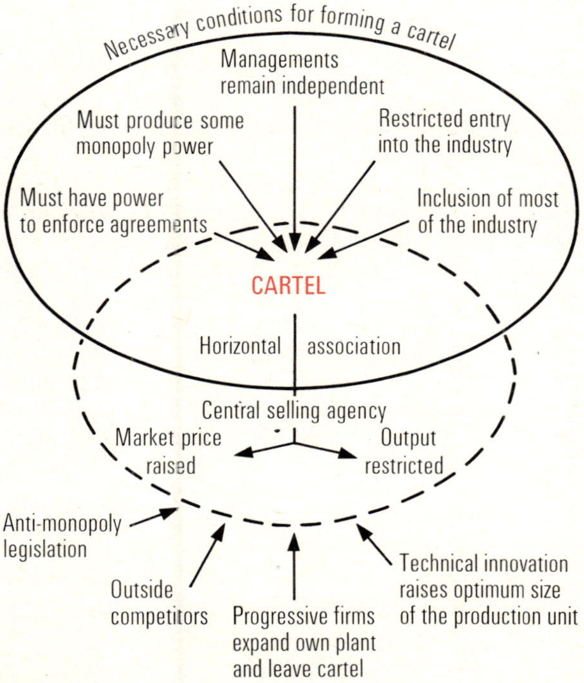

Figure 10·3

iii The holding company. A holding company is a public company whose business is to hold and exercise a controlling interest (51% or more of the voting power) in other firms.

It may be set up when two firms are merged, or it may be used as the means of effecting control over an integrated set of plants or over a conglomerate.

Holding companies usually result in the pyramiding of capital. Pyramiding is a process of holding 51% or more in a number of companies which in turn hold controlling interests in further companies and so on. The real extent of the holding company's control is, therefore, concealed, since each company continues to trade under its own name.

Examples of very large holding companies in the U.K. are Vickers and I.C.I. (Imperial Chemical Industries). Vickers is entirely a holding company, but I.C.I. often shares the investment in firms set up to exploit new materials which I.C.I. make.

10·5

In the table below it is assumed that the holding company invests its capital in 51% of each of two companies, A and B. These two firms each control two subsidiaries, C and D, and E and F. What is the value of the assets controlled by this holding company?

Holding company

£20 000

A £10 000 (£19 610) **B** £10 000 (£19 610)

C £9 805 (£19 230) **D** £9 805 (£19 230) **E** £9 805 (£19 230) **F** £9 805 (£19 230)

(Figures in brackets show the capital of each firm, assuming that the holding is 51% of the shares.)

A £29 610 **B** £76 920
C £59 220 **D** £116 140

The holding company is a very flexible form of organisation. Where necessary it can have tight control over subsidiary firms and so promote reorganisation and integration. On the other hand, it can provide a substantial share of the capital needed to expand a developing firm and provide, if necessary, additional management expertise, while leaving independent the existing management of the company acquired.

Many holding companies control 'conglomerates' which describes a diverse group of companies assembled purely for investment opportunity. There is no other common factor, these companies may produce quite dissimilar products and provide no opportunity at all for integration, horizontal or vertical. Why then should you form a conglomerate company? The holding company controlling the conglomerate organisation specialises not in a product, but in developing investment opportunities. It will buy any likely source of profits.

The great disadvantage, from a public point of view, is that pyramiding is concealed and it may be very difficult to unravel the chain of control, or to identify the directors who are ultimately responsible for decision making.

10·6

Look at the label on any household commodity and by using *Who own Whom* find out if the commodity is produced by an independent company.

iv Trusts. An industrial trust is the name given, especially in the United States, to a company or group of companies which acts in a monopolistic manner. A trust holds the shares of various companies which it then controls for the benefit of its shareholders. A trust is a means of controlling a large number of previously independent firms. Unlike the cartel it brings direct control to bear over the managements of firms owned by the trust. The principal aim of such organisations used to be control of prices but now more subtle questions of power, both political and economic, may be of equal importance.

Since control is effective, a trust can integrate the activities of its members. Usually the full range of vertical integration can be achieved, and the output levels of each plant can be controlled to meet the needs of succeeding processes. Where small specialist component makers supply a whole industry and require capital for expansion, a trust may provide the capital but take over control. The control of the supply of components to the trust's

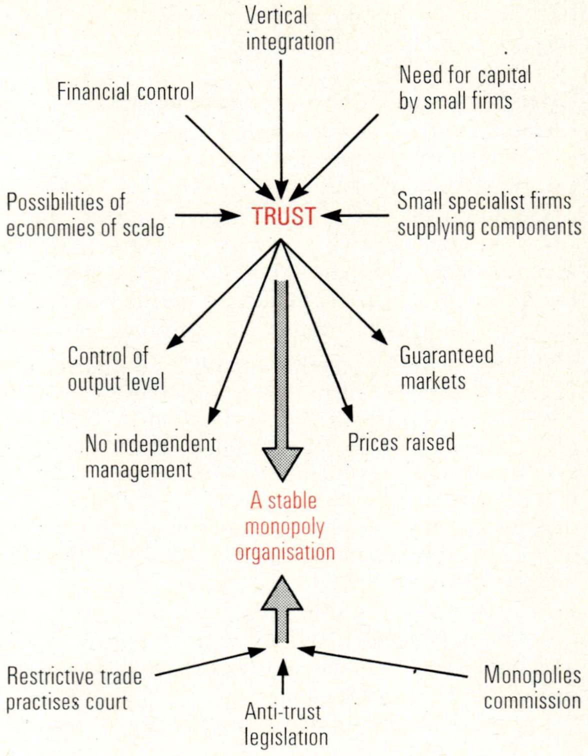

Figure 10·4

industrial rivals is a powerful competitive weapon. Sometimes a new member firm is now guaranteed a supply of raw materials or a market for its output.

The principal advantage of the trust is that, because of its power, it can improve efficiency and gain various economies of scale. This may be the source of profits rather than the use of monopoly power over prices. The temptation to exercise monopoly power is very strong, however, and very complex anti-trust legislation has been enacted, particularly in U.S.A. (*Unit trusts* are relatively new institutions, in the capital market and are not to be confused with the trust referred to above. For further information see satellite *Financial Institutions*.)

Methods of combining firms

Combination leads to increasing industrial concentration, that is, the supply of goods to the market is in fewer hands.

Company A may offer cash or its own shares to the shareholders of company B. If 51% or more accept the offer then company B will disappear, and company A takes control.

The acceptance or rejection of a take-over bid is normally left to shareholders under the guidance of the existing board of directors. The motive for take-overs is to benefit the bidding firm by obtaining additional assets (e.g. for horizontal integration), or, by acquiring management of technical expertise to obtain an increased rate of profits on capital. Consequently take-overs usually imply that the existing management has made some inadequate use of its assets because it is, to some extent, incompetent. Sometimes the reason for the take-over is that, as a combined firm, better results could be obtained than would have been possible for either firm on its own. The takeover is possible because the company bidding for the shares considers that the present market price underestimates the true value of the assets if they were administered by a better management.

Some small or medium sized firms may be taken over simply because they *are* efficient or because they have experience in a new technology. Almost the sole criterion for accepting a take-over is that shareholders are offered more money in the form of promised future profits, or in the form of cash, than they can obtain from the present situation. The only interest taken into account is, therefore, the rather narrow interest of current shareholders, whose links with the firm are often tenuous and temporary. Perhaps the more general public interest, the interest of employees (many of whom may be dismissed after a take-over) and the interest of the firms' customers and suppliers ought to be taken into consideration.

The straightforward take-over is only one of the several forms of merger or combination of firms. The actual method employed will depend upon the advice given to the firm's directors by their accountants and because of the legal and other regulations, many very complicated procedures are involved.

Note that motives other than the purely economic enter into the building of large concerns. Indeed, sometimes inordinate ambition is the driving force leading to the creation of industrial empires: see biographies of Henry Ford, Andrew Carnegie, Cornelius Vanderbilt.

10·7

In various circumstances any of the following advantages may be obtained. Group these under their appropriate technical heading, as used by economists:

i the reduction of competition by achieving a common pricing policy or by market-sharing,
ii the reduction of wasteful duplication of effort in marketing and distribution,
iii the reduction of total production capacity by buying up inefficient competitors and then closing them down. This will permit a rise in the selling price of the remaining output.
iv the purchase of management expertise which is under-utilized in its own plant and which could profitably manage a much larger firm (particularly in reverse take-overs),
v the integration of firms to reap economies of scale or market-control,
vi the diversification of risk by diversification of interest,
vii the unified control over a complete product range.

Why does the small firm survive?

Most small firms are one man businesses, as in the retail trade, or partnerships or private companies. There are about 570 000 registered companies in the U.K., but only about 16 000 are public companies.

Of the new companies registered each year, the majority are small. About half of these new companies will fail for one reason or another, and of the remainder some will never expand.

Small firms seem particularly suitable to any business whose market is limited, or which requires great flexibility of approach and direct control of daily operations. The management optimum is therefore small and dis-economies of a large scale organisation preclude growth. All kinds of professional services require the 'personal touch' which means that the mass production of such services is impossible. In part this is because, literally, every case to be dealt with is different so the service is unique every time. To a slightly lesser extent the same principle applies to a great deal of retail trade and services such as laundries, jobbing builders or window cleaners where products or services are non-standardised, and where local goodwill is very important.

The products of these specialist firms appeal to a small but discriminating market which wants something different from the mass-produced alternative, and, where necessary, is willing to pay slightly more for the exclusive product. Small firms may also survive as clients of large firms, providing special equipment (e.g. a shuttle-making firm in Yorkshire), sub-contracting, or making components).

Imperfection in markets, based on transport costs, 'protects' smaller firms from outside competition. The super-market in the city centre may be cheaper than the local grocer's store, but you have to save the cost of bus fare on every trip or else it is not worthwhile shopping there. The principle of opportunity cost applies here.

Small firms may be able to fill gaps in the market of large firms because the scale of operation is too small to be profitable to the large firm, or because the cost of forcing the small firm out of business may not yield commensurate extra profits.

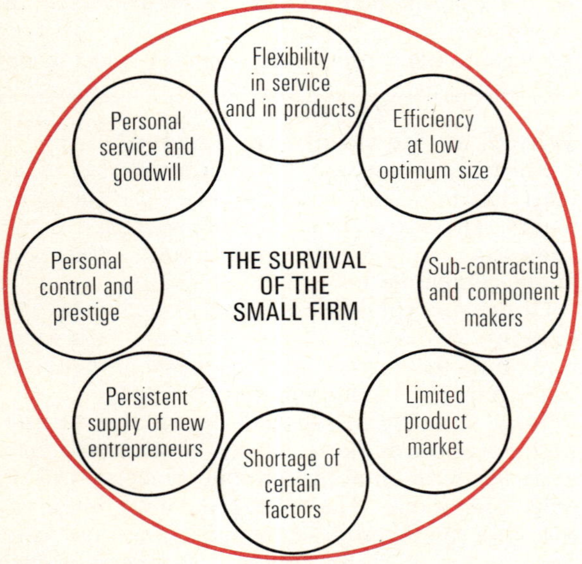

Figure 10·5

10·8

Examine the market for fashion goods, groceries and shoes as part of your study of retail trade, to see how many large firms there are compared with small firms (see satellite *Retail Trade and Distribution*).

The size of firms may also be limited by the supply of entrepreneurial skill; however, small firms may be the teething rings on which young entrepreneurs cut their competitive teeth. Shortages of certain essential skilled workers will also prevent a firm expanding.

One major limitation to the growth of small firms is the lack of capital. A recent investigation showed that 63% of small firms are financed by overdrafts from commercial banks, only 3% had access to merchant bank's money and less than half (48%) used ploughed back profits. The Smaller Businesses Association in the U.K. is aiming to expand the merchant bank supply of capital to members. There are 350 000 small firms employing half the U.K.'s manpower, so they should be a profitable, if risky, market for loans.

Another impediment to the growth of firms is the limited supply of land for expansion, especially in regions such as the Midlands and South East. In these regions it is often difficult to obtain an Industrial Development Certificate.

Finally, one reason why firms may not expand is the entrepreneur's reluctance to increase his profits if by so doing he loses personal contact with employees and customers.

10·9

List all the ways in which a large firm might drive a small firm out of business.

Figure 10·6 shows the factors encouraging or limiting the growth of the small firm. The relative

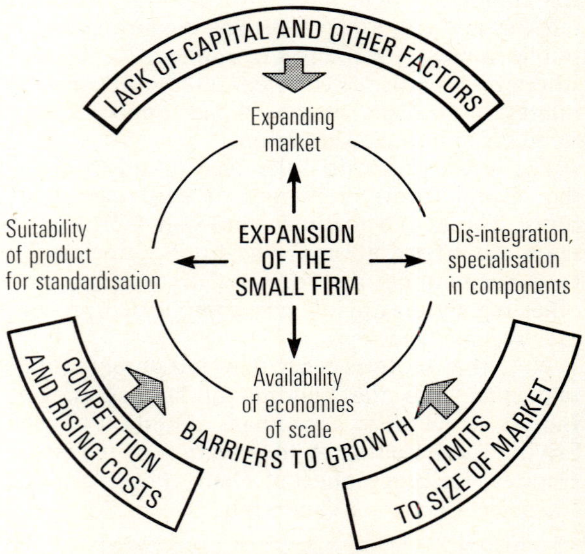

FACTORS ENCOURAGING AND LIMITING THE GROWTH OF THE SMALL FIRM

Figure 10·6

importance of each factor will vary as circumstances change.

10·10

Consider any example of a small firm that you know and list the items in figure 10·5 in their order of importance to the survival of that firm.

10·11

On which of the following may internal economies of scale depend?

A The existence of indivisible factors.
B Standardisation of product.
C The Stock Exchange value of the shares.
D The size of the market.

10·12

Which of the following would give control over subsidiaries supplying components to an assembly plant?

A A cartel.
B A trust.
C Vertical Integration.
D Horizontal Integration.
E Lateral Integration.

The stability of large firms

The management of large firms is usually highly skilled; and, often self-perpetuating. Large companies can offer salaries far in excess of those of senior posts in public service, and can give just as much real power. If they want extra management expertise they can usually buy it.

The use of management information services based on data processing and computer analysis extends the size of unit which management can handle, and postpones the impact of diseconomies of scale. Intense specialisation and effective systems of communication assist management to solve complicated problems.

Marketing, as a systematic approach to production, is often unknown in small firms, which simply make things and try to persuade people to buy them. Large firms can afford to find out what their prospective customers really do want; then they can plan ahead, develop the necessary technology, build the plant and produce the right commodities. Advertising both extends and creates a demand for commodities so that plant is worked to capacity.

If mistakes are made they are usually very costly ones, but large firms have the resources to bear the loss. In most cases a large firm is sufficiently diversified to prevent any single product being more than a small proportion of its output.

Large firms enjoy internal economies of scale, and these economies are a guarantee of stability. However, national stability may easily be disturbed by international competition.

ANSWERS

10·1

a Correct **D**: this is calculated by adding together Col. 1+2+3 and expressing as a percentage of the total.
Mistaken **A, B, C.**

b Correct **D**: this is calculated by expressing Col. 1+2+3 as a percentage of the total for the number of employees.
Mistaken **A, B, C.**

10·2

a Bar diagrams.
b Bar diagrams.

10·3

a

Item	**Decrease in cost from 100 000 to 1 500 000 tons p.a.**	
	U.S. dollars	Percent
Ferrous material	45·24	37·5
Salaries and wages	12·22	78·6
Other costs	5·00	40·7
Total direct costs	62·46	42·1
Capital costs	26·09	60·0
TOTAL COST PER TON	88·55	46·1

b Salaries and Wages	78·6%
Capital costs	60·0%
Other costs	40·7%
Ferrous materials	37·5%

10·4

Yes: they may be so large that the central organisation cannot keep in close touch with the branches. In a large union, different sections of the membership may have conflicting interests.

10·5

Correct **D** (omitting Holding Co. £20 000) : mistaken **A, B, C.**

10·6

Own research.

10·7

Cartel **i, ii.**
Take over **iii, iv.**
Integration **v.**
Diversification, Conglomerate **vi.**
Monopoly **vi.**

10·8

Retail trade study.

10·9

Economies of scale, leading to greater advertising.

'Free' services e.g. car parking, delivery and credits!

Greater range of goods.

Lower prices.

Price cutting and taking a short term loss in order to eliminate competitor.

10·10

Personal research.

10·11

Correct **A, B, D.** Mistaken **C**: unless achieving internal economies depends on raising new capital.

10·12

Correct **B, C.**

Mistaken **A**: cartels do not always have effective power.

Mistaken **D** and **E**: these are not the appropriate forms of integration which apply to the supply of components to assembly plants.

THE THEORY OF THE FIRM

As we have seen in the previous chapters, a commodity is manufactured because someone takes the trouble to organise and co-ordinate, in suitable proportions, the factors of production; land (including raw materials), capital (buildings and machinery) and labour. This 'someone' is called, in the free-enterprise economy, the entrepreneur and it is he (or she) who decides that 'x' units of labour plus 'y' units of capital plus 'z' units of land constitute an input which is sufficient to produce an output of goods of quantity 'o'.

Each factor of production used by the entrepreneur will require a payment: the owner of land or capital will require a fee for selling or lending his field or machine and the factor labour will require a wage or salary. What is the reward for the entrepreneur called? How is it determined? The next section will deal with these two questions, but before proceeding further we must admit that we make at least three basic assumptions.

i We assume that the economy is fundamentally a freely competitive one and that the state does not interfere.

ii We assume that the entrepreneur is motivated by economic considerations alone and that he seeks a monetary reward.

iii Lastly, we assume that he strives to make this reward as large as possible and will therefore produce a level of output which will maximise his profits.

The picture of the entrepreneur drawn above is of a ruthless unattractive person who probably does not exist in reality. Similarly, the free-enterprise economy postulated above is an abstract concept and does not exist, but in setting up this model economic situation, we hope to learn something about the nature of profits. We confine ourselves to studying a 'model', to assume that that model is the 'norm' (i.e. the typical case) and to assume that we can examine the unusual firm by comparing it with our 'normal' model. Later, we shall be able to judge the validity of our assumptions.

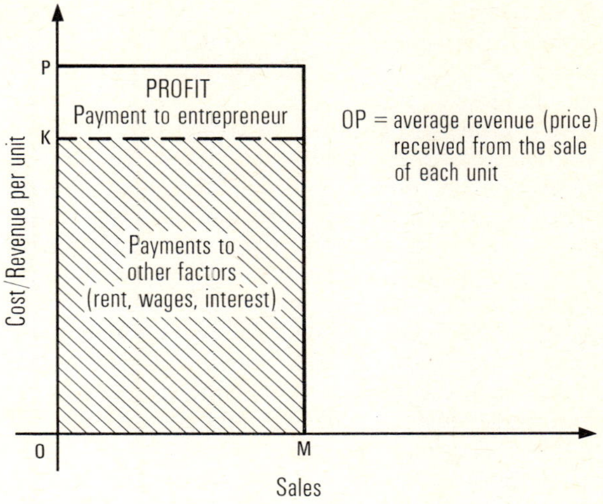

Figure 11·1

We saw in S2 that the payment to the entrepreneur is called profit. Profit is usually regarded by the business man as what is left over after all other factors have been paid. In figure 11·1 the shaded area represents the payments of rent, interest, and wages required to produce an output of OM units. If we assume all of this is sold at price OP per unit, then a profit will be made, because total revenue (OM × OP) is greater than payments to other factors (OM × OK). Hence the reward to the entrepreneur for producing and selling output OM will be profit (KP × OM). Profit is therefore the residual amount left after all payments to other factors have been made. It is important to note that when the entrepreneur gathered together his factors of production he could not be absolutely sure that, at some future date, when he produced output OM, the price per unit would be OP and the payments required by other factors to produce each unit would be OK (figure 11·1). Clearly, anyone who has to guess future prices can be very wrong in his estimates. If our entrepreneur had been over-optimistic he might have allowed cost per unit to exceed OP, expecting that he would receive a price much higher than OP. In such a case, at price OP he would have made a loss. A rather pessimistic entrepreneur may have felt that the price would never reach the level of OP, and thus by carefully controlling his use of the factors of production he may have kept payments to other factors below OK per unit. Careful cost control can increase profits.

Normal profit

Each financial year a firm's accountant will produce accounts set out to meet the requirements of the Companies Act and following the conventions accepted by the accountancy profession. From these accounts it is possible to calculate a firm's costs and profits, but some care must be exercised because accountants and economists often use the word cost to describe quite different items. Economists include in the costs of production an element of profit, which they call normal profit, because unless firms make some profit they will eventually cease production. *Normal profit* can be described as that amount of profit which is just sufficient to keep the entrepreneur in a particular industry. It can be regarded as the supply price of enterprise, just as wages are the supply price of labour.

There are also many different ways of measuring profits. Profit margin refers to the difference between the payments required for the other factors per unit and the selling price. The numerical value of a firm's profits (e.g. £20 000) is obviously of no significance unless we know the size of the firm. For such reasons profit is usually expressed as a percentage return on the capital employed by a firm—the value of a firm's capital indicates its size. The role of profits and their measurement are fully discussed in S18.

The level of normal profit expected varies between industries. Some industries are notably free from risk; in such industries entrepreneurs may accept a normal profit of perhaps 8% on capital employed per year. In other industries economic and political risks may be such that an anticipated return of at least 20% per year is needed before an entrepreneur will set up a business unit.

Therefore normal profit is included by the economist in the costs of production. Any profit above this level is called *abnormal* or *surplus profit*; this can also be described as *monopoly profit* when it arises from a degree of monopoly power in the market.

Fixed and variable costs

Traditionally, economists have tended to distinguish between those costs which are fixed, i.e. unchanged in the short run, even if output changes, and those costs which change or vary as the volume of output changes, and are hence called variable costs.

Given a firm with two factories, machinery and other plant, no matter what the level of output, the cost of those factories and machinery (the fixed factors) has been incurred. If the entrepreneur sells nothing at all, he still has these fixed costs. The only way he is likely to change these fixed costs is by, say, doubling his factories or selling one of his factories, and this alteration of capital content is a long run decision. Hence, fixed costs can change if the *scale* of output changes but not if the level of output changes.

Variable costs change with every level of output no matter what scale of output is adopted. The hiring of an extra bricklayer is a variable cost to both the one-man builder or to the international building construction company. Additional output incurs an additional variable cost: in this case labour and extra bricks will be required. Variable costs will apply to any factors which are variable in the short run.

11·1

Divide the following list into fixed costs and variable costs.

Rent of factory
Local authority rates on factory and land
Normal profit
Wages of weekly workers
Salaries of executive staff
Fuel bills
Raw materials
Transport costs
Oil for machinery
Postage
Painting and repairs to buildings
Interest on bank loan for purchase of machinery
Pensions to former employees
Repairs to machinery

Depreciation

You will have noticed that repairs to buildings and machinery are variable costs, as they vary with the amount of use. It is also necessary to set aside money for the replacement of a firm's capital assets, mainly plant and machinery. The need for replacement is largely due to the wearing out of machinery and plant through constant usage in production; and obsolescence. Capital loses value, i.e. depreciates, for both of these reasons. It is therefore necessary for firms each year to set aside part of their revenue to cover depreciation, i.e. to replace their plant and equipment. When firms set aside a fixed percentage of the original price of the asset to cover obsolescence this money is a fixed cost because the capital will be out of date whether any production takes place or not. The wearing out of capital may be considered a variable cost when it is a function of the productive process.

Fixed and variable cost curves

Let us look at some figures based on an imaginary firm. Schedule A records the changes in fixed and variable costs at various levels of output of J. Enterprise & Co. Ltd., manufacturers of hover-trucks. Whilst the total fixed costs remain, by definition, constant over the range of output levels shown in the schedule, the total variable costs rise rapidly as more and more men are employed to increase the rate of output. Since more hover-trucks are being produced more raw materials are required as well.

SCHEDULE A					
Monthly output of Hover-trucks	Total fixed cost £	Total variable cost £	AFC £	AVC £	ATC £
20	1 000	920			
40	1 000	1 960			
60	1 000	2 540	16·66		
80	1 000	3 000			
100	1 000	3 550			
120	1 000	4 700		39·17	
140	1 000	6 500			

The first thing to do is to examine the contributions of fixed and variable costs to the total cost of producing each hover-truck at different rates of output.

The schedule indicates that, at this stage, we are interested in the cost, *per unit of output*, of producing hover-trucks. To do this we calculate the average fixed cost (AFC) and average variable cost (AVC) at each rate of output per month. For example, when 60 hover-trucks per month are produced the total fixed cost is £1 000. On average this amounts to $\frac{1\,000}{60}$ = £16·66 worth of fixed cost for every hover-truck made, i.e.

$$\text{AFC} = \frac{\text{Total fixed cost}}{\text{Output}}$$

Similarly when the monthly rate of output is 120, the variable costs amount to $\frac{4\,700}{120}$ = £39·17 worth of labour, materials, etc. used on average to produce each hover-truck. (AVC is, therefore, $\frac{\text{Total variable costs}}{\text{Output}}$). Economists normally present AFC and AVC in graphical form.

11·2

a Complete schedule A for yourself. Round off figures to one decimal place.

b Draw the graphs of AFC and AVC (y axis) plotted against output (x axis).

11·3

Which statement below is most accurate in describing what happens to average fixed cost as the monthly rate of output is raised?

A Average fixed cost falls at first and then tends to rise.

B Average fixed cost rises continuously.

C Average fixed cost falls at first and then becomes constant.

D Average fixed cost falls continuously.

11·4

What tends to happen to average variable costs as the rate of output is raised?

A Average variable cost falls at first and then tends to rise.

B Average variable cost rises continuously.

C Average variable cost falls continuously.

D Average variable cost falls at first and then becomes constant.

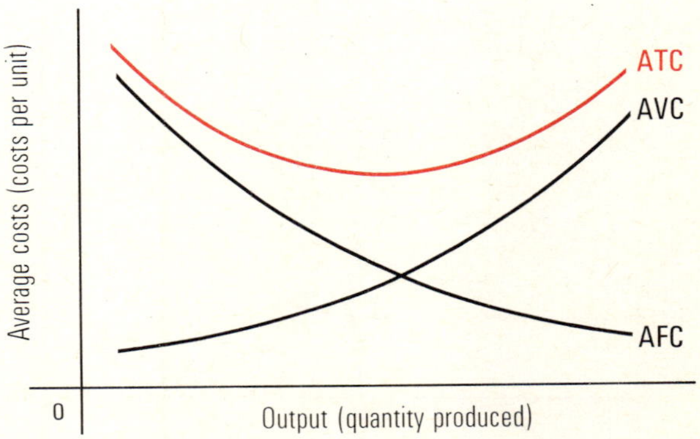

Figure 11·2

The shape of the average cost curve

Since total fixed costs remain unchanged, whatever the level of output, the greater the output, the lower the value of average fixed costs. (Total variable costs rise as output increases, but not at a constant rate.) While output per variable factor is increasing the same outlay on extra variable factors helps to produce a greater number of units, so average variable costs fall. As more and more variable factors are added to the fixed factors the output per variable factor eventually starts to decline (in accordance with the law of variable proportions), so the costs of the variable factors required to produce each unit, i.e. average variable costs, begin to rise. Therefore the operation of the law of variable proportions means that the average variable costs curve is J-shaped.

The addition of average fixed and average variable costs provides average total costs, or simply, average costs. Figure 11·2 depicts the separate AFC and AVC curves, and the effect of their addition to form the average total cost curve (ATC or AC). Therefore the short-run average total cost curve is U-shaped because diminishing returns to the variable factors beyond output OL cause average variable costs to rise. Figure 11·3 depicts the normal shape of the short run average cost curve, and shows that OM is the output at which minimum average cost is achieved. Two remarks can be made about this AC curve. First, the symmetrical U-shaped average cost curve is an economist's model: firms' average cost curves do fall and rise, but they are not symmetrical. Secondly, we cannot tell how much a firm will produce merely by looking at the average cost curve: *firms do not necessarily seek to produce the minimum average cost output* (sometimes called optimum output or optimum capacity): they produce an output which will bring maximum profits, and this may be OM, or above or below OM, depending on market conditions.

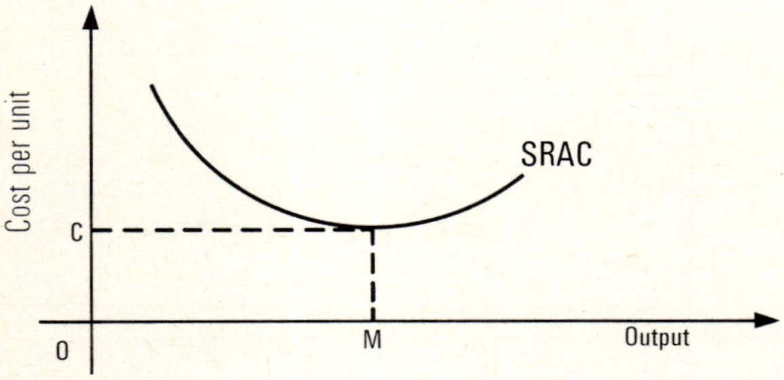

Figure 11·3

11·5

Calculate total cost for each level of output shown in schedule A, and find the values of Average Total Cost = $\frac{\text{Total Costs}}{\text{Output}}$ Complete the figures in the ATC column in schedule A and draw the ATC curve.

11·6

a **i** In figure 11·2 what is the significance of the vertical distance between ATC and AVC at each level of output?

ii In figure 11·2 why does ATC continue to fall for a short range of output beyond the minimum AVC output OL?

b Study the graph drawn for exercise 11·5.

i If 30 hover-trucks per month are produced, how much will each one cost on average:
A £36 **B** £90

ii If the output is increased to 50 per month, by how much will the average cost fall?
A £24 **B** £70

iii At what monthly rate of production is average cost at a minimum?
A 86 **B** 105

Marginal cost

Before we can begin to determine what ouput will bring firms the maximum profits we must examine the concept of marginal cost. *Marginal cost* is the change in total costs which occur as output changes by one unit. Expressed symbolically

$$MC = \frac{\delta TC}{\delta O} \text{ or } MC_n = TC_n - TC_{n-1}$$

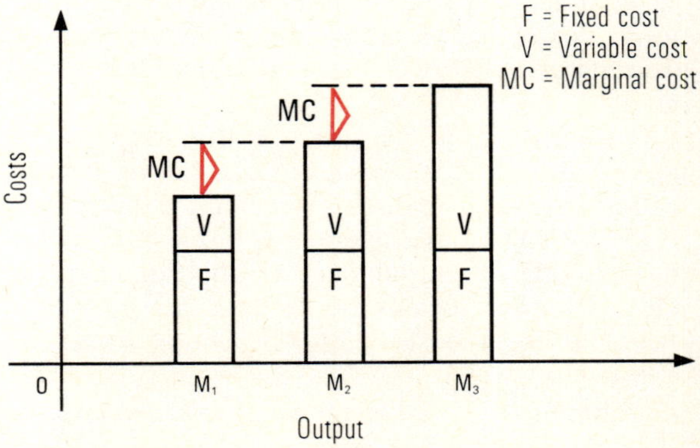

Figure 11·4

Figure 11·4 shows costs of production at three levels of output. Fixed costs remain constant over this range of output. Variable costs increase as output rises. Total costs at each output are (F + V). The increase in total costs is the difference between total costs at OM_1 and OM_2 (or OM_2 and OM_3). This is the marginal cost.

Suppose the information available to you shows the change in total costs when the level of output has risen by 10 units, then you must divide by ten the increase in total costs which subsequently occurs, in order to calculate MC. This is a practical technique which is necessary when the interval is greater than one unit of output.

11·7

Data: the correct answer to exercise 11·5.

Check that you have the correct answer and then write out your data like this:

Output per month	TC	MC
20	1 920	
		$\frac{1040}{20} = 52$
40	2 960	
		$\frac{580}{20} = 29$
60	3 540	
80	etc	
etc		

Notice that the marginal cost is written in between the lines (like other marginal data).

i Now complete this schedule of TC and MC.

ii Graph the MC data (after checking that you have obtained the correct answers). N.B. y axis shows costs, x axis shows output.

iii Add to ii the AC curve calculated in exercise 11·5.

See satellite *Arithmetical and Statistical Methods* for further advice.

The relationship between the AC and MC curves

The average cost curve and the marginal cost curve are the two basic economic concepts used in the analysis of a firm. Marginal cost is the change in total costs arising from a *unitary* change in output.

11·8

To ensure that you know the arithmetical relationship between TC, AC and MC, complete the following schedule and draw two graphs, one of TC and one for MC. You should then be able to answer correctly exercises 11·9, 11·10 and 11·11.

SCHEDULE B

Schedule of output/costs for garments

Weekly output units	AC £	TC £	MC £
200	. . . . .	1 000	
			3·44
400	. . . . .	1 688	
			. . . . .
600	3·42	. . . . .	
			1·34
800	2·90	. . . . .	
			1·40
1 000	2·60	. . . . .	
			. . . . .
1 200	. . . . .	3 000	
			3·20
1 400	2·60	. . . . .	
			. . . . .
1 600	. . . . .	4 640	

11·9

At what output level is MC equal to AC?

A 2·50 **B** 2·52 **C** 1 200 **D** 1 300

11·10

At which of the following levels of output is MC less than AC?

A 1 100 **B** 1 200 **C** 1 300 **D** 1 400

11·11

Suppose the market price for the garments in exercise 11·8 were £2·90. Between what levels of output would both average and marginal cost be lower than the price for which these garments can be sold?

A 750 to 1 600 **B** 800 to 1 270
C 300 to 1 200 **D** 800 to 1 200

Long-run costs

We have dealt so far with the short-run situation where fixed costs are combined with variable costs. In the long run, all costs are variable, for the short-run fixed equipment can now be changed. The tractor has replaced the farm horse, the motor bus the railway branch line service and in truth who knows what may be invented tomorrow. Some commodities like transistor radios have become cheaper in recent years, other commodities have become dearer, so that presumably costs of production have fallen in the case of radios. The cost of air travel fell after 1945 and now shows every indication of rising.

At any point in time, if we examine a firm's costs, then we will see a U-shaped short-run curve displaying the results of the law of variable proportions. A long run average cost curve may be drawn tangential to the series of short-run AC curves.

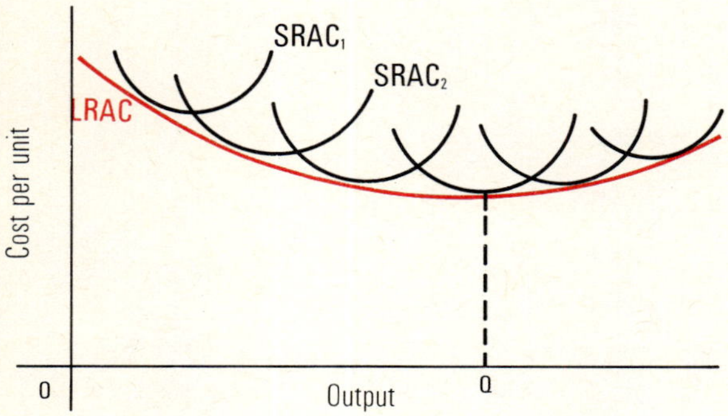

Figure 11·5

This long-run average cost curve eventually rises. The firm can become too large to manage efficiently, and rising administrative costs cause average costs to rise. In this case, we assume that the entrepreneur is the fixed factor. However, like all models, it is of limited application. In the long run, by definition, all things can be changed.

Revenue

At the beginning of this section it was stated that production was the result of the entrepreneur's effort in organising the other factors of production in a business unit. Production will not take place unless there is a demand for the product or a demand can be created. To the firm the demand for its product is shown by the amount of money its customers are willing to spend on purchasing a quantity of units of output at each price. We will continue to use J. Enterprise & Co. as our model as we explore further aspects of the firm assuming, firstly, that the firm operates in an imperfect market and is faced by a falling demand curve; and secondly, that it operates in a perfect market and is faced by a horizontal demand curve.

11·12

The table below shows the relationship between price per unit and the quantity bought for hover-trucks. For each sales level, calculate the total revenue received for each level of sales.

SCHEDULE C		
Price per unit (£) average revenue	Sales per month	Total revenue TR (£)
130	20	2 600
110	40	?....
90	60	?....
70	80	?....
50	100	?....
30	120	?....

The curve DD shown in figure 11·7 is constructed from the data of the first two columns. This curve represents the demand for hover-trucks. It is also the average revenue of J. Enterprise & Co. As average revenue is equal to total revenue divided by total sales, it is also the price of the product.

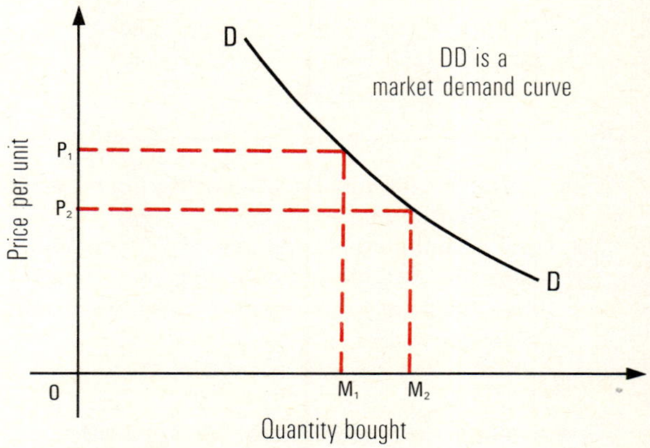

Figure 11·6

11·13

Using the information correctly calculated for exercise 11·12, say which of the following statements is true:

- **A** As the price per unit rises, the total revenue of the firm increases.
- **B** As the price per unit falls, the total revenue of the firm increases.
- **C** As the price per unit rises, the total revenue of the firm falls.
- **D** As the price per unit falls, the total revenue of the firm rises.
- **E** All of these are true but at different price levels.

11·14

Data: correct answer to exercise 11·12. Examine the change in total revenue as prices change.

A Between £30 and £50.
B Between £50 and £70.
C Between £70 and £90.
D Between £90 and £110.
E Between £110 and £130.

In which instance(s) is a price *rise* accompanied by an *increase* in total revenue?

Marginal revenue

A change in the quantity of sales will cause a change in the total revenue received by the person or firm selling the product. The change in total revenue, resulting from a change in sales by one unit is called the *marginal revenue*.

Symbolically $MR = \frac{\delta TR}{\delta O}$, or,

$MR_n = TR_n - TR_{n-1}$

As you have seen above, total revenue can increase or decrease when the commodity price changes, so marginal revenue may be positive or negative.

11·15

The information in schedule D refers to a firm in imperfect or monopolistic competition.

SCHEDULE D

Sales	Total revenue in imperfect market	Marginal revenue	Average revenue
20	2 600		130
		$+\frac{1\,800}{20} = 90$	
40	4 400		110
		50	
60	5 400		90
		....	
80	5 600		......
		....	
100	5 000		......
		−70	
120	3 600		......

a Calculate average revenue (AR) and marginal revenue (MR).
b Plot the average and marginal revenue curves on graph paper. The result should look similar to figure 11·7.

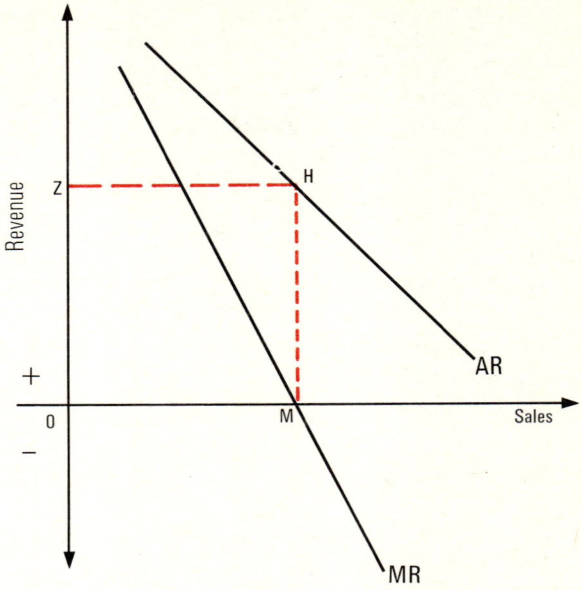

Figure 11·7

The AR curve shows the relationship between price and level of sales. The MR curve shows incremental changes in total revenue as the sales level changes.

At point OM, in figure 11·7, MR is zero. For sales levels up to OM, a fall in price down as far as OZ increases total revenue; MR is positive. For sales levels beyond OM, a fall in price reduces total revenue; MR is negative. The point H on the average revenue curve is the point at which OM is sold at a price OZ. If the price is reduced below OZ the sales will extend beyond OM, and total revenue will fall, as shown by the negative MR. At this stage it is not possible to say what quantity between O and M will be offered for sale, because this diagram does not show the costs of production.

Relationship between average and marginal revenue

Figure 11·7 shows that the firm for which the demand curve is drawn is operating in conditions of imperfect competition, because it is necessary to reduce the price of the article in order to sell more. Therefore in imperfect competition the average revenue will always be greater than marginal revenue (AR > MR); the price (AR) of the last unit sold will exceed the addition to total revenue (MR) from the sale because there has been a price cut on the previous units sold. However, as you already know from S5, in perfect competition each firm accepts that the price is set by market forces beyond its own control. In this case the market price for each firm is constant, whatever the amount (OM_1, OM_2, OM_3) an individual firm offers for sale. The demand curve is a horizontal straight line, as in figure 11·8.

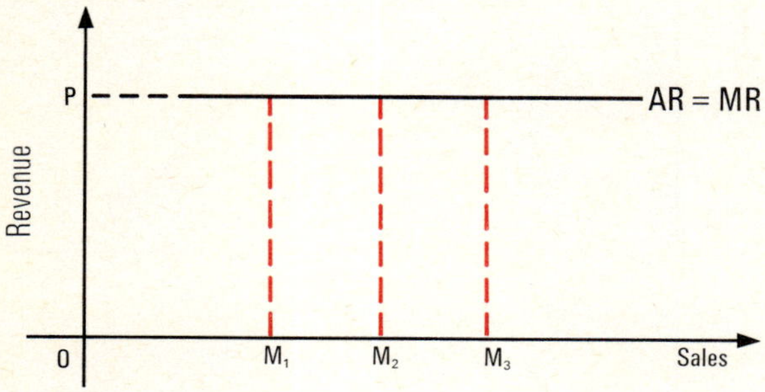

Figure 11·8

11·16

From the following data, plot on graph paper the AR and MR curves. (Ensure that you use scales similar to those fixed for the previous cost and revenue curves for hover-trucks. See exercises 11·2 and 11·7.)

SCHEDULE E			
Sales	**Total Revenue in perfect market**	**MR**	**AR**
20	900		......
40	1 800	......	......
60	2 700	......	......
80	3 600	......	......
100	4 500	......	......
110	4 950	......	......
120	5 400	......	......

The short-run equilibrium of the firm

You now have two basic sets of data about a hypothetical firm J. Enterprise & Co.; the *costs* of production, as determined by the economic structure of the firm, and the anticipated *revenue* pattern, determined by two possible market situations in which the firm assumes it operates.

In schedule D average revenue is falling and so is marginal revenue. If the firm selects a price at which it wishes to sell its goods then it will have to accept a given level of sales, i.e. at £90 it will sell 60 hover-trucks. It can set either price or sales, because this is imperfect competition, but it cannot set both. If it decides to sell 40 hovertrucks then if it charges more than £110, it will not succeed.

Turn to schedule E and as you will have found, MR = AR = £45, so that if our hypothetical firm (which we now assume is operating in conditions of perfect competition), intends to sell hover-trucks at more than £45 each, its competitors, given the conditions of perfect competition, will take all the buyers. Hence £45 is the market price and all our firm can do is to decide how many units it wishes to sell at this given price.

In the exercises which follow, it is assumed that the output and sales figures are identical, that is, the entire output of the firm is actually sold and there is, thus, no problem of stock piling.

11·17

Take two pieces of graph paper. On one plot the AC and MC curves from exercises 11·2 and 11·7 and the AR and MR curves from exercise 11·16. On the other plot the AC and MC curves and the AR and MR curves from exercise 11·15.

11·18

At what output/sales level does J. Enterprise & Co., maximise its profits in both markets? These alternatives refer to your graphs constructed in exercise 11·17.

A Where average costs of production are a minimum.
B Where total revenue is a maximum.
C Where marginal cost equals marginal revenue.
D Where marginal cost is a minimum.
E Where marginal revenue is exactly zero.

The easiest way to arrive at the answer to this question is to deduct total costs from total revenue at each level of sales. Complete this question before reading further. Mark the correct output at which profits are maximised on your graphs as a vertical straight line through the appropriate output figure.

The output where MC = MR is important because this is where profits are maximised, which is the prime aim of entrepreneurs. This output is called the equilibrium output: there is no reason for producers to move from this position.

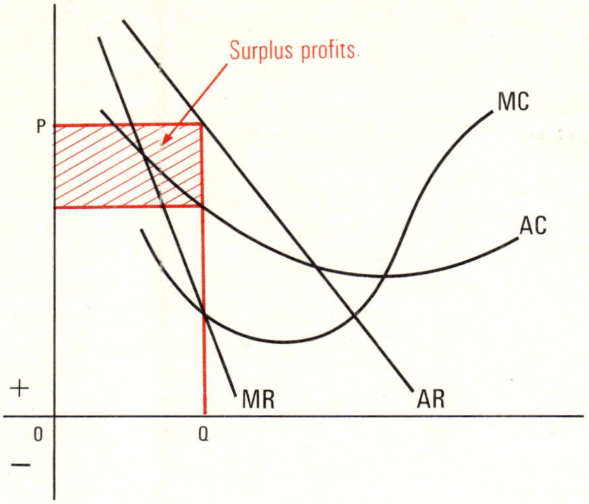

Figure 11·9

Profit maximising under monopoly

Figure 11·9 shows a seller faced with a downward sloping demand curve. At what point will he maximise his profits? At an output less than OQ marginal revenue is greater than marginal cost (MR > MC) and as he increases his output towards OQ, every extra unit of output brings in more revenue than it costs to produce. At an output greater than OQ, each additional unit costs more to produce than it brings in revenue (MR < MC). At outputs less than OQ the entrepreneur, in search of greater profits, will expand production until he reaches OQ the point of maximum profit. The monopolist can earn surplus, or monopoly profits, at output OQ, because AR > AC. Total monopoly profits are shown by the shaded area in figure 11·9.

Equilibrium under monopoly

A monopolist is a firm that can influence either the price or supply of the product in the market. *It cannot do both.*

The position we have just described, where MR = MC, is the point of equilibrium. In figure 11·9 having chosen a price (OP), then given an existing demand curve (AR) it follows that he can sell only the output (OQ) appropriate to that price. If he has an output OQ, then if he is determined to sell all that output, he must select the price (OP) consistent with that demand curve.

11·19

Why can a monopolist not raise his selling price to an unlimited extent?

- **A** The laws of the land make it illegal.
- **B** Even if the commodity was the only one bought, there is a limit to the amount of money which people have available.
- **C** There are always some indirect substitutes for a commodity.
- **D** Apart from water, people can always do without the particular product, so the market will disappear.

11·20

How does the monopolist seek to affect the market price for his commodity?

- **A** By creating artificial scarcity for his product by withholding supplies and so inducing consumers to pay a higher price than would rule under perfect competition.
- **B** Simply by raising the price at which he offers the goods for sale, so that the perfect competition price is exceeded.
- **C** By ensuring that there is no competitor able to offer a close substitute for the monopolised commodity within the market.

The power of the monopolist over supply

Monopolists in theory are single firms, but in practice are defined in the United Kingdom as any firm which sells about one third or more of the total supply of a commodity. The power of the monopolist to control the total supply to the market may rest on a variety of bases, designed to prevent the entry of competitors. Legal monopolies may be granted, based on patents, copyrights or registered designs. In some cases the capital costs of setting up a rival firm may effectively prevent entry of competitors into the market. Sometimes the known market demand is considered to be insufficient to provide a profitable business to more than one supplier. Component firms within an industry have amalgamated in the past to produce a monopoly which has grown in size and in efficiency so that economies of scale resulted in an AC curve at a much lower level than was possible under competitive conditions. There is no prior reason for stating that price under monopoly conditions will be higher than under perfect competition. In fact, the economies of large scale competition may lead to a cost structure which results in lower prices.

Degree of monopoly

The degree of monopoly is the control that a

firm can exercise over a market and is shown by the size of its monopoly profits (see figure 11·9). The larger the monopoly profit, i.e. the greater the excess of AR over AC, the greater will be the control, or the degree of monopoly, that a firm has over the market.

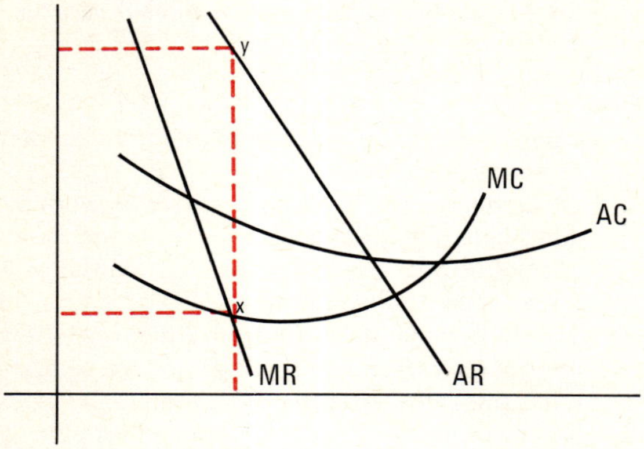

Figure 11·10

The second way of indicating monopoly power is to look at the difference between AR and MR at the most profitable rate of output. In figure 11·10 this difference is clearly shown, and may be measured along the 'y' axis. This depends on the position and the elasticity of demand, which indicates the responsiveness of the level of sales to a change in the price charged by the monopolist. An expansion of sales in this case, will not add much to total revenue because of the relative size of the price reduction needed to increase the quantity demanded. As the average revenue curve falls rapidly it would be expected that MR will also fall rapidly (e.g. the steep MR curve in figure 11·10): hence the distance between MR and AR will indicate monopoly power. Remember that the power of a monopoly to control price increases as the AR curve becomes nearer to a vertical line. In figure 11·10 MC>MR beyond OM, thus further sales become unprofitable.

Our analysis has therefore shown, that when marginal costs are equal to marginal revenue we locate a rational output which achieves maximum profit. We have also seen how marginal costs are related to average costs and how marginal revenue is related to average revenue. The difference between average revenue and average cost, multiplied by output, at each output level, gives the amount of surplus profit.

Price discrimination by a monopolist

It is quite possible for a firm to be a monopolist in terms of a local, regional, or national market, while at the same time there is intense competition between that firm and its rivals in wider markets, particularly in international markets. Consequently the monopolist may face two quite separate demand curves, and under certain conditions he may charge different prices to different groups of consumers.

Where markets are separated, perhaps by legal restrictions, by distance, or, as in some cases, by time, e.g. the demand for telephone services, and demand conditions are such that the elasticity of demand (explained later in more detail) differs in each market, the monopolist will maximise his profits by charging different prices in each market.

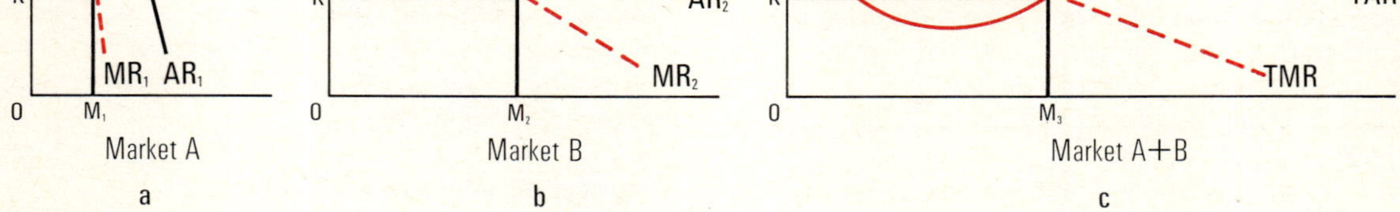

Figure 11·11

As figure 11·11 shows, we assume there is only one MC curve because it is the same firm which produces the commodity for both markets. The monopolist can combine the demand curves in each separate market to form a total average revenue and a total marginal revenue curve, shown in figure 11·11c. Against this he can set his marginal cost curve and produce the output OM_3 at which MC = MR = OK. The total output is then divided between the markets A and B in such a way that the marginal cost OK at output OM_3 equals the marginal revenue in each market, and so he will maximise profits in each market. Reading from the separate demand curves, the monopolist will sell a small amount OM_1 of his total output in market A at a relatively high price OP_1, and sell the larger part OM_2 at a lower price OP_2 in market B, where demand is more elastic. The ability to charge different prices in different markets will depend on whether elasticities of demand differ, and whether there are any extra costs involved in keeping the markets separate, to ensure that, for example, consumers in market B do not resell the product to consumers in Market A at a price lower than OP_1.

Equilibrium of the firm under perfect competition

Under perfect competition the seller believes that he is faced with so many competitors that he must take the market price as given. He can sell as many units as he wants in the market for his commodity and, because his share of the market is so small, he does not expect his sales to affect market price.

If he withholds his supply from the market he will not expect his action to affect the market price. If he raises his selling price above the market price, consumers will buy or substitute the products of competitors, and he will sell none. As a result the demand curve (i.e. AR) for any product under the assumed condition of perfect competition is a horizontal straight line, so AR = MR.

As we know, whatever the degree of competition, a firm will aim to produce its maximum profit output, where MR = MC. Therefore in perfect competition, since AR = MR, maximum profit output will be where MC = MR = AR. But we must bear in mind an additional assumption about perfect competition: *the assumption that factors are completely mobile,* and therefore that new firms will enter the industry if existing firms are making surplus profits, i.e. as long as AR > AC. When new firms enter they increase the total supply of the industry, so the market price available to each firm falls, until all surplus profits are eliminated and AR again just equals AC, meaning that firms are just making normal profits. By a similar argument if firms are temporarily making losses (AR < AC), firms will leave the industry, and the total supply of the industry will be reduced. The market price will rise until it equals AC again and the remaining firms are making normal profits. We can therefore conclude that in perfect competition the equilibrium output of the firm is reached when

MR = MC (profit maximisation)
AR = MR (infinite quantity demanded at market price)
AR = AC (normal profits only)
Therefore AC = MC (output produced at minimum average cost).

This equilibrium position is depicted in figure 11·12. Notice also that at the equilibrium output OM price (AR) equals MC. The price people are prepared to pay must cover the marginal cost of production.

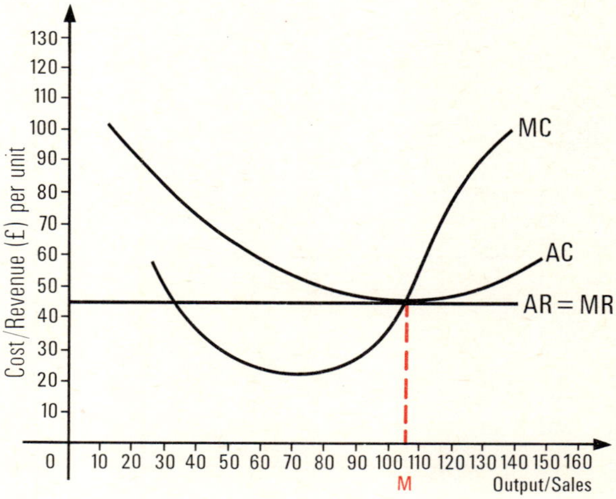

Figure 11·12

Figure 11·13 depicts a situation in which, because of a rise in demand for the product, the market price has risen. The firm reacts by increasing output until MR = MC. Notice that the firm makes surplus profits temporarily (AR > AC), and the maximum profit output OM is above minimum average cost output. Figure 11·14 depicts a situation in which demand has fallen and the market price has fallen below average cost. The firm is making a loss (AR < AC). Notice that the firm still produces an output at which MC = MR, in this case ensuring minimum losses rather than maximum profits. The minimum loss output OM is below minimum average cost output.

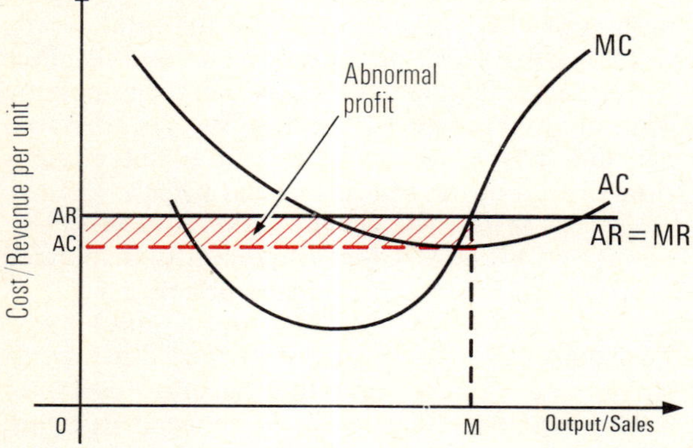

Figure 11·13

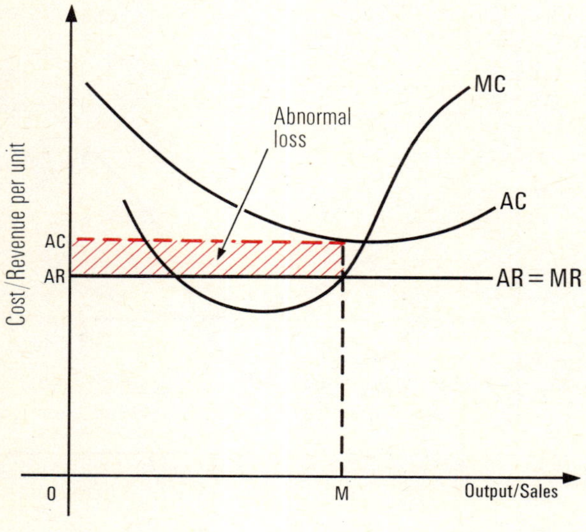

Figure 11·14

11·21

Data: graph above, figure 11·12.

a What sales level would yield maximum profit under perfect competition?

A 75 **B** 90 **C** 105 **D** 120

b What output is AC at its minimum?

A 75 **B** 90 **C** 105 **D** 120

How can a firm continue making a loss in the short run? If a firm's revenue exceeds its AVC then there is some contribution towards his fixed costs. Suppose ATC equal £2 000 per unit, of which 800 is AFC. If he earns more than £1 200 (AVC), say £1 400, then he is covering his variable costs, labour and so on, and getting £200 towards his fixed or capital costs. If he does not produce at all, he does not even earn £200 towards his fixed costs. This is patently a short-run situation, and the firm will only continue production if it is confident that by reorganisation will it reach an equilibrium position where all costs are covered.

In real-life terms, if a firm can pay its workers and buy raw materials it can carry on business in the short-run. How long the short-run will be depends on the willingness of the landlord and other creditors to wait for payment of fixed costs.

Equilibrium under monopolistic or imperfect competition

Monopoly and perfect competition represent opposite market situations. Between the two lies a range of imperfect market activity, at times closely resembling the situation described under perfect competition and at other times approaching a monopolistic market. Any movement through the spectrum of market imperfections necessitates the removal of some and at times all the assumptions adopted in these limiting cases. However, under imperfect competition the equilibrium output of the firm is always given by the equation MR = MC.

The main difference between perfect and imperfect competition is that the outputs of each firm in imperfect competition tend to be differentiated, though the products are close substitutes for one another. As a result each firm can vary the price of its product by varying output. The firm faces a downward-sloping demand curve. The usual method of product differentiation is by marking the product with some kind of brand name or by packaging it in some distinctive way. Once such differentiation occurs, each firm's market is separate from that of its rivals. This separation may be of course, the result of advertising, but so long as the distinction is real enough to the customer, it will be possible for each firm's product price to differ by small amounts. Some firms may then be able to increase their profits by raising the price at which they offer their goods for sale; other firms who are more efficient may keep their prices low and sell proportionately more, and also increase their profits. Customers' loyalty can be obtained, not only by price competition, but also by the use of sophisticated advertising techniques. So long as total revenue rises by more than the cost of the advertising (MR > MC) then it will pay to advertise, because profits will rise.

In conditions of monopolistic competition there is a large number of competing firms within the industry, so that no one firm has control over raw materials or the factors of production. New rival firms cannot be prevented from entering the industry. More efficient firms will tend to compete effectively and depress the current market prices. Alternatively, by offering higher rewards in order to obtain the factors of production which they require, they tend to raise the costs of production (thus shifting the competitors AC curves to the left or upwards). Rival firms who may not be efficient enough to absorb the higher costs may then become marginal, and may go out of business, as their brand name proves insufficiently strong to hold their customers in the face of rising prices. For example, a housewife may buy X detergent at 10p per packet, or 11p per packet, but at 20p she might switch to Y brand, irrespective of the pull of X. Figure 11·15 shows how costs and market prices for some firms may rise and their output fall as a result of such competition. Clearly, the industry as a whole is in a very unstable equilibrium. Even though the total number of firms may remain almost constant, there will be a change in the identity of those who comprise the industry.

In figure 11·15 firm A is most efficient and can make substantial monopoly profit even though it sells at the lowest price of the firms in the industry. For simplicity, the market shown is similar for all firms concerned. Firm B is one of a group of less efficient firms and its unit costs are higher. By branding or advertising it can charge a slightly higher price than firm A, but it still makes less monopoly profit. Firm C is typical of a group of marginal firms who, despite a high selling price, only just cover unit costs.

The effect of increasing competition may alter the market which each firm faces. For those selling at higher price levels, consumers may be more and more sensitive to price changes. The AR curve may be drawn less steeply in the case of firm C than firm B, and firm B less steeply than firm A.

The equilibrium output of each firm in a monopolistic or an imperfect competition will be where MC = MR, but when price (AR) = AC no monopoly surplus or abnormal profit is being made. However, *when* MR = MC *and price is above AC at the equilibrium output, then some monopoly profit must be made.*

11·22

What constitutes equilibrium output under any form of competition?

A AR = AC **B** AR = MC
C MR = MC **D** MR = AC

11·23

Which of the following, *on its own,* would tell you that a particular firm in equilibrium experienced imperfect competitive conditions?

A AR > AC **B** AR > MC
C MR > MC **D** MR > AC

Equilibrium under oligopoly

Oligopoly is a form of monopolistic or imperfect competition which exists where there are relatively

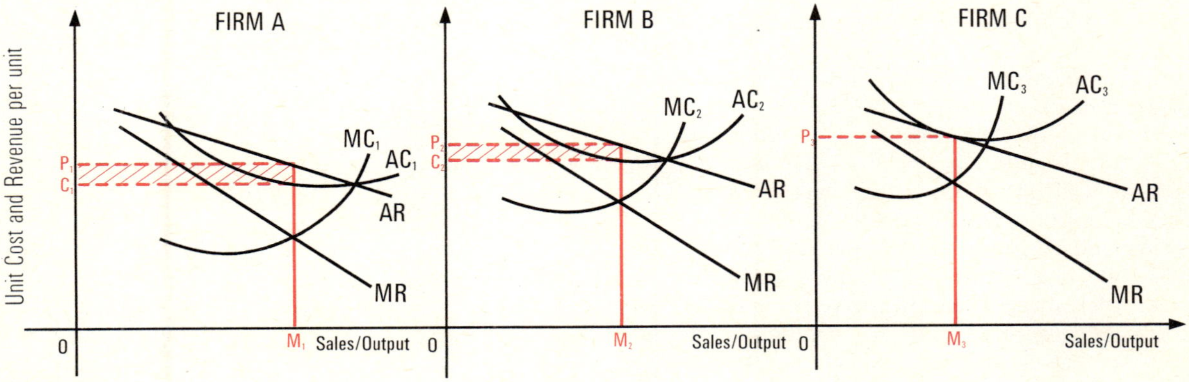

Figure 11·15

few firms competing within a given industry. Each firm's entrepreneurs tend to know the cost and revenue situation of rivals. In perfect oligopoly, where the product is virtually the same, such as petrol, competition tends to take almost any form except price competition. The market price may remain stable and uniform for long periods. This is because price competition between a small group of competitors would tend to be very fierce, and each firm may fear that it would lose the price war which would ensue, and be forced out of business. Any price difference would lead to rapid substitution of one firms' product for anothers'. Consequently there is normally a tacit agreement on a common price, and competition in services. For example, a petroleum company may charge the same price for the same quality of petrol as its rivals, but offer better facilities at its service stations.

However, the greater the ease of substitution of one product for another by consumers the greater will be the tendency to minimise price differentials. If the buying public can remember the names of the producers (or their brand names) because there are relatively few competing in the market, then more substitution of one firm's products for another will take place.

11·24

Make lists of the manufacturers and brand names known to you for the following products: petrol, baked beans, instant coffee, canned peaches.

Which are produced under oligopoly?

The oligopolistic group of competitors may try to reduce the effect of competition by various forms of collusion. Most countries have extensive and complex legislation to prevent such activity whether the agreements are formal or just 'gentlemen's agreements'. (See satellite *Monopolies and Restrictive Practices*.)

Figure 11·16 shows one of the oligopolists who is making an abnormal profit. The collusive price, OP_1, is well above minimum average cost, OP_2, and the output, OM_1, is substantially less than that which might apply under perfect competition, OM_2. Besides this 'restriction' in output, other forms of restrictive practice may be found. Oligopolists may share out markets on a regional or local basis so that every firm can make a 'good living'. An agreement may be made to tender for work

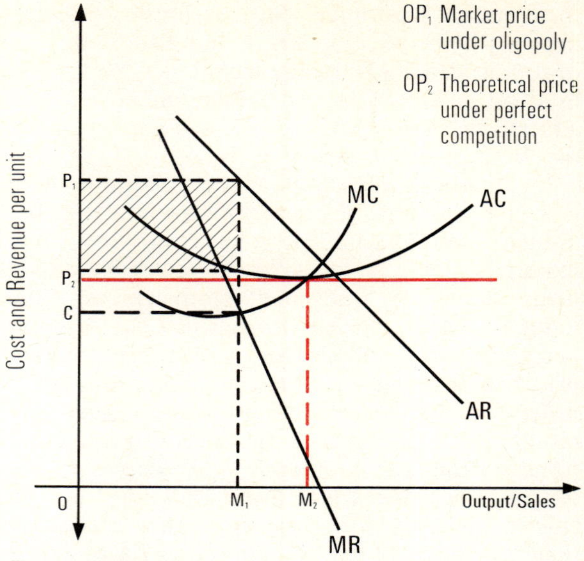

Figure 11·16

from national or local government, so that one firm makes the lowest bid, and is almost certain to be awarded the contract.

Duopoly

A special case of oligopoly is duopoly, where there are two firms. Competition is either very intense or collusion reaches such a pitch that competition is so restricted as to be non-existent.

11·25

Assume the cost data used in exercise 11·8, for which you already have a graph drawn and the revenue data from the table below. What will be the most profitable weekly output at which this firm should produce, assuming all the output is sold?

A 375 **B** 875 **C** 1 100 **D** 1 200

Output of garments per week	Market A AR (£)
200	6·00
400	5·40
600	4·80
800	4·20
1 000	3·60
1 200	3·00
1 400	2·40
1 600	1·80

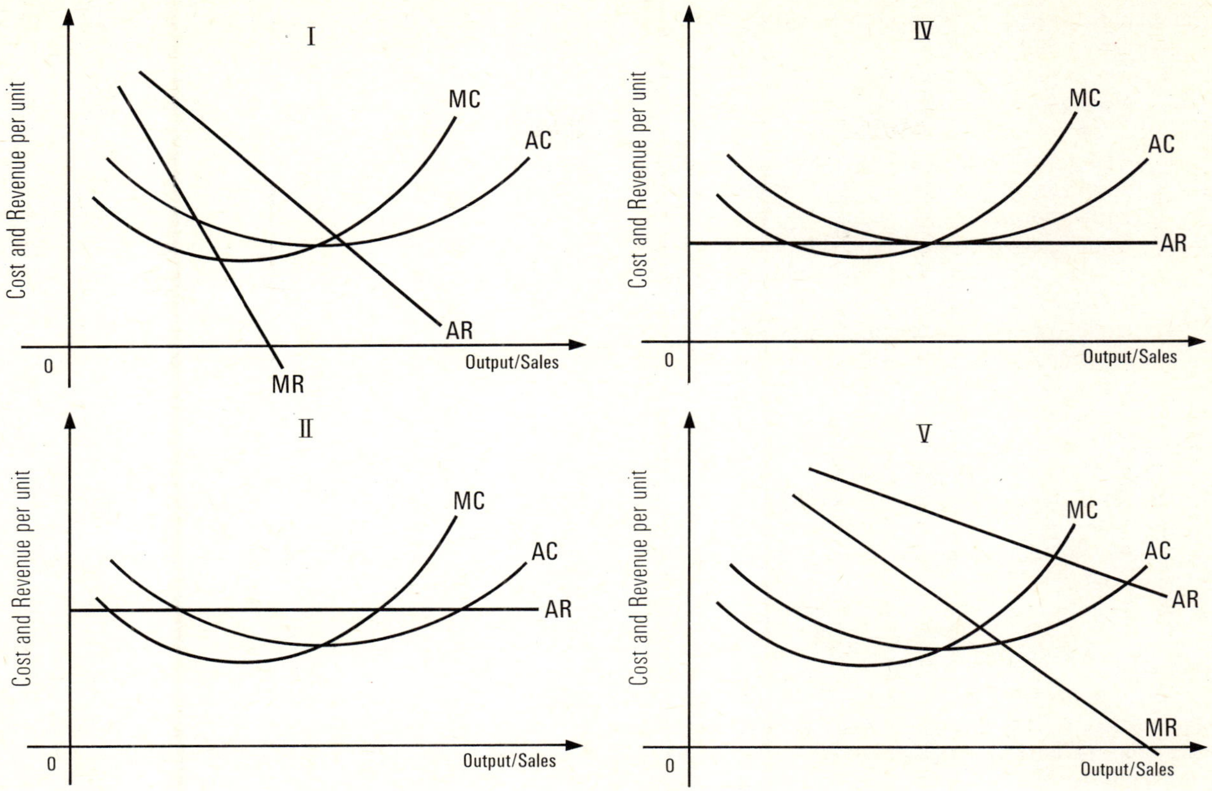

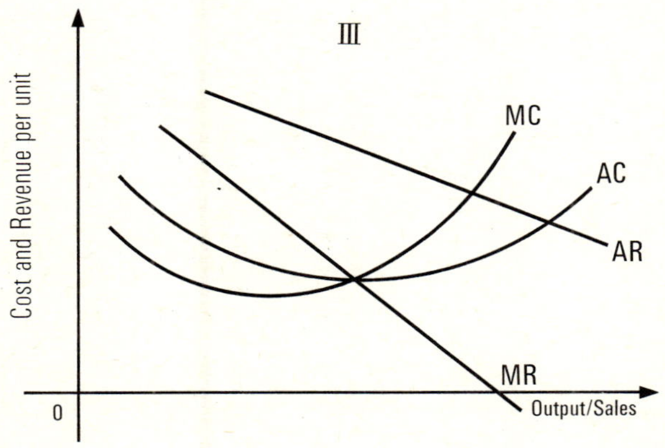

Figure 11·17

11·26

Figure 11·17 shows five market situations (I to V) for a hypothetical firm. Optimum capacity is that at which AC is a minimum, i.e. where MC = AC.

Identify each of the following:

a A firm producing at a level above optimum capacity in an imperfect market.
A II **B** III **C** IV **D** V

b A firm producing at optimum capacity in a perfect market.
A I **B** II **C** III **D** IV

c A firm producing at less than optimum capacity in a perfect market.
A II **B** III **C** IV **D** None of those drawn.

d A firm producing at less than optimum capacity in an imperfect market.
A I **B** III **C** V **D** None of those drawn.

e A firm producing above optimum capacity in a perfect market.
A I **B** II **C** IV **D** V

f A firm producing at optimum capacity in an imperfect market.
A I **B** III **C** V **D** None of those drawn.

11·27

Data as for exercise 11·17, I and IV.

Comparing the perfect competition model with the monopoly model, which of the following general statements is true (unless economies of scale are possible in a monopoly)?

A Under perfect competition, more of the commodity is offered for sale at a higher price than under monopoly.

B Under perfect competition, less of the commodity is offered for sale at a higher price than under monopoly.

C Under perfect competition, more of the commodity is offered for the sale at a lower price than under monopoly.

D Under perfect competition, less of the commodity is offered for sale at a lower price than under monopoly.

11·28

Check the following statements.

a 'Under perfect competition no profit is made.'

A True **B** False

b 'Under perfect competition in equilibrium no profit is made'.

A True **B** False

11·29

Make out two lists, one for similarities and one for differences, to show the difference between a market situation of perfect competition and of monopoly, as they affect the individual firm.

THE THEORY OF THE MARKET

Perfect competition

In perfect competition, all the firms together offer various quantities of a commodity at each price level. Let us see how much will be offered in total at price OP_1. If all the firms are in equilibrium, MC = MR, the quantity supplied equals, in this example a + b. (See figure 11·18.)

Suppose the price goes up to OP_2, then the existing producers will be prepared to increase output quite quickly so that, in the short run a greater quantity will now be offered. In the long run, more firms will join the industry. In response to the abnormal profits which arise when the price goes up to OP_2 individual firms have increased output.

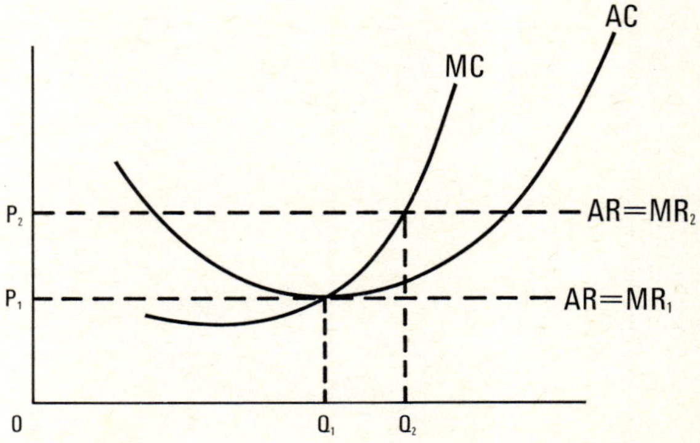

Figure 11·19

The individual firms supply curve is its marginal cost curve and each firm will expand output, given its present capital structure, to the point where MC = MR (see figure 11·19). Therefore, as price changes from OP_1 to OP_2 the point where MC = MR has moved along the MC curve so that in the short run the individual firm offers a greater quantity of output for sale.

If we take an individual firm (see figure 11·20), an increase in price from OP_1 to OP_2 will cause each firm in equilibrium to increase its production from OQ_1 to OQ_2. The sum of all these increases

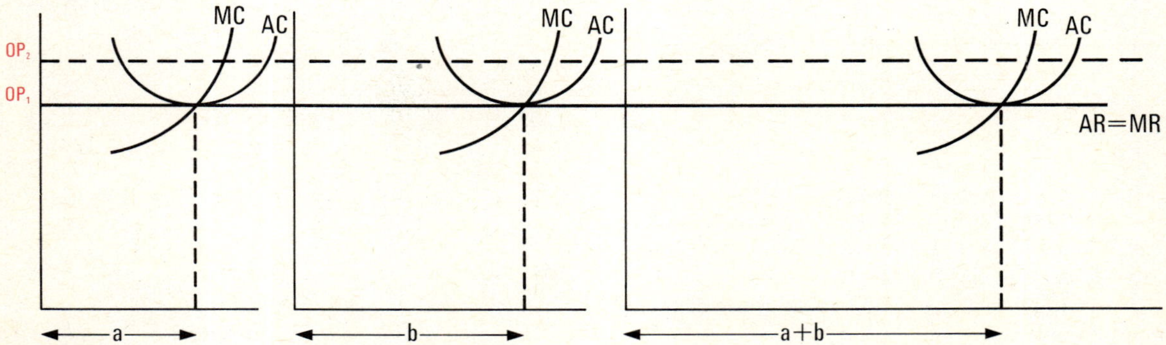

Figure 11·18

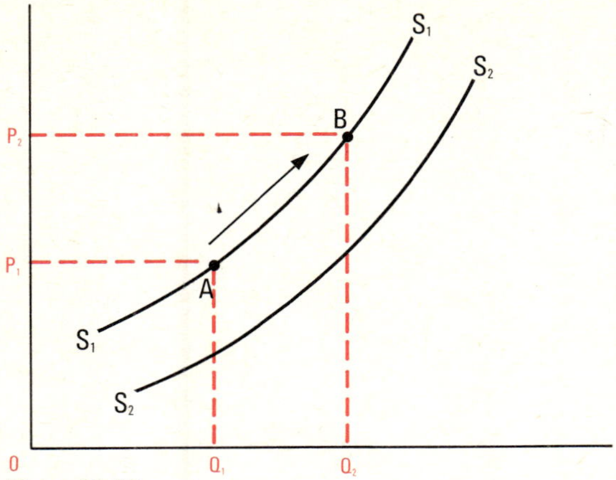

Figure 11·20

constitutes a short run increase in the quantity supplied from that industry from A to B. Since all the firms are now earning abnormal profits (given no change in factor prices) more firms will be attracted to the industry and there will be a further long-run effect increasing supply from S_1S_1 to S_2S_2, i.e. a new situation so that S_1S_1 will be replaced by S_2S_2 (see figure 11·20). Remember that the long-run is the period when *all* factors including capital such as factory size and so on, can be altered.

Monopoly

As there is only one firm, that firm is also the industry. How much it will supply is given by the marginal cost curve intersecting with the marginal revenue curve; hence it can be argued that there is no supply curve in the sense that there is in perfect competition. Quantity bought and sold depends on both MC and MR.

Monopolistic or imperfect competition

Is there a supply curve in this situation? This is very complicated because we have first to decide if soap A and soap B are different commodities or the same commodity. Are we talking about the supply of soap, or of two supply curves, one for brand A and the other for brand B? At this stage in your studies it is easier to treat A and B as two separate commodities and take it that the quantity bought and sold is given by the equation MR = MC. What is most probable is that the two firms will have an unwritten agreement not to charge less than a price at which both make a profit and confine their competition to advertising gift offers, or like the joint stock banks, to services. As competition is non-price competition, we cannot draw a supply curve showing the relation between price and the quantity of soap offered. If these complications are ignored the supply curve of an individual monopoly is its marginal cost curve.

The determination of equilibrium price

Market equilibrium is the bringing together of the firm's supply curve and the consumers' demand schedule in order to determine the amount of units of a commodity that will be bought and sold, within a certain time period and the price that will be paid and received for each unit. Thus we have in figure 11·21 the quantities of a commodity which consumers are willing to buy at any given price, and the quantities which producers are willing to offer for sale at any given price. Demand meets supply in the market, in which there is one price (OP) at which the quantity bought (OM) and the quantity offered for sale (OM) are the same. The price, OP, is the *market price,* or equilibrium price,

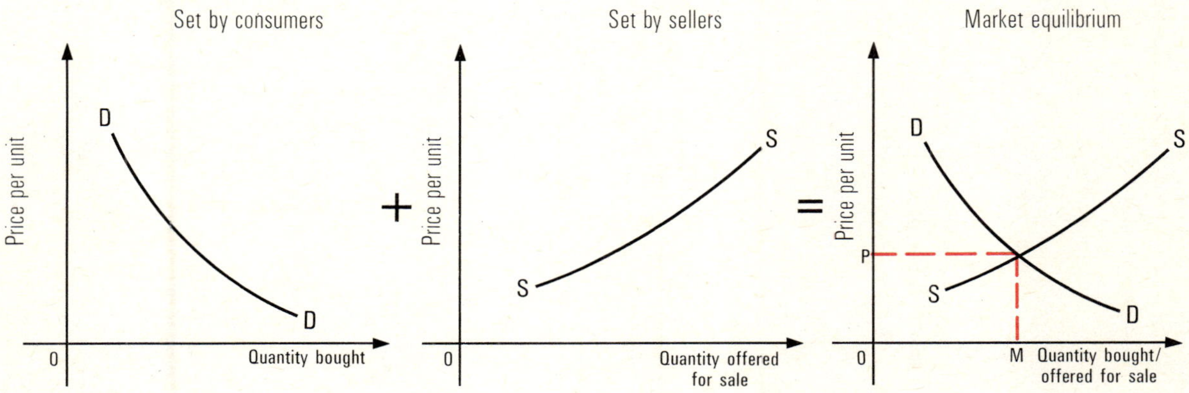

Figure 11·21

because it balances quantity supplied and quantity demanded.

The unit of time referred to must depend on the commodity in which you are dealing. If it is the D and S curves for strawberries, it may be one day; if it is the D and S for motor cars it may be normally a month, for pop records it may be a week.

Changes in equilibrium price will take place if:

i the supply curve shifts, indicating a change in supply conditions. This is described as a change in supply.

ii the demand curve shifts, indicating a change in demand conditions. This is described as a change in demand.

iii both supply and demand curves shift.

It is important to note that any price change must be the result of a shift of at least one of the two separate curves representing supply and demand conditions. We shall now examine the causes and effects of changes in supply and demand.

Changes in demand

As you know, the demand for a commodity is the amounts which consumers will wish to buy at any given price over a period of time. The demand curve depicts the relationship between price and quantity demanded, other things being equal, i.e. assuming other influences on the quantity demanded are unaltered. A change in any of these other influences will cause the demand curve to shift.

Suppose there is an increase in real incomes. The demand for most products will increase. Figures 11·22 and 11·23 show that this can be looked at in two ways. The demand curve shifts to the right, to

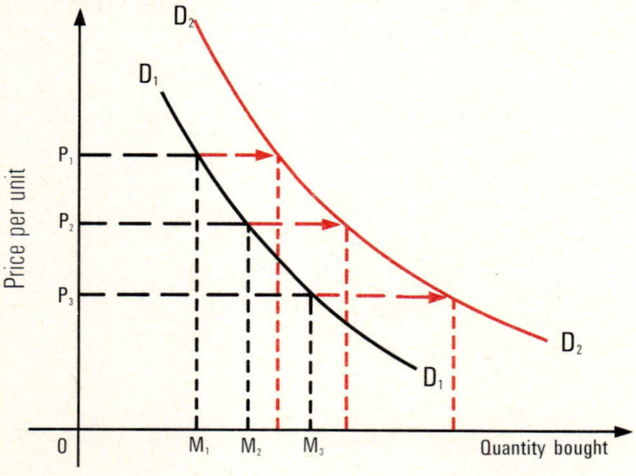

Figure 11·22

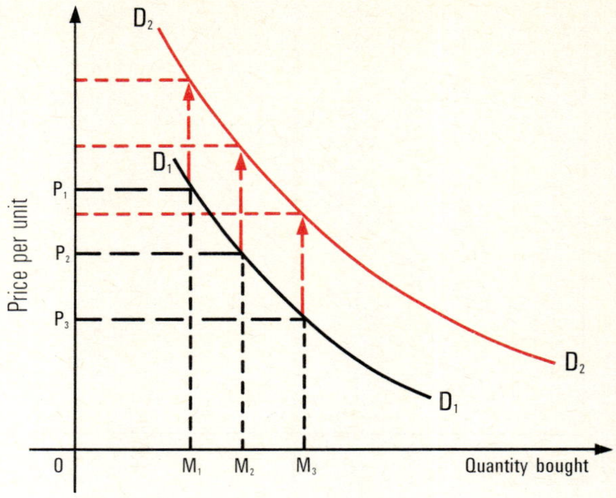

Figure 11·23

D_2D_2, indicating that consumers are willing to pay more for the present quantities of goods offered, or will buy a larger quantity than before, whatever the price. Both of these effects are included in the phrase 'the demand curve shifts to the right'. Similarly, when the demand curve shifts to the left there is a reduction in the quantity demanded at every price.

Causes of changes in demand

A change in any of the influences below will cause a shift of the demand curve to right or left.

i A change in the size and composition of the population.

ii A change in the size and distribution of national income and wealth, e.g. the development of a high-earning teenage population will cause an increase in demand for records and record players. Such changes in income may be caused by alterations in the system of grants and direct taxes, which will change the disposable incomes of various groups.

iii A change in the price and availability of substitutes or complementary goods (goods used with the article in question).

iv A change in the tastes of consumers. The influence of advertising is very important.

The effect of changes in demand

To examine the effect of a change in demand we assume that the original price is OP_1 and sales OQ_1, as determined by the demand curve D_1D_1 and supply curve S_1S_1 as shown in figure 11·24.

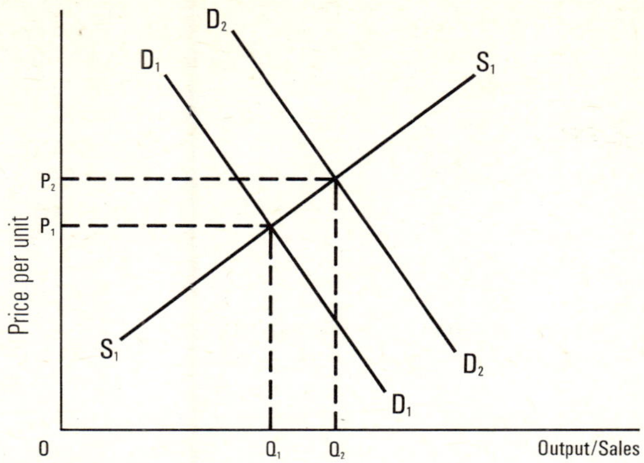

Figure 11·24

After the increase in demand shown by D_2D_2 price rises to OP_2 and sales to OQ_2. We see that quantity supplied increases—a movement along the existing supply curve. This can also be described as an extension of supply. There has been no change in supply conditions, therefore no new supply curve. A fall in demand will tend to reduce market price and reduce sales. This can be seen if we assume demand conditions are originally those depicted by D_2D_2 and then change to D_1D_1. Price will fall from OP_2 to OP_1, and there will be a reduction in quantity supplied to OQ_1—a movement down the existing supply curve. This can also be described as a contraction of supply.

Notice that the actual change in price and sales after a shift of the demand curve will depend on what is later described as the elasticity of supply—the responsiveness of quantity supplied to a change in price. Figure 11·25 shows a situation in which we assume existing firms can quickly alter their output at no extra cost. The supply curve S_1S_1 is horizontal. In such a case an increase in demand shown by D_2D_2 will not cause any rise in price. Price remains at OP_1 and sales increase to OQ_2. Obviously under such conditions a fall in demand will merely reduce sales and price will remain the same.

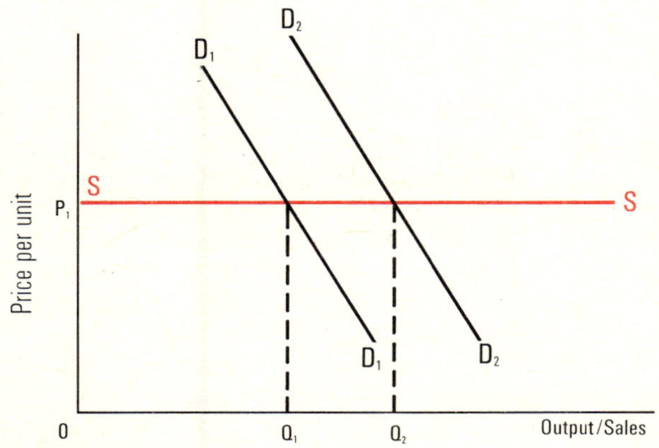

Figure 11·25

11·30

Draw for yourself a situation in which supply is fixed and cannot be altered whatever the change in price. What happens after a fall in demand?

Definitions

A movement along a given demand curve is usually the result of a change in the price of the product, and is known as a *change in the quantity demanded.* A movement to a new demand curve is known as a *change in demand.* A movement along a supply curve is called a *change in the quantity supplied.* A movement to a new supply curve is known as a *change in supply*.

11·31

What is the result of a decrease in demand at all prices?

A More of the commodity is sold at a higher price than before.

B More of the commodity is sold at a lower price than before.

C Less of the commodity is sold at a higher price than before.

D Less of the commodity is sold at a lower price than before.

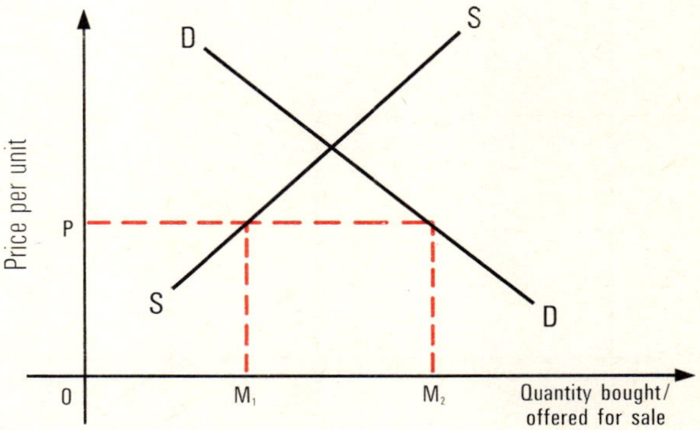

Figure 11·26

11·32

Which of the following does figure 11·26 show at price P?

- **A** A stable position in which demand exceeds supply.
- **B** A stable position in which supply exceeds demand.
- **C** An instable position in which demand exceeds supply.
- **D** An instable position in which supply exceeds demand.

11·33

Given figure 11·26 as a short run situation, what would you expect market price to do?

- **A** Fall to cause demand to contract.
- **B** Rise to achieve a new equilibrium.

Changes in supply

The supply of a commodity is the amount of that commodity a producer offers for sale at any given time at each given price. Supply is a flow measured over a period of time, e.g. so many units per week or per year. We have seen that this flow can be increased or decreased according to price. Once a factory or plant is built any movement in the level of production is a movement within the scale of production of the factory. This change in output is represented by a movement along a given supply schedule. The degree at which a firm can adjust itself in this way is known as elasticity of supply.

Remember that changes in supply as shown in figure 11·27 are changes involving shifts of the supply schedule to the left or right. An increase in the quantity supplied is a movement along the same curve. From an equilibrium position where the firm offers OM_1 units for sale at a price of OP_1, an increase in supply is demonstrated by a shift of the supply curve to position S_3S_3. At this position the firm can offer the original number of units OM_1 for sale at a reduced price of OP_3. If the previous price of OP_1 is maintained then the firm can offer an increased supply of OM_3 units.

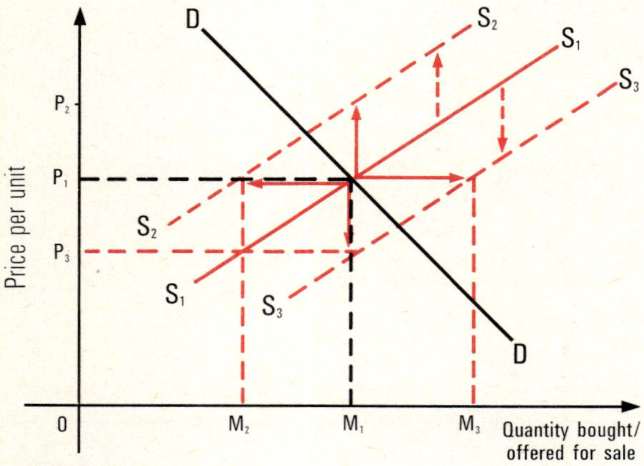

Figure 11·27

Causes of changes in supply

A change in any of the factors below will cause a shift of the supply curve to the left or the right.

i The entry of new firms into the industry or the expansion of existing firms will increase supply. The exit of some existing firms will reduce supply.

ii Changes in the average costs of production brought about by:

(a) a change in the factor prices without a corresponding change in output, e.g. when wages rise faster than productivity.

(b) the achievement of economies of scale, or the introduction of new techniques.

iii Changes in the prices of goods in joint supply or competitive supply. This is explained at the end of this chapter.

iv Changes in the climate, weather, etc. The size of harvests depends on the weather. The supply of primary products will be affected by climatic conditions, e.g. hurricanes can destroy the sugar crop.

v Changes in indirect taxes and subsidies. The imposition of an indirect tax, e.g. purchase tax, will have an effect equivalent to a rise in factor costs, and will raise the market supply curve. Subsidies have the opposite effect—they lower the market supply curve (see satellite *Agriculture*).

11·34

Which of the following would cause the supply curve to shift to the left?

- **A** The merger of the two largest firms in an industry.
- **B** The use of a new capital intensive production technique which reduces unit costs
- **C** The entry of new firms into the industry.
- **D** A shortage of raw materials normally available from overseas.

The effects of a change in supply

To examine the effect of a change in supply we assume that the original price is OP_1 and sales OQ_1 as determined by the supply and demand conditions depicted by the demand curve D_1D_1 and the supply curve S_1S_1 in figure 11·28.

An increase in supply is shown by the new supply curve S_2S_2. We can see that an increase in supply will tend to reduce price and increase sales. The demand curve is unaltered because the demand conditions are unchanged, but the increase in supply causes price to fall, and at the lower price OP_2 there is an increase in quantity demanded (also called an extension of demand), so that sales rise to OQ_2.

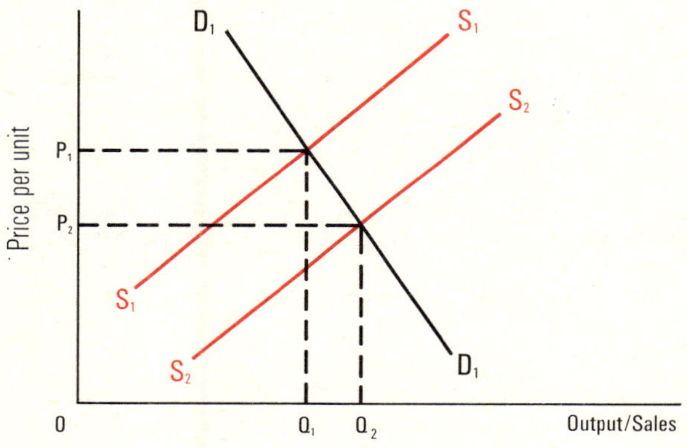

Figure 11·28

The effect of a reduction in supply can be seen if you consider that OP_2 is the original market price and sales are OQ_2. Then supply falls—a shift of the supply curve to S_1S_1 and so price rises to OP_1 and

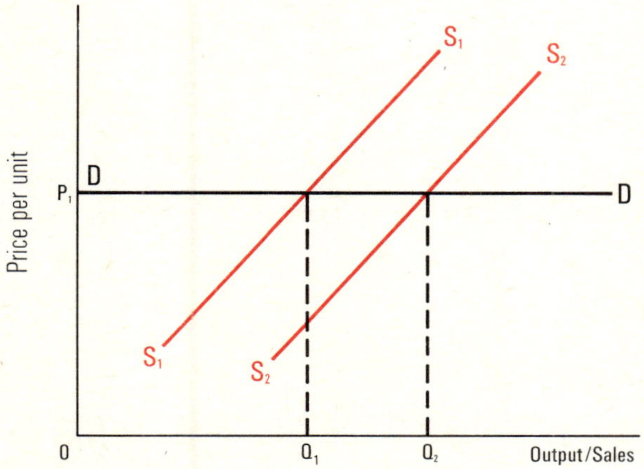

Figure 11·29

there is a reduction in quantity demanded (also called a contraction of demand to OQ_1.

A change in supply will not always cause price to change. Look at figure 11·29 in which the demand curve is a horizontal straight line—what is known as perfectly elastic demand. In this case an increase in supply will not reduce price, but sales increase to OQ_2. Similarly a fall in supply will not raise price.

11·35

Draw for yourself a diagram showing a situation where quantity demanded is constant whatever the price, and supply falls. What is the result of the fall in supply?

From the foregoing analysis we can see that the change in price and sales after a change in supply depends on the degree of the change in supply and the elasticity of demand.

The importance of the time period in the responsiveness of supply

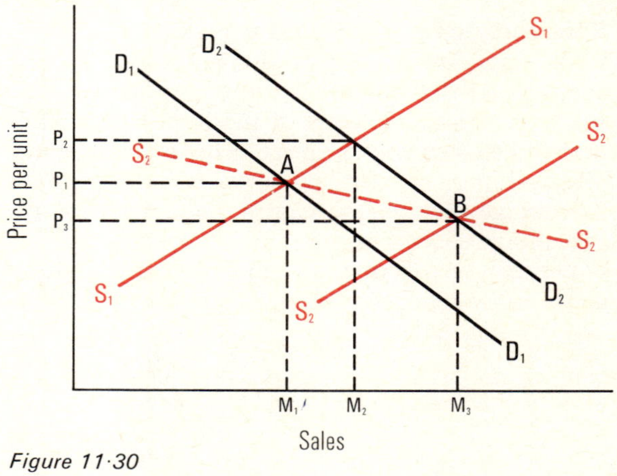

Figure 11·30

Figure 11·30 shows a firm that is offering OM_1 units of output at price OP_1 per unit. There is an increase in the demand for the firm's product, as shown in the movement of the demand schedule from D_1D_1 to D_2D_2. At this new level of demand the firm is able to offer OM_2 units for sale at a price of OP_2. In order to meet this increased supply of OM_2 units the firm finds it necessary to introduce overtime or shift working systems, and possibly to bring back into production obsolete machinery. In order to offer OM_2 units for sale the firm is faced with an increase in costs, but this increase can be passed on to the consumer in the form of higher price at OP_2. Thus, it is only possible for the firm to meet this higher supply at a higher cost, and as this increase in costs is related in higher prices, at this point price tends to equal the highest cost of production.

Faced with an increased market a firm may wish to exploit its own position and gain economies of scale. This will require the firm to initiate investment and shift the supply curve to the right to S_2S_2.

The time taken to increase output from OM_1 to OM_2 units depends upon the flexibility of the firm's cost structure, i.e. the elasticity of supply. In manufacturing industries the movement from OM_1 to OM_2 units is usually accomplished in the short term. The movement to supplying OM_3 units is a long term movement. To move from supplying OM_2 units to OM_3 units a firm must be confident of selling the increased output at price OP_3 per unit. This last movement from S_1S_1 to S_2S_2 represents a change in the fixed capital structure of the firm.

If points A and B are joined to produce S_3S_3 we arrive at the long-run supply curve for the firm.

Elasticity of supply and demand

We must now turn to the concept of price elasticity of demand. It is quite easy to calculate this as a precise measure of the responsiveness of demand to a change in price. This is done at any given point on the demand curve by comparing the percentage change in quantity bought with the percentage change in price.

Let us take a general example first and then try some arithmetic. We start with figure 11·31, in which a very small price change (δy) from OP_1 to OP_2 causes a change in the quantity bought (δx) from OM_1 to OM_2. In part I of the diagram the cause of the price change (the shift in the supply curve) is shown, but it is just assumed in Part II. Part II shows the price and quantity changes enlarged by exaggerating the x and y scales.

In practice elasticity is measured along an arc (section) of the demand curve by considering the effect of a unitary change in price. This is sometimes called *arc elasticity*. If you want to calculate elasticity of demand precisely at one point on the demand curve (*point elasticity*) you can use the mathematical technique for differentiating the formula for the curve (if known).

Arc elasticity

What we want to find out is whether the percentage change in the quantity demanded is more (or less) than proportionate to the small percentage change in price.

A percentage change in the quantity demanded which is exactly proportionate to the percentage change in price will give a result of 1:1 or $\frac{1}{1}$, and hence it is called unitary elasticity of demand. If the percentage change in the quantity demanded is *more* than proportionate to the percentage change in price, demand is said to be elastic at that point on the demand curve and has a numerical value greater than 1. Where the percentage change in the quantity demanded is *less* than proportionate to the percentage change in price, demand is said to be inelastic at that point on the demand curve and

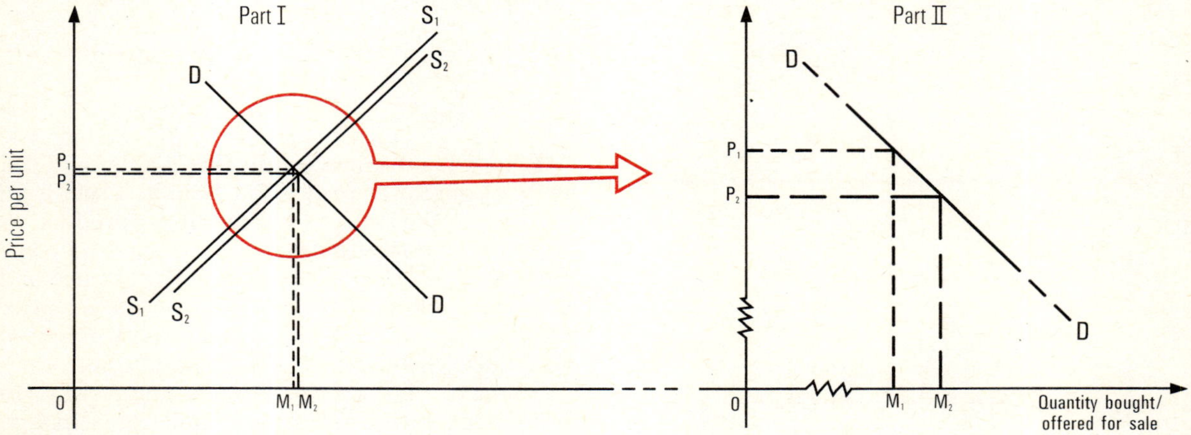

Figure 11·31

has a numerical value less than 1.

The percentage change in demand is measured by:

$$\frac{\text{Change in quantity bought}}{\text{Original quantity bought}} \times \frac{100}{1} = \frac{M_2 - M_1}{M_1} \times \frac{100}{1}$$

The percentage change in price is measured by:

$$\frac{\text{Change in price}}{\text{Original price}} \times \frac{100}{1} = \frac{P_2 - P_1}{P_1} \times \frac{100}{1}$$

The coefficient of price elasticity of demand (E_d) is the ratio of the percentage change in demand to the percentage change in price, i.e.

$$E_d = \frac{\dfrac{\text{Change in quantity bought}}{\text{Original quantity bought}} \times \dfrac{100}{1}}{\dfrac{\text{Change in price}}{\text{Original price}} \times \dfrac{100}{1}}$$

The $\frac{100}{1}$ cancels out.

or, simply,

$$E_d = \frac{\text{Percentage change in quantity demands}}{\text{Percentage change in price}}$$

See satellite, *Arithmetical and Statistical Techniques.*

A numerical example

Assume we are given the following information on the amount of a commodity bought at different prices.

Price	Quantity bought
10p	100
5p	200

You can then draw up the demand curve on graph paper assuming it to be a straight line between these two points, and calculate the elasticity of demand at varying prices (figure 11·32).

Starting at 10p let us assume the smallest possible rise in price—to 11p. By how much does the demand fall? Substituting the information into the formula:

$$E_d = \frac{\dfrac{\text{Change in amount bought}}{\text{Original amount bought}}}{\dfrac{\text{Change in price}}{\text{Original price}}} = \frac{\dfrac{20}{100} \times \dfrac{100}{1} = 20\%}{\dfrac{1}{10} \times \dfrac{100}{1} = 10\%}$$

Coefficient of price elasticity of demand = 2

Since this is greater than one, demand is (over a small arc as near to 10p as we can manage) elastic.

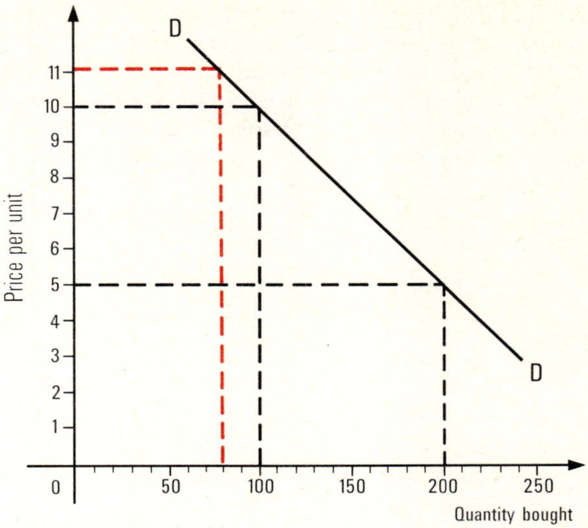

Figure 11·32

The '2' means that the response of demand is more than proportionate to the change in price. We would therefore expect price to move in the opposite direction to total expenditure. To check, compare total expenditure at 10p with total expenditure at 11p.

11·36

Measure the elasticity of demand at each price in figure 11·32. (See satellite *Arithmetical and Statistical Methods.*)

The limiting cases. In figure 11·33 the elasticity of demand is infinite. A small change in price will either cause effective demand to disappear altogether if it rises or it will absorb all of that commodity which is available if price falls. This is usually known as a perfectly elastic demand curve because $E_d = \infty$ at all points on the demand curve. It is the situation faced by a firm under perfect

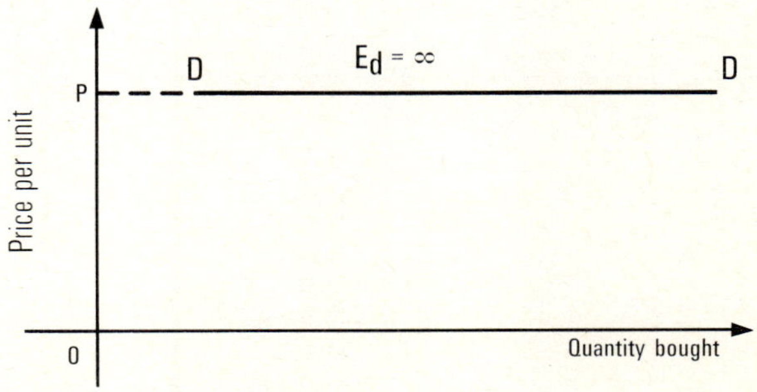

Figure 11·33

competition. In figure 11·34 the elasticity of demand is zero—there is no response of demand to a price change. This is an absolutely inelastic demand curve. Figure 11·35 is a special mathematical case called a rectangular hyperbola, where there is a constant amount spent on the commodity at all

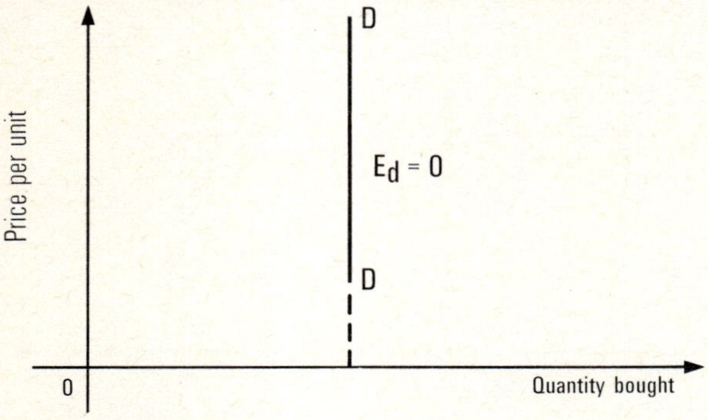

Figure 11·34

price levels and so the elasticity of demand is unity throughout the length of this demand curve. Such a demand curve exists for many government-bought commodities. If the local authorities, for example, are told what their total expenditure is to be in the coming year, the suppliers of their school books are faced with a hyperbolic demand curve.

Differences in elasticity of demand

Let us examine the reason for the change of elasticity of demand along the demand curve, so

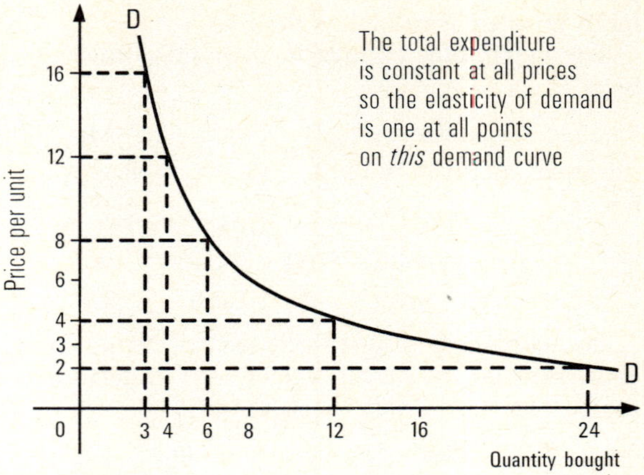

Figure 11·35

that we can derive a general principle showing the relationship between the slope of the demand curve and the elasticity of demand.

11·37

Figure 11·36a is derived from the following schedule:

Price per unit	1	2	3	4	5
Quantity bought	5	4	3	2	1

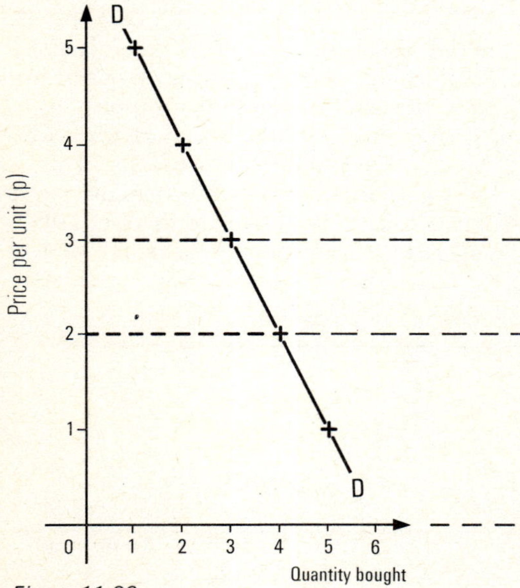

Figure 11·36a

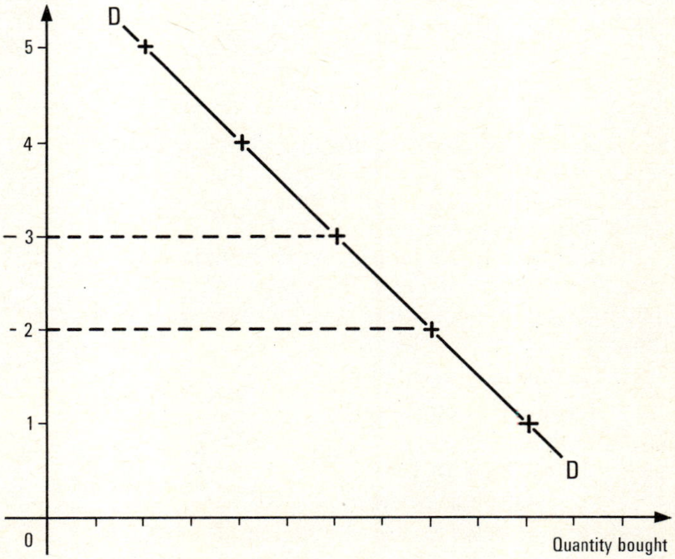

Figure 11·36b

Draw your own copy of the diagram, then:

a measure the arc elasticity of demand at each price, basing your calculations on a one penny rise in price at each level.

b mark on the demand curve on your diagram the answers to part **a**, opposite the appropriate price.

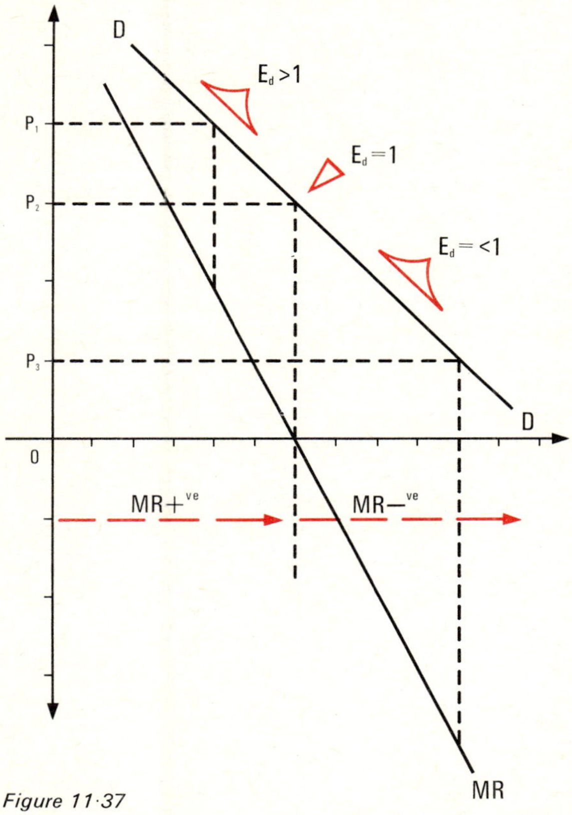

Figure 11·37

In figure 11·37, at prices greater than OP_2 any price reduction will increase total revenue (MR is positive), or elasticity of demand is greater than 1. At prices less than OP_2, total revenue decreases (MR is negative), or elasticity of demand is less than 1.

Now let us turn to figures 11·36a and 11·36b. Can we say by inspection only then at 3p per unit the left hand demand curve is more elastic than the right hand demand curve? Firstly, demand curves themselves are not elastic or inelastic since elasticity varies along the curve. Secondly, one cannot judge elasticity without measuring it. Until it is measured one cannot say whether or not both curves have a range of elasticities which are all greater than one or all less than one. It is quite possible for the elasticity, although changing along a given curve, to be entirely above or below one. It may simply be one section of the demand curve, which is presented for examination. Last but not least, on diagrams or graphs where the scales are not stated, appearances may be deceptive. Figure 11·36b shows exactly the same demand curve as figure 11·36a, except that the scale on the x axis has been doubled. Hence at any given price level, the price elasticity of demand is identical.

Thus the visual comparison of price elasticity can only be done when (a) both graphs have the same scales, (b) the price change is identical in each case and (c) the price at which elasticity is measured is also the same.

Summary

An *elastic* demand has a coefficient greater than one, and occurs where the percentage change in demand is more than proportionate to the percentage change in price; total expenditure and price move in the opposite directions.

An *inelastic* demand has a coefficient less than one: the percentage change in demand is less than proportionate to the percentage change in price, and the total expenditure and price move in the same direction.

A *unitary* elasticity has a coefficient of one; the percentage change in demand is proportionate to the percentage change in price; total expenditure is constant.

It is important to remember that the elasticity of demand varies throughout the length of almost every demand curve, whether it is a straight one or not, except for the three limiting cases. Except for these cases, there is no such thing as an elastic demand curve or an inelastic one. For one thing, *it is the demand not the curve which is elastic*, for another, the elasticity varies at different price levels.

The major factors which affect the price elasticity of demand are as follows.

i The availability of substitutes in a similar price range.

ii Habit and time. Habit delays the process of substitution. People may be slow to react to price changes.

iii The proportion of a consumers income spent on the article. If only a very small proportion is spent, as in the case of matches, a considerable rise in price will not deter consumers, so demand will be inelastic. A £20 increase in the price of cars will not worry the rich man, though poorer people may be driven from the market.

iv The durability of a commodity. Durable goods possessed by the consumer are substitutes for new goods of the same type. A fall in price of new radios will encourage existing radio owners to buy new replacements as well as attracting new buyers. The demand for durable goods will tend to be elastic.

Income and elasticity

Price elasticity is affected by the level of the consumer's income, as we have seen in **iii** above. A different concept is income elasticity of demand.

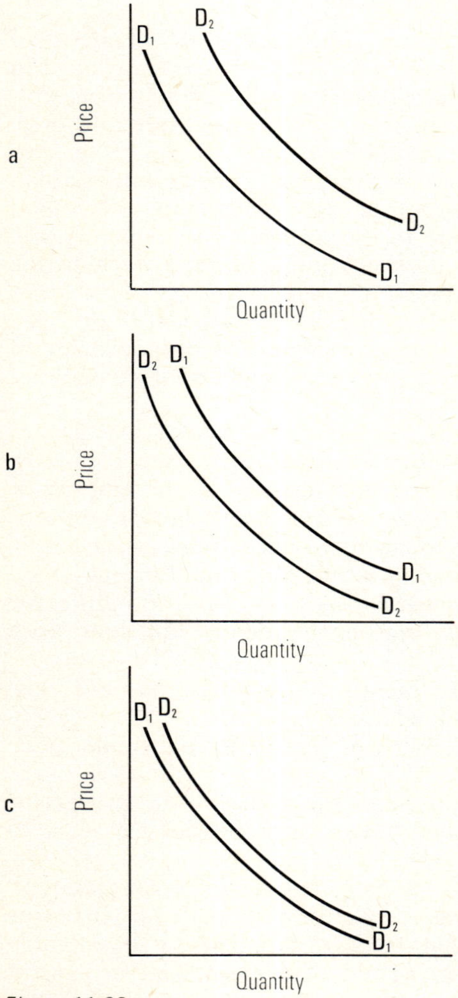

Figure 11·38

This is the percentage change in the quantity demanded resulting from a small (e.g. 1 %) change in income. Income elasticity causes a shift in the demand curve. Figure 11·38 gives three examples.

Assume a consumer's income has doubled. A shows his demand for beer. He has a new curve D_2. At all prices he buys more. B shows his demand for cigarettes. He is now smoking cigars, and at all prices has reduced his cigarette consumption. (Goods for which demand falls as incomes increase, such as bicycles, are often called inferior goods.) C shows his demand for bread. He eats slightly bigger meals, but does not eat much more bread. Income elasticity varies greatly from commodity to commodity.

The practical importance of the concept of elasticity of demand

Each time a firm contemplates a change in the price of its products, it considers the effect of the price change on total revenue. Assuming a normal market demand curve, the effect of a price rise will be to reduce the quantity sold, at least to some extent. This, in itself, may not matter. What does matter is the *proportionate* response of demand, i.e. by how much total revenue rises or falls. It will not always pay a firm to reduce the selling price of its products, because that may result in a lower total revenue (i.e. where MC > MR).

In any case, the rational firm will be concerned with its profits rather than just the changes in total revenue. At any output between that at which MC = MR and that at which MR = O, a price fall will add to total revenue because the elasticity of demand is greater than one (i.e. MR is positive) *but* MC is greater than MR at these levels of output so profits will fall, despite the increasing revenue received.

The price elasticity of supply

This is calculated in a similar way as the price elasticity of demand (see satellite *Arithmetical and Statistical Methods*).

$$E_s = \frac{\dfrac{\text{Change in quantity offered for sale}}{\text{Original quantity offered for sale}}}{\dfrac{\text{Change in price}}{\text{Original price}}}$$

or, more simply

$$E_s = \frac{\text{Percentage change in the quantity supplied}}{\text{Percentage change in price}}$$

Where the elasticity of supply is greater than one, supply is said to be elastic, where it is less than one, supply is inelastic.

The significance of elasticity of supply is that it is, in effect, a measure of the ease and rapidity with which producers can change the supply to the market in response to price changes.

Any straight line supply curve down through the origin has unitary elasticity $E_s = 1$). Check this by drawing such supply curves and finding out whether the proportionate changes along each axis are the same. Completely inelastic supply is represented by a vertical supply curve, completely elastic supply ($E_s = \infty$) is represented by a horizontal supply curve.

Factors affecting elasticity of supply

Frequent confusion of factors which affect elasticity of demand and supply can be avoided by remembering that the price elasticity of supply relates to changes in the quantity *offered* for sale and not to the amount people want to buy. Hence the elasticity of supply relates to the flexibility of producers in supplying their markets in response to changes in price.

To summarise, the elasticity of supply will depend on the following factors.

i The time period considered. In the very short run, say, one day, it is difficult to increase the quantity of any product on the market, so supply is very inelastic. In the short run, say, one month, it is usually the case to increase the output of manufactured goods, but the supply of most primary products will remain inelastic, because the output of crops, vegetable products and minerals cannot be increased quickly. For example, it takes approximately a year to increase the supply of wheat. Note that the supply of oak wood may remain inelastic for a century.

ii The availability of stocks. Stocks may be held to meet fluctuations in demand. Also goods may be imported to add to the domestic supplies.

iii The availability of factors of production. It will be difficult to increase output if there is a shortage of skilled men or specially designed machinery. Therefore, the supply of all goods and services becomes less elastic when there is full employment. Note also that when a shortage of skilled men develops it may take several years for the number to be increased, depending on the time needed for training. However, when there is a shortage of unskilled labour, and the price of such labour is rising, more capital may be used as a substitute.

iv The ease of entry or exit for marginal firms. The long run supply curve of an industry will depend on whether firms can easily leave or enter.

11·38

Which of the following factors are not likely to affect the price elasticity of demand for frozen peas:

A Availability of substitutes.
B Price in relationship to weekly income.
C Perishability.
D Availability of raw peas.

11·39

Cigarettes in general tend to have a low price elasticity of demand. State which of these factors is most important in influencing this tendency.

A Durability.
B Addictive qualities.
C Price in relation to weekly income.
D Availability of substitutes.

11·40

In establishing the likely elasticity of supply of steel these factors are offered for consideration:

1 The existence of long-term contracts.
2 Competition with plastics for domestic equipment.
3 The shortage of skilled labour.
4 The indivisibility of units of production.

Which factor(s) are not relevant?

A 1 **C** 2
B 3 **D** 4

Applications of supply and demand analysis

The effect of indirect taxes. A purchase tax is usually placed on commodities whose demand curve over the range taxed tends to be inelastic, for example cigarettes or petrol. A rise in price does not lead to a large decrease in the quantity bought so that the taxing authority does not lose revenue because consumers buy less. Let us take the case of a 20% tax on retail price.

i The supply curve moves up by 20% at each and every quantity because to receive the same amount per unit the seller must raise his selling price by the full amount of tax.

ii The distance between the new and old supply curve increases because of the proportionate tax.

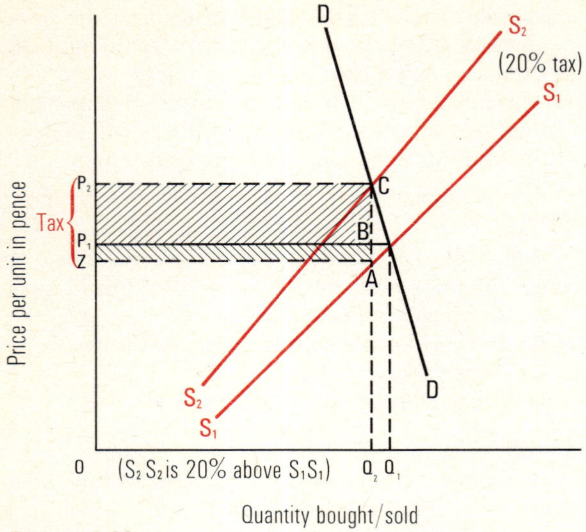

Figure 11·39

The original equilibrium point is given by price OP_1, and quantity OQ_1. The new equilibrium point where S_2S_2 crosses DD is OP_2 and OQ_2.

Let us first look at the effect on consumers. The quantity demanded falls (price has gone up), and for the new quantity OQ_2 consumers pay P_1P_2CB *more* than they did before tax. That shows how much worse off they are. Turn to the producers, who sold OQ_1 at OP_1 per unit. Now they can only sell OQ_2 (less) at an effective price OZ, which is the price the producer gets per unit after paying tax. Thus the area ZP_1BA shows that at OQ_2 he is losing $ZP_1 \times OQ$ pence because of the imposition of a tax.

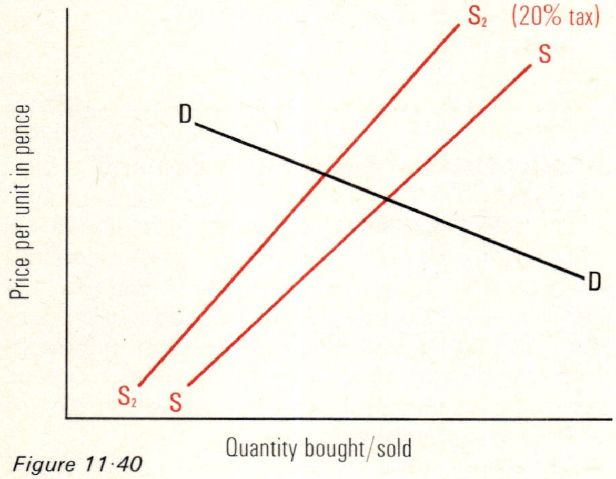

Figure 11·40

Which is hit most by the tax, producer or consumer? In this case the consumer, because area P_1P_2CB is greater than area P_1BAZ. If a government wishes to place the incidence/burden of taxation on the consumer it must choose a market situation where the elasticities of supply and demand approximate to the case given above. The lower the elasticity of demand compared with the elasticity of supply, the greater the amount of tax borne by consumers.

11·41

Who bears the greatest burden of taxation, consumer or producer in figure 11·40?

Subsidies

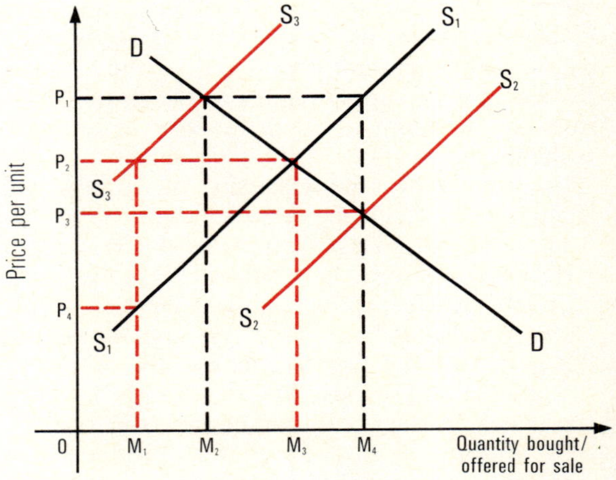

Figure 11·41

11·42

If the original supply curve is S_1S_1 in figure 11.41, and then a government subsidy is introduced, what would be the effect?

A The supply curve would shift to S_2S_2.
B The supply curve would shift to S_3S_3.

11·43

In figure 11.41 what is the new equilibrium price following the grant of a subsidy?

A OP_1 **C** OP_3
B OP_2 **D** OP_4

11·44

What is the extent of the subsidy per unit in figure 11·41?

A $OP_1 - OP_2$ C $OP_2 - OP_3$
B $OP_1 - OP_3$ D $OP_2 - OP_4$

11·45

What is the amount sold in the new equilibrium situation in figure 11·41?

A OM_1 C OM_3
B OM_2 D OM_4

11·46

Draw the new supply curve in figure 11·42 which arises from a 20% ad valorem subsidy.

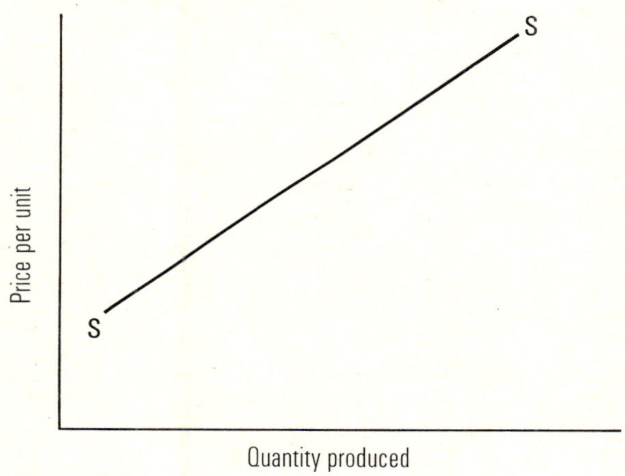

Figure 11·42

Inter-relationships of supply and demand

The complex structure of industry is such that the effects of a change in the supply, demand or price of a single commodity is not confined to that product but has repercussions over a wider section of industry.

Joint demand. Commodities that are demanded for joint use, i.e. electricity and electric appliances, motor cars and petrol; are said to be in joint demand. Any movement in the demand for one of the joint products will cause a change in the demand for the other.

In figure 11·43, we assume that a tax has been levied on sports cars, hence the supply curve moves upwards from S_1 to S_2 and the quantity bought falls from OM_1 to OM_2. As less new cars are bought (we ignore stocks of old cars) the demand for tyres falls (from D_1D_1 to D_2D_2) and only OM_4 quantity of tyres will be produced.

Composite demand. When a commodity has several uses, or can be demanded for several purposes the demand for that commodity is said to be composite. This is the case for most fuels; e.g. electricity is used for domestic purposes, heating, and as an industrial fuel.

Competitive demand. An example of this is where the commodities are very close substitutes as in the case of beef, pork or lamb. A rise in the price of one, caused by changes in supply of one will cause an increase (shift) in the demand for the others.

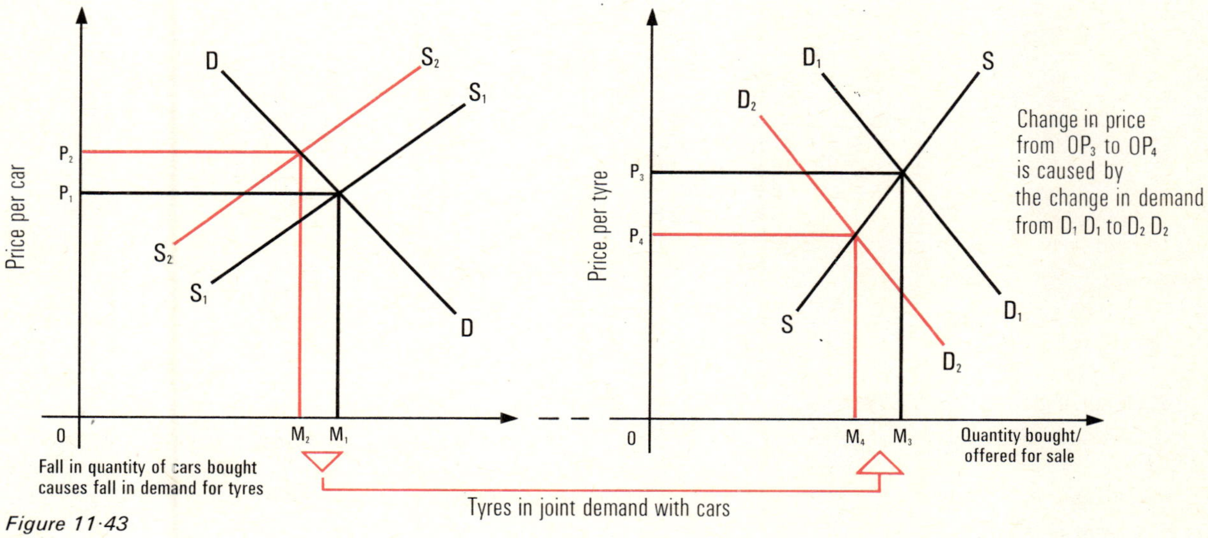

Figure 11·43

Derived demand. Steel is not demanded for its own sake; steel is of no use to the final consumer until it is fashioned into a finished product. Thus the demand for steel is said to be *derived*. The demand for steel is derived from the demand for other commodities that embody steel, for example motor cars.

Competitive supply. This exists when an increase in the supply of one commodity necessitates the reduction in the supply of another. For example, if the quantity of milk available is fixed, butter and cheese are in competitive supply. Housing and playing fields are in competitive supply in a given area. When there is full employment of resources, all goods are in competitive supply.

In this section we have dealt with many technical terms and basic concepts. A useful form of revision for either individual readers or for discussion groups is to look at goods advertised in current newspapers or journals, and to analyse, as far as possible, the conditions of demand and supply for each commodity or service.

ANSWERS

Note—if any of your graphs prove to be inaccurate they should be redrawn.

11·1

Fixed costs
- Rent of factory
- Local authority rates
- Normal profit if calculated on capital
- Salaries
- Painting and repairs
- Interest on loans
- Pensions
- All other costs vary with output

11·2

a

Monthly output hovertrucks	AFC	AVC	ATC
20	50·0	46·0	96·0
40	25·0	49·0	74·0
60	16·7	42·3	59·0
80	12·5	37·5	50·0
100	10·0	35·5	45·5
120	8·3	39·2	47·5
140	7·1	46·4	53·5

b Graph.

11·3

Correct **D**.
Mistaken **A, B, C**: see figure 11·2.

11·4

Correct **A**.
Mistaken **B, C, D.**

11·5

Output	TC	AC
20	1 920	109·5
40	2 960	74·0
60	3 540	59·0
80	4 000	50·0
100	4 550	45·5
120	5 700	47·5
140	7 500	53·6

11·6

i The vertical distance between ATC and AVC shows the value of AFC. This must be added on to AVC to obtain ATC. Notice that the gap narrows as output increases because AFC declines.

ii AFC is always falling, so until OM (figure 11·3) is reached falling AFC more than offsets rising AVC.

i Correct **B.**
ii Correct **A.**
iii Correct **B.**

11·7

Output	TC	MC
20	1 920	
		52
40	2 960	
		29
60	3 540	
		23
80	4 000	
		27·5
100	4 550	
		57·5
120	5 700	
		90
140	7 500	

Note that MC is the difference between successive TC figures, and is written between the TC values shown. Remember MC is the increase in TC *per unit*, therefore when output increases from 20 to 40 per month, TC increases by (2 960−1 920) = 1 040. The increase per unit is therefore: $\frac{1\,040}{20} = 52$.

ii Graph of MC.
iii Graph of AC.

11·8
Graphs from data below.

Weekly output units	AC £	TC £	MC £
200	5·00	1 000	
400	4·22	1 688	3·44
600	3·42	2 052	1·82
800	2·90	2 320	1·34
1 000	2·60	2 600	1·40
1 200	2·50	3 000	2·00
1 400	2·60	3 640	3·20
1 600	2·90	4 640	5·00

11·9
Correct **C.**
Mistaken **A, B, D.**
AC always equals MC when AC is at a minimum: see satellite *Arithmetical and Statistical Methods.*

11·10
Correct **A.**
Mistaken **B, C, D.** At **B,** MC = AC.

11·11
Correct **B.**
Mistaken **A, C, D.**

11·12

Price (£) Average Revenue	Sales per month	Total Revenue (£) per month
130	20	2 600
110	40	4 400
90	60	5 400
70	80	5 600
50	100	5 000
30	120	3 600

11·13
Correct **E.**
Mistaken **A, B, C, D.**
Careful examination of the answer given for exercise 11·12 will reveal that for any price fall between £130 and £70, so many more people buy the trucks that total revenue actually increases. However, when price falls below £70 the increase in sales which occurs is not sufficient to compensate for the fall in price, so total revenue starts to fall.

11·14
Correct **A, B.**
Mistaken **C, D, E.**

11·15

Sales	TR	MR	AR
20	2 600		130
40	4 400	90	110
60	5 400	50	90
80	5 600	10	70
100	5 000	−30	50
120	3 600	−70	30

11·16
MR = AR = £45 at all sales levels. See OP in figure 11·8.

11·17
Cost and revenue curves drawn on a single graph. Note that AR does not *necessarily* = MC = AC.

11·18
Correct **C.**
Mistaken **A, B**: since profit is the difference between total cost and total revenue, these answers ignore one half of the information.
Mistaken **D**: this point has no particular significance in this context.
Mistaken **E**: this is the same output level as alternative **B.**

11·19
Correct **B, C, D.**
Mistaken **A**: laws can always be changed, and the monopolist may be the government!

11·20
Correct **A**: even state run monopolies are usually limited in their powers. It would be rare for any monopolist to have the power to force people to buy as well as to dictate the price. The only power the monopolist has is to say that if consumers are not willing to pay the asking price, they must buy less or even do without altogether.
Mistaken **B**: just because he raises the offer price, does not mean he will sell enough to maximise

profits. It is not sufficient, therefore, to change the asking price for the product.

Mistaken **C**: merely preventing the supply of an alternative product does not necessarily control the market price unless the monopolists' own supply to the market is also controlled.

11·21

a Correct **C**. Mistaken **A, B, D**.
b Correct **C**. Mistaken **A, B, D**.

11·22

Correct **C**. Mistaken **A, B, D**.

11·23

Correct **B**. Mistaken **A, C, D**.

11·24

Petrol and baked beans are probably produced in conditions of oligopoly. Petrol sales are dominated by about five companies and baked beans by two companies. Instant coffee (over 50 brands) and canned peaches are produced under monopolistic competition.

11·25

Correct **B**, i.e. where MC = MR.

11·26

a Correct **D**. Mistaken **A, B, C**.
b Correct **D**. Mistaken **A, B, C**.
c Correct **D**. Mistaken **A, B, C**.
d Correct **A**. Mistaken **B, C, D**.
e Correct **B**. Mistaken **A, C, D**.
f Correct **B**. Mistaken **A, C, D**.

11·27

Correct **C**. Mistaken **A, B, D**.

11·28

Both statements are false. If entrepreneurs do not earn normal profits, under any conditions, they leave the industry.

11·29

The important difference is that under perfect competition, the individual firm is faced by a horizontal demand curve. It can sell an infinite quantity at a given price. Under monopolistic conditions, the firm faces a downward sloping demand curve, and can only sell more by reducing the price. From this it follows that under perfect competition, AR = MR = MC and under monopolistic conditions AR > (MR = MC). In everyday terms, perfect competition is characterised by price competition: monopolistic competition by product differentiation and heavy advertising.

11·30

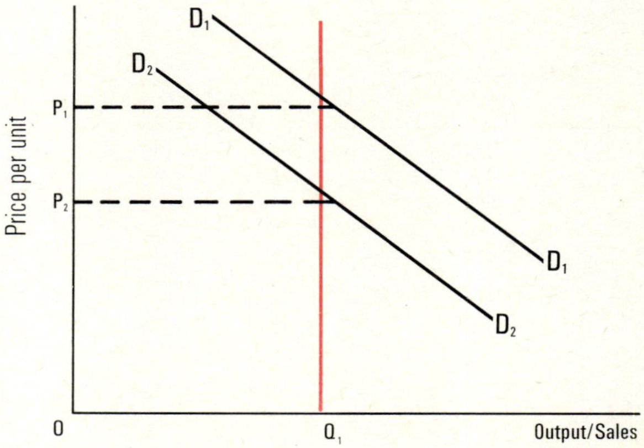

Demand falls, shown by the shift of the demand curve from D_1D_1 to D_2D_2. Price falls to OP_2 but since the quantity supplied cannot be altered sales remain the same.

11·31

Correct **D**. Mistaken **A, B, C**.

11·32

Correct **C**. Mistaken **A, B, D**.

11·33

Correct **B**. Mistaken **A**.

11·34

Correct **D**.

Mistaken **A**: mergers do not necessarily have any effect on the quantity offered for sale. Where it takes place for reasons of market power, it is quite likely to lead to more being offered for sale in order to capture a larger share of the market.

Mistaken **B**: this will shift the supply curve to the right (i.e. more offered for sale at current prices, or price reductions at all levels of output).

Mistaken **C**: this will shift the supply curve to the right, as the output of the new firms is put onto the market.

11·35

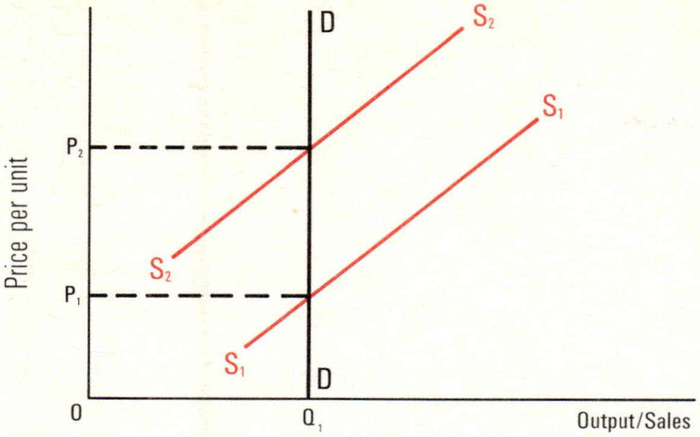

After the fall in supply, from S_1S_1 to S_2S_2 price rises to OP_2, but there is no change in quantity demanded.

11·36

Price	Elasticity of demand
3	0·25 Inelastic
4	0·36 Inelastic
5	0·50 Inelastic
6	0·67 Inelastic
7	0·875 Inelastic
8	1·14 Elastic
9	1·50 Elastic
10	2·00 Elastic

11·37

Elasticity of demand at

P	Ed
1	
2	·2
3	·5
4	1.
5	2.

11·38

Correct **C**: frozen peas are not perishable, so this will affect neither elasticity of demand nor supply. **A, B,** and **D** *do* affect the price elasticity of demand.

11·39

B is *most* important.

11·40

Correct **A**: long term contracts commit suppliers to certain levels of production regardless of price.

Correct **C**: skilled labour takes time to train and hence affects elasticity of supply.

Correct **D**: a steel furnace has a certain output below which it simply will not work. You cannot make 2 tonnes of steel in a furnace designed for 50 tonnes.

Incorrect **C**: availability of substitutes affects elasticity of demand only.

11·41

Refer to figure 11·39, where the consumer bears most of the tax. In the exercise, however, the division is clearly such that the producer pays most of the tax. The consumer pays P_1P_2CB; the producer pays ZP_1BA.

11·42

Correct **A.**

11·43

Correct **C.**

11·44

Correct **B.**

11·45

Correct **D.**

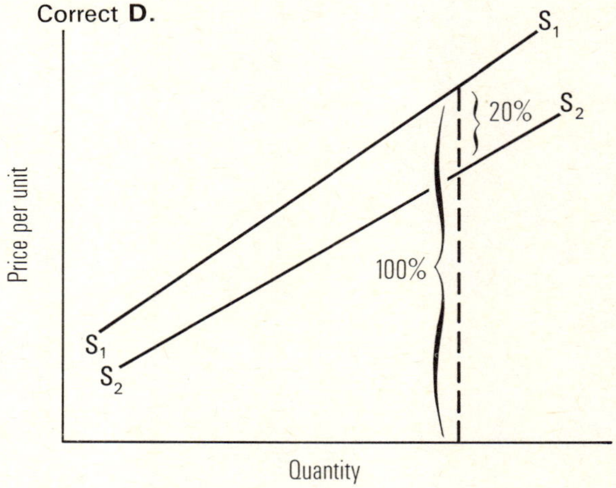

THE QUANTITY AND VALUE OF MONEY

STUDY SECTION **12**

In this section we shall continue the study of money which we began in S6. There we saw what money is, what it does, what qualities it needs to possess to perform certain functions and where it can be bought and sold. We shall also examine the importance of the demand for and the supply of money to the economy as a whole. Rather than consider money in isolation as an item apart from the rest of the economy we shall consider the effects which a change in the total supply of money may have on such important variables as the price level and the rate of interest. You may find it helpful at this stage to re-read S6.

We have in previous sections analysed the market for goods in terms of the demand and supply for them. We discovered that the determination of the price of goods can only be explained in terms of the conditions and changes in the demand and supply of them. So it is with money. If we wish to analyse the value of money we must seek to understand the demand and supply of it. But what do we mean by the value of money? Do we mean the price of a loan, or in other words the rate of interest? Or, do we mean the economic goods (commodities or services) which can be exchanged for a certain sum of money? The values of goods are expressed in terms of the money or price which can be exchanged for them, so it would seem that the value or price of money must be the quantity of goods which must be exchanged in order to obtain it. If the price of goods generally rises then the value of money has fallen. The same amount of money is worth less in terms of goods. So when we talk of the value of money we usually mean the goods it will buy. When we obtain a loan, however, we have to pay a price, the rate of interest. Is not this also the value of money? No, this is the price of a money loan.

It is important to distinguish between the two concepts that we have just discussed. The value of money is expressed in terms of the commodities or services it will exchange for, while the value of a money loan is the rate of interest on loans. We shall firstly analyse the determinants of the rate of interest, or in other words, the price of money loans. The price of a loan is determined by the demand for and the supply of loanable money and it is to these two factors which we now turn for an explanation.

The demand for money

Nearly every individual needs cash in his pocket or purse for the everyday transactions which are a part of daily life. Travelling to work or buying one's lunch involves payment in cash which necessitates the holding of money. When people are faced with the regular payment of bills they may choose to hold the money in cash form awaiting the date on which payment should be made or they may prefer to hold money in their current account at the bank and pay the bill by cheque. If they have a Giro account then of course the bill will be paid through the Post Office's Giro network. Whether the money is held in the form of cash, or a bank deposit which is transferable by cheque, it represents money that is demanded by the public. It is immediately spendable.

Firms will also have a demand for money in order to pay regular bills for their purchases of raw materials and the payment of wages. The fewer assets a firm holds in money form, the better it likes it, since capital held in liquid form cannot be earning a profit.

The desire to hold wealth in money form is usually referred to as *liquidity preference*. You may choose to hold your wealth in the form of rare stamps, paintings, investments or property. These assets are not easily converted into a spendable form and are therefore known as *illiquid*. Perhaps you remember how we noticed in S6 that the commercial banks had to choose between liquidity and profitability. The more of its assets a bank holds in cash form, the less it can invest or lend out as advances to customers. Holding cash therefore incurs for a bank the opportunity cost of the interest it could be earning on the advances. It is the same for people and for firms. Wherever we are forced to hold our wealth in liquid form we incur the opportunity cost of what we could have been earning with it. We may have left it in the deposit account of our bank and earned, say, $3\frac{1}{2}\%$ interest, or we have purchased Savings Certificates for the interest they would yield us.

We may be led to believe, therefore, that people avoid holding their wealth in a liquid form whenever possible and that the demand for money is therefore always very low. This is not quite the case. There are definite reasons for people positively demanding money. Attempts have been made in the past to divide the demand for money into different categories. Some have referred to the *active demand* for money, for instance, which is a demand for money derived from the need to conduct daily cash transactions and pay regular debts. This they have distinguished from the *passive demand* for money which is derived from people's and firms' desire to hold money, not for use at present, but for use at some future date. Active and passive demand are just two terms which have been used to categorise the demand for money.

Another way in which the demand for money has been described occurs where a distinction is made between a *positive demand* to hold money for a purpose which is likely to be profitable to one, and the *negative demand,* where holding money is simply unavoidable. An example of the latter case occurs where a firm has to find the wages of its employees each week. It lets its cash balances build up from payday to payday so that the wage bill can be met. For much of the week, therefore, cash is being held unavoidably and performing no useful or profitable job.

A modern analysis of the demand for money was presented by the late Lord Keynes. In his book *The General Theory of Employment, Interest, and Money,* which was published in 1936, Keynes outlined a new approach that was to transform the thoughts of economists about the control of the economy. His concern was mainly with the causes and the cures of unemployment. Throughout the inter-War years unemployment in the U.K. never fell below 10% of the working population. Keynes was to show that the answer lay in a completely new approach to the problems of the economy as a whole and was to repudiate much of the economics that had been written by the so-called Classical economists, whose main concern had been with the individual elements of the economy rather than with the economy as a whole. Keynes showed that

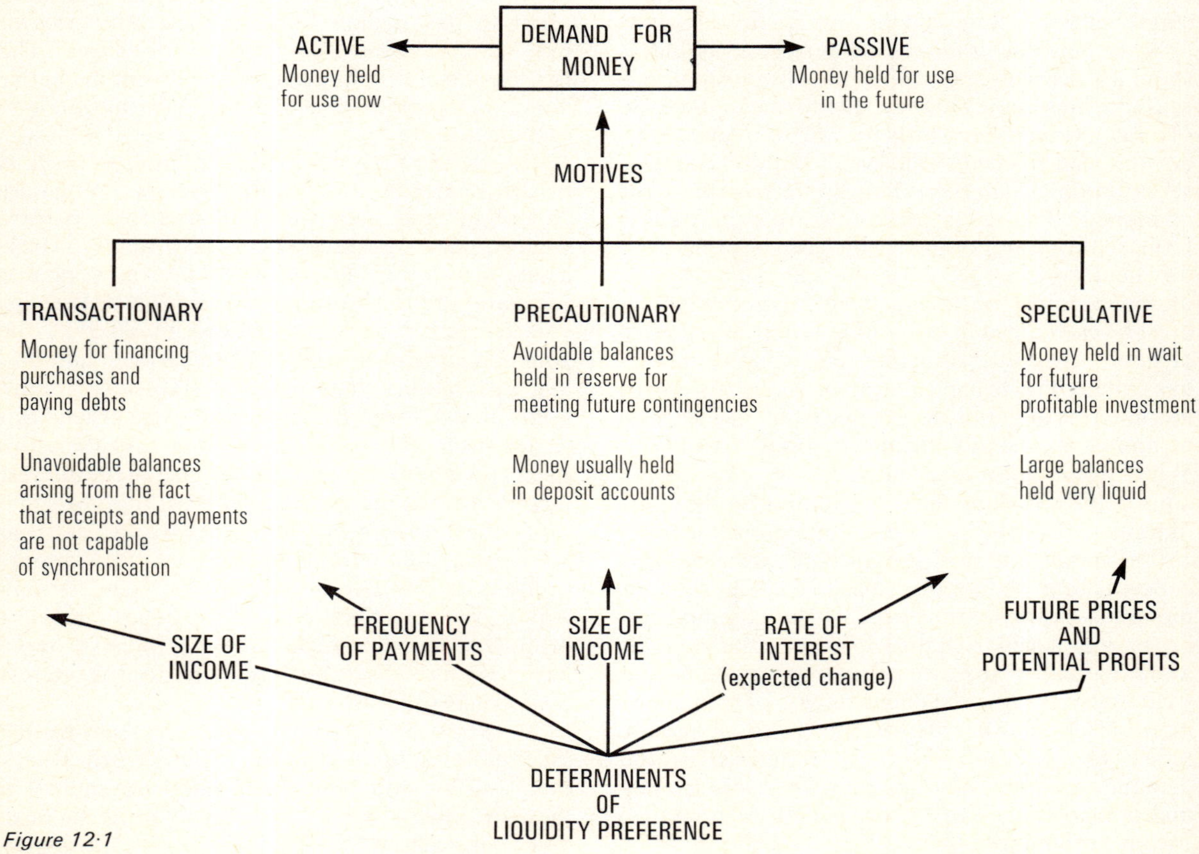

Figure 12·1

the supply of money, and the rate of interest were intimately connected. He concluded that the rate of interest was in fact determined by the demand for, and the supply of, money. He thus analysed the demand for money by describing the motives which prompt people to hold their money in liquid form, i.e. the motives for their *liquidity preference*.

There are three main motives:

i The transactions motive. People derive their spending power largely from their income. In order to satisfy their daily, weekly, or monthly wants they will have to spend their income regularly. If a person is paid monthly, then for much of the month he will be holding a stock of money awaiting payment of the next bill when it falls due. As the month wears on his stock of money will become smaller, until his stock will have fallen to nil just before the next payday, providing he saves nothing. If therefore, you receive £100 on the first day of the month and have nil on the last day of the month, then the average amount you hold during the month is £50. The greater your income, the higher will be the average amount you will hold for transactions.

We all need cash for the purpose of conducting our everyday transactions, but this is only one part of our money. If we have a current bank account then the deposit in this account can be withdrawn in cash or transferred by cheque. Thus our stock of money consists of cash plus our bank deposit. The amount we will hold at any time for the purpose of transacting our regular business will depend upon whether we get paid weekly or monthly, whether we pay our regular bills at the beginning or at the end of the month, whether our income is large or small, and the level of prices of the goods we purchase.

To a large extent firms are in the same position. They receive their money from the sales revenue of their products or other earnings. From these returns they have to make regular payments for the purchase of raw materials or for the payment of wages and so on. The amount of money they have in stock at any one time therefore depends on a whole host of factors; whether wages are paid weekly or monthly, how regularly returns from sales come in, how often bills for raw materials have to be settled and so on.

From the community's point of view, therefore, we can say that the need for a stock of money to be held for transactions purposes arises from the fact that the series of receipts and payments that are regularly arising cannot be synchronised. Balances of money have, therefore, to be kept waiting for a time when the transaction can be made. Two factors will determine the size of the stock of money held for transactions purposes, the size of incomes, and the frequency of payments.

12·1

If you receive an income of £30 per week each week and in spending all of it, you spread your spending out evenly over the whole week, how much on average will you hold as your stock of money?

A £5 **B** £10 **C** £15 **D** £20 **E** £25

12·2

If you are paid a salary of £120 per month, you spend all of it, and you spread your spending out evenly over the month, how much on average will you be holding as your stock of money for the purpose of transactions?

A £20 **B** £40 **C** £50 **D** £60 **E** £80

---

ii The precautionary motive. The second distinguishable reason for people's holding of money is their desire to have a reserve of money to meet unforeseen circumstances. Keynes described this as the precautionary motive for holding money. At any one time people and firms will demand to keep a certain proportion of their wealth in the form of money, rather than in the form of interest-bearing securities which are not easily encashable, in order to meet expenses which could not have been foreseen. Temporary unemployment for an individual, or the loss of sales revenue due to, say, a strike of delivery drivers, would cause an unforeseen demand for money. The amount an individual holds in stock for precautionary motives will remain relatively constant over time, as it will with firms, but it may increase as national income increases.

At this stage we should be quite clear that when we are talking of the demand for money we mean cash and bank deposits *not cash alone*.

iii The speculative motive. The third and final motive for demanding money, according to Keynes, is the desire to have a stock of money at the ready to take advantage of any opportunity for profit which may arise. For example, firms may keep idle balances of money for the purposes of speculation in the product markets. If they anticipate future changes in the price of their essential raw materials they feel inclined to stagger their orders accordingly. It is not uncommon just prior to the annual Budget, when firms may be anticipating, say, increases in the import tariff on a particular raw material, for firms to stockpile goods by buying them before the tax changes so avoiding the higher price that is bound to result. This is a form of speculation. If firms wish to take advantage of such situations they must be prepared to hold a stock of money for the purpose. They must balance the cost of holding their wealth in the form of a liquid non-earning asset against the benefit to be gained from speculating in the manner just described.

In fact, Keynes explained that the speculative motive for holding money arises because people and firms can choose between keeping some of their wealth in the form of money, which will yield no interest, or converting it into income-yielding assets, such as government securities (also called bonds). The higher the reward for surrendering liquidity, i.e. the higher the interest received, the less money people will wish to keep. The yield, or market rate of interest, on government securities, varies inversely with the price of these securities on the Stock Exchange: when the prices of securities are high, yields are low; when the prices of securities are low, then yields are high.

The basic principle underlying this statement may be explained by taking a simple example. If the government wishes to borrow a hundred pounds, it usually issues a promise to pay in, for example, 10 years' time. It also normally states a *fixed* rate of interest, say 5%. If the bond is purchased for £100, the buyer will receive £5 per year for as long as he holds the bond. Suppose, however, that after one year the general rate of interest on loans rises to 10%. The bondholder will not be able to sell a bond earning 5% (or £5) per year for £100 because a prospective buyer can earn £10 per £100 elsewhere. Therefore, the bondholder lowers the price of the bond to about £50, so now the purchaser will receive £5 from the government as he holds the title deed or bond, and this is 10%, or the competitive market rate of interest. Of course, if he holds on to this bond for nine years, he will also gain a capital appreciation of £50, so that the total *yield* will be £5 per year interest plus £50. In practice, the pricing of bonds is complicated because not only is the interest usually calculated at a compound rate, but capital appreciation is also taken into account. Nevertheless, the principle of such transactions is that when security prices are high and yields low, people will prefer to hold their wealth in the most liquid form, money, because it will not be worth buying securities. Instead, potential buyers will hold money, in the hope that the yields on securities will soon rise again. They would be foolish to use their money to buy securities at a high price yielding a low rate of interest, when, if their expectations were correct, they could buy the same security later at a lower price and with a correspondingly higher yield. Similarly, when yields are high, and the market prices of securities are low, people will prefer to buy these income-yielding assets rather than hoard cash.

12·3

You have £1 000 cash which you could use to buy government securities. The market rate of interest is expected to rise in the near future. Will you

A Maintain a stock of money?

B Buy some government securities immediately?

12·4

The current market rate of interest is 5%. You expect it to fall to 3% in the near future. As a speculator will you

A Maintain a stock of money?

B Buy some government securities immediately?

We have said that the demand to hold money, or liquidity preference, arises because there are three distinct motives explaining the public's desire to hold some of their wealth in the form of money. The motives are the transactions motive, the precautionary motive, both of which are un-

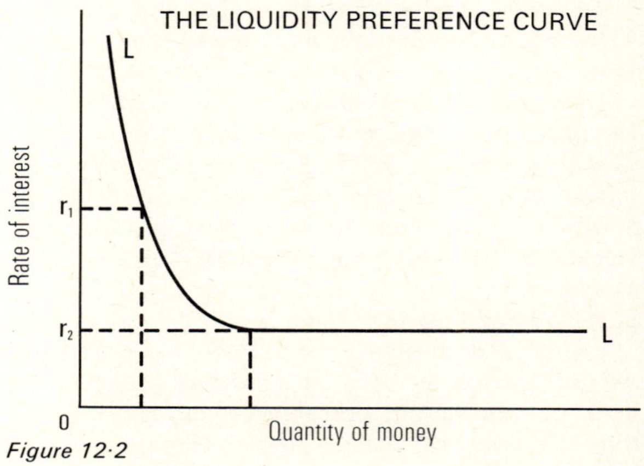

Figure 12·2

responsive to changes in the rate of interest, and the speculative motive. The amount of money held for speculative motives will depend upon the present market rate of interest and also upon the expectations that investors have about the future rate. The market rate of interest is the reward for surrendering liquidity, or, in other words the price paid for money loans.

The liquidity preference curve

From what has been written about the relationship between the rate of interest and the demand for money, we can construct a demand curve for money showing how the quantity of money the public wishes to hold will vary according to the rate of interest—figure 12·2. In this diagram the 'rate of interest' represents the general level of interest rates. (The structure of interest rates is discussed in S16). This demand curve for money is also known as the liquidity preference curve (or schedule).

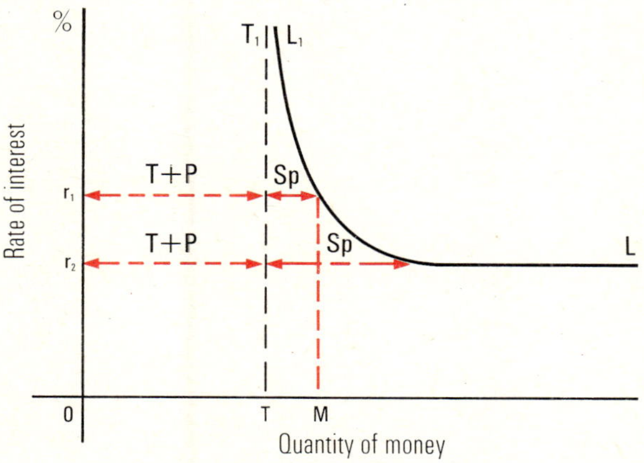

THE LIQUIDITY PREFERENCE CURVE

Figure 12·3

In figure 12·3 the speculative liquidity preference curve is L_1L. The vertical dotted line T_1T shows the quantity of money demanded by the public for transactions and precautionary purposes: we have shown that this is unaffected by variations in the rate of interest, i.e. it is interest inelastic. The gap between the line T_1T and the complete curve L_1L shows how the quantity of money demanded for speculative purposes varies with the level of interest rates. At high rates the amount demanded for this purpose will be minimal; people and firms will prefer to convert any excess cash they receive, above their transaction and precautionary requirements, into securities offering high yields. At lower rates the amount demanded increases, because when the yield on securities is lower, a few more people will hold on to cash, expecting to be able to buy securities later when yields are higher again. Therefore at interest rate Or_1 the demand for money is composed of OT for transactions and precautionary purposes, and TM for speculative purposes. At very low rates of interest the quantity of money demanded for speculative purposes will be infinite, because no one will wish to convert money into income-yielding assets when yields are so low. At Or_2 the demand for money is infinitely elastic; note that the amount demanded for transactions and precautionary purposes will remain the same.

Of course, like any other demand curve, the whole liquidity preference curve may shift if people increase or reduce the amount of money they require to keep for any of the three motives at the same level of interest rate (e.g.Or_1). An overall increase in the demand for money is depicted in figure 12·4. The new demand curve is L_2L. The speculative demand for money becomes infinitely elastic at the same level of interest rate as before.

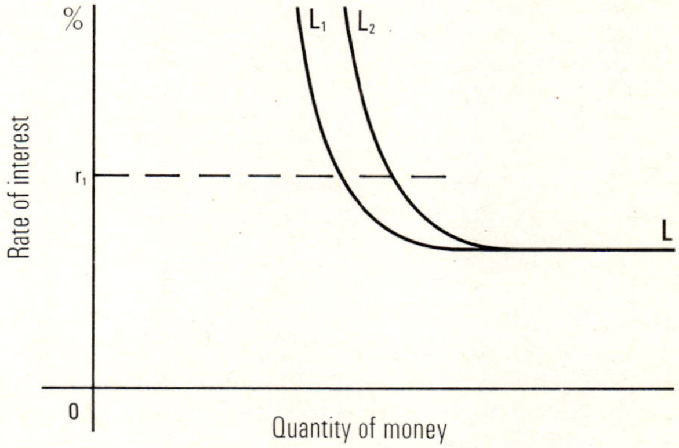

Figure 12·4

12·5

What reasons can you suggest for

i an increase in the transactions and precautionary demands for money at an unchanged level of interest rates?

ii an increase in the speculative demand at an unchanged level of interest rates?

Following the Keynesian analysis of the demand for money, you can see that the level of interest rates, i.e. the price of money loans, will be determined by the interaction of the demand for, and the supply of, money.

The supply of money

As you will remember from S6 the supply of money consists of currency and bank deposits. When we talk of the supply of money we mean the stock of money that is in the country at any one time. Forms of 'near money' which we also discussed in S6 are also very important to the economy, but for the time being we shall concentrate on currency and bank deposits and leave the more complicated analysis of near money until a little later.

In the table below the figures given show that currency (notes and coin) forms just over 20% of the money supply; the rest is composed of entries in the books of the domestic banks, the National Giro, and the discount houses.

THE MONEY SUPPLY IN THE U.K.*

		£ million	
	1964	1969	197–
Currency in circulation with public	2 328	2 903	
Deposits at banks and National Giro:			
(a) current accounts	4 742	5 172	
(b) deposit accounts	3 348	4 973	
Deposits at discount houses	90	96	
Total	10 508	13 144	

Source: *Annual Abstract of Statistics 1970*

* Strictly speaking this should be called the money stock. It is not a flow. The items chosen are those in the Bank of England's second definition of the money stock, M_2.

Consult the *Annual Abstract of Statistics* or *Bank of England Quarterly Bulletin,* add data for the most recent year you can find and compare the proportions of currency and bank deposits for that year with the last year shown above.

The supply of notes and coin in this country is regulated by the Bank of England which is the sole note issuer. The notion that the British currency is backed by gold is now no longer true. The supply of notes and coin is varied by the Bank in accordance with the needs of the general public to make cash transactions. Thus at Christmas time the supply of notes and coin may be increased by as much as £10 million in order to satisfy the needs of consumers who are making more cash purchases than they normally do.

Most of our attention is going to be directed toward the volume of bank deposits, since they represent by far the greater part of the total supply of money, and are especially important because the banks themselves have the ability and the inclination to create deposits. The Bank of England only has indirect control of this process, yet if the supply of money is to be controlled the Bank must take certain measures. Before looking at these measures remind yourself of the process by which the commercial banks can create deposits, by referring to S6.

In S6 we showed that a bank's power to create deposits was limited by the need (a) to preserve adequate cash and liquidity ratios, and (b) to ensure that there was adequate security for their loans. Since liquid assets are easily convertible into cash, it is the liquidity ratio which is the main determinant of bank lending. Given a liquidity ratio of 28%, we saw that the banks collectively could expand deposits by 3½ times any increase in liquid assets, and would have to reduce deposits by 3½ times any fall in liquid assets. Note that we refer to the banking system as a whole: a mere transfer of cash between individual banks will not affect the overall level of deposits, but it would force the banks losing cash to reduce deposits and allow the banks gaining cash to expand deposits.

If the banking system as a whole receives liquid assets, then it can create total deposits to 3½ times the value of these liquid assets, and if it invests in illiquid assets, it must correspondingly reduce its deposits, so as to maintain the 28% liquidity ratio. The size of this 'deposit multiplier', 3½, is determined by the ratio necessary between deposits and liquid assets. If the liquidity ratio were smaller the deposit multiplier would be larger.

Because of developments during the spring of 1971, we need to show that the value of the deposit multiplier can be altered in three ways. The most obvious way is for the Bank of England to decide that the ratio of liquid assets to gross deposits need no longer be 28:100 or 28% but should be, say, 12½%. In this case, the 'deposit multiplier' has changed from 3½ to 8.

Another method of altering the deposit multiplier is to alter the list of acceptable items for inclusion as liquid assets; for example, the Bank of England could decide that cash in the till (about 6% of gross deposits) may no longer be regarded as a liquid item to be included in the 28% liquid assets ratio. By altering the definition of liquid assets, the Bank of England has made the effective ratio 34%, because the banks would have to increase their other liquid assets, say cash at the

Bank of England, to meet the new requirement. The deposit multiplier would in this case be nearer 3 than $3\frac{1}{2}$.

The third method of changing the value of the deposit multiplier is a little more complex. The liquidity ratio is, at present, the ratio of liquid assets to *gross* liabilities or deposits. The Bank of England could decide that the ratio should be of liquid assets to *domestic* liabilities only, and it could require quite a different ratio to apply to overseas deposits.

Suppose the ratio of liquid assets to gross liabilities is 1:10, then the deposit multiplier will be 10; if, however, the definition is changed to the liquid assets to domestic liabilities ratio, and the ratio remains at 1:10, then it is not possible to have a simple deposit multiplier as before, because the overseas deposits may have all kinds of effects; sometimes the deposit multiplier of domestic deposits may be accentuated and at other times this deposit multiplier may be diminished.

It is worth noting that the possibilities we have just described merely make the practice of credit creation more complicated; the principle remains the same. If banks only require a proportion of their liabilities as liquid assets, then there will be a multiple creation of credit.

In fact, during May 1971, proposals were made to implement all three of the measures described above at the same time. The Bank of England proposed to apply a liquidity ratio of $12\frac{1}{2}\%$ to all banks, including deposit-taking finance houses, but excluding the discount houses. Liquid assets were, in this proposal, re-defined to include cash at the Bank of England, other than special deposits, Treasury bills, money at call with the London money market, British Government stocks with under one-year to maturity and commercial bills which qualify for re-discount at the Bank of England. The reader will notice that cash in the banks' tills is not included in the proposed $12\frac{1}{2}\%$ ratio.

All banks would be required to place special deposits, bearing a rate of interest near to that given on Treasury bills, with the Bank of England as required. In the past these special deposits were a certain percentage of gross liabilities; in the future, they would, if the proposals are accepted, be calculated by reference to all, or only some, of the banks' liabilities. Hence, the rate of call could apply to overseas deposits only.

The proposals, therefore, not only alter the numerical value of the liquidity ratio and the deposit multiplier, and change the definition of the liquid assets by excluding cash in the tills, but also, if the special deposit is regarded as a call on the liquid assets of banks, change the simple relationship of a single ratio of liquid assets to gross liabilities.

Suppose the ratio of liquid assets to gross liabilities is set at $12\frac{1}{2}\%$, but a call is made for a special deposit of 5%, based on domestic liabilities only. We may now argue that there will be a series of liquidity ratios; a ratio of liquid assets to gross liabilities, a ratio to domestic liabilities, and as a consequence of the determination of these two ratios, yet another ratio, the ratio of liquid assets to overseas liabilities. Nevertheless, the principle of a deposit multiplier still remains; if there is no special deposit called for by the Bank of England, an addition of one pound to the newly defined liquid assets of the banking system, say, in cash at the Bank of England, will allow the system as a whole to increase their total liabilities by eight times, given the $12\frac{1}{2}\%$ liquidity ratio. A call for a special deposit will reduce this multiplier, but by how much depends on the nature of the special deposit.

Thus, the government has the power to affect the bank's opportunities to choose between liquid and illiquid assets, and thus, through the liquidity ratio, the government can affect the bank's power to create new deposits.

12·6

What would be the value of the deposit multiplier if the liquidity ratio were

a $33\frac{1}{3}\%$? **b** 25%? **c** $12\frac{1}{2}\%$?

12·7

What will be the effect of companies' payments of corporation tax on the level of

a commercial bank deposits?

b liquid assets of banks?

An important factor, which in a free economy will affect the lending power of the commercial banks, is the amount of cash which the public wishes to hold at any one time. If the liquidity preference of the public increases, so that they withdraw cash from the banks, then the banks' ability to lend will be restricted, as by convention the banks have to retain a proportion of their assets in the form of cash in the till, or as a deposit in the Bank of England.

Now let us see how the Bank of England, in the absence of complete control over the commercial banks, controls the total supply of money to the country by influencing the lending power and thus the deposit creation of the commercial banks.

Controlling the money supply

The money market is constantly changing to exploit new opportunities for profits. Thus the government, through the Bank of England, may experience some difficulty in exercising control over the market institutions, for as soon as effective direction is established over one market situation, the structure of the market may change and thus force the Bank or the government to restructure its system of market management. For example, in the period 1960 to 1970, commercial banks found that it was possible to use subsidiary companies to avoid the traditional controls over commercial bank credit expansion.

For these reasons, the government must attempt to answer the following questions before setting out to control the money supply.

i What constitutes the supply of money? Certainly currency in circulation and commercial bank current account deposits are money, but it is generally accepted that deposit accounts must also be included, because they can so easily be transformed into current accounts. Therefore the Bank of England's second definition of the money supply includes deposit accounts. The third of the Bank's definitions includes deposits held at accepting houses and overseas banks. You can find the different totals under the different definitions listed in the *Annual Abstract* or the *Bank of England Quarterly Bulletin.* Refer also to satellite *Sample Studies of Financial Institutions* for further discussion.

ii Which institutions are subject to the control of the monetary authorities? Normally it is the commercial banks and discount houses which come under the direct control of the government (via the Bank of England), but because the public has been making increased use of deposits at other institutions, the Bank of England has had to extend its requests for limitation of lending to acceptance houses and other financial insitutions, such as hire purchase finance houses, which are not directly affected by the traditional weapons of monetary control.

iii How much will interest rates be affected by monetary controls? If money is 'tight', i.e. loans are difficult to obtain, interest rates will be high. If money is 'cheap', i.e. loans are easy to obtain, interest rates will be low. You can already see that the government may sometimes hesitate to restrict the supply severely, because if it does not interest rates rise excessively. Later we shall use the concept of liquidity preference to explain this.

Monetary controls

We shall first look at some of the more traditional controls employed by the Bank of England.

i Bank Rate. The rate at which the Bank of England discounts first class bills for the discount houses is known as the Bank rate. It is announced each Thursday and when changes are announced it usually causes a flurry of activity in the money market as one institution after another rushes to adjust its rates in accordance with the official rate. But why do all the rates in the market change at the same time?

The discount houses borrow at call and short notice from the commercial banks. If the banks call in their short term loans to the discount houses the latter are 'forced into the Bank'. In other words they have to sell some of their Treasury bills or commercial bills to the Bank which will buy them at the discount rate of the Bank rate (although sometimes it may make loans at the prevailing level of market rates).

The Bank of England fixes the Bank rate deliberately at a higher rate than any other short term rate of interest in the money market. Hence as the discount houses know that borrowing from the Bank of England will be unprofitable, it is known as the 'Lender of Last Resort'. As soon as the Bank announces an increase in the Bank rate the discount houses know that it is going to be more expensive to 'go into the Bank'; to cover this eventuality they in turn put up their discount rate. This will increase the margin of profit on the business they are conducting and they will increase their demand for money from the commercial banks. This increase in demand will allow the banks to increase their short term lending rates. If they do not also increase their long term lending rates then the demand for long term funds will also increase. So when Bank rate rises, all other rates of interest tend to rise in step as borrowers chase funds from one source or another.

In fact, several rates are immediately adjusted

upwards or downwards following a change in Bank rate, e.g. 'money at short notice' lent to discount houses is usually 2% below Bank rate. The question for the government, however, is whether an increase in the Bank rate will reduce the demand for bank loans and other credit generally. If it does then the commercial banks will be able to create fewer deposits. The supply of money will thus be restricted.

We must, therefore consider the interest-elasticity of demand for money loans; or, in other words, the responsiveness of the demand for money loans to changes in the rate of interest. This will depend on the use to which the money is being put. If you are a businessman, earning 10% return on the capital you are employing in your firm, you will readily pay 5% in interest on the capital borrowed. If the rate of interest rises, however, you will have to think very carefully and may even cease to borrow until either the rate falls or your returns increase. The average return on capital employed in U.K. industry is approximately 15% and the Bank of England has had to accept recently that a Bank rate of 7% is not a great disincentive to borrowing.

Overdraft rates range from ½% to 4% above Bank rate, so if Bank rate is 7%, a company may be asked to pay 9%. Even at this rate firms are only too willing to borrow. It was for this reason that the Radcliffe Report (*Workings of the Monetary System* H.M.S.O. 1959) suggested that small changes in interest rates had little effect on the demand for money loans. They recommended that large jumps in the rate would have to be made if any influence were to be made on the supply of money. The fact is then, that in the U.K. at the present time the demand for money loans is largely interest-inelastic.

ii Open market operations. The second method by which the Bank of England can attempt to control the supply of money is known as open market operations. The government broker, acting on instructions from the Bank, buys or sells government securities on the Stock Exchange. Open market operations can have three effects:

(a) a direct effect on the supply of money,
(b) 'making the Bank rate effective',
(c) a reduction or increase in the liquid assets of the commercial banks, which will affect their ability to create deposits by making loans.

The sequence of events is as follows.

The commercial banks hold part of their cash as bankers' balances at the Bank of England. If the government broker enters the market and buys, say, £100 000 of bonds, it will pay the sellers of the bonds by cheques drawn on the government's account at the Bank of England. The sellers will present the cheques at their own banks and receive a corresponding increase in their bank deposits; this therefore is an immediate increase in the money supply in the hands of the public by £100 000. However, bankers' balances will also have increased because of the transfer of cash from the government's account to pay the cheques. Most of this extra cash will be converted into other liquid assets, and this increase in liquid assets would allow the commercial banks to increase deposits by making loans. A multiple expansion of deposits can take place. The Bank of England has therefore increased the supply of money by buying securities in the market.

The converse is also true. If the Bank wishes to reduce the supply of money it can do so by instructing the government broker to sell securities. This will cause buyers to draw cheques on their accounts at the commercial banks in favour of Bank of England. This immediately reduces the supply of money in the hands of the public, and to pay the debt to the government, the bankers' balances will be reduced. The banks will replace the lost cash by recalling money at call from the discount houses: as a result the discount houses will be forced into the Bank and will have to borrow at Bank rate, and the Bank rate is made effective in the money market. The third result is that if the banks were already at the minimum liquidity ratio, total deposits must be reduced by reducing advances, in order to restore the liquidity ratio. Therefore if £100 000 of bonds were sold initially, the total reduction in deposits, combining the initial reduction plus the reduction in loans would be, if the deposit multiplier is 3½ times the initial sale, £350 000.

In practice open market operations are not always as effective as this, for several reasons. First, the money used to purchase securities which the government broker sells may not all come from commercial bank deposits: some may be withdrawn from deposits at building societies or from loans to hire purchase companies. If this is so there will not be such a large initial reduction in the supply of immediately spendable money, although the clearing banks, acting as agents through whom final payment is made to the government, will lose cash. Secondly, the banks may have sufficient liquid assets to enable them to avoid the necessity for a multiple contraction of deposits after the initial loss of cash; i.e. if originally they have liquid assets equal to 30% of total deposits, and then lose cash equal to 1% of deposits, they can restore the cash loss and still leave the liquidity ratio at approximately 29%. A third limitation on the effectiveness of open market operations, and also of calls for special deposits (see below), is that the commercial banks will prefer to sell investments (their government securities) rather than reduce loans to their customers, which would cause loss of goodwill and reduced interest income. When the banks try to sell securities, the price of the securities on the market will tend to fall and there will be a corresponding rise in yields, i.e. the market rates of interest will rise. The Bank of England is often unwilling to allow large fluctuations in the prices and yields of government securities, so to prevent the prices falling it may stop selling securities itself, and buy the securities which the commercial banks are selling! Consequently the Bank pays the commercial banks by increasing their bankers' balances, and so the banks gain the cash they need and do not reduce total deposits by cutting loans.

Similarly, when the government broker buys securities, not all the money created will end up as commercial bank deposits: some will be deposited with other institutions in the form of 'near money'. As total deposits increase the public will probably wish to keep a little more of their money in the form of notes and coin, in the ratio of £1 currency to £4 bank deposits, so the commercial banks will lose a little of their increased cash for this reason. Therefore, in practice, open market operations will not cause a contraction or expansion of deposits by as much as 3½ times the initial change in liquid assets.

It is important to note that only open market operations in long-term securities or sales of Treasury bills to holders *other than discount houses or banks* will affect the liquid assets of commercial banks. The commercial banks class Treasury bills as liquid assets, since they can be resold on the money market to the discount houses or some other buyer quickly and without loss of capital value. This is because Treasury bills have a very short life and in fact the Bank of England likes to have stable rates and prices of Treasury bills. Therefore when the banks acquire Treasury bills originally bought by discount houses, they aquire liquid assets, and their lending powers are not reduced but increased. The Radcliffe Report pointed out that the solution lay in the government's reducing the number of Treasury bills sold and increasing the number of longer-term securities sold. Then if the commercial banks bought the longer term debt their liquidity ratio would be effectively reduced. The process they recommended is known as *funding*.

iii Funding. The government has occasion to borrow funds for many purposes. It may borrow from the public during war time in order to finance the purchases of arms and materials essential to the war effort. If this is the case then the debt is known as 'deadweight' debt. It is a deadweight to the government because it does not represent any kind of tangible asset. On the other hand, however, the government may borrow in order to finance some major capital project like the electrification of British Rail or the building of an additional airport. In this case the debt is known as 'reproductive' debt. It is balanced by some real asset which will benefit the community. Unfortunately the greater part of the British National Debt is in the deadweight form.

The British National Debt had its origin in 1694 when William III had reason to borrow to finance the wars against France. During the First World War the Debt increased to £7 800 million. By 1945 it had reached £25 000 million. In 1969 it reached £34 000 million.

The structure of the National Debt is as follows:

(a) Floating debt consists of short term securities, Treasury bills.

(b) Funded debt consists of long term government stocks. You can find a list of these stocks in the financial pages of most newspapers. Examples are, War Loan 3½%, 2½% Consols, Exchequer Loan 5% 1976–1978. The dates referred to are those between which the government will redeem (buy back) the bonds at their face value.

NATIONAL DEBT 1969, A SUMMARY

	£ million
Total Marketable Securities e.g. Conversion Stock, Exchequer Loan. Treasury Loan, B.O.A.C. stock, Funding Loan	19 228
National Savings Securities e.g. N. Savings certificates, Premium Bonds, National Savings stamps	2 015
Floating Debt i.e. Treasury Bills	5 740
Other Debts (including debts to other countries)	6 999
TOTAL NATIONAL DEBT	33 892

Source: *Annual Abstract of Statistics*

12·8
Calculate the proportion of total debt accounted for by floating debt.

Each year the government is obliged to pay interest on the National Debt. The revenue for this comes largely from taxation. It is a considerable burden on the taxpayer, accounting as it does for over 10% of total government current spending each year.

Now we shall return to the question of funding. The process is simply the restructuring of the National Debt from floating to funded debt.

We have seen that the government is continually borrowing money, both to finance major projects, and to bridge day to day gaps between income and expenditure. Short term government borrowing is achieved by the sale of Treasury bills through the discount houses. Long term government borrowing is carried on by the sale of bonds on the Stock Exchange. Every day the government borrows money and repays previous debts: it is a continuous process. The government therefore always has the power to alter its borrowing from long term or short term, or from short term to long term. It can repay a bond and issue Treasury bills, or repay bills and issue bonds. In this way it can alter the banks' opportunities to purchase liquid assets. When the government sells Treasury bills, the banks have the opportunity to purchase liquid assets. In order to maintain their liquidity ratio, banks can create new deposits to the value of $3\frac{1}{2}$ times the liquid assets. On the other hand, if the government restricts the sale of Treasury bills, the banks must reduce their deposits by $3\frac{1}{2}$ times the value of their loss of liquid assets.

To some extent the commercial banks have avoided the restriction imposed by funding on their lending powers. Even though the number of Treasury bills available may decline as the longer term debt being sold by the government is increased, the banks may maintain their liquidity by adding to their holdings of commercial bills. These bills of exchange can be bought from the discount houses, and are just as liquid as Treasury bills and earn the banks a small rate of interest. It is to other measures therefore that the government and the Bank of England have had to look in order to gain effective control over the supply of money.

iv Special deposits. When these are required the Bank of England informs the commercial banks that part of their deposits held at the banks are to be 'frozen' and unusable. You will remember that the commercial banks' deposits with the Bank of England are part of their holdings of cash, so to be told that part of it has been made completely illiquid is the same as being told that part of their cash has been converted into an illiquid asset. In this way the Bank of England affects the lending power of the banks. They restore their cash ratio by converting liquid assets, but they must make up their liquidity ratio again to 28% of their total deposits and this means reducing their deposits by cutting down on advances.

Interest is usually paid by the Bank of England on the special deposits held by it for the commercial banks, but this is no compensation for losing part of their liquid assets which would back $3\frac{1}{2}$ times the amount in created deposits. In 1969 the Bank halved the interest on special deposits because the commercial banks had not reduced advances sufficiently.

Special deposits are usually fixed at a certain percentage of the total assets of the commercial banks: 2% has been the most normal figure used by the Bank.

v Directives. The Treasury can issue directives to the commercial banks to restrict their lending. Some time ago it was fashionable to speak of 'moral suasion' in this respect but, when the banks failed to respond, directives were introduced. If the directives are ignored the Bank threatens to withdraw interest on the special deposits. Directives could require the banks to restrict the increase in advances to a certain percentage, e.g. 5% p.a., and to make loans only to certain categories of business, e.g. exporting.

vi Prescribed liquidity ratios. Many other advanced industrial nations rely on fewer but more direct methods to control the lending of their banks. One such method is for the central bank to prescribe the liquidity ratio maintained by the commercial banks. In the case of Britain the Bank of England would simply decree that the commercial banks must increase their liquid cash assets to, say, 30% of their total assets. This would effectively reduce their lending powers. However, the calling and releasing of special deposits has the same effect.

A credit squeeze consists of several of these measures. It is normal to hear the announcement that the Bank rate has been raised, the Bank has increased its holding of special deposits and has also directed the banks to restrict their lending.

CHANGE IN THE MONEY SUPPLY 1967–1970

Financial Years	Currency in Circulation	Bank Deposits	Total Money Supply
1967/68	+106	+1220	+1326
1968/69	+ 69	+ 846	+ 916
1969/70	+129	+ 152	+ 281

+indicates an increase

Source: *Bank of England Quarterly Bulletin Dec. 1970*

The table above shows just how successful the government's monetary policy can be at times. A high Bank Rate of 8%, strict directives, open market operations and the holding of special deposits by the Bank of England were all used during this period in order to restrict the supply of money to the economy. You can see how important an item bank deposits is when compared to the total money supply.

Domestic Credit Expansion (DCE)

In times when a credit squeeze is necessary, borrowing by the public sector (the central and local governments and the nationalised industries) must be curtailed as well as borrowing by the private sector. The public sector borrows by raising overdrafts and issuing securities (Treasury bills, bonds). However, there is an extra source of funds for the public sector, in addition to the financial institutions we have already mentioned; the government can borrow sterling from the Exchange Equalisation Account. To allow for this a new definition of changes in purchasing power has come into use, known as Domestic Credit Expansion.

Domestic Credit Expansion measures the *increase in credit* during any period. It can differ from the figures for changes in the *money supply* because it includes the effect of public sector borrowing from overseas. When there is a balance of payments deficit the Exchange Equalisation Account accumulates sterling, which is paid in by foreigners who have received sterling in payment for their exports to us, and pays out foreign currencies in exchange. These large sterling holdings of the Exchange Equalisation Account are used by the government to finance its expenditure, so in effect the government is borrowing from overseas; the excess sterling paid in by foreigners comes into the Exchange Equalisation Account because the country is running a balance of payments deficit. When there is a surplus the Exchange Equalisation Account sells sterling and the government cannot borrow from this source; therefore when there is a surplus on the balance of payments Domestic Credit Expansion will be less than the increase in the money supply. The table following shows how the change from deficit into surplus in 1969 affected DCE. Public sector borrowing from overseas was negative.

Controlling the supply of money is not easy. Given that you can successfully control the supply of cash and bank deposits you then have the problem of credit which comes from other sources. Strictly speaking, this is not regarded as 'money', but as it contributes to the total purchasing power of the community, it must be regarded just as seriously. For this reason, as we have already explained, the government may restrict public sector borrowing. Another form of credit which must be controlled is hire purchase. Goods purchased on hire purchase are in fact obtained through the lending of finance companies. These companies lend generally for periods of up to three years. The interest rates charged on the loans are higher to compensate for the relative lack of security offered by customers. The Chancellor of the Exchequer obtained powers in the early 1960s to regulate the repayment time for hire purchase debt, and also to regulate the 'down payment' or initial deposit, that is required before a hire purchase loan can be made. The Chancellor, during a period of domestic credit restriction, will increase the down payment and reduce the repayment term necessary, by law, before hire purchase agreements can be arranged.

Regulation of the money supply involves more

DOMESTIC CREDIT EXPANSION 1967–1970 £ million

	Currency in circulation	Public sector borrowing from overseas	Bank lending to private sector	Bank lending to public sector	TOTAL
1967/68	+106	+1 450	+746	– 26	+2 276
1968/69	+ 69	+ 422	+577	+109	+1 177
1969/70	+129	–1 239	+710	–206	– 606

Source: *Bank of England Quarterly Bulletin Dec. 1970*

than the control of one or two variables in the economy. Measures must be taken to affect the whole network of institutions whose function is to create credit. New institutions may be set up, the functions of old ones may change. The monetary authorities must remain aware of these changes and make efforts to influence them: indeed, in May 1971, a series of proposals were circulated to make the banking system more effective and competitive. The Bank of England proposed that banks should no longer determine, collectively, an interest rate, but that each bank should be free to offer customers its own rate of interest. Another proposal would remove the quantitative ceilings on bank lending so that banks should be free to lend as much as they like deciding policy solely on commercial grounds.

At the time of writing, these proposals were under discussion, but already on 17th May 1971, the Bank of England announced that it would no longer buy, outright, gilt-edged stock which has more than a year to go to maturity. In this way, the banks could no longer simply sell gilt-edged stock to the Bank of England when they needed liquid funds; hence, this new regulation strengthens the Bank of England's power to affect the liquidity of banks and the supply of credit through funding operations. *The Economist* of 22nd May 1971 described these proposals in an article significantly titled 'Yes, at last, revolution for the City'.

12·9

Given that the cost of borrowing on long term is higher than the cost of a short term borrowing, a policy of funding will reduce the cost of paying interest on the National Debt.

True/False

12·10

Commercial bills are just as liquid as Treasury bills.

True/False

12·11

'Liquidity versus profitability' is a phrase which means that the commercial banks are constantly seeking ways of becoming more liquid.

True/False

12·12

Special deposits are a more liquid way of holding one's assets than advances because the special deposits might be released at a moment's notice.

True/False

12·13

In January 1971 the ratio of liquid assets to total deposits held by the commercial banks was 30·5%. Six months previously the ratio had only been 28%. This means that in the six months in question the banks lending powers had increased.

True/False

12·14

You have a choice between borrowing £1 000 at 10% interest and buying a car now, repaying the loan over two years, or saving out of your income for two years and buying the car in two years' time. Prices of new cars are increasing at the rate of 10% per year.

Would you,

A buy the car with the loan?

B save up the money for two years and then buy cash?

12·15

If the rate of interest now rose to 15 per cent per year would you

A buy the car with the loan?

B save the money and pay cash in two years' time?

12·16

Would you conclude from your answers to the previous questions that an increase in the Bank rate during a period of rising prices is likely to be less successful in restricting the demand for bank loans than during a period of stable prices?

Yes/No

This last question leads us on to the final consideration and second aspect of the control of the supply of money. We recognise that there is some relationship between the supply of money and the price level. Thus during a period of rising prices we seek to control borrowing, but during a period of rising prices, borrowing is much more popular. If you can buy an article now which in one year's time will cost say, 10% more, then you will be only too willing to borrow the money at any rate of interest less than 10%. You may even be prepared to pay more than 10% since you will be receiving the satisfaction of your wants for a year, which without the loan you would otherwise have to forego. Thus rising prices encourage borrowing, which in turn encourages increases in the supply of money. Assuming that the increases in the supply of money are spent, this brings us full circle in stimulating increases in prices. For this reason during a period of rising prices less reliance can be placed on Bank rate policy than was once the case.

We have now considered, in some detail, the demand for and the supply of money. True to the pattern of our earlier experience we expect this to explain something to us about the price of money. What is the price of money? We explained earlier in this section that we must distinguish between 'money' and 'money loans'. The price of a 'money loan' is the rate of interest which has to be paid to secure the loan. Thus within the money market there exist short term rates of interest, while in the capital market long term rates are quoted. The price of money, however, is expressed in terms of the goods and services which will exchange for it. Thus during a period of rising prices we talk of the decline in the value of money, since the same unit of currency will exchange for fewer goods and services.

First we shall complete briefly the theory of the determination of the rate of interest, leaving a fuller analysis until S16 when further principles which have not yet been learned can be applied to the analysis. Then we shall look at the value of money as expressed in changes in the Index of Retail Prices.

The monetary theory of interest

We have discussed earlier how the demand for money arises, and we have now shown that the supply of money is controlled by the monetary authorities and so, at any one time, we assume it to be fixed. Figure 12·4 shows the interaction of the two forces of demand and supply. You will see how the monetary authorities can influence the rate of interest by altering the quantity of money supplied at any one time.

Given the existing state of liquidity preference, the authorities can bring about a change in the rate of interest from Or_1 to Or_2 by increasing the supply of money from OM_1 to OM_2. If the money supply is increased further, from OM_2 to OM_3, there will be no effect on the interest rate—all the extra money will be absorbed into idle balances, and none will be used to buy bonds and force down interest rates. The effect on the rate of interest of an increase in the liquidity preference of the public

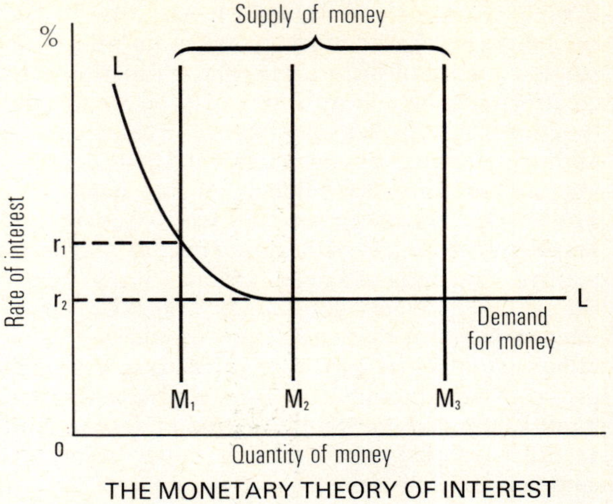

Figure 12·5

when the supply of money is fixed at OM_1 is shown in figure 12·6. As the liquidity preference curve shifts from L_1L to L_2L the rate of interest will rise from Or_1 to Or_2.

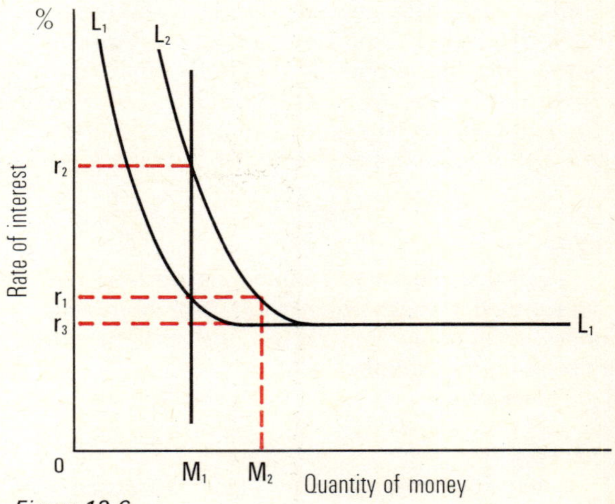

Figure 12·6

12·17

As the LL curve shifts to the right in figure 12·6 more money will be demanded at all rates of interest except at the lowest rate (Or_3). The reason that no more is demanded at interest rate Or_3 is that,

A people are holding less money.
B the price of bonds is low.
C the quantity of money demanded at Or_3 is infinite.

12·18

'An increase in the supply of money will, other things being equal, lead to a reduction in the rate of interest'.

In the above statement, the phrase 'other things being equal' refers to

- **A** the rate of interest.
- **B** the demand for money.
- **C** the supply of money.

12·19

'A fall in the liquidity preference of the community other things being equal, will lead to an increase in the rate of interest'.

True/False

You may question this monetary theory of the determination of the rate of interest, in the light of what has been said previously about the Bank of England's Bank rate policy. We have already stated that nearly all interest rates move in conjunction with the Bank rate and that this in turn is fixed by the Bank of England every Thursday. So, if the rate is fixed, why do we need a theory? The answer to this lies in the fact that when the Bank adjusts the Bank rate it can only affect all rates if it also alters the money supply. Without an alteration of the money supply changes in the Bank rate would have little effect on market rates of interest. Following an increase in the liquidity preference of the community the Bank will either stimulate an increase in the supply of money in order to keep interest rates down or it will keep the supply of money stable and allow the rate of interest to rise.

The manipulation of interest rates by the Bank of England has both internal and external consequencies. Where the demand for loans is interest-elastic the ability of the commercial banks to create deposits will be curtailed by an increase in the Bank rate. On the international front, however, an increase in the Bank rate will attract foreign funds from investors abroad who wish to lend in Britain at a higher rate than they can earn in their home countries. In order to do this they will have to obtain sterling currency and this will provide foreign currency for the nation's reserves to settle international debts, and increase the value of sterling on the international money market. This aspect of Bank rate policy is dealt with in S20.

Now let us turn to the value of money as expressed in the Index of Retail Prices.

The supply of money and the price level

We saw in S6 how money has four functions in an economy. It acts as a medium of exchange, a measure of value, a store of value and a standard for deferred payments. If you can imagine a situation in which there was no money then the value of a commodity would have to be expressed in terms of all other goods which might be exchangeable for it. In this situation the price of one commodity may rise or fall in terms of other goods. Suppose five kilograms of potatoes exchange for half a dozen eggs in November, but for only three eggs in the following May.

12·20

Has the price of eggs risen or fallen?

Thus where no money is used, as the exchange value of one good rises so the exchange value of another good must fall. In this situation we can draw one very important conclusion. *There can be no general increase in the price level where the supply of money is nil.* All that will happen in a 'no money' state is that the exchange values of individual goods will alter in terms of each other. There can be no overall increase in the level of prices. We must conclude therefore that the supply of money has something to do with the determination of the general level of prices. It is this relationship which we will soon examine but before doing so let us be sure what we mean by the price level.

How do we measure price level changes?

When we talk of prices having increased during the previous year we are usually referring to the Index of Retail Prices. This measure of the general level of retail prices is compiled by the Department of Employment and Productivity and published monthly in that Department's *Gazette*. It can be found also printed in the *Economist* and newspapers. A full description of the method of compiling the Index can be found in the satellite *Arithmetical and Statistical Methods*; a summary is all we shall make here.

i Commodities covered by the Index. The Index covers the following commodity groups:

Food	Durable household goods
Alcoholic drink	Clothing and footwear
Tobacco	Transport and vehicles
Housing	Miscellaneous goods
Fuel and light	Services

Each group consists of a number of sections; for Food, for example, there are bread, beef, fish, etc.
ii Collection of statistics. Retail prices are collected by the Department's offices from 200 different areas of the United Kingdom. Care is taken to ensure that a fair representation of all types of towns and rural areas are sampled. Furthermore, seasonal variations are taken into account and eliminated. Prices of the same quality of goods are noted at the same time each month and on the same day of the week. Where possible a representative sample of shops is used including small retail and large multiple stores. Altogether 920 goods and services are monitored from the 200 offices dealing with a total of approximately 2 000 retail outlets.
iii Weighting. The Department considers its job as similar to that of collecting the average price of a basket of shopping. Its 'basket' contains 920 goods and services. Each month it calculates the percentage increase in the total purchase. In practice however it does not calculate the total money cost each month, as it finds it is much simpler to find the percentage change in each good or service and to combine these changes into an all-items average percentage change. Now problems arise here. An example will help us to understand more clearly. If the price of a box of matches were to increase by 50% and the price of a pound of beef were to fall by 50%, then it would be incorrect to assume from this that the one balanced the other out and that there had been no change in the average price of this basket. Account must be taken of the proportion of average household expenditure taken up by each item. The procedure used is called *weighting*. If the total weight of the basket is 1 000 units then each item can be given a weight according to the proportion of the average household's expenditure it takes up. If, for instance, the average household spends 30% of its total expenditure on food then a weight of 300 will be attached to the item 'food', being 30% of the total weight of 1 000.

The following table gives the weights of the groups of items contained in the index.

Group weights used in 1966

	1966
Food	298
Alcoholic drink	67
Tobacco	77
Housing	113
Fuel and light	64
Durable household goods	57
Clothing and footwear	91
Transport and vehicles	116
Miscellaneous goods	61
Services	56
TOTAL	1 000

These weights are a useful guide to the changes in spending patterns of the average family. Details of these changes are derived from the Family Expenditure Survey which is conducted annually.

12·21

Do the changes in spending patterns, as shown in the table correspond with changes in the number of different types of retailing establishments in your area? Try to think what new shops have set up or of those which have recently modified the types of goods they stock.

12·22

The level of average earnings has been rising continuously. Is this the reason for the average family's spending a smaller proportion of its total spending on certain items? If so, which items are so affected?

Once the weights are attached, it is possible to calculate the average price increase, in percentage terms, of the total purchase.
iv Calculation. The percentage increase of each good is multiplied by its own weight. The sum of all of the products is calculated and divided by 1 000. This is the average price increase of the total purchase. For example, suppose the purchase consists of two items only, Food and Housing, with weights of 600 and 400 respectively. Suppose the percentage increase in the price of good is found to be 10% and of Housing 6%. The average percentage increase in the total is calculated as follows:

Food	$10 \times 600 =$	6 000
Housing	$6 \times 400 =$	2 400
Total		8 400

$$\text{Percentage increase } \frac{8\,400}{1\,000} = 8{\cdot}4\%$$

12·23

Using the 1966 weights shown in figure 12·10 calculate the percentage increase in the total basket if the individual increase were as follows:

Food 10%, Alcohol 5%, Tobacco 4%, Housing 5%,

Fuel and light 10%, Household goods 10%, Clothing 1%, Transport and vehicles 3%, Miscellaneous goods 5%, Services 10%.

v Presentation. A base year is chosen and changes in the average percentage increase in the level of retail prices are expressed as changes on that original year. The base year is given the value 100. If in the following year average retail prices have been found to have increased by 5%, then the Index in the following year will have risen to 105. When 1962 was the base year used the Index moved as follows: 1963—102·7; 1964—104·7; 1965—109·5; 1966—114·5. Thus between January 1962 and January 1966 the Index of retail prices had risen by 14·5 points indicating a rise in the level of retail prices during that time of 14·5%.

Changes in the level of retail prices

The rise in retail prices concerns everyone. It is generally thought that a slow rate of increase in prices, of 2 or 3%, is quite a healthy state of affairs. Entrepreneurs are encouraged to invest in the knowledge that the prices of the goods or services they are intending to manufacture will rise in price between the time when they have to pay for the raw materials and the time when they receive the revenue from sales. This is a sort of unearned bonus which encourages investors. Periods of falling prices have always been associated with falling production, austerity and large scale unemployment. Inflation, as we call a general rise in the level of retail prices, is therefore desirable if it can be kept within certain limits.

PURCHASING POWER OF THE POUND 1900–1967
(expressed in new pence)

1900	100							
1913	85	100						
1920	34	40	100					
1931	51	60	1·52	100				
1938	50	59	1·48	98	100			
1946	30	35	89	59	60	100		
1956	19	22	57	37	38	64	100	
1967	15	17	43	28	29	48	75	100

12·24

During which period did prices fall?

12·25

By what percentage did prices rise between the years 1938–1946?

When prices rise by more than a minimal rate of 2% then the effects of such an inflation are not as desirable as indicated earlier. Many other effects can ensue.

i People on fixed incomes suffer most. Old-age pensioners, people living on fixed benefits such as widows, the unemployed, the disabled, or people holding bonds which pay a fixed rate of interest on the original face value, all suffer as their money income remains constant and their real income falls. Those who will be least affected are those whose wages are found from the proceeds of manufacturing. Since the price of the products they are manufacturing have been rising the revenue for their increased pay is more readily available.

ii Saving is discouraged. People soon realise, when prices are rising rapidly, that the money they saved last year is worth less now that it was then, in terms of its purchasing power. If you were to save £100 in a bank and received 3% interest while prices were rising at the rate of 7% per year, then in three years' time your £100 will have depreciated by 12%. Under these circumstances saving becomes unattractive.

iii Borrowing is encouraged. If you borrow £100 at a rate of interest of 8% and have to pay back a year later, then if prices in that time have risen by 7%, the real cost of the loan to you is only 1%. If you had waited a year before buying a particular article, and its price has risen by 8% in that time, then you might just as well have borrowed the money at 8% and had the utility offered by the article purchased for the period of that year.

iv Consumption is encouraged. Obviously you will not want to wait to buy the goods you desire, if you expect their prices to rise rapidly in the future.

v Exports suffer. The price of our exports to overseas buyers will rise and tend to reduce quantity demanded. The amount by which the demand for exports is reduced will depend on the elasticity of demand for our exports.

vi Imports will rise. Foreign goods will become relatively cheaper than British goods. The demand for imports is therefore likely to increase. Both **v** and **vi** will worsen the balance of payments position for the U.K.

vii The burden of the National Debt will be reduced. The government pays a fixed income to holders of the securities which make up the National Debt. This income is the interest rate fixed at the time of issue. During a period of inflation as the value of money falls the real cost of paying the interest on the Debt will fall. Tax returns will automatically rise as earnings and firms' revenue and money profits rise so the burden of the Debt will be reduced. The unfortunate holders of government stock, of course are the losers by this. The purchaser of a bond, in 1960, for £1 000 at 5%, will receive £50 per year in income from the bond. If prices rise between 1960 and 1970, the year of the bond's maturity, to the extent of 50%, then the income of the bond will still be £50 but the purchasing power of that income will have fallen by a third.

We shall return, in greater detail, to the causes and effects of inflation in later sections. Since it is an economic problem which is currently concerning most industrial countries, we shall notice how the existence of inflation is intricately tied up with many variables within an economy. When we examine the U.K. balance of payments, for example, we shall notice the effect of inflation. On the other hand, when we examine how we can maintain a policy of full employment in an economy, we shall discover that such a policy is one of the causes of inflation. Thus inflation is a subject to which we shall return again and again. As we understand more economics in later sections we can apply what we have thus far learned to a deeper analysis than we are yet equipped for.

We have said enough, however, to show that an increase in the Retail Prices Index of 7·5%, as was experienced in the U.K. in 1970, is positively undesirable. We shall now look at one theory which seeks to connect increases in the price level with increase in the supply of money. It is called the Quantity Theory of money.

The quantity theory of money

The Quantity Theory purports to show the relation between prices and the quantity of money. In an attempt to reach mathematical precision, the so-called *quantity theory equation* was formulated.

$$M \times V = P \times T$$

when:

M equals the quantity of money
V equals the average number of times a unit of money changes hands per year
P equals the average price per transaction
T equal the number of transaction per annum

Money includes bank money; V is better known as the 'velocity of circulation'. The quantity of money, multiplied by the number of times each unit of that money performs a task, equals the total number of exchange transactions multiplied by the average price per transaction.

However, since MV is equal to the total volume of cash transactions, and PT equals the total volume of cash payments, MV is identical with PT, and the so-called equation is merely a tautology.

The theory may be queried on two other grounds. Firstly, is each term of the equation capable of statistical computation?

M can be calculated by adding the quantity of currency in circulation (the weekly return of Bank of England Issue Department), to the total bank deposits.

V equals the velocity of circulation. An index based on clearing house turnover has been prepared by the Midland Bank, the Midland Bank Index of Business Turnover (details in *Midland Bank Review*, May 1958).

P is shown by several published indices giving an indication of the level of prices (e.g. Wholesale Price Index numbers by the Board of Trade, and the United Kingdom Index of Retail Prices published by the Department of Employment and Productivity.) It is obvious that there is no homogeneous commodity on which an average price can be calculated. Thus, these index numbers merely show the direction of trends.

T equals the number of transactions per year. There is no way of calculating all these, but the number is assumed to vary with the total output of the country. Therefore the unemployment figures may be an indicator.

Secondly, what is the relationship of the variables?

Suppose M increased by 5%, given V and T remained constant. A strict interpretation of the quantity theory would say that P should increase in the same percentage. Another interpretation would say that P will change by less than 5%, but the change will be in the same direction as the change in M. Thus, an addition to M will affect V and T, but the major effect will be on P, and that effect will be an increase in the level of prices.

Arguments of this kind demonstrate the usefulness of the equation. It is a method of isolating one variable, assuming others remain unaffected. Unfortunately, sometimes it is not only the chosen variables which are affected. A change in productivity could cause a change in prices without any change whatever in the quantity of money. Any version of the Quantity Theory of Money must assume that there is no major technological change.

Further, the theory is limited in that velocity of circulation is not stable. Changes in the velocity of circulation can vary for institutional reasons (a change in the method of paying wages) or velocity can change because of people's expectations.

Any change in the price level leading to an expectation of a further increase must lead to a tendency to buy quickly before the next increase. Thus, formulations of the Quantity Theory which look to a simple connection between the quantity of money and prices assume a static economy.

The quantity of money is not therefore regarded as the most important factor. Movements in velocity are more important, for the opposite to passing on a unit of money is holding on to it. Variations of the Quantity Theory have been built on this inverse relationship.

The importance of money 'held' is that it may lie 'idle' or it may be placed at the disposal of industry as an investment. Thus, £10 not travelling around from hand to hand may hide under the mattress, or it may be added to the £1 000 being used to build a new factory.

In other words, when velocity is high people are not saving but spending, Spending money means, other things being equal, a tendency for prices to rise. A fall in velocity which results in a rise of saving which is used to finance an increase in investment can lead to a fall in prices.

The weakness of the Quantity Theory is now obvious, for savings, investment and consumption enter into the analysis (and will be dealt with in S15–22). What, then, is the importance of the Theory?

i It is a useful means of isolating variables.
ii The development of the inverse of velocity—holding money—led to a further analysis of the demand for money, and the concept of saving.
iii It has a limited application when a large increase in the quantity of money feeds inflation; see the German post-1918 experience described in most economic history books.
iv Action by the central bank which *changes expectations* can change the velocity of circulation and thereby influence the general level of prices.

Nowadays economists recognise that there is no simple formula to explain the relationship between the different causes of inflation at all times and in all circumstances. We must analyse many variables before being able to pin down those relevant to a particular situation. Below are listed some of the more prominent ones but a really thorough investigation of the causes of inflation must be left until further topics have been covered in the text. The satellite text *The Management of the Economy* discusses the causes and effects of inflation in Britain in the 1960s.

Other theories of inflation

Inflation is a situation in which the general level of prices is increasing. It will occur whenever there is a change in the conditions relating to the overall demand or supply of goods and services throughout the economy. Just as the price of an individual commodity is determined in the market by the forces of demand and supply, so the general price level, which is, as we have seen, only an average of all the prices in all the different markets, depends on the demand or supply of goods and services in general. During wartime it is usual for the supply of goods to the market to be restricted as the resources for production are diverted into industries catering for the Armed Forces. Under free conditions the price level would undoubtedly rise since a situation of general excess demand would exist. It is for this reason that governments often resort to rationing during wartime in order to ration out scarce goods which would otherwise rise in price. Rationing is a fairer way of distributing goods to the consumer. Without it prices generally would find their own level and the poorer sections of a community would simply go without.

Inflation can vary in intensity and is usually described in one of four ways.

i *Creeping inflation* is descriptive of a rate of price inflation of about 2% per annum or less. It is generally accepted that such a rate is not undesirable in an economy since it acts as a stimulus to investment.

ii *Moderate inflation* of about 4 or 5% is approaching danger level in that it will encourage itself. Expectation of future price increases will stimulate present demand for goods and services; this will in turn stimulate further price increases. Also the volume of a country's exports and imports is likely to be affected at this rate.

iii *Rapid inflation* in excess of 6% is absolutely undesirable and must lead to great hardship for those on fixed incomes, deterioration in the balance of payments, inflated wage demands from the unions, uncertainty about the future and what amounts to panic buying to avoid future price increases together with a fall in savings.

iv *Hyper-inflation or 'runaway' inflation* occurs when events really get out of control. Prices rise faster and faster until the value of money can be seen to be falling daily. Confidence is lost in the value of money and the money system starts to break down. Before very long people are not prepared to accept money in payment for goods since they know its value can only fall. At this stage the functions of money are beginning to disappear. Money becomes unacceptable as a medium of exchange as people revert to barter. It ceases to act as a store of value and can no longer be regarded as a reliable unit of account or a standard for deferred payments. Thus money, or the unit of currency, ceases to act as money and has to be scrapped, e.g. in Greece after the Second World War.

Whatever the type of inflation the causes are individual to the place of origin. A 4% inflation in Italy, for instance, will not necessarily be caused by the same factors as inflation of the same rate in Britain. In each case the causes must be isolated from a whole host of information about variables within the economy. Analysis of these variables will form the basis of S14 to S22 but the causes can be divided into two general categories.

Demand pull—inflation

We have already said that the general price level will rise if there is a general rise in the demand for goods and services, which is not accompanied by a general rise in the supply of goods throughout the country, e.g. when full employment exists.

In this situation we say that there is a demand pull. Excess demand generally is pulling up prices. The question for economists is 'What is causing the excess demand?' It could be that people were saving less and spending more of their incomes. It could be that people were earning higher incomes. Perhaps credit facilities were so readily available that demand had been increased without reductions in saving or increase in income. There are many possible causes of demand pull inflation all of which are associated with increased spending by either the public, firms or the government.

You will probably notice the similarity between this theory and the quantity theory of money. The link between them is that an increase in the supply of money in circulation will undoubtedly stimulate increased demand. If this is not matched by a similar increase in the supply of goods and services generally throughout the economy then inevitably there will be an increase in the price level.

Cost push—inflation

There is another school of thought which may attribute the cause of inflation within an economy at any one time to a general increase in costs. These increases in costs may have come about through increases in the prices of widely used raw materials, or through increased interest charges on loans, or, more likely, through general increases in average wage rates which have not been accompanied by any increase in output per man/hour. All of these factors might lead to a general increase in costs leading to so-called cost push inflation.

So we see that there may be factors on both the demand side and on the supply side contributing to an inflationary situation. The quantity theory of money takes no account of the supply side dealing rather with an increase in money supply which stimulates overall demand. As we shall see in later sections especially S20 many government measures may be inappropriate to control cost push inflation, since they are measures designed just to regulate the demand side.

ANSWERS

12·1

Correct **C**: on average you will hold half your total.

12·2

Correct **D**: the same reason as the previous answer.

12·3

Correct **A**: wait for the price of bonds to fall and the market rates of interest to rise. You can then invest at a higher rate of interest.

12·4

Correct **B**: buy securities now, with an interest of 5% before the yield falls.

12·5

i a rise in national income and expenditure.

ii a decline in political stability—there might be 'a run on the banks'.

12·6

a $3 = \frac{100}{33\frac{1}{3}}$ **b** $4 = \frac{100}{25}$ **c** $8 = \frac{100}{12\frac{1}{2}}$

12·7

a Fall.

b Fall. Because cash is transferred from bankers' balances to government account at Bank of England.

12·8

Approximately one sixth or 17%.

12·9

False.

12·10

True

12·11

False: they balance safety against earnings.

12·12

False. Both are illiquid assets. Loans are repaid within an agreed period, but there is no certain date for the release of special deposits. Indeed, additional special deposits might be called.

12·13

True. Because the liquidity ratio rose above the minimum, but in fact banks try to keep above the minimum for this part of the year, in order to meet the loss of cash when companies pay taxes, January to March, every year.

12·14

Correct **A**: the real cost of paying interest will be offset by the rise in prices of cars.

12·15

Correct **A**: the real cost of the loan is now 5% per year, but we assume the utility offered by the car for an extra two years outweighs this cost.

12·16

Yes, the demand for bank loans during a period of inflation is interest-inelastic.

12·17

Correct **C. A** refers to a change in LL which does not take place at Or_3. **B** incorrect: when bond prices are low, interest rates are high.

12·18

Correct **B.**

12·19

False, quite the opposite.

12·20

The price of eggs has risen in terms of potatoes.

12·21

Individual answers.

12·22

A smaller proportion is spent on food, household goods, clothing and shoes. People usually spend a larger proportion of their income on luxuries as they become more prosperous.

12·23

6·7% increase.

12·24

1920–1931.

12·25

$66\frac{2}{3}$%. The purchasing power of money fell from 10s. to 6s.—a fall of 40%. Therefore prices rose by the reverse ratio—from 6 to 10—i.e. by $\frac{4}{6} = 66\frac{2}{3}\%$.

THE BALANCE OF PAYMENTS STUDY SECTION 13

We saw earlier in S7 that international trade is in essence no different from trade between any two areas with a single country. In practice, however, complexities arise from the use of different national currencies, and the desire of all governments to exercise control over their monetary systems, particularly their rates of exchange. In order to achieve control, it is necessary to know what is happening, and so each country draws up a balance of payments account, which is a record of all its financial dealings with the rest of the world. The account is normally drawn up annually, and is a sum of all the thousands of individual transactions made by private individuals, companies and governments during that time.

Figure 13·1 shows the transactions which take place between countries. These transactions are divided into current transactions (the exchange of goods and services), and capital transactions.

i The import and export of commodities and manufactured goods. Trade in such goods, which can be seen, is known as *visible trade,* and the difference between the value of visible exports and the value of visible imports is known as the *balance of trade*. In Britain's case the 'trade gap' is usually negative, i.e. the value of visible imports exceeds the value of visible exports, but if the foreign currency needed to pay for the excess of imported goods can be earned by selling services abroad, there is nothing undesirable about a negative balance of trade. You can find out the types of goods Britain exports and imports, and the values of each category, by consulting the *Annual Abstract of Statistics* or the HMSO publication devoted specifically to the balance of payments.

ii The import and export of services, such as insurance, banking, tourism, and transport. This is known as *invisible trade*. This section must also include the government expenditure of foreign currency necessary to maintain military forces and diplomatic staff abroad, and interest, profits, and dividend payments. More than one third of Britain's gross earnings of foreign currency comes from invisible transactions.

For example, Americans who wish to insure their property at Lloyd's will pay dollars for this service, just as an American firm will pay dollars for the British sports cars it imports. British tourists travelling abroad will spend foreign currency on the services of hotels, entertainment, etc. They may buy the foreign currency they need at banks, by paying in sterling, or they may pay a travel agent in sterling to arrange their holiday, and he will be responsible on their behalf for paying foreign currency for the services they enjoy. Therefore the trade in services between residents of different countries creates flows of foreign currencies just as the trade in goods. The tourist industry in Britain and in many other countries is a very important exporting industry because so much money is spent by foreigners travelling in Britain. Thus the tourist industry is said to be 'a major dollar earner'. The tourists actually pay in £ sterling, but the Bank of England receives the dollars which they exchanged for these £ sterling.

Government expenditure is a major debit item

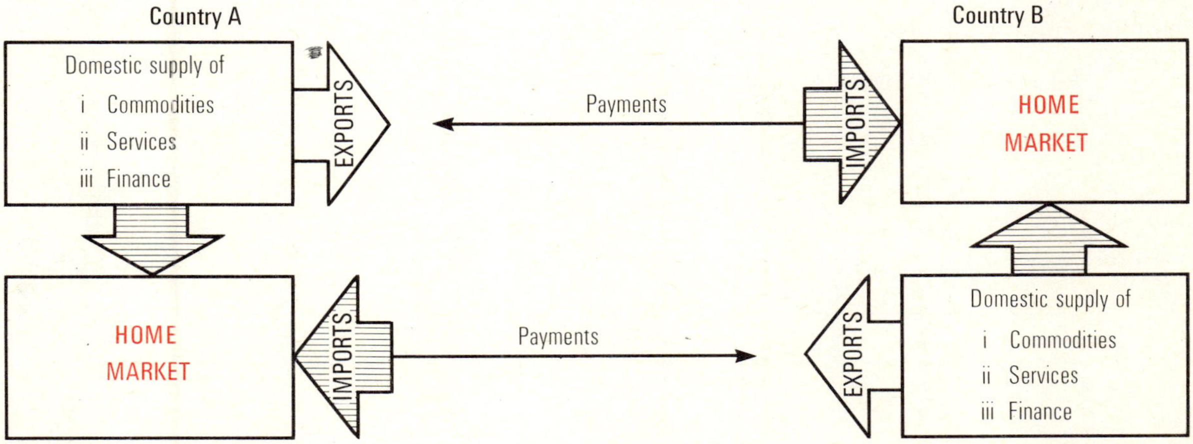

Figure 13·1

in British invisible trade, because the British government spends so much more abroad than foreign governments spend in Britain. The large expenditure abroad is caused by the need to maintain a network of embassies, consulates, and advisory staff, the requirements of defence policy, and overseas aid commitments.

Interest, profits and dividends is another major item—in this category British earnings exceed outpayments. Interest is received on loans made to foreign governments or private institutions, profits from British owned companies overseas, and dividends from shareholdings in foreign companies. Corresponding outpayments arise when the British government, local authorities, or firms pay interest to foreign lenders, when foreign-owned companies, e.g. Ford of Britain, remit profits to their parent companies, and dividends are paid to foreign shareholders. You can see that large investment abroad in previous years can give rise to regular annual incomes of interest, profits and dividends. An initial capital outflow, as described in the next section, is likely to earn a series of annual returns, payments for the services of capital, which will be recorded as inflows, i.e. credit items, in the invisible trade section of the current account.

The item *private transfers* in the invisible account refers to any legacies, gifts, etc., which are sent abroad or received from abroad. The composition of Britian's invisible exports and imports is shown in figure 13·2. Notice that *shipping* is the biggest single credit item (earning foreign currency) and the biggest single debit item.

When the figures for both visible and invisible trade are combined, we obtain the *balance on current account*, see figure 13·3. We can see that in 1969 the surplus on invisible trade more than offsets the negative visible balance, so a surplus is registered on the current account as a whole.

Just as a person who earns more than he spends on day-to-day living (current expenditure) is able to put money aside for investment, so, for a country, a surplus on current account makes it possible for investment in foreign countries to take place, or for reserves of foreign currency to be built up. In these two ways a country can increase its wealth, by adding to its assets.

13·1

a Is either of the two forms of assets mentioned above preferable to the other?

b Is it better to use a surplus to build up reserves of gold and foreign currency than for the purchase of property overseas?

CURRENT ACCOUNT 1969		£ million
1 VISIBLE TRADE	Exports (f.o.b)	+7 061
	Imports (f.o.b.)	−7 202
	Visible Balance	− 141
2 INVISIBLES	Government (net*)	− 458
	Private services and transfers	+ 564
	Interest, Profits and Dividends	
	Private sector	+ 780
	Public sector	− 329
	Invisible Balance	+ 557
CURRENT BALANCE (1+2)		+ 416

* this is the balance—inflow and outflow taken together.

Source: *Economic Progress Report Sept. 1970*

Figure 13·3

THE MAKE-UP OF INVISIBLES, 1969

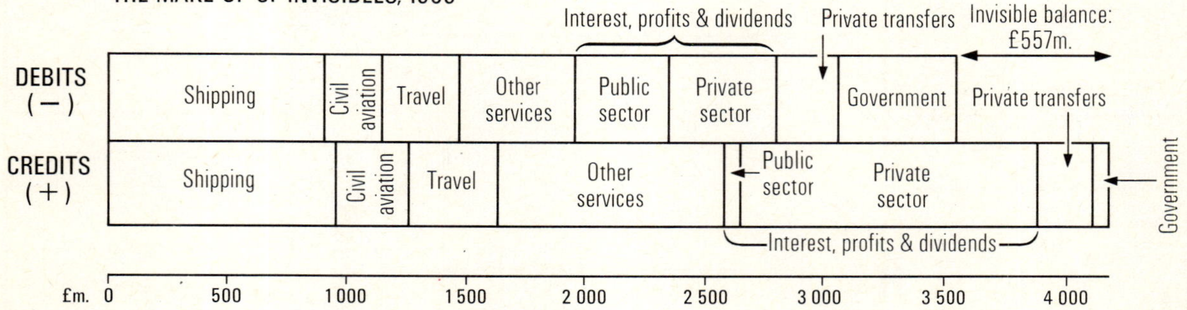

Figure 13·2

Source: *Economic Progress Report Nov. 1970*

13·2

A party of British schoolchildren go to Italy for 2 weeks. Is this:

A A visible import.
B A visible export.
C An invisible export.
D An invisible import.

13·3

Which of the following are debits on the shipping account?

A Port dues paid by a Royal Mail Line's ship docking in Los Angeles.
B Handling charges paid by a Panama registered ship docking in London.
C Single fare from Southampton to New York on s.s. 'United States', paid on embarkation in dollars by a U.S. tourist.
D Freight charges paid by an importer to an Italian shipping company for cars brought to the U.K.

13·4

Divide the following into visible and invisible exports and imports.

A Sale of long-playing records to U.S.A.
B Shipping of records to U.S.A. on Greek ship.
C Sale of music copyright to Italian record company.
D Sale of sheet music to Australia.
E Payment for singer's concert tour in Bolivia.
F Government-promoted trade exhibition in Poland.
G Royalties from U.K. to British composer officially resident in Switzerland.

iii Investment and other capital flows. If foreigners lend money to a U.K. firm, buy shares in a company, or purchase a company completely, there is an inflow of capital into the country. The Bank of England receives foreign currency in exchange for the sterling required for use in the U.K. The same happens if a local authority (such as the Greater London Council), or any other firm or institution, borrows Eurodollars to finance expenditure. Such movements of funds are taking place all the time, including, as figure 13·4 shows, both long-term and short-term borrowing in both directions, that is flows into the U.K., shown by a '+' sign, and investment or lending in foreign countries by U.K. residents, shown by a '−' sign.

In any one year investment abroad is an outflow, but it is hoped that in future years the effective use of these capital investments will give rise to inflows of interest, profits, and dividends on the current account.

TOTAL CURRENCY FLOW AND OFFICIAL FINANCING 1969

		£ million
1	BALANCE OF TRADE	−141
2	INVISIBLE BALANCE	+557
	CURRENT BALANCE (1 + 2)	+416
3	INVESTMENT and OTHER CAPITAL FLOWS	+ 48
	made up of:	
a	Official long-term capital	− 98
b	Overseas investment in U.K. public sector	+ 63
c	Overseas investment in U.K. private sector	+621
d	U.K. private investment overseas	−617
e	Euro-dollar borrowing in London for investment overseas	+ 70
f	Import credit	+256
g	Export credit	−333
h	Balances (gross) of sterling area countries	+258
i	Balances (gross) of non-sterling countries	− 50
j	Foreign currency transactions of U.K. banks	−106
k	Other short-term flows	− 16
4	BALANCING ITEM	+279
	TOTAL CURRENCY FLOW (1 +2 +3 +4)	+743
	*(Allocation of Special Drawing Rights. . . . .)	
	*(Gold subscription to I.M.F. . . . .)	
	TOTAL	+743
5	OFFICIAL FINANCING**—made up of Net drawing from (+)/net repayments to(−):	
	IMF	− 30
	Other monetary authorities	−669
	Drawing on (+)/additions to (−) official reserves	− 44
	TOTAL OFFICIAL FINANCING	−743

Source: *Economic Progress Report Sept. 1970*

Figure 13·4

** decrease in assets +, increase in liabilities +, increase in assets −, decrease in liabilities −.

* in those years when it applies, these items will be here to show the effect of all transactions on the reserves and debt position. For comment on these see satellite *International Trade and Finance.*

The idea of 'inward flows' being '+' and 'outward flows' being '−' needs some further comment.

It is easy enough to see that expenditure on

imports is an outflow of money, shown by a minus figure in the Balance of Payments Accounts. Less obvious is the use of the + and − signs in the official financing section. A repayment to the I.M.F. (a decrease in the liabilities of the U.K.) should be shown as a minus, whilst increasing the debt to the International Monetary Fund would be a plus. Similarly, a fall in the reserves—using them to finance a negative total currency flow—is a '+'. It may be helpful, in understanding this, to imagine two civil servants, one responsible for keeping the account of money going in and out of the reserves, and the other keeping the Balance of Payments Account. Money transferred from the reserves to pay for an excess of imports over exports, for example, would be an outflow (−) from the point of view of the Keeper of the Reserves' while it is an inflow to the Keeper of the Balance of Payments'—a '+' to him.

Remember that *any official financing necessary to balance a negative total currency flow will be marked by a plus,* although this can be considered an undesirable change, whereas a positive total currency flow will be balanced by negative items in official financing, so *a rise in reserves, or a reduction in liabilities, will be marked by a minus.*

13·5

What did the government do with the £743 million surplus in the total currency flow for 1969?

The balancing item

If you have understood the principle of drawing up the Account so that it balances (note that in figure 13·4 the +£743 m is exactly balanced by a −£743 m), you should have little difficulty in understanding the Balancing Item. The flow of money in should (and does) equal the flow of money out, but some of the figures cannot be collected accurately—remember that the accounts should record *every* transaction with a foreigner by *every* individual in the country. In practice there are errors and omissions; smugglers and tax dodgers do not render exact returns of their operations, but also perfectly legitimate businesses may be inaccurate, months behind, or mistaken. As time goes by, mistakes are discovered and the figures for a particular year may be adjusted a year or two later: a discovery of some £10 million unrecorded exports, for example, would mean a change of +£10 m on the Balance of Trade and of −£10 m off the Balancing Item. The account still balances, and those accounts kept by the government, which they know to be accurate, such as the extent of our official borrowing, will be exactly the same.

13·6

Which of the following could be shown by a '+' sign in the Balance of Payments Accounts?

A A rise in the Reserves.
B Private investment by a U.K. resident in a German firm.
C A repayment of £100 million to the I.M.F.
D Credit given by a British exporter.

Changes in layout

Until 1970, the Balance of Payments accounts were designed to distinguish between long-term and short-term capital. Items a to d in figure 13·4 were lumped together in a section called 'Long-term Capital Account', and this, and the Current Account (which has not been altered see figure 13·2) were combined to give the so-called 'Basic Balance'. This reflected the belief that permanent investment is a respectable means of borrowing or lending, representing funds attracted by the sound state of the economy and not liable suddenly to be withdrawn. Short term capital was indicated, under the old system, in a section called 'Monetary Movements'—including items e to k plus 'Official Financing'. The reason for the change was that in practice it became impossible to distinguish the genuine long-term investment from the short-term: stocks and shares (classified as a long term investment) could be re-sold within a few weeks, the whole transaction being financed by a Euro-dollar loan. The 'Basic Balance' was found to be an unsatisfactory indicator of the economic health of the economy, and the new form draws attention to the *Current Balance* or signs of whether the U.K. is 'paying its way' by trade in goods and services and building up the nation's international wealth, and to the *Total Currency Flow* which, if in surplus, shows the amount the government can add to the reserves or use to pay off debt.

Balance of payments problems

As figure 13·5 shows, there were large minus Total Currency Flows from 1963 to 1968, necessitating official government borrowing and reduction of the reserves. It was necessary to borrow foreign

U.K. BALANCE OF PAYMENTS SUMMARY 1963–69							£ million
	1963	1964	1965	1966	1967	1968	1969
A Current Account							
Visible Balance	− 80	−519	−237	− 73	−552	− 643	−141
Invisible Balance	+194	+124	+160	+116	+240	+ 324	+557
CURRENT BALANCE	+114	−395	− 77	+ 43	−312	− 319	+416
B Currency flow and official financing							
Current balance	+114	−395	− 77	+ 43	−312	− 319	+416
Investment and other capital flows	−103	−289	−308	−564	−560	−1 010	− 48
Balancing item	− 69	− 11	+ 32	− 26	−201	− 81	+279
TOTAL CURRENCY FLOW	− 58	−695	−353	−547	−671	−1 410	+743
Gold subscription to I.M.F.				− 44			
Total of above	− 58	−695	−353	−591	−671	−1 410	+743
Financed as follows:							
Official borrowing	+ 5	+573	+599	+625	+556	+1 296	−699
Official reserves	+ 53	+122	−246	− 34	+115	+ 144	− 44
Total Official Financing	+ 58	+695	+353	+591	+671	+1 410	−743

Figure 13·5

currencies because the gold and foreign currency reserves were insufficient by themselves to meet the demands upon them. The 1962 level was £1 002 million, and the government continues to keep reserves at about this level by borrowing when necessary from the I.M.F. and central banks.

13·7

Taking the value of reserves to be £1 000 million, express them as a percentage of 1969 imports.

The 'problem' from 1963–68 arose out of borrowing the money—if there were unlimited funds available there would be no problem. Whether the money was obtained from a variety of central banks or from the International Monetary Fund, (i) it has to be paid back in the form of foreign currency (mostly within 3–5 years) and (ii) the lenders attached conditions to their loans. These conditions were explicit, in that the I.M.F. laid down the way the economy should be run (the amount the banks could lend, the amount of purchasing power to be left in the pockets of consumers, etc.) and implicit in that the government in its foreign policy had to bear in mind that it could not afford to upset those countries from which it wished to borrow.

The borrowed funds, however, were not used directly to buy goods and services, or to invest in the industry of other countries—this was being done by the thousands of private persons, companies and corporations who make up the economy. As they did so, they were selling sterling in order to buy foreign currency, so by their actions they were putting pressure on the exchange rate (see S20 and satellite *Contemporary Problems of Foreign Exchange and Trade*). If there is a heavy demand for U.S. dollars, then the price of them will tend to rise. If the normal price is 36p to \$1 (£1 to \$2·80), it might rise to 37½p to \$1 (£1 to \$2·40). If it is decided to maintain the exchange rate at \$2·80 then the government must make available dollars at that rate of exchange, taking from its reserves of foreign currencies or by borrowing from other central banks large quantities of dollars and other currencies which were in demand, and selling them on the foreign exchange market in order to keep the rate of exchange up to about \$2·80 = £1.

In November 1967, the pressure got so great that the U.K. decided to fix a new rate of exchange (to devalue the pound), lowering it from \$2·80 to \$2·40:

this made imports more expensive but made it possible to reduce the price, in terms of what the foreign customer paid, of our exports. A £40 overcoat, for example, selling at $40 \times \$2{\cdot}80 = \$112$, could be reduced in price to $40 \times \$2{\cdot}40 = \$96$, although the British manufacturer still received £40. The object of the exercise was to sell more overcoats (and other things, of course), as a result of the fall in price to the overseas buyer and so earn more foreign exchange than before to eliminate the need for borrowing: its success depended mainly on the elasticity of demand for exports—if demand proved to be elastic (see S11) it would be effective. Devaluing the pound, however, means a loss in value for those who were keeping their purchasing power in this form—especially those central banks who keep their countries' reserves in sterling—which is one reason why the rate of exchange is kept fixed. The balance of payments problem is that of keeping a fixed rate of exchange, at the same time maintaining a reasonable reserve, given certain domestic policy objectives.

It would not have been necessary to make British exports more competitive by devaluing the pound if it had proved possible to avoid domestic price increases (including invisible exports such as the cost to foreigners of a holiday in Britain). If there is inflation in the U.K. exports will be too highly priced. On the other hand, whenever the U.K. tries to increase output, to reduce unemployment in order to reduce the waste of unused resources, and avoid the social evil of having men and women willing and able to work but without jobs, that is, whenever the government aims for growth of the national product, there is a tendency for the rate of inflation to increase. Wages rise, industrial costs rise, exporters' costs rise and so British exports are too highly priced and, again there is what is called a balance of payments problem, as current balance becomes negative, and has to be balanced from other sources.

The problem, of course, is to reconcile the aims of: growth, full employment, a fixed rate of exchange backed by reasonable reserves and a rising standard of living. Borrowing is acceptable if the time it buys and the capital investment it permits are used effectively: it is no permanent solution for sooner or later debts must be repaid.

The terms of trade

Imagine a simple economy: tractors are exported and oranges are imported in exchange. In Year 1, one tractor exchanges for 200 cases of oranges; in Year 2, one tractor exchanges for 225 cases of oranges. In this case the terms of trade have moved against the orange-producing country and in favour of the tractor producing country. The points to notice are (i) that it is a comparative concept (the terms get better or worse—one cannot say they are 'high' or 'low', only compare with some earlier period) (ii) that it is the rate of exchange that matters: this means that if the price of tractors goes up while the price of oranges stays the same, the terms of trade would be said to have improved or 'become more favourable', for the country exporting tractors. In one sense this is true: for the same amount of effort, more oranges are now received but the *quantity* of tractors sold may fall (they are now more expensive), and this may lead to unemployment in the tractor industry.

Our imaginary simple economy was involved in trade in only two goods. However, international trade today covers an immense variety of goods, so how can we establish what changes in the terms of trade have taken place when a country such as the U.K. imports and exports so many products? The answer is that we can record how the *prices* of exports and imports change. If prices of exports rise and import prices remain unchanged it follows that a given volume of exports will now earn currency enough to buy a larger volume of imports than before. This is called a *favourable movement* in the terms of trade, simply because the *same volume of exports* could buy a *larger volume of imports*. To measure changes in export and import prices we use the system of index numbers, as explained in S12 and the satellite *Arithmetical and Statistical Methods*. From these two indices we construct the terms of trade index in the following way:

$$\frac{\text{Index of Export Prices}}{\text{Index of Import Prices}} \times \frac{100}{1} = \text{Index of Terms of Trade.}$$

Therefore favourable movements in the terms of trade will be indicated by a rise in the index, e.g. from 96 to 99, or from 100 to 102. A favourable movement will be recorded if:

export prices rise faster than import prices, or
export prices rise and import prices remain constant, or
export prices rise and import prices fall, or
export prices remain constant and import prices fall, or
export prices fall more slowly than import prices.

Remember that we cannot predict the effect on the *balance of trade* of a favourable or unfavourable movement in the *terms of trade* without further information about whether export or import prices changed, and the elasticities of demand for exports and imports. The elasticities of demand will determine the changes in total revenue which follow changes in export and import prices. Also the cause of the changes in prices is important. For example, if export prices rose due to increased foreign demand, we could expect an increase in the volume of exports even at a higher price, so a favourable movement of the balance of trade will result. However, if export prices rose due to rapid rises in the costs of production, we would expect exports to decline in volume, and if demand is elastic, the rise in export prices would cause an unfavourable movement in the balance of trade, i.e. export earnings would fall.

In practice, a country producing agricultural products would view with dismay a fall in export prices, because the demand for such commodities is usually inelastic, whereas the U.K. in 1967 deliberately worsened her terms of trade (by devaluation), hoping that a fall in export prices, in terms of foreign currency, would result in a proportionately greater increase in quantity sold and so lead to an increase in the total earnings of foreign currencies.

Methods of control of the balance of payments: Visible trade

Imports may be altered by:

i Imposing or altering quotas (i.e. stated annual limits on the physical quantity of specified commodities which are imported), e.g. 4 million yards cotton cloth from country X; 200 tons coffee from country Y.

ii Imposing a pattern of tariffs which raises the domestic price of imports. These may be levied on classes of goods as a means of protecting domestic industry, especially new industries with temporary high levels of costs. Alternatively, they may be levied against imports from certain countries.

iii Various temporary schemes may be devised to affect the quantity or price of imports, for example, an overall surcharge may be made on all imports for a specified period. This raises the price in domestic terms and raises revenue for the government at the same time as reducing the amount which domestic purchasers have to spend on other products.

Any means of affecting prices or quantities of goods in international trade must be used with caution, firstly, because the U.K. is a member of G.A.T.T. (see satellite *Contemporary Problems of Foreign Exchange and Trade*), and secondly, because our exports may be affected by other nations operating similar schemes designed to control *their* imports.

iv The need for imports may, in the long run, be reduced by encouraging the production of import substitutes in the home country.

Export earnings may be increased by raising the price of exports if the price elasticity of demand in overseas markets is inelastic. Alternatively if the price demand overseas is elastic the home prices should be reduced so making the products more competitive in the international market and raising the level of earnings. Therefore after a devaluation, not all exporters should reduce their foreign currency prices. They should maintain the previous foreign currency price if they think that the demand for the product is inelastic.

Methods of control of the balance of payments: Invisible trade

For many countries the invisible items have very much less significance than they do for the U.K. The surplus on the U.K. invisible account has, traditionally, more than covered the deficit on the visible account. The size of individual items is small compared with imports or exports of commodities but the revenue earned is vital to our balance of payments.

Government expenditure overseas is subject mainly to political considerations rather than economic, because political policies and international defence agreements largely determine the level of expenditure. Any reduction of this item involves an opportunity cost which cannot be calculated in the marketplace.

Spending abroad can be controlled by setting a maximum which may be spent overseas, both by private citizens and companies. Exchange control regulations are often stricter in the U.K. than overseas.

Control of interest, profit and dividends, is partly a matter of regulating the extent to which firms may repatriate their earnings to overseas parent companies. Such controls may be avoided by invoicing components or semi-finished goods at less than cost to other sections of a multinational firm. Profits may then be shown where taxation is least. Although controls on invoicing do exist they are very difficult to operate effectively.

Control of capital flows

When a U.K. firm sets up plant overseas, e.g. a new oil refinery, it is exporting capital. A single firm may export say £80–£100 million in a single instance. This may not be much compared with the total of over £10 000 million of overseas assets owned by U.K. firms and citizens. However, it is a large sum compared with the annual amount of new investment, and even more so compared with the net balance of credits and debits on the capital account. Under certain conditions, the single investment by the U.K. of £100 million abroad may contribute to a negative currency flow, or if it is, say, an American firm investing a new aluminium smelter in Scotland, it could result in a positive currency flow. However, an outflow of dividends will eventually occur as the plant makes profits, and will increase the debit items on the invisible account. Investment abroad by British companies is subject to exchange control, i.e. a firm has to apply for permission to buy the foreign currency required. The government can also encourage or discourage foreign firms which wish to set up branches in this country.

Now that you have studied the balance of payments accounts, you should have realised that the payments and receipts give rise to a supply of, and demand for, the £ sterling on the international money market. As with any commodity the pressures of supply and demand affect the price or value of that commodity.

The international prices of currencies—the foreign exchange rates—merit a study section to themselves, S7. They are also discussed in the satellite text *Contemporary problems of foreign exchange and trade*.

13·8

Which of the following techniques could be used to help increase export earnings?

A A domestic credit squeeze.

B Provision of tax concessions to exporters.

C Introduction of new marketing techniques.

D Provision of additional credit facilities.

13·9

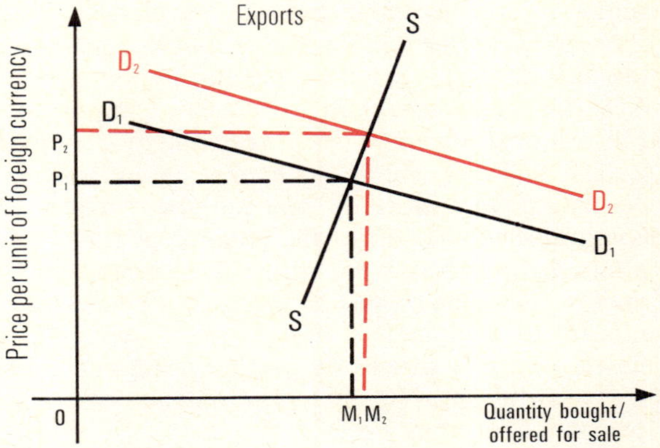

Figure 13·6

What are the likely causes of a movement of the demand curve for a country's exports from D_1D_1 to D_2D_2?

13·10

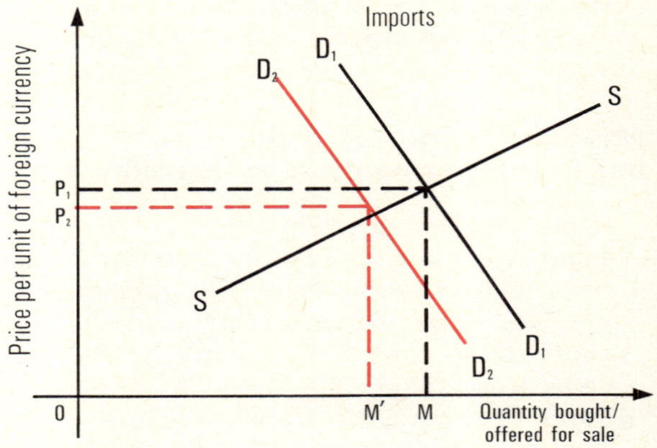

Figure 13·7

What are the likely causes of a movement of the demand for imports from D_1D_1 to D_2D_2?

ANSWERS

13·1

No single form of asset is preferable to any other, because each serves a different purpose. Reserves of gold and foreign currency are required to pay out to foreigners at the fixed exchange rate when foreigners sell sterling, but gold holdings yield no interest, and foreign currency holdings, when lent for very short periods, will earn very little. Property overseas should yield a higher return, but the enterprise may fail, or be nationalised without compensation.

13·2

D is correct, money is going out of the country in exchange for some benefit—an 'import'.

13·3

Correct **A, D.**

Mistaken **B**: this is a credit, paid by an overseas resident to the U.K. for services provided.

Mistaken **C**: this is a domestic transaction between a U.S. resident and a U.S. company.

13·4

Visible export	Invisible import
A, D	**B, F, G**
Invisible export	
C,E	

13·5

The government paid back £30 m to the IMF, £669 m to other monetary authorities, and put £44 m into its own reserves, so that the reserves increased by £44 m (see footnote to figure 13·4).

13·6

None of them, they are all 'minus' items. Read the paragraph after figure 13·4 carefully.

13·7

$$\frac{£1\,000}{£7\,202} = \text{approx. } \frac{1}{7} = 14\%.$$

13·8

Correct **A**: in so far that any products which are largely sold on hire purchase or other credit will not tend to be bought so readily on the domestic market. This then makes more available for export, or diverts resources to export products. This may also reduce purchases of imports where these are financed by credit.

Correct **B**: although against the rules of G.A.T.T. this could be used temporarily, especially by various forms of rebate of tax. This would make exporting more profitable.

Correct **C**: where these are not in use, the development of additional official marketing assistance, possibly with the aid of consular information services, should increase exports.

Correct **D**: the mere provision of credit does not guarantee that it will be used but the 'Export Credit Guarantee Department' (E.C.G.D.) guarantees for a fee to repay loans made by banks to exporters, should the buyers default. These facilities have helped with very large export orders, for example, of atomic power stations.

13·9

The other countries may have increased their national incomes so that they have an increased demand for imports, or there may have been a change in taste leading to an increase in the demand for the exporters' particular products.

13·10

There may have been a change in tastes so that the country demands less imports. Home food production may have increased, reducing the need to import.

THE CIRCULAR FLOW OF INCOME STUDY SECTION 14

This second half of the study course embarks upon the analysis of the national economy. The emphasis is largely upon the national totals of consumption, saving, investment and employment.

Expenditure and income

'What one person spends is another person's income.' This very simple idea can be seen in any everyday exchange transaction. For example, if you buy a transistor radio set, your expenditure becomes income to the shopkeeper. The shopkeeper then spends the money which he receives on new stock. This money then becomes income to the wholesaler and thence to the producer. You, perhaps, may be employed by the producer of transistor radios who has paid you the money with which you bought the transistor radio. This simple relationship is a circular flow of income and expenditure.

We have, in fact, already seen much of this kind of relationship in the earlier part of this course. We showed that resources are used for production (S2), and that population is both the supply of labour and the consumer of output (S3). The employed population work in firms (S4 and S10) in which they produce goods and from which they earn wages (S9). The output from the manufacturers is sold under various degrees of competition (S5) in exchange for money (S6), as facilitated by banks and other institutions and the principle of the exchange of goods satisfying consumers' wants (S8) which takes place in home and overseas markets is examined in S7 and S13.

From the producer's side, the output of goods and services depends on maximizing his profits according to the various market conditions. The need to respond to changes in demand and supply conditions was examined (S11), as was the general level of prices at which market equilibrium for goods and for factors of production is reached, which depends partly on the supply of and demand for money (S12). The profitability of employing factors of production will determine the numbers of those factors employed and therefore the income from which consumption is financed. Hence we have a circular pattern of relationships starting with people as producers and ending with people as consumers, creators and users of real income or money income.

Money income and real income

Money income is income in terms of wages, dividends, profits and rent which can be spent on (i.e. exchanged for) goods with which to satisfy human wants. Real income is the flow of actual commodities and services with which human wants are satisfied. The concept does not depend on current price levels: for example, if wages and salaries doubled and at the same time the prices of commodities and services also doubled, there would be no general change in real income even though money income had increased.

Money income is, therefore, the gross flow of money which you receive as a payment for work done or services rendered, or as the owner of land or capital.

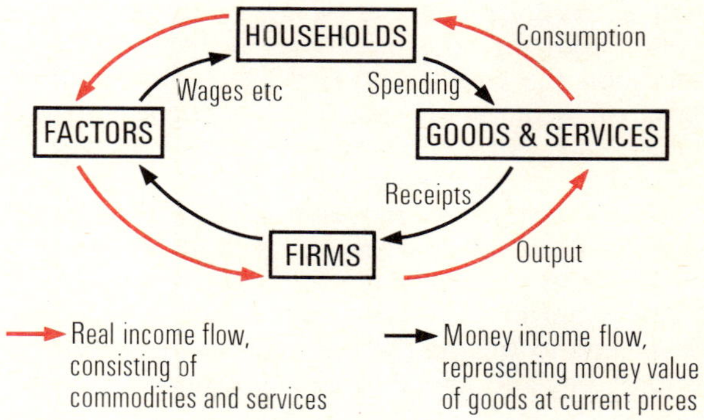

Figure 14·1

You can see in figure 14·1 a simple model of the circular flow of income. In this, households provide the factor services, that is, the services of factors of production, to firms whose output is in turn sold and consumed by members of households. As a reverse flow, firms pay the factors for the work done or services rendered and these are paid out in the form of wages, profit, rent or interest. The households then spend their incomes upon the goods which have been produced by the firms. These payments are in fact the receipts which firms receive.

What is your money income really worth? Your money income represents a transferable claim on commodities and services. Its real value is, therefore, its purchasing power in terms of goods and services which can be bought at current price levels.

In practice, indices of prices can be used to measure price levels and so to calculate changes in real income (*Satellite 1, section 9*).

Models of the circular flow of income

You will notice in figure 14·1 above, that no reference is made to imports and exports. In other words, this is the case of a closed economy. In this particular, rather over-simplified, version there is no public sector either, so that households spend all the money income which they receive on satisfying their wants. So long as firms disburse in factor incomes all that they receive from the sale of their goods, then their goods will continue to be bought. It does not matter how much firms pay the factors of production as incomes since they will receive exactly that amount of money back as receipts from the sale of their goods. In this example whatever the level of prices, the money spent by firms will be received back as payments for the firm's goods and thus any price level is appropriate to maintain the circular flow. Whatever the money level of incomes, the real level of income to the households will remain the same since this consists of real goods and services.

In this very simple model all income is spent on satisfying consumer needs: there is no holding on to the money. This model is in a simple form of equilibrium because each householder's spending is income to the firm which, in turn, employs the households and the factors they own, that is, land capital and their own labour. So long as all money paid to the households is spent, and all the receipts which come into the firm are spent on the factors, then there is nothing to prevent this system going on and on. The model of course assumes that production takes place at the same *rate* as sales (no changes in stocks can therefore occur). We can therefore say that the market for these goods is in equilibrium because supply and demand are equal at current market prices. Savings in the context of this study section is defined in the same way as it was in S1, that is, as income not spent on consumption. In this model, where all income is spent on consumption, no saving can take place.

We can make the model (figure 14·2) a little more realistic now by assuming that there is more than one firm and more than one household. The principles which are applied are exactly the same. In this model we assume that firm A takes raw materials, that is, from the factor land, and makes semi-manufacture goods or components which are, in turn, processed by firm B to make the final product. Whilst the circular flow of income is a little more complicated it is, in principle, undisturbed. One point which should be noted is that payments to the factors by firm B is equivalent to 'value added'. 'Value added' is a very important concept not only here but in the later study of the national income. It simply means that the contribution to the flow of real income by a firm is not the gross sales value of its output. From this sales value must be deducted the cost of components and services bought from other firms. Hence firm B pays to its factors of production its total sales value minus the cost of its components which it obtained from firm A. In all subsequent models it is assumed that the total value of sales by firms is the aggregate sum of values added. The model in figure 14·2 is in equilibrium because as long as the

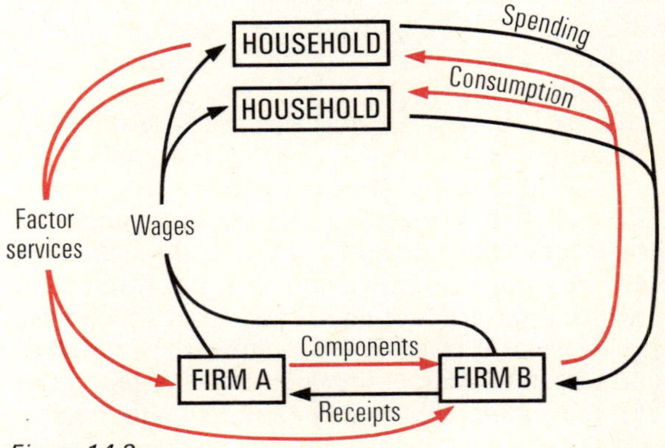

Figure 14·2

flow of factor incomes (represented by 'wages' in the diagram) is equal to the sum of the values added by each firm this model of a simple economy will remain in equilibrium.

We have now to acknowledge that the circular flow of income is not quite as perfect as these models suggest. There are at various points a number of leakages from the system as well as a number of injections into it.

In the model in figure 14·3 we are going to concentrate on the flow of *money* in the economy, and examine the variables which it is most easy to measure in real life. Households do not receive all of the factor incomes which are paid out by firms since nearly all governments impose some form of *taxation* on incomes. The income which is left after tax is called disposable income but not all of this is spent. Most households save a certain amount, at least, in so far as not all their income is spent on consumption. Firms also save by retaining some of their profits. Hence *savings* represents a further leakage from the system. All of the money spent on consumption is not received by the firms which made the goods. Part, at least, of this flow of expenditure by consumers is taxed. Various kinds

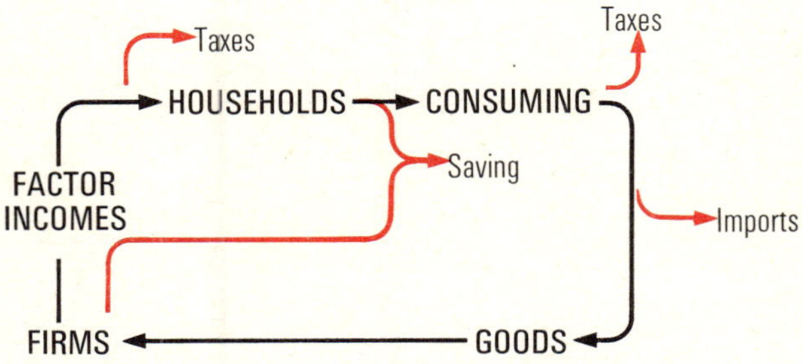

Leakages from the circular flow

Figure 14·3

of expenditure tax may be imposed by governments (such taxes as purchase tax, sales tax or value added tax).

There is yet one more leakage from the system. Not all of the money spent on consumption is paid to the firms within the national economy since a certain amount of goods, especially raw materials, are imported. This money spent on imports represents a flow to overseas firms. On the other hand there is an income from the sale of exports abroad. You can see therefore that it matters very much what happens to the taxes once they are collected, to the saving, and to the balance of imports and exports, visible and invisible.

You can think of this model as something rather like a waterpipe system. The total flow of water within the water system represents the flow of money, representing real goods and services available to the national economy. Each leakage from the system, that is, savings, taxation and imports, represents a diminution of the total flow which eventually will become the next round of incomes. It matters very much, therefore, what happens to this taxation and to savings and to the Balance of Payments. Only if these 'leakages' are balanced by some kind of inflow will the economic system remain in equilibrium. As you will discover in a moment, the principle inflows are investment, central and local government spending, and the inflow of earnings from exports and capital from abroad.

The circular flow in a national economy

In figure 14·4 we have developed a more complex version of the previous set of diagrams. Basically the idea is the same, namely, that there is a circular flow of income expenditure throughout a national economy. In the past, traditional economic thought has concentrated on the flow which exists between firms and households. In particular, emphasis has been laid on the effect of the consumption by households which results in a demand for consumer goods which are produced by the firms. In the 1930s the work of Lord Keynes emphasized the crucial nature of the role of savings and investment in maintaining this circular flow of income. In a modern mixed economy such as that of the U.K. the role of the public sector is also very important.

The flow of income and expenditure

Let us look at figure 14·4 in detail. Firms pay the factors of production for their services. Part of this flow is taxed by the government. Although the payments made to factors are based on the respective values of these factors to the production process, the money is actually paid to the owners of the factors of production, namely households. Of the gross income due to households, part is taxed on the basis of income, so that we now have both firms and households paying their share to the public sector, which will itself pay factors of production, consume, invest and save. The total (aggregate) expenditure of households is the basis of the demand for consumer goods. At this point we have a critical division in the flow of income and expenditure. Households can decide whether to consume or whether to save. Of the money spent on consumption, part will go to the public sector as a tax on expenditure as an additional alternative method of raising revenue. The goods bought by households are mostly produced by firms in the domestic economy. However, some of the goods which people wish to buy are imported from overseas so there is a leakage at this point. The demand for consumer goods as expressed in the domestic market then becomes the revenue for firms which produce those goods.

By definition, *saving is income not spent on consumption.* Hence saving tends to diminish the flow of demand for consumer goods in the domestic market. This leakage from the flow may be offset by an increase in the demand for capital goods if there is an increase in investment. However

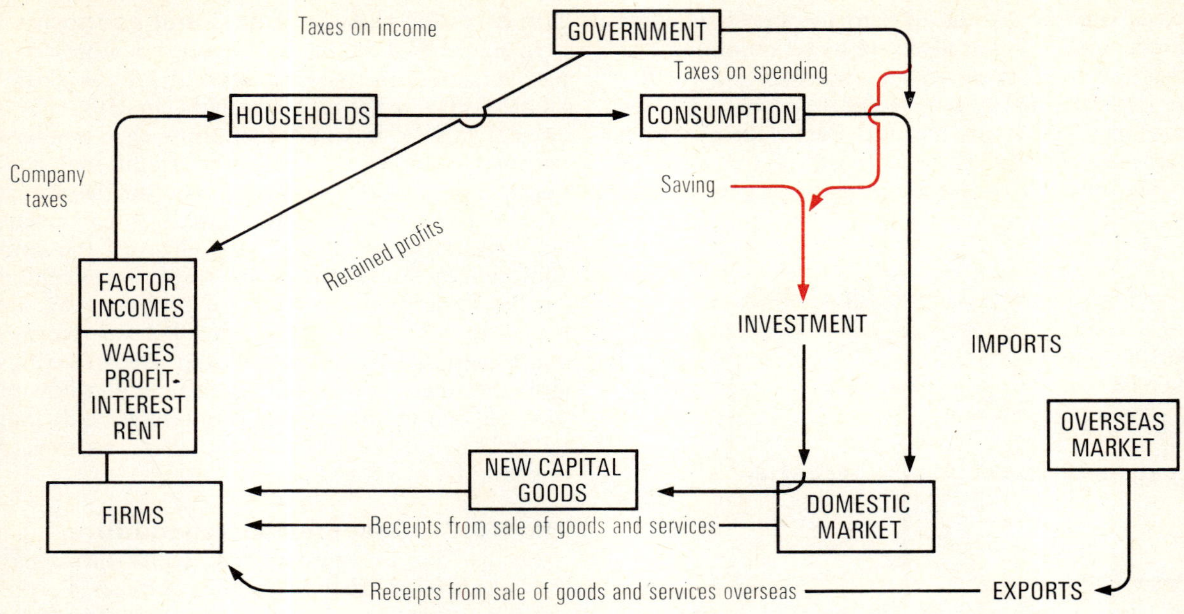

CIRCULAR FLOW OF INCOME/EXPENDITURE

Figure 14·4

savings are not necessarily equal to investment. The connection between savings and investment is a difficult and important part of economic theory, and it will be explained in S17. Capital goods go partly to increase the real capacity of industry to supply future goods and services. There are, therefore, at least two demand flows within the economy, that for consumer goods and that for capital goods based on savings.

Now we can turn for a moment to the public sector and note that among the principal sources of income which are at the disposal of the government are taxes paid by firms, by households on their income and by households on their spending. Government expenditure has two main effects upon the economy. First of all it reallocates resources, since the government will buy a different set of goods and services from those which private consumers might decide to buy. This, in turn, leads to a demand for the use of the factors of production on different kinds of projects and a supply of a different range of goods and services. Instead of being based on private decisions to satisfy consumer wants, the government's decisions will be based on social or political criteria (library books not television sets). The total size of the government's expenditure compared with the total of household expenditure is most important. The second effect of government expenditure is to divert part of the demand which is flowing in the economy, towards investment in social projects which would not otherwise take place. Such investment is an addition to that which is made by private companies and made possible by the savings decisions of households.

We can now see that the total demand for goods and services within the economy is composed of demand for consumer goods and for investment goods by both the private and public sectors.

Now we turn to the overseas market. Any demand for imported goods is clearly a leakage from the total disposable income which could be used on goods and services supplied by the domestic producers. On the other hand, there is an inflow of demand for our goods and services when we provide exports to overseas markets. Again, the size of the balance between imports and exports may be critical in maintaining the flow of demand within our economy. Hence the importance of the balance of payments on current account. We have omitted from this diagram the outflow demand for our investment abroad and inflow of foreign investment to us. This, of course, is part of the total Balance of Payments problem which you have studied in S13.

So far we have worked our way round figure 14·4 as far as 'domestic market'. One final point on this diagram; the inflow of demand for capital and consumer goods from the domestic market to the firms represent the total national expenditure on goods and services. The precise selection of goods and services which people want to buy at present market prices will determine in the end how the factors of production are allocated.

Even in this relatively simple analysis you will notice that any interruption in the flow of expenditure and income tends not only to increase or to decrease that flow but also to redirect the flow towards specific ends. When this system is in balance or equilibrium the total outflow of factor incomes from the firms will equal the total inflow of receipts for the goods and services which firms produce. At any point where there are leakages from or inflows to the system, the total system can move out of equilibrium or move towards a new equilibrium position.

We have seen the effect on the domestic economy of the overseas payments in S7 and S13. We shall now turn to look at two other key areas where decisions are taken which affect the flow of income and expenditure. Firstly there are households which decide to consume or save, and secondly (in S21), there is the public sector.

The propensity to consume and save

When people are considering how to use their income, they may either decide to spend it on consumer goods, or to save it. How much of our income, on a national scale, do we consume? Figure 14·5 shows the figures for consumers' expenditure and total personal incomes in years 1960, 63 and 66.

The *average propensity to consume* is the proportion of our disposable income spent on consumption. Hence for figure 14·5 we have deducted taxes on incomes from the total personal incomes for the years shown. The resulting figure is the total amount which consumers have to spend or to save.

14·1

For each of the years shown in diagram 14·5 calculate the proportion of personal incomes which consumers spent. We shall assume for the purposes of this discussion that the balance was saved.

U.K. total	1960	1963	1966	197?
Consumer's expenditure	17 000	20 000	24 000	
Personal disposable income*	18 000	22 000	26 000	

Figures in £ millions
* Total personal income less income tax, national insurance, etc.

Figure 14·5 Source: *Annual Abstract of Statistics*

The average propensity to consume (APC) is measured by dividing the total amount of consumers' expenditure (C) by total personal disposable income (Y). This may be written as a simple formula.

$$\text{APC} = \frac{\text{C}}{\text{Y}}$$

If we look at groups of individuals we generally find that people with small incomes tend to consume all of their disposable income, but at higher income levels people can both afford to save, and do save, a much larger proportion of their disposable income. This is simply because at low income levels there is nothing surplus to the expenditure required to maintain a basic standard of living. At higher income levels not only can basic standards of living be met but luxuries can also be afforded, still leaving a surplus income, which by definition, is saved.

The *average propensity to save* (APS) is the proportion of disposable income which is not spent on consumption. From income we therefore deduct consumption to obtain the figure for saving.

$$\text{APS} = \frac{\text{S}}{\text{Y}} \text{ or APS} = \frac{\text{Y}-\text{C}}{\text{Y}} \text{ or } 1-\frac{\text{C}}{\text{Y}}$$

These formulas are two ways of looking at the same thing. The average propensity to save is either the proportion of income which is saved, that is, $\frac{\text{S}}{\text{Y}}$ or we can say that it is 1 minus the average propensity to consume.

14·2

Use both methods for calculating average propensity to save for each of the three years shown in figure 14·5. You should get precisely the same answer for each method.

14·3

Suppose you won in a lottery a sum yielding an income of £10 000 per annum. How much would you spend on consumption? What would be your average propensity to save at this income?

The marginal propensity to consume and save

The *marginal propensity to consume* (MPC) shows by how much consumption will increase when money income increases. If we use the symbol δY to show a marginal increase in income then the marginal propensity to consume

$$MPC = \frac{\delta C}{\delta Y}$$

Look, for example, at figure 14·6 which shows imaginary total consumption and total income figures of three successive years.

14·4

In figure 14·6, calculate the increase in consumption between year 1 and year 2 and between year 2 and year 3. Put your answers in the marginal consumption column. Calculate similar figures for the marginal income column.

14·5

Using figure 14·6 calculate the marginal propensity to consume for the time period year 1 to year 2 and for the time period year 2 to year 3. The results of this exercise demonstrate how much of any increase in income is consumed.

If you think in terms of the flow of income/expenditure shown in figure 14·4 and imagine that there is an annual flow of this income expenditure, then a measurement of the marginal propensity to consume will tell you how much of each increase in incomes will be spent on consumption, and therefore how much of the increase in income will be saved. This in turn tells you what proportion of any increase in the national income will be devoted to consumption, and therefore to the production of consumption goods, and how much will be devoted to savings and how much *could* be used eventually for investment in new production goods.

The *marginal propensity to save* shows how much of any increase in disposable income the nation will tend to save. If we use the symbol δS to represent the increase in savings and δY to represent the increase in incomes then

$$MPS = \frac{\delta S}{\delta Y}$$

The marginal propensity to save is therefore the increase in savings expressed as a proportion of the increase in income.

You should note carefully that when we use the term 'disposable income' we are talking only about the effect of decisions made by households and firms on the consumption and saving (as in figure 14·4). If instead of disposable income we use the term 'income', then we imply the inclusion of both public and private sector decisions. Where the average propensity to consume and the marginal propensity to consume are calculated on the basis of national income figures (as in the *National Income Blue Book*), then this tells us about the total flow of demand for consumption and for saving.

Savings do not come only from households; in fact companies save more than private persons. In 1968 personal saving was £2075 million;

Year	Total income	Marginal income	Total consumption	Marginal consumption
1	16		15	
		....		....
2	19		17	
		....		....
3	24		20	

Figure 14·6

Figures in £1 000 millions.

company saving £2747 million; government saving £2196 million; public corporations £800 million. The source of company saving is the undistributed income of firms.

The consumption function

When we say that expenditure is a function of income, then we simply mean that the amount we spend *depends on* the amount of income we have.

When we come to draw the graph of the consumption function we shall be dealing in aggregate income and aggregate expenditure. The term 'aggregate' means the national total of something, for example, aggregate consumption means the national total of spending on consumption goods at current market prices.

The graph of the consumption function

The graph of the consumption function shows the relationship between changing income levels and the resulting changes in consumption, i.e. it shows how consumption will vary as income changes.

14·6

From the data given in figure 14·7(a) and 14·7(b) you should plot two graphs on the same axes. Income (Y) should be plotted on the horizontal (x) axis.

Y = C		Consumption function	
Y	C	Y	C
4	4	3	5
8	8	7	8
12	12	12	12
16	16	16	15
20	20	19	17
24	24	24	20

(a) (b)

Figure 14·7 Figures in £1 000 millions

If you plotted a graph showing that all income had been consumed, you would find that you had drawn a straight line 45° to the x axis (as shown in your line derived from figure 14·7(a). Any point on this line shows that all the available income is spent on consumption and so none is saved. At all incomes, expenditure equals income (Ex = Y), so this 45° line can be called the 'Ex = Y' line (See points Y_1C_1 and Y_2C_2 in figure 14·8). Most diagrams of consumption functions show consumption function partly above the 45° line and partly below it. At any point above the 45° line people are spending more than their current incomes, that is, they are living partly on past savings or on credit. At any point below the 45° line, not all incomes

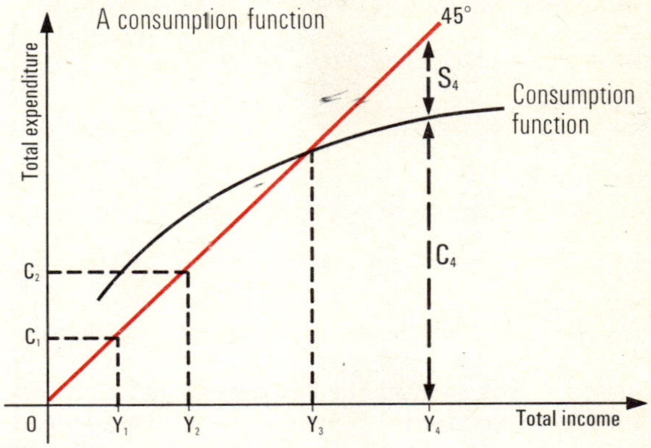

Figure 14·8

are being spent on consumption, so, by definition, some is being saved. At low aggregate income levels the consumption function is normally above the 45° (Y = C) line. There will normally be one point where the consumption function cuts the 45° line at point Y_3 in figure 14·8. This point is a break-even point where all the income is spent on consumption. At income levels above Y_3 not all of the aggregate income is spent on consumption, and hence, aggregate saving occurs.

Measuring the MPC and APC on the graph of the consumption function

You have already seen how to calculate the marginal propensity to consume and the average propensity to consume from arithmetical data. It is quite easy to measure the APC and MPC on any consumption function.

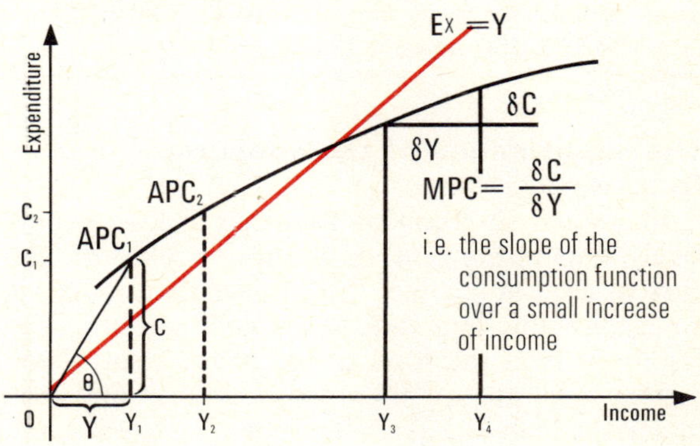

Figure 14·9

In figure 14·9 the techniques for measuring the APC and MPC are illustrated. The average propensity to consume at any level of income can be simply calculated by calculating the slope of a line through the origin to the income level on consumption function. For example, at income level OY_1 the average propensity to consume is $\frac{OC_1}{OY_1}$ or $\frac{C}{Y}$. Now, $\frac{OC_1}{OY}$ is the slope of a line drawn from 0 to the point APC_1. In the right-angled triangle formed by the origin, O, APC, and Y_1, the slope is given by the tangent of angle θ. Tan θ is $\frac{OC_1}{OY_1}$ and $\frac{OC_1}{OY_1}$ is also the formula which you learned earlier in this section for calculating average propensity to consume. Similarly, the average propensity to consume at income level OY_2 is $\frac{OC_2}{OY_2}$

The marginal propensity to consume is the slope of the consumption function between any two successive small incremental points, for example, the marginal propensity to consume between income level OY_3 and OY_4 is $\frac{\delta C}{\delta Y}$, that is, the increase in consumption expenditure divided by the increase in income level.

14·7

You should now calculate from your own graph of the figures given in figure 14·7b the average propensity to consume at any income level of £4 000 million, at an income level of £8 000 million, and at an income level of £24 000 million. Also, using the techniques shown in figure 14·9 you should calculate the marginal propensity to consume between £20 000 million and £22 000 million. Check your answers.

The significance of the consumption function

In a static situation we find that at low income levels the amount of consumption exceeds the current level of income; this implies that savings is a negative, that is, a state of dis-saving occurs. The family will eat the food stored in the pantry; the factory will use up its stocks of parts and raw materials. Here the average propensity to consume is greater than 1. Any increase in income will be entirely consumed, though the amount of dis-saving will tend to diminish as income levels rise.

At higher levels of aggregate income the average propensity to consume tends to fall below 1, that is, not all of the aggregate income is spent on consumption. Since consumption and saving are part of the circular flow of income, any decision to add to savings and to diminish the amount of consumption will, through the circular flow, lead to a change in income in the next time period.

The marginal propensity to consume shows the change in the propensity to consume between one year and another. Decisions to consume or not to consume (that is, to save) made in any one period of time will subsequently affect the demand for consumption goods. If the demand for electricity is rising, then an investment in generating stations is likely to take place, so that changes in consumption may affect investment decisions. Hence, any change in the marginal propensity to consume in one period of time will lead, ultimately, to changes in incomes in a future period of time.

Now we can return to figure 14·8 for a moment, and take account of changes in the aggregate income levels over time.

The consumption level C_4 in one time period will lead, in the next time period, to a demand for consumer goods; similarly S_4 leaves resources available for an entrepreneur to use to produce capital goods. If the saving is matched by investment then these two together amount to the aggregate demand in money terms for the factors of production, but any given aggregate monetary demand (AMD) does not necessarily mean that all the factors of production will be employed. the position of full employment. In figure 14·8, if S_4 is matched by investment then, some people will be employed providing consumer goods, C_4, others will be employed building capital goods to the amount equal to S_4. If a country's labour force is 20 million people, C_4 could occupy 16 million and S_4 2 million. As total expenditure equals total income the flow of cash proceeds leaving 2 million unemployed. It is sufficient to note, at present, that OY_4 need not mean that every resource is fully employed.

As one moves from one income level to another over time, the marginal propensity to consume tells us the proportion of income which is consumed and the proportion which is saved. Thus the MPC shows us how much of the next increase in output of goods and services in the economy will be used for consumption and what proportion will be available for investment. (Look again at figure 14·8). Generally we find that the marginal propensity to consume tends to fall as the aggregate income level rises and the curve gradually becomes less steep. As the MPC changes then so does the relationship between consumption and savings and therefore between the demand for consumption goods and the availability of resources for investment. Will investors use the resources released by the savers? Since capital goods wear out there is, in any economy, a minimum investment level which is needed to maintain the supply of real capital which is required for the production of future goods. Thus capital replacement requirements suggest that at least some of S_4 (non-consumption, or unused resources) will be used by the investors. Suppose, however, investors do not use all the resources then set aside by the savers? The answers to these questions are very important as they determine income levels. Meanwhile, see if by using figure 14·8 you can work out what would happen to total income or expenditure.

Aggregate monetary demand (AMD)

In terms of figure 14·8 we have now looked in some detail at the relationship between consumption and saving by households, and added to it the consumption and savings done by the public sector. Together the aggregate demand for consumer goods and the aggregate demand for investment by both public and private sectors constitute the aggregate monetary demand (AMD) for goods and services within the economy, taking into account the overseas market. In diagram terms we are measuring the flows across the bottom of figure 14·8. So far we have ignored the possibility that savings might not equal investment and that the overseas market situation may not be in balance. These two points will be taken up in later sections. Bearing in mind our restricting assumptions in regard to savings and investment and the balance of payments, we have shown the critical importance of the marginal propensity to consume in determining the aggregate savings and consumption at each level of income or expenditure and in turn, the determination of the aggregate factor incomes.

In our next study section, we shall study in detail the aggregate incomes, expenditure and output (or product) of the national economy.

14·8

Suppose Y_1 (income in the present period) = 100
and S_1 (savings in the present period) = 20.
Then what level of Investment in period 1 will produce a level of Y_2 (income in the next period) of 100

a 0 **b** 10 **c** 20 **d** 30 **e** 40

14·9

Assume same data as for 14·8
If $I_1 = 30$ will Y_2 be higher or lower than Y_1.

14·10

Assume same data as for 14·8.
If $I_1 = 10$ will Y_2 be higher or lower than Y_1.

14·11

Given that $Y_1 = 100$; $S_1 = 20$; $I_1 = 20$; what is the size of the Average Propensity to consume

a $\frac{2}{5}$ **b** $\frac{3}{5}$ **c** $\frac{4}{5}$

14·12

Now suppose I_1 is 30 (but Y_1 and S_1 remain the same) what will be the level of Y_2?

a 100 **b** 110 **c** 120

14·13

Study the following table: The marginal propensity to consume is $\frac{4}{5}$.

Y_1	Y_2	Y_3	Y_4	Y_5	Y_6	Y_7 etc.
C 80	80	84				
S 20	20	21				
I 20	25	25				
$Y_2 = 100$	Y_3 105	Y_4 109				

You will see that the Y in one year is made up from the C+I of the preceding year. Also the annual increase in C is $\frac{4}{5}$ of the previous year's increase is Y.

Notice that as Y increases so does C and S but I remains constant. Eventually S will increase to a level equal to I and then Y will rise no more.

Find the ultimate level of Y, C, S and I either by completing the table or by a quicker method if you know one.

ANSWERS

14·1

$\frac{17}{18}; \frac{10}{11}; \frac{12}{13}$. Our research for current data.

14·2

	1960	1963	1966
$APS = \frac{S}{Y}$	$\frac{1}{1} = 0{\cdot}06$	$\frac{1}{11} = 0{\cdot}09$	$\frac{12}{13} = 0{\cdot}08$
$APS = 1 - \frac{C}{Y}$	$(1 - \frac{17}{18}) = 0{\cdot}06$	$(1 - \frac{20}{22}) = 0{\cdot}09$	$(1 - \frac{24}{26}) = 0{\cdot}08$

14·3

Own data.

14·4

YEAR	δC	δY
1		
	2	3
2		
	3	5
3		

14·5

$MPC = \frac{2}{3} = 0{\cdot}67$ for Year 1/Year 2

$MPC = \frac{3}{5} = 0{\cdot}60$ for Year 2/Year 3

In other words 0·67 of the increase in money income which occurred between year 1 and year 2 will be used for consumption. Similarly, 0·60 of the year 2 to year 3 increase in money income will be consumed.

14·6

Graph of consumption function.

14·7

At an income level pf £4 000 million, the $APC = \frac{5{\cdot}8}{4} = 1{\cdot}45$

At an income level of £8 000 million, the $APC = \frac{8{\cdot}8}{8} = 1{\cdot}1$.

At an income level of £24 000 million, the $APC = \frac{20}{24} = 0{\cdot}8$

The MPC between £20 000 million and £22 000 million $= \frac{\delta Y}{\delta X} = \frac{1{\cdot}2}{2} = 0{\cdot}6$

14·8

Correct **C**: the economy will remain in equilibrium when I = S.

14·9

Higher, because injections exceeded withdrawals.

14·10

Lower, because withdrawals exceeded injections.

14·11

Correct **C**: $\frac{80}{100} = \frac{4}{5}$

14·12

Correct **D**: C(80)+I(30) = Y(110).

14·13

Y = 125.
C = 100.
S = 25.
I = 25.

NATIONAL INCOME

STUDY SECTION **15**

Before reading this section, the student is advised to look again at S1 which discusses the basic problem of deciding how to allocate income. We saw in S1 that an individual distributes his income amongst a series of goods and services in such a way that he maximizes his satisfaction. Thus, given an income in the form of a wage, salary, rent interest or profit, we saw that an individual would firstly decide how much to spend on consumption and how much to save and then, secondly, he would decide how to distribute his expenditure on consumption amongst the goods and services offered in the market. Just as the national income is the sum of the separate factors' incomes, so is the total expenditure of the community the result of the total, or aggregate, of all the separate expenditure decisions.

Expenditure produces income

Furthermore, whenever an individual spends money on a commodity or service, he is providing income to another, and thus since the expenditure of all the individuals in the community creates the income of that community, then the decisions on the expenditure side should result in a total figure exactly the same as if one added up the community's total income. The aggregate national income, that which has been earned by the community, equals the aggregate national expenditure, (because of our concept of a circular flow which we explained in S14). If the members of the community earn and are paid in money, they have been paid for producing real goods and services and they will spend their money on real goods and services.

National income and expenditure

National income and expenditure accounts are prepared annually, and an example, with explanatory notes, is given in *Documentary Sources*. You should examine this now, and refer to it throughout this study section.

The aggregate or the total addition of all goods and services represents the total output of the nation or the national output. If the nation produces three goods A, B and C, which are produced by labour alone, and each is valued at £100, then the national income for the producers will be £300. As there are only three commodities to be purchased, the total national expenditure in this simple model will also be £300. How do we value this national output in this very simple model? The only possible way to value the products A, B and C is to find out how much they fetched in the market or, find out how much the community was prepared to pay for them. In this case, the community was prepared to pay £300 so that we have three identities: the expenditure of the community as a whole equals the income of the community as a whole, and that in turn must equal the value of the national output.

It is worth noting at this early stage that as real income is expressed in monetary units, if the three goods had been valued at £200 each, national income would equal national expenditure which in turn would equal national output at the figure of £600. Nevertheless, no-one in the community would be one bit better off than they were before, even though the monetary value has doubled. This illustrates quite clearly the difference between a change in real income and money income.

The importance of national income studies

Our simplified model enables us now to see that a decision to spend money on a new motor car for the family will affect the income of the motor car producers and attract raw materials, capital and labour from the production of, say, refrigerators, to the motor car industry in order to satisfy the consumers' demand for a further motor car. Conversely, if an industrialist decides to anticipate the future pattern of expenditure on motor cars, and therefore builds an addition to his factory, he will be taking resources from perhaps the domestic appliance industry in order to build his factory. In so doing, he is creating, for those people employed in building his factory, income which will in turn become expenditure. (In this model we have assumed that there are no unemployed resources and, therefore, that the decision to build more motor cars or build a motor car factory necessitates a switch of resources.)

The example above indicates the importance of studying the national income and expenditure accounts, because these accounts show how the nation is allocating and re-allocating its real resources. They also show the aggregate effect of decisions made by the community as a whole.

There is a further reason for emphasizing the importance of understanding these accounts. The managing director of an individual firm can, on the best evidence available to him, decide quite correctly the economic policy of his company. All his prognostications can, nevertheless, be completely negated by the imposition of an indirect tax on his goods; a tax which is, of course, imposed by the government. The reasons for the imposition of this tax can be that the government considers that our managing director (and others in his industry) is taking and using too much of the community's resources for his productive processes and, therefore, should be discouraged, because either the government itself wishes to use those resources for a community project or that the government for some purpose, for example, an export drive, wishes to encourage the transfer of those resources to other industries. The requirements of the national reserves of foreign exchange sometimes cause the government to interfere with the plans of a particular firm. We have already seen (S13) that no country operates a closed economic system. To the extent that it trades overseas, part of its economic life is interwoven with the political and commercial systems of other countries, which are largely beyond its control. Hence the national income accounts in conjunction with the balance of payments indicate to both the student of economics and to the industrialist the economic context within which each individual firm or person or household, operates. It is not enough, therefore, to study how the latter allocate resources without understanding thoroughly the economic policy of the community as reflected through its government, whose policy is, in turn, shown in its published accounts.

Measuring national income: three methods

Before we turn to the three methods of calculating national income it is worth noting the practical difficulties of gathering national income statistics. If one asked a householder if he had a bathroom this would appear to be a perfectly reasonable and easy question. However, the householder may count as a bathroom, a living-room with a curtained-off shower. He may count as a bathroom any room in which there were some washing facilities or he may only count as a bathroom, a room with a bath tub and a shower. Thus, what appears to be a simple question can lead to all sorts of difficulties and a perfectly honest person could deny having a bathroom simply because he had not understood the question. Hence, in every questionnaire, the government specifies precisely what its terms mean and there has to be an arbitrary definition of the facilities which constitute a bathroom. So it is with income questionnaires, and schedules. Quite often it is a matter of convenience, for the income tax authorities or for computational purposes, that determines whether a person is regarded as self-employed or employed by a firm. We know, for example that business men usually try to get as much of their real income on expenses (and therefore allocated to the firm) as possible. Hence, the national income accounts suffer from the usual difficulties of gathering information, and very great care has to be taken by students of economics to examine the footnotes and appendices to published tables to ensure that they understand precisely what each definition encompasses. Although in the national accounts the totals of income and expenditure should always be the same, in practice this rarely occurs and there are, therefore, 'balancing items', which are accounting devices to bring into balance the three methods of computation. Their size is some indication of the margin of error, which government accounting systems in practice need to accept. You should not, therefore, imagine that the national accounts are more accurate than we have described.

In the last study section you examined the concept of the circular flow of income. Now we are going to try and measure this circular flow at various points. In figure 15·1 we have a rather simplified version of the figure 14·4. This diagram emphasises the three main sources of expenditure in any national economy that is, expenditure by the government (the public sector), expenditure on consumption, and expenditure on capital investment. If we ignore, for the present, overseas trade, we can say that these three flows of monetary demands for the products of firms can be measured as the gross national expenditure on goods and services. (This is labelled GNEx in diagram 15·1.)

$$GNEx = C + I + G$$

The sum total of all payments made to the factors of production is called national income (in the diagram 15·1 it is labelled NY).

The money value of the gross national product, or the output of capital goods, consumption goods and services, both for individuals and for the

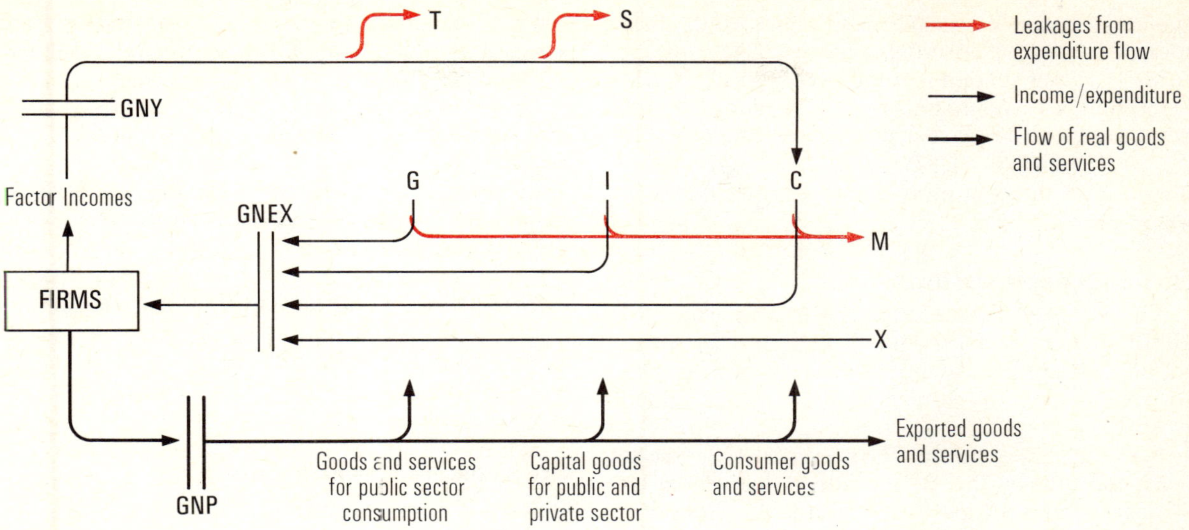

GNY — Gross National Income
GNEx — Gross National Expenditure
GNP — Gross National Product
C — Consumption expenditure
G — Government expenditure
I — Investment expenditure
X — Export expenditure (by foreigners)
S — Savings
T — Taxation
M — All sectors' expenditure on imports

Figure 15·1

government, is shown by the gross national product (GNP). The GNP is always calculated in terms of money—there is no other way of aggregating different commodities.
(See also figure 14·1).

$$GNP = C + I + G$$

We can say that the national income equals the national expenditure for two reasons; first because we have assumed that all income is consumed, or saved or, in the form of taxation, is reallocated by the government. These sectors create the demand for the national output of goods and services which are sold in the economy.

Therefore $GNY = GNP$

Secondly, the money demand for the national output becomes receipts which are then paid out again by firms as factor incomes, that is, the amount paid for goods and services represents payments to factors to produce the goods. Thus $NEx = NY$, therefore, if

$GNY = GNEx$ then it is also true that

$GNY = C + I + G$

We can therefore see that the following identity holds true, given our assumptions

$$GNY = GNEx = GNP = C + I + G$$

So far we have ignored overseas trade, assuming that the economy is a closed one. It is now time to account for the addition of imports and exports on figure 15·1. There is, in the form of exports, an outflow of real goods and services for which there are incoming payments which are in addition to total domestic expenditure. We assume, for the moment, that this is balanced by an outflow of payments made by consumers, firms and the government in return for an inflow of real imports, that is, that the balance of payments is in equilibrium.

Therefore

$$GNY = GNEx = GNP = C + I + G - M + X$$

Here M is expenditure on imports and X is receipts from exports. In the above equation, M must be deducted because the gross figures for $C + I + G$ include expenditure on imports. X must be added because it represents goods and services produced domestically. For the sake of simplicity we include capital goods in X and M.

These three ways of looking at the national income must, in the end, add up to the same amount since what is earned is spent and represents the value at current market prices of the goods and services produced, including overseas trade. The money received by firms is paid out again in the form of factor incomes in the next period. In S14 we found that aggregate monetary demand was composed of the same items so we can say that

$$GNEx = C + I + G - M + X = AMD$$

Now let us turn to a more detailed examination of the accounts.

National expenditure

The national expenditure is the total value of all the goods and services bought by the community during a year, both for consumption and for investment. Investment includes goods added to stocks.

National Expenditure = Expenditure by persons + expenditure by the private and public sector of industry + expenditure by the local authorities and central government (for the contemporary definitions of these terms see the appropriate government accounts).

National income

The national income is the total of all factors' incomes in a year. Since some inhabitants of the country will have income which is earned abroad this must be added and any income which is due to overseas residents which is earned in this country must be deducted. The national income is therefore regarded as the net aggregate product of and the sole source of payment for, all the agents of production. Incomes which are transfer payments, such as family allowances, will not be included, as there is no corresponding contribution to production.

National output or national product

In concept this is the total output of all the factors of production, that is, all the real goods and services which people are paid to produce. Since one cannot add together a house, a car, some carpets, a warm coat, some vegetables, and so on, in any meaningful way other than in money terms, the national output has to be measured in terms of market prices. We can, therefore, think of the national product as the money value of all goods and services which flow into being during one year. A rather formal definition is to say that *the national product is the aggregate joint product of the resources of land, labour and capital over a given time period, normally one year*. Unless these goods and services are normally exchanged for money they will not be included in the aggregate total for national product.

The principles of the national income accounts

In the National Income accounts (see *Blue Book*) you will find tables at the beginning which show a summary for the national income and expenditure accounts and also a table showing personal income and expenditure. Before examining these accounts in further detail, you should carefully consider the main items set out in the tables below which show the principles of the accounts.

The gross national product

Table A **EXPENDITURE** (which purchases GNP)

1	Consumers' expenditure	C
	plus	
	Public authorities' current expenditure on goods and services	G
	plus	
2	Gross domestic fixed capital formation	I
	plus	
3	Value of physical increase in stocks and work in progress	I
	equals	
	Total Domestic Expenditure at Market Prices	
	plus	
4	Exports and property income from abroad	X
	minus	
5	Imports and property income paid abroad	M
	equals	
6	**Gross National Expenditure at Market Prices**	
	minus	
7	Taxes on expenditure (indirect taxes)	
	plus	
8	Subsidies (e.g. to farmers)	
	equals	
9	**Gross National Expenditure or Product at Factor Cost**	
	minus	
10	Capital consumption	
	equals	
11	Net National Expenditure at Factor Cost (see table B, item 10)	

Table B **FACTOR INCOMES**
(which show their share of the GNP)

1 Factor incomes Income from employment Income from self-employment plus 2 Gross trading profits of companies plus 3 Gross trading surplus of public corporations or other public enterprises plus 4 Rent equals
Total Domestic Income
minus 5 stock appreciation equals
6 Gross Domestic Product at Factor Cost
plus 7 Net property income from abroad i.e. net income from overseas (income receipts from abroad less income payments to overseas people or firms) equals
8 Gross National Product at Factor Cost
minus 9 Capital consumption equals
10 National Income (see table A, item 11)
plus 11 Transfer payments to individuals minus 12 Profits which have not been distributed to shareholders etc. minus 13 surpluses of nationalised industries etc. equals
14 Personal Income
minus 15 Direct taxes on persons, e.g. income tax equals
16 Personal Disposable Income

You should refer to these tables continually when reading the explanations below. We must emphasize that there are variations in the actual national accounts from year to year so that the student should pay particular attention to the footnotes and explanations of definitions, but the major aggregate terms given above should help you when looking at the more detailed tables in the government publications.

We can now deal in further detail with the particular items. The numbers in brackets refers to the number on the left-hand side of the table and the prefix A or B indicates the table in which you will find the item.

15·1

Which of the following changes is necessary to obtain the gross national product at factor cost from the gross domestic product?

A Add exports, deduct imports, then add stock appreciation and deduct subsidies.
B Add exports, deduct imports, then deduct stock appreciation, add subsidies and deduct subsidies.
C Add the net property income from abroad only.
D Deduct capital consumption only.
E Deduct stock appreciation only.

15·2

Which of the following items marks the distinction between the gross national product and national income?

A Capital consumption.
B Exports and imports.
C Stock appreciation.
D Transfer payments.
E Subsidies.

Some problems of measuring the national income

A The national product (A9 and B8)

1 The gross national product may be calculated by aggregating all the expenditure (A9) which generates the gross national product. In practice there are two ways of measuring the money value of the national product. Firstly, one can measure the national product in terms of the selling prices and quantities of all the goods available in the market. This may, however, involve a certain degree of double counting, a feature which will be examined a little later. Alternatively, national product may be measured at 'factor cost', that is, the total output of goods and services may be measured in terms of the payments which are made to the factors of production in return for having produced these goods and services (B8). To some extent services raise a problem here, for

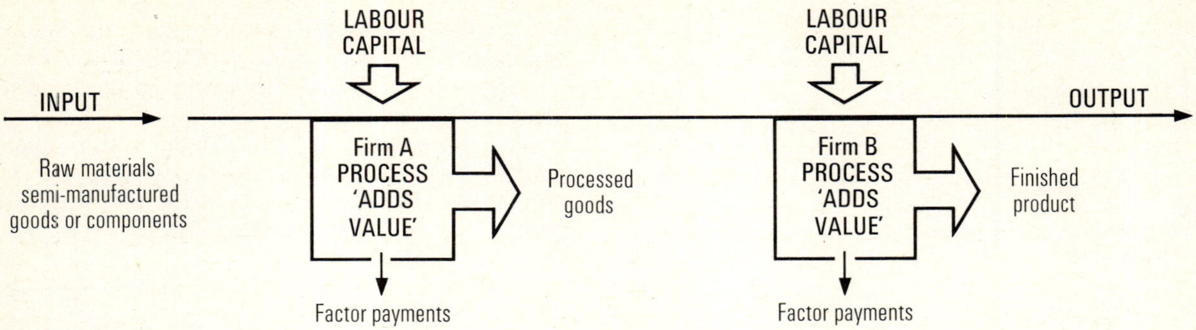

Figure 15·2

their value is usually measured by the current prices which are paid for them. Such prices may be rather arbitrary, particularly when services are bought by the public sector, because there are no normal market forces in operation.

2 The national product may be calculated by using a statistical sample throughout all industries. If, however, one adds together the total value of all firms' outputs, double counting would occur, since part of the value of any firm's output is the value of the raw materials or components which have been used. These have already been counted as the value of the final products of the firm supplying them. Therefore only the 'value added' by each stage of production is included as part of the total national product (A11).

Figure 15·2 illustrates, as an example, part of the processing of materials for the car industry. Iron ore is sold to the steel works which in turn produces raw steel which is then sent to rolling mills, to the car-body makers, and finally to the car assemblers. If the gross value of the output of each stage was added together we would end up counting the value of the raw materials five times. The difference between the buying price of raw materials plus the cost of the other factors of production, and the selling price, after processing, is termed the 'value added'. This difference is what, in effect, is produced by the separate firms. National product is therefore the aggregate of the 'value added' of each firm in the country.

3 Capital consumption (B9) is the deduction necessary to allow for the fact that part of the national output must be used to replace worn-out capital. This is known as depreciation. The true value of national income is equal to net national product (A11).

4 Stock appreciation is deducted because some money income will arise merely from the sale of stocks which have risen in price during the accounting period. For example, if the price of shoes rises, a shopkeeper's income can increase if he sells existing stocks at a higher price.

5 The value of an *existing* asset, when sold, is not included in the national product because it does not represent new assets coming into existence nor does it create new income, so it is not included in national income nor in national expenditure. For example, when a second hand car is sold, only the dealer's income will be included in the national income, because only this represents a service provided for the customer. It is just a transfer from one person to another, but the sale, for example, of a *new* house is included in the national expenditure when sold, and in the national product, since it represents a new asset flowing into being, and since incomes are generated by its creation it is included also in national income.

B National expenditure (Table A)

1 Only expenditure on final goods and services provided must be included, for if intermediate transactions were counted, duplications would occur.

2 To be included, an expenditure must be in return for work done or services rendered or else it does not represent an income to anybody nor does it represent an increase in goods produced or services rendered.

3 The actual amount which individuals can consume depends on the relationship between the market price of goods and services and their incomes in money terms. Therefore, any measure of national expenditure which is based upon market prices may be rather suspect, because a rise in national expenditure may simply reflect a general upward trend in prices and not an increase in the real supply of goods and services.

Although practical measurements of national expenditure have to be done in terms of market prices it is possible to calculate a set of indices through which one can measure national expenditure in terms of constant prices, and thus to reflect the growth, in real terms, of the national expenditure (and, by implication, of national income).

The important thing here to remember is that in national income accounting we are always trying to measure physical goods and services in terms of another commodity, that is, money, which is itself of changing value. Part of this change in expenditure due to rises in prices is taken account of when the appreciation in the value of stocks is deducted from total national output of goods and services.

C National income (Table B)

1 National income includes only those goods and services normally exchanged for money. Any items not so exchanged are excluded, for example, personal characteristics and skills, work done by a mother for her family, and geographical and other natural facilities. However, part of our standard of living depends on these and other services not paid for, for example, the work of voluntary organizations and services we do for ourselves.

2 The services industries are a rapidly growing source of employment (and therefore of income) but they are taking OVER, as paid services, things we previously did for ourselves, for example, childrens' nurseries, launderettes, market gardens, etc. These latter increase the national income and also the share of national income attributed to services but it does not necessarily increase our standard of living. However, as services are increasingly paid for, the national expenditure will show a rise and the national product is similarly increased as the output of services increases.

3 Income tax returns are the main source of accurate information about the gross incomes paid to the factors of production. However, although these cover nearly all incomes, they do not cover all personal assets. Note in this context the difference between personal incomes and personal wealth.

4 The incomes of citizens of overseas countries who are temporarily resident are not included in the national income because these people are not part of the national community. For the same reason overseas-owned investments which are held within the national boundaries are not included. This is because the national income is an attempt to measure the total income of all the residents, that is, the citizens of a particular country.

5 Most governments provide some kind of social security and unemployment benefits to appropriate citizens. Such payments are known as *transfer payments* (B11). Other examples in the U.K. are unemployment benefits, children's allowances, old-age pensions and redundancy payments. These are not included in the national income even though they are part of people's disposable income, because there is no equivalent in the national product as these payments do not represent work done or services rendered by the recipient.

6 Another group of transfer payments which are excluded is the interest on public authority debts, for example, the payment of interest by local authorities on government loans, and the payment of interest on national savings or development bond or the winnings on Premium Bonds. Again, these payments do not represent goods produced or services rendered and so have no equivalent in the national product.

7 The allowance for capital consumption (A10 and B9) is only an estimate and subject to quite arbitrary measurement. Since in a developed economy this is often a very large sum, it may be a source of inaccuracy.

National income and the standard of living

The national income is simply a monetary measurement of the real flow of goods and services available to the community. As such, any increase in the national income may simply reflect a change in the value of money. Individually we may be no better off because the increases in money incomes may be swallowed up by rises in prices. If everybody's money income is raised their standard of living is not, therefore, necessarily increased. If, however, we raise the level of employment or productivity of labour then the standard of living will rise. This is because the rise in the level of employment implies that there are fewer factors being wasted and that the total output of goods and services will increase. In the same way, a rise in the productivity of labour implies an increased output per man employed. In consequence both of these changes will lead to an increase in the national product.

Changes in the money level of national income over the years does not therefore mean an automatic increase in the real income per head of the community i.e. GNP ÷ population. This is so because:

(a) There may be changes in the value of money.

(b) There may have been changes in the size of the population which may tend to absorb the additional real income.

In most countries it is important to set any increase in the national income against the growth in population. In some cases in recent decades the entire growth of the national income has been offset by increases in population. (See the discussion of Malthus in S9.) Changes in the distribution of age groups will also affect the pattern of national expenditure as demand changes for different classes of goods. This means a reallocation of national resources to meet specific wants (see S3 Population).

(c) Some items not previously included in the national income may now be included, such as work previously done for oneself and therefore not usually exchanged for money. Where these services are not bought as a result of growing affluence, the national income will show a rise without any real rise in the standard of living enjoyed by the whole community.

(d) As productivity increases, people may chose to work shorter hours.

(e) For some people an increase in the money level of national income may in fact mean a lower standard of living or detrimental effects on some sections of the community. When both parents are out at work there may be a deterioration in the standard of child care. The increasing use of shift working may adversely affect a whole family or it may be at the cost of health, freedom or leisure time. One should therefore be careful to investigate the circumstances of any change in the national

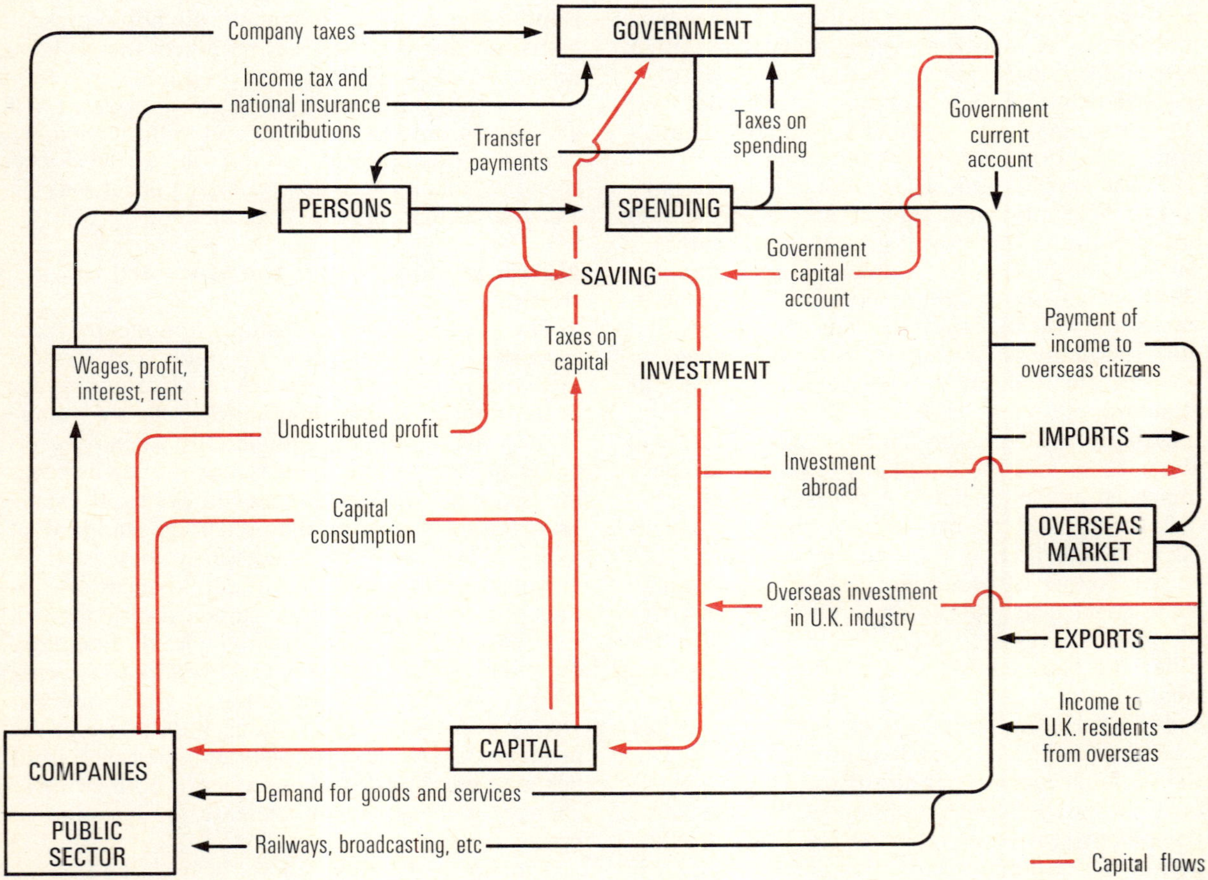

Figure 15·3

income though it frequently means trying to measure the many variables which make a given quality of community life.

National income and the standard of living

National income statistics are frequently used for international comparisons of the standard of living. Apart from problems of defining 'the standard of living' it is well to beware of making simple comparisons even when they are based on the average national income per head (called the *per capita* national income.) That one country has a higher per capita national income than another does not necessarily mean to say that the standard of living of its inhabitants is also higher. Similarly, a rise in the measured national income of any given country does not of itself imply that the inhabitants are any better off in real terms.

Always consider the relationship between the real income and the money income when using the national income statistics, for changes can be recorded simply because of a change in the value of money, or because of a change in definition. For example, when the Republic of Ireland ceased to be part of the United Kingdom, there was a sudden fall in the total national output and population. Further, the student must note that definitions of income are important. We have already emphasized the difference between real income and money income. Similarly, we must not only consider the total national income of any particular country but also the way in which it is distributed: Remember that the *per capita* income is an average and may conceal gross inequality of distribution. Similarly, the distribution of ownership of wealth can effect national spending patterns, the propensity to consume and the resultant propensity to save.

You should compare the distribution of the ownership of private wealth as shown in figure 15·4 with the distribution of personal incomes shown in the *National Income and Expenditure* Blue Book, section 4 *The Personal Sector* in the table headed *Distribution of Personal Income before and after tax*.

The standard of living depends not only upon the material goods consumed by the community but also on the non-material environment in which people live. The national income only measures the cultural and educational facilities which the community values in money terms. The standard of living is a question of quality as well as of quantity. *Per capita* measures of national income do not directly show the burden or incidence of taxation nor directly do they show the personal welfare provisions made through systems of transfer payments. In all these cases one has to look carefully at the contents of the national income accounts before drawing even very tentative comparisons.

The spending pattern of parts of the community are not revealed in any of the summary tables of the national incomes; and yet is it the spending pattern which accounts for much of the difference between the assessment of the individual standards of living. Within any given *per capita* measurement of the national income very large regional differences in money earnings may be concealed. National income per head is often measured on the basis of gross national product, but this in itself may be misleading if the element of capital consumption is high, as it is in well-established industrialized economies.

The *per capita* national income is, by definition, an average figure, and, as in the case of all averages, it tends to hide very wide extremes. For example, a small number of people in one country may be very wealthy while the majority are relatively poverty stricken, whereas in another country the same per capital national income may be shown and yet reflect a much more even distribution of income with few people near the poverty line but rather fewer people in the very high income brackets. *Per capita* national income does not reveal the range and availability of goods for personal consumption, nor does it indicate quality of education or literacy. All these other

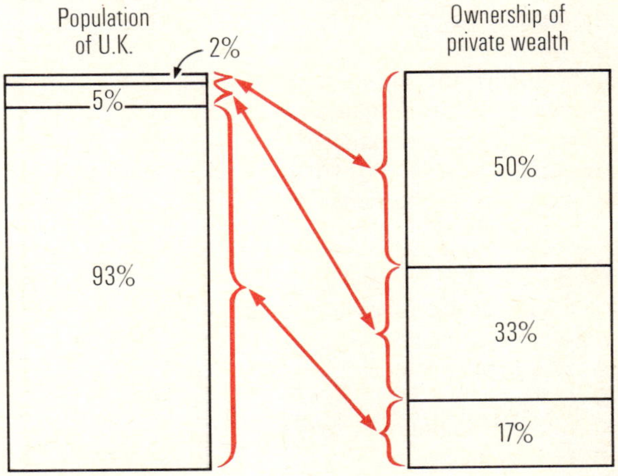

Figure 15·4

factors are in real life just as important as the average income per head.

National Income Account

A copy of the important summary tables from the *United Kingdom National Income and Expenditure* Blue Book is included in *Documentary Sources*. Only matters of principle will be dealt with in this volume as notes are provided with the copy of the accounts.

Transfer payments and the propensity to consume

If a payment is made which is not in return for goods produced, or for services rendered within the accounting period, this payment is a transfer payment which takes money from one group and presents purchasing power to another group. There has clearly been no increase in national output but there has been an important re-distribution of income which may effect the community's propensity to consume, for if the money is given to lower income groups who have a high marginal propensity to consume and taken from the higher income groups, which tend to have a lower marginal propensity to consume, then the average propensity to consume of the community is likely to be greater. The aggregate monetary demand (AMD) for consumption goods and services is likely to be raised and, if there is full employment, a potentially inflationary situation may be created. Such payments illustrate the difference between an individual's income and the community's income. To an individual state pensioner the money he receives is crucial in maintaining his livelihood, but as far as the state is concerned as a nation this individual's income is of no consequence to the aggregated national income, and if it were counted the same income would be counted twice, firstly as earned by the taxpayer and secondly, as given to the pensioner.

15·3

Which of the following items are included in the national income?

A Widows' pensions.
B Gifts.
C Interest on national savings.
D Local rates.
E The purchase price of a new house.

15·4

Would you include all of the following items in gross national product? If not, identify those which you would include.

A Car bodies.
B Headlamps.
C Batteries for fitting into new cars.
D Tyres supplied to car manufacturers.
Petrol.

15:5

Of the following items, which one accounts for the difference between an open and closed economy?

A Savings.
B State-owned industries.
C Capital consumption.
D The balance of payments.
E Payments of contributions to the United Nations.

Increasing the national product

Every government whatever its political complexion seeks to increase the total national product of the nation. If the national product is increasing then it is easier to deal with the problems of the distribution of income amongst each group within the population, for, with an increase in national product, it is possible to give each and every group more. If, on the other hand, the national product is not increasing or decreasing then the problem of the distribution of the national product amongst the various groups which form the community are very much greater. Of course in this context we are referring to an increase in national income per head of population. Let us now turn, therefore, to a discussion of the means and ways of increasing the national product.

You will notice that there is a leakage into savings before spending which, of course, illustrates that either persons spend or they 'not spend' or save. If this savings were to be totally used for investment purposes by manufacturers, then you can see that the circle is maintained. If we assume that this simple case is true it follows that the creation of capital will eventually lead to an additional supply of consumer goods and to an increase in the national product.

The source of increased capital is not only savings by persons, but also by companies (by undistributed profits, see figure 15·3) and by the government. The government invests in industrial infrastructure, that is, roads, railways, docks and harbours, airports etc., and in public enterprises such as the nationalised industries. Personal savings are channelled through financial institutions to be made available as investments by the process of buying new share issues, by loans and debentures and so on. (Bank advances are mostly used for current expenditure and not for capital investment.) Companies may make self-financed investment by withholding dividends from their shareholders and investing these funds themselves, together with depreciation funds which have been set aside for financing capital consumption.

Some new capital comes from overseas investment in the domestic economy; for example, American car and computer companies invest very heavily in Europe. To some extent this is balanced by U.K. investors buying shares in overseas enterprises. Such investment provides flows on the capital account in the balance of payments as well as reverse flows of dividends and interests on the current account of the balance of payments at some future date.

In aggregate, the balance in the national economy between the flow of demand for consumer goods and the creation of new capital is crucial. On one hand there must be enough capital to provide the production capacity to meet the demand for goods and services in both the right quantities and proportions. If the aggregate monetary demand is greater than the capacity of output (that is that maximum output which the current national capacity will provide), then market prices tend to rise in order to 'ration out' the supply among competing buyers. On the other hand, any capacity which is unused results in unemployed capital and possibly the tragedy of unemployed people.

If we assume that the increased capacity is used to produce additional goods then we can see that part of this additional supply of goods and services may be exported and part will be used for an increased domestic consumption. The exports yield an increase in income, in the same way as an increase in the domestic supply of goods and services will yield extra income. The increase in the flow of extra wages will maintain not only the increase in demand for goods and services but also an increase in savings which will finance the original investment (see figure 15·5). As we move from M_1 to M, savings increase. Hence the circular flow of income and the real supply of goods and services will tend to increase.

As the economy grows, that is, as demand for goods and services increases, then so must the capacity to produce both now and in the future. The keys to the private sector are the marginal propensity to consume and to save. These determine the proportion of any current increase in national income which will be consumed or saved in the future. In all economies the role of the public sector (government departments and nationalised industries) is important, though the extent to which it is so, varies. In the United Kingdom about one-half of the total demand for

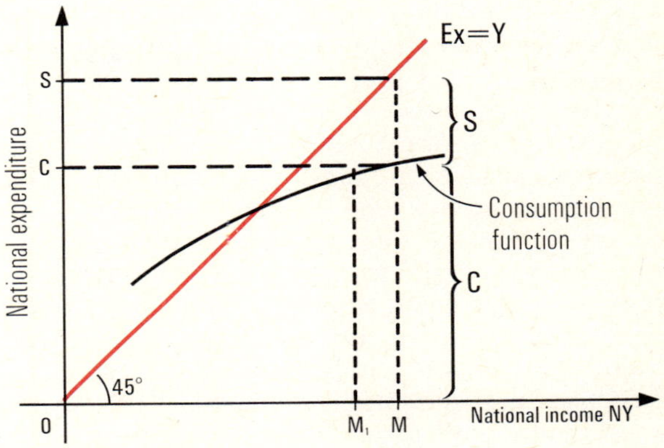

Figure 15·5

consumer goods and services and for capital is determined by public authorities (central and local government).

We can now look again at a national consumption function as in figure 15·5.

The national consumption function

Assuming national income is OM in figure 15·5 then you can see that consumer expenditure is OC and savings is CS. This does not imply that at OM all the factors of production are employed at the given level of expenditure. There are various ways by which the national product may increase other than by an increase in investment in the private sector. These other methods of increasing the national product can be just as important as the mathematical model we have just described.

1 Increasing the physical productivity of labour or capital. It may be possible in conjunction with wage and salary negotiations to alter working practices or techniques in order to increase the productivity of labour. Consequently each unit of labour or capital will produce more, or output per man has increased. This should increase the flow of goods and services on which a given amount of national income is expended and hence the real income of the community should arise.

A similar effect will occur if new capital-intensive industries tend to replace old labour-intensive industries. This will tend to increase the real output relative to the monetary demand for goods and services. Provided that the substitution of capital for labour does not produce unemployment, then the whole community will be better off.

2 Redistribution of income. Most taxation systems tend to take more from those with higher incomes and less from those with lower incomes. As a general tendency those with higher incomes have a higher marginal propensity to save, and when they are taxed and the money transferred to lower income groups there tends to be a rise in the national marginal propensity to consume because low income groups tend to spend all or nearly all of any increase in their incomes. As the national marginal propensity to consume tends to rise then so will the aggregate monetary demand for goods and services tend to rise, because what everyone spends is somebody else's income.

3 Increase in government consumption. Collectively, the various government departments purchase a considerable variety of consumer goods, ranging from army boots to banquets for visiting dignitaries. It is comparitively simple to permit an increase in departmental expenditures.

4 Increase in government investment. Research projects, road works, motorways, docks and harbours, and such like, create an immediate demand for large quantities of labour and, in a modern economy, for substantial amounts of capital equipment. If this is financed by taxation on incomes or expenditure there will be a tendency to reallocate resources away from consumption goods and into investment. This will, in turn, increase the future capacity of industry to add to the supply of goods and services available to consumers. The relationship between increases in investment and increases in income or output can be calculated numerically and is known as *the multiplier*. (See S16.)

Government action in attempting to increase the national product has a freedom denied to private enterprise. Entrepreneurs can spend only what they have, or can borrow. The extent of their borrowing ability is limited by several factors, including the general climate of opinion about trade prospects. Governments, on the other hand, can *always* raise money, either by taxation, or by creating it, through control of the financial system.

However, it is important to note that although the real national income can be increased at any time by an improvement in the physical productivity of labour or capital, it can only be increased by government action if these are unemployed resources available to be called into production. If there is already full employment, and the government tries to increase the real national product by any of the last three methods; it may run into serious difficulties, as we shall see in S21.

15·6

Which of the following items would you not include in the personal disposable income account?

A Income taxes.
B National Insurance benefits.
C Taxes on expenditure.
D Net income to shopkeepers.
E Dividends from shares.

15·7

Which of the following policies would you recommend as a means of increasing the national income?

A Increase old-age pensions.
B Increase the wages of government and local authority employees.
C Reduce unemployment by embarking on investment in public works.
D Reduce taxation.
E Impose import restrictions.

15·8

An increase in children's allowances would be shown as:

A An increase in total personal incomes.
B An increase in the gross national product.
C A reduction in taxation.
D A reduction in capital consumption.
E An increase in incomes from employment.

15·9

The following table is in alternative form to help you revise. The figures in this table are hypothetical. You should look up the current *Blue Book* and insert the appropriate figures to ensure complete understanding of these essential concepts.

EXPENDITURE

Consumers'	Spending (goods and services)		73
Govt.	Spending (goods and services)		15
Firms *Govts.*	Spending on capital goods and stocks		15
Exports	Spending by foreigners on on U.K. goods and services	25	
Less	Spending by U.K. residents on foreign goods and services	20	
			5
GROSS NATIONAL EXPENDITURE (at Market Prices)			108
Add	*Subsidies*	2	
Deduct	*Indirect Taxes*	10	−8
GROSS NATIONAL EXPENDITURE (at factor cost)			100

INCOME

Wages and Salaries	68	
Income from self-employment	8	
Profits—Companies	15	
Public Corpn's	3	
Rent	5	
TOTAL DOMESTIC INCOME	99	
		99
Less stock appreciation		0·5
GROSS DOMESTIC PRODUCT		98·5
Add NET INCOME FROM ABROAD		1·5
GROSS NATIONAL PRODUCT (at factor cost)		100

OUTPUT

4	Agriculture
3	Mining
34	Manufacturing
6	Construction
3	Gas/electricity
8	Transport
13	Distribution
3	Insurance, banking, finance
12	Other services
10	PUBLIC OUTPUT (Health, education, defence, etc.)
3	Ownership of dwellings
99	TOTAL DOMESTIC PRODUCT

DEDUCT CAPITAL CONSUMPTION TO OBTAIN NET NATIONAL INCOME AT FACTOR COST

ANSWERS

15·1

Correct **C**: Mistaken **A, B, D, E**: Look again at the national income accounts.

15·2

Correct **A**: Capital consumption is deducted from the gross national product to give the net national product or national income. Mistaken **B, C, D, E.**

15·3

Correct **E**: Mistaken **A, B, C, D.** These are all forms of transfer payments.

15·4

Correct **E**: Mistaken **A, B, C, D.** These are all components and it would be double counting to include these in the gross national product, except as part of the final price of a car.

15·5

Correct **D**: Mistaken **A, B, C, E.** An open economy is one which includes the full effects of the balance of payments which results from overseas trade. A closed economy is one which has no overseas trade.

15·6

Correct **C**: Mistaken **A, B, D, E.** Note that it is the personal income account and not the national income account to which reference was made.

15·7

Correct **C**: Mistaken **A, B, D, E.**

15·8

Correct **A**: Mistaken **B, C, D, E.** Children's allowances are included on the personal income and expenditure account under the sub-heading 'National Insurance Benefits and other current grants from public authorities'. Any increase in children's allowances would increase therefore the total personal personal income, but as a transfer payment it would not be included on the gross national product account.

15·9

Own work.

INTEREST, SAVINGS, AND INVESTMENT

STUDY SECTION **16**

Interest as a factor payment

Interest is the payment received by the owner of money capital for the use of that capital by the borrower. Suppose you lend £1 000 to a local shopkeeper to buy a delivery van. The shopkeeper calculates that he can pay for the loan out of the increased profits which will come from the extra trade his delivery service will bring. If you are businesslike, you will go to a solicitor, and have a formal agreement drawn up, specifying all the details of the transaction, and you will make arrangements with his bank to see that the repayments are regularly made.

Thus apart from the repayments of the sum lent, you will expect an additional sum, called *gross interest*. Gross interest is composed of three elements:

- **i** Payment for the use of funds. This is *pure interest*.
- **ii** Payment to cover the book-keeping and other office work caused by administering the loan. In the example just quoted this might amount to £8 solicitor's fees and £6 bank charges. In larger loans for long periods (perhaps 20 years or more), the administration costs would be correspondingly greater.
- **iii** Payment for the risk involved. Our shopkeeper may be honest, his calculations may be accurate, but most business contains an element of risk. All lenders run some risk that their debtors will default.

In times of rising prices, you would, if you were wise, add a fourth element to the gross interest on your loan.

- **iv** Payment to compensate for the decreased purchasing power of money. When your £1 000 has been repaid, you will want it to buy you as much as it did when it was first lent. If this is not the case, you will expect a payment to make up this lost purchasing power.

Pure interest is therefore the payment which would be made for a completely riskless loan, for which there were no costs of administration, i.e. it is the payment made to the lender to compensate him for the loss of use of his cash—the sacrifice of liquidity, as explained in S11. The longer the duration of the loan, the less liquid it is, and therefore the higher the rate of pure interest necessary to attract lenders. Some long-term loans, such as those made to companies by the purchase of a *new issue* of debentures, or to the government by the purchase of a *new issue* of securities, are made more liquid because the claims can be transferred to other people by sales on the Stock Exchange. Interest is therefore a price paid by borrowers to lenders, and will depend on the supply and demand for loanable money for various purposes.

The structure of interest rates

Economists often speak about 'the rate of interest' as if there were only one rate. In fact there are very many rates: look at the financial advertisements in your local or national paper, or in the windows of building societies or finance companies. The rates in this interest rate structure vary from low on short-term, low-risk loans, to high on long-term, high-risk loans, and the whole structure itself may rise or fall. Economists refer to a single rate for simplicity, to represent the whole structure. Loans to the British government are practically riskless and very liquid, because there is no suspicion that the government will default and the securities can be resold to another buyer on the Discount Market or the Stock Exchange. The large size of the National Debt makes the cost of administration per unit very low. Therefore the rate of interest on Treasury Bills is taken to indicate the short-term pure interest rate, and the yield on Consols (non-redeemable government securities) is taken to indicate the long-term pure interest rate.

Let us examine some rates in the interest rate structure. First, remember that a rate of interest should usually be expressed as a percentage return each year (p.a.). Interest and discount rates are also explained in the satellite *Arithmetical and Statistical Methods*.

16·1

What is the annual rate of interest if you receive

- **i** £10 per quarter for a loan of £800?
- **ii** £1 per week for a loan of £520?
- **iii** 50p per month for a loan of £30?

---

i Bank rate. This is maximum rate of interest chargeable by the Bank of England for 7 days loans or rediscounts to the Discount Houses. Bank rate influences the Treasury Bill rate, deposit account rates are always 2% below Bank rate, and overdraft rates for private borrowers are $2\frac{1}{2}$% above. (See S6 and satellite *Financial Institutions*.)

ii Treasury Bill rate. This is the rate of discount on Treasury Bills. The purchase of Treasury Bills at a discount represents a 91 day loan to the British government. The difference between the maturity value of the Bills and the discounted price represents the interest paid for the loan. Details of the weekly changes in rates can be found in the financial columns of papers and on the back pages of *The Economist*

iii The nominal rate of interest on government securities (gilt-edged). Government securities (also known as government stock or bonds) are called gilt-edged (because the original certificates were so decorated). Also, in times before inflation reduced the purchasing power of any sum of money lent, they were as good as gold because, unlike shares, a fixed sum is assured at maturity, when the government redeems (repays) the loan at par value.

Stock is issued in units of £100 nominal or par value, bearing a nominal rate of interest, e.g. 5%, which means that the holder of each 5% bond receives £5 per year income, whatever the market price of that bond on the Stock Exchange. These nominal rates reflect the level of interest rates prevailing at the time when the government first issued the stock.

iv The market rate of interest (yield) on government securities. The market rate of interest or yield on government securities is the relationship between the income received from holding a bond and the market price of that bond on the Stock Exchange.

Suppose that the government makes a new issue of bonds, and fixes the nominal rate of interest on these bonds at 5%. If the economic situation is such that the prevailing rate of interest for long-term, low-risk loans is 5%, people will buy these new 5% bonds for £100. Now suppose that a severe credit squeeze is introduced and the cost of borrowing money long-term rises to 10% p.a. What price would buyers on the Stock Exchange now pay for the existing 5% bonds, i.e. paper claims providing an income of £5 p.a.? They would pay only £50, because anyone making a new loan of £100 could receive 10% p.a., i.e. £10 per year, so an income of £5 p.a. would be worth only £50. £5 p.a. from a payment of £50 is a return, or *yield*, of 10%.

Suppose interest rates fell, so that the long-term rate was $2\frac{1}{2}$%. The existing 5% bond would now be worth £200, because, if current rates of interest are $2\frac{1}{2}$%, you would have to lend £200 to obtain an income of £5 per year.

The formula for finding the yield on bonds is

$$\text{Flat Yield (\%)} = \text{Nominal Rate (\%)} \times \frac{\text{Nominal Value}}{\text{Market Price}}$$

If the bond is held until maturity the holder receives not only the annual income but also a capital gain if he bought the bond at a price below nominal value. The yield including the eventual capital gain or loss is known as the *redemption yield.* Consols (Consolidated Stock) are not redeemable, so the yield on Consols shows the long-term interest rate. Details about the types of government securities and their yields can be found in the financial columns of papers.

v The yields on shares. Yields on shares are calculated in a similar manner, either with reference to the dividend per share—which is the amount actually distributed to shareholders—or earnings per share—the total amount which could have been distributed if the company had not retained any profits. The dividend declared each year is expressed by the company as a percentage of the nominal value of the share. The actual market price of the share is usually above the nominal value. The formula is

$$\text{Dividend Yield \%} = \text{Dividend Declared \%} \times \frac{\text{Nominal Value}}{\text{Market Price}}$$

Therefore, if a 20% dividend is declared on a £1 share, of which the market price is £2, the shareholders receive 20p per share, and the dividend yield is 10%. During periods of inflation the average yield on shares may be below the yield on government securities, despite the greater risks involved in holding shares. The reason for this is that people wish to buy shares because they hope that the market price of their shares will rise to keep pace with rising prices, whereas the redemption value of securities cannot rise above £100.

16·2

a How much income per year is received by a holder of a 4% bond which cost £80 on the Stock Exchange?
 A £3·20 B £4 C £5

b What is the yield (flat yield) on this bond?
 A 3·2% B 4% C 5%

c If the price of the bond fell to £40, what would be the flat yield?
 A 8% B 10% C 16%

d If the market rate of interest fell to 1%, what would be the market price of the 4% bond?
 A £25 B £200 C £400

Prices and yields of securities

From the previous exercise you can observe the very important relationship between the market price and the yield of securities. When the prices of securities rise, the yields (market rate of interest) fall; when the prices of securities fall, the yields rise. The same relationship exists between the yields and prices of shares.

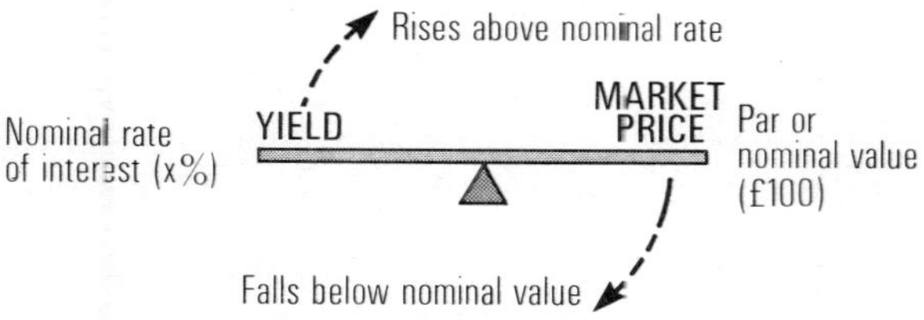

Figure 16·1

This inverse relationship is very significant for monetary policy. If the government wishes to reduce the supply of money by selling securities to the public in exchange for money, it has to lower the price of the securities which the Government Broker sells during open market operations. Yields on securities automatically rise, and eventually the rise will be extended to all interest rates. Therefore if the government wishes to alter the supply of money it cannot keep prices and yields of securities stable ('an orderly market').

The determination of interest rates

Many theories have been put forward to describe exactly what determines the level of the rate of interest at any time. The two main theories provide different explanations of the supply and demand curves which jointly set the price paid for the use of capital. The classical theory states that the supply of savings provides the funds available for lending, and the demand for funds to borrow depends on the demand for real capital. The monetary theory states that the rate of interest balances the supply of actual money and the demand for money to hold. We will examine these theories further.

The supply of savings

Saving is abstaining from present consumption, i.e. not spending all your current income on consumer goods or services. This may be done by individuals (personal saving), or companies which retain profits (corporate saving), or by the central government, local authorities, and nationalized industries (public sector saving). Excesses of current revenue over expenditure, i.e. budget surpluses, and the surpluses of nationalized industries compose public sector saving.

SOURCES OF SAVINGS 1968

	£m	% of total
Personal Saving	2 200	26
Corporate Saving	3 304	38
Public Sector Saving	3 012	36
Total Saving	8 516	100

Figure 16·2 Source: *Annual Abstract of Statistics.*

The reasons for saving

Personal, corporate, and public sector saving arise from different motives.

Personal saving

i) Future consumption. Most people save from time to time for a specific purpose, e.g. for a holiday, to acquire a deposit for the purchase of a house, to help finance their children's education etc. The need to save before the purchase of consumer durables and houses has been reduced by the rapid development of hire purchase finance.

ii) Precautionary purposes. People save 'for the rainy day', i.e. to guard against the misfortune of unemployment, ill health, and to prevent poverty in old age. The extension of social security benefits to all workers since 1948 has somewhat reduced the need to save for this purpose. However, it is important to realize that the life insurance premiums which many people pay must be included in this form of saving. Such regular payments are *contractual saving.*

iii) Habit or accident. Many people save from

habit—the Victorians extolled the virtues of thrift—and some people's incomes are large enough to leave a surplus unspent. This may happen particularly after rises in income, before people adjust their level of expenditure upwards.

iv) Speculative purposes. Some people save rather than buy goods or securities now, if they expect prices to fall. If they actually keep their money in cash form, and do not lend it even temporarily to a bank, such saving is called *hoarding*.

16·3

What is the effect of inflation on the desire to save?

A The desire to save rises because people need more money to buy goods in the future.

B The desire to save falls because the purchasing power of any sum lent declines.

16·4

Does hoarding, **A** increase, or **B** decrease, the amount of money lent?

Corporate saving

The reasons for company saving also apply to unincorporated businesses (partnerships, etc.), and public corporations, although savings of the former will be included in personal saving, and savings of the latter in public sector saving.

i) Future capital expenditure. Firms retain profits to help finance their purchases of machinery, raw materials, etc. (fixed and working capital).

ii) Payment of taxes and to maintain dividends. Taxes are paid on the previous year's profits, so companies accumulate funds for this purpose. In years of low profits companies may maintain the level of dividends by drawing on reserves.

iii) Precautionary purposes. A delay in payment by an important customer, or a reduction in sales, can create difficulties, unless a company has sufficient liquid reserves to make its regular payments (e.g. wages). For this reason large companies often purchase Treasury Bills because they are such a liquid asset.

iv) Speculative purposes. Companies which purchase raw materials may vary the timing of their purchases in order to benefit from price fluctuations. If they have cash and can pay immediately, it is often possible to pick up a bargain.

Public sector saving

Public corporations will aim to achieve surpluses for the same reasons that companies retain profits. The surpluses of local authorities and the central government will depend primarily on the central government's policy regarding the control of public expenditure and the level of tax revenue.

Methods of saving

The method chosen for keeping savings will vary according to the desire for liquidity and risk-bearing. If people desire complete liquidity they will hoard cash. If not, they may lend their savings to commercial banks, building societies, or to the state by making deposits in the Post Office Savings Bank. Most of these deposits can be easily withdrawn.

To encourage longer-term regular savings higher interest rates are offered, as in the 5 or 7 year Save As You Earn (SAYE) scheme, in which the yields are 12–12½%. Contractual savings via insurance companies are illiquid, because a loss is made if policies are cashed before the agreed term has elapsed.

Some people purchase shares as a means of saving, partly in the hope that the capital value of their shares will keep pace with inflation. Shares are liquid if they can be sold on stock exchanges, but selling may involve a capital loss.

Companies will buy government securities, particularly Treasury Bills, and sometimes shares of other companies.

It is very important to remember that the initial effect of all savings is to reduce expenditure, whatever finally happens to the money saved. It is also important to distinguish the everyday use of the word 'investment' from the economist's use. If we 'invest' our savings in existing stocks and shares, we merely have a paper claim on a company's profits, and the previous owner of the claim now has cash to spend. Even if we buy a new share, the company issuing it may use our money to buy existing real capital. Neither of these cases is a real investment. Real investment is real capital formation, i.e. the bringing into existence of new production goods. Real investment is not equivalent, or automatically equal, to saving.

Saving and the rate of interest

How much do variations in the rate of interest affect the volume of saving? If the classical theory is true, the volume of saving should be highly responsive to the rate of interest—rising as interest rises. However, if we examine the reasons for saving, we shall see that much saving is unresponsive to variations in the rate of interest, for the following reasons.

Interest is a reward for lending, not for saving itself. The various rates of interest will influence the form in which savings are held, but the total volume of savings is determined mainly by the level of incomes received and the propensity to consume.

Some types of saving will be unaffected by changes in the rate of interest, e.g. habitual and contractual saving. Companies and public corporations also have to save certain amounts to build up reserves, whatever the rate of interest.

If people save to accumulate a certain sum of money, the higher the rate of interest, the lower their initial deposits need be. In this case, a high rate of interest discourages saving.

16·5

How much would you need to deposit in a savings bank now, in order to obtain £110 in a year's time,

a if the rate of interest on the loan were 5% p.a.?

A £100 **B** £104·76 **C** £105

b if the rate of interest on the loan were 10% p.a.?

A £90 **B** £100 **C** £105

The demand for funds for real investment

Firms therefore purchase new machinery, buildings, and so on, both to replace obsolete, worn-out equipment, and to expand their capacity to produce, because they hope that they will make greater profits.

Thus, the demand for real capital as a factor of production is derived from the demand for goods and services. In order to finance this real investment, firms both in the public and private sectors require money, which they obtain partly from retained profits (in the U.K. this is the most important source), and partly by borrowing, by the issue of shares and debentures. The firm expects the real capital purchased to yield a series of annual returns during its lifetime, which more than cover the annual maintenance and depreciation charges. What remains after such charges have been met is the *net yield*, or *net productivity, of the capital investment*, which is expressed as a percentage rate of return, or rate of profit, on the initial cost of the investment.

Discounted cash flow and investment appraisal

The income from an investment project will be received in a series of annual cash flows, not necessarily equal amounts in each year. Since these expected cash flows will take place in the future, they are worth less than the equivalent sums at the present moment. If you are offered £100 now, or £100 in a year's time, which will you prefer, assuming prices are constant, and you can lend money to a borrower at an interest rate of 10%? Obviously £100 now is worth more than £100 in a year's time, because by lending the £100 received now for a year you can increase it to £110. So £100 now is worth £110 in a year's time, and vice versa, £110 in a year's time is worth only £100 now. Similarly £121 in two year's time is worth only £100 now, if the interest rate is 10% p.a., because at 10% compound interest, £100 lent now will rise to £121 in two years. In such circumstances, we say that the *present discounted value* of £121 received in two year's time is £100.

The formula for finding the present discounted value of any cash flow in the future is obtained from the normal compound interest formula, which states

$$A = P(1+r)^n$$

A is the final amount received, P is the principal lent, n the number of years the loan lasts, and r the rate of interest p.a. applicable. Therefore the formula

$$P = A \times \frac{1}{(1+r)^n} = \frac{A}{(1+r)^n}$$

tells us how much we would have to lend(P) at a given interest rate (r), in order to obtain a certain sum (A) after n years. In other words, we can find the present discounted value (P) of a cash flow (A) which is expected in n years' time by discounting (reducing) A by the chosen rate of interest. For example, the present discounted value of £100 received in one year's time (at a rate of 10% p.a.) is

$$P = £100 \times \frac{1}{1+\frac{10}{100}}$$

$$= £100 \times \frac{100}{110}$$

$$= £90{\cdot}9$$

16·6

What is the present discounted value of £242 received in two years' time, using a rate of discount of 10% p.a.?

A £292·82 **B** £200 **C** £121

The present value of a series of annual cash flows can be obtained using this formula. The cash flows are converted into a capital sum: by summing the discounted values of each annual cash flow during the project's life, the present value of the whole series of expected future returns is obtained. In this calculation appropriate deductions must be made to allow for the annual maintenance charges, etc. Thus the present value of four years of cash flow is:

Net Present Value

$$= \frac{A_1}{(1+r)} + \frac{A_2}{(1+r)^2} + \frac{A_3}{(1+r)^3} + \frac{A_4}{(1+r)^4}$$

The rate of discount used will be the minimum rate of return (yield) which a firm requires from the project.

The sum of discounted cash flows can be compared with the initial cost of the capital. If the present value of the cash flows exceeds the initial cost of obtaining them, the project is worth undertaking. The discounted cash flow (DCF) method is considered the most accurate method of investment appraisal. DCF and other methods of investment appraisal are discussed in a booklet published by HMSO, *Investment Appraisal.* The government has asked nationalized industries to use DCF techniques when considering investment projects, and the various ministries use such techniques combined with Cost Benefit Analysis (see Satellite 8), when considering investment projects such as motorways. A final point to note is that the forecasted cash flows for each future year depend upon expectations about the development of the economy. The more distant the year, the lower the probability that a forecast is correct.

Figure 16·3 shows the present discounted values of a £100 cash flow received in ten successive years, using a discount rate of 10% p.a. By summing the discounted cash flows we discover that 10 annual incomes of £100 are worth only £616·46 now, and not £1 000. Therefore you should pay no more than £616·46 for a project yielding £100 p.a. net for 10 years, if you want at least a 10% p.a. return.

If the rate of discount used is lower, each annual £100 will not be reduced by so much, and the sum of the discounted cash flows will be higher.

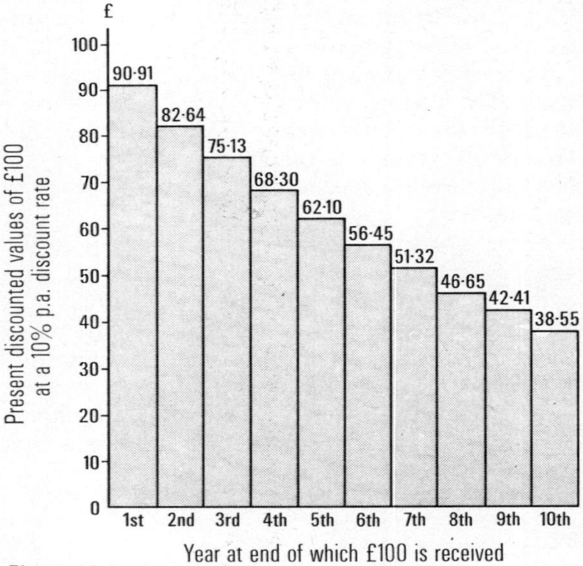

Figure 16·3

The marginal productivity of capital

The marginal productivity of capital (MP_k) is the expected net percentage yield per year from an extra £1 worth of real investment. The concept is similar to the marginal revenue product of labour, discussed in S9, although you should note that, in fact, capital goods are not divisible into £1 units. MP_k was called by Keynes the marginal efficiency of capital. He described the marginal efficiency of capital as the rate of discount which would make the present value of a series of annual returns expected from an investment project just equal to the supply price (initial cost).

Capital investment will be subject to the Law of Varying Proportions (Diminishing Returns), other things being equal, i.e. if we assume that the state of technology, the level of consumer demand, etc., are unchanged. Unless production methods are changed, or demand rises, as more of a certain type of capital is used in production, the return from that type of capital will eventually diminish. This relationship between the volume of investment and MP_k in a given period is illustrated in figure 16·4, which shows the investment demand curve, i.e. the demand curve for real capital. Compare this with the marginal revenue product curve of labour.

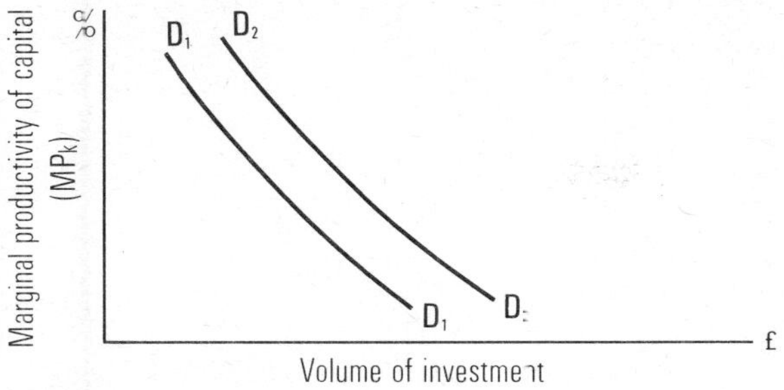

Figure 16·4

In a static situation, as the volume of investment increases, MP_k falls. If the economy expands and businessmen expect greater profits, or technological improvements increase the productivity of each unit of capital, the demand for real capital will increase, shifting the demand curve to the right (D_2D_2). Compare this analysis with the causes of an increase in the demand for labour.

Real investment and the rate of interest

What determines the volume of investment in any period, given the situation pictured by D_1D_1 in figure 16·4? Investment will continue as long as the return from the real capital (MP_k) exceeds the cost of borrowing money to purchase the real capital. This cost is, of course, the rate of interest (r) necessary to attract lenders, bearing in mind the risk and the sacrifice of liquidity. Remember that the dividends paid on shares are a mixture of interest and profit. Therefore investment will increase up to the level where the declining MP_k becomes equal to the rate of interest. In figure 16·5, if the rate of interest is Or_1, the volume of investment will be only OK_1. If the rate of interest is Or_2 the volume of investment will be OK_2. (This would be true in a static situation, but since, as explained in S17, investment opportunities are

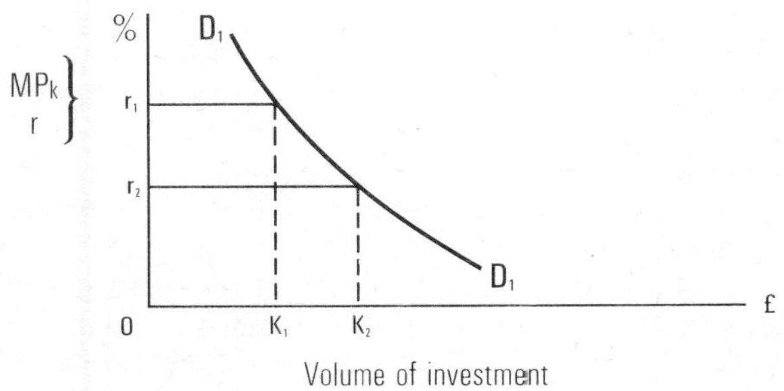

Figure 16·5

always changing, firms do not invest in absolutely marginal projects, where $MP_k = r$, but cease to invest in projects where MP_k is just 2–3% above r.)

Rational use of retained profits

16·7

Real investment projects costing £100 000 and yielding a return of 10% are being considered by two small firms. Firm A has already accumulated £100 000 in its reserves for new capital investment, but firm B will have to issue debentures on the Stock Exchange, and the return on Consols is currently 10%. Which of the following statements are true?

A Only firm A should undertake the investment, because it does not have to pay anything to attract funds.

B Both A and B should undertake the investment, assuming they do invest in completely marginal projects.

C Firm A should not invest in the project, because there are better alternative uses for firm A's money.

D Firm B should not invest in the project, because the cost of raising money will exceed the expected return.

If you answered question 16·7 correctly, you will realize that, even if a firm has accumulated profits to use, the *opportunity cost of any real investment project undertaken is the rate of interest on a loan which could have been made.* A company accountant must consider which use of funds provides the higher income after adjusting for risk, lending, or new capital investment.

Investment and the rate of interest

Interest is only one of the variables which affect the volume of investment. As mentioned already, changes in the level of business confidence about the level of future profits, and technological improvements, are far more important. In a boom interest rates will rise, but the rising demand for goods and services will encourage firms to expand production and increase investment. Of course very high interest rates will deter investment, but such high rates are most likely to be part of an economic policy which discourages investment directly, by reducing the level of total expenditure on goods and services.

In any case projects with a short pay-off period will hardly be affected by small changes in interest rates, because interest charges will be only a small part of the annual charges; depreciation charges, to recover the cost of the equipment, will be the largest part. Changes in the rate of interest will have more impact on long-term investment, because depreciation charges, being spread over a longer period, are a smaller proportion of the annual charges.

The following example shows that a rise in the interest rate from 4% to 5% will cause a larger rise in annual charges, the longer the pay-off period.

	A: 5-year project £	B: 25-year project £
Annual interest charge 4%×£10 000	400	400
Depreciation charge p.a. (taking equal amounts per year)	2 000	400
Total costs to be covered each year	2 400	800
Rise in total costs p.a. if interest rate rises by 1%	100	100
Percentage change in total costs p.a.	4·2% ($\frac{1}{24}$)	12·5% ($\frac{1}{8}$)

Two investment projects of £10 000 are being considered. The costs of project A must be covered in 5 years; the costs of project B can be spread over 25 years.

16·8

Why does a rise in interest rates affect annual mortgage charges more adversely than hire purchase charges?

Criticisms of the classical theory of interest

Figure 16·6 illustrates the classical theory: the rate of interest (Or) is determined by the interaction of the demand for real capital (DD), and the supply of savings (SS). However, careful analysis shows that savings, even savings defined as savings actually lent, do not rise as the rate of interest rises in the pattern shown by the normal supply cuve SS. Also, although higher interest rates will cause a fall in the demand for capital, other influences on investment are far more important. We shall see in S17 that the major influence on both savings and investment is the level of incomes. The classical theory also ignores two facts: banks can create money, so firms' investment may be indirectly financed by bank credit, and not from savings; secondly, not all borrowing is to finance real capital investment. Therefore the theory that the rate of interest is the price that balances the volume of savings and the volume of real investment is inadequate.

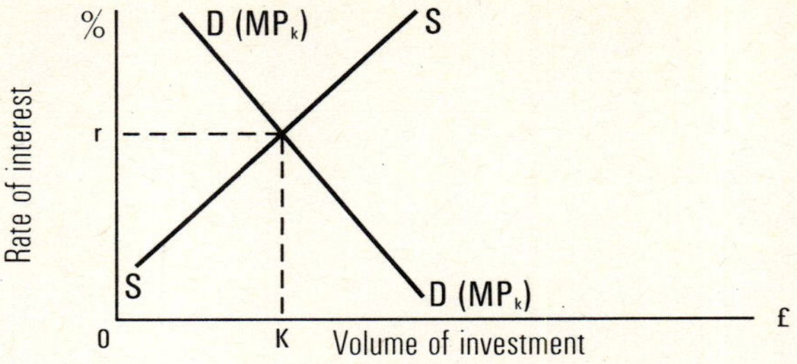

THE CLASSICAL THEORY OF INTEREST

Figure 16·6.

16·9

Why is bank credit considered to be only an indirect method for financing long-term investment?

The monetary, or Keynesian, theory of interest

Criticisms such as those above led Keynes to put forward the theory, explained in S12, that the rate of interest is the price which balances the desire to hold wealth in the form of money and the available quantity of money.

Money which can be spent immediately (coins, notes and bank deposits) is the most liquid asset possible. (S6 and the satellite text *Sample Studies of Financial Institutions* discuss exactly what is included in the money supply.) The public, i.e. ordinary persons, firms, local authorities, and the central government, will wish to hold money for transactions, for precautionary purposes, and for speculative purposes. 'Speculative purposes' refers to the choice between holding wealth in the form of money, a sterile, non-income-yielding asset, or in the form of securities which will yield interest, because of the sacrifice of liquidity.

The quantity of money demanded for transactions and for precautionary purposes (active balances) will not be affected by variations in the rate of interest, but the quantity demanded for speculative purposes (idle or passive balances) will be affected. At low rates of interest a large quantity of money will be demanded, because the low yield from holding securities will not be a sufficient compensation for the loss of liquidity, and will hardly cover the cost of converting money into securities. Also, at very low yields, no-one will wish to buy securities, because everybody will expect the yields to rise later. In other words, the prices of securities will be very high and everybody will expect prices to fall: it is therefore worth while to convert securities into money and to hold money until security prices fall to a lower level.

For the above reasons Keynes stated that at a very low rate of interest, e.g. between 1% and 2% p.a., the quantity of money demanded for speculative purposes will be infinite. This analysis is demonstrated in figure 16·7.

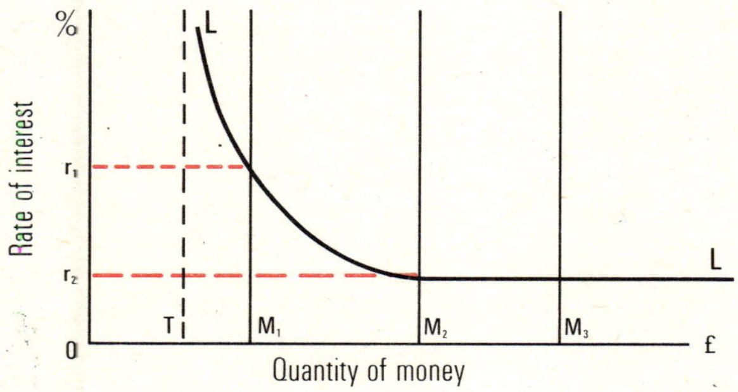

Figure 16·7

LL is the complete liquidity preference curve, or the demand for money curve. At high rate of interest the quantity of money demanded for speculative purposes is minimal, because of the high yields (low prices) of securities. The demand for money is therefore composed of the quantities demanded for transactions and for precautionary purposes (TT), which are interest-inelastic.

M_1M_1, M_2M_2, and M_3M_3 are three separate supply curves of money. The supply is fixed at any one time by the monetary authorities.

Given the current state of liquidity preference, the authorities can lower the rate of interest from Or_1 to Or_2 by increasing the supply of money from M_1M_1 to M_2M_2. As the extra money is supplied and the public's money holdings rise, the public will convert some of the extra money into securities. As the demand for securities rises, prices of securities will rise, and yields (market rates of interest) will fall. Eventually, when the rate has fallen to Or_2, the increased supply of money M_2 will be balanced by the increase in quantity of money which the public desires to hold—a movement down LL. However, a further increase in the supply to M_3 will not lower the interest rate below the minimum Or_2, because any extra money created will not be used to purchase securities when the prices are so high and the yields so low. All the extra money will be absorbed in idle balances.

Shifts of the liquidity preference curve

The whole liquidity preference curve may shift, indicating an increase or decrease in the desire to hold money at all rates of interest. An increase in overall liquidity preference is shown in figure 16·8. The increase may be caused by a rise in prices or an increase in incomes, causing an increase in transactions demand, or by an increase in political or economic uncertainty, when the higher risks may cause people to prefer to hold more money in speculative balances, even when yields from securities are high.

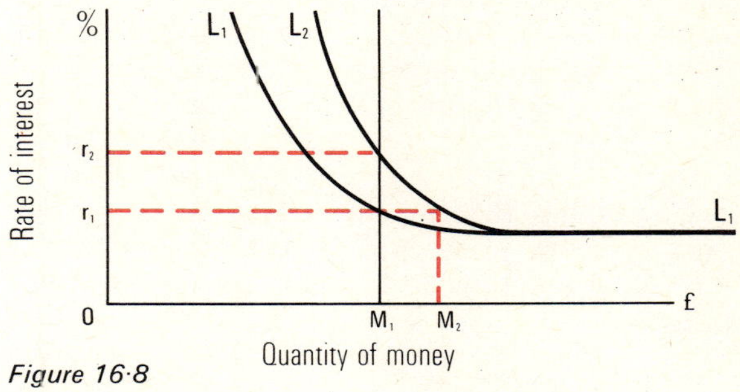

Figure 16·8

The liquidity preference curve shifts from L_1L_1 to L_2L_1—the minimum rate of interest remains the same. Originally, with the supply of money M_1M_1, people desired to hold OM_1 cash at the interest rate Or_1. When liquidity preference rises to L_2L_1, at rate Or_1 people would desire OM_2 money to hold, but with a fixed supply of money, the rate of interest must rise from Or_1 to Or_2. This is because, when the overall demand for money rises and the authorities are unwilling to increase the supply from OM_1, people will attempt to turn securities into money. They can only sell to each other, since the Bank of England will not buy, because by doing so it would increase the supply of money. The fall in demand for securities lowers the price and raises the yield, until the market rate of interest is sufficiently high to reduce the actual quantity of money demanded to OM_1 (a movement up the new demand curve L_2L_1). At Or_2 the reduced quantity of money demanded balances the existing supply.

The monetary theory of interest states that a change in the supply of money, or a change in the overall liquidity preference, will cause changes in the rate of interest. It also demonstrates that the government cannot manage the supply of money and the rate of interest independently, and must consider the effect of one on the other.

A synthesis of the classical and monetary theories of interest

Despite the previous criticisms, the effect of the real forces of saving and investment cannot be completely excluded. Changes in the money supply and liquidity preference are the main causes of short-term fluctuations in market rates of interest, but in the long term the supply of funds from saving and the profitability of real investment are also important. One link is that the yield on government securities (paper claims) will be affected by the prices and yields on alternative paper claims, i.e. the shares and debentures issued by companies. The yields on shares do depend on the profitability of the real capital investment carried out by the firms which borrow money.

Combining the two theories, interest can be said to be the price paid for the use of loanable money. The supply of loanable money can come from:

i current savings out of income;
ii past savings which have been hoarded and not yet lent;
iii proceeds from the sales of stocks;
iv new money, created either by the monetary authorities directly (currency or Bank of England deposits) or by banks (by making loans).

The demand for loanable money arises for the following reasons:

i real investment, either to add to the stock of capital (net investment), or to replace stocks and equipment;
ii borrowing to finance consumption, e.g. by hire-purchase finance companies;
iii liquidity preference.

Sometimes the borrowers and lenders are the same persons, e.g. a company using its retained profits to finance investment, or a person hoarding cash.

In a free market the interest rate would move to balance the quantities of loanable money demanded and supplied, but in fact the monetary authorities do not allow this to happen. Commercial bank loan rates are not allowed to rise sufficiently to reduce the amount of credit demanded to the level desired by the authorities. Instead credit is rationed, e.g. prior consideration is given to exporters. Similarly building society rates are not allowed to rise, although people want to borrow more than the funds which are available.

ANSWERS

16·1

a £40 per year for £800 = 5%
b £52 per year for £520 = 10%
c £6 per year for £30 = 20%

16·2

a **B** is correct. £4 p.a.

b **C** is correct. $4\% \times \frac{100}{80} = 5\%$ p.a.

c **B** is correct. $4\% \times \frac{100}{40} = 10\%$ p.a.

d **C** is correct. You would buy a £4 p.a. income for £400.

16·3

Both **A** and **B** could be correct, but B is predominant, so during an inflationary period people tend to spend past savings and reduce current savings.

16·4

B is correct.

16·5

a **B** is correct. Check by increasing £104·76 by 5%.
b **B** is correct.

16·6

B is correct. £200 deposited at 10% p.a. now would rise to £242 in 2 years' time. A is wrong because you have increased £242 by 10% p.a. instead of reducing it.

16·7

C and **D** are correct. Firm A can obtain a risk-free return of 10% p.a. by purchasing Consols. If the yield on Consols was 10% p.a., firm B would have to pay more than 10% p.a. to attract buyers for debentures, because of the risk involved.

16·8

Mortgages are usually repaid over 15 to 25 years. Hire-purchase payments are usually made over 3 years.

16·9

Bank loans are regarded as an indirect form of financing investment, because, in theory, banks lend only for short terms, e.g. 6 months. However, by lending, they allow firms to use their own capital for fixed investment, and in practice many overdrafts are renewed period after period.

THE EQUILIBRIUM LEVEL OF NATIONAL INCOME

In the last section we noted that the level of savings and of real investment which take place in an economy may depend partly on the rate of interest, but that the major influence on savings is the level of incomes, and that the major influence on real investment is the level of incomes expected in the form of profits. However, since the act of saving reduces the total expenditure on goods and services (by reducing consumption), and real investment increases total expenditure, we can see that savings, real investment, and the level of national expenditure (or national income) per year are all interdependent. In this section we shall examine this relationship in detail, and show how changes in national income are caused by changes in the level of savings and other leakages from the flow of expenditure, and by changes in the level of real investment and other injections into the flow of expenditure.

It is very important to understand what causes changes in the level of national income, because fluctuations in expenditure on goods and services cause fluctuations in the demand for factors of production, resulting in the social and economic problem of unemployment. Also, if expenditure rises faster than output, inflation results, yet governments in most countries aim to encourage the growth of real national income per head.

Injections into and leakages from the flow of expenditure

In S14 the circular flow of expenditure into income was explained. The flows of income or expenditure, savings, investment, exports, etc., which are referred to in this section and elsewhere, are flows per year. For simplicity the words 'per year' are usually omitted, but you should remember that these variables are money values recorded or expected during a year, not a stock existing at any one time.

Figure 17·1 will remind you of the conclusions reached in S14 and S15. Total expenditure, or Aggregate Monetary Demand (AMD), generates the income received by the country's factors for their contribution to production. Out of this income most will be spent on consumption, but part will be saved (S), part spent on imports (M), and part absorbed by taxation (T). Therefore

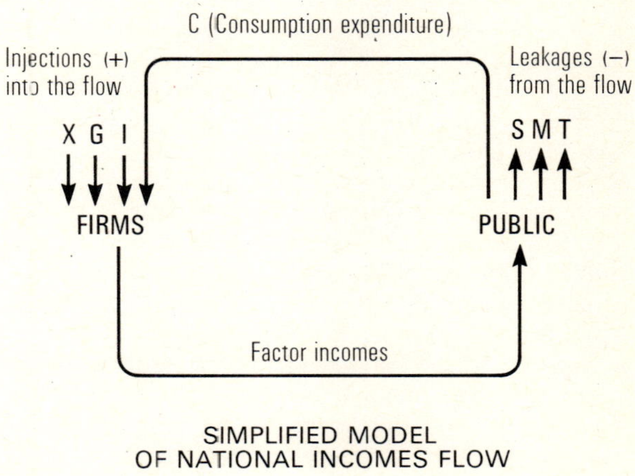

Figure 17·1

savings, imports, and taxation are leakages from the flow of national income into expenditure. However, investment in both the public and private sector (I), exports (X), and current government expenditure (G) are injections into the flow. Therefore AMD is composed of $C+I+G+X-S-M-T$.

$C+I+G+X-S-M-T$ actually add up to the money value of Gross National Product, but in this section we shall use the term national income to mean AMD, ignoring the fact that capital consumption, the depreciation of machinery and so on, should be subtracted from GNP to leave national income.

Equilibrium of national income

A preliminary statement can be made to describe how the level of national income is determined: the rest of S17 will explain the separate stages of the theory put forward here.

The meaning of equilibrium is 'a balanced state', so national income will be in equilibrium when no changes occur in the level of national income from year to year. This equilibrium does *not* imply that all resources are *fully* employed. National income can be in equilibrium when there is considerable unemployment, for example, during the 1930s in Britain and other countries.

Remembering that income is a flow, we can see from figure 17·1 that national income will be in equilibrium over a period of years if, during each year, the leakages from expenditure which take place at that level of income are exactly balanced by the injections generated by that level of income. Compare the flow of national income with the flow of a river. If water is taken away for a town's water supply, the flow will drop, unless an equivalent amount is put back each day. Similarly, for national income equilibrium, each year S+M+T must balance, i.e. equal, I+X+G. This statement does not mean that the first item on the left, S, automatically equals the first item on the right, I, and so on. We are saying that the balance could be achieved in this way: 2+5+4 = 1+4+6. For national income to remain in equilibrium:

a the sum of the leakages from expenditure must balance the sum of injections,

b the values of the separate items must correspond with what people wish to save, import, etc., at that level of income.

(The word 'people' in this section refers to the nation as a whole: it includes individuals, private firms, and the institutions in the public sector.)

17·1

If in a certain year leakages exceed injections, (S+M+T) > (I+X+G), what will happen to the level of national income?

National income will
- **A** remain unchanged.
- **B** rise.
- **C** fall.

Obviously there is no guarantee that in any one year people's plans to save, spend on imports, and pay taxes* will balance people's plans to invest, foreigners' plans to buy the home country's exports, and the government's planned expenditure. Yet, to restate the equilibrium conditions for national income, national income will only remain in equilibrium year after year if the aggregate values of savings, imports, and taxation which people plan at the given level of income exactly balance the investment, exports, and government expenditure planned at that level of income. If planned (S+M+T) does not balance, i.e. equal, planned (I+X+G), national income will change until they do balance. This is the essence of national income theory.

* 'Plan' is a peculiar word to use about paying taxes, but since people can plan, to a certain extent, how much to earn and spend, their decisions on these matters will determine how much tax they pay, e.g. in income tax and purchase tax, and the government also may 'plan' to alter its tax revenue.

A simple model: the closed economy

It is usual to demonstrate how the level of national income is determined by using a model of a closed economy, where there is no foreign trade, with the additional assumption that there is no public sector. Therefore the only leakage from the flow of expenditure is saving, and the only injection is investment. Therefore in such a model national income will reach an equilibrium only when planned saving equals planned investment. We will now show why this is true.

Planned savings and consumption

Much confusion is caused by the failure to distinguish between people's intentions to save, which vary according to the level of incomes received, and the actual, or realized, amount which is recorded in any one year.

Aggregate planned savings at any level of national income can be depicted by the gap between the consumption function and the 45° line (all income spent) in figure 17·2, or by a graph of level of planned savings plotted against income, as in figure 17·3.

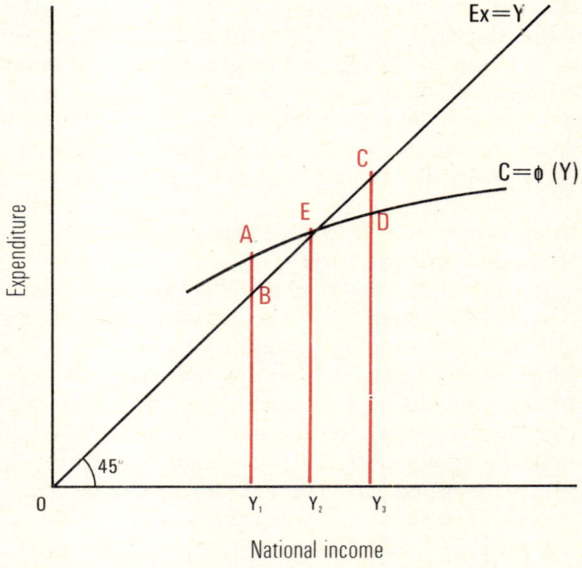

Figure 17·2

Figure 17·2 shows the general shape of the consumption function for a nation, drawn on the assumptions explained in S14 and S15. The vertical and horizontal axes are drawn to the same scale, so the 45° line shows all points at which expenditure would equal income. $C = \phi(Y)$* means that people's intended consumption expenditure varies as income changes: planned expenditure is assumed to rise as income rises, but it rises at a diminishing rate. This last point is shown by the lower gradient ($\delta C/\delta Y$) of the consumption function at higher levels of income. In other words the marginal propensity to consume declines as income rises.

How does the nation dissave or spend more than it has earned? Firstly, by spending past savings. Secondly, by selling or not replacing capital equipment, in much the same way that a farmer can spend more than he earns in a year by selling his tractor. Thirdly, by borrowing; for example, many poor, developing countries borrow from richer ones.

At income OY_1, intended consumption expenditure Y_1A exceeds income $Y_1B(= OY_1)$. Dissaving AB is the cause of this divergence. At income OY_2, people wish to spend on consumption exactly what they receive, so at this level income is exactly regenerated by expenditure, and national income is in equilibrium. At income OY_3, intended, i.e. planned, consumption expenditure is Y_3D, and since, if all income was spent, expenditure would be Y_3C, planned saving must be CD.

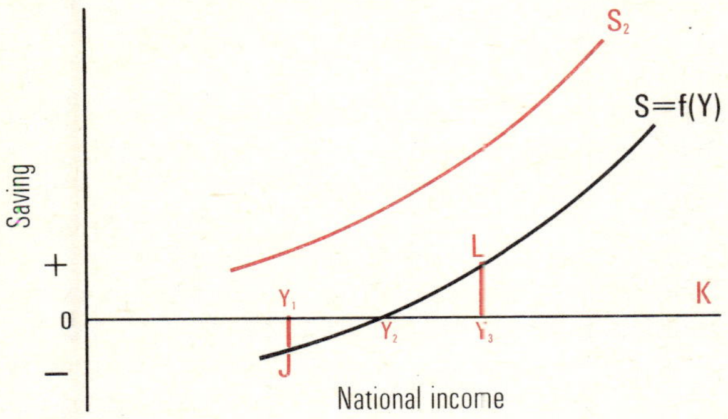

Figure 17·3

Figure 17·3 illustrates the same process as figure 17·2. We have assumed that planned savings, income not spent during any period, will vary with income, rising as income rises. The graph of the savings function $S = f(Y)$ shows this relationship. The marginal propensity to save rises as income increases, as is shown by the steeper gradient ($\delta S/\delta Y$) of the savings function as income increases. The average propensity to save at any level of income is S/Y: i.e. the vertical distance indicating savings divided by the horizontal distance indicating the corresponding level of income.

At income OY_1 people wish to dissave, when possible, to boost their consumption expenditure above their income. Dissaving is Y_1J, = AB in figure 17·2. At income OY_2 there is no saving or dissaving, all income is spent. At income OY_3 saving is Y_3L, = CD in figure 17·2.

17·2
Why does MPS = 1 − MPC?

17·3
If MPS is assumed to be constant, how must the graph of the savings function be altered?

A The graph would be a straight line sloping downwards from left to right.
B The graph would be unchanged.
C The graph would be a horizontal straight line.
D The graph would be a straight line sloping upwards from left to right.
E The graph would be a straight line starting from the origin, O, sloping upwards from left to right.

17·4
What is the average propensity to save at income OY_2 in figure 17·3?

A 0 **B** 1 **C** Impossible to say.

Divergence of realized savings from planned savings

The consumption and savings functions show how planned (or ex ante, before) savings vary with income. However, people may not realize their initial plans, and at the end of any year their realized (or ex post, after) savings may be above or below the level they intended. For example, people may have accumulated larger money balances than they need, or they may have run down their money balances below the desired level (see liquidity preference, S12). Realized savings are also called actual savings.

17·5
If a new savings function is drawn a constant distance above $S = f(Y)$ in figure 17·3 (the curve S_2), what information does this show?

* The symbols ϕ, f, and v used in this section mean that there is a discoverable mathematical relationship between the dependent variable, e.g. C, on the left-hand side of the equation, and the independent variable, Y, on the right-hand side. We say that C is a function of Y, and the symbols ϕ, f, and v represent different functions.

A An increase in the average propensity to save at all levels of income.
B A decrease in the average propensity to save at all levels of income.
C An increase in the marginal propensity to save at all levels of income.
D A decrease in the marginal propensity to save at all levels of income.

17·6

If the new savings function is drawn a constant distance above S = f(Y), what alteration must be made to the consumption function in figure 17·2?
A The consumption function must rise above its present position.
B The consumption function must fall below its present position.
C The gradient of the consumption function will increase at all levels of income.
D The gradient of the consumption function will decrease at all levels of income.

Shifts of the consumption and savings functions

The positions and gradients of the consumption and savings functions depend, as we have seen, on national spending habits. Suppose there is a general increase in the demand to spend. The whole consumption function will shift upwards, and the savings function downwards, to indicate a rise in planned consumption expenditure at all levels of income. Such upward shifts of the consumption function can be caused by two factors:

i Anticipation of a period of rising prices. People will increase their expenditure in a given year in the hope of buying before prices rise.

ii A redistribution of income towards lower-paid groups. The higher-paid groups whose incomes are reduced will absorb the effect partly by reducing consumption and partly by reducing saving. The lower paid who now have higher incomes will both spend and save more. However, the reduction in consumption by the higher-paid will be more than offset by the increase in consumption by the lower-paid, since experience shows that the marginal propensity to consume of the lower-paid groups is higher. For this reason total consumption expenditure will rise whatever the level of national income.

17·7

Suppose tax changes reduce by £1 the income of each of one million people in a higher-paid group, and increase by £1 the income of each of one million people in a lower-paid group. What will be the change in total consumption expenditure (C), if the MPC of the higher-paid group is 0·5, and the MPC of the lower-paid group is 0·9?
A C will be unchanged.
B C will rise by £100 000.
C C will rise by £400 000.
D C will rise by £500 000.
E C will rise by £900 000.

The determinants of planned investment

A careful distinction must also be made between planned (ex ante) and realised (ex post) investment. Realized investment can also be called actual investment.

Investment is carried out mainly by firms, in order to replace or increase capital equipment or stocks, and by local authorities and the central government (e.g. investment in social capital: roads, schools, hospitals, etc.). Private individuals do not carry out much real investment, except, for example, people who build their own houses.

The volume of planned investment in any year will depend on the following influences.

i The level of national income. We saw in S16 that the major influence on firms' investment was the level of profits expected. A situation in which AMD is rising rapidly, and the rise is expected to continue, is likely to cause increases in the volume of investment planned. This part of planned investment, which rises as national income rises, is called induced investment, and is a function of income. I = v(Y). Quite simply, if you are selling your commodity, and the signs are that people are prepared to buy even more than you are currently selling, you will use profits to pay for investment goods *and* because you expect the goods produced by your machinery to sell. Thus you are likely to plan to invest when income is rising.

ii Political stability. Changes in the governing party and in government policy will cause investment plans to be altered at a given level of income. If there is an increase in risk and uncertainty, for example about the future system of aid to development areas, investment plans will probably be cut back. Economics cannot really be divorced from politics. A government whose declared policy is expansionist is more likely to encourage investment.

iii Technical progress. The discovery of new products and processes will stimulate investment. For example, the discovery of natural gas in the North Sea caused an increase in the demand for drilling equipment, steel pipes, terminal buildings, etc.

The volume of investment planned in any year is subject to so many influences that it is likely to change frequently. However, for purposes of explanation we shall assume that planned investment is either determined principally by forces outside the economic system such as new scientific discoveries (autonomous investment), and is assumed to be constant (I_1), whatever the level of national income, or rises (I_2) as national income rises (induced investment). 'Autonomous investment' illustrates the difficulty of studying the economic aspect of human activity in isolation from other aspects. For example, a country could decide to build a large number of nursery schools for educational reasons only. Nevertheless, the existence of these nursery schools may allow mothers to go to work and thereby increase the labour force which is also, of course, of interest to economists. At the same time this building programme could lead to the building of a new brick factory, which is a further investment. As the original motive was educational rather than economic we have to deal with this type of problem by assuming a constant I line because it is not a function of income. Figure 17·4 depicts these two possibilities.

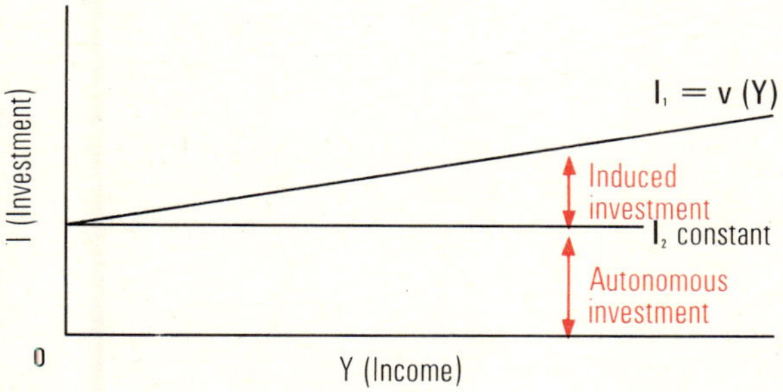

Figure 17·4

Divergence of realized investment from planned investment

Figure 17·4 shows possible investment functions, depicting what people will plan to invest at various levels of income. However, in any one year, realized investment may not correspond with plans. Supposing consumption expenditure has been lower than the level forecast by producers: in such a case producers will find their stocks accumulating. An increase in stocks of goods is classed as investment, although the increase in stocks (also known as inventory investment) is unplanned. Similarly, if in a certain year consumption is higher than forecast, stocks will be run down, and there will be unplanned disinvestment, reducing the realized investment below the originally planned level.

17·8

If in a certain year stocks are reduced below the desired level in relation to firms' output, how will firms tend to react in the following year?

A Firms will increase their output to increase their stocks.

B Output will not be changed.

C Firms will reduce their output because consumption has fallen.

Equilibrium in the simple model economy

We have shown that planned savings are a function of income, and that planned investment is either constant or a function of income. We can expect to discover a certain level of income at which planned S and planned I balance, and we can also deduce that any other temporary level of national income cannot be maintained, because people's plans to save or invest are not fully realized, and their consequent adjustments to their savings or to their investment expenditure (N.B. question 17·8) will either reduce or increase national income in the following year.

The directions in which national income will change are the following:

if planned I exceeds planned S, injections exceed leakages, and national income will rise;
if planned S exceeds planned I, leakages exceed injections, and national income will fall.

These statements, and the consequent equilibrium of national income, are illustrated in figures 17·5 and 17·6. The volume of planned investment is assumed to be constant for the sake of illustrating the principle behind the theory.

Figure 17·5 shows that planned savings equal

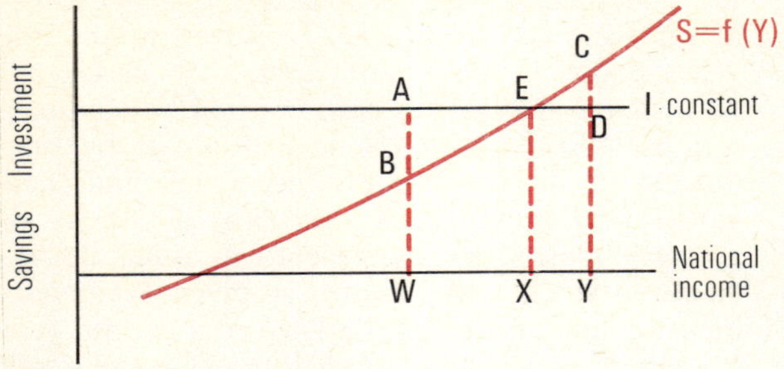

Figure 17·5

planned investment at E. Therefore OX is the equilibrium level of national income, and unless plans change (a shift in the investment or savings functions), national income will remain at OX year after year. Consumption expenditure absorbs exactly that part of output which is produced for consumption, and planned savings, which, unless offset, would reduce the level of expenditure below OX, are exactly balanced by planned investment expenditure (including investment in stocks). Planned I = planned S = XE.

However, if national income is temporarily OW, planned I exceeds planned S. Suppose that in this particular year planned S (WB) is realized. This means that producers' plans to invest (including accumulation of stocks) cannot be realized, because savings are too low—in other words, consumption is higher than producers expected. Stocks will be run down, with the result that, at the end of the year, realized I will be brought down to the level of realized S. Therefore in the next year producers will expand production in order to rebuild their stocks or stocks of wholesalers and retailers. More men will be employed and national income will rise. By this analysis, it becomes clear that as long as planned I exceeds planned S, national income will rise.

If national income is OY, planned saving will be YC, and planned investment YD. If people realize their planned saving during the year, this higher level of saving will result in an unplanned accumulation of stocks because by saving (not consuming) people have not bought up the amount produced. At the end of the year, actual, or realized, I will be composed of unplanned I (DC) in addition to planned I (YD). Therefore in the next year producers will reduce their output in order to run down excessive stocks; labour will be dismissed, or work shorter hours. This reduction in expenditure will cause a fall in national income. This analysis shows that, whenever planned S exceeds planned I, national income will fall.

Using the above assumptions about the behaviour of planned savings and planned investment, we can also show that the equilibrium level of national income must be OX by using the consumption function diagram. The equilibrium income will be such that total planned expenditure on consumption and investment (C+I) equals income received in that year, which is used either for consumption or saving (C+S). The 45° line in figure 17·6 shows all the possible equilibrium positions where planned expenditure equals received income, so that each year expenditure recreates the same level of income.

To plot total expenditure as a function of income, we must add planned I, assumed constant, to $C = \phi(Y)$. Therefore (C+I) is a constant distance above $C = \phi(Y)$. (N.B. The axes in figures 17·5 and 17·6 are not drawn to the same scale.)

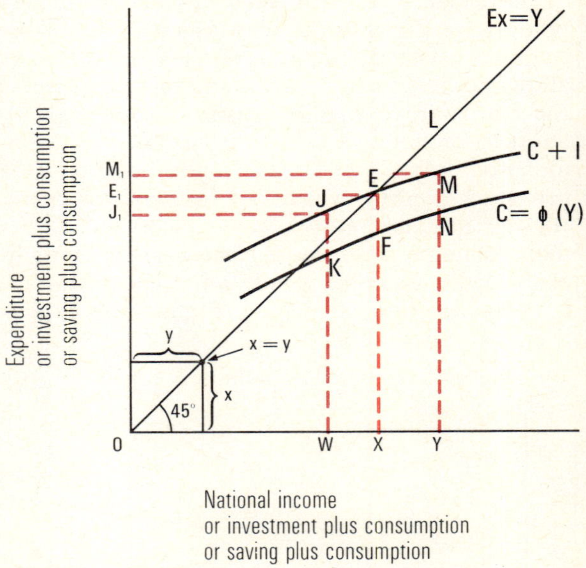

Figure 17·6

Figure 17·6 shows that at income OX planned C+I expenditure exactly recreates income OX (OE_1 expenditure = OX). Unless the C+I function shifts national income will remain at OX every year. We can see that planned S, which is shown by the gap between the 45° line and $C = \phi(Y)$, is exactly offset by planned I (EF).

At income OW, C+I plans (WJ) exceed current income: OJ_1 exceeds OW. People wish to purchase more than the national product at current prices. Therefore output and employment will rise in each successive year, until national income reaches OX.

17·9

Can you think what could possibly result if, at income OW, there is already full employment?

Measure, on figure 17·6, OM_1 and OY. Which line is longer? What does this difference in length mean? At income OY, C+I plans (YM) are less than current income, so the income recreated will be OM_1, which is less than OY. Therefore output and employment will fall until national income reaches OX.

17·10

How can you tell from figure 17·6 that planned S exceeds planned I at income OY?

Fluctuations in the level of national income

We have shown that the necessary condition for an equilibrium level of national income is that planned savings should balance planned investment. However, it is very unlikely that this balance happens, because, as was demonstrated in S16, those who save and those who carry out real investment are usually different people, and furthermore the motives causing saving are quite unrelated to the motives for real investment. Every income earner may decide to not consume or save, but only certain people exercise the power to make an investment decision. Is it likely that the investment planners in the brick industry know that you plan an addition to your house next year and therefore will require bricks? Clearly not. For these reasons we can expect the level of national income to be unstable—rarely settling down to an equilibrium, because the determinants of the equilibrium keep changing. Of course, since improvements in productivity take place, we can expect an upward trend of national income at constant prices (economic growth), but if this were the only change, and planned savings usually equalled planned investment, then the level of employment would remain quite steady, and there would be little fluctuation of income around the growth path. In reality, there are frequent fluctuations in the level of national income and employment simply because economic life is bound to be subjected to constant change. No new invention can be exploited without change, no new taste can be satisfied without change.

Injections and leakages in the more complex economy

It is quite unlikely that a steady equilibrium level of income will be achieved in a more complex economy, where the other leakages from expenditure, imports (M) and taxation (T), and the injections, exports (X) and current government expenditure (G), must be included. The equilibrium condition must be that planned $(S+M+T) = (I+X+G)$.

For a simplified analysis we can assume that imports and taxation increase as income increases. Therefore total planned leakages (S+M+T) rise steeply as income rises—in other words marginal propensity to consume is low, and so the gradient of the consumption function is low. If we also assume that exports and current government expenditure are constant whatever the level of income, figure 17·5 can be adapted to show how the equilibrium is determined where planned $(S+M+T)$ = planned $(I+X+G)$. We do this by taking the constant level of I to represent, instead, all injections, and the savings function to represent all leakages.

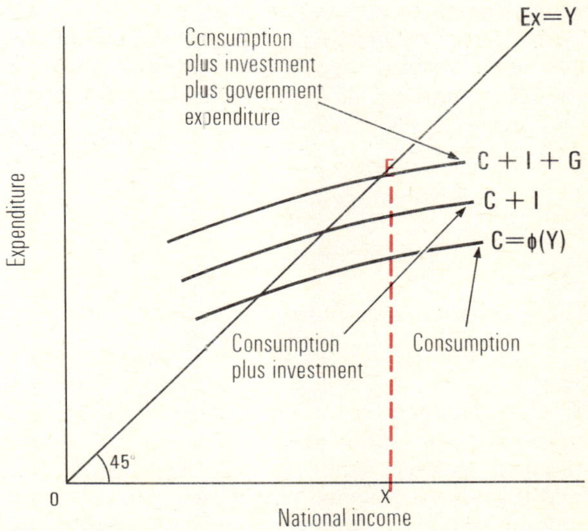

Figure 17·7

To show the equilibrium level of national income on the consumption function diagram, additions must be made. In figure 17·7 to depict planned total expenditure (Aggregate Monetary Demand) the constant additions of planned I and planned G are added on top of $C = \phi(Y)$. If we assume that the balance of payments is in

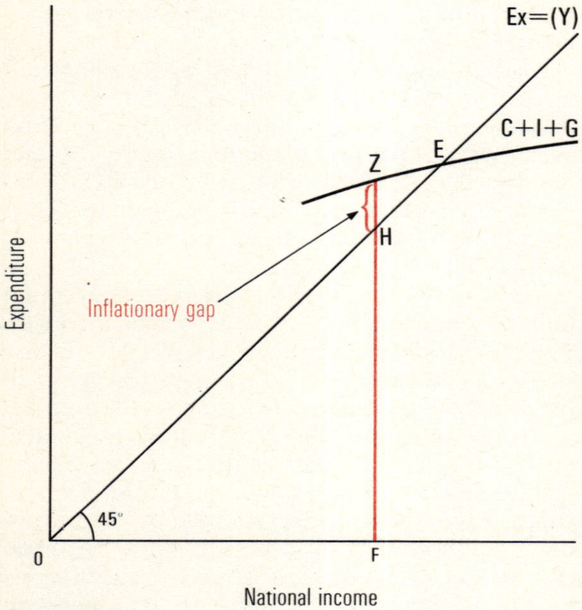

Figure 17·8

balance, then the leakages and injections arising from foreign trade exactly offset each other, and so they can be omitted. If there is a balance of payments surplus then another addition must be made to planned AMD. Remember that AMD = C+I+G+(X−M).

AMD (Aggregate Monetary Demand) = C (Consumption) + I (Investment) + G (Government expenditure) + (X (Exports) − M) (Imports)

From figure 17·7 we can see that the equilibrium, where planned AMD recreates the same level of income, must be income OX. At any income below OX planned injections exceed planned leakages (the gap between the 45° line and $C = \phi(Y)$: planned AMD exceeds the current income, so national income will eventually rise to OX. At any income above OX, planned AMD is insufficient to recreate the current income, so national income will eventually fall to OX.

17·11

The graph of C+I+G function in figure 17·7 is drawn on the assumption that payments are balanced. What would be the effect on the graph of the C+I+G function if we assume that a balance of payments deficit develops?

A The graph would rise above its present position.
B The graph would remain in its present position.
C The graph would fall below its present position.

Inflationary and deflationary gaps

It must be emphasized that there is no guarantee that the equilibrium level of national income will correspond with that level of income and expenditure which assures full employment. In figure 17·8 the full employment level of national income is depicted by OF. We know from S14 that this level of national income will be equivalent to the value of output at current prices. In figure 17·8 planned Aggregate Monetary Demand is shown to exceed the value of full employment output, hence the gap between planned AMD (FZ) and the value of output at current prices (FH) is known as the inflationary gap. In such a case, the excess demand will cause prices to rise, and the apparent equilibrium E can never be reached, because the economy cannot produce such a level of real output and income.

Figure 17·9 depicts a situation where, at full employment level of income and output (OF), planned AMD is insufficient to recreate that level of income. The shortfall of planned AMD (FZ) below the value of output at full employment (FH) is known as the deflationary gap. The deficiency of demand will cause output to fall, and an equilibrium will be established at income OY.

Policies designed to eliminate inflationary or deflationary gaps will be discussed in S21.

It is worth pausing at this point to remind ourselves of the reality underlying this theory. If a man or woman is unemployed for a day, then that day's production is lost for ever and the community has lost that productive effort. Furthermore, unemployment which is protracted causes a loss of morale and in many cases is a personal tragedy; our simple mathematical analysis is ultimately about the lives of human beings. The general unemployment rate, for Great Britain in 1931, 1932, and 1933 was 21·1%, 21·9%, and

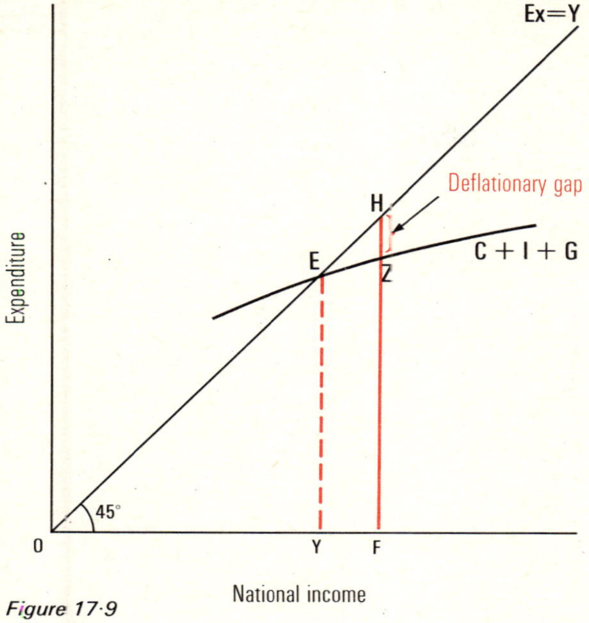

Figure 17·9

19·8% of the employable population. Beveridge quotes the evidence of a skilled wire-drawer aged 32 in his report: 'Any long spell of unemployment leaves you with little to be proud of and much to be ashamed of. Our child is still too young to realize that it is her mother who works. We carefully keep her from knowing it.'

Similarly, inflation can cause personal misery. The person who has worked and saved hard has a justifiable pride in being independent. To these people the erosion of their savings by a rampant inflation sours their years of retirement. Let us remember that as we move the position of the point F on figure 17·8, the terms deflationary or inflationary gap refer to the financial security of real people.

The equivalence of realized savings and realized investment

In the analysis of figures 17·5 and 17·6 we have emphasized the distinction between planned and realized quantities. It is important to remember that, though plans often do not balance, at the end of any year (our conventional time period) realized S+M+T always equal realized I+X+G. Taking the simple economy as an example, realized S at the end of any period always equals realized I, for the following reason.

In the simple economy, at the end of any year, the national income (Y) received in that year must have been spent on consumption goods or saved. This can be expressed by the statement:

Y	=	C	+	S
(Income)		(Consumption expenditure)		(Realized savings)

The national income received by the factors of production will be identical with the value of the national output (O). This can be expressed by the statement:

$$Y \equiv O \quad (\equiv \text{ means is identical with})$$

The national output in the year must have been produced for consumption, or for real investment, including investment in stocks. This can be expressed by the statement:

Output = Consumption goods output + Investment output

or

O = (C+I) output

Since

$$Y = O$$

(C+I) output = C expenditure + Realized S

Supposing C expenditure does not correspond with producers' intended output for consumption. If C expenditure is less than expected, there will be an unplanned increase in stocks (unplanned I), in addition to the planned investment output.

Therefore,

C output bought + Planned I + Unplanned I = C expenditure + Realised S

but,

C output bought ≡ C expenditure

and therefore, at the end of the year,

Realised I = (Planned I + Unplanned I) = Realised S

i.e. the crucial equation,

Realized I = Realized S

This analysis shows that every year realized I equals realized S, because of the definition that any output not brought for consumption must be included in realized investment. Since at the end of the year any income not spent on consumption must be realized saving, realized S always equals realized I. The same will be true if we imagine a higher level of realized consumption than producers expected (lower realized savings), and the consequent unplanned decrease in stocks.

Therefore each year realized S equals realized I, but this does not mean that national income will be in equilibrium every year. For equilibrium in the simple economy planned S must equal planned I, and in the complex economy planned leakages must equal planned injections, because only then can each group's plans be realized, and unless plans are realized, national income will change in the next year, and continue to change until plans do balance. Balance is achieved because if S>I output will tend to fall, if I>S output will tend to rise; changes in output take place until S = I.

The multiplier

We have shown how changes in expenditure cause changes in the level of income. For example, an increase in S (fall in C) will cause national income to fall, or an increase in I will cause income to rise. However, the impact of a change in I, or any other change in expenditure, on national income, is not confined to the initial value of the expenditure. An increase in expenditure by one group will cause an increase in other people's incomes. Out of their increased incomes they in turn will spend a proportion, which creates incomes for a third group. Therefore several rounds of expenditure will follow the initial increase, and the final increase in national income will be a multiple of the initial increase in expenditure. Similarly, if some people reduce their expenditure, other people's income will fall, and they in turn will spend less. National income will fall by a multiple of the initial decrease in expenditure.

To find the size of the final increase or decrease in expenditure and income, we need to know what proportion of extra income people will spend, i.e. we need to know their marginal propensity to consume (MPC).

17·12

Suppose investment increases by £100, and the MPC of all groups is 0·5.* Fill in the table below, figure 17·10, and find out what is the total increase in income after six rounds of expenditure. Can you guess what the approximate figure will be for the final increase in national income as a result of the initial increase in investment of £100?

* The assumption that MPC and MPS are constant, whatever the level of income, is necessary for simplicity, but very unrealistic, as has already been shown.

		Increase in expenditure	Increase in incomes
1st round	I	£100	£100
2nd round	C	£50 (£100×MPC)	
3rd round			
4th round			
5th round			
6th round			
		Total increase in incomes after six rounds of expenditure	——

Figure 17·10

17·13

If the MPC were 0·75, would the final increase in national income be higher or lower?

A Higher **B** Lower **C** Impossible to tell.

The final increase in national income following an initial increase in expenditure is found by adding the successively diminishing rounds of expenditure. The MPC shows how much each round is less than the preceding one. The sum of a diminishing series is found by multiplying the initial number by $1/(1-r)$, where r is the common ratio between successive items in the series. Here the common ratio is the MPC, so the multiplier is $1/(1-\text{MPC})$. Since $1-\text{MPC}$ is also MPS (the proportion of extra income not spent must be saved), $1/(1-\text{MPC})$ can be written as $1/\text{MPS}$. Often the symbol c is used instead of MPC, and s instead of MPS, so alternative ways of writing the multiplier are $1/(1-c)$ or $1/s$.

Therefore the *multiplier, l/MPS, is the number by which any initial increase or decrease in expenditure must be multiplied in order to find its total effect on national income*. The greater the MPC, the smaller the MPS, and so the larger the multiplier: a large proportion of income is respent in every round of expenditure. Similarly, if a large proportion of extra income is saved, the higher MPS, and the smaller the multiplier.

17·14

What will be the final effect on the level of national income if there is an initial reduction in consumption expenditure of £400, and the MPC of all groups is 0·8?

A National income will fall by £500.
B National income will fall by £2 000.
C National income will fall by £3 200.
D National income will fall by £6 400.

The effect of foreign trade and taxation on the multiplier

What are the other leakages from the circular flow of expenditure, in addition to savings? Obviously, expenditure on imports will create incomes for foreign factors of production; the more income spent on imports, denoted by m) must be be generated at home. Therefore the *Marginal propensity to import* (the proportion of extra income spent on imports) (denoted by m) must be included in the multiplier. The multiplier including the effect of import expenditure is $1/s+m$.

A third leakage from the flow of expenditure is taxation. The effect of taxation and the other leakages is depicted in figure 17·11. Direct taxes reduce disposable incomes below the gross amount received, and taxes on expenditure (indirect taxes) must be subtracted before establishing how much gross income sellers of goods and services receive.

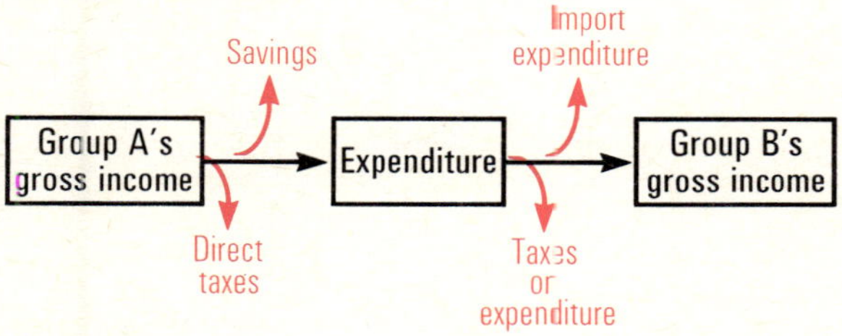

Figure 17·11

To allow for the effect of taxation, the symbol t, denoting the marginal liability to taxation (the proportion of extra income absorbed by taxes), is included in the multiplier. Therefore the complete multiplier is $1/(s+m+t)$.

It is quite useful to consider, at this stage, what the importance of figure 17·11 is to any government planning the creation or diminution of income. Suppose the government decides to increase expenditure in one section of the economy (group A). What will be the total result of this expenditure on the economy as a whole? The diagram shows the leakages which have to be taken into account in deciding how much of this income will be passed on to group B.

17·15

What is the value of the multiplier if, out of each extra £1 received, people save 15p, spend 20p on imports, and pay 15p in taxes?

A $\frac{1}{2}$ **B** 2 **C** 5 **D** 10 **E** 50

Graphical illustration of the multiplier effect

Taking the simple multiplier, 1/MPS, as an example, we can illustrate the multiplier effect on a graph. A large MPS will mean that the gradient of the savings function is high, and the multiplier low, and a small MPS will mean that the gradient of the savings function is low, and the multiplier high.

First look at the table, figure 17·12, showing planned C, S, and I at various levels of national income (figures in £m).

Income	Planned C expenditure	Planned savings	MPS	APS	Planned investment Year 1	Planned investment Year 2
5	5	0		0	10	14
			>0·4			
10	8	2		0·2	10	14
			>			
15	11	4		0·27	10	14
			>			
20	14	6			10	14
			>			
25	17	8			10	14
			>			
30	20	10			10	14
			>			
35	23	12			10	14
			>			
40	26	14			10	14

Figure 17·12

17·16

A Fill in the details for MPS and APS.
B State the equilibrium level of income in year 1.
C State the equilibrium level of income in year 2.
D Draw the graphs of the savings and two investment functions.

Your graphs should look like those in figure 17·13. You can see that in year 1 the equilibrium level of national income is £30m, and in year 2 the equilibrium income is £40m. What is the cause of the rise in the equilibrium income? Planned investment has risen, but only by £4m. The additional £6m rise in income is due to the extra rounds of consumption expenditure—the multiplier effect. We have assumed that MPS is 0·4 at all levels of income: this is shown by the constant gradient ($\frac{2}{5}$) of the savings function. Therefore the multiplier, 1/MPS, is 1/0·4, i.e. $2\frac{1}{2}$. So the extra £4m investment generates a total increase in incomes of £10m.

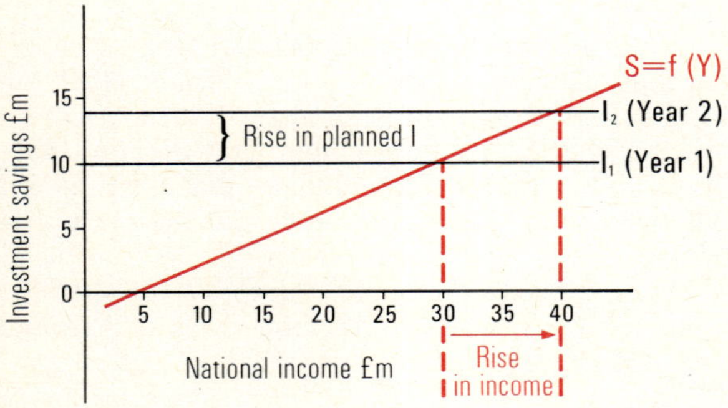

Figure 17·13

The effect of a rise in the marginal propensity to save

What would be the effect of a rise in the MPS? If income were already at the equilibrium, there would be no effect until there was a change in the level of planned expenditure. The gradient of the savings function would change, and the value of the multiplier would be altered, but the multiplier will be effective only when there is a change in expenditure. To clarify this point, answer questions 17·17 and 17·18.

17·17

Suppose the economy is at the original equilibrium level of national income, £30m, where planned S equals planned I at £10m. What would be the effect in year 2 of a rise in planned I from £10m to £14m, if, in year 2, the MPS was 0·8 at all levels of income (i.e. out of every extra £1 received 80p is saved)?

The new equilibrium level of income would be:

A £32m **B** £34m **C** £35m **D** £38m **E** £40m

17·18

Draw the graphs of the new savings function and the two investment functions corresponding to the detail in question 17·17.

Your graphs for question 17·18 should look like those in figure 17·14. We can see that, since the multiplier is $\frac{5}{4}$ (i.e. 1/0·8), after the £4m rise in planned investment, income will rise by a total of £5m, so the new equilibrium level of national income is £35.

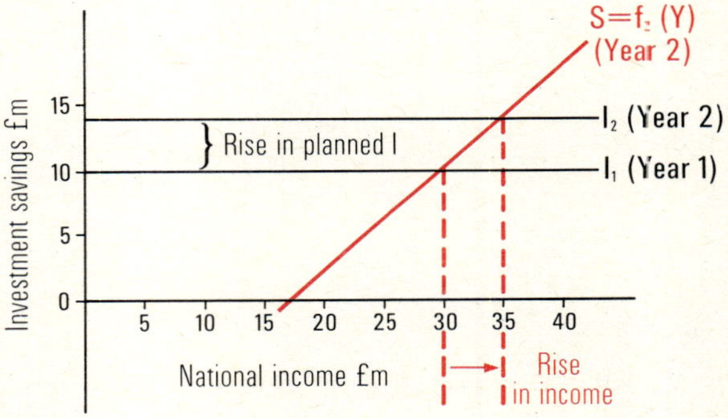

Figure 17·14

The last three exercises have shown that, the *lower* the marginal propensity to save, the *greater* the multiplier, and therefore the greater the change in national income which will follow a given increase, or decrease, in expenditure. Thus a government faced with a relatively high multiplier need only make a relatively small injection of expenditure into the economy to achieve a relatively large increase in total national expenditure.

17·19

Draw the graphs of the consumption and investment functions, as in figure 17·6, which correspond with

a) the savings/investment diagram figure 17·13;
b) the savings/investment diagram figure 17·14.

The effect of a rise in the average propensity to save

If there is a rise in the average propensity to save, this means that people attempt to save a greater proportion of their incomes at all levels of income. We know now that, unless there is a corresponding increase in planned investment, the effect of an increase in planned savings is to cause a fall in expenditure and income: national income will fall, and as it falls, the volume of planned saving will decline, although it may remain the same proportion of national income. This situation is depicted in figure 17·15.

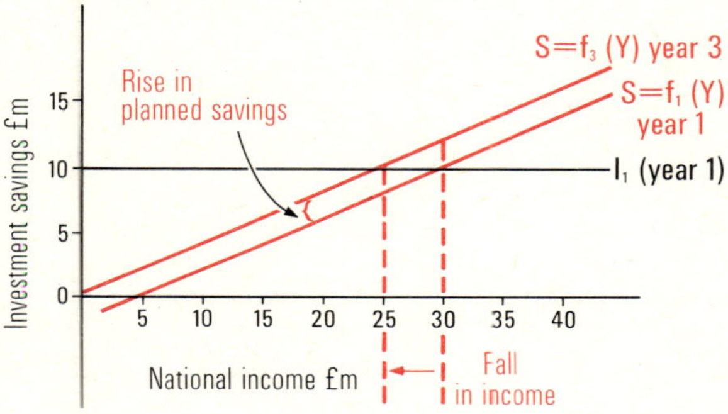

Figure 17·15

Figure 17·15 shows that, from an original equilibrium income of £30m, at which planned S equals planned I at £10m, in year 3 people increase their desire to save by £2 at each level of income. APS (S/Y) rises and becomes a constant proportion of income, $\frac{2}{5}$, since the savings function* $S = f_3(Y)$ starts from the origin. The result of this rise in APS is that equilibrium national income falls to £25m, because only at an income of £25m does planned S, £10m, equal the constant value of planned I.

Notice that the MPS and the multiplier remain unchanged in this example. The gradients of the two savings functions are the same. Using the multiplier, we can calculate that national income must fall to the new equilibrium of £25m, if APS rises by £2m. At the original level of income people increase S by £2m. This means that C falls by £2m, and since the multiplier is $2\frac{1}{2}$, the total fall in incomes must be £5m.

* In this example we have a simple value for f_3 in the savings function, and so it is very easy to establish the equilibrium by algebra. For equilibrium planned S must equal planned I: planned I = £10m, and planned $S = \frac{2}{5}Y$, so equilibrium Y must be £25m.

17·20

Draw the graphs of the consumption and investment functions which correspond with the savings/investment diagram figure 17·15.

The paradox of thrift

In our discussions of the multiplier effect, we have made two very unrealistic assumptions. One is that MCP and MPS remain constant at all levels of income, whereas, in fact, as income increases, MCP falls and MPS rises. The other assumption is that planned investment is constant at all levels of income. We have already learnt that it is more realistic to assume that there will be considerable induced investment as national income rises. By incorporating this assumption into our diagrams, we can depict a situation in which an attempt by all people to save more results in a reduction in realized savings; this is the phenomenon known as the paradox of thrift, illustrated in figure 17·16.

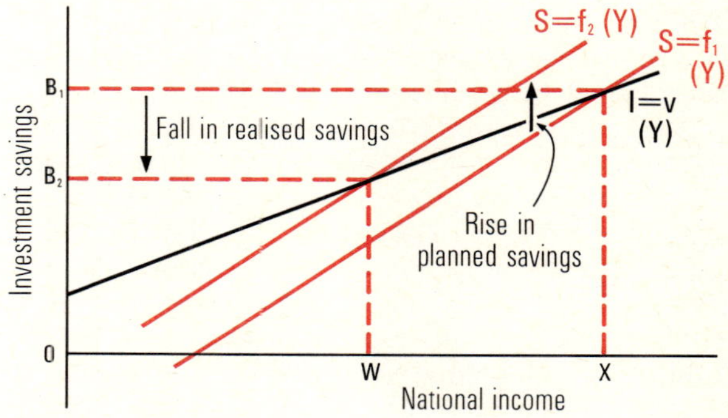

Figure 17·16

In figure 17·16 investment is shown to be a rising function of income, $I = v(Y)$. MPC and MPS still assumed to be constant, but this does not alter the analysis. The original equilibrium level of national income is OX, the income at which the values of the investment function $I = v(Y)$ and the savings function $S = f_1(Y)$ balance. Plans are realized when savings and investment equal OB_1. However, a rise in planned saving takes place, shown by the vertical distance between the two savings functions, and the new savings function is $S = f_2(Y)$. The reduction in consumption expenditure causes a fall in income, and since planned investment is a rising function of income, when national income falls, there is a fall in planned I. When people are planning to save more, they are cutting their consumption plans. Thus a manufacturer of, say, domestic electrical equipment will find that the consumer is tending to buy less, or that sales are increasing at a slower rate than before. It is difficult to persuade shareholders that a new factory or an extension to the present factory is necessary when sales are becoming more difficult. A hairdresser in a similar situation may decide not to open another branch. So we see in figure 17·16 that not only does national income fall to OW, where $S = f_2(Y)$ and $I = v(Y)$ have equal values (plans balance), but the plans are realized at a lower level of savings and investment. Plans are realized when saving and investment equal OB_2.

Figure 17·16 depicts what may happen in a country if a recession develops. If incomes start to fall for some reason, e.g. a fall in export earnings, there may be an increase in saving, for example from $S = f_2(Y)$ to $S = f_1(Y)$ in figure 17·16, so depressing national income further. Planned investment also falls, so the recession deepens. We can therefore conclude that savings are not always desirable. During a depression attempts to increase savings will worsen the situation and delay the recovery of the economy. However, when all resources are fully employed, extra savings *may* prevent excess demand developing, and free factors which can be used for increasing the output of exports or capital goods, especially as the demand for capital goods is likely to be high when the economy is prospering and there is full employment. The use of the word 'may' in the preceeding sentence is quite important. In economics, it is often the case that one influence can be cancelled out by another. We cannot be more definite without listing many assumptions.

Conclusion

In this section we have shown the level of national income depends on the levels of planned savings, imports, and taxation, and of planned investment, exports, and current government expenditure. We have shown that a higher level of injections (I+X+G) will cause a rise in national income, and this rise will be greater than the initial increase in expenditure, because of the very important multiplier effect. Similarly, an increase in leakages from the flow of expenditure (S+M+T) will be magnified by the multiplier effect, and the final reduction in national income will be greater than the initial reduction in expenditure. We have also discussed some of the influences causing changes in plans to spend. Finally we have noted that plans may often change, and there is no guarantee that national income will reach an equilibrium position at a level consistent with full employment without inflation. At full employment there may be inflationary or deflationary gaps, and so the government must attempt to lower or raise planned Aggregate Monetary Demand, always bearing in mind the multiplier effects of its initial actions. These problems concerning the regulation of the economy are discussed further in S21, and in the satellite *The Management of the Economy*.

ANSWERS

17·1

C is correct: more leaks out of the flow than is fed in.

17·2

Extra income must be either spent or saved. Therefore if we subtract what is spent (MPC) from the whole (1), what remains is the part saved (MPS).

17·3

D is correct, although **E** would be correct under certain conditions, i.e. if savings started as soon as national income rose above zero, and **C** would be correct if savings were constant at all levels of income. In such a case MPS = 0.

17·4

A is correct. All income is spent.

17·5

A is correct: people attempt to save a greater proportion of their incomes at all levels of income. An alteration in MPS would alter the gradient of the savings function.

17·6

B is correct. The gradient of the consumption function would only change if MPC and MPS changed.

17·7

C is correct. For every £1 lost the members of the higher-paid groups reduce consumption by 50p, but for every £1 gained members of the lower-paid group increase consumption expenditure by 90p. so there is an increase in **C** by 1m(90p−50p) = £400 000.

17·8

A is correct.

17·9

Prices will rise, because demand exceeds supply (demand-pull inflation), or exports will fall, or imports will rise. All three results are probable.

17·10

Planned S is NL, but planned I is only NM.

17·11

C is correct. The extra imports, unbalanced by extra exports, will cause AMD to fall.

17·12

Increase in incomes

	£
1st round	100
2nd round	50
3rd round	25
4th round	12·5
5th round	6·25
6th round	3·12½
	£196·87½

The approximate total increase in incomes will be £200.

17·13

A is correct. Read the text which follows the question.

17·14

B is correct. The multiplier is

$$\frac{1}{1-0{\cdot}8} = \frac{1}{0{\cdot}2} = 5.\ 5 \times £400 = £2\ 000.$$

17·15

B is correct. Total leakages are 50p out of every £1, so the MPC and the MPS are each ½.

17·16

A MPS is 0·4 at all levels of income

At income	£5m	APS is	0
,, ,,	£10	,, ,,	0·2
,, ,,	£15	,, ,,	0·27
,, ,,	£20	,, ,,	0·3
,, ,,	£25	,, ,,	0·32
,, ,,	£30	,, ,,	0·33
,, ,,	£35	,, ,,	0·34
,, ,,	£40	,, ,,	0·35

B £30m. See text.
C £40m. See text.
D See text.

17·17

C is correct. See text.

17·18

See text.

17·19

a Graph of consumption and investment functions:

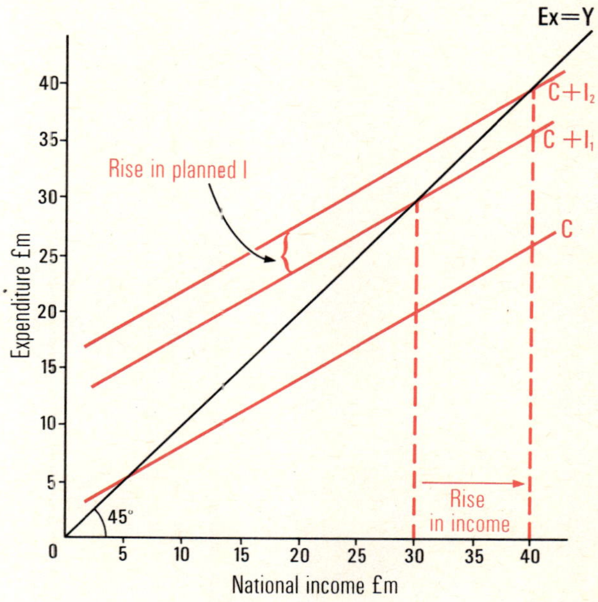

N.B. Gradient of C function is ⅗. (0·6) since MPS is 0·4.

b Graph of consumption and investment functions:

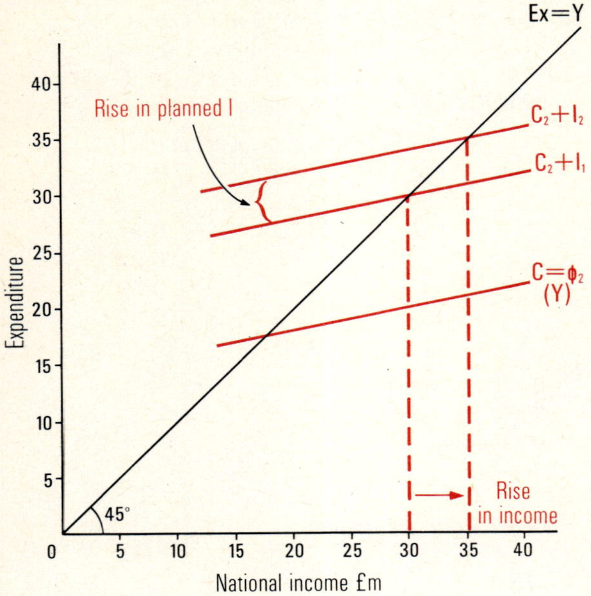

In this case, because MPS is higher (0·8), the gradient of the C function is lower ($\frac{1}{5}$).

17·20

Graph of consumption and investment functions:

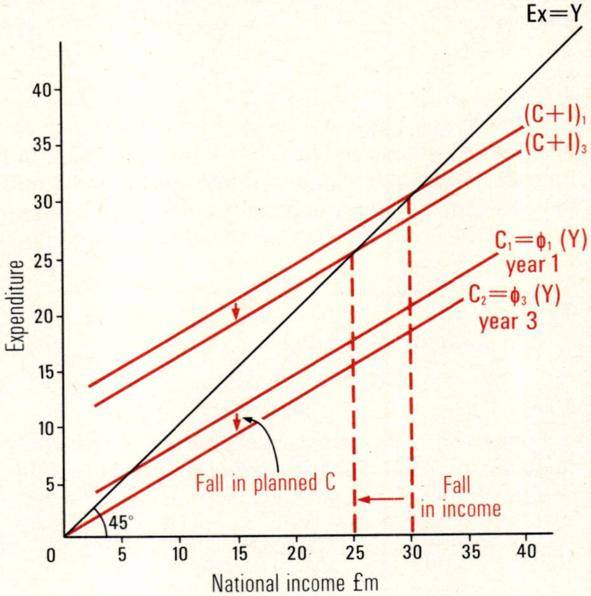

The C function falls by £2m at all levels of income.

PROFIT AND RENT

You have read in S15 that the National Income is made up of the returns to all of the resources for production which have been engaged in economic activity. Labour receives wages and salaries, while capital receives interest. In this section we are going to deal with the returns to the remaining factors, land and enterprise. Land receives rent, while enterprise receives profit. It is profit which we will examine first.

What is profit?

Since profit is the return to enterprise, before going any further we should be sure what we mean by enterprise. The production process can be compared with cookery. You take certain ingredients, mix them together in the correct proportions and the result satisfies a want. With only land and labour as the ingredients output would be restricted to goods like wild fruits which can be picked without the use of any capital. The addition of capital, however, adds a new dimension to the process. It is similar to the addition of eggs to the basic cookery ingredients of flour and fat. New and more exciting wants can be satisfied. We can use capital to combine with land and labour to produce houses, vehicles and a host of other economic goods.

Enterprise comes into the picture at this point. If land, labour and capital are the ingredients of the recipe, then the entrepreneur is the chef. It is he who decides on the ingredients, and the proportions in which each shall be used, and it is on his initiative that the success or failure of the whole project depends. The more adventurous he is, the more likely is the project to result in spectacular success or in disastrous failure. The more experienced and skillful he is, the more certain will be the reward of his enterprise. He may profit by his initiative or he may lose. Without the chef nothing can be cooked: without the entrepreneur no production take place.

The entrepreneur may be an individual, as in the case of a one-man business, or his function may be performed by a group of shareholders in a public company who elect a board of directors to act on their behalf in the running of the business. Essentially the entrepreneurial function is performed by any body which organises the factors of production in order to satisfy wants, for a profit.

18·1

In the case of a state-owned industry, which of the following do you think is acting as the entrepreneur?

- **A** The trade union of the industry.
- **B** The Board of Directors.
- **C** The Chairman of the Board of Directors.
- **D** The Select Committee on Nationalized Industries (a committee composed mainly of Members of Parliament in the House of Commons).
- **E** The government acting on behalf of the public.

Profit is what is left after the other factors of production have been paid (see S2). Every firm draws up accounts at the end of the financial year in order to consider its financial position. The first account to be drawn up is the Trading Account and it looks like this imaginary example.

TRADING ACCOUNT FOR YEAR ENDING 31 DEC. 1970

Debits		**Credits**	
Stocks at at 1 Jan. 1970	£2 000	Sales	£100 000
Raw materials/ purchases	£25 000	Stock at 31 Dec. 1970	£5 000
Fuel	£5 000		
Wages	£50 000		
	£82 000		
Gross Profit	£23 000		
	£105 000		£105 000

You can see from this account that *gross profit* is the excess of sales over the cost of production; it is a residue.

18·2

Calculate the gross profit from the following figures: Purchases £200 000. Sales £1 000 000. Stock at 1 Jan. £200 000. Stock at 31 Dec. £100 000. Wages £400 000.

The firm will next draw up its Profit and Loss Account in order to discover its *net profit*.

It is this net profit (gross profit less other expenses) that will be shared between partners or distributed to the shareholders or simply ploughed back by the company and used as capital to increase that company's future earning power.

Indicators of profitability

As a guide to their progress, or as a comparison with other firms, many firms use the ratio $\frac{\text{Net profit}}{\text{Turnover}}$ to give them a running guide, where turnover = total sales. This ratio answers two questions.

(a) For a given level of sales, how much profit will accrue?
(b) To achieve a given profit, how much must be sold?

Both these questions are fundamental to most practical business decisions.

PROFIT AND LOSS ACCOUNT FOR YEAR ENDING 31 DEC. 1970

Debit		Credit	
Salaries	£5 000	Gross profit (carried forward)	£23 000
Rent and rates	£500		
Other overheads (including fixed capital charges)	£1 500		
	£7 000		
Net profit	£16 000		
	£23 000		£23 000

18·3

In the example of our imaginary firm, what would this ratio have been?

A $\frac{16}{82}$ B $\frac{23}{105}$ C $\frac{16}{100}$

D $\frac{16}{105}$ E $\frac{23}{82}$

Another guide to the profitability of the firm is the ratio of net profit to capital assets employed. This is of great interest to potential investors, since it represents the return on the original investment of capital. A company with a high ratio of profit will find it easier to raise new capital.

The function of profits

The economic problem, as described in S1, is one of unlimited wants and scarce resources. Each society must ensure that its resources are used in such a way that the greatest number of wants are satisfied, without waste. To achieve this, the wants of consumers must be communicated to potential suppliers who will organize the resources for production in order to satisfy demand. The problem is the same whether the society is organized along centrally planned lines or according to private enterprise principles.

In a centrally planned economy, where the factors of production are owned by the state, the allocation of resources to particular industries is determined largely by a central economic planning committee. Decisions are made as to what area shall be devoted to one crop or another, what amount of capital should be devoted to consumer goods or capital goods, and the distribution of labour.

In an economy where the majority of the nation's assets are owned privately, it is the price system or profit motive that provides the stimulus to firms to supply goods demanded by consumers. Consumers indicate their wants to firms by being prepared to pay a higher price for the same quantity of a particular commodity (an increase in demand). Entrepreneurs managing firms producing this commodity will be encouraged to expand supply, with the prospect of a higher selling price, increased sales revenue and higher profits. In turn the increased profits being made by firms in this industry will attract new firms into the industry, which will further swell the supply of goods on to the market. More resources will be attracted into the industry, with the offer of higher rewards, away from other firms producing different goods.

On the other hand, where demand for goods has fallen, their price is also likely to fall, as will sales revenue and, therefore, profits. Falling profits will act as a disincentive to expansion to firms in the industry and a discouragement to entrepreneurs who may have been considering opening new firms in the industry. Resources will be laid off, and, providing that they are mobile, will tend to move into other lines of production.

You can see then, that it is the prospect of profits which leads to increases in the market supply of certain goods, thus satisfying the wants of consumers, and determining the allocation of resources. The exceptions to this are, of course, resources which are needed to provide 'free' services such as defence, roads and medical care. In a mixed economy, like the U.K., the government provides these services out of tax revenue.

In a capitalist economy, then, we have seen how profit can be regarded as:

(a) the reason for making investment
(b) the reward to successful enterprise

(c) the source of dividends to shareholders who provide capital for firms to expand and thus meet the demands of the consumer.

Characteristics of profit

i Profit is a residue. We saw in the trading account of the firm how profit is the remainder after all the other expenses have been paid. Since it is a residue it will fluctuate as the costs of production or the sales revenue vary. Profit is therefore unique among the returns to factors of production in that the entrepreneur is uncertain of his return until after the production process is completed, whereas all the other factors know what the return will be before they start work.

ii Profit can be negative. A loss is a negative profit. If profit is the reward to successful enterprise, then loss is the return (negative) to poor enterprise. Whereas the returns to all other factors are positive and contracted for before production, the return to enterprise is uncertain and can result in losses when risks do not pay off.

ii Profit is the return to uncertainty. The function of the entrepreneur is to organize the other factors of production. In doing so he must take decisions with regard to the proportions in which they should be mixed. The owner of a retail shop, for instance, may decide to invest in supermarket-type shelving, trolleys, baskets and checkouts. This he predicts will enable him to reduce his wage bill, increase his turnover (since more people can be served in the same amount of time) and thus increase his profit. On the other hand, his customers might reject the lack of personal service offered by his new-style shop and prefer to transfer their attentions to one of his competitors. Thus he stands to gain or to lose.

This uncertainty is fundamental to the activities of the entrepreneur. Costs of raw materials, and the volume of his sales, both important influences on profit, can only be influenced to a limited extent. Most large firms employ market research experts to give them more accurate predictions of market behaviour, and skilled buyers to purchase raw materials, but their judgement can be wrong. Generally speaking, the greater the uncertainty the greater must be the prospective profits.

18·4

Rank the following economic activities in order of prospective profitability or loss-making, from high to low.

A A 'Do-it-yourself' shop on a new housing estate.
B Drilling for oil in the North Sea.
C A Discount House.

(N.B. By profitability we mean net profit as a proportion of capital assets.)

Profit as a cost of production

All factors must be rewarded in order to induce them to take part in the production process. There is a certain level of return, below which factors will refuse to work in one occupation and will probably transfer to another line of production: to this the entrepreneur is no exception. When the profits of a particular firm, or a particular industry, fall below a certain level, entrepreneurs will switch their activity to other forms of enterprise. In other words, the entrepreneur must earn, or expect to earn, at least a *normal profit* to enter or to stay in business. This was referred to in S11. It is a minimum return and, since it is essential to attract the entrepreneur, must be regarded as cost of production.

Any profit over and above this normal profit is usually referred to as *abnormal* or *monopoly* profit; it is a residue and we cannot regard it as a cost of production.

Abnormal profits may come about through:

(a) the successful anticipation of changes in market demand.
(b) the innovation of new techniques of production or marketing or organization,
(c) the restriction of competition.

All of these activities will give an entrepreneur an advantage over his competitors, and although the high returns may only be short lived (since new competitors will be attracted to set up business) they will represent abnormal profits in the short run. Remember that this abnormal profit is not a cost of production. Thus you can see that Net Profit − Normal Profit = Abnormal Profit. The word 'abnormal' means in this context a profit which is above that level of profit normal to that particular industry. It is thus only present in the short run, for, except in a pure monopoly, in the long run competitors will enter the industry and profit will become normal.

18·5

The normal return expected by entrepreneurs in the retail grocery business is 15% of capital assets employed. If a firm with £10 000 worth of assets earns a net profit of £3 000 in a year, what is the abnormal profit earned?

A £1 500 **B** £2 000 **C** £2 500
D £3 000 **E** £3 500

The determination of profit in imperfect competition

You saw in S11 how, in order to maximize their profits, firms concentrate on reducing their costs and increasing their revenue. Here, we will first refresh your memories on the cost and revenue curves of the firm and then relate it to what we have said in this section.

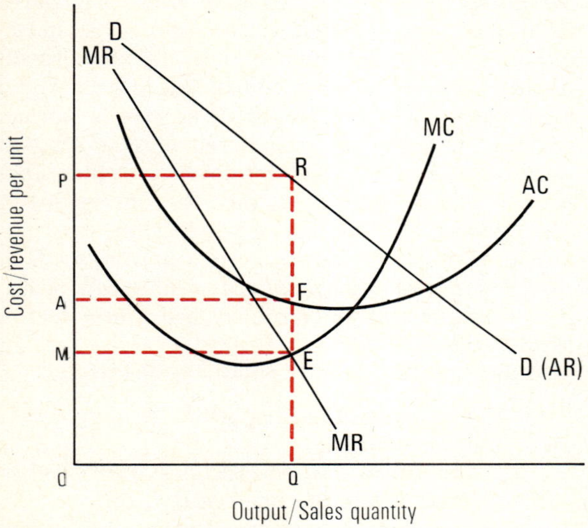

Figure 18·1

18·6

The firm represented in the figure above is operating (in the short run) in what form of competition?

A Perfect **B** Imperfect **C** Monopoly

18·7

It is making a maximum profit where MR = MC (see S11 if you do not remember this), at price OP and output OQ. Which area on the graph represents the firm's abnormal profit?

A OMEQ **B** OAFQ **C** MAFE **D** APRF
E MPRE

In imperfect competition this will be only a short-run position, since in the long run new firms may enter the industry and reduce the demand for our firm's product. The demand curve of *our firm* (shown in figure 18·1) will therefore tend to shift downwards and to the left to result in the position shown in figure 18·2, where MR = MC and also AR = AC.

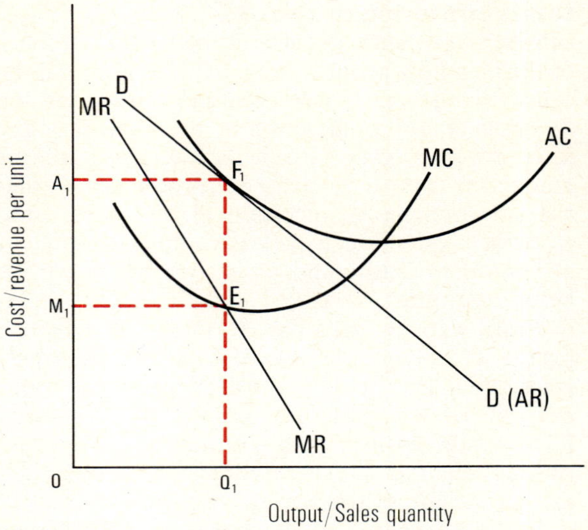

Figure 18·2

Here demand has fallen so that the best profit position is now at output OQ_1 where MR = MC (the first necessary condition). The price at which OQ_1 (which may equal OQ if MR = MC where $OQ = OQ_1$) can be sold has fallen (OA_1) and is equal to the average cost (also OA_1). Since price is equal to average cost this means that total revenue is equal to total cost. The only profit that the firm is making must therefore be a normal profit (which is a cost of production and is included in total cost).

In the long run then, we have seen, abnormal profit (or pure profit as some economists describe it) may disappear as new firms enter an industry. Firms will only earn a minimum or normal profit, providing other firms can set up in competition. In the case of pure monopoly, however, there is no competition for the firm: the firm is the industry. Thus it is with monopoly that abnormal (or monopoly) profit will occur. In the case of perfect competition, a single firm may make abnormal profits in the short run. In the case of monopoly the short-run position is the same as the long-run one. Thus, imperfect competition lies between the extreme of monopoly and the extreme of perfect competition where the demand curve for a firm is horizontal, i.e. AR = MR.

Effects of the profit motive

From the previous paragraph we can see that it is in the interests of firms to reduce the competition facing them and thus increase their share of the market. As you saw in S11 it is also in their interests to restrict output to a position where profits are maximized, and they can only do this if they know that no new competitors will enter the industry. It is not surprising therefore that mergers, take-overs and restrictive practices have been stimulated by this desire. In many cases this has worked against the public interest by causing higher prices. Legislation has been necessary to set up the Restrictive Practices Court and the Monopolies and Mergers Commission which between them attempt to ensure that firms act in the interests of the public as well as in the interests of their shareholders.

The profit motive must not be overstated. Although many firms have been founded by entrepreneurs seeking profit, most large, complex corporations are controlled by directors who are salaried employees. (They may also be shareholders, but this is not essential.) Their behaviour is influenced by many considerations besides profit: they may seek the welfare of their employees or political ends, be troubled by questions of conscience, or perhaps just want a quiet life. Provided that the company makes enough profit to satisfy the shareholders, the board of directors can usually look forward to indefinite re-election.

Profit—a summary

Profit is the return to enterprise.

Profit is a residue left after other factors have been paid. It can be *estimated* in advance of a trading period, but *calculated* only afterwards.

Gross profit is the excess of sales revenue over variable costs.

Net profit is the excess of sales revenue over total costs (variable costs + fixed costs). It may be taken as income by the entrepreneur or by shareholders, or it may be ploughed back into the business.

The main function of profit in a capitalist economy is to stimulate entrepreneurs to move resources into those activities which will supply the goods demanded through the market by consumers.

The minimum level of profit necessary to attract an entrepreneur to a particular industry, and to keep him in it, is normal profit. (This is a cost of production to economists, but not to accountants.)

Profits are normally higher when there is a strong element of uncertainty, or when there is a long period of waiting before investments bear fruit. Profit can be negative.

The earnings of profits normally is dependent on:

(a) the taking of risks,
(b) the successful anticipation of changes in market demand, and the introduction of new products,
(c) the successful introduction of new production techniques,
(d) the restriction of competition in order to increase control of the market.

The effect of the profit motive can be against the public interest, by the restriction of competition, but on the other hand, can lead to the constant innovation of new products, processes and marketing techniques which are decidedly in the public interest.

Rent

Labour receives wages, or salaries; entrepeneurs, profits; capital, interest. However, we use the term rent for payments to land, and sometimes for equipment. The theory of *economic rent* was derived from the earnings of land, so we will first examine the rewards to land, and then show how the concept of economic rent can be extended to other factors.

18·8

Make a list of five goods commonly rented rather than purchased.

Land is the only factor of production that has no cost of production. It will produce goods such as wild fruit, which are capable of satisfying wants without the addition of other factors. It contains mineral resources and supplies water which man has done nothing to create. Furthermore the yield from the land can fluctuate without any change in effort on behalf of the other factors. This is a very important feature, as you will see later in this section. You may argue of course that the output of land can be increased by adding more fertilizer (capital). This is a fact; but it is also true that the output can rise and fall given the same input of other factors. It is this which makes land unique among the factors of production.

18·9

Which of the following would you classify as land?

A Trees
B Untapped reserves of coal
C River water of Birmingham
D The surface of the City
E All of them

The demand for land

The demand for land is usually a derived demand. It will be demanded in conjunction with the other factors to supply the economic goods demanded through the market. The strength of the demand for land will therefore depend upon its usefulness in a particular production process. Its marginal revenue productivity (the revenue resulting from the sale of the product of the land) will determine the quantity of it demanded for production.

The supply of land

The total supply of land in any one country is relatively fixed, but the quantity of land for a particular use can be increased in supply through transfer from a different use. For example, the quantity of land for housing can be increased by transferring its use from agriculture. Only land which is completely specific is unable to transfer its use. Thus a park in the centre of a city might be suitable as a factory or car park, shopping centre or housing estate. A Dartmoor sheep farm, on the other hand, is unsuitable for many other forms of economic activity given the present distribution of population and state of technology. Thus the opportunity cost of the sheep farm is low.

The shape of the supply curve of land for a specific use depends on the ease with which land can transfer to that use on being offered an increased return. The supply of land for building purposes in central London is practically fixed since nearly all the land is built on already. It is almost completely inelastic. The supply of land for building in Lincolnshire, on the other hand, is more elastic since farm land can be transferred readily to another use on being offered a higher return. (We are, for the moment, ignoring planning controls.)

Determination of ordinary rent

The rent of a particular plot of land will be determined by the market forces of demand and supply. Demand is represented by the marginal revenue productivity curve. If the level of ordinary rent were any lower then less would be supplied (it would transfer to another activity). If the rent were any higher more land would be attracted into the market from other activities. In the above diagram, therefore, the level of rent (which we shall at this stage call *ordinary rent*) is sufficient to keep a plot of land in a particular activity and prevent its transfer to another. It is thus equivalent to the land's *transfer earnings*. This is an important term which we are now going to use in a discussion of *economic rent*.

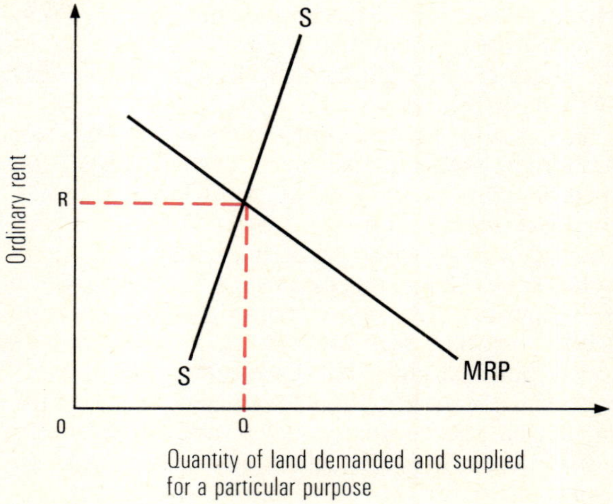

Figure 18·3

Economic rent

Economic rent is not the same as ordinary rent. Although it was first conceived as a return to land, it is a return which may be received by any factor of production.

So far in this section we have confined our attention to returns to factors which have been earned through the activity of those factors. The essential point to remember about economic rent is that it is any payment made to a factor over and above that payment necessary to keep it in its present use. It is therefore an income to any factor, but it is not anticipated by the factor when it enters production. It is interesting to find out just how this can come about.

The supply price of factors

Most factors have to be offered a reward before they will engage in any form of economic activity.

We have already seen that normal profit is necessary to attract entrepreneurs. Similarly a man who is skilled as a welder, living in Birmingham for instance, will expect to receive, say, £30 per week or he will transfer to another job. Capital which is invested in one form of activity will, providing it is not completely specific, transfer to other industries if it is offered a higher reward. This is inevitable as people's spending patterns change. The return which must be offered to a factor to keep it in its present use is called its *supply price,* or its *transfer earnings.*

Determination of the supply price

You have seen in S2 how some factors can transfer more easily than others.

18·10

Which of the following factors are highly specific (i.e. unable to change their use easily):

A A blast furnace.
B A warehouse.
C An unskilled labourer
D A Dartmoor sheep farm.

18·11

If a factor cannot transfer to any other activity, the supply price necessary to keep it in its present form of activity is:

A High **B** Low **C** Nil

18·12

The less specific a factor is, the *greater/less* will be its supply price.

18·13

Consider the figure 18·4:

a Could the supply curve shown here apply to the supply of unskilled labourers in an area of high unemployment?

b Could the supply curve apply to the supply of land on a newly discovered island in the Pacific Ocean which is unsuitable for building on?

c Could it apply to the supply of capital in an economy where production is at a standstill and prospects for investment look poor?

It is, of course a completely elastic supply curve. It will apply to any factor whose supply can be increased easily and without additional cost in response to an increase in demand. This

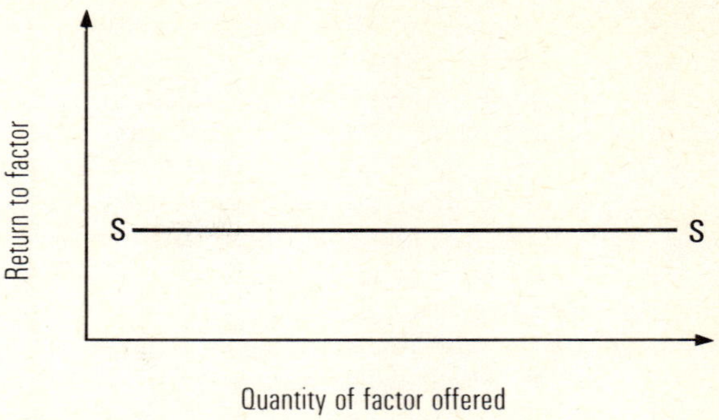

Figure 18·4

means that the entire earnings of such a factor will be its supply price. No more has to be offered to attract more of the factor into production.

In the short term firms often have to offer higher than current rates in order to attract more factors quickly when they wish to expand. In the long term, however, supply can be increased without offering higher rates. An increased demand for labour, for instance, in the short term can only be satisfied by working overtime at higher rates of pay. In the long term, however, more school-leavers will come on to the market and inflate the supply without the offer of overtime rates of pay, and other workers, attracted by the prospect of high wages, will move from other industries.

Now consider figure 18·5 below. Suppose that the demand for the factor increases from DD to D_1D_1. In the short term the return to the factor will rise from OREQ to $OR_1E_1Q_1$ (that is, the

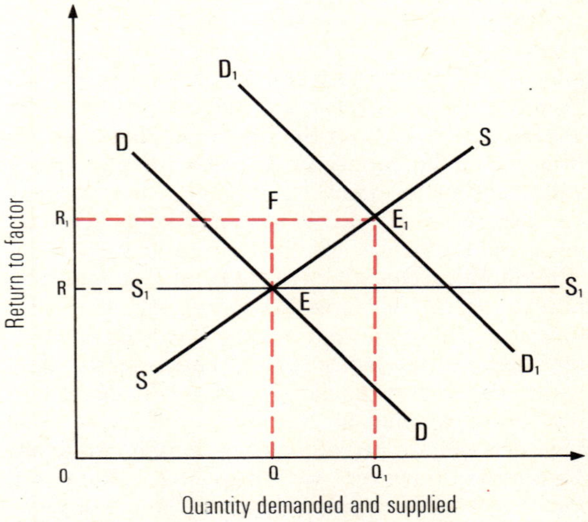

Figure 18·5

return which rises from OR to OR_1 multiplied by the quantity of the factor being employed).

Now we must remember that those units of factor represented by OQ were already being supplied at a return of OR. In order to call into production more units of the factor $(OQ_1–OQ)$ employers have to increase the return offered to OR_1, to all units. So all units of the factor OQ have had their return increased. Thus there is a difference between their actual earnings and those earnings which were necessary to keep the factors in that production process. Therefore OREQ represents their original returns, whether it be wages, interest or ordinary rent, for which they were prepared to work (i.e. their supply price), while area RR_1FE represents a 'windfall' surplus.

This surplus is called *economic rent*.

18·14

Now, what is it that has caused the economic rent in the case above?

A The increase in demand.
B The inelastic supply.
C The inelasticity of the supply curve combined with an increase in demand.

The economic rent has come about because the supply is relatively fixed as the demand has increased. You can see from the graph that in the long term the supply curve takes on the shape of S_1S_1: a perfectly elastic supply curve. Perhaps it might apply to land which takes a full season to be transferred into another form of activity, or perhaps it is the supply of skilled workmen who take several years to train. Once the supply has become elastic the returns to the factor fall to the level required to keep this factor in that occupation, or to the supply price below which factors will transfer to other uses. The economic rent has disappeared, since it was only being received while the factor was relatively fixed in supply.

Economic rent which is only of a temporary nature, as this is, is called *quasi-rent*. The only time that economic rent proper is earned is when the supply of the factor is fixed permanently. This is the reason that the early economists referred to the return to land as economic rent, since they regarded the supply of land as completely fixed. Nowadays, however, we know that where *any factor* is fixed in supply then its income will be in the form of economic rent. This applies especially to persons with extraordinary talents. Thus a famous actor may receive £1 000 per week. What would he be paid if he were not an actor? Perhaps he would teach English in a seconday school and earn £40 per week. If this were so, the producer need only pay the actor £41 to persuade him to act. Why, then, does the actor receive £1 000? The reason is that our famous actor is unique. There is only one of him, and the producer must compete with other producers to engage his services. The supply of this actor is fixed at 1, competitive demand forces his price up, and so he receives a rent of £959 more than he would require as the minimum necessary to persuade him to act. You will notice that ordinary actors, who are in plentiful supply, receive very low wages.

Some applications of the theory

Consider the following figure which shows a short-term supply curve (three years).

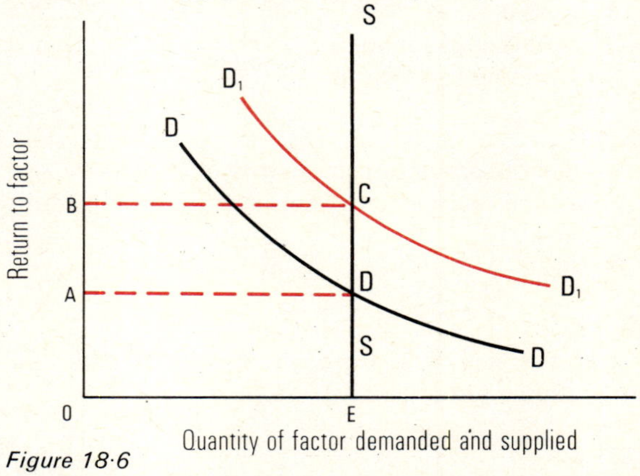

Figure 18·6

18·15

To which of the following factors could the supply curve in figure 18·6 apply?

A The supply of semi-skilled workers in the North-East.
B The supply of capital in the motor industry.
C The supply of qualified doctors.
D The supply of grazing land.
E The supply of enterprise in the fashion clothes industry.

18·16

Which area on the graph represents economic rent?

A OADE **B** ABCD **C** OBCE

As we have seen, economic rent is a surplus over and above what the factor could earn in an alternative occupation. It is due to the inelasticity of supply of that factor and not anticipated by the factor on entering the occupation. Since it is related to the conditions of supply of the factor, it must in turn relate to the nature of the factor itself. The more specific the factor is, the more will its income be in the form of economic rent.

18·17

Say whether you think the incomes of the following have a high or a low economic rent content.

A A successful barrister.
B £1 000 cash invested in liquid assets.
C A lorry driver.
D An acre of vacant land in a Development Area.
E The copyright of a 'pop' record.

Since economic rent is related to the supply of factors, it follows that the supply of factors may be deliberately restricted to force up their income of economic rent. Such is the case with the 'closed shop', operated by many trade unions and professional bodies, where only members of the particular body are allowed to perform certain jobs. Entry to the trade or profession is strictly controlled and thus any increase in the demand for that particular skill will inevitably result in an income of economic rent for the owners of such a skill.

Another example of economic rent in practice occurs where the supply of a factor is controlled by a firm which has a monopoly. In S11 you saw how it was often in the interests of the monopolist to restrict output to maximise his profits. Now the firm is controlling the use of factors of production in the production process, and when it restricts their use it does so to increase their income of economic rent. All monopoly profits can thus be regarded as a form of economic rent. Furthermore, since normal profit is that part of the return which attracts the intrepreneur into that line of production (i.e. his supply price), *any* surplus over and above this is economic rent to the entrepreneur. Again, it is caused by inelasticity of supply and is a short-run phenomenon. In the short run fixed capital cannot be altered, so that a new expanded level of production cannot be established until new machinery and so on is installed. Similarly in the short run new firms cannot set up their factories. In the long run supply will be more elastic and the economic-rent element in profit will be less.

Summary

Ordinary rent is the return to land. It is determined by the demand (marginal revenue productivity) and the supply of the factor.

Economic rent can be a return to any factor. It is a surplus in excess of what the factor needs to attract it into that occupation.

Economic rent results from scarcity. If the supply of factors were completely elastic then no economic rent would exist.

Quasi-rent is temporary economic rent.

All profits above normal are in the nature of economic rent to the entrepreneur.

ANSWERS

18·1

E: none of the others are taking the ultimate risk or have to decide on the overall policy.

18·2

£300 000

18·3

C: $\frac{16}{100}$; turnover is equal to total sales.

18·4

B, A, C: there is room for debate here, but the Discount House is taking a negligible risk since all the bills it discounts have been guaranteed by an accepting house.

18·5

A.

18·6

B or **C**: the shape of the demand curve tells you this (see figure 11·12).

18·7

D: this is the area of total revenue OPRQ less the area of total cost OAFQ.

18·8

T.V. sets, radio sets, cars, concrete mixers, spray guns, tents, caravans, surfboards, boats, evening dress.

18·9

E: land is any gift of nature.

18·10

A and **D**: the others can easily transfer their efforts from one line of production to another.

18·11

C: nil, e.g. value of most bombers after a war.

18·12

Greater, e.g. a person qualified in both law and engineering.

18·13

a Yes. This graph shows that at the current rate of return to the factor there is an unlimited supply. It is completely elastic.

b Yes. The same reason applies as in the previous answer.

c Yes. Same reason.

18·14

C.

18·15

C: the supply of doctors cannot be increased within three years.

18·16

C: OBCE. All the returns to this factor are in the form of economic rent. The quantity supplied would still be OE if the rent is nil.

18·17

A High **B** Low **C** Low
D Low **E** High

EMPLOYMENT

Despite the title of this section it is unemployment that we are now going to consider. We have seen in previous sections how the 'economic problem' of scarce resources and unlimited wants necessitates the use of our resources in the most effective way. The use of resources involves the employment of not one but all of the factors of production. So when we talk of employment, strictly speaking, we mean the employment of labour, capital, land and enterprise. Similarly, unemployment applies not only to labour, but to all of the factors. The reason we usually emphasise the human factor when studying unemployment is that great physical, psychological and social distress is associated with unemployed labour which, it is generally agreed, should be avoided whenever possible.

Employment and the circular flow of income

The need for a separate study of employment has been recognized by economists only relatively recently. Many economists in the nineteenth century, with the notable exceptions of Marx and Malthus, were not prepared to recognize that general unemployment could ever exist other than as a 'temporary derangement of the markets'. They accepted that workers in one industry might, for a time, be unemployed, but they could not conceive a situation where unemployment was spread across all industries. It is not surprising, therefore, that when general unemployment persisted in this country between 1920 and 1938 the economists of the day were completely unequipped to deal with the situation. It is interesting to discover how the 'traditional' view came about.

It was a Frenchman, J. B. Say, who originally put forward the view that general unemployment could never occur. His views were widely followed in this country throughout the nineteenth century and were virtually unchallenged until the 1930s. The argument which follows has come to be known as 'Say's Law'.

Say argued that one man's spending is another man's income. Every time production takes place income is created for the owners of the factors of production; this income is the source of spending power and must become the sales revenue of firms. The greater the level of production, the greater will be the level of income and thus spending. Supply must create its own demand. Since the demand for goods in turn determines the demand for labour it follows that unemployment cannot occur. The effect of any increased supply of goods would be to reduce the level of prices, which would in turn increase the quantity demanded. Thus full employment would be maintained.

This theory conforms to most of the traditional economic theories. It is an attempt to use demand and supply analysis to explain not the determination of the price of a commodity in the market, but something which needs a different analysis. Say's answer to unemployment was a cut in wages (the price of labour). Conforming to the laws of demand and supply, this would increase the quantity of labour demanded. What he, and many others, failed to see was that lower wages caused a fall in the demand for goods and inevitably in the demand for labour.

The problem of unemployment was never really considered seriously until it took this country by storm after the First World War. At no time between the two wars did the percentage of the working population unemployed fall below 9·7%. It averaged approximately 14% and at its height during the Great Depression rose to 21·9%. One man in five was without work. Millions of human resources were idle. What sort of solution to the economic problem was this?

Out of human misery, the economic waste and the uncertainty of successive governments came a man who provided the answers so desperately needed by much of the western world. John Maynard Keynes was first a philosopher and secondly a mathematician. He turned his mind to the study of contemporary problems in the early 1920s and refuted a great deal of the current writings of economics as it then stood. So great was his impact on the understanding of economic problems that the science is now classified into pre-Keynesian and post-Keynesian thought. His main contribution lay in the publication of his book *The General Theory of Employment, Interest and Money* in 1936. Yet years before this he had been urging governments to take the measures which he knew would solve the economic difficulties of the time. His contribution to economics can be compared to that of other great thinkers who have challenged all the existing knowledge and opinion within a particular sphere, and have produced new truths. Let us see what his basic ideas on employment were.

Keynes saw that the analysis of individual markets was inadequate for dealing with the overall economy. It was adequate for analysing, say, prices in the market and their determination, but misleading when it came to aggregate (total) demand. He wrote a general theory which is a theory of equilibrium relating to aggregate demand, aggregate supply, employment, the price level and so on. These concepts were introduced to you in S14 and S15.

Keynes began by attacking Say's Law. He argued that there was absolutely no reason why the income created by firms and paid to the factors of production should necessarily become income for the firms in the form of total spending. He pointed out that if there were 'leakages' from this circular flow of income (see S14) then the total aggregate monetary demand would fall unless they were supplemented by corresponding 'injections'. The leakages he spoke of were saving, imports and taxation, all of which represented income which would not find its way back to the firms who created it. Say had ignored these considerations. As Keynes had shown, there was absolutely no reason why supply must create its own demand. In fact the 1920s had shown that aggregate monetary demand could fall woefully short of the level needed to sustain full employment.

This was the crux of Keynes' argument. The level of employment depends on the level of aggregate monetary demand. This in turn is the sum of consumer spending, investment spending and government spending. So to discover what determines the level of employment, find out what determines consumption, investment and government spending. If unemployment exists the remedy lies in expanding aggregate monetary demand through increased consumption (less saving), or increased investment, or increased government spending. The most immediate and direct of these three methods is the last: government spending. Keynes therefore urged the governments of his time to embark on programmes of public works and thus expand the level of aggregate monetary demand. We shall return, later in this section, to study his ideas in greater detail, but it would be wise at this stage to answer the following questions:

(a) Why should we be so concerned about unemployment?
(b) How do we define unemployment/measure the level of it?

Public concern for the unemployed

It is right that people should be concerned over unemployment. It represents a waste of economic resources, great human distress and a high opportunity cost. Labour is essential to the production process. The wants of the population can only be satisfied through the activity of the factors of production. If any of these factors is unemployed, therefore, the ability of the population to produce is diminished while its appetite for consumption is not. Unemployed labour thus represents a waste of economic resources. On the human rather than the economic side there is concern for the personal suffering experienced by the men and their families whose income is reduced. There is the loss of self-respect and the respect of others that a man feels when he has to recognize that his skills are no longer needed. He is forced to live on charity, on the state, on 'the dole'. He no longer provides for his family's needs. Where is his self-respect, his social status now? They are replaced by feelings of inferiority and uselessness which inevitably lead to a deterioration in a man's confidence in himself and the system which has created this suffering. Finally there is the opportunity cost to the country as a whole, of resources unemployed. At the time of writing this section there are 628 000 registered unemployed in the U.K. In a full year these men, when combined with the other factors of production, might produce an output of, say, £2 000 per annum each. (This is probably a very conservative estimate.) This means a total of £1 256 000 000 worth of goods at present-day values. This is the opportunity cost of the level of unemployment. It represents about 3% of the gross national product, the total value of houses built in this country in a year, or 14% of the total value of visible exports of the U.K., depending on what opportunity costs you care to consider. It follows that if the unemployed could be suitably employed they would be capable of doubling the rate of economic growth, solving the housing shortage or contributing materials to export earnings. Such is the seriousness of unemployment to an economy. Why does the government not take steps to end it? We shall return to this question later in the section.

Measuring unemployment

Suppose you were given the task of calculating the number of unemployed people in the United Kingdom at any one time; how would you set about it? Presumably the first thing you would do is to decide whom to include in your total. Would you include everyone in the population who is not gainfully employed? Of course not; pensioners and children engaged in full-time education are not unemployed, nor are housewives who work at home bringing up a family. You would probably decide that rather than say who you would include it is easier to distinguish who you would not.

19·1

Which of the following groups of people would you not include in a register of unemployed people?

- **A** University students and college students (full-time).
- **B** Housewives.
- **C** Children at school.
- **D** Pensioners.
- **E** People who have left one job and are looking for another.
- **F** People who have been made reduntant through the closure of their time.
- **G** People who are off work through illness.
- **H** People who are disabled and unable to work.
- **I** School-leavers who have not found jobs.
- **J** People who will not work, yet are capable of working.
- **K** People who are working part-time, say mornings only.

You should find that the only groups you are left with are people who are fit and able and want to work but for whom there is no work available. The only questionable one among this group is **J**: people who will not work. There is undoubtedly within our society a section of people who, although they are physically fit, are unwilling or unable to hold down a job for any length of time. Usually this results from emotional or other psychological reasons, but occasionally it may be due to the fact that with unemployment benefits and social security payments a man with a few marketable skills may be better off out of work than when he is earning a regular pay packet. Perhaps in truth, however, the situation that needs remedying is not a cut in social security benefits, which would only serve to handicap blameless wives and children, but an increase in the level of wages paid to such workers so that such a situation could never occur. At any rate this group only comprises a very small proportion of the total number of unemployed.

Having decided which groups to include in your total you must now decide from where it is best to obtain the statistics. Since every unemployed person is entitled to a state benefit once he has registered as unemployed, the task of collecting statistics is simple. The Department of Employment and Productivity carries out its functions through local offices in the form of 'employment exchanges'. Each unemployed person 'signs on' before being entitled to his benefit. Every employment exchange thus has a constant register of the unemployed.

REGISTERED UNEMPLOYED IN THE U.K.
(thousands)

	1963	1965	1967	% change from 1965 to 1967
Total	516·0	305·0	539·0	77
Agriculture	16·9	12·3	15·0	25
Mining	9·8	6·0	9·3	50
Manufacturing (total)	176·0	84·0	190·0	125
Food	18·6	10·3	16·9	
Chemicals	7·6	5·5	8·2	
Metal manufacture	15·3	4·8	20·1	
Engineering	31·3	15·9	36·9	
Shipbuilding	18·8	6·0	10·2	
Vehicles	10·1	6·4	17·4	
Other metal goods	11·6	5·2	14·1	
Textiles	21·7	9·7	22·8	
Leather	1·5	0·7	1·3	
Clothing	12·5	5·2	12·7	
Bricks	7·4	3·8	7·6	
Timber, furniture	6·4	3·5	7·4	
Construction	75·7	46·0	93·9	
Gas/Elec/Water	3·8	2·5	4·3	
Transport/ Communication	30·5	23·2	34·2	
Distributive trades	58·6	34·2	55·8	
Insurance/Banking Finance	6·1	6·6	9·0	
Professional/ Scientific	13·0	8·8	13·2	
Misc services	51·3	33·2	50·4	

Figure 19·1

Unemployment in the U.K.

Figure 19·1 gives the statistics for the registered unemployed in the U.K. for three years 1963, 1965 and 1967. The figures are broken down into occupational groupings and by analysing them we can see which occupations suffer the most violent fluctuations. You should analyse them in the following way.

i Column 4 shows the percentage change in the numbers employed between 1965 and 1967.

ii The first few percentages have already been calculated.

iii Only approximate percentages need be calculated.

iv Calculate the percentage increase in the following way:

$$\frac{\text{Change in unemployed (1967–1965) totals}}{\text{Original total (1965)}} \times 100$$

For example, the percentage increase in the numbers unemployed in the food industry is calculated as follows:

$$\frac{\text{Change in numbers unemployed (16·9–10·3)}}{\text{Original total}}$$

$$= \frac{6·6}{10·3} \times 100 = 65\% \text{ app.}$$

When you have completed the table you can begin to analyse the results. (A slide rule is helpful to the economist, as such calculations often occur.) The best way of presenting this information is in the form of a horizontal bar-graph which is shown in figure 19·2. Construct such a graph for yourself in which the most affected industry is drawn as the top bar and the least affected industry at the bottom. Insert the 77% line, which represents the increase in total unemployment from 1965 to 1967.

Having drawn the graph you are now in a position to draw some important conclusions.

19·2

Are they consumer goods industries?

19·3

Are they service industries?

19·4

Are they industries which supply goods for other industries?

What do you notice about the groups which experienced a decline in employment of more than 77%?

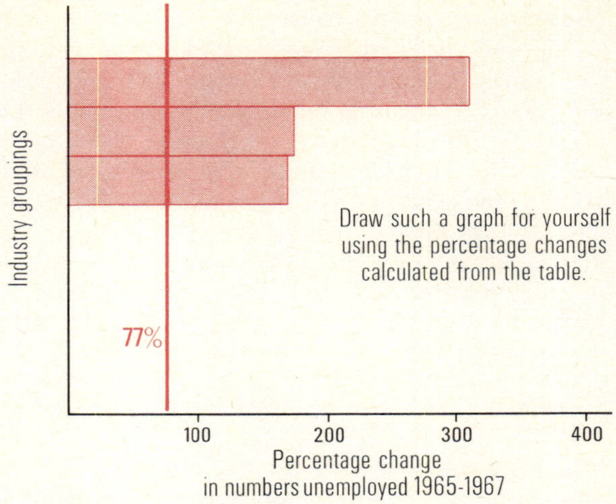

Figure 19·2

From the answers you will conclude that fluctuations in employment occur more violently in producer goods industries. Why is this? Let us take the industry of 'Metal manufacture', for example. Unemployment increased in excess of 300% between 1965 and 1967, while the average increase was only 77%. It is not difficult to see how this could have happened. Suppose the demand for vehicles, washing machines and other goods which have a high metal content had fallen by 10% in each case. The immediate reaction of entrepreneurs in these industries would be to reduce their orders of metal raw materials, presumably by 10%, but they would also need to review their orders of replacement tools and machinery, which are also made of metal. If they thought the fall in demand were to continue they would be encouraged to reduce their orders of machines by an even greater percentage. The industry which bears the brunt of these decisions is, of course, the metal manufacturing industry. The same argument applies to any industry which is supplying the needs of other industries. Thus you will have noted that vehicles, engineering and textiles all have a higher than average fluctuation in employment following a general reduction in the level of demand.

Geographical variations in in unemployment

It is in no way surprising to discover that unemployment rates vary geographically. If they vary occupationally and affected occupations tend to be localized one must inevitably suffer localized unemployment. To add to the problem, it is just those industries which suffer the greatest degree of fluctuation in employment which tend to be localized. The iron and steel industry tends to be localized near the coalfields, the motor vehicles industry is still largely concentrated in the Midlands along with engineering, while cotton textiles are manufactured largely in Lancashire.

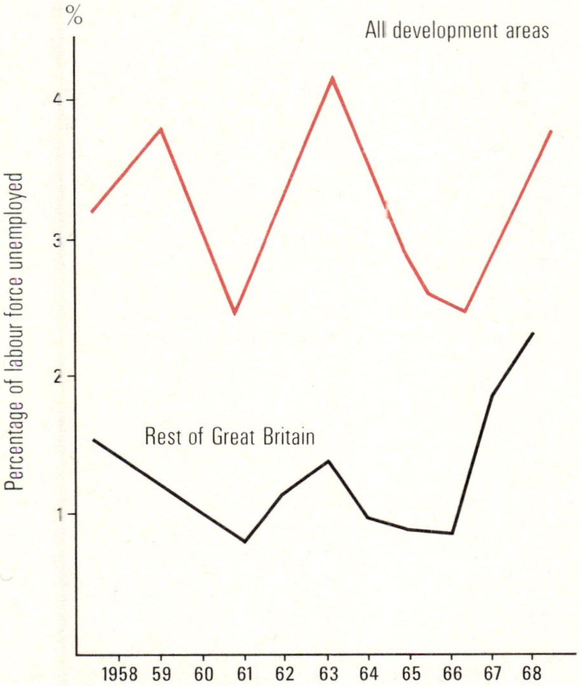

Figure 19·3

Figure 19·3 shows the regional variations in unemployment in the U.K. between 1958 and 1968.

Notice that general fluctuations in economic activity, which cause the level of unemployment to fluctuate nationally, affect the Development Areas more seriously. The Development Areas—Scotland, Northern Ireland, Wales, Northeast and Northwest—have been defined by the government as areas which need special consideration because of their higher than average level of unemployment. Recently North Cornwall was granted Development Area status along with North Devon, while Plymouth lost its claim through an increase in employment.

There is another factor which needs to be noticed from figure 19·3. Whereas the national level of unemployment fluctuated in much the same pattern as the level in the Development Areas, the level in those Areas never fell as low as the highest level in the country as a whole. This means that within the total number of unemployed in certain regions there is a permanent element which cannot be explained by factors which are general to the economy as a whole. In fact there are many different types of unemployment, and it is these which we are going to examine now.

Structural unemployment

A man might find himself thrown out of work for one of many reasons. The first reason we will examine is termed structural change. The demand for labour is derived from the demand for goods and services, and so if the demand for the goods produced by any one industry falls it follows that unemployment in that industry may follow. One of the economic facts of life in a free-enterprise economy like ours is that the wants of consumers are constantly changing. Through the price system manufacturers experience changes in the demand for their product, their total revenue and their profits. This is a sign to them to change the amount they are supplying to the market and their demand for the factors of production, notably labour. At any one time, therefore, there will be firms in some industries expanding while in other industries firms are contracting, that is, there are changes in the structure of industry. In theory the factors laid off by the contracting firms will be taken on by the expanding ones. In practice, however, there are many factors which prevent such a swift reallocation, and cause immobility of resources.

NUMBERS EMPLOYED BY INDUSTRY (thousands)

Industry	1959	1966
Agriculture, forestry and fishing	642	467
Mining and quarrying	831	576
Engineering and electrical goods	1 909	2 308
Vehicles	860	853
Textiles	841	757
Shipbuilding	267	201
Metal goods	505	593

Figure 19·4

A small selection of industries has been chosen to illustrate the point we are considering.

19·5

Which of the above industries experienced a decline in the demand for their products between 1959 and 1966? (Answer this from your general knowledge and check with the answer, as it is possible for the number of employees to fall because of increased productivity, rather than because of a fall in demand.)

19·6

Have these industries suffered a decline in the numbers employed?

19·7

Are these industries localized?

19·8

Which industries experienced an increase in numbers employed?

19·9

Would you think this was as a result of an increase in the demand for the products of these industries?

19·10

Are these growth industries located in the same areas, generally speaking, as the declining industries?

19·11

Are factors therefore likely to be immobile between industries?

We have discovered our first type of unemployment—where structure of consumer demand has changed (and it is changing constantly), and where labour is in any way immobile, the result is called *structural unemployment*.

Now refer to figure 19·4 again.

19·12

Can you find two industries which suffered a fall in the numbers employed yet experienced an increase in the demand for their products?

Factor substitution

A decline in the demand for labour, which is accompanied by an increase in the demand for the product it is engaged in producing, clearly indicates that the labour has been replaced by some other factor. Factor substitution of this kind has been continuing since the beginning of specialization. The Luddites, a group of workmen led by Ned Ludd at the beginning of the eighteenth century concentrated on smashing the machines, which they feared would replace them. Industries which were once labour intensive are now capital intensive. We have seen in earlier sections how an entrepreneur will always tend to substitute factor A for factor B when

$$\frac{\text{Marginal revenue product of A}}{\text{Price of A}} > \frac{\text{MRP of B}}{\text{Price of B}}$$

As the cost of labour increases compared with the cost of capital, which could do the same job, so the demand for labour will decline. Alternatively, as the marginal productivity of labour declines, or the marginal productivity of capital increases relative to that of the other factor, capital will be substituted for labour.

Technological unemployment

In a technological society which depends for its livelihood, in a competitive world, on the constant improvement of its methods of production, new techniques, inventions and new forms of capital equipment are an essential feature of economic life.

Thus it appears inevitable that unemployment must result from this form of technological change. In fact, however, since the beginning of the exchange economy the overall demand for labour has been constantly increasing. New techniques of production have created new products and new materials which have all enjoyed an increasing demand. For example, when the assembly-line system was introduced in the motor vehicles industry in the early part of this century it might have been thought that the demand for labour would fall. Quite the opposite, however, occurred. The reductions in cost which the new system brought about reduced prices, expanded the quantity demanded and maintained the total demand for labour in that industry. Furthermore with the growth in the demand for capital equipment in the motor industry there followed an expansion of the engineering industry which necessarily expanded the demand for labour even further. Cheaper vehicles meant cheaper transport costs and thus cheaper priced goods. There was an expansion in the demand for all goods and services and a further growth in the demand for labour.

We have seen, then, how the general level of unemployment is, in the long term, not necessarily reduced by technological changes. Individual industries, however, must be affected where technical improvements lead to the substitution of capital for labour. Vehicles and agriculture have both experienced a declining demand for labour, obviously a result of factor substitution. Our farms are more capital intensive, and a glimpse in any car factory will show the advanced, computerized assembly lines which require less labour. We hope, of course, that the workers laid off one job will be required on another. Immobility has to be reckoned with, however, this time across the occupation barriers. If labour is occupationally immobile then *technological unemployment* is likely to result. This is the second type of unemployment and is due to a change in techniques, whereas structural unemployment is caused by a change in the structure of industry in response, for example, to a change in demand from coal to oil.

Localized unemployment

Where structural unemployment occurs in a localized industry a particular area will suffer more than other areas. Again where technological unemployment occurs in a localized industry the same consequences can be expected. The difference here is that whereas technological unemployment may only be relatively short-term, dependent upon the time it takes to retrain redundant workers, structural unemployment arising from a change in demand is a long-term phenomenon.

Changes in demand are in many cases permanent. This is particularly the case with industries producing goods for export. If the demand for British exports is price elastic, then if one of our export industries were to suffer an increase in costs resulting in an increase in price of, say 5%, the quantity demanded abroad may be reduced by as much as 15%. An export market lost once to a foreign competitor may be lost for good. If we take the British shipbuilding industry, for example, we can see a situation of increases in cost, lost markets overseas, a localized industry and therefore localized unemployment. Even where a change in the demand for an export commodity is not permanent, export industries tend to be generally more prone to fluctuations in demand.

Short-term unemployment

Any employment exchange, at any one time, is likely to have on its register of unemployment a group of people whom it can reasonably expect to place in employment within a short period. It is these workers we shall look at now.

i Seasonal unemployment. Any one who lives in a seaside resort knows how the demand for labour fluctuates during the year. Hotels, restaurants and other services all require large amounts of labour during the summer season with consequent unemployment during the winter. In many industries, where the demand for the goods or services fluctuates seasonally, the same problem of seasonal unemployment exists. Alternatively, where the vagaries of the weather prevent production, the same problem occurs. The construction industry is always particularly badly hit by a hard winter.

ii Casual unemployment. Many jobs carry with them the unenviable feature of irregular lay-offs for the workers engaged. Road-building contractors usually hire men for the duration of the particular contract. When the work is finished the men are paid off, although some may be rehired immediately for the next job. However, the remainder will find themselves unemployed. Actors are in a similar position, and film extras work from day to day.

Any worker who is employed on a day-to-day basis is a casual worker. Usually they are employed as labourers in jobs which are likely to suffer irregular changes in demand. When they are unemployed they form a definable group—casual unemployment.

iii Strike lay-offs. The next category in this section of short-term unemployed arises from the wide-ranging consequences of a strike. Where those employed in manufacturing of, say, glass for the windscreens of cars, are involved in strike action they are likely to create unemployment in motor-assembly firms and the firms which supply them. The more specialized an industry's firms become the more one firm becomes dependent on others. A strike by a dozen workers in a factory making carburettor needle valves could result in thousands of car-industry workers being laid off for a short time.

iv Frictional unemployment. This is simply people out of work whilst in the process of changing their jobs. Getting another position may take a week or so, even with forewarning.

Long-term unemployment

Inevitably on the register of unemployed at the local employment exchange there will also be a group who are unlikely to be placed easily or quickly for reasons of personality or ability.

i The unemployable. Anyone who is unable to obtain work under normal conditions through being physically disabled or mentally unable to face the work situation falls into this group.

ii Voluntary unemployment. Inevitably there will always be some people within a Welfare State who find that the income derived from being unemployed together with increased leisure yields a greater benefit than that gained by working. In order to claim unemployment benefit a man must present himself at the employment exchange twice a week as fit and ready to work in any job available. Otherwise he must present a medical certificate to the local office of the Department of Health and Social Security in order to be entitled to Social Security benefit. Fortunately for society, numbers within this group are very small indeed. There are very few people who would choose to be unemployed.

Cyclical unemployment

In 1944 Lord Beveridge published *Full Employment in a Free Society*. It represented the first comprehensive survey of different types of unemployment and helped to reshape the thinking of post-war governments in their attitude to the unemployment problem. In his book Beveridge examined fluctuations in economic activity throughout the nineteenth century in this country. The regularity with which high economic activity, full employment and rising wages gave way to a slackening off of production and the inevitable unemployment was staggering. Boom was followed by slump with disastrous regularity. The average length of time between the peak of each boom was about eight years. It is this cycle of activity which has come to be known as the *trade cycle*. The unemployment that resulted from this situation is known as *cyclical unemployment*.

Before we examine the causes of the trade cycle we will trace the different phases that have been distinguished.

Boom

The boom phase is a period in which there is full employment and industry is working to full capacity. Usually it is accompanied by rising wages and rising prices, caused by the increasing shortage of labour and certain key raw materials. Economic activity is very profitable and entrepreneurs feel optimistic about the future prospects of investment. Investment is therefore high and the demand for funds pushes up interest rates. Sooner or later the boom ends. The upper turning point has been reached and a recession has set in.

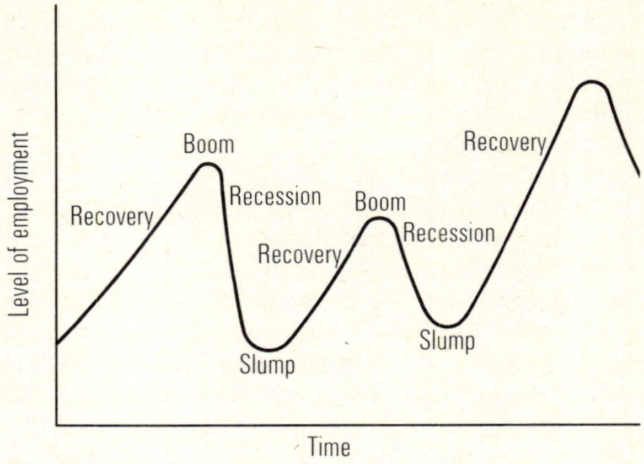

Figure 19·5

Recession

Once the recession has begun it inevitably gathers momentum. Consumption falls off, thus reducing the profits of businesses. These firms have borrowed money at high rates of interest in anticipation of high returns, but they now find that they are experiencing losses. Further investment is discouraged. Unemployment rises, the excess supply of labour tends to force down wage rates and prices fail to rise and may in fact fall in some cases. When prospects are at their bleakest we have reached the slump.

Slump

The slump is a phase which is categorized by heavy unemployment, unused capacity in industry, low profits or losses, very low expectations of future profit, no desire to invest, falling prices and surplus funds available for lending. When the lower turning point is reached a recovery has begun.

Recovery

Recovery can happen quite quickly. As soon as consumption, wages, employment and prices start to rise the prospects of future profits look more hopeful. Firms find it easy to expand supply by calling into production unused resources.

This pattern was repeated time and again throughout the nineteenth century. Since the Second World War, however, we have managed to avoid a major slump. The methods we have used to combat the onset of a slump all stem from the adoption of 'Keynesian' policies, which we shall refer to again now.

The problem of the turning points

To prevent the trade cycle from taking its full course it is necessary to know what factors are responsible for the upper and lower turning points. If the government wishes to follow a full-employment policy then it must prevent the onset of a recession. What is it then that ends the boom? Several theories have been put forward to explain the phenomenon, and we will look briefly at some of these.

One theory concentrates on the length of time capital takes to wear out. If, for example, all capital employed in industry had a life of ten years, then on average each year one-tenth would be replaced. If, then, something were to occur, such as a war, which increased the demand for capital goods for a limited period, industry would be left with spare capacity. Much of the capital in use would be new and therefore would not need replacing. The demand for capital would therefore fall dramatically until the new capital needed replacing, when demand for capital goods would be restored to its former level.

Other theories have tried to explain the trade cycle in terms of fluctuations in agricultural output. It was believed at one time that as harvests fluctuated from good to bad, so the economy was bound to be affected through the effects on prices and wages and the supply of goods.

Another theory tried to explain the phenomenon of fluctuations in business activity in terms of the time lags experienced in some industries between an increase in demand and the resultant increase in quantity supplied. Agriculture was taken as a case in point. Here, if the demand for a crop were to rise, thus forcing up the price and the returns to farmers, so more land would be put under that particular crop. The following year an excess supply would be likely to appear on the market due to the fact that perfect competition existed in agriculture. The excess supply would force down the market price and thus the returns to farmers. Thus very little land would be put under that crop the following year and a gross shortage would be experienced the year after that. Each year the fluctuations would be likely to get greater owing to the time lag between a fluctuation in market price and the time when goods would come on to the market in response to this.

It was inevitable that such a puzzling phenomenon as the trade cycle should promote so many theories concerned with its origins. Beyond those we have mentioned, there have been theories put forward in terms of the supply of money, the rate of interest, the level of consumption and the level of production. Most of the theories put forward, however, have one thing in common. They all recognize the part played by investment in the trade cycle. Investment plays a key part and therefore if one is to fully understand the trade cycle one must turn to the determinants of investment and the factors which are likely to cause it to fluctuate.

The key role of investment

A potential investor has two considerations. 'What is the investment going to cost?' and 'What is it going to yield in return?' Most funds for investment purposes are borrowed. The cost of this is the current market rate of interest. Even if the funds are already held by the investor then he incurs an opportunity cost. This is equal to the interest he could have earned with his funds if he had lent them to some other investor. The yield on the investment is the profits earned during the life of the asset. But how can one know what an asset is going to be earning in, say, six years time? How can one judge?

Let us take the example of a shipping company which is considering investing in a new passenger vessel. The liner is estimated to cost a total of £40 million pounds which will have to be borrowed at the current rate of interest. If it can carry, say, 2 000 passengers to the U.S.A. every ten days at a cost of £100 each then the revenue from one trip will be £200 000. Suppose the cost of a trip is £100 000, leaving a gross profit of £100 000. This represents a profit of £10 000 for every day the ship is in service. Over a year, if the ship is working for 300 days, £3 million profit is earned. This is a gross return of $7\frac{1}{2}\%$ on the initial outlay of £40 million. If the original outlay had to be borrowed at an interest of 8% obviously the investment is not going to be worth while. But there are so many other factors to worry about. Will the costs of running the ship remain constant over the life of the vessel? Will the price of other forms of substitute transport remain constant? What assumptions can be made concerning the demand for places on the ship? These and many other problems must be resolved before the investment will take place. Business decisions of this sort can only be based on careful estimates. The basis for these estimates can only be the trends that can be seen at present taking place. If, say, the demand for places on board passenger liners is increasing and has been increasing for the past ten years then it is not unreasonable to feel optimistic about the future. But what if the trend over nine years was upward yet in the year immediately preceeding this one demand fell? It only needs one bad year to upset forecasts. This is the nature of investment. A recent increase in the cost of fuel, harbour fees or wages, or a recent fall in the price of air travel, might prevent the investment from taking place. What matters is not what the investment will earn but what the investor *expects* it to earn.

If this example is expanded on to a national scale you can see how if demand generally throughout the economy is seen to fall or increase more slowly investors might all feel pessimistic. Acting as one they could easily create the conditions favourable to a recession. What we need to explain now is why, once it has begun, the recession gathers momentum and hastens the slump.

Cumulative effects

i During the recovery phase employment, income, wages, prices and profits are all rising. All this is encouraging to investors. More investment takes place, and since this represents an injection into the circular flow of income, income increases still further. When investors act together in increasing investment they are in fact creating the climate in which they can expect future profits to increase. The recovery, once started, gathers pace under its own momentum. It feeds on itself. If enough people think that the future for profits is good then it will be good.

The same happens in reverse during a recession. As profits fall so the expectation of future profit declines. Investment will be reduced and this in itself will create a fall in income and therefore in total expenditure. Investment is thereby further discouraged. Thus the expectations of investors explain, in part, the cumulative nature of the recovery and recession phases of the trade cycle. But there are other factors to be taken into account.

ii The investment multiplier, which you examined in S16, expresses the relationship between increases in investment and the resultant increases in income. A £100 million increase in investment will bring about a £300 million increase in income if the size of the multiplier is 3. Thus whether we are in the recovery or recession phases of the cycle the changes in investment will result in a multiplied effect on income. This will increase the cumulative effect.

iii Another factor is the effect that rising prices have on the real value of debts. During a recovery, for example, as the economy reaches full employment, prices will rise. This reduction in the value of money penalizes lenders but benefits borrowers. £100 borrowed at 5% involves an annual payment of £5 interest. If prices were to rise during that year by ten per cent then the borrower would only be repaying £90 in real terms. Furthermore, the £5 interest, in real terms, only represents £4·5 owing to the reduction in the purchasing power of the money. Investors who borrow funds during a recovery know therefore that the real rate on interest is less than the market rate that they are being asked to pay. This acts as a further incentive to investors and increases the cumulative nature of the trade cycle.

iv The fourth factor to be considered is a phenomenon called the *accelerator*. This must be explained in some detail.

The accelerator

You have seen how the investment multiplier expresses the effect of changes in investment on the resultant change in the level of income. The accelerator expresses the relationship between a change in the level of income and the resultant level of investment. Thus we have interdependent relationships, in which income and investment feed on each other. We must explain how this happens.

In a closed economy the level of national income is equal to the level of national expenditure in the form of consumption, investment and government spending. $Y = C+I+G$. If the level of national income remains constant, then each year part of the capital which has produced the gross national product will need replacing. This is the only investment that will take place. As soon as income rises, however, new capital will be needed to satisfy the increased demand for goods and services. The impact of an increase in income on investment can be quite startling, hence the term 'accelerator'.

Suppose we return to our previous example of the shipping company. Imagine that the liner is working at full capacity. What will happen if the demand for places on the liner increases by 50%? The company will need a new vessel at a cost of £40 million. An increase in consumer expenditure (a part of national income) of £3 million per year has resulted in an increase in investment of £40 million. The shipping company is, of course, banking on the fact that the ship has a life of thirty or forty years and in that time will more than recover the original investment. Thus a £10 000 machine with a life of ten years may only be capable of producing an output of £2 000 per year. If expenditure/income increases by £2 000, investment must increase by £10 000. The accelerator in this instance is 5.

The value of the accelerator can be calculated from the following formula:

$$I_n = a\delta Y$$

where I_n is the new investment
a is the accelerator
δY is the change in the level of income

19·13

If the level of income increases by £1 000 million and the value of the accelerator is known to be 1·5, what will be the level of new investment?

This accelerator is the fourth factor we have examined which has its effect on the cumulative nature of the recovery and recession phases of the trade cycle. We have not yet explained, however, why a boom should end or a slump turn into a recovery.

The turning points

There must come a time during the boom phase when all the existing resources for production are fully employed. After this point the only way in which real income can be increased is through an increase in output per unit of resources employed. Thus the rapid expansion of income is naturally checked as full employment is reached or approached. We say that the ceiling has been reached. But why must a recession follow?

As full employment is approached so the increases in income, which come about through successive increments in investment, will get progressively smaller. This is because the marginal propensity to save rises as income increases. This means that the size of the multiplier will be getting smaller, and therefore each increase in investment will affect income in a reduced way. Now consider the effects of the accelerator. As the increases in income get smaller so the effect on the level of investment will become adverse. An example will help to explain this point.

Suppose the accelerator is constant at 2. Figure 19·6 shows the effect of changes in the level of income and the effects on investment resulting from these income changes.

Year	Level of income	Change in level of income	New investment (from accelerator only)
1	100		
2	200	100	200
3	300	100	200
4	400	100	200
5	480	80	160
6	540	60	120
7	580	40	80
8	600	20	40
9	610	10	20
10	610	0	0

Figure 19·6

Suppose equilibrium demand for consumer product x is 1 million units per annum, that 1 machine makes 1 000 units, that each machine lasts 10 years. The equilibrium capital replacement is 100 machines per annum. If in 1970 demand for x rises 10%, i.e. by 100 000, its manufacturers place orders for 100 new machines. To meet this the capital goods industry must double its capacity. In 1971 the capital goods industry may be back to the 100 replacement demand: unless consumer demand increases by *another* 100 000, the capital goods industry must work to less than capacity: it lays off men, dividends go down and recession is on the way.

How then can a slump turn into a recovery?

During the slump investment is falling, which leads to greater falls in income through the multiplier process. As income falls so the level of savings will also fall.

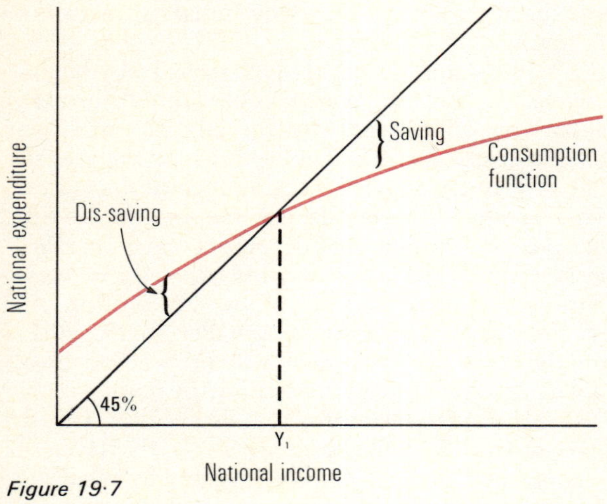

Figure 19·7

Once savings have fallen to nil income can fall no more since dis-saving will take place. This will in turn increase the level of income. In figure 19·7 dis-saving takes place once income falls below Y_1 and this forces income back up to the equilibrium level of Y_1.

We can see, therefore, how income can never fall to zero. Once it has fallen to its minimum level, the output of goods can be produced by the capital available without any need to replace machines that wear out. This is because industry is working with excess capacity and has capital to spare. Eventually, however, there must come a time when some machines will need replacing. As soon as this happens the new investment undertaken will, through the investment multiplier process, create extra increases in income. The recovery is at last under way. Once begun it will feed upon itself as we have seen already.

We have seen how the turning points are arrived at. The inevitability of the trade cycle is apparent, but it is important to realize that we have been considering a free economy in which the government plays no active part in influencing the course of economic events. From 1946 to 1971 this country has experienced no slump and it is the role which the government has played which has been responsible for this.

How have slumps been avoided since the war?

The answer to this question is now within your scope to discover. In S17 you saw how the government can determine the level of aggregate income through its influence on consumption, investment and government spending (C+I+G). In this section you have learned how the level of employment is determined by the level of aggregate expenditure. Thus the government has it in its power to determine the level of employment.

The mass unemployment experienced in this country and many others during the 'depression' or 'slump' of the late 1920s and early thirties was the result of a chronic deficiency of aggregate demand. To make matters worse countries reduced government spending (even cutting civil servants' pay), and went in for restrictionist policies in respect of their international trade. Aggregate monetary demand was thus reduced in more ways than one. Policies were followed which aggravated a situation in which unemployment was about 22%. The recovery in the U.K. was encouraged by a scheme of public works in favour of the construction industry, popularly called the 'building boom'. This programme, combined with the onset of rearmament in the late 1930s, stimulated the recovery of the economy.

Since the Second World War one of the declared aims of government policy has been full employment. This has been attempted through policies called 'demand management'. Through adjustment of taxation, changes in the rate of interest, and altering levels of government spending, aggregate monetary demand has been kept at a level thought to be sufficient to maintain full employment.

Has the trade cycle been abolished?

The answer to this question is very complicated. There have been small cyclical fluctuations since 1945. Governments have attempted to intervene as soon as a recession appeared probable. However, the difficulty of predicting economic trends has sometimes led to governments taking too vigourous action, and this has sometimes intensified fluctuations. In any case the period since 1945 has been one of great technological change, causing unemployment from time to time. It would therefore be wrong to assume that a depression could not occur in the future, and that the trade cycle can be controlled by governments, and by the controls of aggregate demand only.

19·14

Examine the statistics of employment, annual increase in wages and prices can be seen. Plot these statistics on a graph using the axes as shown in figure 19·9. When you have done this, group years together into those of 'recession', 'recovery' and 'boom'.

Year	Unemployment (thousands)	Annual percentage weekly wage rates	Increase in retail prices
1958	457	2	2·8
1959	475	2·5	0
1960	360	2·8	0·8
1961	341	5	3
1962	463	3·6	2·8
1963	573	7	1·8
1964	381	5	2
1965	329	5	4
1966	360	6	3·5
1967	560	2	2·6
1968	564	12	5
1969	580	9	6·5

Figure 19·8

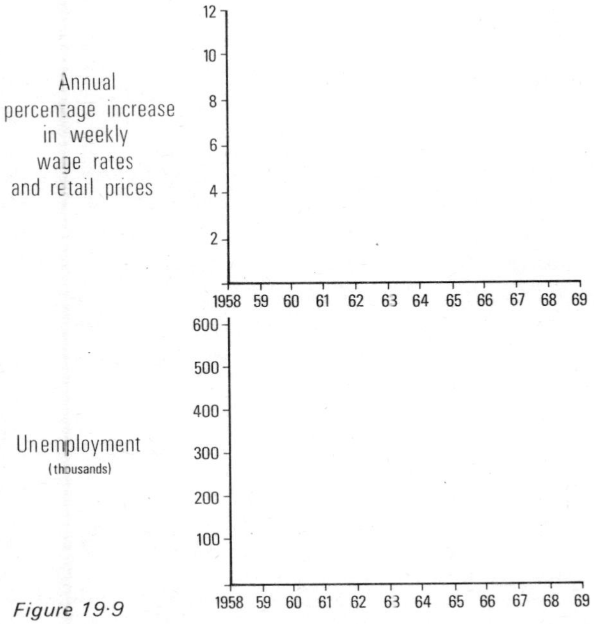

Figure 19·9

19·15

	Recovery	Boom	Recession
1959			
1960			
1961			
1962			
1963			
1964			
1965			
1966			
1967			
1968			

Why has the boom not been maintained?

We know how a recession comes about. As full employment is approached so the increases in income become smaller. Through the accelerator this brings about a decline in new investment, thus turning a boom into a recession. The government in its role as manager of the economy attempts to step in and avoid the decline in investment. It has done this by attempting to influence aggregate demand through monetary and fiscal measures, and by stimulating investment directly in the public sector and indirectly in the private sector. The problem has been to know how much influence to exert and when to exert it. How do you tell when a recession is about to set in? Do you keep a close watch on the level of investment, on wage rates, on prices or profits? Of course you must do all of these things. But with the best will in the world you cannot accurately predict the onset of a recession until it is actually happening. With the best statistical techniques available the data take time to collect, and by the time it has been analysed it may be too late to affect the trend that is then in progress. Generally speaking the actions of successive governments in the post-war period have been 'too great, too late'. In other words action has been taken after the event rather than in anticipation of it.

Let us take a practical example to simplify the argument. Suppose the economy is in a boom phase with all the characteristics of such a phase. In June, say, of the year under consideration, investment is seen to have declined below the monthly average in April. Does this mean that a recession is about to set in (or has set in)? We look at the long-term trend in investment and find that it is increasing but at a declining rate. Predictions based on this present knowledge indicate that if nothing is done to stimulate the level of investment then a recession is likely to set in shortly. What action should be taken? What is the cause of the declining rate of investment? Is it the accelerator at work? Are increases in income proceeding at a slower rate? Suppose they are. Should steps be taken to increase income through measures designed to increase aggregate monetary demand? Do we have the resources available to supply the increased money demand with real goods?

19·16

What would happen if aggregate monetary demand were to be increased when resources were fully employed?

A A recession **B** A fall in investment

C Inflation **D** A fall in wage rates

The only solution to our problem, if we are fully employed, is to attempt to maintain the level of investment without creating excessive aggregate monetary demand, which in a fully employed economy will probably lead to an increase in the price level. Increases in money income must be linked with increases in output per unit of resources employed. If we fail to achieve this the result will be an excess demand which will pull up the price level, and then because of the fact that our exports become too expensive steps will have to be taken to reduce AMD.

This has in fact been the pattern of the British economy since 1945. The movements that you plotted from the figures in figure 19·8 are the result of policies designed to stimulate and then to restrict annual increases in AMD. It has been impossible to predict the exact effects of a specific measure or package of measures taken at any one time. To know the effect of, say, increased public investment on the level of national income we must know the size of the multiplier. This will be based on an estimate of the marginal propensity to consume. Then we must estimate how long the multiplier effects take to work through the system. Then we have to face the fact that other things may not 'remain equal' and there may be other forces at work besides the ones which the government has deliberately created. There is therefore bound to be a large margin of error in any prediction of the effects of measures taken to influence the level of investment, expenditure or income. You may take one set of measures and think they are not working because visible signs are slow to show themselves. Thus you may take more measures to strengthen the first ones. If the first ones *were* working, however, you may have precipitated a recession, or you may have stimulated a boom beyond where resources are fully employed, thus creating an inflationary situation.

Gone then are the days when the Budget was the chief instrument for influencing the economy. Nowadays, as you will see in later sections, constant adjustments are made to the variables we have been discussing. We recognize that the trade cycle is at work and that we must try to dampen the oscillations which would take place in a freely working economy. The following paragraphs show, in model form what can happen in a free economy with no government intervention. If you find that you are unable to follow the mathematical symbols then pass on to the verbal description which follows.

A model of cyclical fluctuations

We start with the proposition that

i $$Y = C+I+G$$

(Income = Consumption + Investment + Govt. spending)

ii $$Y_t = C_t+I_t+G_t$$

where 't' is the present time period.

But:

$$C_t = mY_{t-1}$$

where Y_{t-1} is the income of the previous year. Consumption in this year depends on the income of the previous year, where 'm' is the average propensity to consume.

So:

iii $$Y_t = mY_{t-1}+I_t+G_t$$

substituting mY_{t-1} for C_t in **ii**

Now:

$$I_t = a(C_t-C_{t-1})$$

where 'a' is the accelerator and C_t-C_{t-1} is the increase in consumption.

Investment in the present period depends on the increase in consumption, and the accelerator.

Thus we can rewrite the original equation as

follows by substituting for C_t and I_t:

iv $$Y_t = mY_{t-1} + a(C_t - C_{t-1}) + G_t$$

Substituting again for C_t we get

v $$Y_t = mY_{t-1} + a(mY_{t-1} - mY_{t-2}) + G_t$$

where Y_{t-2} is the income of two time periods ago. Which is the same as

vi $$Y_t = (1+a)mY_{t-1} - maY_{t-2} + G_t$$

We shall now show how the level of income in the present period Y_t depends upon income in previous years, the propensity to consume and the relationship between a change in consumption and the resultant change in investment.

Suppose

$$G_t = 1;\ m = 0{\cdot}5;\ a = 1$$

Substituting these values in (6) above

$$Y_t = (1+1)0{\cdot}5Y_{t-1} - 0{\cdot}5 \times 1(Y_{t-2}) + G_t$$

or $$Y_t = Y_{t-1} - 0{\cdot}5Y_{t-2} - G_t$$

From this equation we can now see what will happen to the level of income over a period of time.

Period	Y_{t-1}	$-0{\cdot}5Y_{t-2}$	$+G_t$	$= Y_t$
1	0	−0	+1	= 1
2	1	−0	+1	= 2
3	2	−0·5	+1	= 2·5
4	2·5	−1	+1	= 2·5
5	2·5	−1·25	+1	= 2·25

Figure 19·10

Notice how the level of income has risen and then fallen. Government expenditure has remained constant, so has the propensity to consume and the relationship between the change in the level of consumption and the resultant level of investment. We have thus built up a mathematical model of the cyclical fluctuations within an economy.

Complete the table for yourself, taking into consideration the next five time periods.

19·17

Is income in period 6 rising or falling?

19·18

Is income in period 9 rising or falling?

Now let us see what happens if we alter the relationship between changes in consumption and the resultant level of investment. Suppose that a change in consumption now brings about a greater change in investment such that the change in I is twice that of the change in C. Thus a = 2. The original equation was

$$Y_t = (1+a)mY_{t-1} - maY_{t-2} + G_t$$

With the old value of m = 0·5, G = 1 and the new value of a = 2 this becomes

$$Y_t = 1{\cdot}5Y_{t-1} - 1Y_{t-2} + G_t$$

We can thus construct a new table with the new value of 'a' from the above equation:

Period	$1{\cdot}5Y_{t-1}$	$- Y_{t-2}$	$+G_t$	$= Y_t$
1	0	−0	+1	= 1
2	1·5	−0	+1	= 2·5
3	3·75	−1	+1	= 3·75
4	5·625	−2·5	+1	= 4·125
5	6·19	−3·75	+1	= 3·44
6	5 16	−4·125	+1	= 2·03

Figure 19·11

Complete the table, taking into account the next four time periods.

Notice how the cyclical fluctuations are in this model greater than in the previous one.

19·19

If the value of 'a' were, say, 4, would you expect the fluctuations to be greater still?

Construct a table to show the effect on Y_t if the value of a = 4, m stays at 0·5 and G stays at 1.

You now have three tables showing the effects upon income of different values of a, the relationship between changes in consumption and the resultant changes in investment.

19·20

Construct three graphs on the same pair of axes showing the fluctuations in the level of income Y_t over different time periods. Graph 1 will plot values of Y_t from the first table we drew where the value of a = 1, graph 2 the values of Y_t when a = 2, and graph 3 when a = 4.

We have shown how the cyclical fluctuations in the economy will depend for their intensity upon the value of the accelerator, which is the relationship between changes in the level of consumption and changes in the level of investment. You can see also from the equations we formed that if the marginal propensity to consume and therefore the multiplier alters again this will bring about changes in the intensity of the cyclical fluctuations. If we knew the values of the multiplier and the accelerator we could thus predict the pattern of income over future time periods. Economists have been engaged in attempting to do this, but the task of calculating these values is exceptionally difficult and little credence can be given to predictions at present.

We have been studying the interaction of the accelerator and the multiplier in this section because of its relevance to the effects on the level of employment with which we are mainly concerned here. The level of unemployment will fluctuate with the level of income, that is expenditure. In order to maintain full employment, the government must anticipate the cycle and take steps to maintain the level of aggregate expenditure when they anticipate it is likely to fall. These policies will be investigated in a later section in more detail.

Now we must turn from the problem of cyclical unemployment to a consideration of the problem of the other forms of unemployment which we have been considering. We have examined regional, structural, technological, localized, short-term and long-term unemployment. We have seen how the problem of cyclical unemployment can be tackled. We will now look at the solutions to the remaining forms of unemployment.

Redeployment

Most unemployment other than cyclical arises from the fact that either capital or labour is immobile. Perhaps labour is occupationally immobile even though capital is geographically mobile. Perhaps the reverse may occur. The fact is that if capital and labour were completely mobile (both geographically and occupationally) few problems of unemployment would arise in the long term. As old industries declined and were replaced by growing industries capital and labour would be reallocated with a minimum of disturbance.

Let us examine the measures which can be taken to increase the mobility of capital and labour.

i More national resources can be allocated to areas of high unemployment. In the recent past priority has been given to the Development Areas in an effort to plan the future location of industry. Cash grants have been offered to firms in respect of their land and plant costs incurred in setting up in Development Areas. These come under the system of Investment Grants. Industrial Estates have been built by local authorities with the assistance of the central government to provide firms with the local facilities they need. Advance factories have been built for prospective firms to rent or buy, and in some cases rent-free terms are arranged for the first few years of a firm's settling-in period. Road communications to these estates have been improved. Setting up away from the Development Areas has been strictly controlled by the issuing of Industrial Development Certificates. Every firm which has to set up a premises of any size must obtain this licence to build. It will be withheld if in the opinion of the Board of Trade it is against the public interest.

19·21

Are these policies designed to increase the mobility of labour or capital?

---

ii Government training centres have been set up throughout the country in an effort to ease the transition from one job to another. Training grants are payable to firms that are prepared to retrain workers from other industries.

iii Redundancy payments are now payable to people whose jobs cease to exist. They are related to a man's wage and the length of time he has spent with a particular firm.

19·22

Is measure (iii) designed to improve the mobility of labour geographically or occupationally?

---

iv The employment exchanges operated by the Department of Employment and Productivity have widened the scope of their responsibilities. Whereas they were at one time only concerned with one locality and, generally speaking, manual labour, they now take a wider view of the situation in increasing the scope of their register of jobs and co-operating with employment exchanges in other areas.

v Declining industries may be offered the protection of a tariff on competing imported goods. This allows the industry to contract slowly, while incurring high costs, and therefore contracting its labour force more slowly. 'Natural shrinkage' is achieved when those who reach retirement age are replaced by fewer entrants to the industry.

vi A regional employment premium has been payable to firms in Development Areas. This has operated within the framework of the Selective Employment Tax. S.E.T. can be payable by all firms, refunded to manufacturing firms, but for firms in Development Areas not only can the tax be repayed but a premium per man employed may also be added.

vii The development of a regional approach to economic planning in this country through Regional Economic Planning Councils has given more voice to those areas with special needs. The planning of new industry, ports, roads, towns, etc., is now carried on with special reference to the problems of localized, regional and other short-term forms of unemployment.

Full employment

One of the main aims of government is the maintenance of full employment. Why, you may ask, is it therefore prepared to tolerate a situation in which over 600 000 men may suffer from enforced unemployment? The answer to this question is that the existence of full employment creates pressures within the economy which act adversely upon other aims of government, such as the maintenance of stable prices and the earning of a surplus on the balance of payments. Aims can and do conflict. A choice therefore has to be made between the achievement of one or another aim. Perhaps a level of unemployment, despite our abhorrence of the thought, is necessary in order to achieve the other aims. This decision is beyond our scope at the moment and we must wait for a later section before seeing how this conflict of aims can be resolved.

ANSWERS TO S19

19·1
Do *not* include **A, B, C, D, G, H, K.**

19·2
No.

19·3
No.

19·4
Yes.

19·5
Mining and quarrying, textiles, and shipbuilding.

19·6
Yes.

19·7
Yes.

19·8
Metal goods and engineering and electrical goods.

19·9
Yes.

19·10
No.

19·11
Yes.

19·12
Vehicles and agriculture.

19·13
£1 500 million.

19·14
See p.282.

19·15

	Recovery	Boom	Recession
1959			√
1960	√		
1961		√	
1962			√
1963			√
1964	√		
1965		√	
1966			√
1967			√
1968			√

19·16
C, inflation.

19:14

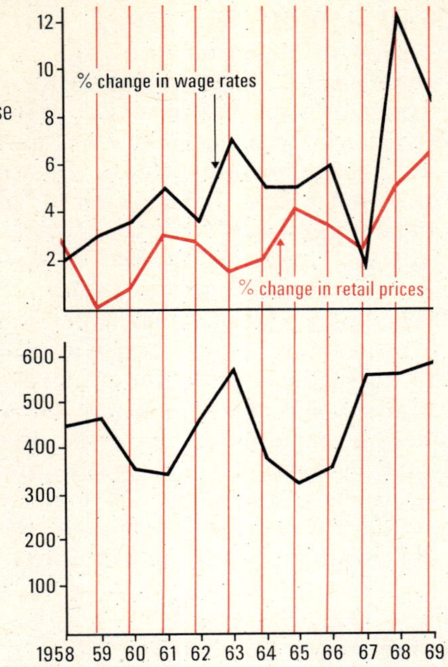

Figure 19·12

19·17
Falling.

19·18
Rising.

19·19
Yes.

19·20

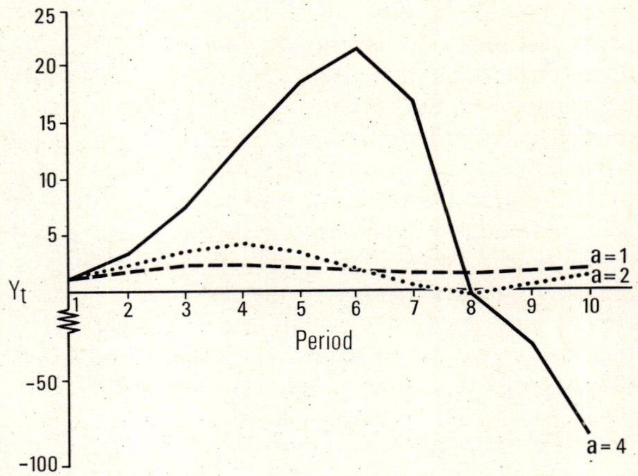

Figure 19·13

19·21
Capital.

19·22
Both.

FOREIGN EXCHANGE

STUDY SECTION **20**

We saw in the last section how the government assumes responsibility for maintaining a high level of employment in the economy. It does this by attempting to ensure that the level of aggregate monetary demand is sufficiently high to call into production all of the nation's resources. We saw, also, the cycle of business activity that is constantly at work causing fluctuations in the levels of investment and employment and in the annual increases in gross national product (G.N.P.), prices, profits and real incomes.

In this section we shall see how this internal economic activity within the U.K. affects the external position of the country with regard to its balance of payments and the value of the £ sterling. For example, government measures designed to prevent a recession might, through the multiplier and accelerator effects, lead to such great increases in aggregate monetary demand that our home resources could not meet the demand. The natural inclination of consumers and firms who cannot get the goods they want supplied by British firms is to turn to those supplied by foreign firms. Thus imports increase. Again, if the level of retail prices in the U.K. rises more quickly than those of other countries with whom we are in international competition, we in the U.K. tend to buy more foreign and fewer home-produced goods. Foreigners will tend to buy less of our goods and more goods from other countries. Not only are our imports adversely affected then, but our exports also tend to decrease. It is this relationship between internal causes and external consequences that we shall now examine in some detail.

Importing and exporting

In S7 and S13 we considered simple models of international trade. Only in the cases of centrally directed economies, where all importing and exporting is done by government agencies, do such models come near the truth. In most cases, the pattern of international trade is the sum of many thousands of individual decisions by private persons and firms, and nearly all countries have trading relations with each other, even if only indirectly.

The main problems in considering international trade arise through the fact that different countries use different currencies. If you buy a Japanese camera you expect to pay for it in pounds while the firm that manufactured it in Japan expects to earn yen to pay for the factors of production that were employed in its manufacture. Somewhere along the line, therefore, pounds must be exchanged for yen. Figure 20·1 explains the process.

In figure 20·1 you will notice that the British bank buys the foreign currency by selling pounds. But who will want to buy pounds? Well, it might be that a Japanese citizen has bought a British article for £15 and the Japanese importer will need to buy pounds and sell yen. The demand and supply for different currencies is thus determined by the activities of individuals firms and governments in different countries.

The problems most commonly encountered by students are answered below.

Q. What happens to the earnings of foreign currency made by British firms?

A. They are held by British banks, in particular the Bank of England, and form part of the nation's reserves of foreign currency.

Q. What happens if the total earnings of U.K. firms abroad are less than the amount spent by people and firms in this country on goods from abroad?

A. British banks will have been selling more pounds to get foreign currency than foreign banks will have wanted to buy for their own importers.

Q. Who, then, will have bought the extra pounds?

A. The Bank of England will have bought them and sold its reserves of foreign currency that it had built up in previous years.

Q. But suppose so little has been earned abroad in previous years by U.K. firms that we have no reserves of foreign currency?

A. In this case the Bank of England will seek to borrow from other central banks on behalf of the British banking system.

Q. Could not British firms and banks simply sell sterling on the foreign exchange markets in return for foreign currency?

A. Yes, they could, but since few people would desire or need sterling to buy U.K. exports the tendency would be that the price of sterling would fall.

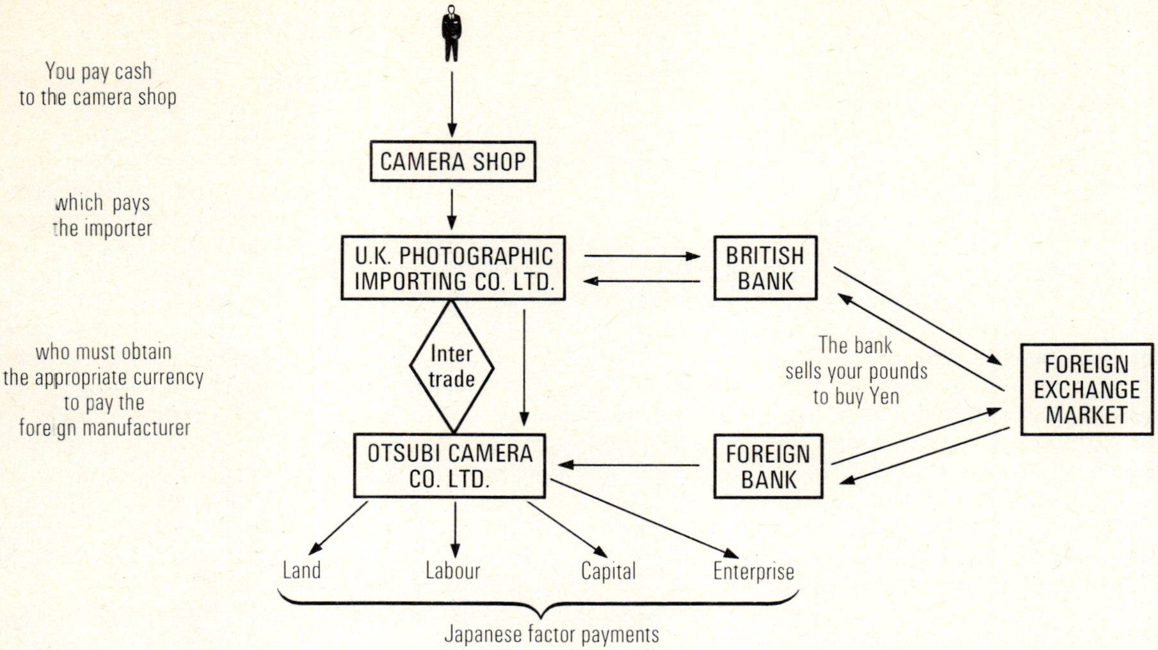

Figure 20·1

Q. Why should this be a problem to us?

A. The fact that the Bank of England operates what is called a Fixed Exchange Rate system, under which it guarantees to fix the value of sterling in respect of other currencies, means that we cannot lower the price of sterling without officially devaluing sterling. If we do this we now have to export more U.K. goods to buy the same amount of foreign goods. If we increase our exports there will be fewer resources available for the production of resources for the home market.

Q. So there is really no alternative to paying our way internationally?

A. No. The U.K. as a whole must earn enough foreign currency through the exports of its firms, to provide importers with the currency they need.

You can see from the above conclusions that it is vital for a country, in the long run, to earn enough foreign currency through its exporting to pay for its imports. It is to the balance of payments that we must look therefore to see how the U.K. in particular has been faring.

The U.K. balance of payments

The balance of payments is a record of what has been earned and what has been spent by British residents, firms and the government over the period of one year, in their transactions with people, firms and governments abroad. These transactions include the buying and selling of

U.K. BALANCE OF PAYMENTS 1969
(£ millions)

Item	Difference between Payments and Earnings	
CURRENT ACCOUNT		
Visible goods	−141	
Government Services and Transfers	−458	
Private Services and Transfers		+564
Interest, profits and dividends in the public sector		+780
Interest, profits and dividends in the public sector	−329	
	−928	+1 344
	£m.	
CURRENT ACCOUNT SURPLUS	+416	
Investment and capital flows	+ 48	
Balancing item	+279	
TOTAL CURRENCY FLOW	+743	

Figure 20·2 Source: *Annual Abstracts of Statistics*

goods and services, investing abroad on short and long term, and investment in the U.K. by foreign firms. You can see the complete picture for 1969 in the table figure 20·3.

If there are any items in the table that you cannot understand, refer back to S13, where each item is described in detail.

Notice from the table how in 1969 Britain received an inflow of foreign currency to the amount of £743 million which was in fact used to repay loans borrowed in previous years from the I.M.F. (£30 million) and other monetary authorities (£669 million), and to add to our reserves (£44 million).

Figure 20·3 below shows the figures for the U.K. balance of payments on current account, and the combined current and capital account balance, for the ten years 1960–1969 inclusive. Look carefully at the table and notice how during these years the U.K. had a fundamental weakness in the accounts.

U.K. BALANCE OF PAYMENTS 1960–68
(£ millions)

Year	Current balance	Overall balance (current+long-term capital account)
1960	−265	− 325
1961	− 4	− 339
1962	−112	+ 192
1963	+114	− 58
1964	−395	− 695
1965	− 77	− 353
1966	+ 43	− 547
1967	−312	− 671
1968	−319	−1 410
1969	+416	+ 743

Figure 20·3 Source: *Annual Abstract of Statistics*

20·1
From the figures showing the total currency flow calculate:
- **i** Total surpluses for the ten years.
- **ii** Total deficits for the ten years.
- **iii** The net demand for foreign currency. (i.e. over and above what British firms had earned during the ten years).

As you will see, we have hardly been paying our way. We shall now analyse how this situation occurred and arrive at conclusions concerning the remedies to such a situation.

How does a deficit occur?

We can see from the table above that the worst year for the U.K. balance of payments was, without any doubt, 1964. The deficit on current account was £395m, while the outflow capital account was £300m. This gave an overall deficit of £695m. Let us try to answer the following questions: 'Why was 1964 such a calamitous year?', 'What brought about the improvement between 1965 and 1966?', 'What caused the decline in 1967?', and finally, 'Why was there a persistent tendency to go into deficit?' You can answer these questions for yourself, using the data from figure 20·4 *Changes in the U.K. Balance of Payments*. In this table each item in the balance of payments has been listed. Any improvement from year to year has been shown as + and a decline is shown as −. The changes have been calculated from the table *Balance of Payments in the U.K. 1969* which you can find in the *Annual Abstract of Statistics*.

We can see how the table works by considering a specific example. If you look at the invisible account for 1964 in figure 20·4 and in particular at interest, profit and dividends for the public sector for that year you will see a figure of +£13m, in the first column, which tells us that in 1964 we earned £13 million more from this activity than in the previous year. In 1965 earnings from this source were £15m worse than in 1964, while in 1966 they were £28m worse. What we have done is to compare the change in the net balance on each item in each of the years.

At the foot of each year column you will see the total improvement or decline on the overall balance or currency flow. We therefore have the information we need to sort out which item or items are the real culprits in causing the balance to deteriorate. In answering the following questions you will analyse the problem.

20·2
Considering 1964 only, which of the following items helped worsen the balance of payments?
- **A** Imports rose too much.
- **B** Exports rose too slowly.
- **C** Private investment abroad was too high.
- **D** Foreign investment in the U.K. fell too much.
- **E** All of these.

CHANGES IN THE U.K. BALANCE OF *PAYMENTS 1964–1969
Changes in £ million: + improvement: − decline

	1964	1965	1966	1967	1968	1969
	+204	+331	+365	− 60	+1 151	+788
IMPORTS	−643	− 49	−201	−419	−1 242	−286
INVISIBLES						
Government services and transfers	− 50	− 15	− 23	+ 6	+ 2	+ 4
Private services and transfers	− 23	+ 4	+ 39	+130	+ 133	+ 95
Interest, profits and dividends in private sector	− 10	+ 67	− 34	0	+ 9	+229
Interest, profits and dividends in public sector	+ 13	− 15	− 28	− 12	− 60	− 95
CAPITAL						
Investment and other capital flows	−186	− 19	−256	+109	− 304	+711
TOTAL CURRENCY FLOW	−637	+342	−206	−124	− 739	+667

Figure 20·4

Source: *Annual Abstract of Statistics*

* Balancing item not included

20·3

Which of the following causes of the 1964 deficit seem likely to you?

A People in the U.K., and firms, spent too much on both home-produced goods and on imports.
B British prices were higher than those of comparative goods and services abroad.
C British firms could sell most of what they wanted to at home without having to bother about exporting.
D 1964 was an election year and the government dared not cut consumer spending for fear of political unpopularity.
E All of these could have been contributory causes.

Check your answers before proceeding.

20·4

What measures would you have suggested if you had been the new Chancellor of the Exchequer in November 1964?

A Stimulate exports
B Discourage imports
C Encourage foreign investment into the U.K.
D Discourage U.K. investment abroad
E All of these

Here are some of the measures actually adopted by the government during the years 1965 and 1966.

i An import surcharge of 15% was levied on all but essential imports of food and raw materials.
ii An import deposit scheme was introduced whereby all importers had to lodge 50% of the total value of their imports, in cash, with the Board of Trade. This discouraged buying on credit.
iii Bank Rate was increased to 8%.
iv Restrictions were placed on commercial bank lending.
v Hire purchase facilities were restricted.
vi Reductions were made in government spending abroad.
vii Reductions were made in government spending at home (to help reduce aggregate monetary demand).
viii Increased Purchase Taxes were placed on many goods.
ix Income tax was increased by 2½%.
x Selective Employment Tax was introduced. This tax was paid by employers on each of their employees. Manufacturing firms received a rebate and a premium. It was thus a tax on services.
xi A £50 limit was placed on traveller's expenditure abroad.
xii Overseas investments in areas other than the Sterling Area were prohibited.

20·5

Each of the measures listed above (items i–xii) will affect some part of the balance of payments. Consider each in turn. Will it increase or reduce visible exports, invisible exports, investment into or out of the U.K.? Check your answer.

Now refer again to the figure 20·4 *Changes in the U.K. Balance of Payments* and we will continue with our analysis of the U.K. balance of payments problem.

20·6
Notice how the measures we have just described brought about an improvement in the U.K. balance of payments in 1965. Which item improved most?

1967 was again a very bad year for the accounts. You can notice two definite causes. While every other item in the balance was improving, visible exports actually fell for the first time in ten years and visible imports rapidly increased. We must therefore ask ourselves what factors might have caused both events. Why should people and firms abroad buy fewer British goods while at the same time British people and firms were buying more foreign goods? The obvious conclusion is that foreign goods were relatively cheaper than U.K. goods. This was the conclusion reached by the British government in November 1967 when they devalued the £.

After devaluation £1 exchanged for 2·4 dollars rather than its former exchange value of 2·8 dollars. Thus a foreigner could get the same British goods 14% cheaper in terms of his own currency. A British person on the other hand would find that his £1 would buy 14% less foreign currency. Foreign goods were thus 14% dearer to him. This also meant that British firms had been given a 14% price advantage over their foreign competitors.

Look again at figure 20·4, *Changes in the U.K. Balance of Payments* to see how devaluation had its effect on the British balance of payments in 1968. Visible exports improved by £1 151m while import payments worsened by £1 242m. Now there is a very good reason why exports should react more quickly than imports. It is explained by the content of U.K. imports and by their higher price. Roughly a third of our imports consist of essential foodstuffs, the demand for which is price inelastic. Another third consists of essential raw materials, which are also price inelastic. Again, these imports are necessary for the production of exports, so if the demand for our exports rises it follows that the demand for imported raw materials must also rise. The demand for our exports, on the other hand, tends to be price elastic. Exports of vehicles, machinery, engineering products of all kinds are all competing with foreign substitutes. A reduction in their foreign price is bound to attract custom away from the rival makes.

The improvement in the balance of trade continued into 1969 and 1970. A surplus was achieved in the third quarter of 1969 and on the whole of 1969 the surplus amounted to £502m. Was this the result of devaluation or was it the result of the measures we have been discussing? It was the result of both. Without restrictions at home, firms would have been unable to have produced the increase in exports that was a feature of the recovery. Home demand would have soaked up the increased production without allowing a surplus for export.

So Britain's balance of payments problems are cured? Or are they? In the short term perhaps, but what about long term solutions?

Long-term solutions

Devaluation gives a country a breathing space. Restriction of aggregate money demand at home affects the demand for imports, but in the long run is bound to have a depressive effect on investment and production. The long-term solution to a country's competitive position abroad depends on the rate at which its costs, and therefore prices, increase compared with those of its international competitors. This in turn depends upon the rate at which output of goods and services can be increased each year in real terms. In the long term then, economic growth is the answer. Such growth can come about in either of two ways. Either you must use more resources, or you must use the existing resources more efficiently. These problems will be dealt with in detail in later sections.

Exchange rates

We shall now see how changes in the balance of payments affect the value of a country's currency. At the time of writing, the value of the pound on the foreign exchange markets is as follows:

£1 = 2·39 dollars, 13·19 French francs, 8·68 marks, 855 yen

You can find the exchange value of the pound in terms of other currencies for yourself by looking in the financial pages of most national daily papers, or in *The Economist*. How did such prices get fixed in the first place? A simple numerical example will help us to understand.

If we take a very simple model involving only two countries, France and Germany, who both have internal currencies, the franc and the mark, circulating in their respective countries, we can see how the exchange rate between those currencies will be fixed. We should further assume that there is no trade between the countries to begin with, in which case the prices of two goods, shoes and saucepans, are as follows:

	France	Germany
Shoes	10 francs	16 marks
Saucepans	2 francs	8 marks

Now assume that trade starts up between individuals of the two countries, that there is no restriction on their trading and that no transport costs exist in carrying goods from one country to another. You will see a little later why we need to make this final assumption however unrealistic it may seem.

Individuals who are seeking to maximize their standard of living soon find they can do this simply by buying goods in their own country, carrying them to the other, trading them for another commodity and returning to their own country once again. Can you see where there are profits to be made through trade?

20·7

It will pay people in France to buy shoes/saucepans in francs and sell them for marks in Germany. (Indicate which word is correct).

20·8

It will pay people in Germany to sell shoes/saucepans in France and spend their francs on the other commodity. (Indicate which word is correct.)

As you can see, the possibility of gain arises through the fact that in France one pair of shoes exchanges for five saucepans, while in Germany one pair of shoes only exchanges for two saucepans. People in France will therefore buy two saucepans (4 francs), and sell them in Germany where they will receive 16 marks. They will then buy a pair of shoes and return to France. A pair of shoes has thus cost them 4 frances instead of 10. On the other hand, people in Germany will be busy selling shoes in France where they will receive 10 frances for which they can buy five saucepans.

'This cannot go on for ever,' you are saying. You are quite correct. The increased demand for saucepans in France and the increased demand for shoes in Germany will, other things being equal, push up their respective prices. In fact, prices will continue to adjust until no further possibility of gain arises. The final situation might look like this:

	France	Germany
Shoes	10·5 francs	17·5 marks
Saucepans	3 francs	5 marks

Once this position has been reached the two exchange rates and the two opportunity costs bear the same ratios to each other. In other words, sellers in both countries will have become aware of the prices they can expect to receive for their goods. An equilibrium has been reached.

20·9

What is the exchange value of 1 franc in terms of marks?

A 1·5 marks **B** 1·66 marks
C 0·6 mark **D** 3 marks

20·10

What is the exchange value of 1 mark in terms of francs?

A 1·5 francs **B** 1·66 francs
C 0·6 franc **D** 3 francs

In our very simple model of two countries trading two commodities under limiting conditions we have seen how the exchange rate has been determined by the relative purchasing power of each currency in their respective countries. This is, in fact, the proposition put forward by the 'Purchasing Power Parity' theory. It cannot be accepted as an explanation of the determination of exchange rates, however, since the conditions which must be imposed are so unrealistic. In the real world there are restrictions on trade, there are transport costs and people in different countries have vastly different tastes. We must look to further explanations of the determination of exchange rates, therefore.

The demand and supply of currencies

In view of the time we have spent discussing balance of payments deficits it may seem odd to find that in fact the balance of payments must always balance. This is why it is called a balance. The situation arises from the use of accounting methods. The balance of payments is, of course, only a record of what has happened in terms of transactions between members of one country and another. If a British company has built a factory in a foreign country it will have bought building materials and services and labour in that country. It will have paid for them in the currency of that country. When the event is recorded in the British balance of payments for that year an outflow of private investment will be recorded in the capital account (i.e. shown as a minus entry). But the money must have come from somewhere. Let us say that foreign currency was provided by the British banking system for the firm by simply converting part of its deposit account from sterling into the foreign currency. The foreign currency will have thus come from the country's reserves and we must credit these reserves with having provided it. This will appear in the Official Financing section as a '+' entry. It will be a '+' because the reserves have been credited with paying out the foreign currency. Thus the deficit on Total Currency Flow is matched by a surplus on the Official Financing Account. In this way the balance of payments must always balance. (See satellite *Contemporary Problems of Foreign Exchange and Trade*). Consider the table below.

EXTRACT FROM U.K. BALANCE OF PAYMENTS 1969

	£ million
Current account balance	+416
Balance of long-term capital transactions	+327
Total currency flow	+743
Repayments of loans:	
(a) To IMF	− 30
(b) To other countries	−669
Additions to reserves	− 44
Total official financing	−743

Figure 20·5

Thus we see that the surplus in trading and investment was used largely to repay loans from the I.M.F., and to add to our reserves.

20·11

'In 1969 the demand for sterling by foreigners exceeded our demand for foreign currencies.' True or false?

The value of the pound on the international foreign exchanges is its price in terms of other currencies. As a price, therefore, it will be determined by the opposing forces of demand and supply. We must analyse what it is that decides the demand and the supply of a currency in order to see how the exchange rate is determined.

In 1969 the demand for sterling was relatively high, compared to the supply. It is foreigners who demand sterling with which to buy British goods, or invest in the U.K. We supply sterling in order to get the foreign currency with which to buy imports and invest abroad. If, as in 1969, the balance of current and long-term capital accounts is a surplus then it follows that less sterling is being supplied than demanded. We have a case of foreign currencies. Under free market conditions, on the other hand, this excess demand would force up the price of sterling in terms of other currencies.

A balance of payments deficit is inevitably followed by what is normally called 'pressure on the pound'. You will often read in your papers that the 'pound came under pressure on the foreign exchange markets today'. This simply means that pounds were being sold in exchange for foreign currencies, probably by firms who needed the foreign currency for import payments, or by holders of sterling who were frightened that the value might fall and were selling it to buy dollars in order to anticipate that fall.

So we see that under free market conditions the price of the pound will not be determined by anything more or less than the forces of demand and supply. These forces in turn depend upon the activities of traders and investors as shown in the U.K. balance of payments.

Exchange rates, however, are not allowed to fluctuate freely. The Bank of England, for example, operates the Exchange Equalization Account for the express purpose of evening out the demand for and supply of sterling and thus maintaining a fixed price for sterling. To understand why we wish to fix the price of the pound it is necessary to trace past developments and see the historical perspective behind this decision.

The Gold Standard

Prior to the First World War Great Britain and most other major industrial countries were on the Gold Standard. This meant that the value of their currencies was expressed in terms of a specific weight of fine gold. Internally the currencies of these countries were either gold coins or paper currencies which were convertible into gold. Externally international payments would be made in gold.

The main feature of the Gold Standard which concerns us here is the way in which the system ironed out surpluses and deficits between different trading countries. To understand this procedure you must appreciate that when one country enjoys a surplus on its international earnings and payments this must mean that some other country has suffered a deficit. Another way of putting this is that the total value of world imports of goods and services and capital outflows equals the total value of exports of goods and services and capital inflows. Total balance of payments surpluses will equal total balance of payments deficits. This is shown in the following table.

20·12

Countries A, B, C, D, E, F are engaged in multilateral trade.

WORLD TRADE

Deficit £438m	A	B	Deficit £186m
Surplus £212m	C	D	Surplus £50m
Surplus £140m	E	F	?

Calculate the balance of payments for country F. Is it a deficit or a surplus? How much is it? (N.B. These countries engage in no other international trade.)

It follows, then, that if one country has a deficit on its balance of payments, another must be enjoying a surplus. The same countries, however, cannot go on running deficits for ever, so some mechanism or measure must be taken to turn a deficit into a surplus. How did the Gold Standard do this? The table below shows the mechanism. You should appreciate two facts in order to understand the workings;

- **i** Each country's internal note issue depended on the value of gold in its reserves.
- **ii** Deficits or surpluses on the balance of payments result in movements of gold out of or into a country's reserves.

THE GOLD STANDARD

Country A in deficit ↓	Country B in surplus ↓
Gold flows out as gold is the reserve currency ↓	Gold flows in ↓
The internal money supply reduced, as this supply was linked to the amount of gold held as a reserve in the Gold Standard system. ↓	The internal money supply increased ↓
Aggregate monetary demand falls as the amount of money and credit is reduced ↓	Aggregate monetary demand increases ↓
Employment, earnings, costs and prices tend to fall; this system assumes a competitive market situation ↓	Employment, earnings, costs and prices rise ↓
Export prices fall ↓	Export prices rise ↓
Demand for exports rises as A's goods become cheaper; Demand for imports falls as A's population has less money to spend on imports ↓	Demand for exports down; Demand for imports up ↓
Country A in surplus ↓	Country B in deficit ↓
Gold flows in	Gold flows out

. . . and so on.

The system appears so self-regulating and simple that you may be wondering why countries ever left the Gold Standard. Can you see anything in the events which occur following a deficit which are distinctly undesirable? You will probably decide that any system which aims to cure a balance of payments deficit by creating unemployment is less than perfect. This is just what the Gold Standard mechanism did, however. By forcing the deficit country to reduce its internal money supply in relation to the amount of gold it has lost it created unemployment in that country in the hope that costs will be reduced. But there are other reasons why the Gold Standard worked less than perfectly.

The system only works properly if all countries abide by certain rules. Imagine what would happen if the U.K. had a balance of payments deficit and as a result gold flowed out of Britain, and into the U.S.A. which was enjoying a surplus. Britain then reduced its internal money supply, thus reducing aggregate monetary demand. In theory the resultant fall in costs and prices in the U.K. plus the increased aggregate monetary demand in the U.S.A. should increase the U.S. demand for U.K. exports. Suppose, however, that the U.S.A. did not expand its supply of money as gold flowed into the country. U.S. demand for U.K. exports could only rise if it were price elastic. If the demand for U.K. exports were in fact price inelastic then the U.K. balance of payments would not benefit from increased exports to the U.S.A. What about imports? Demand in the U.K. for goods produced in the U.S.A. should in theory fall, because of the fall in aggregate monetary demand in the U.K., but if in fact the demand for imports in the U.K. is income inelastic then again the balance of payments will fail to benefit. The U.K., therefore, would be carrying out deflationary policies and incurring high levels of unemployment while no benefit to the balance of payments was being experienced. The U.S.A. would remain in surplus and gold would continue to flow out of Britain into the U.S.A. Thus there are three conditions which are necessary for the Gold Standard to work:

- **i** The demand for exports must be price elastic.
- **ii** The demand for imports must be income elastic.
- **iii** All countries must stick to the rules, which implicitly assume free competition in the factor market.

Even when these conditions are met, the levels of unemployment which have to be endured by countries during their enforced periods of deflation are considered to be totally unacceptable. In the years between 1925 and 1931 when the U.K. had returned to the Gold Standard, unemployment never once fell below 10% and at its peak reached 22%. It is because of these high social costs, which are inevitably incurred, that the Gold Standard has been compared to the use of a sledgehammer to crack an egg. It does not allow a country to pursue a policy of full employment by conducting an independent monetary policy.

What then were the alternatives facing countries who wished to leave the Gold Standard? During the First World War the Gold Standard was suspended and countries turned to policies of free exchange rates.

Free or floating exchange rates

Under the system a currency is let to find its own value on the foreign exchange markets, being determined solely by the forces of demand and supply. When a country enjoys a surplus on its balance of payments, the demand for its currency will rise when foreigners have to obtain it to pay for their imports. The supply of the currency will fall as residents need to purchase less foreign currency to buy their imports. Thus the value of the currency of a country in surplus will rise, while the value of a country in deficit is said to 'depreciate'. Thus the system is known also as exchange depreciation.

This system also has a self-regulating feature. If the U.K. were in deficit then the value of the pound would fall in terms of other currencies. In 1919 the value of the pound in dollars fell from 4·76½ to 3·40. Thus an American could buy more pounds for his dollars and U.K. export prices would fall to him. A citizen of the U.K., however, would be able to obtain less foreign currency with his pounds, and the price of imports to him would rise. Given that the demand for foreign goods in the U.K., and that the demand for U.K. goods overseas, was price elastic, U.K. exports would rise and U.K. imports would fall, thus correcting the balance of payments deficit. In this way, therefore, the balance of payments can be left to look after itself.

Since the balance of payments is looking after itself a country is then left free to adopt an internal monetary policy as it sees fit. A country could follow an inflationary policy designed to bring about full employment. Let us examine the consequences of such a policy by answering a few questions.

20·13

Which of the following measures would increase aggregate monetary demand in a country?

- **A** An increase in government spending.
- **B** Measures designed to increase the propensity to save.
- **C** An increase in the level of investment brought about by lower rates of interest.
- **D** Increased taxation.
- **E** Restrictions on imports.

20·14

What are the likely effects of an expansion of aggregate monetary demand?

A Increased production and therefore increased exports.

B Increased home spending and therefore increased demand for imports.

C As full employment is reached so costs will rise and therefore prices will tend to rise. Thus demand for exports will tend to fall and the demand for cheaper imports will rise.

D Increased investment abroad.

E All of these.

20·15

Is an expansion of aggregate monetary demand, in order to secure full employment, most likely to tend towards a deficit or surplus on the balance of payments?

20·16

If a deficit results and the currency is allowed to find its own level, will the international value of the currency rise or fall?

20·17

Would you expect a fall in the value of a country's currency to improve or worsen a country's balance of payments position?

20·18

'If the value of a country's currency is allowed to float, then inflation within the country will be matched by depreciation of the external value of the currency in terms of foreign currencies' True or false?

The preceding questions followed a definite line of argument, coming to an inevitable conclusion. With freely fluctuating exchange rates a country can follow an internal policy designed to increase employment, and if this leads to inflation and a balance of payments deficit then matters will be put right by an adjustment (depreciation) of the rate of exchange.

Free exchange rates were in operation during the period 1919–25. In some countries high levels of inflation were experienced while in others, notably Germany, runaway inflation was incurred. Terrific loss of confidence in a currency and devastatingly harmful effects are experienced when inflation reaches these proportions. It is probably because of these events that countries have always been shown to be unwilling to return to a situation of freely floating exchange rates. Basically, no country will deal solely in other countries' currency. Each country insists on holding some gold in its reserves, and hence maintained enough control over the exchange rates to ensure a minimum surplus to acquire gold reserves.

But there are other disadvantages of a system which allows the value of a country's currency to be decided in the international foreign exchange markets. Fluctuations in the value of a currency is bound to lead to speculation, and speculative activity reflects the anticipations of dealers in foreign exchange markets and takes place without necessarily having any consideration of the basic economic trends in costs or employment of any country.

The market in foreign exchange

The foreign exchange market consists of nearly all of the banks together with a few firms who specialize as foreign exchange brokers. There is no meeting place for the market, since nearly all business is conducted over the telephone and Telex. Banks throughout the world conduct business with each other in this way, buying and selling currencies in exactly the same way as they might buy wheat or rubber or any other commodity. It is therefore an international market where the value of the 'commodities' being bought and sold will be determined, under free conditions, by the forces of demand and supply. These free conditions existed in many countries before the Second World War when there were no restrictions on a firm or an individual who wished to switch his entire assets from one country and one currency to another. Since the War, exchange control has become the order of the day, but we will look at this control a little later. Let us consider a situation in which the foreign exchange market would buy currencies for anyone, regardless of the purpose for which it was required.

Given freely fluctuating exchange rates, it is easy to see how a holder of a currency, or someone who might in the future need to hold a currency for any length of time, would become very conscious of fluctuations in the value of that currency. It would be natural for him to seek to protect himself against loss if he anticipated a depreciation of the currency he was holding. Similarly, there are always speculators who see the potential gains to be made from holding a currency which is likely to appreciate in value. During the 1930s French capitalists with large holdings of francs were constantly living in fear of a depreciation of the franc. It was not uncommon, therefore, during this period for enormous amounts of francs to be sold for dollars and held in American banks. 'The flight from the franc' was the popular term used to describe this movement of money, which came to be known as 'hot money'. It would flit from one country to another as its owners either feared loss or anticipated a profit by holding it in another currency.

Now if a large number of speculators think that the value of a currency is going to fall, they sell it. Few people at this time would want to buy it and the result would be a fall in its value. The fear of a fall in value thus causes it to lose its value. The effects of this can also be very serious, both for the country whose currency has increased in value and for the country whose currency has depreciated.

When the value of a country's currency falls, the price of imports rises, and the price of exports falls. Unless the demands for its exports and imports are both price elastic no benefit need be experienced in the current account of the balance of payments. In the capital account, however, money (short-term capital) will have been transferred into other countries in panic proportions. The nation may therefore have to follow a deflationary policy when it least wants to. On the other hand, the country which is receiving the 'hot money' will be forced into an inflationary policy. Money will be entering the country, so the value of its currency will rise, thus increasing the price of its exports and reducing the price of its imports. To make matters worse the money may leave the country at a moment's notice.

Yet another disadvantage of the wild fluctuations in currency values is the adverse effects they will have on traders throughout the world. You may sell goods to a foreign firm for payment in three months' time. In the meantime, however, the value of the respective currencies may change, leaving you without any profit whatsoever. Suppose the exchange rate between pounds and dollars is £1:2·4 dollars and you contract to buy a consignment of cars from an American firm for 2 400 dollars. If, before you make payment, the value of the pound were to fall so that £1 = 2·0 dollars, you would have to pay £1 200 for the cars instead of the £1 000 you anticipated paying. How many importers are willing to take these risks?

Buying and selling at spot and forward rates

It is possible to minimize the risks of holding one currency or making contracts in another by the process of buying or selling at forward rates of exchange.

On the foreign exchange market it is possible not only to buy and sell at the present, 'spot', market rate, but also to buy and sell at a 'future' rate. In other words you can buy or sell now for delivery in the future and in this case you will pay a known price in the futures market.

Suppose we take the example of the car importer again who has to pay 2 400 dollars for the consignment of cars in three months' time. He could buy the dollars now and keep them in a bank in the U.S.A. or he can contract to buy the dollars now but not receive them or pay for them for three months. He is thus faced with the choice of buying 'spot' or 'forward'. Obviously if he does buy them at the current, spot rate of exchange, he gives up the interest he could earn on his pounds. However, he could transfer his dollars to, say, a New York bank and earn the current rate of interest in the U.S.A. If, therefore, the interest he could earn in the U.S.A. on short-term lending is higher than the interest he could earn on short-term lending in the U.K. he will be inclined to buy and pay for and receive the dollars now. He could then switch them to New York and lend them for three months until he had to pay for the cars. You may think that this is a great deal of trouble to go to in order to earn a small profit, but the foreign exchange market is seething with people who are prepared to work on very narrow margins for a small profit.

A numerical example will explain more clearly. If the current short-term rate of interest in the U.S.A. is 8%, while the rate in the U.K. is 6%, then over three months the difference will be $2\% - 1\frac{1}{2}\% = \frac{1}{2}\%$. This may not seem much, but on £1 million $\frac{1}{2}\%$ is £5 000.

Suppose we reverse the situation and assume the interest rate in the U.K. to be higher than in the U.S.A., then it will obviously be to the advantage of our importer to contract to buy the dollars forward, at the forward rate of exchange, and so keep his money in pounds to be invested short term in this country.

The main factor determining the spot or forward rates of exchange, therefore, is the short-term rates of interest that can be earned in different currencies. A few questions will improve your understanding of this point. Check your answers after each one.

20·19

The spot rate for dollars is \$2·46 = £1. The forward rate for dollars is \$2·39 = £1. By how much must the U.S. short term interest rate exceed the U.K. rate in order to persuade people to buy at the above forward rate?

A At least 1% **B** At least 2%
C At least 3% **D** At least 4%

20·20

If you had £1 000 and the short-term interest rate in the U.K. was 3% and in the U.S.A. 2% for three months' lending, by how much at least would the spot rate of exchange have to be lower than the forward rate to persuade you to buy dollars now at spot and invest them in the U.S.A.?

A 1% **B** 2% **C** 3% **D** 4%

20·21

'When the forward rate is lower than the spot rate for dollars in terms of pounds this implies that the short-term rate of interest is higher in the U.K. than in the U.S.A.' True or false?

Another point a holder of currency has to consider is the likely fluctuations in the exchange rates in the near future. If, for instance, you think that the value of the pound is likely to fall in the near future then you will be encouraged to sell pounds now and buy dollars. This will push up the spot rate for dollars and the spot rate for pounds will fall. If you think that in the future you will be able to buy pounds more cheaply, then you will be even more encouraged to sell pounds forward (pounds which you do not possess in fact), knowing that you will be able to buy them cheaper when you have to deliver. Thus it was in France in the 1930s when a devaluation of the franc was feared, that Frenchmen sold their francs for spot pounds and with their pounds bought forward francs. The forward francs were cheaper than the spot francs because it was feared that they would lose their value. Considerable fortunes were made out of this sort of trading or speculation.

20·22

Suppose the spot price of pounds is 2·50 dollars and the forward price is 2·00 dollars. Would it pay you to sell pounds at spot and buy at forward? Yes or no?

So we see that the difference between the spot and forward rates of exchange depends upon not only the relative rates of interest in different countries for short-term investment but also on expectations of future changes in the value of a currency.

You can see now how during the 1920s and 1930s, when many currencies were allowed to float in value on the foreign exchange market, fluctuations in the value of currencies caused large-scale movements of short-term capital from one country to another. Whether this was done by speculators who were seeking short-term gains or by holders of currencies who were seeking to avoid losses is unimportant. The fact remained that these large-scale capital movements could bring about the very fluctuations that speculators desired. The more traders feared changes in the value of currencies the less likely they would be prepared to involve themselves in trade which involved them in holding currency for any length of time. It was thus disruptive of trade to allow exchange rates to fluctuate freely.

It will be no surprise to you to learn, therefore, that after the Second World War, when all countries were conscious of the need to expand international trade and follow independent monetary policies, steps were taken to fix the values of currencies in respect of others and also to control the activities of speculators in foreign exchange. The system adopted by most countries was one of a fixed exchange rate. The world had therefore passed from the Gold Standard, through freely fluctuating, to fixed exchange rates. We shall now examine the system of fixed exchange rates and the machinery necessary for its efficient functioning.

Fixed exchange rates

The first essential for a country wishing to stabilize the exchange value of its currency is an agency for equalizing the demand and supply of its currency in the foreign exchange market. Thus the Exchange Equalization Account which was set up in the U.K. in 1932 was copied by other countries in following years.

In order for the Exchange Equalization Account to work properly it had to have a reserve of gold and foreign currencies that it could use to buy pounds when their value appeared to be falling. In order to guarantee the value of the pound, therefore, the U.K. had to have adequate reserves. These reserves would be increased when the balance of payments on current account was in surplus and reduced when in deficit. Now suppose a deficit for a couple of years led to the complete exhaustion of the reserves, then the country would either have to take immediate and drastic steps to convert deficit into surplus or borrow from someone the foreign currency necessary to protect the value of the pound. The immediate steps referred to could mean severe deflation and the resultant heavy unemployment so familiar under the Gold Standard. So a far more satisfactory solution would be to borrow the foreign currency until such time as the balance of payments could be brought into surplus in a less drastic way. Thus it was that the two institutions, the Sterling Area, which consisted of a changing association of nations with close commercial associations with the U.K., and which kept their reserves in London and in the International Monetary Fund, have both served to help the Bank of England to protect the value of sterling.

The Sterling Area

The origins of the Sterling Area lie in the period before the First World War. Great Britain during this time was the foremost trading nation in the world. Her dominions conducted their trade with the U.K. or at least financed it through the money market of London. It was most natural for them to hold their accounts with London banks in sterling. Furthermore this was the period of substantial U.K. balance of payments surpluses on current account. These surpluses were invested within the British Empire and again quite naturally sterling became acceptable as a trading and a reserve currency for the countries of the Empire. The Bank of England continued to act as central banker to the banking systems which were developing throughout this area. Sterling was the natural currency in which to hold the reserves of these countries.

When in 1931 the U.K. left the Gold Standard for the last time it took the Sterling Area with it. The association was completely voluntary, with the Bank of England serving the interests of the whole area. At this time there were other countries who wished to keep their currencies stable and they too felt inclined to convert their reserves into sterling, hold them in London and thus become members of the Sterling Area. Japan and France both joined in this way.

Now consider the strength this combination of reserves offered to the Exchange Equalization Account. Instead of each country trying to maintain the value of its currency independently, the several countries each used the same currency and pooled their reserves to achieve their common object. In fact the stability of prices in the U.K. during the period following 1931 compared with other countries encouraged others to join the association. To understand the principle behind this 'mutual protection society' a diagram will help.

THE STERLING AREA

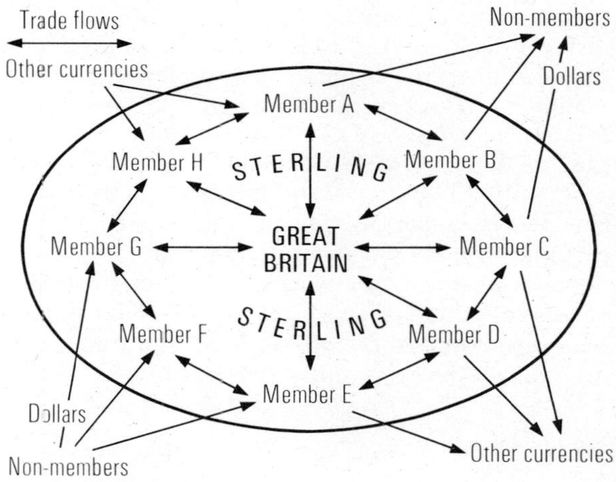

Figure 20·6

The Sterling Area became *officially recognized* after 1945 when the Bank of England became the legal holder of the reserves of the Area. In order to protect the value of sterling the Bank of England needs reserves of gold and foreign currency with which to buy sterling when others sell it, thus keeping up its price. When any member of the Area earns currency from abroad it pays it into its account with the Bank of England, which is then free to use it in the Exchange

Equalization Account. Any member who needs foreign currency to pay international debts can draw them from the 'central pool' in return for sterling. Providing therefore that the Area as a whole earns more foreign currency than it has to pay out there will never be any need for the Bank of England to sell sterling on the foreign exchange market in order to obtain the foreign currency needed. But in another way, the Area as a whole must remain in surplus and the value of sterling is safe. An individual country can go into deficit with another member and the debt can be settled in sterling (no selling of sterling, therefore no fall in its value). Any member can also go into deficit with a non-member and the foreign currency will be provided from the earnings of the rest of the Area.

After 1945 Britain was faced with the task of post-war reconstruction with the inevitable falling-off of exports and an increased demand for imported raw materials. It was inevitable that the balance of payments should go into deficit. Now the remainder of the Sterling Area were producers of primary products which were in great demand. The U.K.'s deficit was therefore financed by the surpluses earned by the other members. In this respect, therefore, the Area was a great help to the U.K. Furthermore the earnings of the City of London financial institutions in handling the trade and finance of the Area brought in a considerable amount of 'invisible earnings' for the balance of payments.

Nevertheless it became necessary for members to agree voluntarily to restrict to the utmost their demand for dollars in terms of trade and investment. More recently the value of the Area has been questioned here in Britain, since one or two new developments have taken place.

Firstly, not all members have been complying with the agreed rules. It is a voluntary association and members lodge their earnings of gold and foreign currency with London completely voluntarily. If certain members do not put their earnings of foreign currencies into the common pool then the system breaks down. It has recently been felt preferable by some members to hold an ever-increasing proportion of their reserves in dollars, thus reducing the size of the pool.

Secondly, the Area as a whole has been finding it increasingly difficult to earn a surplus with the rest of the world. As we noted before, the Area consists of mainly primary producers. A fact of life which these countries have had to face in recent times is that through world over-production of primary products prices have been falling. The terms of trade have thus been becoming less favourable for the members of the Sterling Area

$$\left(\text{Terms of trade} = \frac{\text{An index of the price of exports}}{\text{An index of the price of imports}}\right)$$

and thus the same volume of exports has been buying fewer imports. Similarly an increasing volume of exports has been necessary to buy the same volume of imports.

The result of these two trends has thus been to weaken the arguments in favour of the Sterling Area as far as Britain is concerned. If the Area as a whole earns a deficit, then the U.K. is still commited to protecting the value of the pound. She must therefore earn a balance of payments surplus to counteract the Area's deficit or she

U.K. RESERVES AND LIABILITIES 1962–68
(£ million)

	1962	1963	1964	1965	1966	1967	1968
U.K. reserves, gold and foreign currency	1 002	949	827	1 073	1 107	1 123	1 009
Liabilities in sterling with Sterling Area countries	2 430	2 592	2 591	2 594	2 599	2 453	2 311
Liabilities in sterling with non-Sterling Area countries	733	670	714	781	895	1 353	1 649
Total liabilities	3 163	3 262	3 305	3 375	3 494	3 806	3 960

Figure 20·7 Source: *Annual Abstract of Statistics*

must borrow the foreign currency demanded by the Exchange Equalization Account if it is to function effectively. This last alternative is the one to which Britain has had to turn increasingly over the last fifteen years. The table figure 20·7 shows what a precarious position the Exchange Equalization Account could find itself in. It shows on the one hand the holdings of gold and the reserves of foreign currencies held in the U.K., and on the other hand, the deposits of sterling held by the U.K. for overseas Sterling Area countries. Notice that during the period 1962–68 while the reserves rarely exceeded £1 000 million the deposits of Sterling Area countries were constantly running in excess of £2 000 million. Add to these the sterling balances held by countries who are not members of the Sterling Area and you find the total liabilities in sterling held by foreigners in the form of accounts, with our banks and in the form of short- and long-term investment in Treasury bills and British government stocks.

20·23

What was the ratio of reserves to liabilities
a in 1962? **b** in 1968?

20·24

What fraction of the total holdings of sterling, by foreigners, would need to be converted into other currencies in order to force the Bank of England to borrow in 1968?

20·25

Was the Bank of England in 1968 getting stronger or weaker in its position of defender of the pound than in 1962?

We said there were two institutions which have developed to help the Exchange Equalization Account hold enough foreign currency to be sure of providing a demand to meet the supply of pounds at any time. We have also examined the development of the Sterling Area. Now we will look at another institution which was set up with the express purpose of enabling countries with temporary balance of payments deficits to maintain the value of their currencies.

The International Monetary Fund

As the second World War was drawing to a close many countries considered how together they could achieve certain joint objectives. These were as follows:

i To promote international trade and to get away from the restrictionist attitudes of the inter-war years. This would be done by a continual reduction of tariffs.

ii To stabilize the value of trading and reserve currencies since it was recognized that fluctuations in their value led to speculation and uncertainty which was damaging to the first aim.

iii To pursue independent monetary policies which would allow countries to achieve full employment.

iv To stimulate economic growth through increased specialization and trade.

Now in considering these aims one or two facts were obvious. The international monetary authorities needed to co-operate more than in the past. Thus a conference was held in 1944 at Bretton Woods in New Hampshire, U.S.A., to formulate a plan that would be acceptable to all. The aim was to find a system without the disadvantages of the Gold Standard or of the system of freely floating exchange rates.

The outcome of the conference was the setting up of the International Monetary Fund, which began its work in 1947. The rules of membership were as follows:

i All members had to declare the value of their currencies.

ii All currencies should become freely convertible with each other.

iii The value of a currency should only be changed after consultation with the fund.

iv A pool of reserves was to be set up. Each member would contribute to the pool according to her holdings of reserves. Each member could in any one year withdraw foreign currency up to one-quarter of the value of the amount it had initially deposited. The initial deposit was called its quota. Three-quarters of the quota could be placed in the country's own currency and the remainder had to be placed in gold or foreign currencies. A country could therefore draw foreign currency year after year to protect the value of its currency. The only restriction placed on its borrowing was the rule that the Fund should never hold more of a country's currency than twice the value of that country's quota.

Let us take the U.K. for example. Her initial quota was 1 300 million dollars. She declared the value of her currency to be £1 = 4·03 dollars. She could thus draw up to 325 million dollars in any one year until the Fund found itself holding

$$\frac{1\ 300}{4{\cdot}03} \times 2 = \text{app. £650 million.}$$

The purpose of the I.M.F. is thus not to provide countries in balance of payments with an easy way out of their problems, but to provide a temporary loan so that such a country might rectify its deficit less harmfully than may have happened under the Gold Standard system. Savage deflationary policies could be avoided and full employment maintained.

If the Fund considered that the problems of a country were not of a temporary but of a permanent nature then it would recognize that a 'fundamental' disequilibrium existed in that country's balance of payments and would probably recommend a devaluation of that country's currency. Thus such a country would no longer need to borrow so heavily on the Fund to protect the value of a currency that was over-valued. It is to devaluation that we now turn, since Britain has experienced two devaluations of the pound since the Second World War. We shall see why they became necessary and whether they were successful or not.

Devaluation

Quite obviously if a country fixes the value of a currency and makes it freely convertible with other currencies it must select a value that is not too high. If this occurs then foreigners will have to pay too high a price for it and they will be discouraged from importing from or investing in that country. On the other hand, residents of that country will find foreign currencies relatively cheap and will be encouraged to buy foreign goods and invest in foreign countries. The demand for the country's currency would thus be low while the supply of it would be high. Market pressures would try to force the value of the currency below that at which it had been fixed. In order to prevent the value from falling an Exchange Equalization Account would have to buy the currency with foreign currency from the country's reserves. Once the reserves had been exhausted borrowing would become necessary from other countries or from the I.M.F. Once the country can no longer borrow there is no possible way in which the value can be maintained. The country thus declares a lower exchange rate for its currency. A devaluation such as this has been experienced by the U.K. in 1949 when the currency was devalued from 4·03 dollars to 2·80 dollars, then again in 1967 from 2·80 dollars to 2·40 dollars.

We shall examine the circumstances of the 1967 devaluation a little more closely. As you have seen earlier in this section, the U.K. incurred total currency outflows in 1963, £58m; 1964, £695m; 1965, £353m; 1966, £547m; and 1967, £671m. Traditional deflationary methods had failed to turn the deficits into a surplus. Borrowing from the I.M.F. had been so large that special arrangements had to be made for the so-called special case of the U.K. Eventually, however, it had to be recognized that there was a fundamental disequilibrium in the balance of payments. The

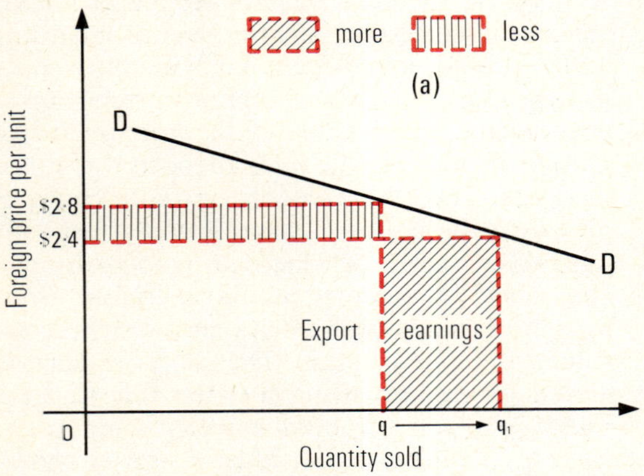

ELASTIC DEMAND FOR U.K. EXPORTS

Figure 20·8a

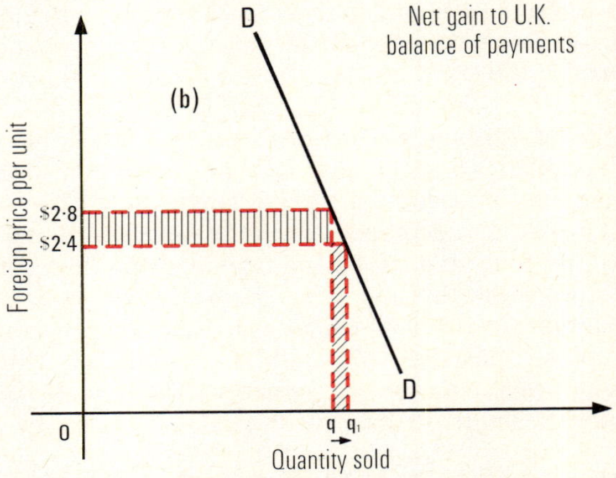

INELASTIC DEMAND FOR U.K. EXPORTS

Figure 20·8b

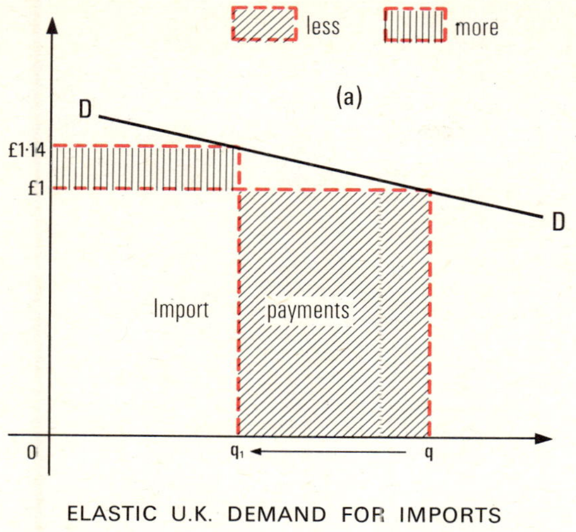

Figure 20·9a

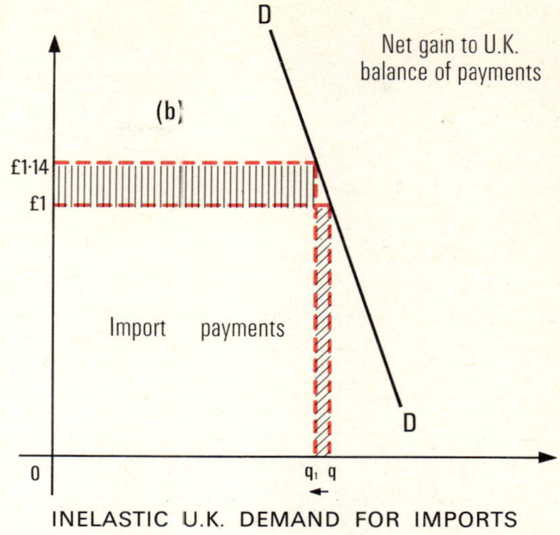

Figure 20·9b

currency was over-valued. Devaluation was the only step remaining. It was regarded as the last resort. But would it prove to be successful.

In theory, devaluation brought about a 14% reduction in the foreign price of U.K. exports and an increase of 14% in the price of foreign imports. Whether or not this would lead to an increase in the earnings of U.K. exports depended on the price elasticity of demand for those exports. Figure 20·9 illustrates this point.

Figures 20·8 and 20·9 show the effect of devaluation on the import payments of a country. In *both* cases demand must be price elastic if the U.K. balance of payments is to benefit from the relative price changes following devaluation.

Given that the above conditions were met there were other considerations that had to be borne in mind before being able to predict whether the devaluation would bring the required improvement in the balance of payments. These considerations are listed below:

i Would other countries also devalue? If they did then the U.K. would have gained no price advantage for her international trade with those countries.

ii Was the devaluation large enough? If it was not then a further devaluation would eventually become necessary. This would probably be anticipated by holders of sterling, who would seek to sell it and thus force the Bank of England to take protective measures.

iii Would the high import content of U.K. exports iron out the price advantage offered to British exporters? In fact this was reckoned to reduce the 14% advantage to a 10% one.

iv Could costs be kept down for long enough at home to give British manufacturers a good opportunity of increasing their share of overseas markets? This depended on the rate of wage inflation at home. Of course if other countries' costs increased at the same rate then we had less to worry about.

v Was there enough spare capacity among U.K. manufacturing exporters to expand to meet the increases in quantity demanded without great increases in costs? In other words, was the supply of U.K. exports price elastic?

In figure 20·10a, where the supply of U.K. exports is seen to be elastic, an increase in demand from DD to D_1D_1 leads to nearly a doubling of output but only a small increase in price from OP to OP_1. British exports thus retain much of their competitive advantage from the devaluation.

In 20·10b where the supply is inelastic, an increase in demand for a similar price fails to lead to a large increase in quantity supplied. Thus any advantage gained from devaluation is reduced.

It is important, therefore, that not only should demand for British exports be price elastic but so also should be the supply. Similarly the U.K.'s demand for imports must be price elastic if the balance of payments is to benefit.

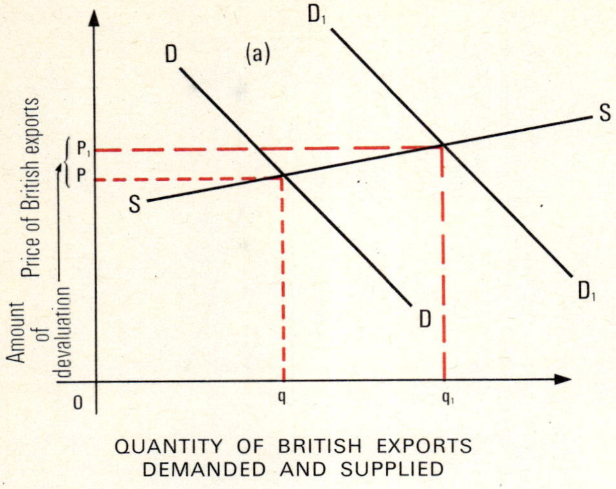

Figure 20·10a

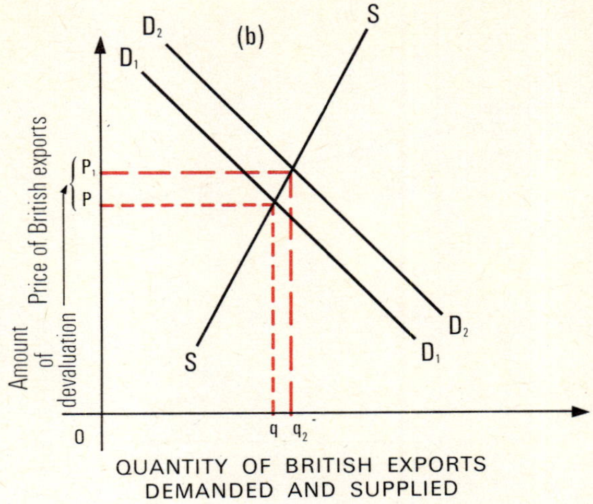

Figure 20·10b

20·26
See if you can list the conditions under which a country would find it profitable to revalue (i.e. increase the value of its currency in relation to other currencies).

Germany revalued the Deutschemark in 1969 in response to exhortations from the I.M.F. and other major trading nations. Germany had for many years up to this point been earning a huge surplus on her balance of payments which had resulted in an enormous inflow of foreign currency into her reserves. Without running a large deficit on her capital account this meant that currencies were leaving the world circulation flow. The only way they could re-enter the flow was for Germans to spend them either on imports or in investing abroad. This they were not doing, since German goods were relatively cheaper and therefore more attractive than imports. Eventually, however, Germany was persuaded to revalue, thus increasing the value of the mark and the price of German exports to foreigners. Foreign goods became cheaper to German residents, whose standard of living rose, as a result. The balance of payments moved from surplus into deficit and the much wanted currencies began to leave the German reserves and play their part again in the world money system.

This shortage of world trading and reserve currencies has been becoming increasingly more series over the past few years. We shall examine what has come to be known as the 'world cash crisis' in the following paragraphs.

International liquidity

If an Indian merchant wishes to buy ivory from an African exporter what currency does he use to pay the bill? He cannot use rupees because the African will not accept them. He may be unable to obtain the African currency, so he must obtain a currency which is internationally acceptable. If a small underdeveloped country wishes to hold its reserves in a stable currency whose value is protected by a major industrial nation, which currency will it choose?

In both of the above cases some form of international money is necessary which will be stable in value and acceptable throughout the world. Gold, sterling and dollars have these properties and have come to be recognized as three forms of international liquidity.

Gold performs all the traditional functions of money on an international scale. It has all the qualities necessary to perform as an international form of money. It is rare, acceptable everywhere in payment, portable, divisible, durable and recognizable. The only problem as far as its use as an international currency is concerned is that there is not enough of it. What there is comes mainly from two sources, South Africa and Russia. The gold mined in Russia fails to find its way on to the international market and that from South Africa is bought in return for dollars largely by the U.S. Federal Reserve Bank, which then uses it to back its supply of dollars. Until August 1971 the United States was the only country which would sell gold in return for dollars at an official rate of $35 per fine ounce.

Sterling became internationally known and acceptable during the nineteenth century, when British businessmen were investing heavily in their Empire. An Indian merchant had the choice of holding his wealth in the form of gold or in the form of a currency. The value of the rupee was too unstable to risk holding too many, but sterling represented a form of liquidity which was stable in value, easily exchangeable for any other currency and readily obtainable. Thus throughout the world sterling came to be thought of in terms of being 'as good as gold'.

After the Second World War the economic damage suffered by the U.K. handicapped her ability to maintain a surplus in her balance of payments. In 1949 she was forced to devalue, and thereafter the 'golden' image was seen to have left sterling for ever. The Gold Standard had been left behind in 1931 and the value of the pound depended solely upon Britain's ability to earn a surplus in her balance of payments. This event seemed to be becoming increasingly more difficult, and so world bankers, trader and governments sought new forms of international liquidity.

The dollar had been kept pegged to gold even though other countries had adopted a fixed exchange rate standard. Thus it was inevitable as people looked for a currency that was in reasonable supply, stable in value and easily convertible that they should turn to the dollar. The dollar thus became unofficially recognized as a world currency.

The crisis we spoke of earlier arises from the fact that the supply of international forms of liquidity falls dramatically short of that demanded. International currencies are needed if multilateral trade is to expand at its fastest rate possible. It is similar to the need for money within an economy: without money trade is restricted to barter; barter demands a double coincidence of wants (i.e. the buyer must want what the seller has and the seller must want what the buyer can offer in exchange); therefore trade is restricted; if trade is restricted then specialization is of necessity restricted also. On an iternational scale countries need to specialize in order to benefit from the principle of comparative advantage. The more countries specialize the more they need to trade with each other. Unless trade is going to be restricted to bilateral agreements, akin to barter, an international medium of exchange is essential. Thus the supply of international currencies is of great importance. We shall examine the conditions of supply of gold, sterling and then dollars.

i The supply of gold increases only in accordance with the volume mined each year. In 1970, 1 280 tonnes will be mined, while by 1974 this is expected to have fallen to 1 200 tonnes per annum. In 1974 it is anticipated that demand will exceed supply by at least 400 tonnes. In 1967 in response to a very heavy demand for gold a two-tier gold market was created. This allowed the Central Banks to buy and sell gold amongst themselves only at the official rate of 35 dollars per ounce, while the free market could find its own price for gold. In 1969 the free market price of gold reached 44 dollars an ounce, but since then it has steadied at around 36–37 dollars. The supply of gold is thus relatively fixed, for unless more dollars are offered per ounce of gold, mining companies cannot afford to incur greater costs in extracting that metal.

ii The supply of sterling depends upon the spending abroad and the investment abroad by U.K. residents. In other words, the only way in which sterling can find its way into other countries' reserves is for the U.K. to run a deficit on her balance of payments, in other words, to export capital. This she did for many years throughout the nineteenth century, which led to sterling being adopted as a world reserve and trading currency. Since the Second World War, however, sterling has been devalued twice. Its value clearly cannot be relied upon as much as it once could. At times, therefore, people are loath to hold sterling, since they fear that its value will fall. Furthermore, since the Second World War the U.K. has had a persistent and fundamental balance of payments problem which has resulted in her having to take measures to restrict the outflow of sterling. Owing to the pressure on the pound, the Bank of England has on numerous occasions had to borrow foreign currencies and enter the foreign exchange market to but sterling. Thus the supply has been reduced.

iii The supply of dollars similarly depends upon the U.S.A. running a balance of payments deficit. Since 1945 there has been little to worry about here with the large programmes of aid, overseas investment in foreign countries, post-war reconstruction loans, etc., which have all increased the

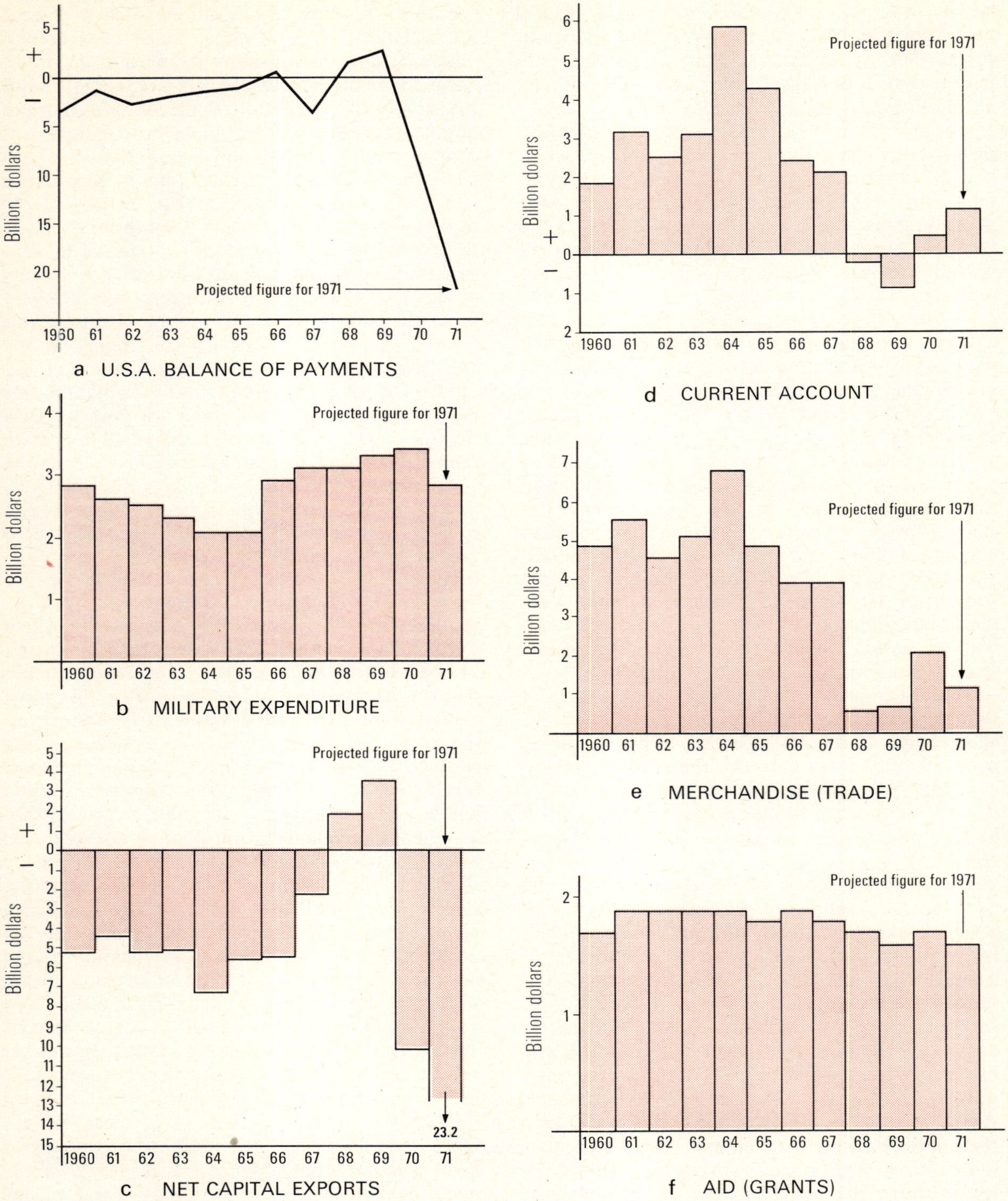

Figure 20·11a-f

supply of dollars to the world outside America. The Korean War also resulted in the spending of dollars overseas which swelled the world supply. The Vietnam War has served to maintain the supply of dollars in a similar way.

The crisis

The expansion of world trade since 1945 has proceeded at a pace much faster than the supply of currencies to finance that trade. If one measures the value of world imports in total one finds that the increase since 1950 is four times as great as the increase in international liquidity. World trade has expanded at the rate of about 300% during the period 1950–70 while the output of gold has increased only by 40%. The difference has been met mainly by the supply of dollars. Thus the international monetary system has been propped up by the dollar. The success of the system rested on two basic asumptions:

i That dollars were backed by gold and therefore were as good as gold.

ii That the supply of dollars would continue to increase indefinitely.

In the mid-1960s both of these assumptions could no longer be taken for granted. First, France chose to convert her dollar holdings into gold. In 1965 400 million dollars were exchanged for gold with the U.S.A. and 600 million dollars in 1966. If other holders of dollars had rushed to do the same then the price of gold would have been forced up and all faith in the dollar would have gone.

Secondly, there were signs recently that the supply of dollars might be drying up. The situation in Europe is less tense than it was a few years ago and therefore the Americans feel less inclined to spend dollars there for defence or for aid. The value of overseas aid has been questioned more closely in the U.S.A., with the result that the aid programme has been pruned. Finally, the possibility of a lessening of the war in Vietnam means that fewer dollars will find their way in that direction. Thus the world supply of dollars seems to be drying up, there is no other currency ready to step in, so we have a crisis. What is desperately needed is the means to settle trading accounts internationally and also some means by which a nation can store her wealth in the form of reserves. If it is not found then the result must be reduced trade, less specialization, less economic growth, which would be catastrophic for the developing countries, and thus a lower standard of living for all.

As a result of a chronic balance of payments deficit and overpriced exports, in August 1971 the United States decided to force a re-alignment of exchange rates; in essence by keeping stable the gold value of the U.S. dollar, and forcing those countries with large and growing reserves (particularly Japan) to revalue their currencies upwards. What happened to the dollar is summerised in figures 20·11 and 20·12. Examine them carefully and apply the principles just discussed.

PRICE INDICES

Country	1963	1965	1967	1969	1970
U.S.	**100**	**104**	**109**	**114**	**121**
Japan	100	98	99	105	111
France	100	105	107	114	126
Germany	100	102	102	102	104
Italy	100	101	99	102	108
Holland	100	104	104	104	108
U.K.	100	105	110	123	131

These show the rise in prices of goods for export, as measured in the currency of each exporting country. The devalations by Britain (14% in 1967) and France (11% in 1969) do not therefore pull down the lines for the U.K. and France, as they would if the index were shown in dollars.

Figure 20·12

Plans for international monetary reform

Different solutions have been put forward by various people. These are described in the satellite *Contemporary problems of foreign exchange and trade*. New proposals are described in the financial press from time to time.

A scheme of Special Drawing Rights (SDRs) was introduced at the beginning of 1970. Under the scheme credit is created at an agreed annual rate by the International Monetary Fund. These credits (SDRs) are to be allocated to countries in accordance with their quotas. They can be drawn by a country at any time and therefore constitute an addition to that country's reserves. One member country can use them to pay another. Thus additional international money has in fact been created.

The fascinating thing about this scheme is that the economist Keynes was arguing for a scheme such as this in 1943 prior to the setting up of the I.M.F. As far back as 1920 Keynes wrote that the Gold Standard was a 'relic of a barbarous age'. He envisaged an International Clearing Union within which the necessary supply of international money could be increased or restricted according to the world's needs. Payments between countries within the union would simply be made by the transfer of a deposit from one account to another. The Americans, who were so much against it at the time, have recently been instrumental in getting similar arrangements in the Special Drawing Rights scheme.

In all probability the future supply of international liquidity depends on the second scheme; the development of SDRs. Whether this can meet the future needs of the world's monetary system remains to be seen. Whatever system is finally adopted, it must be flexible enough to expand the supply of world money in step with the growth of the world's trade.

ANSWERS TO S20

20·1

Total deficit	£4 073m
Total surpluses	£1 260m
Net demand for foreign currency	£2 813m

20·2
E.

20·3
E.

20·4
E: to correct all the items showing a worsening position listed in 20·2.

20·5
See page 305.

20·6
% change in imports.

20·7
Saucepans

20·8
Shoes

20·9
B

20·10
C.

20·11
True

20·12
Surplus £222m.

20·13
A, C, and perhaps E, because these would be an increased demand for domestically produced goods.

20·14
B, C.

20·15
Deficit

20·16
Fall.

20·17
Improve; given that exports are price elastic

20·18
True.

20·19
C.

20·20
B.

20·21
True.

20·22
Yes.

20·23
a 1002: 3163, i.e. approximately 1:3.
b 1009: 3960, i.e. approximately 1:4.

20·24
$\frac{1}{4} \simeq \frac{1009}{3960}$: we have only sufficient reserves to cover $\frac{1}{4}$ of our liabilities.

20·25

Weaker.

20·26

When a country's currency is undervalued, its exports are cheap. This may lead to large orders which encourage producers to bid up the price of factors, thereby leading to an inflationary pressure. An under-valued currency is usually accompanied by a persistent balance of payments surplus, which tends to cause balance of payments deficits for the country's trading partners. They will exert political pressure for a re-valuation.

20:5

	Increase exports	**Reduce visible imports**	**Increase invisible exports**	**Reduce invisible imports**	**Increase investment into U.K.**	**Reduce investment out of U.K.**
Import surcharge		√				
Import deposit scheme		√				
Increased Bank Rate			√		√	
H.P. restrictions	√	√				
Reduced government spending at home		√		√		
S.E.T.	√					
Reduced government spending abroad				√		√
Ban on overseas investment						√
Increased income tax		√				
Increased purchase tax	√					
Travel allowance				√		

REGULATING THE ECONOMY

STUDY SECTION **21**

Sections 18 and 19 have shown us the problems involved in maintaining full employment and balancing export earnings and capital inflows against import expenditure and capital outflows. Such problems involve the control, as far as is possible, of the level of demand for labour, and the demand for exports and imports. The government can also influence the type of labour supplied, and can take measures to encourage firms to export, but measures of this kind to influence supply require a long time to be effective. For example, if it takes two years to train men of certain skills, any measures taken now cannot be effective until two years have elapsed. Similarly, it may take several years for firms to build up export markets. Salesmen need to develop contacts and need time to organize their marketing procedures: it is not sufficient to sell motor cars without organizing servicing centres, with adequate stocks of spare parts.

21·1

Refer to the following list.

A Devaluation.
B An increase in purchase tax.
C A reduction in income tax.
D Measures to encourage investment in development areas.
E An agreement between all countries to reduce tariffs.
F A reduction in the volume of bank lending.

a Which of the above measures are likely to increase imports?
b Which of the above measures are likely to increase exports?
c Which of the above measures are likely to increase employment?
d Which of the above measures are likely to reduce imports and employment?

From your answers to the questions you should have noticed a possible conflict between the policies designed to maintain full employment and policies designed to achieve an equilibrium on the balance of payments. We are now going to examine more closely another possible conflict, between full exployment and price stability. It is this problem which in recent years has worried the governments of all advanced countries, particularly those of the U.S.A. and U.K.

Inflation

The meaning, causes and effects of inflation, and other material in this chapter, are discussed more fully in the satellite *The management of the economy*. The word 'inflation' has a variety of uses. Refer back to figure 17·8 depicting an inflationary gap: in this case, inflation means the excess of aggregate money demand (AMD) over output at current prices. Inflation is more commonly used to describe the *result* of such an excess of demand over supply, i.e. it describes a situation in which prices are continuously rising. Therefore, when we say that Britain has suffered seriously from inflation since 1960, we mean that during the period prices have risen steadily and the economic effects of this rise have been undesirable.

21·2

Suppose a retailer spends £1 000 a year on toys, which cost him £1 each. How many can he buy if the wholesale price rises by 10%?

A 900 **B** 909 **C** 1100

21·3

Suppose the price of British-made toys rises by 10% per annum from £1, and the possible imported alternatives originally cost £1·10 and their price rises by 1% per annum. After how many years will the retailer start buying imports?

A After 1 year **B** After 2 years
C After 3 years

21·4

If you are thinking of buying a motor scooter for £100, and you expect the price to rise by 10% per annum, would you save up for a year, or try to borrow some money in order to buy the motor scooter now?

The answers to the question above demonstrate some of the undesirable effects of inflation. As prices rise the purchasing power of money falls. The retailer in question 21·2 would probably raise his selling prices to raise his money income, but people on fixed incomes—widows, or the elderly, who receive pensions, or students receiving grants—will find that they can buy less. Their real income falls. During inflation producers can maintain or increase their real incomes by raising prices, and employees can bargain for higher wages—out of which they can pay the higher prices. Therefore, during inflation people on fixed incomes suffer most.

If prices rise faster in one country than in others, the country with the higher rate of inflation will find that more imports are being bought as substitutes for dearer home-produced goods, and dearer exports reduce the quantity demanded abroad. Rising prices are likely to cause balance of payments problems.

A third undesirable effect of inflation is that 'inflation feeds on itself'. We have already noted that if people expect prices to rise, they try to raise their money incomes to compensate for the rise in prices. This rise in wages or profit margins without a corresponding increase in output will cause a rise in costs of production and therefore a rise in market prices. This is known as the wage price spiral—refer also to cost-push inflation, page 309, and the satellite *The management of the economy*. Moreover, we can also see that during inflation saving becomes unattractive. If the purchasing power of any sum saved falls every year, people are likely to reduce their annual savings, and increase their consumption expenditure. An increase in consumption expenditure increases AMD. If AMD is already excessive, then extra consumption will worsen the situation.

We have noted three undesirable effects of inflation:

i A fall in real incomes of those people whose money incomes are fixed. (Even without inflation, most people in this group have a low standard of living.)

ii The tendency for the balance of trade to run into deficit, which will probably lead to a deficit on the balance of payments.

iii The probability that, once started, inflation will get worse, i.e. prices will rise faster each year, because AMD continues to rise and rising costs push up prices.

Why does the government not take stringent measures to prevent inflation, or, if prices are already rising, to stop the price rises? You may be able to see the conflict of policy already, but before we explain the conflict we must examine the apparently opposite situation—deflation.

Deflation

Figure 17·9 depicts a deflationary gap.

To have the exact opposite of the usual meaning of inflation, deflation should mean a situation in which prices are falling, but in fact it means a situation where AMD is insufficient to absorb the total output of the country. We shall see that the government may introduce a deflationary policy (measures to reduce AMD), in order to prevent inflation, but in an advanced economy prices do not respond quickly to reductions in demand. Producers are more likely to reduce output and accumulate stocks than cut prices. One reason why prices do not fall is that, when output is reduced, mass production industries lose the benefits of economies of scale, so average costs rise when output falls. Therefore the initial results of a deflationary policy will be a fall in output and employment, and then a fall in investment. Only if AMD was kept very low for a long time would prices in general begin to fall.

21·5

Why will the initial reduction in AMD cause a later fall in investment?

The conflict between full employment and price stability

Section 17 showed that a level of national income which brings full employment will not happen automatically. If the government aims to maintain full employment, it must attempt to regulate AMD at a sufficiently high level to cause producers to employ all, or nearly all, those people who seek work. Ideally, it must ensure that planned AMD just reaches that level which ensures full employment, but does not become excessive. However, for many reasons it is impossible to make such fine adjustments to planned AMD. As explained in S19, precise adjustment of total expenditure in any one year is impossible, because no one can predict exactly how people will react to changes in taxation, investment incentives, a credit squeeze, or any of the other measures discussed later. For example, predictions about the effects of an increase or decrease in income tax will depend on the estimates of the marginal propensities to consume of all the people affected by the tax change, and the time lag between the change in tax and change in consumption habits. Similarly a credit squeeze may not become effective for several months, by which time the economic situation may have changed. In this way booms and slumps may be aggrevated and not eliminated by government action.

However, even if the government could regulate the level of AMD precisely, experience has shown that full employment and price stability tend to be contradictory aims of policy. We shall see that the maintenance of full employment leads to demand-pull inflation, and probably encourages the development of cost-push inflation, but while prices have been rising only slowly (2–3% p.a.) governments have been prepared to allow such creeping inflation, as a by-product of full employment. Indeed, gently rising prices in so far as they indicate rising demand, encourage businessmen to expand capacity, and so promote full employment and the growth of real output. For such reasons, governments are unwilling to introduce deflationary policies when annual price increases are moderate.

Demand-pull inflation

Section 19 showed that regional unemployment rates vary widely. When the government raises AMD in order that more labour will be employed in producing goods and services, it is most unlikely that the extra labour demanded will correspond both in type and region with the unemployed labour available. As AMD rises, labour, particularly skilled labour, becomes scarce in the Midlands and the South-East of England, while unemployment rates in regions such as Scotland, Wales, and North-East and Northern Ireland remain well over 3%. Producers in the Midlands and South-East who find the demand for their products rising will bid up wages to attract the necessary labour, and will be able to raise their product prices because of the rising demand; they may even welcome a slight reduction in orders resulting from a higher price if it enables them to fulfil the remaining orders more quickly.

Rising demand will also cause the prices of some raw materials, particularly primary products, to rise. We can therefore see that shortages ('bottlenecks') will develop as AMD rises, although in certain areas unemployment will remain high. As the national unemployment rate falls, more shortages of certain types of labour and capital occur, and prices rise faster, i.e. *demand-pull inflation* develops.

The ratchet effect and the Phillips curve

Suppose the government decides that a certain level of AMD is excessive and attempts to reduce demand. We have already seen that the initial results of such deflationary policies will be to reduce output and employment, particularly in certain regions, while prices still rise, though perhaps at a slower rate. It seems that the price level can be changed in one way only—upwards. This effect is known as the *ratchet effect*. One suggested relationship between the level of unemployment and the rate of price increase is depicted by the graph shown in figure 21·1, and is called, after its inventor, the Phillips curve.

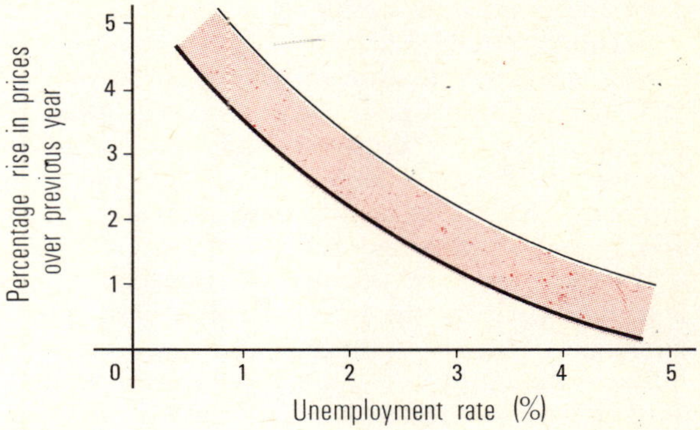

Figure 21·1

The Phillips curve illustrates that in economies such as the U.K., prices will tend to rise slightly even when the national unemployment rate is high (4–5%) so the government cannot adjust AMD so as to achieve full employment and price stability at the same time; i.e. if it plans to reduce unemployment to about 2% it must accept an annual increase in the price level of 3–4%. The curve is drawn in the form of a band because a range of price increases has been observed at any given level of unemployment.

21·6

Would the shape of the Phillips curve be different if factors were perfectly mobile?

In the latter half of the 1960s this simple relationship between the rate of change of prices and the level of unemployment in the U.K. was disturbed. Prices rose more rapidly even at relatively high levels of unemployment (for example $2\frac{1}{2}$%). This indicates that there may be another cause of inflation, apart from excess demand.

Cost-push inflation

Cost-push inflation means that prices may be forced up by rising costs, even though demand is not excessive in all industries. There are many possible causes for the initial rise in prices:

i a rise in import prices (possibly caused by devaluation);

ii a rise in factor incomes, without a corresponding rise in the output from that factor (e.g. wages rising faster than productivity);

iii government action, such as the removal of price controls (for example on rents, or food prices), or the imposition of higher indirect taxes (for example purchase tax).

Before the devaluation of sterling in November 1967 British import prices were relatively static, so the major cause of cost-push inflation in Britain has been increases in incomes exceeding increases in productivity. One man's wage increase can be another man's price increase.

If there is no excess demand in the economy as a whole, a rise in the price of a few products is likely, according to traditional analysis, to cause a fall in the quantity demanded, which will lead to a reduction in profits and a decline in employment in the trades concerned. However, the full employment policy removes some of the competitive pressures which restrain producers from raising prices. If AMD is kept at a high level by government policy, so that there are some trades and regions where labour is very scarce, the wages of certain groups of employees will rise. Employees in other industries and in other regions will try to gain increases in wages and salaries comparable with those already granted due to scarcity. Employers will not wish to risk strikes when there is a high demand for their products, especially if expensive equipment will remain idle during a strike. Large, integrated companies can suffer heavy losses during a strike by a few men. Moreover, powerful unions will gain similar increases for all their members, whether or not wage agreements are negotiated nationally: therefore each employer knows that, after a wage increase has been granted, he and his competitors will all be faced with similar increases in labour costs. Our conclusion is that, in a complex economy, where there are many interdependent stages in the production process, and AMD is kept at a high level, employers are likely to lose more by forcing strikes than by granting large wage claims.

If all those who claim wage increases obtain them, without corresponding increases in output per man, labour costs and hence prices will rise. However, if the wages of most employees in the country rise there will not be a significant fall in demand for many products. People will be able to pay the higher prices out of their higher money incomes. Increases in wages, or profit margins, will create the higher money incomes, out of which the extra money expenditure can be met. The only people who cannot keep up with rising prices are those on fixed incomes and groups with little bargaining power. Therefore, in an inflation the weakest, in terms of economic power, suffer most.

However, suppose the government adjusted the incomes of poor people at reasonable intervals, by changes in taxes and benefits. Surely then no-one would suffer from inflation (whether cost-push or demand-pull)! Two initial objections are that the weaker groups would always be losing purchasing power, until such time as their money incomes were raised, and that tax changes, such as an increase in income tax, may have undesirable effects. The more important problem concerns the effect of inflation on foreign trade, especially for countries such as the U.K. where exports form about 20% of GNP.

Inflation, the balance of payments, and the level of employment

In an open economy demand cannot be continually regenerated by an increase in money incomes, even if pensions and other transfer payments are increased regularly. Assuming a fixed exchange rate, the quantity of exports demanded will fall when prices rise faster in the exporting country than in others. If exchange rates are fixed and demand for exports is elastic, export earnings will decrease and import expenditure will increase, because rising domestic prices make imported substitutes more attractive. A balance of payments deficit will result: severe restrictions on the growth of AMD will be imposed to correct this; as shown later in this section, such measures will reduce employment and deter investment and economic growth.

From this brief survey of the causes and effects of demand-pull and cost-push inflation we can see that there is frequently a conflict between the desire to maintain full employment, the desire to keep prices stable, the need to balance international payments and the desire for economic growth. These conflicts are discussed further in S22. However, the government and the people, in a democracy, must choose policies to fit their preferences. Unless people adjust their own economic behaviour, for example in wage bargaining and price fixing, and government controls are effective, full employment is likely to lead to inflation, which will hurt people living on fixed incomes. If inflation is faster than in other countries, this will eventually result in a balance of payments crisis, and restraints on economic development. In the rest of this section we shall discuss the range of controls which a government may use in its attempts to regulate the economy, and the diverse effects which various controls may have.

21·7

Suppose an article sells at a price of £1·00. Of this £1·00, 20p is absorbed by the cost of imported materials, 60p by wages and 20p by profits. Then assume import prices rise by 25% (perhaps due to a devaluation).

a What will be the new selling price after the rise in import prices has been incorporated?
A £1·02½ **B** £1·05 **C** £1·25 **D** £1·45

b To what level will the selling price rise after both wages and prices are raised by a percentage equal to the initial rise in selling price (in **a**)?
A £1·09 **B** £1·24 **C** £1·25 **D** £1·75

The range of possible controls

The level of AMD will determine the level of employment and demand for imports. It will influence the rate of growth of prices (demand-pull inflation) and a high level of demand is important in order to encourage the growth of output. Therefore, most government measures to regulate the economy are designed to affect the level of AMD and the relative proportions of C, I, X and G within AMD. Other measures are designed to encourage greater and cheaper output. We showed at the beginning of the study section that such measures to influence supply directly take a long time to become effective. The controls used can be divided into the following categories:

i Fiscal policy. This is the variation of the level of taxation and government expenditure. Changes in fiscal policy are usually announced in a Budget, but some changes can be made at other times during a year. The Chancellor of the Exchequer and his civil service department, the Treasury, are directly responsible for fiscal policy. The collection of taxes is the responsibility of the Board of Inland Revenue and the Board of Customs and Excise.

ii Monetary policy. By this we mean variations in the price (interest rates) and supply of money. Since bank deposits are the main form of money in the U.K., the Bank of England is responsible for application of monetary policy, but it receives instructions from the Treasury. Chancellors may announce changes in monetary policy in a Budget speech, or at any other time.

iii Direct controls. Fiscal and monetary policies affect the level of AMD and output mainly via the market mechanism. For example, changes in taxation alter the supply or demand conditions for various products, but there is no direct government intervention to fix the amount supplied or demanded. However, in some cases, either for speed, or because the market mechanism will be too slow or unpredictable, it is considered desirable to impose direct controls. For example, Industrial Development Certificates are used to regulate the supply of land for factory building, import quotas are imposed on a few products, or a wages and prices freeze can be imposed. It is often debated how much the government should use its powers to control the nationalized industries in 'pegging' the prices of their products. This problem is part of the wider problem of what criteria should guide the nationalized industries' behaviour, which is considered in the satellite *Industry in the public sector*.

iv Voluntary campaigns. These include campaigns designed to boost savings, and to encourage firms to export. A voluntary prices and incomes policy is also in this category.

We shall now examine each category in turn. You should also refer to the relevant satellites, Nos. 2, 6, 8, 10. You should consider which measures affect AMD directly, and which are designed to increase the supply potential of the economy. It will become clear that most measures vary AMD, and so may be inappropriate for the control of cost-push inflation.

Public expenditure

Fiscal policy will affect total public sector expenditure. At the end of the 1960s this amounted to half of total national expenditure; it appears that out of every £1 spent, 50p was spent by the

	Current expenditure £m			Capital expenditure £m			
	Goods and services	Transfer payments (net)	Debt interest	Gross fixed capital formation	Other	Totals	as percentage of total public expenditure
Central government	4 461	4 023	1 112	392	536	10 524	60
Local authorities	2 602	303	487	1 587	86	5 065	29
Public corporations	(not included)		172	1 661	122	1 955	11
	7 063	4 326	1 771	3 640	744	17 544	100

Figure 21·2. Public expenditure 1967 Source: *National Income Blue Book*

government. However, this statement, like many other apparently simple statistics, is misleading. Figure 21·2 shows that total public expenditure includes capital expenditure by the nationalized industries, current and capital expenditure by the local authorities, and current and capital expenditure by the central government. The last item accounts for 60% of total public expenditure. However, net transfer payments, including payments of debt interest, total about 34% of total public expenditure. These transfer payments are received and spent by persons and firms, so much of the government's fiscal activity is concerned with reallocating income, and *direct* public expenditure therefore amounts only to about 33p out of every £1 spent.

The national income in 1967 was £34 292m. Note that the item G in the statement AMD = C+I+G denotes the current expenditure on goods and services by local authorities and the central government. Public sector capital formation is included in I.

Even if it is not finally responsible for half of final expenditure, surely the government, with so much money passing through its hands, can easily control AMD by variations in fiscal policy? To explain why this is not so we will concentrate on central government expenditure. Here it is sufficient to point out that if nationalized industries are to plan ahead and achieve their financial targets, it is not possible to vary the level of AMD in one year by altering the capital expenditure of nationalized industries. It is slightly easier for the government to regulate local authority expenditure, but the flow cannot be turned on and off like water from a tap. Many items of expenditure,

vices, cannot be stopped immediately, and regular annual sums are required for the maintenance of basic services, such as education, police, sanitation, etc. The central government exercises two main forms of control over local authority expenditure: first, central government departments must approve various major items of expenditure, and second, local authorities together have to negotiate the level of the rate support grant which they receive every year from the Treasury to supplement their income from the rates.

The Budget

The original purpose of the Budget was to raise revenue to cover annual expenditure by the central government. Now it has two purposes: to regulate the economy and to redistribute income between various sections of the economy. It is no longer considered necessary to balance current tax revenue against expenditure. Indeed the regulation of the economy may require current expenditure to exceed revenue, a Budget *deficit*, or revenue to exceed expenditure, a Budget *surplus*.

A Budget statement is usually made every April. The Chancellor of the Exchequer presents a Financial Statement to the House of Commons, which shows the estimated revenue and expenditure of the last financial year (ending March 31st) and the forecasts for the next year. Here any alterations due to tax changes will be shown.

Figure 21·3 shows the Budget estimates for 1968–69.

Figure 21·4 lists the main items of current expenditure covered by the Budget statement. This excludes National Insurance Fund expenditure.

Referring to figure 21·3 again, the National Loans Fund shows mainly what loans, net of repayments, are to be extended to nationalized industries and local authorities. Any surplus or deficit from the Consolidated Fund is carried over to the National Loans Fund, so a surplus reduces the government's need to borrow from the public, and a deficit increases the need to

BUDGET ESTIMATES 1968–69 (£m)

	Before Budget changes	After Budget changes
Consolidated Fund		
Revenue		
Taxation	11 552	12 475
Miscellaneous receipts	400	499
Total	11 952	12 875
Expenditure		
Supply services	10 548	10 725
Consolidated fund standing services	764	764
Total	11 312	11 489
Surplus	640	1 386
Loans from the National Loans Fund (net)		
To nationalized industries	921	921
To local and harbour authorities	505	505
Other	318	318
Total	1 744	1 744
Less Consolidated Fund surplus	640	1 386
Net borrowings of National Loans Fund	1 104	358

Figure 21·3 Source: *Broadsheets on Britain, DEA, No. 19*

CENTRAL GOVERNMENT CURRENT EXPENDITURE COVERED BY THE BUDGET 1968–69

	£m	Sub-totals £m	Percentage of total
Current expenditure on goods and services			
Military defence	2 317		(24)
National Health Service	1 269		(13)
Finance and tax collection	163		(9)
External relations	101		
Other	531		
		4 381	46
Subsidies			
Housing	121		
Agriculture and food	247		
Nationalized transport undertakings	166		
Employment premiums	152		
Other	29		
		715	8
Current grants to personal sector			
Education	201		
Supplementary benefits	392		
Family allowances	161		
Other	285		
		1 039	11
Current grants to local authorities		1 701	18
Current grants abroad		171	} 5
Current grants to National Insurance Fund		310	}
Debt interest		1 175	12
Total expenditure		9 492	100

Source: *National Income Blue Book*

Figure 21·4. Central government current expenditure covered by the Budget

borrow. The amount the government needs to borrow is called the *net borrowing requirement*—it indicates an increase in the National Debt. The size of the net borrowing requirement is very important, because the means by which the money is borrowed, whether by issue of Treasury Bills, Savings Certificates or long-term securities, will have a considerable impact on the economy, as it will affect the government's monetary policy. The importance of the net borrowing requirement is often overlooked.

Control of the economy by fiscal policy

i **Budget surpluses and deficits.** An increase in government expenditure without any offsetting taxation will cause a rise in AMD. If the Budget was previously balanced, the increase in expenditure will cause a Budget deficit. A Budget deficit will therefore increase AMD, and because of the multiplier effect, the final increase in expenditure will exceed the initial net increase in expenditure. The multiplier effect of an increase in G (i.e. including local authority expenditure) can be expressed by the following statement:

$$\delta Y = \frac{\delta G}{1-c}$$

If the Budget is originally balanced and taxation is increased without a corresponding increase in expenditure a Budget surplus is created, which will reduce AMD. The fall in purchasing power will cause a multiplier effect reducing national income. It is important to note, however, that an increase in taxation, δT, will not cause a reduction of people's expenditure by the same amount, because the increase in taxation will be partly offset by less saving. For example, if a person's MPC is 0·8, and his disposable income falls by £1 a month, his expenditure will not fall by £1, but by 80p per month. So an increase in income tax will cause a reduction in expenditure of $c\delta T$, i.e. the increase in taxation multiplied by the MPC.

The sections of the Budget

The Budget statement is divided into two sections, Consolidated Fund and National Loans Fund, which roughly correspond to the division between current items and capital items. Reading figure 21·3 downwards we see that taxation provides nearly all government revenue. Consolidated Fund expenditure is absorbed mainly by the supply services; such expenditure requires annual approval from Parliament. The main items are defence, the health service, grants to local authorities for education and other services, and various aids to industry, including subsidies and grants. Grants and other transfer payments comprise about half of the budget expenditure.

The other item of expenditure is Consolidated Fund standing services, which do not require annual approval. The main item here is debt interest, especially when interest rates are high. Therefore the multiplier effect of an increase in taxation on expenditure is the following:

$$\delta Y = -\frac{c\delta T}{1-c}$$

In this case δY will be negative, and the expression means that national income will fall by a multiple of the reduction in expenditure.

Suppose the government increased expenditure and taxation by the same amount, so that $\delta G = \delta T$. The budget would remain balanced. Would there be no change in expenditure? G would increase expenditure by $\delta G \times \frac{1}{1-c}$ or $\frac{\delta G}{1-c}$, but δT ($= \delta G$) would reduce expenditure by $\frac{c\delta G}{1-c}$.

The result would be that *national income would change.*

$$\delta Y = \frac{\delta G}{1-c} - \frac{c\delta G}{1-c} = \frac{\delta G - \delta Gc}{1-c}$$

$$= \frac{\delta G(1-c)}{1-c}$$

Therefore $\delta Y = \delta G$!

The odd result of equal increases in taxation and expenditure is that national income will increase just by the amount of the increase in expenditure. This effect is often called the balanced budget multiplier, and it arises because the increase in taxation will not cause an equivalent reduction in consumption expenditure.

21·8

Suppose the government wished to reduce government expenditure and cut taxes in such a way as to leave AMD unchanged. If the government cut the income tax yield by £400m and the MPC of income tax payers was calculated to be 0·75, by how much should the government cut expenditure so as to leave AMD unchanged?

A £425m **B** £400m **C** £375m
D £325m **E** £300m

21·9

If the government cut both taxation and expenditure by £400m in the above example, what would be the net effect on AMD?

A AMD would rise **B** AMD would fall
C No effect

In the late 1960s the government tried to maintain large Budget surpluses in its efforts to restrain AMD and reduce inflation. Notice in figure 21·3 the surplus estimated for 1968 was £1 386m; in fact the surplus was higher and in 1969–70 a surplus of nearly £2 500m was recorded, yet prices rose 5·4% in 1969.

ii Control of particular sectors. Any measure to change AMD must necessarily affect particular sectors. The government may seek to increase consumer demand by reducing income tax, or it may seek to raise investment expenditure by bigger tax allowances, higher grants, or cuts in corporation tax. It could reduce the purchase of imports by raising purchase tax or income tax, or directly by imposing tariffs, although in most cases the latter is contrary to the General Agreement on Trade and Tariffs. It is obviously difficult to predict the precise effect of such changes in policy, partly because the time lag between tax change and effect may be considerable. We have already noted that people will try to offset a rise in purchase tax or income tax by reducing savings. They may also spend past savings. Any change in investment incentives will not be fully effective for a year or more, because of the time firms need to adjust their investment plans. The control of particular sectors of the economy will involve redistribution of income by means of grants and taxes. For example, if the poor receive more in grants than they pay in tax, national income is being redistributed in their favour.

Direct and indirect taxes.

Taxes can be divided into two classes— direct and indirect. Direct taxes, such as income tax, corporation tax, capital gains tax, are levied on a person's or firm's income or wealth. Nearly one-half of government revenue is raised by direct taxes, including about one-third from income tax and surtax. The impact and incidence of direct taxes are usually on the same person: this means that the person directly responsible for paying the tax cannot pass on the effect of the tax, the incidence, to anyone else. For example, only in rare cases can a group of people pass on to others the effect of a rise in their own income tax, by forcing up their own wages and the prices of the products they produce. Direct taxes cannot be legally evaded, though considerable skill and effort may be put into devising means of avoiding them, by adjusting the timing of receipts and by qualifying for the maximum exemptions.

Indirect taxes are taxes on goods and services, which raise the price above the factor cost. They are paid only when people buy the taxed goods or services. Therefore they are also called *expenditure taxes,* and they can be avoided in the sense that people can reduce their purchases of the taxed goods and services.

21·10

Refer to the table of Central Government Revenue in the *National Income Blue Books,* or the table of Exchequer Revenue in the *Annual Abstract of Statistics.* Make a list of the category and volume of tax receipts in a recent year.

The impact of indirect taxes is on those people responsible for paying the tax: in the case of purchase tax, wholesalers or retailers; in the case of selective employment tax—a tax on labour employed in service industries—the employers. However, the incidence of such taxes is spread between producers and consumers. If the market price of a product is raised consumers bear part of the tax, and in so far as producers' revenue is reduced, and the public buys less of their product, producers bear part of the tax. The proportions of an expenditure tax borne by producers and consumers depend on the relative elasticities of supply and demand. The less elastic demand is relative to supply, the greater the incidence of the tax on consumers.

Imagine a case where demand is completely inelastic. As shown in figure 21·5 the imposition of a tax will raise the supply curve. The vertical distance between the two supply curves shows the amount of the tax. After the tax increase the price rises from OP_1 to OP_2.

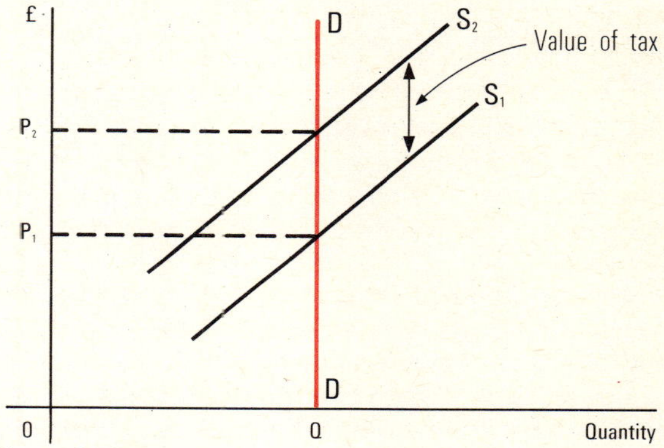

Figure 21·5

Where demand is completely inelastic the price will rise by the amount of the tax, and there will be no reduction in quantity demanded. Consumers bear the full incidence of the tax. You should now draw some supply and demand curves of varying elasticities, and find out how the effect of a tax will be spread between producers and consumers.

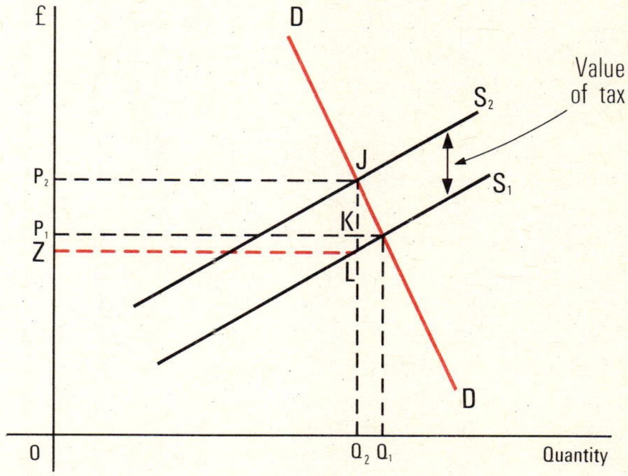

Figure 21·6

21·11

Refer to figure 21·6, which shows the effect of the imposition of a tax.

a What is the amount of the tax per unit of the product?

A P_1P_2 **B** OZ **C** ZP_2

b What shows the total tax payments by consumers?

A P_1P_2JK **B** ZP_2JL **C** ZP_1KL

21·12

If the government wishes to impose an expenditure tax which will be certain to raise a large revenue, why will it tax a product for which demand is inelastic?

The principles of taxation

The general principles governing tax policies are discussed here. The effects of particular taxes are examined in the satellite, *The management of the economy*.

No tax is ideal, especially as many people object to paying taxes, although at the same time they clamour for government action to provide certain services. Taxes, like the Budget as a whole, serve two basic purposes. They raise revenue, and changes in taxation will affect AMD. Also they have a specific impact on particular sectors, and alter the distribution of expenditure and income. Some taxes which are effective in controlling AMD may have undesirable effects on the distribution of income. The following are some desirable attributes of a tax.

i Equity. This is a vague concept, but it refers to the fact that taxes should not be imposed regardless of the ability to pay. Taxes which require the same payment by the poor as by the rich are inequitable in the sense that the lower paid pay a higher proportion of their income in tax than the higher paid do. Such taxes are called regressive taxes, whereas progressive taxes take a larger proportion of people's incomes the higher their incomes are. In Britain the income tax system is progressive whereas expenditure taxes on beer, on tobacco and to a certain extent on petrol are regressive because lower-paid people often spend as much on these products as the higher paid.

ii Certainty and clarity. This attribute may seem strange, but imagine a system in which you did not know from one year to the next how much tax would be levied on your income or on the goods you bought. Tax arrangements which are difficult to understand may not have the effect the government desire. Businessmen often criticize the frequency of tax changes as much as the tax changes themselves, because firms (and individuals) wish to plan for the future, and frequent tax changes will prevent them from making realistic plans. Changes in purchase tax and other expenditure taxes will reduce sales of certain products, and alter production costs. The selective employment tax raises the costs of production in service industries.

iii Ease of payment. This attribute is related to the previous one. The Pay As You Earn system by which employers deduct the income tax due from employees' pay is convenient both for the Inland Revenue and for the employee, because he knows that he is not building up a tax bill. Self-employed people and companies have to put aside money reserves to pay the tax due when they are assessed.

iv Cheapness in relation to revenue raised. Many taxes may sound sensible, but be very expensive to administer. Taxes such as capital gains tax fall into this category. It seems fair that people who buy and sell securities and other assets in order to make a profit should be taxed on their net gains, but the valuation of assets and the checking of transactions requires many man-hours of work. Capital gains tax and surtax raise relatively little revenue compared with the cost of collection. People who oppose the introduction of a value added tax say that it will be complex and very expensive to administer.

v Consistency with the government policy. When the initial rate of tax on taxable income is 38·75% (1970–71), as soon as a person becomes liable to income tax, just over 30% of every extra pound he earns will be absorbed by tax. The percentage is reduced by the effect of the earned income allowance. Over a wide range of income, up to about £4 000, the marginal rate of tax remains at the level of 30%; after that it increases steeply, especially when surtax is added. Many people suggest that the income tax structure in Britain begins at too high a level and is too steeply progressive beyond incomes of £4 000 p.a. They say this structure encourages absenteeism and discourages people from working harder and taking posts of greater responsibility, because a lot of the extra income they may gain is absorbed in tax. It is difficult to find clear evidence for these statements, because the tax structure cannot be suddenly altered for the sake of experiment.

However, if these arguments are correct, a very progressive direct tax system, although it is a means of narrowing the gap between rich and poor, will discourage the production of extra goods and services. Therefore higher income taxes, as well as reducing demand, can reduce supply.

If higher tax revenue is necessary in order to reduce the demand on resources, the government may decide to raise expenditure taxes instead of income taxes. However, if the goods taxed are consumed mainly by the higher income groups the tax yield is likely to be low: for example, a tax on yachts will have a low yield because there are relatively few yachts, and a rise in price might cause a considerable reduction in the number demanded. People would switch expenditure to other goods and there would be little, if any, reduction of the demand on resources. The tax yield will be higher and more certain if a tax is placed on something which is consumed by all sections of the community and for which demand is inelastic, for example cigarettes. More expenditure will be absorbed in the purchase of cigarettes, leaving less for the purchase of other products. Unless people can raise their money incomes, real incomes and the demand for resources will fall. However, in this case the tax will be regressive, and will cause a rise in prices, which will in turn stimulate higher wage claims. In this way higher expenditure taxes can promote cost-push inflation.

A basic objection to the British system, in which expenditure taxes are levied only on certain categories of goods, is that it distorts the relationship between costs of production and the selling price. As a result the pattern of consumption and investment expenditure does not reflect the real costs of production of different products. A practical effect of this is that high expenditure taxes on products such as cars will slow down the growth of important export industries. A sales tax, such as that levied in the U.S.A., spreads the impact of taxes over a wider range of goods. If the same percentage rate of tax was levied on all goods and services there would be no distortion effect. One reason for the introduction of the selective employment tax in 1966 was that until then there had been hardly any taxes on services.

The limitations of fiscal policy

We have shown that it is difficult to make sudden changes in the overall level of expenditure. It is easier to alter taxes, especially as the Chancellor has the power to alter expenditure tax rates by 10% in any year without the formality of a Budget (the regulator power); however, tax changes designed to reduce demand may have undesirable side effects, and it is difficult to predict how soon tax changes will be effective.

Monetary policy

Monetary policy is more flexible than fiscal policy, since changes in policy can be made at any time. Also the effects are less obvious to most people and so the introduction of a credit squeeze is less unpopular than higher taxes, although a credit squeeze will result in a rise in the cost of hire purchase finance and in the interest charged on loans for house purchase.

Monetary controls are designed to affect total expenditure by altering the cost of borrowing and the availability of loans. In regulating the availability of loans the authorities attempt to control the supply of money, so controls must extend to whatever is considered to be money.

One part of the money supply which is not strictly controlled is cash, i.e. notes and coins. The whole note issue is now a fiduciary issue, i.e. backed by government securities, and not by gold. The value of the fiduciary issue can be altered, subject to the formal approval of Parliament, and the amount of notes and coins issued is determined by the public demand for cash. Bank deposits form over 80% of the money supply and this proportion is increasing, so controls are intended to regulate the growth of this major form of money, and to allow the public to decide for themselves how much cash they wish to use at any time. If the note issue were limited, a shortage of notes would result in an increase in payment by the transfer of bank deposits.

The traditional monetary controls apply only to the banking system. They are alterations of Bank Rate, open market operations, the use of special deposits, and directives.

i Bank Rate. Changes in Bank Rate are designed to alter the cost of borrowing, and to attract or discourage the inflow of 'hot-money'—short-term deposits moved from one international financial centre to another in search of a high interest rate.

When Bank Rate is raised all short-term interest rates rise. The Discount Houses fear being 'forced into the Bank', i.e. having to borrow funds from the Bank of England at Bank Rate (see S12). To offset this danger they raise the rates at which they are prepared to discount Treasury and commercial bills. The commercial banks raise the interest charged on their loans to the Discount Houses. Therefore, all money market interest rates rise to follow the change.

21·13

By referring to past issues of *The Times Business News or The Economist,* find out the level of Bank Rate and the Treasury Bill discount rate at those times.

Longer-term interest rates follow the change. Commercial bank deposit account rates have been fixed at 2% below Bank Rate, and their overdraft rates vary from $\frac{1}{2}$% to $2\frac{1}{2}$% above Bank Rate, according to the status of the borrower. Hire purchase rates also follow the change. If a higher Bank Rate is expected to last for a long time building society loan and deposit rates will rise. Also, the yields on gilt-edged securities will rise and the prices will fall—see S16.

21·14

Why will the yields on gilt-edged automatically rise when short-term interest rates rise?

A change in Bank Rate is usually part of a 'package deal' with other measures. The immediate effect is slight since bank loans are one of the cheapest forms of credit, and during a boom small rises in interest rates will not deter expenditure; similarly a small reduction will not stimulate investment in a depression. However, a rise in interest rates will raise costs of capital investment and stock holding, and deter long-term investment (see S16). Therefore a weapon designed to restrain demand-pull inflation may stimulate cost-push inflation. Another disadvantage of a higher Bank Rate is that a 1% rise can add about £100m to the annual cost of servicing the National Debt. Of this about £40m will be paid to foreign holders of debt, and so adds to the balance of payments outflow.

ii Open market operations. The Government Broker, acting on instructions from the Bank of England, will buy or sell government long-term securities on the Stock Exchange. Open market operations can also be conducted in Treasury Bills on the money market, but to have any effect on the structure of bank assets, the Treasury Bills must be bought or sold by institutions other than the Discount Houses.

21·15

Why will the purchase of Treasury Bills by the Discount Houses have an effect on the structure of bank assets?

Open market operations have two effects; first on the prices and yields of government securities, second on the supply of money.

If securities are sold to the public, the public pays money to the Bank of England. As explained in S11 the Bank of England will settle its claims by reducing the bankers' deposits of the commercial banks. The results of the sale are the following.

(a) The price of securities will have been reduced to attract buyers. Therefore, the yield on securities and the long-term rate of interest will have risen (refer to the passage about the long-term rate of interest in S16).

(b) The amount of money held by the public falls as money is exchanged for securities.

(c) The commercial banks suffer a reduction in cash, and therefore a fall of liquid assets. They will restore their cash to the required level by recalling money at call. This may 'force the Discount Houses into the Bank' and so open market operations 'make the Bank Rate effective'.

(d) If the liquid assets ratio has fallen below the required percentages, the commercial banks will have to reduce their deposits until the required ratio of liquid assets to deposits is restored. The banks can reduce their deposits either by selling the securities they hold (investments) to the public, or reducing advances. If this happens, the amount of money held by the public will contract by a larger amount than the original reduction caused by the sale of securities. There will be a multiple contraction of credit. Purchase of securities by the Government Broker will have the opposite effects—reducing the long term interest rate and increasing the supply of money.

21·16

The commercial banks' liquid assets are already at the minimum required level (28% of total deposits), and the Bank of England reduces liquid assets by £100m. By how much, approximately, must total deposits fall in order to restore the required ratio?

A £28m	B £72m	C £100m
D £280m	E £350m	

If the banks can acquire extra liquid assets by any means, or if, despite the original sale of securities, their liquid assets remain above the required ratio, open market sales of securities will not cause a multiple contraction of credit. We shall see later that, paradoxically, the Bank of England may provide the extra liquid assets the banks search for by buying the securities which the banks sell and so raising bankers' deposits. Another source of alternative liquid assets is an increase in the holdings of discounted commercial bills.

Funding is an aspect of open market operations. It means lengthening the age structure of the National Debt, by issuing less short-term debt, for example Treasury Bills, and more long-term debt, for example 20-year bonds. This will reduce the liquid assets created by the public sector which can be obtained by the commercial banks; consequently the banks must seek alternative liquid assets or reduce deposits.

iii Special deposits. The Bank of England can call for special deposits equivalent to a small percentage of the commercial banks' total deposits to be lodged with the Bank of England. These special deposits are not to be counted as part of liquid assets, and the Bank of England pays interest on them at the current Treasury Bill rate. Special deposits are called or released in $\frac{1}{2}$% or 1% stages. They were first called in 1960.

A call for special deposits reduces liquid assets, and release increases liquid assets, so the special deposits control is equivalent to varying the liquid assets ratio. The aim is to reduce or increase the banks' ability to lend, but if commercial banks can find alternative liquid assets the aim of calling special deposits is frustrated.

iv) Directives (credit rationing). Open market operations and calls for special deposits designed to reduce the availability of loans have often failed to be completely effective, because banks have preferred to sell their investments rather than reduce their advances. Therefore, it has frequently been necessary for the government and the Bank of England to use their power to issue directives to the commercial banks to restrict loans. Usually the instructions concern both the volume and direction of loans. For example, in May 1965 a call for special deposits was followed by a request from the Bank of England that the commercial banks should not increase their advances in the year up to March 1966 by more than 5% of the existing level. Loans for exporters were to receive preference, and loans to finance private consumption were to be kept at a minimum. The banks were also asked to apply a similar limit to their purchases of commercial bills. At this time the Bank of England also requested other financial institutions to restrain their lending activities, although the Bank has no power to issue directives to them.

Even directives have not always been obeyed by the commercial banks, because the banks are reluctant to enforce a restrictive policy so severely that they drive some of their customers into bankruptcy. The banks themselves also suffer when a customer goes bankrupt, because a loan may not be repaid. In 1969 the banks' failure to reduce advances sufficiently caused the Bank of England to halve the rate of interest payable on the special deposits for one year.

Hire purchase controls

Apart from the controls on commercial banks, the other main instrument of monetary policy is a direct control—the variation of hire purchase regulations. The minimum deposit and the period in which the loan must be paid off have been altered many times. A higher minimum deposit and a shorter pay-off period deter borrowers and so reduce the amount of credit-financed expenditure. More details about the operation of monetary policy are included in the satellite *Sample studies of financial institutions*.

A credit squeeze

A combination of several or all of the restrictive measures will introduce a *credit squeeze*. It will become difficult to borrow money, even at high rates of interest. Some debtors may be unable to renew the loans they have negotiated, and some firms may become bankrupt because their current cash flow is insufficient to meet the payments required from them. This can happen even though the future prospects of the firm are bright. New expanding firms with low current earnings and firms whose sales are financed by the hire purchase system will be the major sufferers in a credit squeeze. The difficulty and higher costs of borrowing will force firms to raise prices in order to finance their expenditure.

It is clear that an effective reduction of the supply of money is no easy alternative to higher taxes as a means of restraining inflation. Like fiscal policy it is designed to slow down expenditure, but like fiscal policy the immediate impact may push up some prices, and slow down the growth of real output, before the change in people's expectations and downturn of expenditure are achieved. Though less obvious than higher taxes to the man in the street, a credit squeeze may also be less desirable, since the effects spread right through the economy, whereas fiscal policy can be more discriminating. For example, consumption of some products can be discouraged by higher taxes, while certain types of investment can be encouraged by grants or allowances. Scarce money will inhibit all forms of expenditure.

Difficulties in the enforcement of monetary policy

The main reason why open market operations and special deposits have been ineffective in restraining the growth of bank advances is that such operations lead to a conflict with the Bank of England's traditional policy of preserving an 'orderly market in gilt-edged', i.e. avoiding frequent and wide fluctuations in the prices of gilt-edged securities, so that potential buyers will not be deterred by the fear of large capital losses. The Bank is responsible for managing the National Debt in such a way that the government has little difficulty in covering its net borrowing requirement (see study section S6) by the issue of securities. Aggressive selling of securities to reduce the volume of money in the hands of the public would require a significant drop in the prices of securities, and so the yields, market rates of interest, would rise (refer to S16).

The Bank is unwilling to allow this to happen. For the same reason the Government Broker will be asked to purchase securities if sales by the commercial banks appear likely to cause a considerable fall in prices and rise in yields. By doing so the Government Broker provides the commercial banks with the cash they want and so the policy of maintaining an orderly market frustrates the policy designed to force banks to reduce their deposits. It is quite clear that a choice must be made: the Bank cannot at the same time 'peg' interest rates and effectively control the supply of money. Refer to figure 16·7.

Another development reducing the effectiveness of traditional monetary measures is the development of alternative sources of credit, or the *parallel banking system*—so called because many other institutions are now offering the facilities traditionally provided by the commercial banks. Merchant banks and hire purchase companies are providing increasing opportunities to borrow, so they increase the supply of money. Building societies, too, are providing a cheque transfer service, and so building society deposits have become increasingly more liquid. Such competition for the commercial banks has developed partly because borrowing from commercial banks has been restricted. The Chancellor has been forced to extend his requests for a limitation of loans to other financial institutions, but it has become increasingly more difficult to define what is included in the supply of money and to control all sources of credit, as is shown in the satellite *Sample studies of financial institutions*.

Limitations of monetary policy

There is considerable debate as to how important it is to control the money supply. Followers of Professor Milton Friedman, who base their arguments on sophisticated developments of the 'old' equation of exchange, $MV = PT$, argue that the aim should be to allow the money supply to grow by a steady rate, say about 5% per year, to encourage growth, and at the same time restrain inflation. A more rapid expansion will force up prices unless output grows at a rate about 5%, and a slower increase will be unnecessarily restrictive. Many advocates of such a policy disapprove of frequent adjustments in monetary policy, as practised in Britain, and point out that despite the credit squeezes the money supply rose by well over 5% per annum in the 1960s.

Other criticisms of monetary policy have been explained: a credit squeeze inhibits the growth of new and expanding firms, and higher interest rates raise costs of production (by raising the costs of overdrafts to finance stock holding, etc.). The main item of expenditure which is effectively deterred by higher interest rates is long-term investment in housing, roads, etc., which is very important for the long-term growth of the economy. Higher interest rates also raise the cost of servicing the National Debt, which means that higher tax revenue is necessary, and some of the higher interest payments go to overseas holders of debt. It has been calculated that a 1% rise in Bank Rate can add £40m in a year to the invisible account outflows.

Alternative methods of controlling the economy

In addition to the limitations of traditional monetary and fiscal policies discussed above, it should also be noted that such policies for the most part affect AMD, and do nothing, or very little, to encourage the growth of supply. Measures to encourage the growth of supply would be as useful as measures to restrict demand, if the government is trying to control demand-pull inflation, and more appropriate if cost-push inflation is the problem.

Of the alternative methods of control already mentioned, the one which seeks to regulate demand and at the same time stimulate the growth of supply is a productivity, prices and incomes policy. The difficulties involved in applying such a policy are fully discussed in Satellite 8, Chapter 5. Past experience has shown that while it is easy to give lip service to such an ideal as keeping the growth of incomes in line with the growth of productivity, individual groups of employers and employees will be unwilling to follow the policy when it applies to their own incomes.

Several measures to encourage savings have been introduced in recent years. If successful they would reduce the proportion of income devoted to consumption expenditure, and so free resources which could be diverted to the production of exports or capital goods. An additional result would be that less taxation would be necessary if the average propensity to save rose, since the extra saving would be a voluntary reduction of consumption. However, the measures introduced, such as Premium Bonds, the Save As You Earn scheme and various tax concessions, have not been sufficient to offset the disincentives to saving presented by inflation. Personal saving in Britain is lower, as a percentage of income, than in many European countries.

The imposition of direct controls, for example import quotas, is often an admission of failure, because they usually do nothing to remedy the situation, and are difficult to administer in a complex economy. Moreover, when the controls are removed, the original problems reappear. For example, when the wage freeze was ended in 1967, employees began to demand very high wage increases to 'catch up lost ground'.

Conclusion

It seems clear that governments have less immediate control over economic development than they claim to have, and of the many controls which can be used none are perfect. All seem to have defects in the sense that they cannot simultaneously promote full employment, stability of prices, a balance of payments surplus and economic growth. In particular, the imposition of many restrictive measures raises costs, and hampers the growth of output and productivity. In the next section we shall examine this problem of the government's role further, and in particular examine policies designed to promote economic growth.

ANSWERS TO S21

21·1

a C, D (imports of machinery), E.
b A, E.
c A, C, D, and possibly E.
d B, F.

21·2

B is correct. After a price rise of 10% each toy costs £1·10.

$$\frac{£1\ 000}{£1{\cdot}10} = 909.$$

21·3

B. After two years the price of British toys will be £1·21, but the price of imports will be just over £1·12 each.

21·4

Unless the interest charges were very much higher than 10% p.a., it would seem preferable to borrow and buy now.

21·5

The fall in AMD reduces firms' sales and profits, so they are likely to cut their investment plans, **a)** because demand has fallen, **b)** they have less cash to finance the investment.

21·6

If factors were perfectly mobile, prices would not rise until all factors were fully employed, so there would be no curve. The variation of the rate of growth of prices with unemployment would be depicted by an L-shaped graph going along the horizontal and vertical axes.

21·7

a) B. 25% of 20p is 5p.

b) C. Add 5% of 60p and 20p.

21·8

E is correct. If MPC is 0·75, out of an extra £400m disposable income people will spend £300m and save £100m.

21·9

B. Consumption would rise only £300m, but G would fall by £400m.

21·10

Exercise about tax receipts.

21·11

a C. **b** A.

21·12

The rise in price caused by the imposition of a tax will cause little fall in quantity demanded, so the total tax revenue, quantity demanded multiplied by the value of the tax, can be easily predicted by examining the total sales before the tax is imposed. For this reason taxes are imposed on articles of 'mass consumption', for example cigarettes, petrol.

21·13

Exercise on relationship between Bank Rate and Treasury Bill rate: rate changes in 1971.

21·14

When short-term interest rates rise, some people who have been holding gilt-edged securities will wish to purchase shorter-term securities, such as Treasury Bills. They sell gilt-edged, and as gilt-edged securities are sold their price falls and the yield on the securities rises. The supply of securities on the market increases, but there is no change in demand.

21·15

If the Discount Houses purchase Treasury Bills they eventually pass into the possession of commercial banks, for whom they are liquid assets, easily exchangeable for cash.

21·16

E. Deposits must contract by $\frac{100}{28} \times £100\text{m}$ = £350m approximately.

PROBLEMS OF ECONOMIC PLANNING AND POLICY

STUDY SECTION **22**

The purpose of our work so far has been to show that the easy common sense answers to economic problems are often quite inadequate. We have attempted to show that economics is a science, albeit a relatively new and imperfect one. We have done this by suggesting that the first thing an economist does is to examine carefully the existing situation. Having described and analysed this existing situation, most economists then attempt to apply their science to suggest how conditions may be changed to achieve a desired aim. In normal circumstances there is a variety of ways by which one can travel from the present situation to the achievement of the future goal. Which route one takes will depend very much on the body of knowledge existing at the time. Both firms and governments have to take decisions within this limitation.

We have dealt, so far, with some of the basic parts of this economic theory, but we must re-emphasize that our knowledge of this theory is continually changing, and is likely to continue to change in the future. Governments face the same problem. They have always attempted to control economic events in such a way as to maximize the welfare of the nation, and how they have set about doing this has depended on their knowledge of economics at the time at which these decisions were made.

For example, after the First World War the government of the United Kingdom believed that unemployment would lead to a reduction in costs and prices. This would make us more competitive with other countries and so lead to an increase in our exports. When the decision was taken to allow unemployment to grow in this period, the state of economic theory was such that this seemed to be the best method of maximizing the welfare of this nation. The work of Keynes in the period of the early 1930s has led to a new body of theory which suggests that an increase in unemployment will not necessarily lead to a fall in prices and will not, therefore, lead to an increase in our competitiveness with other countries.

As both the circumstances in the real world and our knowledge of it are constantly changing, the problem of planning is particularly complex. In this chapter we can only suggest some of the questions that one should ask, and indicate some of the applications of economic theory—as it stands at present—to the attainment of some of the objectives of economic policy.

This is not to say, however, that your study of economics to date is inadequate. On the contrary, because most economists are attempting to apply scientific methods to social problems, they are building up not only a body of theory, but a method of approach towards the control of the economic environment. Fundamentally, this method is the scientific method of investigation (using statistics), model building and predicting future events, followed by further investigation of those predictions to see how accurate they turned out to be.

This is very much like the procedure in the natural sciences. One has a theory, say, that if water is boiled in a sealed container it will sooner or later explode. Therefore, one takes a sealed container, applies heat to it and sees whether this is so. The fact that 1 000 sealed containers explode may lead the scientist to predict that, in the same conditions, all sealed containers will explode in the future. However, this is not necessarily so. The 1 001st sealed container may not explode and, thus, the scientist has to start all over again constructing a new theory. If this is the case with such a simple example, then how much more complex is the model-building theory of the economist who is seeking to predict human behaviour and who is unable to subject human beings to the test conditions of a laboratory.

The desire to control events has always been a characteristic of any society, and of the government controlling that society. But there have been periods in English history when the government felt that the best way of maximizing the nation's wealth was to take the decision to interfere as little as possible. This policy was known as 'Laissez-faire'. It was based upon the acceptable economic theory of the early nineteenth century. In Adam Smith's words, 'each individual in seeking his own gain is led by an invisible hand to promote an end which was no part of his intention. By pursuing his own interest he frequently promotes that of society more effectively than when he really intends to promote it.'

The theory implied that individual employers and employees, producers and consumers, should be left free to make their own decisions and bargains. A free market in which wages and other prices could vary up or down would ensure that surpluses and deficits of labour or commodities were automatically corrected.

This laissez-faire attitude was not always observed in practice. Despite criticism by some economic theorists of the Victorian era many Factory Acts and Public Health Acts were passed in order to protect individuals against exploitation by those with greater economic power: the length of the working day was reduced and minimum standards imposed for house building and for the preparation and sale of many goods.)

Moreover, as the nineteenth century came to a close it became more and more obvious that the decision of the government to stand aside was not solving contemporary problems. It had been assumed, amongst other things, that there was a state of perfect competition, that prices were flexible and that factors of production were mobile and would re-deploy themselves in response to price changes. These assumptions were becoming more and more questionable. For example, when from 1870 onwards the state decided to intervene in the educational system and make a major stride towards some form of compulsory education, the state had the problem of deciding precisely how much to pay its teachers and this decision was not simply a matter of supply and demand. The state not only demanded teachers but was also to some degree responsible for the supply of teachers. It was also found that such schemes as roads, sewers, water supply, were not well provided by free market forces, and that state intervention was necessary. So that the simple view of a supply and demand situation obviously no longer applied. At the same time, because of the legal system of inheritance, wealth could be concentrated in the hands of a few people who might use their economic power in a way contrary to the interests of the rest of the population. In fact, towards the end of the nineteenth century a body of socialist economic theory came into being which argued vehemently that private ownership was inimical to public welfare. It was argued, for example, that if the public at large were to be cared for in their old age, then this could only be done through state intervention, and that if people were to know of job opportunities in other areas, or even in their locality, that this information could only be provided through employment exchanges, for how would workpeople go to jobs in new expanding industries which were able to offer higher wages, if they did not know of their existence?

Moreover, firms do not necessarily produce in response to consumer demand, but through advertising may induce demand after they have decided to produce. You can see examples of this in the cosmetics and toilet preparations industry. In many different ways, advertisers attempt to persuade consumers, not that the product will serve a particular purpose, but that it will enrich their lives. The advertisers attempt to create a new demand, or to modify the consumers' previous scales of preferences.

Furthermore, market forces take no account of social cost. The cheapest way to make saucepans may be in a noisy factory which belches out smoke, and pours its waste into the nearest river. The purchaser of saucepans may prefer that they be produced in such a way that the environment is not polluted by waste or noise, but since his relation to the entrepreneur is simply that of a consumer of saucepans, he has no way of expressing his preference in economic terms.

This idea of consumer sovereignty, whereby the spending of consumer's income on certain goods encourages the production of those goods to the maximization of personal and social benefit, has proved to be a gross over-simplification. Manufacturers have banded together to defend their product regardless of the consumer's interest. Labour has organized itself in the form of trade unions to defend its position, and, indeed, consumers in recent years have also formed associations in an attempt to defend their interests, so that the simple idea of the market price of a commodity indicating its value, in terms of anything more than a short-run supply and demand equation, has proved to be an inadequate explanation of the world as we know it.

In an attempt to equate personal and social interests communist countries have tried to control, through the state, both the means of production and the process of distribution. They attempt to use the voting system, which creates the social authority, to plan an economy which will be just to both producer and consumer. Like all other societies, they find that they have to establish a scale of preferences to allocate scarce resources amongst competing ends. They determine in their plans what their resources are and how they shall be used to achieve certain goals. The price system is still used, but it is a tool of the central plan by which they attempt to control the consumption of each commodity. Thus, a communist society may decide on the production of, say, one million family motor cars. This decision means that the production of other goods is such that there are only the resources left for this quantity of motor-car production. The factories producing the motor cars are given this figure as their goal, and a process of costing and pricing takes place with the intention that consumers will demand no more than a million motor cars and the inputs of labour and material in those factories will be costed to produce this quantity of motor cars at a minimal cost. The difficulty, however, is that the economic situation is always changing and, therefore, if there has been a change in the social structure of a communist country, which leads to a change in the demand for cars, or if planners under-estimate the numbers willing and able to buy them, the plan will go awry. Similar errors have occurred in this country. For example, it was thought in 1946 that the cost of producing electricity would be so low that consumers in general would prefer electricity to gas. Quite able and reputable economists were predicting the early demise of the gas industry. In fact, the cost of producing electricity per unit has not fallen as much as expected, the gas industry has produced cleaner and better domestic cookers and fires, has advertised these utensils imaginatively and has found a new source of fuel in the form of natural gas. Hence, the gas industry shows not the slightest sign of disappearing. It is such problems as these which have led some communist countries towards the use of the market economy and price system in certain areas of economic planning. They allow the market mechanism to indicate that, for certain goods, an increase in price may reflect a strengthening demand for those goods and, therefore, the producers of those goods are given more resources to meet the increase in demand. Despite its obvious imperfections, the price system is often the best way of allocating scarce resources to meet consumers' demand.

Whilst some communist countries have moved towards a market economy, those countries which have tended in the past to depend almost entirely on a market economy have moved towards greater state intervention. Laws have been passed to regulate the conditions of production and the marketing procedures for many products, in order to protect the consumer. Other laws state the correct procedure for the formation of companies, and give the government powers to influence the location of industry and provide financial assistance to firms. Institutions such as the Monopolies Commission and the Restrictive Practices Court have been set up to examine the degree of competition between firms. Although there are some direct controls, in most cases the profit motive and the market mechanism are left to operate; government measures such as grants, subsidies and tax allowances just alter the prices on which producers and consumers base their decisions. However, in Britain some basic industries which have a large degree of monopoly power and have had difficulties in financing necessary capital expenditure have been transferred from private to public ownership. It is a matter for continual debate how far these nationalized industries' actions should be guided by the profit motive, and how far by considerations of social benefit, if actions of the latter kind generate losses which have to be covered from tax revenue (see satellite *Industry in the public sector*). The other development is that the state (the central government and the local authorities), particularly in Britain, has undertaken to provide certain services to a standard which might not be available for everyone under private enterprise. Public corporations provide some goods and services at a loss if any form of commercial accounting procedure is applied.

22·1

Name some services which local authorities provide **a)** with no direct charge to the user, **b)** at a price which does not usually cover the full cost of the services.

The change in economic objectives

The above modifications to the working of the market mechanism have not been sufficient to solve all economic problems. Theoretical work such as that by Keynes has shown that, even if the market mechanism were working perfectly and factors were completely mobile, a country would not automatically arrive at the ideal position of full employment and balanced payments. What were formerly ideals to be achieved without government intervention are now accepted aims of government policy. The list of aims has gradually increased.

During the Depression in the 1930s some governments (e.g. in U.S.A. and Germany) took direct action to reduce unemployment. After experience of managing the economy during a war, the British government accepted, in 1944, the responsibility of maintaining full employment (then defined as keeping unemployment below 3%). In the 1950s and 1960s the problems involved in maintaining stability of prices and balanced payments have received more attention, mainly as a result of the success of the policies designed to reduce unemployment. However, we have seen that many of the measures taken to correct a deficit or slow down inflation also deter investment and the growth of real income: politicians and others have begun to emphasize that economic growth (the increase in real income per head of the population) is an aim of equal importance with the other three. There are now four generally accepted aims of economic policy: full employment, price stability, balanced payments (or a surplus), and economic growth.

The emphasis on economic growth has led to arguments about the way in which the growing national income should be distributed. The government has a direct influence on the distribution of income by its choice of taxes, transfer payments, and through the provision of services for which the user does not pay the full cost. The introduction of an incomes policy in place of a less controlled system of wage bargaining is another way in which the government can attempt to influence the distribution of income.

Therefore the list of economic aims about which people expect political decisions continues to grow, although the recent history of the British economy (see satellite *The management of the economy*) shows that the government has little influence by itself on many of the economic variables (the level of wages, prices, exports, imports, etc.), and *many policies designed to achieve one aim prevent the achievement of another*. For example, restraints on the growth of AMD which are introduced in order to control inflation and reduce a balance of payments deficit raise unemployment and slow down economic growth. Political efforts to achieve a more even distribution of income per head may prevent the faster growth of national income in which all can share. (Moreover, looking beyond national interests, you should realize that all countries cannot simultaneously achieve a surplus balance of payments, because if some countries have surpluses others must have deficits.) This problem of choice between various aims of policy exists for all governments, and for this reason all governments, whatever their political opinions, are now involved in some sort of economic planning, the meanings of which we shall discuss later in this chapter.

Economic growth as an aim of policy

Before we deal with the problems of achieving a high growth rate, let us pause for a moment to question the very concepts of continual growth as an aim in economic policy. Growth cannot be pursued for its own sake without regard to some of the inevitable costs which must arise from giving this aim too great an importance. Suppose we asked the car industry to increase car production by 20% p.a. Would this make sense if the results were to be simply a lack of space in which to put these cars? Would an economic policy which encouraged the creation of highly paid workers in the car industry be appropriate if, by so doing, there were created a lack of resources for the building of new schools and hospitals? Would these affluent car workers really be better off if there were a lack of facilities for public education and health? Furthermore, would the continual growth in the number of motor cars produced, and the roads for these motor cars, lead to a reduction in the countryside and to a pollution in the environment causing such heavy social costs that the gain from the extra cars would be completely cancelled out? It is quite obvious that no single aim should be pursued without taking into consideration the opportunity cost. It is also worth mentioning that any system which assesses the cost of economic activity and the benefits which thereby accrue must take into consideration not only private profit, but social advantage or disadvantage.

Thus, in S15 we noted that an increase in money national income per head did not necessarily mean that a nation is better off. Improvements in the material standard of living in a country can be measured by the increase in real prices) per head, but even this measurement can be unreliable. It does not indicate what kind of goods and services are being produced (the country may be directing a large proportion of its resources to the production of armaments), and since GNP per head measures just the average income it does not show whether all groups are better off, or whether the benefits of higher production have been confined to a few. Also, as output increases, people may work shorter hours, and prefer more leisure time rather than even higher incomes. In such a case the growth of GNP per head will under-estimate the increase in welfare.

As long as we do not forget these qualifications, we can see that economic growth is desirable because it means that the material standard of living of the population improves. In economically advanced countries, especially since governments have undertaken the responsibility to maintain full employment, people have become accustomed to expect, year by year, increases in private affluence, while at the same time they expect better public sector services as well (e.g. health, education, road and rail services). In developing countries the need for improvements in food and clothing, transport, health, and education services is obvious. Mass communications, especially television and films, have shown millions the standard of living of the richest communities, so it is not surprising that the governments of developing countries aim for rapid economic growth.

Unless the output of a country grows faster than the population, one group of one sector can obtain more goods and services only at the expense of another. If a country's output per head is static, redistribution of income to enable the poor to buy more, or greater expenditure on education and other welfare services provided by the public sector, are possible only if the majority of consumers accept the reduction of their disposable incomes caused by higher taxation. Redistribution is obviously easier to achieve if peoples' real incomes are rising, and the measures taken allow the incomes of the poorer section of the community to rise more rapidly than those of the richer. Similarly, when output and expenditure are rising, a greater proportion of the nation's expenditure can be devoted to the public sector without actually reducing the amount of expenditure by the private sector.

The causes of economic growth

Assuming that the population is growing only slowly, some increase in GNP per head can be achieved in any one year if unemployed labour and capital are utilized, but if full employment is maintained, annual increases in output can only be achieved if the labour force is growing, or if the output per head of the existing labour force is increased. Therefore, ignoring changes in the terms of trade, the long-term growth of real income per head depends on the rate of growth of labour productivity, measured in terms of output per man hour. In a country where the working population is static or is growing only slowly, e.g. in Britain, measures to promote economic growth are those which are designed to increase the output of the existing labour force.

22·2

The non-working population of a country is rising faster than the working population, and workpeople are working shorter hours. Which of the following is true?

A The rise in GNP per head will be greater than the rise in output per man-hour.
B The rise in GNP per head will be equal to the rise in output per man-hour.
C The rise in GNP per head will be less than the rise in output per man-hour.

The main method of increasing labour productivity is to provide labour with better equipment to work with, by greater capital investment. The improvement can be either in quantity, or quality (due to technical progress). The more capital per man, the greater the productivity per man. One explanation of the fact that real wages are higher in the U.S.A. than in Britain is that more capital is employed per man. Countries with the highest investment ratios (investment expenditure as a proportion of GNP) have achieved the fastest growth rates. Between 1955 and 1964 West Germany spent 23·7% of GNP per year on investment and output per head grew by 5% per year; the contrasting figures for Britain were 15·8% and 2·6% per year.

A higher investment ratio is not, by itself, sufficient to cause faster growth. Some long-term investment projects, such as the construction of motorways and power stations, require expenditure for several years before any benefit is felt, and a considerable proportion of investment expenditure will be devoted to the replacement and increase of social capital, houses, hospitals, schools, etc. An improvement in the social capital of the country, however necessary, will not cause an immediate increase in output per head, although in the long run the growth of labour productivity will be affected by the health, skills and attitudes of the population.

The effectiveness of investment in plant and machinery in raising output per head will obviously depend on whether new techniques are applied, and whether any economies of scale are realized. If existing equipment is merely increased, and methods of production remain unchanged, extra investment will not raise output per head. Even if new types of equipment are introduced, they may not be efficiently used. The efficient use of new machinery and buildings usually requires changes in working practices by all employees, including management. A national measure of the effect of extra investment on output is the marginal capital/output ratio (the amount of extra investment needed to produce an extra £1 worth of output). The marginal capital/output ratio will rise if more investment is directed to the improvement of the social capital of the country, if extra capital is less efficiently used, or simply if the marginal productivity of capital is declining (see S16).

Restraints on growth

To increase the proportion of GNP devoted to investment, the present rate of growth of consumption, exports, or current government expenditure must be reduced. The balance of payments situation may preclude any reduction of exports, especially as faster growth will probably cause a rapid increase in demand for imports. The rate of growth of consumption will be cut if the public's desire to save increases (the average propensity to save rises), or higher taxes are imposed. However, people may be unwilling to accept a slower rate of growth of private consumption now in return for a promise of a faster rate of growth of consumption later. By maintaining consumption expenditure at its current high level they will prevent resources being switched to capital formation. Similarly there will be much resistance to a reduction in public sector consumption expenditure on goods and services, especially if reductions in welfare services, or higher charges, are involved. For all these reasons it may be very difficult to increase the proportion of national income devoted to investment.

Some methods of increasing productivity can have undesirable long-term effects. Swifter transport systems lower unit costs of production, but people will object to the construction of new motorways and airports when these threaten to alter the nature of the area in which they live. Certain processes of production, particularly those involving the use of chemical products, lead to air and water pollution. Action taken to prevent pollution will raise costs of production and so slow down the growth of real income per head: the conservation of the environment may be preferred to cheaper goods. For example, the use of lead-free petrol and the modifications of exhaust systems designed to reduce the emission of harmful exhaust gases will raise the cost of buying and running a car. As mentioned above, growth involves changes in working practices and rationalization of industry: some employees become redundant, and most, whether redundant or not, have to learn new skills and patterns of work. By disturbing the established way of life of families and communities rapid change can cause psychological stress.

We can see that the achievement of faster growth of real income is not an unmixed blessing. Faster growth can result in the sacrifice of other policy aims, such as full employment, or a balance of payments surplus, and it also involves certain other costs to the community, which are difficult to value in money terms. The technique by which economists try to assign money values to social costs and benefits in order to compare the advantages and disadvantages of certain policies is known as cost-benefit analysis. Suppose you intend to create better transport facilities for London. On a narrow basis you would cost the building and operation of an underground railway against the possible income from passengers. Cost-benefit analysis is more complex: it would compare alternative systems, undergrounds, buses, etc., and consider wider benefits such as the benefits to industry ensuing from good transportation for employees, access to a wider labour market, and the effects on housing and health. Only after all these considerations would a particular system be chosen.

Economic planning

Monetary policy

This is the policy that is normally pursued through the Bank of England and is designed to alter the supply of money in order to change the amount of purchasing power available to the community, to alter the cost of that money by affecting the interest rates, and to alter the ease with which various sections of the community may borrow that money. These processes are described in satellites, and in the study sections 6 and 12. The point to make here is that since 1946 the Bank of England has been nationalized and there is no question of the government ever allowing these means of monetary control to fall into the hands of any private group of individuals.

Fiscal policy

Fiscal policy in this country is exercised through the Treasury, and usually refers to those decisions announced by the Chancellor of the Exchequer in his Budget speeches to Parliament. The government normally announces its future plans for expenditure on commodities and services and its decisions on transfer payments between one section of the community and another. To meet the expenditure, it also announces its plans for gathering income by direct and indirect taxation. All states, whether communist or not, consider that the fiscal policy is a matter for the elected representatives of the members of that state, whatever the form of election. It is worth recognizing that, such is the size of state expenditure, fiscal decisions can affect the market fortunes of individual industries or firms. Thus, changes in purchase tax levied on motor cars can affect the output and, therefore, the costs of the motor industry. Furthermore, the levels of taxation and the ways in which taxes are imposed affect the individual ownership of wealth and the individual's propensity to accumulate wealth. Hence death duties may make the distribution of wealth more even and high family allowances may change the distribution of wealth and alter the power to consume away from the higher income groups towards the lower income groups. Such redistribution in wealth can again affect individual firms and industries. As a thinking point you might consider the effect on the manufacturer of prams of an increase in the purchase tax levied on prams which came into effect at the same time that there was an increase in family allowances.

Foreign exchange policy

This is implemented by the Bank of England and the Treasury working together to control the rate at which the pound sterling is sold overseas. It basically controls the amount of exports which a country must exchange for a given quantity of imports that it requires from overseas countries. Much depends on the proportional importance of foreign trade to the country in question. It is interesting to note again that there is no case of any state leaving the value of its currency to a completely free foreign exchange market. All states use their reserves to stabilize or to interfere in the market price of their national currency. Again in this sphere, there are varying degrees of state interference.

Other forms of governmental intervention

These range from the activities of the weights and measures inspectors ensuring that proper scales are used in commerce and that proper descriptions are given to commodities, to the setting up of a Board of Enquiry to adjudicate a wage settlement. It is particularly thought-provoking to note that in a wage dispute between power-station workers and their employers in 1971, the government insisted that the 'national interest' should be borne in mind, and this simply shows explicitly that the wage rate of one section of the community is of concern to us all.

The growth of state influence in all matters has caused all governments, of whatever parties, to become involved in government planning, although the word 'planning' was formerly associated with centrally controlled economies, such as those in communist countries. Economic planning, as fractised in Britain, was described in 1969 as involving:

- **a** Analysis of the existing economic situation and of past trends.
- **b** Projection of those trends, taking account of known changes in the situation, and an attempt to foresee the probable outcome. This includes analysis of the uncertainties and the possible results.
- **c** Discussion by all parties concerned, principally government and industries, of the analysis and projections.
- **d** Study and discussion of the constraints preventing better performance and of how they can be overcome.
- **e** Action by those concerned to overcome the constraints and so to improve performance.

This description omits any indication of how better performance is measured, but we must assume that it refers to the achievement of the four generally accepted aims of economic policy listed on page 120. The description also glosses over the need for political choice between alternatives when the aims of policy are incompatible. Different governments may use different terms in their description of the planning process, but few, if any, would reject the need for analysis of trends and discussion of the constraints which prevent better performance. Where disagreement arises is over section (e), the action which follows such discussion. It is the nature of the action taken which distinguishes market and planned economies.

The typical procedure in centrally planned economies is that the government constructs a forecast of the changes in output required from the various state-owned industries, say for the next five years, and each industry and firm is allocated the factors which are considered sufficient to enable them to fulfil their required output. Prices are fixed by the government, usually on the principle that necessities such as basic foodstuffs should be relatively cheap, and less necessary items more expensive. Therefore the price of a product gives no indication of the scarcity of that product or its factor cost. In market economies, by definition, the state does not control the allocation of all resources, so the action which follows planning discussion is a mixture of persuasion, and manipulation of the market mechanism, plus some direct controls. For example, if the British government wishes to reduce the imports of chemical products, it can stimulate an increase in the output of the chemical industry in Britain by special negotiations with firms in the chemical industry, backed up by grants, in order to encourage them to build new plants in Britain rather than elsewhere. The negotiations may include the placing of orders by nationalized industries and some government departments which may otherwise be placed elsewhere. In more general terms an economic planning exercise must be conducted before every budget, to determine whether an increase or reduction in AMD is required, what components of AMD (C, I, G, or X) need to be changed, and what particular mixture of tax and expenditure changes will assist in achieving the aims of policy. The distribution of incomes can be changed, and market prices, set by the forces of supply and demand, can be raised by the imposition of expenditure taxes and reduced by subsidies. Once the monetary and fiscal changes have been made, the government relies mainly on the market mechanism to make people act in the way that has been forecast.

Attempts have been made in Britain to construct longer-term forecasts of the development of the economy (e.g. the National Plan, 1965), starting from the basic assumption that faster growth of labour productivity was possible ($3\frac{1}{2}\%$ p.a. instead of the actual $2\frac{1}{2}\%$ p.a.). Industries and firms were expected to adjust their production plans to conform with the higher expected growth rate of GNP (3·8% p.a.). However, such 'indicative' planning was not successful. The rapid growth of AMD during 1965 caused balance of payments difficulties which were countered by severe deflation (including a 'wages freeze') in 1966. To a certain extent the false expectations aroused by the plan's forecasts caused reactions which reduced the chances of the plan's success: for example, the rapid growth of public sector investment aggravated inflationary pressure. The details of British planning and its effects are discussed in the satellite *The management of the economy*.

The effectiveness of planning

Experience in both centrally planned economies and market economies has shown that neither form of planning is very reliable. The basic difficulty of central planning is that it is impossible to make accurate long-term forecasts about the pattern of consumption expenditure, especially when incomes are rising and people begin to require greater variety of choice. If the forecasts are wrong, surpluses of some goods develop and shortages of others, but if prices are fixed the surpluses and shortages cannot be removed until the government decides it is necessary to alter the range of relative prices. Due to the delays in adjustment, when price changes are made they are often large. Some communist countries, particularly Yugoslavia and Hungary, have modified their economic system to allow market forces to have some effect. For example, factories whose goods sell well are allowed to retain some of the revenue in order to expand their productive capacity and to pay bonuses to employees.

The same difficulties in forecasting economic behaviour, due to the inadequacy of statistics and the complexity of the influences affecting consumers' and producers' decisions, have caused problems for governments attempting to influence the development of market economies. Promises by politicians that the rate of inflation will soon decrease, or that the balance of payments will move into surplus in the next year, frequently turn out to be false. In countries like Britain, which export a considerable proportion of their output and import an equivalent amount, the difficulties of forecasting and control are increased, because events in foreign countries are beyond the control of the home country's government. When the usual monetary and fiscal measures prove ineffective, the use of more direct controls has been suggested, e.g. the implementation of a prices and incomes policy.

Of course some progress has been made in controlling the economic environment; the period since 1845 has been one of increasing real incomes in all countries, although the distribution of income is very unequal. However, neither central planning nor reliance on the market mechanism can be expected to solve all economic problems of a country, partly because human wants are unlimited—as incomes rise and new techniques and products are discovered, new demands arise—and partly because the aims of macro-economic policy are determined by political decisions, about which there is usually considerable difference of opinion.

22·3

Indicate whether the following statements are true or false.

- i In a free economy workers are able to change jobs as they wish and to decide whether to work or not, so that there will always be some unemployment.
- ii Government intervention to ensure more competition is inconsistent with the operation of a free-enterprise market economy.
- iii If there is full employment, then any attempt to increase consumption will lead to inflation unless there is an increase in productivity.
- iv The price system is a rationing system which favours those who have more money to spend.
- v Real national income can be increased by expanding total monetary demand, hen resources are fully employed.
- vi The impersonal working of the free market always results in the greatest good for the greatest number of the population.
- vii Competition and the profit motive always ensure the best distribution of resources.
- viii In real terms to achieve a high rate of economic growth we have to remove productive resources from such social services as education or health.

ANSWERS TO S22

22·1

- **a** Education, rubbish collection.
- **b** Housing (rented accommodation).

22·2

C is correct.

22·3

- i True.
- ii True. Logically, you cannot have it both ways.
- iii True.
- iv True.
- v False. If all resources are employed you normally experience inflation.
- vi False.
- vii False. Social costs?
- viii False. In real terms health and education count.

Index